Creative Industries

Creative Industries

Contracts between
Art and Commerce

Richard E. Caves

Harvard University Press

Cambridge, Massachusetts, and London, England | 2000

First Harvard University Press paperback edition, 2002

Library of Congress Cataloging-in-Publication Data

Caves, Richard E.
    Creative industries : contracts between art and commerce / Richard E. Caves.
        p. cm.
    Includes bibliographical references and index.
    ISBN 0-674-00164-8 (cloth : alk. paper)
    ISBN 0-674-00808=1 (pbk.: alk. paper)
    1. Arts—Economic aspects—United States—History—20th century.
I. Title.
NX705.5.U6 C38   2000
338.4′77′00973—dc21   99-086569

Contents

Preface

The organization of "creative industries," in which the product or service contains a substantial element of artistic or creative endeavor, has received surprisingly little attention from economists, with a sole exception: the question whether public subsidy is warranted for the performing arts. Reflection quickly suggests several explanations. Economists, proud of their theoretical apparatus and facility with statistical tools, are put off from industries such as these that yield few congenial data sets. Also, in a field that deserves its nickname of "dismal science," frivolous activities can hardly exert the intellectual pull of serious industries such as steel, pharmaceuticals, and computer chips. The idea for this project came to me about two decades ago, but for these reasons I thought it best postponed to a time when my reputation for professional seriousness could more comfortably be placed at risk.

When I began to gather information and reflect seriously on this project, I discovered that while systematic data are scarce, copious information on deals and trade practices is available in trade journals and general newspapers, as well as in books by nontechnical observers of these activities. If one settles for information that is heterogeneous and largely qualitative, but nonetheless abundant, a great deal can be learned of the economic organization and behavior of these sectors. I also discovered that sociologists have made important progress on several lines of empirical observation. In particular, they have exposed the networks of informal contracts that knit together the participants in most creative industries. Their empirical findings complement nicely the analytical resources of contract theory, a rapidly evolving branch of economics.

Indeed, the theory of contracts and the logic of economic organization—the question of why and how some transactions are internalized within the firm while others take place between independent economic agents or firms —provide the analytical framework of this book. At the start I introduce several bedrock or axiomatic properties that pertain either to all creative industries, or to some in contrast to others. The book then applies economic analysis to these structural properties in order to explain many features of organization patterns and contracts observed in creative industries. Succeeding chapters hopscotch across a range of industries providing entertainment and culture: the visual and performing arts, cinema and TV films, sound recordings, book publishing, even toys and games. The strategy is to deal with each behavior pattern in the context of the creative activity that best illustrates it. Readers with interests confined to a particular sector can direct their reading by means of the table of contents and index, but the introductory chapter is required reading for comprehension of all that follows.

As this study came together, I realized that most of its conclusions can be stated quite simply. Further, in this case data sets are not available to support sophisticated statistical methods. Some theoretical problems hinted at here may invite serious formal development, but other economists have more skill and affinity for that task than I do. As a result, I chose to write the book as simply as I could, and I hope that the bulk of the text will be clear to readers with only an introductory familiarity with economics. Some slightly more technical points and the results of a few simple quantitative analyses appear in the notes.

The markets and institutions under study are chiefly those of the present-day United States. Earlier times and other places yield many valuable empirical illustrations of conceptual points, however, and I have drawn on them freely. Indeed, keeping the book's length within reason required the regretful exclusion of a good deal more historical material. The book almost completely ignores issues of public policy toward the arts. Most economists who have written about the high-culture creative industries obviously care deeply about them, and have naturally warmed to public policies that would advance them. I have resisted the temptation to follow these scholars, if only to keep attention focused on the behavioral issues that preoccupy this study. After all, effective public policy depends on the policymaker's understanding of the economic behavior that the policy affects. Such an understanding should certainly embrace the knowledge of why creative activities are organized the way they are.

This project has benefited over the years from many friends, acquaintances, and assistants, including Philippe Aghion, Charles Booth-Clibborn, Darlene Chisholm, Gil Einstein, Tom Eisenmann, Steve Harris, Barbara Krakow, Anita McGahan, Doug Price, John Sutton, and Lois Torf. Valuable feedback came from presentations made at Harvard, MIT, UCLA (Anderson Graduate School), and the British Academy of Management. Splendid research assistance was provided by Amy Erenrich and Jung Oh. Ann Flack (aided by Elin

Lee) looked after the assembly of a large and complex manuscript. Michael Aronson of Harvard University Press provided encouragement and help over a long time period. Two referees for the press supplied valuable input, and special thanks are due to one of them, an anonymous sociologist, for extensive notes and suggestions.

Bibliographical materials useful for this book came from widely scattered sources. A list of selected references is not included, due to the publisher's constraints on the length of the volume. Such a list can be obtained by contacting the author (Department of Economics, Harvard University, Cambridge, Mass., 02138; rcaves@harvard.edu).

Introduction: Economic Properties of Creative Activities

Economists have studied a number of industrial sectors for their special and distinctive features: pharmaceuticals and computer chips for competition to innovate; chemical process industries for rivalry to install new capacity; food processing for product differentiation and the rise of dominant brands. Indeed, few sectors have escaped notice that display some distinctive form of competitive behavior or pose distinctive problems for public policy. One has been largely missed, however—the "creative" industries supplying goods and services that we broadly associate with cultural, artistic, or simply entertainment value. They include book and magazine publishing, the visual arts (painting, sculpture), the performing arts (theatre, opera, concerts, dance), sound recordings, cinema and TV films, even fashion and toys and games. So far, economists exploring this area have mainly focused on public subsidy for the elite performing arts.

While economists have been game to think about public policy toward creative activities, they have largely ignored questions about why those activities are organized the way they are. Artists of all types engage in creative processes and tasks that come to completion only with the collaboration of "humdrum" (or "ordinary") partners, and perhaps of other artists as well. The painter needs an art dealer, the novelist a publisher. The cinema film requires a number of actors, a director, screenwriter, cinematographer, production designer, make-up specialist, and many others who see themselves in some measure as artists (along with teamsters and accountants, who likely do not). These collaborations rest on deals and contracts—perhaps of the "handshake" variety, perhaps elaborately drawn. Some artistic production occurs within continuing organizations—a major symphony orchestra, or a Hollywood film studio in the 1930s. Other creative wares emerge from one-time deals. This book is about the organization of creative activities: why deals and contracts are structured the way they are; why some creative activities occur in ongoing organizations ("firms"), and others in one-off deals ("the market").

Economic analysis has tools for answering these questions, but they have seen little application to the creative industries. The theory of contracts addresses why self-interested parties structure their deals as they do. The field of industrial organization studies (among other questions) why transactions occur within continuing firms or between independent parties and why those firms are few or many, operating in one market or several. In this book, I attempt an integrated attack on the organization of creative activities using these tools. There is much to be done, and the goal could be pursued in several ways. We could identify a few choice, distinct questions and wring them dry. Or we could block out the bedrock properties of creative activities and show how they drive organizational patterns in the many markets with substantive creative elements. The latter procedure is the weapon of choice. This chapter proposes some fundamental properties and sketches how they will be used throughout the book to explain why creative activities are organized as they are. A final section provides a primer on contract theory, the most important branch of economics for this study and the one least well represented in most introductory courses.

Economists writing about the arts (for example, William D. Grampp in his *Pricing the Priceless*) often take up the burden of proving that artistic workers make the same sorts of economic choices as do humdrum mortals who profess no creative urge or skill.[1] Here I assume that creative workers are purposive and intendedly rational in their activities—like everyone else. They may have different tastes. They may be less entrepreneurial or less skilled in negotiation, but that remains to be seen. What I stress instead is that creative goods and services, the processes of their production, and the preferences or tastes of creative artists differ in substantial and systematic (if not universal) ways from their counterparts in the rest of the economy where creativity plays a lesser (if seldom negligible) role. These differences rest on the bedrock properties of these activities that distinguish them from other sectors of the economy, and in some cases distinguish creative activities from one another.

Basic Economic Properties of Creative Activities

Demand Is Uncertain

There is great uncertainty about how consumers will value a newly produced creative product, short of actually producing the good and placing it before them. It might meet acclaim and bring in revenue far exceeding its cost of production, or it might find few customers who place any positive value on it. If the creative product is costly to produce (a movie, rather than a painting), producers will try however they can to learn whether buyers' valuations will be high or low, before all of the product's costs have been incurred. Research and pretesting are largely ineffective, however, because a creative product's success can seldom be explained even ex post by the satisfaction of some pre-existing need.[2] The problem worsens when the costs are sunk, as they usually are, and cannot be retrieved once a disaster is evident. This property implies that the risk associated with any given creative product is high, and that ways of allocating or sharing it will be important for the organization of production. This is what one Hollywood observer called the *nobody knows* property.[3] One study of the success of TV series demonstrated it dramatically. The TV networks use a number of signals about new programs to attract advertisers, and the networks themselves heed those signals in deciding which pilot series to select for the season's schedule. Nonetheless, none of these signals has any statistical ability to predict what series will actually succeed.[4]

Economics pays a great deal of attention to sellers and buyers who are stuck with problems of asymmetrical information: the buyer of a used car who suspects that the seller conceals his superior knowledge about its defects; the seller of a gourmet food product who can prove its excellence only by begging customers to buy and try it. A creative product is an "experience good" like these, but the buyer's satisfaction will be a subjective reaction. The producer's intimate knowledge of the good's production process still leaves him in the dark about whether customers will like it: *nobody knows*. The organizational problem is to deal with symmetrical ignorance, not asymmetrical information. A different sort of asymmetry, however, proves very important. Complex creative products (cinema films, popular music albums) proceed from conception to finished product in a series of stages, with costs at each stage completely sunk when the product moves to the next stage. But fresh news does arrive along the way about the good's market prospects. When Joe hands the unfinished good along to Mary, Joe's input to the project is a sunk cost, but Mary can still adjust or even withhold her input. If Joe and Mary at that moment both receive fresh news about the project's ultimate success, it is efficient for Mary to hold decision rights about whether and how to proceed (Joe has no more choices open).[5] This asymmetry explains the pervasive use in creative industries of the option contract, by which Mary buys from Joe the option to proceed if she wishes, once she has digested any fresh news.

Creative Workers Care about Their Product

Economists normally assume that workers hired for some job do not care about the traits and features of the product they turn out. They care about their pay and working conditions and how much effort they must exert, but not the output's style, color, or features. Skilled craftspersons often do express pride in or concern for the quality of their work and the goods they turn out, but economists seldom see this interest as affecting the organization of production. In creative activities, however, the creator (artist, performer, author) cares vitally about the originality displayed, the technical prowess demonstrated, the resolution and harmony achieved in the creative act. While these concerns with artistic achievement bear some relation to consumers' ultimate reception of the product, the relationship need not be close. The musician may value the achievement of some finesse of execution that will elude the typical concertgoer, although it *will* be noticed by fellow music professionals. Hence, the artist may divert effort from aspects of the task that consumers will notice (thus affecting their willingness to pay) to those they will neither notice nor value. Throughout this book we distinguish sharply between creative and humdrum inputs. Wherever they work, humdrum inputs demand a wage at least equal to what they earn in the outside market for inputs of their type. They do not care who employs them or what task (within their competence) they are asked to undertake. They are just in it for the money.

The problem of coupling creative effort with humdrum commerce goes still deeper. The view of creative inspiration inherited from romanticism holds that the artist creates out of inner necessity. Imagination and passion carry their own warrant and should not compromise with reason and established practice. Successful imitation of a master, once considered a worthy achievement, becomes an act of cowardice and sloth. Art claims a superior reality that separates the artist from the craftsman.[6] Asked to cooperate with humdrum partners in some production process, the artist is disposed to forswear compromise and to resist making commitments about future acts of artistic creation or accepting limitations on them. The rub is that resources are scarce, and compromise is hence often unavoidable. Rejecting it on principle distracts one's mind from making the best deal available.

The artist's tastes bear not only on how the creative task is performed, but also on how much effort is allocated to creative work. The artist typically has the alternative of a day job, and indeed is likely to possess valuable skills that could command high pay. A taste for creative work increases the amount of effort supplied by diverting it from humdrum tasks: the "starving artist" syndrome. The prevalence and strength of tastes that affect the qualities and quantity of creative effort we call the *art for art's sake* property.

This property implies that artists turn out more creative product than if they valued only the incomes they receive, and on average earn lower pecuniary incomes than their general ability, skill, and education would otherwise warrant. Less obviously, when the worker cares deeply about the traits of the product, the problem of organizing its production is fundamentally changed. The entrepreneur who organizes purely humdrum production faces this problem: Can I recruit inputs needed to turn out a given product at a cost less than what buyers will pay for it? In creative activities the good news for the entrepreneur is that creative inputs come cheaply. The bad news is that the traits of the product and the terms of employment of the creative inputs must be negotiated at the same time, and with persons unwilling and perhaps unable to precommit their creative choices. Artists find it difficult after the event to explain their aesthetic choices, let alone stipulate them in advance.[7]

The fact that the artist works outward to realize and reify an inner vision partly explains why *nobody knows*. The artist does not know and cannot pre-test whether her creative vision will prove equally compelling to others. Still worse, she cannot tell whether her conception has been successfully extracted from her inner vision and turned into an external creative product. The quality of the vision and the effectiveness of its realization are both up for grabs.

Some Creative Products Require Diverse Skills

Some creative outputs need only a single creative worker: the artist who paints a canvas. Many, however, require diverse skilled and specialized workers, each bringing personal tastes with regard to the quality or configuration of the product. A cinema film results from the efforts of many different artists, each with different skills and aesthetic values and thus with potentially conflicting priorities and preferences that are pressed upon the director who coordinates their efforts. The diverse tastes and preferences obviously complicate the deal for organizing the activity, as implied by the *art for art's sake* property. Formal contracts are largely infeasible, and we find in complex creative activities that conflicting preferences of collaborating artists often get resolved by the rank-order mechanism of "muscle."

A further vital complication results, however, if all of these inputs must perform at or above some level of proficiency and conformance for a viable product to result. The creative activity then involves what economists call a multiplicative production function. A production function is simply a recipe for combining specified inputs to obtain an output. We usually suppose that inputs are substitutable: you can produce a gadget with two units of labor and one of capital, or one of labor and two of capital; perhaps four units of labor and no capital will do the job. In a multiplicative production relationship, however, every input must be present and do its job—or at least perform at or above some threshold level of proficiency—if any commercially valuable output is to result. A large number multiplied by zero is still zero. This is what Michael Kremer called the O-rings theory of production.[8] Here we call it the *motley crew* property. It has a number of implications about selecting the team of inputs for a given creative product and sustaining all team members' cooperation while production is under way.

Differentiated Products

When a creative product goes to consumers for their assessment, they typically value it in comparison to similar creative products. Seeing a movie and reading a book are alternative ways to spend the evening. More important for the organization of creative activities, one movie gets chosen among all those that are playing (or on rental at the video store). No two are identical, but they can and do differ in two ways that themselves have diverse consequences. Once they have experienced both, buyers may agree that product A is better than product B, what an economist calls vertically differentiated. If A and B are sold at the same price, nobody will buy product B. Cultural outputs also can differ in their traits, moods, styles, whatever, in ways independent of buyers' overall judgments about their quality levels. Two songs, two paintings, two "action" movies may be quite similar in the character and quality that consumers see in them, but they are not identical. In economic terms they are horizontally differentiated. When horizontally differentiated products are sold at the same price, some people will prefer one, some another. Creative products generally exhibit some mixture of vertical and horizontal differentiation. Most creative products can differ from one another in many ways: paintings, for example, may vary in size, color, type of imagery, skill of draftsmanship. The more dimensions, the more likely it is that differentiation is horizontal: everyone might agree that the leading actor's performance was better in film B than in A, but some people like A better for other reasons.

This is the *infinite variety* property. We use it to invoke either the universe of possibilities from which the artist chooses, or the array of actual creative products from which consumers or intermediaries choose. The paintings that could be painted are infinite. The canvases that have been painted are very numerous, and many pairs of them can be found that most people would regard as quite similar in style and about equal in merit. That is, they are differentiated, but not much differentiated. The *infinite variety* property has many implications for organizing creative activities. For instance, when many examples of a creative product are available for consumption, most consumers may be nearly indifferent, yet somebody must choose which Scarlatti sonata to play, or which low-budget slasher film to show. The choice may no longer matter to Domenico Scarlatti, but it matters a lot to holders of copyrights in slasher films.

While creative possibilities are always abundant, creative realizations are sometimes not. Songs are cheap to compose, but productions of Wagner's *Ring* cycle are very costly (relative to opera lovers' bankrolls) and hence few. When the fixed (and sunk) costs soar to a level approaching consumers' combined willingness to pay, a different organizational problem arises.[9] Possibly no ticket price that the impresario can charge will cover the *Ring*'s costs, even though music lovers' total willingness to pay will suffice (because what some pay for tickets is less than their valuation of the experience). This problem accounts for the deficits bemoaned in the nation's opera houses and concert halls. It explains the nonprofit donor-supported organizations that arise to manage and finance these activities (addressed in Part IV).

Vertically Differentiated Skills

Cultural products differ unpredictably in the quality levels that consumers see in them. The artists who supply individual creative inputs also differ in skill, originality, and/or proficiency, though less unpredictably. These talent differences are observed when the skilled agent performs in turning out the creative product, when the finished product goes on display, or both. One artist's skill may be apparent to peers trained to supply the same creative input, to persons specialized in the coordination of this and other creative inputs, and perhaps to others qualified as teachers, critics, and the like. Artists may raise their skills by training and/or practice, but nonetheless trained and mature creative agents settle on different plateaus of proficiency. That artists (however proficient) can have good days and bad days does not undercut this ranking process, although it does wrap some uncertainty around it. For example, Hollywood's screenwriters, directors, and producers will largely agree at any one time on who are the "A list" and the "B list" screenwriters. In the terminology of economics, these creative inputs are themselves vertically differentiated. This is the *A list/B list* property.

Quality-differentiated inputs raise a number of questions about the organization of creative activities. Why do the B-list inputs get used at all? Can a film producer successfully economize with a B-list composer after paying a star's ransom for an A-list screenwriter? To what extent do consumers make their own A lists and B lists, and are these the same as the artists' and producers'? One may also wonder why the ranking of talents absorbs so much of the small change of conversation in many creative circles. Must we invoke a human propensity to establish pecking orders, or is there a clear economic explanation? A potential B-list artist with a good pedigree has something to lose from refining the ranking. Howard Becker argued that the ranking of artists and their work is intrinsic to the problem-solving process that underlies all forms of creativity.[10]

One reason why rank matters is the money at stake. The relevant economic concept is the differential rent—the extra total amount that people will pay to see a movie with an A-list star over the same film with a B-list star.[11] That differential rent limits the maximum pay that the A-list star can demand. To ask less is to leave money on the table. The rent concept also explains why the B-list artist might find it difficult to sell her services at any price. No matter how cheaply she works, the resulting film's revenue might not cover its other costs. Or, given *infinite variety,* she may face long waits between films in which her services can be a cost-effective substitute for an A-list artist.

Time Is of the Essence

The performing arts and creative activities involving complex teams—the *motley crew* property—obviously require close temporal coordination of their activities. The concert must be announced and prepared to take place at a particular time. The cinema film is efficiently shot in a certain sequence over a few weeks, during which all creative inputs must be available when needed. Although they might expect actors' performances to suffer, directors usually shoot scenes of a film out of sequence in order to group together those involving particular sets, locations, or actors. This problem of coordination in time flags the fact that the selection of a creative input depends not just on its qualities but also on when it is available. A less competent performer who is free at the right time might get the nod. Along with the *motley crew* property, temporal coordination implies a hold-up problem: an indispensable input demanding better terms on the threat of withholding its services at the last moment.

The problem of temporal coordination interacts with the conventional effect of time's passage on the value of a project. An investment that costs $100 and will bring revenue of $200 tomorrow is of course more profitable than one that will bring $200 in ten years. When a motion picture with a $100 million budget is first being organized, its expected profitability need not suffer much if the start is postponed. No substantial costs have yet been incurred, and besides, the movie might flop. But with the project under way and $95 million already spent, any delay that postpones the influx of revenue is very costly. That reliance of the economic profitability of creative activities on close temporal coordination of production and the prompt realization of revenues I call the *time flies* property.

Durable Products and Durable Rents

Many creative products are durable: not the symphony performance itself, which dies with the last reverberation in the hall, but the symphony's published score, and its performance recorded by a particular orchestra and conductor. Long after its composition, orchestra managers may be willing to pay royalties to perform the score, or music lovers to pay a royalty-inclusive price for the classic recording. The legal duration of the copyright determines how long the original creator or performers can collect these royalties, which are rents to the creator.[12] This durability is the *ars longa* property.

That some of these streams of rent arrive as numerous small "lumps" is important for organizing creative activities. When a recorded song is played by a radio station, on a jukebox, or by a background-music service in a public space, not many people hear it, and each may value the experience at most in pennies. Yet those pennies may add up to "real money"—that is, an amount worth pursuing if collection costs permit. The efficient collection of numerous small-value rents poses an organizational problem for owners of copyrights. It also creates a problem of contracting with the creative inputs when the durable creative product is first produced: shares in expected future rents must be defined and bargained over, and some agent assigned the responsibility for collecting and distributing them.

The other group of issues raised by the *ars longa* property concerns the warehousing and retrieval of creative durables. Some repose in public or nonprofit organizations—museums and libraries. Others, such as cinema films or master tapes of music recordings, remain in the hands of their creators or those firms' commercial successors. The Metropolitan Museum holds a vast inventory of Old Master paintings; the Wildenstein Gallery's inventory is much smaller though still impressive. How tasks are divided between them is an economic issue.

Notice that the preceding seven properties make no distinction between what Herbert J. Gans called "popular culture" and "high culture."[13] That distinction is treasured in the realm of high culture, exemplified by Clement Greenberg's famous essay on "Avant-Garde and Kitsch."[14] Serious producers of high culture engage in a cutting-edge process of problem solving and experimentation in which form transcends and dissolves content, and the consumer's direct, subjective response matters for little or naught relative to her appreciation of the creative product's formal relation to the aesthetic frontiers of yesteryear. Kitsch is the easy-to-like mature products descended from previous creative innovations, enjoyed by consumers who have made no intellectual investment to engage with the frontiers of creative advance. What stands unclear in Greenberg's distinction is the mapping of avant-garde and kitsch to economic and social realms of high culture and popular culture. Is all popular culture kitsch? Or does each line of cultural products—novels, popular songs, cinema films—have its own ecology of avant-garde and kitsch products and purveyors? Gans, a sociologist, argued for the latter position. The social processes and organizational structures surrounding high and low forms of culture do not fundamentally differ. The sophistication and self-awareness of avant-garde artists, their number relative to producers of routine creative goods, and the distribution of consumers' interests between experimental products and the equivalent of "easy listening" may vary from one creative realm to the next, but all of these elements appear in each realm. If this complex ecology does prevail in each creative activity, it should certainly imprint itself on the organization of firms and contracts, so it is a working hypothesis for this study.

Plan of the Book

This book addresses the play of these properties of creative industries as factors explaining the structures of organizations, deals, and contracts found therein. The empirical focus is on the here and now, but some telling evidence arrives from distant shores and long-ago times. The focus jumps freely from one creative activity to another, exploiting the fact that we all have a working sense of how movies are made and exhibited, books published, concerts organized, and the like. Each creative sector makes its appearance where its special features stand out most sharply for displaying some pattern, or to provide contrast and comparison.

Part I uses simple creative goods (one artist's product) to explore the economic situations of the artist striving for recognition and the gatekeeper who might select her work for development and promotion. Their relationship exposes the many difficulties of contracting on creative activities. Part II switches to complex creative goods—motion pictures, plays—that require teams of artists with diverse talents. They are assembled through contracts that try to harmonize their interests in the face of the constraint that *nobody knows*. Part III turns to consumers of creative goods and the certifiers on whom they rely for advice. Consumption decisions about creative goods share some distinctive properties. The consumer's benefit increases with accumulated experience, and consumption choices are made in a social context. Part IV addresses markets in which *infinite variety* fails, and the supplier of a single creative good is hard-pressed to cover costs. Nonprofit organizations play a major role in resolving the problem. Part V focuses on *ars longa*, the survival of creative goods or their templates to pursue rents over time and through space.

The Theory of Contracts

Most of the economic tools and terms used in this book are quite simple and presume previous exposure to the subject only at the level of the introductory course. Some mildly technical points are buried in notes so the squeamish can pass over them without courting confusion. One group of issues important for this book, however, lies in a relatively new subfield of economics known as contract theory. Much of this book is about why contracts and deals are structured the way they are, and so simple contract theory plays a considerable role. Since this subject has not yet percolated down to the introductory texts, this section provides a rudimentary account of the field's key insights.[15]

A contract is the agreement that governs the conduct of any economic transaction, defining what each party brings into (you supply the lettuce, I bring 89 cents) and takes from (I get the lettuce, you keep the money) the transaction. The problem gets interesting as the exchange grows more complex, perhaps with numerous parties taking actions and receiving rewards at different times, and with the actions and rewards depending on developments that occur after the contract is signed. The decisions and actions controlled by a contract proliferate rapidly as the number of parties to it increases; the problem is simpler for artist and art dealer than it is for the producer assembling a motion picture. Contracts also get more complex when the actions they govern occur over a long period of time, during which more new developments can intrude; the motion picture will be finished in a year, while the artist and dealer might hope to collaborate for the artist's whole career.

Parties enter into a contract, each hoping to get maximum benefit from it. More benefit to one seems to mean less benefit for the other, and indeed the division of benefits between contracting parties ultimately depends on their bargaining power and cannot otherwise be explained. Sometimes bargaining power is a trivial factor, as in the lettuce purchase: many grocers sell lettuce, and many households buy it, so the going price of 89 cents is the only one agreeable to both parties. Contract terms are not so tightly determined, however, when at least some parties lack close alternatives and enjoy an expected net benefit to divide among them. A fundamental principle, then, is that they should mutually agree to arrange their individual tasks and contributions so as to generate maximum value from the project as a whole, then bargain over the division of the net benefit. If defining a participant's contribution and setting its benefit share get confounded, the project will generally yield less than maximum value to all participants.

When the venture governed by a contract has an intrinsically uncertain outcome, or an outcome depending on uncertain future events, the parties face a formidable problem in writing a *complete contract* that pins down every action that each will take and the reward received. These things must be specified for every possible "state of nature"—that is, every set of circumstances that might emerge over the venture's duration. We can imagine and often prepare for many contingencies that will affect a contract's outcome. Still, nothing resembling a complete contract ever emerges in practice. Nature is always springing surprises that we failed to anticipate. Even "states" that we can imagine often defy formal description in a contract. Moreover, we have limited patience and powers of concentration for reaching a complete and mutually satisfactory contract—*bounded rationality*, in the language of contract theory. Once the ink is dry, problems of incompleteness likely emerge. The parties can fall into haggling over their response to some unanticipated state of nature, each hoping to slant the response to its own benefit. Ensuring that one's partners honor their commitments entails monitoring costs. All contracts that emerge in practice hence are highly incomplete. Still, they often work quite well for us, thanks to devices that attain much of a complete contract's objective without all of its apparatus.

A good alternative to the elusive complete contract is the *incentive contract*. Rather than specify a party's exact contribution (say, hours worked at some task), the contract can link the party's reward to the value it adds. This is not easy, for two reasons. First, each party's cost of taking part in a project is the effort or other input that is supplied. This cost often is not directly observed by the project's manager or other participants, and so cannot serve as the base for the party's reward. That payoff must turn on the project's overall value, or the output that results. The observed total payoff depends on each party's efforts, but also on other unforeseen and unobservable random factors. The party paid on the basis of the project's outcome has an incentive to work hard, but also gets stuck with the risk that its earnest effort appears, because of some random misfortune, to create little value. To absorb this hazard willingly, a risk-averse participant must be offered higher expected pay at the outset. This premium for risk-bearing provides a reason for weakening the incentive compensation. The weaker the incentive, however, the less the party's input of effort. Parties to a contract seek out some best compromise between strengthening incentives and keeping risk premia down, but the problem still makes the incentive contract underperform a hypothetical complete contract. Contracts in the creative industries encounter this problem, although it is mitigated by the fact that creative participants often behave as if they were risk loving rather than risk averse.

In creative industries, complex projects require the collaboration of several parties, each providing different but complementary inputs or resources. Such joint ventures have their own problems of effective incentive contracting—the *motley crew* problem. The project's net benefit or surplus is the fruit of these complementary inputs. Each might be necessary for the project to create any value, which makes it impossible to identify and reward the contribution of each one individually. Subtract one input, and there is no project: each participant "makes" the whole project. In the optimal incentive contract, each party's reward needs to be tied to what it contributes to the combined value created by the project, to induce it to exert the best effort for the project overall. When shares of the project's benefit are divided among the participants, however, the incentive for each is generally too weak: if I get the whole benefit from the project, I exert effort to the point where the last dollar's worth of effort I contribute brings in just a dollar of gross revenue; if I get only a 50 percent share, I quit short of that effort level.[16] Most contracts that we find in the creative industries have strong though incomplete incentive provisions. The contracts are commonly simple, and they evade a complete contract's need to describe each input or action ex ante and monitor it ex post. They accommodate pervasive uncertainty about the prospective buyers' valuation of the project's output, which mocks the idea of enumerating future states of nature.

Simple incentive contracts also benefit from heavy reliance on commonplace but effective enforcement mechanisms. Enforcement indeed is conceptually difficult in incomplete contracts. Not only do parties tend to slack on their contributions in the absence of monitoring or strong incentives; they also may try to hold up their partners in the midst of the project, refusing to supply their input (necessary for any valuable output to emerge) unless dealt a larger share of the benefit pie. People writing contracts anticipate hold-ups, of course, but without a good enforcement mechanism they can only avoid them at a cost. For example, they might forgo project technologies involving sunk and specific inputs—exactly the venture possibilities that make complex contracts attractive. What saves the day is the force of *reputation*. Suppose that we belong to a community of creative workers whose members regularly enter into contract-governed projects that are expected to be profitable but are subject to potential hold-ups. Suppose that some of us (not parties to a given contract) can observe when party Z attempts a hold-up, that we can costlessly pass on this news to all our fellows, and that nobody ever forgets Z's transgression.[17] Z will be excluded from all future deals. Any potential Z, knowing that this fate awaits, will face future losses that will more than offset the gains reaped by one successful hold-up.

Many complex creative deals occur in communities that are very efficient at maintaining and adjusting reputations for contract fealty. This efficiency in turn reduces the costs associated with writing and enforcing contracts, because it makes feasible highly incomplete contracts that are renegotiated on a "good faith" basis when unanticipated contingencies turn up. The theory of contracts employs the notion of an *implicit contract* that involves no written terms at all, only an informal understanding that the project will be governed by practices that are common knowledge in the community. Related to it is the concept of a *relational contract,* in which the enforcement mechanism of reputation does not even depend (explicitly) on community-wide reputations. Suppose that Z and Y have complementary endowments of skills or assets that can support a series of expected profitable projects. No other parties fit together with Z or Y so well as the two do with each other, or a comparable fit can be achieved only after the parties incur *switching costs.* Those switching costs create room for a hold-up in any particular Z–Y deal, because any party will pay the switching cost in order to avoid it. One party's hold-up, however, will likely induce the partner to incur those switching costs, rather than risk still more hold-ups, which would deprive the transgressor of a future series of expected profitable cooperations. The transgressor's reputation for good behavior with its natural partner may suffice to sustain cooperation in a series of profitable projects, even if the surrounding economic community cannot observe or costlessly verify the behavior of Z and Y under their deals. Such relational contracts are said to create value because they let the partners commit (that is, sink irrevocably) resources into *transaction-specific assets* that hold their full value only when used in Z–Y projects.

Contract theory emphasizes problems that arise from asymmetrical positions of the parties, most notably *asymmetrical information,* leading to the "lemons" problem. If one party (the current owner of a used car) has better information about its quality than does the prospective buyer, the buyer naturally suspects that the seller will overclaim that quality or fail to mention known defects. Two sorts of contract failure can ensue. The unwary buyer who has undervalued the seller's exploitation of information asymmetry can wind up owning a lemon, or the suspicious buyer can forgo the purchase of what is in fact a good used car. Remedies to the lemons problem exist in guarantees and independent appraisers (as well as reputations, if the seller deals regularly), but the problem seldom goes away. In fact asymmetrical information plays little role in creative industries' contracts, exactly because of the property that *nobody knows* the value of a project until most or all resources have already been committed to it. Rather than asymmetrical information, there is symmetrical ignorance.

Another problem that does pervasively affect creative industries' contracts, however, is that of efficiently allocating *decision rights* under an ongoing contract. When a contract is left incomplete, the parties must agree on how to decide their common course of action, after some unanticipated development occurs or an uncertain outcome is resolved. Given whatever deal they initially struck to share the project's benefits, they will commonly have conflicting preferences about how to revise or fill out the terms of their deal. At this point, it may matter greatly who is better positioned to observe, diagnose, and act on the resolved outcome. Maximizing the value of the venture calls for assigning the right to decide on the responsive adjustment of the project to the party better suited to act (Z). Giving Z the decision right at some interim stage, however, poses for Y the problem that Z's decision will be bent toward maximizing value for Z and not necessarily for Y and Z together. Y can preserve an acceptable contract, however, by demanding compensation up front for Z's expected opportunistic behavior in making such interim decisions.

This problem of allocating decision rights turns out to be pervasively important in the creative industries, because complex creative projects regularly involve sequences of actions, each one a sunk and irrevocable cost for the party incurring it. The writer prepares the movie's screenplay; the producer mobilizes the actors and other inputs to make the film; the editor edits it and the composer prepares the soundtrack music; the studio plans the film's advertising and distribution. At each stage one party makes a decision about sinking more resources into the project, while the previous contributors' investments are wholly sunk. Decision rights efficiently lie with the party about to contribute still-fungible resources. That is because the project should go ahead if and only if its currently expected value exceeds the still-avoidable cost of these fungible resources (even if not the costs previously incurred). This allocation of decision rights is achieved by an *option contract*. Party Y, in a position to decide the next move, negotiates a contract with predecessor X that specifies how X will be rewarded if Y decides to go ahead with the project. Y also purchases from X the opportunity for a specific time interval in which to investigate the current omens and resolve whether and how to proceed with the project. Once Y exercises its option to purchase and sinks its own input into the project, decision rights are handed on to Z, who takes an option to consider the next step.

This book relies on contract theory, but also on the field of industrial organization, which seeks to explain the sizes, activity patterns, and numbers of firms that we find competing in particular markets. For this task contract theory and industrial organization come together. From the viewpoint of contract theory the firm can be regarded as a *nexus of contracts*—between the owning shareholders and the chief executive, the chief executive and the vice presidents, and on down to the factory manager and the workers. Contracts in force within the firm may not differ fundamentally from those between independent parties. Still, there is a difference between the firm's hiring workers on a presumed long-term basis and the workers coming together for circumscribed projects. Long-term employees get their marching orders from a supervisor each day, under a flexible continuing contractual arrangement and usually without any fresh or recurring contract costs. Every project outside the firm involves a separate contract, although it may benefit from relational practice. Which mode of organization works best varies from situation to situation; the motion picture industry demonstrates this dramatically in the sharp transition that occurred in the 1950s from one mode to the other (see Chapter 5).

Drawing on contract theory's contribution, the field of industrial organization brings its own techniques to explaining why the production of creative goods is organized as it is. Why are some markets served by a single seller (for example, a city's major symphony orchestra), others by many (commercial art galleries in New York)? The answer is that each market's technology and activity patterns dictate that participating firms incur some fixed cost, or produce subject to some economies of scale. Relative to the amount of market demand that the firm faces (and the aggressiveness with which the firm competes with its rivals), these fixed costs determine the maximum number of competitors that can "fit" into the market and still earn normal profits. The number may be shriveled further in some industries by first-mover advantages that incumbents enjoy simply from having already arrived. To explain why an industry contains only a few firms, we look for these scale and first-mover factors. The high concentration of cinema film studios, for example, turns out to be due to the fixed cost of maintaining an apparatus for distributing and promoting films. Movie production takes place as one-shot deals on a much smaller scale.

The number of firms occupying a market is important for industrial organization, because it strongly influences how competitive and efficient they are, but it is not the only important question about how the marketplace is organized. Firms in a market, like the products they offer, are rarely homogeneous. Directly competing firms fall into groups differing in the product varieties that they turn out or the way they organize those goods' production. In the creative industries these diverse groups of market competitors turn out to reflect the basic properties of creative goods. For example, the inner and individualistic aspect of creative production mixes badly with the orderly, rule-driven routines of the large, bureaucratic firm. Creative industries tend to be organized so that the most delicate dealings with artists concentrate in small firms specialized to this task, while other firms (usually much larger ones) undertake to combine creative work with large teams of humdrum inputs.

Another question about industrial organization often carries the tag "firm versus market": explaining why some transactions take place at arm's length between independent parties while others get "internalized" within the firm. The question most commonly takes two specific forms. Why are firms sometimes vertically integrated, supplying their inputs internally and/or distributing their product through their own sales organizations, while elsewhere these transactions take place at arm's length? Why does the firm operate in several different product markets, perhaps using some inputs or facilities in common, when those markets could each be served by independent, single-market firms? The answers to these questions depend heavily on the theory of contracts, already outlined. Where a firm and its major supplier can build up a relational long-term contract that permits efficient transaction-specific investments, they may get along perfectly well as independent organizations. Where such contractual dealings are soured by opportunism, haggling, and monitoring costs, vertical integration comes to the rescue. These choices of organization are discrete. Contracting problems certainly exist within the integrated firm as well, but it has a trump card in the flexible, long-term employment contract, which lets it retain an experienced team of inputs and deploy them flexibly in light of the day's fresh news. Hence, especially where different organizational arrangements are about equally effective, we may find quite different organizational forms coexisting, or observe dramatic shifts from one to another.

I

Supplying Simple Creative Goods

The chapters of Part I address creative activities in their simplest setting, where one artist deals with a simple firm that promotes and distributes her creative work. It starts with artists' training, the values and objectives that it instills, and the subsequent apprenticeship phase (Chapter 1). It then follows the aspiring, apprentice artist to her encounters with "gatekeepers" who decide whether the prospective value of her creative output warrants the cost of humdrum inputs needed to place it before final buyers. Even the simplest setting—the visual artist and the art dealer—exposes the litany of woes that betide contracts with artists in creative activities (Chapter 2). That chapter also introduces the problem of explaining the ecology of gatekeeper firms: how many art galleries are in operation, where they locate, and exactly what they do. A distinction appears in art galleries—and subsequently in other industries that distribute artists' creations—between those specialized in selecting and developing artists' work and those primarily concerned with promoting it to a wide public.

Chapter 3 explores the deal between artist and gatekeeper in three other realms—publishing books, recording popular music, and organizing concerts. A common pattern appears in the structure of contracts. The gatekeeper offers an option contract that assigns to himself the right to decide whether to commit additional resources to the project. The artist is compensated by a promise of royalties, anticipated by an advance, if the gatekeeper picks up the option. The royalty rate splits the profit between artist and gatekeeper, while the advance induces the gatekeeper to expend appropriate effort on the project. Chapter 3 also addresses the role of the agent as intermediary between artist and gatekeeper. The agent serves an obvious function of bargaining agent for the artist and a less obvious one of making the gatekeeping process work more efficiently.

The gatekeeping function denies many willing artists the opportunity for commercial exposure of their work. This fact predicts a highly skewed distribution of artists' incomes, abetted by another process, the superstar effect. The data agree well with these predictions (Chapter 4).

1

Artists as Apprentices

In the visual and performing arts, the number of students graduated each year from qualified programs of specialized study greatly exceeds the number who can become income-earning professionals. Although starving artists are numerous, starved artists are not. Many of them eventually settle for some way other than their artistic calling to keep bread on the table. Those who persevere continue to hone their skills and attempt to establish themselves as capable and recognized professionals and (with that) earn enough to keep them in the game.

Each creative realm has its set of intermediaries who select artists. The intermediaries' choices serve their own mixtures of motives. Dedication to advancing the arts is often present, but profit is usually sought, and the costs of humdrum inputs must be covered. Sociologists call these intermediaries "gatekeepers," which is apt given that the market for aspiring artists does not clear at a positive price: many are excluded at the gate, although they would gladly sign the contract that the gatekeeper offers to those who pass. The following three chapters will develop several economic features of the interaction of artists and gatekeepers: what motivates gatekeepers and thereby determines which artists are chosen; why the gatekeeper's contract takes the form that it does; and what consequences arise from the excess supply of would-be artists.

This chapter starts with the salient features of young artists' training. School training defines or reinforces the budding artist's standards and personal goals, setting attitudes that color the artist's subsequent dealings in the marketplace. It imparts skills through specialization and intense practice, thereby closing off other career lines and limiting the artist's alternatives to supplying creative inputs. It continuously filters talent and sets up the basis for *A list/B list* rankings. After formal full-time schooling ceases, artists enter an apprenticeship period of refining skills and competing for the attention of gatekeepers and others who can advance their careers. The apprentice's living and working styles set the scene for her dealings with gatekeepers and contribute to determining agglomeration and location patterns that are important for the organization of markets for creative goods.

Schooling and Artists' Tasks and Values

Visual Arts Students

Social scientists' studies of artists' schooling depict the idealized creative process held out to students and the values that they tend to adopt. A study of students at the School of the Art Institute of Chicago shows how the romantic ideal of the creative artist is embedded in the curriculum.[1] Students decide early in their school careers whether they will pursue the high arts, industrial or advertising art, or art education, and they gain competence only in their specialties. The commercial track does not supply a fallback for the unsuccessful fine artist. High-level creative achievement, here and in the visual arts generally, is associated with creative problem-solving: the original and talented artist is the one successful at spotting novel problems and solving them in fruitful and compelling ways. Thinking up creative ideas and the craft of making artistic objects have to some extent become separate specialties. The priority of creative problem-solving deters budding artists from servicing consumers who want decoration. Instead they ally themselves with the cultured tastes of those who know the tradition within which the artist works and can thus recognize the problem posed for solution, link it to its foundations, and identify related problem-solving efforts. This problem-solving process is both task and reward for the artist. Students asked why they make art invariably invoke "rewards not *from* the work but *in* the work, rewards derived not from the *product* but obtained in the *process* of production."[2] Concessions to commercial taste are discouraged, because they impugn the artist's seriousness about rigorous pursuit of the creative problem-solving process. Commercial art students, by contrast, expect to be handed their problems, and the solutions should respond to an employer's wishes.

This problem-solving paradigm closely resembles that in scientific inquiry and research: what new discovery will create the most perceived value, and what research strategy will realize it? In the visual arts, of course, the artist formulates problem and solution internally, in a way that is perhaps not really self-articulated. The problem is certainly not posed with scientific precision. The sophisticated onlooker has the task of interpretation, which involves working backward from the end result to the problem/resolution process that generated it. Viewers need not extract the same interpretation that the artist thinks she instilled into the work, nor need they agree on the importance of the problem or the fullness of the solution. Indeed, an important role of critics and dealers is devising such interpretations (with or without verbal assistance from the artist) and pressing them upon the general public (see Chapter 12). Thus, the quest for innovation proceeds similarly in the fine arts and in science, although innovations of the visual arts are subjective and meet with diverse valuations.

Comparisons of Chicago art students' performance on various tests and exercises confirm these impressions. They differ from students in other fields in being serious and introspective, socially reserved, relatively indifferent to accepted standards of behavior and morality, imaginative and unconventional in outlook, intensely subjective, and highly self-sufficient. A young person's conviction of calling to an artistic career often provokes conflicts with parents and apartness from peers, so that the conviction and the preoccupation with internal problems are all one package. Students on the fine-art track do not differ from other art students in performance on cognitive or perceptual tests, but they have high aesthetic and low economic values and (relative to art-education students) low social values. Teachers' subjective valuations duly reward students for asking novel questions. Overall, the results indicate, the artistic calling requires the rejection of goals widely valued in the culture and the embrace of "personally felt problems of an existential nature which the artist tries to confront on his own terms."[3]

The study followed Art Institute School students over time to compare professional success with their student records. In preparation for this, the fine-art students were asked to make drawings of self-selected objects under experimental conditions. These drawings were evaluated by both professional and lay-judge panels on technical quality and originality. The lay judges tended to equate overall aesthetic quality with technical quality, the professionals to equate it with originality—an ominous difference for young artists seeking to establish themselves in the commercial realm.[4] A group of students were scored on the extent of their success in the art world after five to six years. Indeed, success was positively correlated with problem-finding success revealed in the drawing experiment, as well as grades in studio courses and scores on tests measuring cognitive originality. Overall, success rides on the ability "to relate conscious tasks to deeply felt subconscious issues in novel ways."[5]

The Chicago study covered one art school in the 1970s, so generalizing it is hazardous. Its generality stands as a hypothesis, one consistent with casual evidence on art education at other places and times. It is also consistent with the subsequent evidence on artists' contractual dealings in the art market.

Music Students

Young artists are thus prepared to pursue careers more as a priestly calling than as a professional activity, and they are discouraged from compromise between external commitments and the inner necessity of artistic creation. Somewhat similar patterns appear in the training of young musicians, as shown in a study of a major eastern U.S. conservatory. A student musician's talent is judged on both proficiency and "musicality" or expressiveness. The core of instruction is one-on-one lessons with individual teachers in which the development of expressiveness is a key concern. Musicality is cultivated in the context of the solo performer, the star, the Heifetz or Rubenstein, the role that students idolize. Despite the central place of a student's musicality, its evaluation is highly subjective (proficiency is easier to judge), and musicians frequently disagree in their judgments of it. Teachers' qualifications for developing it are equally subjective, a fact reflected in the emphasis on whom the teacher studied with—a chain of apostolic succession leading ideally back to Orpheus. The student's soloist-oriented training culminates in the "degree recital." Students participating in this conservatory's orchestra were filled with dissatisfaction, partly from superficial and administrative problems festering at the time of the study but partly because the musical values that it cultivates are not those of individual expressiveness.[6]

Music students must pass successive gatekeepers who judge talent by increasingly stringent standards. The judgment is always based on performance given whatever training the student has already received, and talent is never deemed a pure "gift." Nonetheless, students and many who help them with their career judgments regard talent as God-given. The student readily adopts the attitude that talent demands as its price the budding musician's dedication to its full realization, and the conservatory reinforces the attitude of a priestly calling to cultivate an art rather than to prepare for a career.

A vital feature of the training regimens for visual artists and musicians is that they treat the highest career aspirations—dreams of being an artist of renowned originality, or a musician of the highest calibre—as the sole focus of training and attitudes. Lost from the calculus is the very low probability that any randomly selected "talented" student will indeed pass through successive gates and come even within sight of the avowed career goal.[7] In terms of its economic implications, the training-supported attitudes of artists are in effect highly risk-loving. This may be partly a matter of limited information: everybody knows about the big successes and the glory rained upon them, while the failures and disappointments—and the opportunity cost that they exact—are far less evident. Teachers reinforce this attitude for its motivational value; in the words of one voice teacher, "without the fantasy of being great you could not even begin."[8] Neither the student's motivation nor the teacher's employment prospects will benefit from harping on the student's low chances for big-time success. In the visual arts the process is further reinforced by the artist's thralldom to an inner truth, which devalues the relevance of others' opinions about the work.

Creativity and Craft

The tension between creativity and craft in artists' training runs through the whole modern history of the creative (distinguished from performance) arts. In Europe, guilds with a strong orientation toward craftsmanship and proficiency gave way to academies with official standing that elevated the creative element but retained a strong regimen of accepted practice. The modern art school and conservatory are nineteenth-century innovations that in their values reflect the romantic idea of an artistic calling, but enjoy humdrum economies of scale in the use of facilities and equipment. They also put the student in continuous contact with numerous peers, to facilitate mutual learning coupled with a subtle competition for rank and distinction that anticipates the overt competition ahead in the creative marketplace. University-based creative training blends in another element—giving the aspiring artist general training that provides backup for the highly risky investment in artistic training. Incidentally, it also provides a general audience for the arts resembling the nonspecialist audience that the artist will later face.

The conflict in artists' training anticipates the same conflict in artistic practice, which is most evident in fields such a ceramics and photography that attract practitioners with both fine-art and craft orientations. Craftspersons working in ceramics value virtuoso technical skills, accept the constraint of practical usefulness of the object, and place less weight on uniqueness and formal innovation. Fine-arts orientation points to the opposite values and attitudes. In the case of photography, news publications or advertising agencies impose their own exacting requirements on commercial assignments. Fine-art photographers generally show little interest in advanced technical facility and work without any baggage of externally imposed constraints.[9] Fine-art photography has gone through a number of paradigm shifts in which various elements of craft and creative objectives solidify and regroup.

The Apprentice Stage and the Selection Process

With full-time schooling completed, the aspiring young artist proceeds into an apprenticeship mode. In many lines of creative work this involves physically locating in some center close to other artists, prospective employers, and the writers, critics, and other impetus-givers in the field. Sometimes the agglomeration economies stem from the complex production process that requires coordination of many creative and humdrum inputs—Hollywood and the production of cinema and TV films. In other cases agglomeration arises in order to facilitate artists' training and development processes and the gatekeepers' filtering activities. The visual arts provide vivid evidence— Montmartre, Greenwich Village, SoHo. We consider the pursuit of the artistic career first, then return to the agglomeration process.

Getting One's Work Known

The young visual artist rents a loft as a workplace to prepare and store her work. It is not just a physical space but also an informal institution to accommodate the visits and parties that put the artist in touch with other artists and participants in the commercial art world. A body of work must be assembled and honed, and opportunities found to bring it to the art world's attention. But where should this loft be? This question can be put at two levels: why New York? and why SoHo, the East Village, or whatever is the current loft neighborhood? The logic of agglomeration comes clear from the nature of the apprentice's task and search procedure.

The apprentice artist's tasks are to build her body of work and the skills and sensitivity needed to produce it, and to get it known and accepted. Both tasks involve extensive interpersonal contacts. The artist spends time looking at the work of other artists—both established and apprentices. Artists apparently do not give each other much criticism; rather, each tests the cogency of the problems she addresses and the elegance of the solutions against those pursued by her peers. Equally important, a continuous dialogue takes place to establish what are the major issues and new ideas—about art philosophies and attitudes as well as techniques and materials. This is a key point to explain the clustering of young artists. Continuous and extensive contact with other young artists is not just for *la vie bohème*. One must see other artists' work— illustrations in contemporary-art magazines are not a good substitute. Still more important, one must be plugged into the latest ideas about what is valid and important, even before this dialogue is embodied in new works of art on view in the galleries and glossy magazines.[10]

A loft gives the apprentice contact with not only other artists but also, she hopes, collectors, writers, and dealers. Dealers dominate the intermediation between artist and collector, for reasons that will become apparent. Nonetheless, many serious collectors of contemporary art seek out direct contact with artists, for several reasons. They share the artist's own interest in new ideas and developments, and want to catch them at the source rather than to wait for dealers and writers to filter them. Insofar as collecting is a competitive activity, spotting the cutting-edge art puts the collector ahead in the scramble; furthermore, diligent search substitutes for large cash outlay in building a distinguished collection. The joys of discovering a hot new artist early are augmented by the joys of buying her work not only cheaply, but also from a stock not yet picked over. Critics and writers compete with others of their kind for success in trend-spotting, and thus have a similar reason to clamber through artists' lofts in quest of the new. However advantageous and necessary for the artist may be a relationship with a dealer, these direct contacts underscore the romantic notion of the artist as a visionary who pushes back the frontiers of consciousness.[11]

Also, art-making takes place today with hardly any settled conventions or defining traditions, or at least none that have lasted for more than a decade. Art world "groupies" are much more rudderless than in the past in terms of interpreting new art and deciding which artists have opened up promising avenues to creative success. When unmediated direct contact with new works of art yields less evidence than ever about the art world's ultimate judgment, the evidence from personal contact with the artist by default grows more important. The apprentice artist gains from personal qualities suited to engage this world of art enthusiasts. Andy Warhol, both early and late in his career, invested most of his evenings in circulating through gallery openings, cocktail parties, dinners, benefit galas, fashion shows, wherever he might be invited. Not particularly gregarious or articulate, he took along his to-be-famous young associates to absolve himself from the burden of being entertaining. Alice Goldfarb Marquis, remarking on the present-day role of the artist's persona, observed its dependence on modern information and entertainment media. Marcel Duchamp executed the strategy impeccably but drew little attention. Barnett Newman delivered thunderous pronouncements on righteous ways of making art, but these did not travel beyond the art insiders.[12] Successful art-world reputations have been built by self-promotion as the essence of creativity and by satirizing the idea that works of art should be fabricated to the preferred specifications of persons sampled randomly from the general public.[13]

Most of all, the artist seeks public exposure for her creations, ideally in a well-established gallery that will understand the work and promote it suitably. One avenue is to enter various juried exhibitions, which requires the preparation of slides and/or the shipment of works themselves. Another is to pursue various noncommercial spaces where work can be exhibited and sold. Sunday morning hangings on the park fence are left to the hobbyist painters. Cooperative galleries, however, are a helpful outlet; a group of artists share expenses and provide labor inputs, with the members picking newcomers for admission from a continually renewed list of applicants. Around 1980 Charles Simpson identified 14 of these in New York's SoHo art belt, 36 in other east coast cities.[14] These co-ops give exposure for the artist, but members lack the entrepreneurial ability of a capable dealer and the knowledge of what works of art likely will find customers.

Most desirable is to form a relationship with a commercial gallery. The artist acquaints herself with the styles of art exhibited by various likely galleries to learn which would have the most affinity for her own work. Artists recognize a vertical differentiation of galleries based on the quality as well as the style of the art that they offer. The apprentice artist might regard one-tenth of New York galleries with respect, and feel stylistic affinity to a smaller number of them.[15] The artist then makes the rounds, leaving slides or lugging her portfolio. The odds are heavily against her. Some contemporary art dealers do not routinely consider new artists at all. Those who are receptive may see as many as 50 artists a week, perhaps pursuing several of them further through studio visits. One dealer spoke of seeing a thousand artists' slides each year, visiting 50 studios, trying out five artists in group shows, and adding one of those to the gallery's regular stable.[16]

The dealer is concerned with what will sell, of course, but commonly uses two filters that matter greatly for the apprentice artist. First, dealers rely heavily on established artists (particularly those whom they regularly show) for suggestions about new artists to represent.[17] This pattern appears in other times and places, such as Raymonde Moulin's study of the French contemporary art market between 1945 and 1960 and Liah Greenfeld's report on Israel.[18] New York artists successful in the avant-garde movements of the late 1960s and 1970s attributed nearly all of the gatekeeping function to the evaluations that arise within the artist community; running one's slides around to galleries was felt to be next to useless.[19] The dealer's knowledge of immediate commercial prospects presumably excels that of most established artists, but the artist holds the advantage in detecting basic creativity and originality. In this sense the artist community forms its own *A list/B list* ranking, and the dialogue among artists over changes and new directions is itself a filtering mechanism of peer review. Second, dealers consider not just the artist's current achievement but also her fundamental resilience and seriousness. Dealers observe that many artists can generate work that will sustain one or two good gallery shows, but lack the potential for long-run development. According to dealer John Weber, "I'm not interested in artists who haven't paid their dues . . . A dealer must know that this person will go on being an artist for some time down the pike."[20] Another dealer observed that most artists have worked for at least a decade before attaining the craft and maturity to support a significant one-person exhibition. It is common for several dealers to be watching an artist's work as it crystalizes, raising the question of who ultimately commits first.[21] This long-haul investment component of the dealer-artist relationship is central to their problem of striking a deal, discussed in Chapter 2.

Apprentices' Economic Choices

The young artist faces certain cold realities of economic choice. The artist without a gallery is hard-pressed to make any net income (after materials and other expenses) from her art, yet the table must be graced with a certain amount of bread. A spouse's career or the support of a generous family may be the answer. Lacking these, she faces a trade-off between time spent making art and that spent generating income. Most persons who credibly aspire to artistic careers have skills and qualities that fit them for success in other occupations. A serious career pays better than casual jobs. Yet casual jobs can be taken for any desired amount of time, while the serious career leaves little time or energy for the artistic calling. Fine artists, both successful and aspiring, agree that they cannot take the obvious route of working at commercial art while building a fine-art career; the clash between serving external and inner needs is seen to preclude this seemingly natural solution. Besides, commercial art is a nine-to-five job.[22] Despite the low pay, routine but flexible jobs have considerable attraction, especially if they are art-related (museum guard, art shipper, framer). A common choice is to postpone the serious career well into middle-age for fear of lost focus on the artistic career, even if external recognition of artistic skill has been minimal.[23]

The same trade-off has a spatial dimension in the artist's decision to locate in the high-cost New York center. Among Chicago Art Institute School graduates, those with the most promise and early success were most likely to make this investment. The alternative of settling in a smaller art center or university portends a scene that the young artist might find slow and inbred, with the creative denizens either defensive or self-satisfied.[24] Secondary centers do have their artists' lofts and galleries, indeed with the important advantage of costs much lower than New York's. Some yield easier sources of income from one's own or one's spouse's jobs. A few St. Louis artists, for example, made major investments to establish a presence in New York, renting space and spending substantial time there. The New York gallery show finally landed by one artist was thought to have cost him $75,000. Serious St. Louis artists visit New York and are well aware of the advantages, costs, and risks of locating there.[25] The pull of the art center has a life-cycle element: once an artist either becomes successful or throws in the towel and shifts to another career, she has less interchange with other artists and is apt to relocate away from the center.[26]

The Logic of Art Centers

Opportunities for contact with other artists and their work, and for interchange of ideas about the process of defining and resolving creative problems, clearly attract most artists. Other centripetal forces are also at work and interact with these.

Creative Work and Centripetal Pull

Why New York or Paris should house a large dealer market for art (contemporary or other) has its own explanation. The economist's standard model of retailers' locational choices focuses on why they should disperse: to be the only seller convenient to nearby customers, and to avoid vigorous price competition with proximate dealers. This centrifugal force can be overridden, however, if two conditions hold. First, when customers choose their purchases by making the rounds of competing dealers, their shopping costs are minimized when the dealers cluster. Second, the more differentiated are the dealers' wares, the less does proximity foment price competition, offsetting that disadvantage of proximity. The art market certainly shares both properties. Because art purchases are major expenditures for most customers, the cost of travel to a distant center does not offset the advantage of access to numerous dealers upon arrival. Hence, important art centers may be few in number and spaced widely.[27]

Low-cost access to auxiliary services needed by artists and dealers is another centripetal force. In a large and active center, specialized auxiliaries find enough business to cover their fixed costs. Otherwise their functions must be performed by less specialized (and hence less proficient) agents. This force probably plays some part in art-market agglomeration, due not so much to the shippers and framers as to the writers and publications. The art market, compared to humdrum markets, surely suffers from high information costs: the works offered are unique and numerous, making the customer's search intrinsically costly *(infinite variety)*. Furthermore, the qualities of much contemporary art do not easily reveal themselves, supporting an interpretive role for writers (as well as dealers) to help potential buyers to match the works available to their tastes. (Critics and other certifiers will be discussed in Chapter 12.)

These factors suffice to explain the art center without any reference to the artists themselves. The artists are tied to it by the processes already discussed. Access to gallery shows provides much of their information network; one survey found that 40 to 60 percent of New York gallery-goers were either artists or art students.[28] The dealers similarly minimize their costs of selecting artists to represent when the artists cluster nearby.

Still more centripetal forces arise from the artist's particular needs for space. The loft should be big (given the large scale common in contemporary art) and cheap. Artists first drifted to New York's SoHo in the late 1950s when it was a fag-end manufacturing area of doll makers and waste-paper processors. Landlords found artists to be useful scavengers of upper floors in poorly maintained buildings that nobody else wanted. They would pay some rent and make their own repairs. The artist ghetto soon attracted dealers, often new entrants who had been staff members in uptown galleries. New contemporary galleries had space requirements similar to the artists' own (uptown spaces better served the secondary market in older art), plus the advantage of on-the-spot access to the latest creative innovations.[29] The gallery-hopping advantage of clustered dealers drew customers to the neighborhood. Also, *art for art's sake* closeness to the creative process gave utility, and some serious collectors were bent on seeking out the artists directly.

Art Centers' Built-in Turnover

The trendiness of SoHo and the surfeit of moneyed customers in turn attracted restaurants and other retailers, exposing an interesting instability in art agglomeration. Rents began to rise sharply, pricing out the artists. The galleries also began to disperse, because they were sensitive to the high rents and had lost the attraction of the artists' presence. The trendy boutiques and their customers remained, in a precarious locational balance. There is thus a certain self-destructing property in the spatial location of the market for contemporary art.

This process has repeated itself in New York several times. Starting around 1982, the East Village went through the cycle in less than a decade. The area was seriously run down and its previous low-income community disrupted by crime, which opened up low-rent space to artists. Lightly capitalized contemporary art galleries quickly followed. With the joys of *le premier cri* freshly recalled from SoHo, the arts and culture media immediately arrived at the scene. Shoppers and tourists followed, gentrification was set in motion, and the neighborhood businesses and cheap clubs that supported the artists' communication and interchange were squeezed out. At the end of the decade an art-market recession eliminated many of the galleries, the more successful ones moved out, and the artists sought their next vibrant slum, a largely empty district of factory buildings in Brooklyn known as Down Under the Manhattan Bridge Overpass (DUMBO). Art hangers-on are still catching up, but developers have noticed the area's splendid views of the Manhattan skyline. The process has been repeated in other cities—note Venice in the Los Angeles area and SoMa (south of Market Street) in San Francisco. Local-government developers in down-at-the-heels cities (Peekskill, New York; Providence, Rhode Island) have set out to attract artists as a catalyst for urban upgrading.[30]

Location among Cities

This spatial adjustment occurs between as well as within cities. The New York art center's strong centripetal forces are not those of a black hole. Limiting factors in New York City include high Manhattan rents, the economic choices of some serious artists to live in other places, and some art collectors' preference to deal with local galleries and artists. Indeed, as Stuart Plattner noticed, U.S. population census data suggest that the big centers' share of the U.S. artist population has been declining. Nonetheless, the forces centralizing exhibition spaces remain powerful: New York's art exhibition spaces are four times as numerous as those in Los Angeles, five times as numerous as Chicago's.[31] A large city is (other things equal) better suited for an art center than a small one, and both the number of artists and the number of exhibition spaces apparently increase more than proportionally with U.S. cities' populations.[32] In the 1960s it was estimated that two-thirds of America's better-known artists lived in New York, and that pattern has not obviously changed.[33]

Similarly interesting differences may appear in patterns of art centers over time. Certainly the importance assigned nowadays to creative originality in the visual arts, as against the development of craft, has worked its effect. In the 1960s Bernard Rosenberg and Norris Fliegel noticed a contrast between older artists who had patiently cultivated their skills and younger ones in quest of originality more than finesse in execution. One wins—or loses—more quickly in the new game, implying that the artist population of a high-voltage art center turns over more rapidly.[34]

Apprenticeship and Gatekeeping in Other Art Worlds

The contemporary-art community performs three economic functions: it helps artists to develop their skills at formulating and executing works of art, grades and ranks their contending talents, and matches them to galleries able to display and promote them. Each other line of creativity has its own "art world" (Howard S. Becker's felicitous phrase) that performs these functions. They share some properties with the visual arts. The number of candidate artists greatly exceeds the number who can earn as much as humdrum jobs would pay. A diffuse sorting and grading process works to produce the *A list/ B list* ranking. The gatekeepers base their selections not just on some ineffable kernel of talent but also on the artist's personal qualities, which are important for collaborating with other artistic and humdrum inputs and for developing her career as a promotional investment. The art worlds also show important contrasts. When the manuscripts of first novels compete for the publisher's acceptance, what matters is more the creative product at hand than the likelihood that a still-better second novel will follow. While the visual artist faces a thorny problem of contracting with her dealer, her skills at public performance and collaboration are only incidentally important; for the performing artist they matter much for the gatekeeper's decision.

Writers, Agents, and Publishers

In Virginia Woolf's famous formulation, the writer needs only a room of one's own and an income of £500 a year. Some of the advantages of agglomeration to visual artists, however, also accrue to aspiring writers. New York has long served as a writers' mecca for its high density of publishing houses, periodicals, and other outlets for the written word. For the aspiring writer their proximity matters less for shortening the trip to the gatekeeper's barrier than for offering a variety of fruitful day jobs. These jobs afford some practice in writing skills and yield contacts that help identify the most promising gate or even cajole a gatekeeper. Incidental evidence comes from Richard Fine's study of 40 established east coast writers who worked in Hollywood during the 1930s. Only six of them were native New Yorkers, but 29 resettled in New York some time before their Hollywood sojourn. Thirty worked on the staffs of New York magazines and newspapers, but only one continued this work once a substantial royalty income began to flow. The extensive social life accessible to the New York writer obviously had its professional benefits in the interchange of information and opinion. Traditional publishers fancied the role of presiding over literary salons, which enhanced the social benefits to writers of living nearby. Once some success was gained, the New York writer benefited from a circle that accorded respect and even adulation for the writer and inviolate status to the written word. In Richard Fine's words, "friendships, marriages, writing collaborations, grudges, and feuds abounded among and between writers."[35] The only recent study of writers' agglomeration (in Cologne, Germany) confirms this pattern. The leading writers who live there know each other but do not interact closely. In an *A list/B list* pattern, they are known to writers of less renown or who are earlier in their careers, and master-disciple relationships exist. There is no coherent elite group, and little interchange occurs among the B-list writers.[36]

In Malcolm Bradbury's longer perspective, the writing profession has shown only sporadic tendencies to agglomeration.[37] Clustering means "big city" and high living costs, a disadvantage to those who for art's sake would minimize the hours denied to the muse by humdrum work. Without specific creative advantages, the call of cheap living is strong, and literary bohemias have attracted mainly those with independent incomes. The urban bohemias, Bradbury thinks, have nurtured waves of success, both in popular writing and in the coteries of the literary magazine and the small press, but these have been transient. While journalism and teaching offer employments congenial to free-lance writing, they have also become more professionalized, making casual dips into gainful employment harder and relatively less remunerative. His investigation of careers of earlier English authors suggests that a high proportion of them did succeed in making literature their sole profession by early middle age, but this depended on their willingness to undertake many types of writing.[38]

Popular Musicians, Managers, and Record Companies

The training of modern-day popular musicians runs to the informal; they learn to imitate the sounds that they hear on favorite recordings. High-school students in large numbers "fool around" in garage bands, most of them quitting short of any serious run at a career. The sorting and grading function begins only when the musician or group seeks paying engagements (gigs). For individual free-lance musicians, the *A list/B list* distinction begins in earnest as musicians listen to each other and interact in paid sessions and jamming on the side. The rankings that result depend mainly on playing skill, but also adaptability, versatility, and the interpersonal skills that are valuable for seizing the unpredictable and fluid opportunities open to these musicians. Showing up on time, knowing all the conventions that allow popular musicians to perform in groups with little or no rehearsal, and behaving cooperatively are all necessary to sustain a good reputation. A musician unable to take up an offered gig may recommend an alternate, but thereby puts her reputation on the line if the alternate falls short. A lot of contacts take place outside the context of paid performance (such as at auditions and openings), where mutually beneficial information is shared and skills are tested and honed.[39] Successful professional free-lancers have incentives for watching new talent and integrating it selectively into the market; this process is described in Chapter 7.

Groups serious enough to acquire expensive amplification equipment and a van for hauling it start to get engagements in the least pretentious clubs, where they fine tune their skills in both performing and songwriting as well as test their ability to collaborate and endure low pecuniary rewards. Drive and self-confidence may matter as much as talent, but the self-confidence overflows into ego problems that commonly cause groups to break up. An aspiring group accepts jobs for low pay, playing songs that are popular while trying to write and develop their own compositions. Day jobs remain essential as the group seeks to build its playing and writing skills to the point of attracting a record company.[40] They come to need managerial services in the early steps of professional development, yet their current earnings are modest and their small chances of ultimate success complicate engaging a manager whose compensation must come from low-probability future earnings (see Chapter 3). As the band pursues a recording contract, its demonstration tape joins the many that fill the mailbags delivered to recording companies (like artists' slides arriving at art galleries). The tape arriving over the transom seldom produces a recording contract directly, but it may alert the record company's talent scout, the A&R (artists and repertory) person.

Classical Musicians and the Contest Circuit

A classical musician such as a concert pianist faces a notoriously small probability of a big success, making the sorting and ranking mechanism particularly draconian. For a typical comparison, American music schools each year graduate about 14,000 students with performance degrees, while 250 to 350 jobs in symphony orchestras become available.[41] Joseph Horowitz noted that the 1990 *Musical America* directory listed 572 solo pianists available for engagement, up from 199 twenty years earlier. More than half of a year's opportunities for performances with North American symphony orchestras went to just ten pianists, while another 125 to 150 picked up one or two each.[42] An industry of management firms exists to match musicians with engagements (Chapter 3). But a major gatekeeping function is performed by competitions that have proliferated around the world—five dozen in the United States alone, and overall ten times as many in 1990 as in 1950. These are nonprofit operations sited in particular cities, funded partly by ticket sales but mostly by private and (outside of the United States) government donations. Clearly a large number of donors gain satisfaction from fostering the discovery of talent and increasing the stock of cultural capital.

Horowitz's study centers on the Van Cliburn International Piano Competition, its namesake himself having leapt to fame in the Tchaikovsky International Competition in 1958. His resulting triumph playing Tchaikovsky's

Concerto No. 1 and Rachmaninoff's Concerto No. 3 on the world concert circuit precipitated the organization of citizens of his hometown, Fort Worth, Texas, to fund and manage the Van Cliburn competition. Applicants competed for places by submitting tapes; but because these vary in quality and may have benefited from editing, the contest shifted to videotaped auditions at selected sites around the world. In 1997 it sent itinerant juries out to hear applicants in short public recitals, to screen them for the main competition. Contestants play an assortment of solo works and concerti before live audiences, and the Van Cliburn and other competitions clearly sort their contestants on the basis of not only keyboard skills but also audience appeal and the ability to perform under pressure.[43] Winners are guaranteed a number of public performances. At first these were mostly with second-rate orchestras (not a clear advantage for career-building), but the competition later upgraded the orchestras and offered concerts at locations dispersed more widely around the world.

Pondering the subsequent careers of the Van Cliburn competition's winners and runners-up, Horowitz concluded that it performs (as do its rivals) a valuable gatekeeping function, but that the greatest beneficiary is not always the contest winner. That is not just because competition judges sometimes disagree strongly (especially those who are established pianists with firmly held views about how a piece should be interpreted). It is also because the elements of tenacity and dedication are not fully revealed on the competition circuit. The competition's management recently took this pattern to the heart and recast it somewhat as more a showcase of talent and less a horse race of thoroughbreds. The Van Cliburn and other contests have in any case become trade shows attracting representatives of artist management firms, orchestras, and concert presenters. The competition ceased to demand that all contestants choose works from required lists. Competitors now select music to suit their own skills and personalities, indeed making few overlapping choices in the 1997 round and moving well outside the nineteenth-century showpieces that are the traditional battleground in music competitions.[44]

2

Artists, Dealers, and Deals

Much of this book is about the industries that mediate between the artist and the consumer of artistic creations. Some, such as art galleries and concert booking agencies, distribute creative goods and services directly with no elaborate apparatus of their own. Others, like book publishers or cinema and TV filmmakers and distributors, combine diverse creative inputs and/or processes and distribute them in large-scale operations. Contemporary art galleries' dealings with artists expose starkly the problem of mutually satisfactory relationships between the two parties as well as the turnover of artists and of the galleries that select and promote them.

Relationship between Artist and Dealer

Dealers in contemporary art place artists' work before potential purchasers and those who might influence them, through exhibitions (galleries) and direct representation (other, private dealers). The dealer is much more than an order-taker, because for many reasons the art does not speak for itself. Purchasers seriously interested in the evolving art market—collectors and museums—care not just about the work at hand but also about the artist's trajectory of development. The collector has a strictly economic reason for this—the future market value of the art object enters directly into the purchaser's effective cost (or, possibly, profit) from the acquisition. Aesthetically, serious collectors see contemporary art-making as a process evolving out of a historical context, so their valuation of a purchase depends on the likely stylistic evolution of the artist and, indeed, of the school or movement in which she works.

Promoting the Artist's Career

The dealer thus not only offers art works but also serves as the artist's agent and promoter in a career that (both parties hope) will evolve fruitfully. The promotion takes many forms. The dealer spends time with prospective clients articulating the artist's intent, providing context for her work, and formulating a best case for its significance. Shows are organized and promoted. An active contemporary gallery may have a stable of 18 to 25 artists. Each gets a one-person show roughly every year and a half, with advertisements, mailed announcements, and a reception (white wine in plastic glasses). The dealer promotes the artist with such certifiers as art writers and museum curators, supplies illustrations to art publications, tries to place the artist's work in museum exhibitions and encourages purchases by museums and major collectors, whose judgments provide counsel to less well-informed buyers. He arranges loans to museums and other exhibitors and seeks representation for the artist with friendly galleries in other cities.[1]

The effectiveness of this promotional effort obviously depends on the artist's performance as well. Her work must emerge steadily enough to be ready for shows that are scheduled well in advance. The artist's personal touch in interacting with collectors (and various certifiers) and involving them in her creative process affects the payout of the dealer's promotional efforts (Chapter 1).

The artist does have an alternative to the prevalent exclusive relationship with a single dealer: selling her works *à la carte* to whatever dealers wish to resell them. Such a system offers a superficial attraction. Competition among dealers maximizes the prices that they pay for her work. It also tends to keep down the prices at which dealers offer her art to collectors, thus enlarging their purchases. If the dealer's promotional investments are important, however, competition among dealers need not work in the artist's favor. Without exclusive representation, any one dealer's promotional efforts spill benefits over to other dealers offering her work, depressing his incentive to promote.[2] A clear example of this spillover problem lies in protection of the prices that the artist's work commands in the secondary market (for example, previously sold works coming up at auction). If—as is surely true—the market's valuation of an artist's works is subjective and buffeted by shocks and reconsiderations, the artist benefits from the dealer's diligence in averting low prices in the secondary market (for example, by bidding in the auction) and thus blocking negative signals. The dealer's incentive to sustain market prices shrivels if he cannot expect future profit from selling her work at the preserved high prices.[3] The only artists observed to choose nonexclusive representation are already well established.

The artist-dealer relationship illustrates starkly the problems that parties face in managing collaborative economic relations. The artist does not simply hire a dealer to market her work. Although the art gallery is a small business, it more efficiently represents two dozen artists than a single one. The artist's creative spark may be necessary to the dealer's success, but so is the dealer's promotional effort to the artist's renown, and each party's actions affect the benefit flowing to the other. As a contract, their relationship resembles a joint venture more than a principal-agent relationship. Furthermore, it is barnacled with all the difficulties that afflict such contracts.

Ideal and Attainable Contracts

Consider the best imaginable contract that artist and dealer could devise. The artist's work should become widely known and respected, so that many collectors and museums will follow the artist's development and pay high prices to possess her work. The young artist and the dealer ideally agree that each will exert optimal effort to bring this goal about—the dealer in his various promotional activities,[4] the artist by producing work of a character and at a pace that is ideal in light of the number of potential purchasers interested in her work and her fecundity in devising new problems and effective solutions.[5] Once committed to these efforts, artist and dealer then expect a certain inflow of revenue over time, and they must agree on how to divide the joint profit after subtracting the costs that each has separately incurred.[6]

Suppose that artist and dealer can define their goal in economic terms: the maximum present value of revenues from sales of the artist's work, including the dealer's share, minus the direct costs incurred by both dealer and artist. They still face a vexing problem to reach a complete contract (defined in the Introduction). Each works independently to advance the shared career goal. Each should push any such investment to the point where the last dollar's cost of that effort adds just one dollar of gross revenue to this stream. To achieve that, each must commit explicitly to the efforts he or she will exert. With that commitment infeasible, the dealer and the artist can reach the simpler agreement that each takes 50 percent of every revenue dollar, but then each underinvests. The dollar cost that adds the last dollar to the revenue stream brings only 50 cents to the party who spends it. Each therefore has an incentive to exert less effort than would maximize the value of the deal for both together. Thus, a profit-sharing contract beats one that lacks a profit-incentive component, but it does not maximize the deal's value unless the parties can negotiate and commit to ideal levels of individual effort.[7]

If the parties do try to commit their levels of effort in this and other creative activities, they will face formidable difficulties. On the *nobody knows* principle, the market's future valuation of the artist's work is highly uncertain at the opening of the first solo exhibition, not to mention twenty years hence. Suppose that artist and dealer agree on a best guess. Can each party commit in advance to "best efforts" under the contract? The dealer cannot plausibly commit to a number of hours spent chatting up the artist's work to collectors, a number of phone calls to writers and curators, and so on. Even if he could prespecify these actions, the artist cannot hang around the gallery continuously to monitor the commitment. Likewise, *art for art's sake* precludes the artist's even thinking about committing the character of her future work, let alone setting forth a plan in quantitative detail. If the artist's output cannot be contracted, the intensity of her future effort is just as problematic a commitment, and one that cannot be plausibly monitored by the dealer. In short, for both parties there are problems with noncontractable and hidden effort. The problem would be vexing enough if the parties each knew exactly what actions they would best perform, but could not write down commitments to undertake them. Even worse, in reality the effects of their actions are intrinsically uncertain *(nobody knows)*. The artist may fail to develop a valuable long-run reputation either because her work fails to catch the market's fancy at the outset, or because it appears too flashy and facile, hence without potential for long-run development.[8]

Even if best efforts could be specified and enforced on both parties, formal contracts can be infeasible because of outcomes that one party can observe but the other cannot. Because the artist's whole production process is internal and nonobjective, only she can say whether the creative result realized her intention. The dealer, specialized in knowing what will sell, is the one who observes whether collectors brighten or glaze over as he extols the beauty or distinctiveness of the work. That is, on both sides of the deal, outcomes are observed by one party but hidden from the other.

Finally, even if artist and dealer could write a contract that surmounts problems from hidden efforts and outcomes, the problem remains of opportunism—selfish actions that exploit the other party's costs of monitoring or enforcing the contract. For the dealer to exert best efforts at promoting the artist's work, he must expect to receive compensation for any sales that the artist might make directly to collectors whose interest is stirred by the dealer. Artist and collector, however, have an incentive to deal directly and divide the dealer's cut (which might be as high as 50 percent), and stories are common of artist-dealer relationships falling apart when unreported direct sales are detected.[9] Opportunism also occurs on the dealer's side. The artist does not readily observe when sales take place at the gallery and payment of the profits becomes due. What works remain in stock she can check readily at a gallery nearby, but not at one in a distant city. Dealers have been known to conceal sales and postpone payments as long as possible. Furthermore, lightly capitalized art galleries frequently go out of business, leaving the artist as a major unsatisfied creditor and/or unable to retrieve her unsold works from the vanished establishment.[10] The artist's ideological disinclination to drive a hard commercial bargain and stronger interest in having her work seen than sold underlines the relevance of the dealer's opportunism.[11]

Cooperation in Practice

Despite this litany of woes, artists and galleries do cooperate. What devices work? First, formal contracts are simply avoided. Dealers speak of informal shared understandings that continue until and unless the parties' interests drift apart. The infeasibility of explicit contracting leads the parties into the language of moral obligation, with reputation the insurance of reasonable performance in the absence of legally binding obligations.[12] The most common arrangement involves nothing more than a dealer's "handshake" commitment to promote an artist and show her work periodically in exchange for exclusive representation and a share of the proceeds of sales.

An important term of this implicit contract is the sharing not of profits but of gross revenues. The dealer deducts a commission that has apparently drifted upward over the years from 33.3 to 40 to 50 percent. The higher figure tends to prevail in New York and in galleries that provide extensive services and have well-established clienteles.[13] Some promotional outlays—announcements and catalogues, framing costs—may be charged partly to the artist. Sharing revenues rather than profits has two effects. First, unless the artist's and dealer's shares of combined costs happen to equal their agreed shares of gross revenues, the resulting division of net revenue will differ from a profit-sharing agreement. Second, when revenues rather than profits are shared, neither party gets credit for the costs that they incur, giving an incentive to skimp on them. Expanding promotion outlays by a dollar costs the dealer that dollar but increases the dealer's earnings only by his portion of the induced increase in sales revenue.[14] With revenue sharing, each party benefits disproportionately when the other party incurs revenue-increasing costs.[15] This fact predicts haggling under the contract and explains why all artists with revenue-sharing contracts believe that their dealers underspend on promoting their work. Compared to profit-sharing, each party to the contract does indeed underspend unless they can write their promotional obligations directly into their contract.

Independent of this problem is that of the contract's duration, because the absence of an enforceable long-run commitment limits efforts that advance future but not current sales. Here, the dealer's outright purchases of the artist's work potentially make an important difference. They can reward the dealer with capital gains to offset the myopia induced by a short-term contract. Such purchases are very risky investments, however. They become especially so in art booms when current prices are high and the dealer faces a growing potential opportunity loss if he holds works rather than putting them on the market.[16] The dealer's purchases for investment also can provoke conflict with the artist, who has an incentive to retain her own best works. This action by the artist generates potential rewards to support the artist's own investment in her career, but it shrinks the flow to market that supports the dealer's promotional efforts.[17] Stipends paid against expected future sales address the artist's problem of covering the costs of her apprenticeship, and they improve the dealer's incentives (because he gets the full pecuniary benefit of sales for which the artist has received prepayment in stipend), but they are also risky for the dealer and invite haggling problems and moral hazard for the artist.

The evidence available on how these practices work out is only impressionistic and likely biased toward experiences of the more successful and famous galleries and artists, since the losers expire without leaving a record. The helpful but risky devices of stipends and investment purchases by dealers seem to get only limited use. Those dealers who employ them have been well financed and filled with deep personal conviction about the importance of the artists whom they supported. For example, D. H. Kahnweiler, Picasso's early dealer, drew on the resources of his wealthy banking family to help whom he thought to be the important emerging artists of his time. He never worked on consignment but relied on stipends and outright purchases (based on a contractual formula tied to the size of the painting).[18] Of the Parisian dealers central to modernism in the visual arts, Paul Rosenberg came to wealth after World War II only by virtue of works by Picasso, Braque, and Gris bought in the 1920s that had until then been unsaleable. Paul Durand-Ruel died in 1922 with little pecuniary wealth but 1,500 Impressionist and Postimpressionist canvases, which his grateful heirs sold over the next two decades.[19] In New York, Leo Castelli's combination of personal wealth and dedication to advancing the visual arts permitted him to pay stipends to the leading pop artists, for whom Castelli had high (and, in the end, justified) hopes.[20] In general stipends seem to go only to artists whom dealers regard as especially promising and/or who stir up competition to represent them.[21]

The course of artist-dealer relations can also be viewed from the artist's perspective, with Pablo Picasso the premier twentieth-century example in the commercial as well as the aesthetic sense. His arrival on the art scene was well timed, because a solid dealer market for contemporary art had emerged in late nineteenth-century Paris in the wake of the Impressionists. The French art market continued to broaden in the early twentieth century, influenced importantly by a well-known speculative investment group organized in

1903 by André Level. Level bought astutely among then-contemporary French artists. When his so-called La Peau de l'Ours collection was (by precommitment) sold in a widely publicized auction in 1914, it earned a rate of return in the neighborhood of 8 percent a year.[22]

Picasso may have had little regard for dealers, but he was never less than commercially astute. His first show in Paris at Ambroise Vollard's gallery (1901) included portraits of three backers of the exhibition, and he gave two works to critics who wrote complimentary reviews. He switched to dealer D. H. Kahnweiler, who energetically and effectively supported Cubism as a movement and promoted Picasso's work through connections with other galleries in Germany, Switzerland, and Eastern Europe. Kahnweiler's efforts were crushed during World War I when the French government expropriated the German national's stock of art. Dealer Léonce Rosenberg then seized the Cubist banner, proclaiming Cubism as the only viable style of painting and lauding Picasso as the head of a Cubist army. Rosenberg's efforts were over-reaching for Picasso, who had little respect for some of the second-string Cubists and preferred to keep his stylistic options open. In 1918 Picasso in-gratiated himself with two of France's leading dealers—Paul Rosenberg, who specialized in nineteenth-century French art, and Georges Wildenstein, who focused on Old Masters—an alliance consistent with Picasso's then-reviving interest in classical styles. Picasso gave them informally the right of first re-fusal to purchase his paintings, an arrangement that lasted twenty years. Rosenberg was willing to play a long-run game, positioning Picasso as an art-ist whose work was marked by openness and exploration. He arranged for important and costly international exhibitions of Picasso's work (in Munich, New York, Chicago, and at a pioneering museum show at Hartford), setting high prices and selling little. Drawing on his experience as a successful dealer in Impressionists, he encouraged Picasso to paint works in series that would capture the art world's attention.[23]

The course of the artist-dealer relationship naturally depends on the un-predictable curve of the artist's own development. With the dealer's promo-tional effectiveness tied to his ability to support the artist's work and articu-late its virtues, the parties naturally tend to part company if her style takes a direction that the dealer does not fancy. A major shift in style might carry the artist away from the gallery's aesthetic habitat.[24] Short of that, conflict can arise between the dealer eager for work similar to what has already enjoyed commercial success and the artist attuned to the conquest of new creative problems. Some ruptures in dealer-artist links of course result from dealers' competition to represent successful artists, an aspect of the population and turnover of galleries to which we now turn.[25]

The Ecology of Art Galleries

Among the commercial intermediaries in the creative industries, contemporary art galleries are relatively simple firms. Their degrees of success and rates of turnover mirror the success of the artists whom they choose to represent. The gallery population also responds to changes in the number and tastes of potential buyers. Economists apply a simple ecological principle to explain the size and composition of a market's resident population of firms. Any niche that a firm can fill profitably (that is, in a way that at least covers its costs) will get filled; any niche that grows unprofitable will eventually be vacated. The number of resident firms then depends on several factors, two of which interact: the size of the market to be served, and the amount of fixed costs that each firm must cover in order to survive. Another factor is how firms compete. The higher they set their prices, relative to their costs, the more readily are fixed costs covered, and the more firms can potentially fit into the local market.[26] Finally, the motivation of business owners makes a difference. Many dealers appear to share *art for art's sake* preferences and hence are willing to settle for less profit than humdrum entrepreneurs. That factor probably makes for a denser population of galleries than if they were run by profit-seekers.[27] The art market embraces both newly made contemporary art and a secondary market in which older art of all types and vintages turns over. The focus here is on contemporary art. The secondary market is considered in Chapter 21 in the context of the turnover of existing stock.

Dealers' Qualifications

Think of the economic problem of allocating potential small-scale entrepreneurs among the tasks of art dealing, furniture retailing, shoe repair, accountancy, and many other such tasks. Many persons' choices may be accidental or random, but some are determined by the skills and tastes relevant to the particular trade. The anecdotal evidence on art dealers' backgrounds suggests that a taste for art plays a large role, although well-suited entrepreneurial skills are also evident. The dealer may be a now-and-former collector or certifier in the art market, or an artist whose creative career did not take off. A common combination is a strong taste for art coupled with a cushion of personal wealth from family sources or previous occupations; the word "dilettante" suggests itself, but there is no clear boundary between the serious dealer and the dabbler.

Among the dealers important in the modern development of the contemporary art market, Peggy Guggenheim came from a wealthy, art-collecting family and spent the 1920s and 1930s in Paris in contact with leading artists.

After briefly operating a gallery in London in 1938, she returned to the United States and opened her New York gallery in 1942. Her real goal was to establish a museum, and Art of This Century was a cross between a gallery and an art museum. Two New York dealers important after World War II were Betty Parsons and Sam Kootz. Parsons was trained in art and had spent a decade soaking up the art world in Europe and the years 1938–1946 working for other galleries. She was wrapped up in artists' development and clearly more interested in nurturing an artist's success than in exploiting it once in hand. Kootz, in contrast, was trained in law and had worked in management and advertising. He had given himself a fine education in art and saw his commercial skills as a suitable basis for promoting artists.[28] Sidney Janis had enjoyed a successful career as a manufacturer of shirts, then took a decade to tank up on knowledge of the art world before opening his own gallery. Leo Castelli had successfully pursued various businesses while collecting art and hanging out with contemporary artists. Martha Jackson had been a collector who fancied dealing directly with artists, while John Bernard Myers had held editorial and other culture-related jobs that brought him extensive art-world contacts. Charles Cowles had behind him a family fortune as well as employment with an art magazine and as a curator. Arne Glimcher of Pace Gallery and Larry Gagosian both began modest gallery operations outside of New York, then worked their way up through various collaborative dealings with New York galleries before emerging as important New York dealers.[29] The dilettante element seems more evident in galleries in smaller art centers, where it manifests itself in a high turnover of galleries as the thrill wears off for the dealer lacking a career motive.[30]

Hazards and Strategies

Although galleries require modest start-up investments, even those that ultimately succeed expect to and do run losses for several years. A leading New York dealer in the mid-1980s estimated that a gallery would require a $250,000 start-up investment and the capacity to lose that sum again before cash-flow turns positive. These shake-down losses result either from the dealer's trial-and-error efforts to find successful artists or just the repeated shows and exposure needed before initially chosen artists catch on. All of the outcomes are highly uncertain, so it is not surprising that 75 percent of contemporary art galleries are estimated to survive no more than five years.[31] In her more selective sample of galleries, Diana Crane observed somewhat better odds: of 290 New York galleries handling contemporary American art in 1977, 60 percent were founded after 1965; of such galleries operating in 1949, 26 percent remained alive in 1977.[32]

These extended periods of negative cash-flow underline the investment element in the artist-dealer relationship and the force of the contract failures noted previously. Because of this hazard, collectors have been an important source of financing for some ultimately successful galleries. The serious collector might gain several advantages by becoming the dealer's not-so-silent partner. If the gallery shows artists already in the collection, capital gains and validation of taste follow the gallery's (and artist's) success. When the gallery represents an artist who is already "hot," the partner-collector buys first place in the queue to consider new works for purchase.[33] When Ivan Karp left the Castelli Gallery, within twelve hours he had received calls from many Castelli clients and others who offered backing for a new gallery, but Karp deemed all of the offers tainted by desires for a voice in the work to be shown.[34] In the 1920s American collector Chester Dale bought a large block of stock in the Galeries Georges Petit in Paris, in order to get first pick of major contemporary works and avoid paying the dealer's mark-up; this private interest led to serious conflicts with his dealer-partners.[35]

The contemporary art gallery can employ several strategies for recruiting and nurturing viable artists. One may be called horizontal differentiation: the dealer attempts to spot new trends in the work of artists, ideally a group of capable artists working in a related style. The dealer gains a critical-mass advantage in drawing the attention of art writers, curators, and collectors to an innovative style. Indeed, the innovative dealer may gain when other galleries hop on the bandwagon—the advantage of creating more interest in the style offsets the disadvantage of more rivalry for clients and artists.[36] Dealers sometimes make large and risky investments in promoting innovations, a reflection of the contemporary art market's preference for transcending existing conventions over pursuing other dimensions of artistic achievement.[37] The aggressive pursuit of trends, however, leaves its own ecological niches: the successful Pace Gallery began with a stable of "oddball" artists who fitted into nobody's taxonomy.[38]

Trend-setters or not, galleries representing successful artists leverage their assets through collaboration with galleries in other cities. Except for a substratum offering purely decorative art, contemporary art galleries are strongly constrained to the single, proprietor-managed location. Successful artists' reputations are national or worldwide, however. Many galleries consign or sell works to other galleries in one-shot deals, but trend-setters have an incentive to forge more substantial alliances. Just before World War I, Kahnweiler established regular relations with (among others) Alfred Flechtheim's gallery in Berlin and the Washington Square Gallery in New York.[39] Leo Castelli exploited his success with Pop Art by developing a network of friendly galleries in the United States and abroad, supplying them at a 30 percent discount from retail prices (which left Castelli with a margin of up to 20 percent). These outlets grew increasingly important as Castelli's New York collectors found their wall space glutted with the large-size canvases favored by Castelli's artists, and approximately 70 percent of Castelli's sales for a time were to other galleries. In Europe, Ileanna Sonnabend's lock on Pop Art through her association with Castelli bestirred other dealers to invest in promoting minimalist art, and John Weber's New York gallery was built on the diffusion from Europe of minimalist artists and Arte Povera.[40] Paris dealer Denise René started with Victor Vasarely and built a position as home base for the Op Art movement.

Because a contemporary art dealer handles a small number of artists in relationships that (if successful) tend to be durable, the turnover of galleries is associated with the turnover of successful artists and styles. This turnover pattern is not inevitable, of course, and fate might be evaded by a dealer who repeatedly picks promising new styles or excellent young artists. After Kahnweiler's holdings of Cubist art were expropriated during World War I and subsequently disposed of at auction, he re-established a gallery in the 1920s, adding some new artists (including Paul Signac), but judged perceptively that no dealer can hope to spot more than one or (at most) two new generations of artists. Before his big success with Pop Art, Leo Castelli had little luck with second-generation Abstract Expressionists or young European artists.[41]

Vertical Differentiation

Galleries for new art also display something akin to vertical differentiation. Many galleries sell contemporary art that is decorative but makes no claim to innovation. They operate beneath the radar of the certifiers of high art, and they serve interior decorators and homemakers whose interest is in agreeable and harmonious surroundings ("the swatch people"). This demand is local and not so subject to agglomeration pulls, and so galleries offering decorative art are proportionally more prevalent in cities with little standing as art centers.[42] Some artists who fail to establish themselves in the high-art segment retreat for profit (if not necessarily pleasure) to supplying decorative art.

Within the fine-art segment, however, another sort of vertical differentiation prevails. Superficially, it distinguishes galleries by the price of the art, reputation of the artist, opulence of the premises, and range of services offered by the gallery. Artists of talent if not of genius find willing buyers if the price is right, and the right price cannot cover costly premises and elaborate promotional services.[43] More fundamentally, galleries that focus on the screening of artists and their care and feeding in personal relations are distinguished from galleries that focus on their promotion to collectors and the art world at large.[44] A gallery that is especially astute or lucky sometimes migrates from the former status to the latter as its artists' successes warrant increasingly ambitious and large-scale promotion. This distinction between the "pickers" and the "promoters" reflects both differences in the talents and interests of the dealers and differences in the scales and fixed costs of operation. For example, Arne Glimcher's Pace Gallery employs 50 to 75 persons and benefits from the accumulation of clients among the rich and famous. It publishes extensive catalogues and mounts shows of museum-type scholarly quality. Nowadays its artists are successful ones attracted from other galleries by Glimcher's prowess at shaping high-level careers.[45] Promoters and pickers will turn up in several other creative industries, where they differ greatly in scales of operation.

Dealer-Artist Links and Turnover

The other mechanism of turnover among the linked dealers and artists is of course the migration of artists between galleries. Much turnover flows from the random forces noted previously: disputes that arise from incomplete dealer-artist contracts, and shifts that occur when the artist changes her style or the dealer repositions the gallery's prevailing style. For artists who are gaining or have achieved extensive recognition, however, turnover also occurs through migration from the galleries that specialize in selecting and nurturing new artists to those specialized in major promotional activities. When the American realist artist Andrew Wyeth burst on the scene in 1948 with the sale of his *Christina's World* to the Museum of Modern Art, he was represented by the Macbeth Gallery, a modest picker of new artists, which sold his tempera images at $300 to $600. He switched to the high-profile Knoedler Gallery in 1951, as his success brought sold-out shows and prices that by 1959 had escalated to $100,000. Knoedler staff member Coe Kerr took Wyeth along when he left to start his own gallery. Wyeth's prices continued to rise rapidly in the 1980s, and he could afford to withdraw from exclusive gallery representation and hold back many of his works—an astute choice in light of collectors' enthusiasm coupled with the poor critical reception that Wyeth's work received for lying outside the currently fashionable styles.[46] Artists' changes of gallery affiliation place a great strain on the informal contracts that seek to implement forward-looking and long-term relationships. For successful artists the sums involved are not small; after a legal dispute, artist Peter Halley apparently paid his former gallery $162,500 for expenses it had already incurred in anticipation of a canceled show (Halley had been receiving a stipend of $40,000 a month).[47]

The persistent but not eternal links between dealer and artist, the continuous shakeout of artists seeking success, and these diverse roles played by galleries together explain the turnover (entry/exit and success) that occurs among the galleries. Some bet on winning artists and prosper, while others back losers and vanish along with their protégés.[48] Some float to the top by backing new styles that gain wide recognition: Betty Parsons with Abstract Expressionism, Castelli with Pop Art, Denise René (Paris) with Op Art, Virginia Dwan with minimalists, Mary Boone with figurative painters reacting to minimal art. Charles Cowles, with a west coast background, relied on bringing to New York strong west coast artists not well known or represented in the east.[49] Some galleries with strong promotional skills (such as Pace and Marlborough) have flourished by attracting successful artists from other galleries. Betty Parsons was pressed by her most successful Abstract Expressionist artists (Mark Rothko, Barnet Newman, Clyfford Still, Jackson Pollock) to drop her other artists and promote them more intensively; oriented toward artists rather than promotional strategies, she refused and lost them to promoters such as Sam Kootz and Sidney Janis. Peggy Guggenheim's gallery, Art of This Century, had scored a major early success with Jackson Pollock, who received a stipend from the gallery; Robert Motherwell and William Baziotes were then lost to Kootz, because Guggenheim would not match Pollock's stipend arrangement.[50] Even a highly successful trend-setting gallery is limited in its ability to capture the benefits by the number of artists it can feasibly promote: Leo Castelli passed up Andy Warhol and James Rosenquist, and several other successful Pop artists went to Richard Bellamy's Green Gallery (Bellamy was by general agreement a highly skilled picker of artists but not a successful gallery manager).[51] An implication of these turnover processes is that the lifespan of the typical contemporary gallery is short. The growth of the art market obscures this (because many galleries hence are young in any case), but the pattern seems clear.

Diana Crane studied the linkage between stylistic turnover and the gallery population in New York.[52] She identified the artists who worked actively in the first generation of each of five styles and the galleries that had shown them. A gallery was defined as committed to a style if it showed more than five artists working in that style. The 36 galleries that committed to a style were 27 percent of all the galleries who exhibited these artists (only five galleries ever committed to more than one style). The committed galleries were marked as leaders in two senses: they had commonly been the first to exhibit the artists whom they represented, and their artists had achieved more success on the test of retrospective museum exhibits and museum purchases. Their artists were more likely to have had works sold at auction, and they accounted for a comfortable majority (but only that) of the artists whose works commanded top auction prices for that style. In sum, success with stylistic bandwagons accounted for much of the upper tail of gallery successes, but not all.

Further insight into the relation between the turnover of galleries and of art styles comes from Liah Greenfeld's study of the Israeli art market. For a new style to be disseminated, it must command enough economic (humdrum) resources to keep its artists from starving and the dealers in business. The origins of these resources may vary, however, from one style to another. Greenfeld drew a sharp contrast between the fonts of resources that in the 1970s supported Conceptual Art, on the one hand, and Surrealism and Expressionism, on the other. Conceptualism did not appeal widely to collectors, but it did to museum curators, art writers, and sophisticated dealers engaged in the dialogue of innovation and development in contemporary art. With extensive publicity and exhibitions in museums and other noncommercial public spaces, and with active purchases by museum curators, Conceptualism established itself solidly despite a paucity of sales to private collectors. It was supported by galleries willing to sacrifice commercial profits for prestige, and it benefited from the artists' collaboration in jointly promoting the movement, especially in international exhibitions outside of Israel. The artists also made their personal resource commitment: Conceptual artists are more likely to rely on other employment than artists working in more commercial styles. Expressionism and Surrealism, "mature" styles by the 1970s, by contrast found favor with collectors and hence with more strictly commercial galleries, and artists practicing them were more likely to make their livings solely from art.[53]

This difference in the resources supporting various styles evidently prevails in the New York market as well, although it is not well documented. Pop Art quickly found favor with collectors, while the certifiers and museums were slower to warm to it. Conceptualism has apparently relied on the certifiers, supportive dealers, and a small but determined band of collectors. Pattern Art never attracted strongly either collectors or certifiers in New York, but in U.S. regional art centers it appealed to both groups, especially corporate collectors.[54] Earthworks, costly to execute and usually not appropriable by the collector, depended on a few enthusiast collectors and galleries. Sophisticated art writers were notably important for promoting noncommercial styles such as Conceptual Art and earthworks; both schools appealed to an ideology that saw virtue in art being immune to appropriation and ownership by the individual collector.[55]

The turnover processes evident in other art centers are qualitatively similar to those in the New York market, but the role of stylistic bandwagons is surely less. Where art markets are smaller, galleries perforce represent a wider array of styles and rely less heavily on commitments to cutting-edge contemporary art. In France, provincial galleries similarly depend on discounted purchases from Paris galleries for well-known artists while making what modest investments they will in showing and developing local artists. Greenfeld documented the Israeli art market's development to the point where it shared fully in the international turnover of art styles and hence of galleries and local artists.[56] Provincial dealers in the United States suffer the reverse of agglomeration effects: the top artists work somewhere else, and art consigned to them by art-center galleries has already been picked over. Their costs of gallery space may be low, but they lack the resource of a local set of media and promoters, and must themselves spend more in time and resources to promote contemporary art to local clients.[57]

3

Artist and Gatekeeper: Trade Books, Popular Records, and Classical Music

The filtering of artists by gatekeepers and the promotion and distribution of their works goes on in all the creative sectors, leading to trouble-prone relationships between artists and the firms that link them with humdrum inputs. Authors and trade-book publishers offer a useful comparison to the visual artist and gallery. Whereas the gallery seeks to promote an unpredictable career, the publisher addresses a problem that is usually simpler. The manuscript of the book is in hand; even if not, as with celebrity authors and blockbuster novelists, the prospective development of the artist's career is not such a central concern. While that smooths the contracting process, it raises the stakes for the gatekeeper, who has more information to work with and hence a more complex task of processing it. The record album is the unit of transaction between the pop performing group and the record label, just as is the gallery show for the artist and dealer. Each team, however, hopes to launch and sustain a career for the artist. The deal again runs into problems already seen in the visual arts: hidden actions and information, incomplete contracts, the uncommitable nature of artistic inspiration, and moral hazard. The tweedy author and the grunge musician face very similar issues of contracting with gatekeepers. It proves convenient to explore some issues in the author's context, others in the musician's.

These problems of gatekeeping and contracting open several distinctive issues of industrial organization. Agents commonly serve as business representatives for artists, but their role in allocating creative resources goes much farther. They perform their own gatekeeping function in deciding which artists to represent, and along with this undertake the matching of artists to jobs or humdrum partners. Some of these tasks have natural-monopoly elements, others need one-on-one relationships to artists, so the organization patterns of agents vary greatly among art realms. Another issue of industrial organization, demonstrated in trade-book publishing, is the informal but extensive information networks that link editors in different publishing houses. The creative-industry firm is no fortress of proprietary information.

Author, Agent, and Publisher

Like classical musicians and cinema and TV film artists, trade-book authors employ agents as intermediaries, to match author with publisher and bargain the best terms. The agent deals proximately with an editor, who becomes the manuscript's champion or manager within the publishing firm. Because all functions that a publisher performs—copy-editing, printing, distribution, and so forth—can be subcontracted, the tasks performed by the publishing-house editor and the small-scale entrepreneurial publisher differ only in governance relationships among the parties.

Agent as Intermediary

The creative act of authorship has its sociable side, but compared to visual art and pop musicianship it is a solitary and individual calling. The typical beginning author cannot follow the visual artist and build a reputation outside the realm of commercial gatekeepers. There does exist a marketplace for literary reputations in the high-minded circles of the university campus and the little magazine, but it has separated itself from the mainstream of commercial writing in books and magazines.[1] There is, then, no marketplace for early reputations of emerging authors ("celebrity" books aside). The author simply prepares a manuscript and presses it into the hands of a gatekeeper, either the publishing-house editor or an agent. The chances that the gate will open are small. The president of Doubleday once stated that three or four of the 10,000 submissions received "over the transom" each year were accepted. Novels face even worse odds (one in 15,000), while scholarly and textbook publishers net many more fish from the stream of submissions.[2] These odds understate the author's chances, since they pertain to any single publisher's acceptance rate, whereas many manuscripts find homes after multiple submissions.

The publisher might decline a particular manuscript for many reasons: it fundamentally lacks quality and originality; it shows promise that could be realized only with substantial further work by the author; it is too specialized to be profitable; it fails to fit well into the publisher's portfolio of books; or it arrives at the wrong time, when the publisher's pipeline is full. Because any novice's manuscript has a tiny chance of acceptance, the publisher either incurs a high cost (per acceptance) of filtering out the losers, or chances many errors of omission (rejecting manuscripts that are worth publishing). There is room for an intermediary who can efficiently match up publisher and author. The agent does that job. Publishers once shunned agents as collectors of rents that an inexperienced author might leave on the bargaining table. Agents are now welcomed for reducing the publisher's recruitment costs. Just when and how this attitude shift occurred is not clear. But a logically sufficient explanation lies in the growth of the literary marketplace and the total supply of manuscripts available for screening by any one publisher.

The agent's skill as intermediary lies in sensing the threshold quality a manuscript needs in order to interest a publisher and knowing the sorts of manuscripts sought by various publishers. The agent who selects from the "slush pile" of unsolicited submissions a would-be author to represent thus serves as a first-stage gatekeeper. The agent may press the author to change or improve the manuscript enough that an editor can see its potential. The agent then submits the manuscript to appropriate publishers, not so much to foment an auction as to identify the most fruitful author-publisher match. To this task the agent brings both superior knowledge and a reputation asset grown from repeated interactions with publishers. The experienced agent seeks a reputation for truthful assessments—not overclaiming either the quality of submitted manuscripts or the collaborative capability of the author. The quest for this reputation is propelled by the agent's own compensation structure. The agent's conventional 10 percent of the author's royalty does not provide a compensatory total income (that is, one matching other job opportunities) unless he "hits" with a reasonably large proportion of submitted projects.[3] Agents nurture relationships with editors rather than with the publishing houses that employ them, and the editor's claim on the publisher's resources may be more important than the publisher's identity. Editors, who frequently change jobs between publishing houses, function as in-house entrepreneurs with concentrated incentives to produce successful books. They hence value accurate assessments and astute matchmaking by agents, including theory-of-the-case ammunition for getting promising projects accepted by the publishing house. Editors with projects in mind may turn to agents representing authors who have done similar books. Indeed, switches in occupation between agents and editors appear common.[4]

The importance of agents' matchmaking function is affirmed by evidence on the origins of literary agents in the nineteenth-century Britain. At the outset the services were informal and unpaid; persons with *art for art's sake* tastes often performed a good-offices function solely for the pleasure of seeing a fruitful deal completed. The growth of the literary marketplace (provincial newspapers, for example) encouraged the emergence of author-paid agents such as A. P. Watt, who served as not only a bargaining agent but also a counselor and legal advisor to authors. Watt began by charging fees for services, but authorial poverty and the power of well-tuned incentives soon led him to contract on a revenue share of 10 percent, a figure that (with some upward perturbations) persists to this day.[5] The origins of the agent's role underline a reason why the agent is efficient for performing the gatekeeping function. As the author's employee, the agent can elicit information from the author on components of her "reservation price"—willingness to cooperate, make manuscript changes, and the like—that the author bargaining directly with the publisher might strategically conceal. The presumed nonnegotiability of the conventionalized agent's fee keeps this strategic consideration from inhibiting the transfer of information from author to agent. The elicited information might tell the agent that no deal is likely, but the publisher is spared wasted haggling costs.

The author-agent relationship does tend to destruct when the author succeeds and becomes well-known to publishers. The agent's talents for shaping manuscripts and interceding with publishers become less valuable. The 10 to 15 percent commission implies a high charge for negotiating and monitoring contracts, services that a lawyer could perform for a fee.[6] Agents, like others who help develop an artist's career, find it difficult to write contracts that award them the expected value of their contribution to the artist's lifetime income without creating a strong incentive for the artist once successful to demand renegotiation. The committed duration of artist-agent contracts is commonly short and often open-ended. The downside hazards of long-run commitments must be too great: for the agent, being stuck promoting a burned-out author; for the author who achieves major success, overpaying for the agent's current services.

A good test of agents' function comes in the traits of publishing segments where they are not used, or just falling from or coming into use. The last is illustrated by Christian publishing, which has recently seen much turnover of firms, cutbacks of lists, movement of authors from house to house, and increased prizes for the most successful authors.[7] Each factor favors or reflects agents' services. The turnover of firms and cutback of lists both increase the magnitude of the publisher's filtering problem and make the agent's gatekeeping more valuable. Meanwhile, enlarged top prizes raise the value to the author of the agent's bargaining skills, and mobility of authors likely reflects the agent's matching function. The agent plays little or no role in book publishing outside of trade books, because his advantages in lubricating the process of selecting authors do not carry over. The scholarly author holds professional qualifications and a reputation that have no counterpart for writers of sensitive first novels. The gatekeeping publisher has easier access to information beyond the manuscript itself. Textbook publishing, for example, with high fixed costs for both author and publisher, requires at least informal precommitment between author and publisher at the outset, and peer review supplies a cost-effective evaluation. For scholarly books the publisher is apt to use other gatekeepers than the agent, such as the well-known academic who, as series editor, takes on the gatekeeping function for a 2 to 3 percent royalty. The academic author desires the quality signal broadcast by a distinguished series imprint, and the series editor's reputation certifies this. The series editor's own reputation suffers if weak or partisan manuscripts get published. Most scholarly authors rationally expect little pecuniary gain, so that the agent's bargaining prowess has little payout. The scholarly publisher runs little risk from accepting manuscripts submitted through a series editor, and need not commission costly evaluations. The selection of the series editor, however, is a serious investment for the publisher.[8]

Author and Publisher

Publisher and author of a finished manuscript face an easy contracting task. The manuscript removes most issues of opportunism and hidden actions on the author's part and makes the publisher's actions easy to specify. For established authors or celebrity books, however, publishers may participate in an auction based on just a twelve-page prospectus; if the remaining 500 pages on arrival lack the lapidary quality of the prospectus, the publisher generally can back out.[9] That is, the deal takes the form of an option contract obligating the author to deliver the manuscript to the publisher, but the publisher need accept it only if it is "satisfactory." Many disputes arise over decisions to decline manuscripts. Insufficient quality or a missed deadline are contractually valid grounds, though they can be abused as makeweights for opportunistic factors. Contracts frequently entitle the publisher to retrieve an advance for a declined manuscript. Exercise of the privilege leads to bitter disputes and often proves infeasible, leading to such compromises as partial recoupment from the author's royalty income when the manuscript is placed elsewhere.[10] The general implications of option contracts are discussed in the next section.

The royalty contract gives the publisher only an attenuated incentive to promote the book. For a trade book correctly expected to enjoy moderate sales, the typical royalty contract, which offers the author 10 percent of the book's retail price, splits the gross profit (that is, the difference between the publisher's marginal cost and wholesale unit revenue, before deducting the publisher's fixed costs) about 58–42 between publisher and author.[11] As was shown in Chapter 2's discussion of profit- and revenue-sharing contracts, the author's royalty based on sales leaves the publisher with an underinducement to promote the book (the author, correspondingly, wants more promotion than would maximize author's and publisher's joint profits). The author's advance, though, strengthens greatly the publisher's marginal incentive to promote—he gets roughly the full resulting gross profit—until the advance is earned back, which increases the efficiency of the contract.[12] Another conflict arises between publisher's and author's interests in keeping a book in print once its sales fall to a low level. Keeping a book in print and in stock imposes a fixed cost on the publisher, while the author gets royalty income without sharing that cost.

The publisher's standard contract enjoys widespread use, with little variation in its terms. Why does it so dominate the alternatives, especially since many rejected authors would happily sign if they could? Why does the author receive nearly half of the gross profits? In fact some publishers require only that the author cough up the cost of publishing, distributing, and promoting the book. Completed book manuscripts in a sense go unpublished because the author is unwilling (unable) to throw good cash after time that was badly invested (aside from the pleasure of literary toil). The "vanity press" sector does not appear to do a large business.

Suppose that the standard contract were less generous to the author—say, 5 percent rather than 10 percent royalties. Publishers, gaining a larger share of the profits, would choose to publish more books, and the threshold of commercial prospects would fall. Weaker or more specialized manuscripts would get published, but also some potential authors capable of writing good books would divert their energies to more rewarding activities. Here we find for the first time a pattern that appears throughout the creative industries. Creative inputs are vertically differentiated *(A list/B list)*, but also subject to pervasive horizontal differentiation *(infinite variety)* and uncertain reception in the market *(nobody knows)*. There is a collective interest in keeping enough artists in the game to ensure ample candidates for random success in book publishing (or, in motion-picture production, availability of just the right bit player for a role). That interest is advanced when the author allowed through the gate receives a large prize. We call this the *lottery prize* phenomenon: many keep buying tickets despite the rational expectation that their chances of winning are tiny. Readers benefit if more good books get written, and publishers who gain utility from publishing putatively good books also will not regret liberally compensating the author who is allowed through the gate.

The lottery-prize arrangement may serve the common good, but why does each party individually stick with it? Why does no trade publisher prosper by fishing from the "slush pile" the few promising manuscripts that have slipped past the 10 percent publishers, and offering these rejected authors smaller prizes? Authors have no minimum-wage contract, unlike many performing artists (Chapter 7). The ample supply of parties willing to become 10 percent publishers by itself tends to make this "deviation" unprofitable.[13] Perhaps an informal standard evolves, widely shared among readers, publishers, and successful authors, as to how good is a "good book," and how deserving of reward is an author capable of passing through a good publisher's gate. This standard discourages bottom-fishing in the manuscript pile, even if it proves (marginally) profitable. That is, the 10 percent royalty publisher who cuts to 5 percent certainly loses the good authors. He also loses some marginal authors who would rather continue searching for a 10 percent publisher rather than "slum" for 5 percent. He loses respect among publishers and potential employees. These factors may deter trade publishers from cutting the royalty below a conventionalized rate, although the argument does not explain exactly why that convention took root in the first place—beyond the focal power of round numbers.[14]

Because most authors complete books only infrequently, career-building investments dwindle in importance. Nonetheless, a successful first book raises readers' interest in the next, just as a successful second book increases demand for the first. The publisher can internalize this benefit only with contractual first refusal of the author's next manuscript. The author has an interest in committing subsequent books to the publisher in order to lift his incentive to promote the first. Such a lock-in has pitfalls for the author, however. On what terms will the next book be published? A right of first refusal leaves the author free to accept any better offer for her next book. When the next manuscript comes around, the original publisher's bid anticipates some of the second book's expected spillover profits from promoting backlist sales of the first, in order to meet the highest outside bid. A firm commitment of the author's subsequent works denies her this leverage. In the first contract she can try to bargain favorable terms for subsequent books, but at that time *nobody knows,* and her bargaining power hence is weak. With the contract terms on future books left incomplete, the locked-in author assumes that the publisher will exploit any opportunity that arises. She either demands up-front compensation for being locked in or underinvests in effort on the next manuscript. In practice, lock-ins are not seen, and first refusals prevail but apparently cause few problems. One survey of authors found that not only did they typically take the first contract offered to them, but that over 60 percent repeated with the same publisher by default.[15]

The history of contracting practice holds interest, because the changes reflect changes in the technology and organization of publishing, changes that have not always improved the incentive structures of contracts. In England in the nineteenth century and before, either the author received a fixed payment from the publisher, or the two parties shared the net profits from the publishing venture. Up to the 1830s and 1840s, the deal covered only a single printing of the work. Printing type was too costly to be set and retained for possible reprintings, so that any reprint was technically a fresh start for the publisher. The development of stereotype and later electrotype plates eased reprinting and allowed an open-ended deal dependent on the book's sales. Open-endedness increased the uncertainty of the venture, however, encouraging the publisher to share the risk with the author (especially the novice).

The royalty contract with an advance improves efficiency until the advance is recouped, but then generates discord as the author benefits more from the publisher's actions that enhance gross revenue, while the publisher with a revenue-sharing contract underspends. In any case, Victorian novelist George Eliot was the first major writer to receive a royalty contract (in 1860 for *The Mill on the Floss*), and by 1900 it was standard in both Britain and America. At first the royalty kicked in only after the publisher recovered printing expenses, but that feature disappeared.[16] The royalty contract was probably associated with the rise of the large publishing house and the practice of successive differentiated editions of successful novels. A profit-sharing contract needs the account-keeping process (whoever performs it) to be transparent to both parties and free from "judgment calls" that allow opportunism. As publishing firms became larger, with overheads spread among many projects, and as the publisher's costs became a stream incurred over time, accounting opportunism arose of the sort that Hollywood later made famous (Chapter 6). The practice of temporary purchase of copyright by the publisher had strong efficiency advantages (the publisher faced the full cash-flow consequences of his decisions), with one exception. As the time of reversion of copyright to the author approached, the publisher's incentive was to run the presses nonstop and flood the market.[17]

Editor and Publisher

The gatekeeping process in book publishing affects the relationship between the editor and the publisher who employs her. The editor plays an entrepreneurial role inside the firm, starting with the decision to accept a manuscript. Editors in scholarly publishing have substantial authority to sign manuscripts on their own, as quality and breadth of interest are relatively easy to determine, and the firm's risks are correspondingly small. In trade publishing uncertainty is greater, and success is more dependent on the efforts exerted by other specialists within the firm (design, advertising, marketing). The editor assumes the role of advocate, supplying impetus and staking her own reputation on her conviction of a manuscript's commercial worth.[18] One asset that the editor deploys in this contest for resources is her status as the key link between the firm and the author.[19] The editor's entrepreneurial role diverges from the formerly central copyediting function, now spun off to specialists. Despite their entrepreneurial roles, editors' compensation apparently contains little pecuniary incentive.[20] Bonuses may be growing more common, however. Highly successful trade editors are commonly rewarded with their own publishing imprint, which at least enlarges the reputation capital that they can glean from producing successful books. As head of an imprint, the editor also has the discretion of offering larger advances and taking a more active role in the book's design, marketing, and publicity.[21] The mobility of editors among publishing houses is high and increased by the goodwill asset built up between editor and author, which allows a publisher to bid for an editor's services with the hope that her authorial ducklings will waddle along behind. The *nobody knows* outcome of editors' efforts allows reputations to swing unpredictably between dud and star status, which also increases mobility.[22]

Editors' circulation among jobs flags a pattern of behavior that appears throughout the creative industries. Regular employees who play a creative role (for example, engineers in semiconductor firms), or who hold goodwill assets with independent artists (such as trade-book editors), maintain extensive contacts with their counterparts in other firms. The contacts involve the exchange of copious information and deal possibilities in the form of favors given and returned. Economists normally assume that proprietary information is an asset used intensively within the firm and guarded vigilantly against leakage to the outside world, so this interfirm "networking" needs an economic explanation. Through these industries surge large, amorphous flows of new information. With constantly changing data, new information is costly to obtain, nobody knows it all, and employees with similar professional interests can benefit by sharing on a reciprocal basis. An employee of firm A may have some bit of information about a failed project of A's that is useful to firm B, yet its leakage imposes no cost on A. When an employee of A passes it to B's employee, the two firms taken together are better off. Furthermore, A's employee (and therefore the firm itself) acquires a call on some future reciprocation. One-third of editors reported having had projects referred to them by other publishers.[23]

This process of exchanging information complements the mobility of personnel between firms. The network not only facilitates job switching; it also widens individuals' circles of contacts and speeds the dispatch of information toward its points of greatest usefulness. The role of informal reciprocity and reputation is underlined: the better connected the network, the faster the news of defection travels, and the longer it is remembered.[24]

Dealings between Artist and Record Company

Young pop musicians (introduced in Chapter 1) seek work at local clubs, schools, and the like, honing their performing skills and (likely) writing a body of songs that they hope will eventually attract a record company ("label"). A band recruits a personal manager to help with both its creative development and business management. This role is both complex (in terms of the mixture of skills and the personal congeniality required) and risky (because of the large proportion of performing groups who break up or fail ever to earn substantial revenue). Managers accordingly demand a large share of a successful group's income, 15 to 20 percent of gross earnings (and thus a large bite of net earnings), excluding advances from labels for recording costs, support of tours, and the like. The contract's duration is clearly a sensitive issue. It generally runs from three to five years, with the artists holding the right to cancel if their earnings fall below some threshold. The manager receives a continuing share of royalties from any records made under the contract.[25]

Performers and labels pursue each other in various ways. The labels employ talent scouts ("strange noctavagants," *Fortune* once called them) to seek out talent, and in-house producers become advocates for groups that they record in the manner of publishing-house editors.[26] Musicians employ attorneys in the manner of literary agents to shop demonstration ("demo") tapes around to labels. A label may receive three to four hundred tapes a week, so only those backed by a competent certifier are likely to get attention.[27]

Terms of Recording Contracts

The principles behind the typical contract for a present-day popular music composer-performer resemble those in the visual arts. The artist (group) provides the creative inputs through songwriting and performing to create master tapes of songs suitable in quality and quantity for release as an album. The label produces and distributes the album on compact discs and cassettes and advertises the artist and album through videos, by supporting performance tours, and by promoting the album to broadcasters and record buyers. The artist collaborates not just in producing the master tape and video but also in touring and associated direct promotion.

Like the visual artist (and less like most trade-book authors), the musician and label seek to promote an extended career and gain a long-lived earnings stream. The payout is highly uncertain, however. *Nobody knows:* casual estimates suggest that roughly 80 percent of albums and 85 percent of single records released fail to cover their costs (the "stiff ratio").[28] The chances for a successful second album are not high even given a successful debut album. The artist who had her whole life to ready the first album now has six months for the second. Apart from that, among all the world's possible record albums, randomly excellent, okay, or terrible, the musician's first released album might be a lucky draw of excellence that is unlikely to be repeated.[29]

For artist and label the issues of contracting essentially duplicate those faced by visual artists and authors. Royalty contracts based on sales revenue again dominate, with a more efficient profit-sharing deal likely ruled out by the difficulty of monitoring the label's bookkeeping. Contracts also reflect both the uncertainty of success and the inability of young performers to supply inputs other than their time and talents. The artist can commit to produce an album that the label might find acceptable to release, but of course cannot predict or guarantee the public's response. The label cannot efficiently guarantee in advance what promotional effort it will undertake: this depends on the album's character and how much (if any) public interest it initially elicits.

In the standard recording contract, the artist commits to deliver exclusively to the label master tapes for a series of albums. The label holds an option to distribute these records for a period of time, and commits to pay royalties based on revenues generated by each recording. For each album the label provides an advance to the artist that at least covers the cost of recording the album (including union-scale wages to the session musicians) and may provide income that anticipates earnings from royalties. The advance against royalties is an absorption of risk by the label and a guarantee of minimum royalty income for the artist. Royalty rates fall in the range of 11 to 13 percent for a new artist (as low as 9 percent for a small, independent label), 14 to 16 percent for artists in the middle range of success, and 16 to 20 percent for superstars.[30] The rate on a given album may escalate with the number of copies sold.

The effective value of these nominal royalty rates is reduced by what Donald Passman called a series of "cheats" by the labels that have crawled into the standard contract. The royalty is based on the album's suggested retail list price, but this is reduced by an arbitrary "packaging charge" for the record's container, 20 percent for cassettes and 25 percent for compact discs. The count of records shipped (for determining the royalty payment) is reduced by genuinely donated copies used for promotion, but also by phony donated copies (15 percent) conventionally generated by boosting the wholesale price quoted to the retailer but shipping an offsetting number of free copies. Until recently the count of records shipped was reduced 10 percent to allow for breakage, although fragile shellac records disappeared from the market 50 years ago. The breakage and free-good allowances together knock the artist's royalty base down to 76.5 percent of actual shipments.[31]

A vital feature of the recording contract—one that appears throughout the creative industries—is its option structure. An option in this context gives the gatekeeper an exclusive right (for some period of time) to consider acquiring the artist's creative product on pre-agreed terms; if the gatekeeper declines, he has no further obligation to the artist, and she keeps any payments already made to her (in some art realms that includes payment for the option itself). The label, having advanced to the artist the cost of recording an album, is not required to release it, if the tape disappoints sufficiently to kill expected profit.[32] That means gross profit (without deducting the advanced recording cost) from the record at hand plus net profit expected from future albums. If the label continues to release tapes delivered to it, the contract then obligates the group to supply further albums. Nowadays the terms commonly require the artist to deliver a second album within some number of months after the first. The label's acceptance carries an increased advance and royalty rate, but it also commits the artist to ready yet another album, the cycle continuing for a total of eight to ten records.[33]

The artist receives royalties on a record only after the advance is recouped. No necessary relation exists between profit to the label and the recoupment of the advance. Likewise, an artist might issue a series of apparently successful records and yet receive no royalties except for any excess of the advance over recording costs. These outcomes depend simply on the size of the negotiated advance relative to the maximum joint profit actually available to artist and record company together. The label insists on "cross-collateralizing" the artist's albums issued under a contract. Cross-collateralizing pools revenues from independent projects (or markets) for the purpose of recouping advances for any of them: if the first record fails to earn back its advance, the deficit becomes a claim on the royalty stream of the second record, and so forth.[34]

The option contract looks unfair to guileless young musicians, yet its form has a compelling logic. Many creative goods proceed through stages of production with costs completely sunk at each stage, yet with the final payout remaining highly uncertain. At each stage, fresh news regarding the ultimate payout likely emerges, and additional costs are incurred. The efficient contract allocates decision rights at each step to the party about to sink liquid purchasing power and able to test its expected payout against the project's current prospects. If would-be superstar musicians became much scarcer relative to the public's demand, the new equilibrium contract would likely provide the musicians with more favorable advances and/or royalty rates, but preserve the option structure. This proposition does depend on the two parties' attitudes toward risk; if artists are risk averse, the label might give a firmer commitment to release even in the presence of fresh bad news. In fact highly successful artists bargain for somewhat stronger obligations for the company to release; for example, the master tape need only be "technically satisfactory" or "in the artist's previous style" rather than "commercially satisfactory."[35]

Implications for Incentives

This contract has a number of salient incentive features. By guaranteeing terms of access to the artist's future albums, it bolsters the record company's incentive to promote the artist's first album despite the high expected stiff ratio. A successful group is under exclusive contract long enough for the label to recoup on later albums any losses run on earlier ones. Promotion of one album generally has positive spillover effects for the artist's previous albums, and this is also internalized. If the artist is successful enough, the contract's built-in schedule of royalties may not escalate fast enough to deny substantial rents to the label. But the contract is then prone to renegotiation: injustice perceived by the performer in her current contract does not favor the timeliness and quality of the next album delivered. The label has only limited ability to collect its biggest contractual jackpots in full. The label's incentive to promote a successful artist withers as the contract's expiration date approaches, shrinking the rents expected to fall into the label's hands from subsequent albums. For the artist the multiyear option contract does not provide much downside protection. Even if the label continues to pick up its options, unsuccessful albums may cause it palpably to "lose interest" in the artist. While it might be obligated by contract to issue the artist's next album, it is not obligated to promote it. The label's ability to terminate a contractual arrangement is quite complete, and the artist's ability to sustain the forward motion of a best-efforts commitment quite limited.[36]

The royalty contract based on the label's sales revenue diverges in some ways from the terms under which authors and visual artists get paid. While the label funds the physical production and distribution of the album, large components of promotion costs (as well as all recording costs) are recoupable from the artist's royalties. Because each party to a royalty contract benefits from the other's promotional outlays, the label might even overpromote an album, relative to the outlay that would maximize parties' combined profits. The incentive's strength increases with the company's confidence that the label will recoup all costs that it has advanced. The incentive decreases with the artist's effective royalty rate. The higher the rate, the less of a promotion-induced extra dollar of revenue lands in the company's pocket. There is no easy way to test empirically for overpromotion, beyond noting the industry lore on promotional expenditures charged to artists' royalties that have little function save gratifying the artist: vanity billboards on Sunset Boulevard and "limousines to take you to the bathroom" might attest to either an overinducement to promote or the strong appeal of ego gratification to the immature.[37]

The artist may have little control over the promotion outlays chosen by the label, but the costs of recording the album depend directly on the artist's quest for quality (and degree of organization for achieving it). The royalty contract seemingly induces the artist to underinvest in studio time and resources, because the company pockets a large share of the additional revenue once the advanced recording costs are earned back. Nonetheless, record executives commonly complain of the artist who out of indiscipline or perfectionism takes up far more studio time than necessary.[38] Such a concern by the artist with creative success over income can be written off to *art for art's sake*. The uncertainty of the album's success, however, supplies an economic reason why the performers might rationally overinvest in studio costs. If the album fails to recover its costs, the artist receives no royalties while the loss—whether large or small—falls entirely on the label. The artist's royalties increase dramatically, however, when album is a big success—indeed, the royalty *rate* commonly escalates. If inflating the studio costs raises the chances of a big win, while the downside loss falls entirely or mostly on the label, the artist could select a heavier investment in album production costs than the label would prefer.[39]

Governance of Contracts

Recording contracts encounter various problems of opportunism as they run their course. Previously mentioned was the erosion of label's incentives to invest in the artist's career as the contract's expiration date approaches. From the artist's viewpoint, a problem of moral hazard arises because the label keeps the books that determine the earnings remitted to the artist. This problem festers at some level in all of the creative industries, reaching its peak in the motion-picture industry. Recording artists face less commonly the problem that afflicts visual artists (Chapter 2) of bankruptcy and disappearance of the commercial partner, but a greater hazard of opportunistic transactions. In a long dispute between the Beatles and EMI and its U.S. subsidiary Capitol, undercounts of sales for royalty calculation were alleged, as were transfers of "free" promotional records to subsidiaries that released them for commercial sale.[40] Music videos are a valuable tool for promoting albums, although their high fixed cost warrants their preparation for a new artist only if an album has already shown substantial public appeal. A video therefore is not committed in the contract initially and involves renegotiation. The video itself generates a royalty stream for both artist and label, apart from its promotional benefit. Usual practice is apparently for the label to recoup 50 to 75 percent of the video's cost from the artist's royalties—from the video, from the record, or from the two cross-collateralized.[41] Overall, the recording contract seems peerless in the scope that it offers for governance disputes. With the recent consolidation of several record companies these have reached fever pitch, causing many artists to consider managing their own promotion and record distribution over the internet. But one website among the endless horde, with no mediating gatekeeper, is probably an inadequate substitute for an established label.[42]

Artists' concert tours raise their own set of complications. Concerts on the road bring in substantial revenue streams while also incurring heavy direct costs as well as personal stress for the performers. They promote record sales, just as records increase the demand for concert appearances. This interdependence provides an example of an economic relationship that appears here and there throughout the creative industries. Assume that an artist's recordings and concert tours are each profitable, taking just their own respective costs and revenues into account. Because each increases demand for the other, each profit stream's recipients would willingly spend to induce an increase in the scale of the other activity. When a deal is worked out, it is not clear whether (in this case) the label will contribute to touring expenses, or the tour's beneficiaries (artist and promoter) will sacrifice to increase the stream of recordings. A mutually acceptable deal could send payments flowing in either direction. Labels have supported tours to a degree varying over time, cutting back when music videos emerged as an effective competing promotion technology. New and unknown groups can benefit greatly from opening for established groups at concerts; indeed they might willingly pay for the privilege and have been known to do so.[43] In the 1960s touring pop groups were paid very little, but their recordings received extensive local airplay. British artists found that to build a base of fans large enough for a high level of success with recordings they had to make several money-losing tours of the United States—clearly a high cost for establishing a group.[44] Gradually the concert circuit evolved into a spectacular "show" and a way to "break" (that is, promote into widespread recognition) new groups and advertise new albums of well-established ones. The revenues from concert tours have increased greatly, but so have their costs and promotional benefits, and taken by themselves they apparently are profitable only for the most popular groups.[45]

Contracts between performers and local promoters and venues suffer their own epidemic of failures. A profit-sharing arrangement is common: the performers get a guaranteed minimum payment; before any further distribution to the performers, the promoter recovers expenses and a "guaranteed" profit; and the remaining net revenue is divided between performer and promoter in a ratio between 60/40 and 90/10. Large venues (stadiums) with local spatial monopolies capture some rents (often partly absorbed in union wages and feather-bedding agreements); local promoters, however, lack any rent-yielding unique assets. Scope for opportunism arises as performers move rapidly from one venue to the next, while accounts arrive only months later, when the expenses and gross revenues are costly or impossible to audit. One booking agency, Frank Barsalona's Premier Talent, rose rapidly in the late 1960s to dominate the scheduling of rock concerts partly through forming continuing informal partnerships with local presenters. The agency would guarantee that the local presenter broke even if a concert unexpectedly lost money; the presenter presumably sustained the relationship by rendering honest accounts. Enforcement of contracts in the creative industries depends heavily on the power of repeated interactions among parties who value their reputations for cooperative behavior.[46]

Agents and Job-Matching

Agents play several roles in the creative industries. Literary and concert-booking agents perform a job-matching function—lining up trade-book authors with publishers and popular musicians with performing venues. The gatekeeping role assumed by the literary agent results from excess supply due to *art for art's sake,* but the job-matching task would remain even if every manuscript found a publisher and every publishing house issued its preferred number of titles. Creative outputs such as book manuscripts differ pervasively *(infinite variety);* in the short run that matters for the matching process, publishers are likewise heterogeneous—in their fields of interest, backlists, current congestion of the publication pipeline, promotion methods, and so on. Indeed, most creative activities have to solve some job-matching problem— allocating vaudeville acts among theatres, big bands among ballrooms, classical pianists among concert series, actors among movie projects. The organization of matchmaking agents varies greatly. In classical music (this section's empirical focus), the agency function at times has been nearly monopolized.

Hence, we need to pin down the basic functions that agents perform—which side of the market they represent, and what forces determine their number relative to the parties whom they represent.

Whose Side Are You On?

Why do matchmaking agents represent the side of the market that they do? We usually see them representing sellers. But that arrangement is not universal (think of executive search firms and other such independent purchasing agents), and for some matching problems it is hard to see any case for attaching the matchmaker's services to one side rather than the other. Why should marriage brokers represent would-be brides rather than potential grooms? The gatekeeping role suggests one way to explain which side is represented. With potential authors vertically differentiated *(A list/B list)*, and a cost incurred to assess the quality and prospects of any given author, it would clearly be inefficient for every publisher to read every manuscript that tumbles over the transom. Publishers, we assume, cannot themselves divide up the stream of submissions and share their assessments with each other, while an agent who finds a good manuscript knows which publisher will find it most attractive. Agents, as they decide which authors to represent, "pool" the task of assessment, performing it once for the benefit of the several publishers to whom the agent refers promising manuscripts. All gain from this pooled screening.[47] The gain increases with the number of writers who never find a publisher.

Matching is a two-sided process: publishers need to find out about writers, and writers about publishers. Suppose that publishers' policies are readily revealed by their backlists and reputations with their authors for capability and integrity; authors' qualities are more costly to expose. If the transacting parties on one side of the deal are represented by agents who pool information and economize on its transfer to the other side, pooling the more costly assessments of authors and their manuscripts beats pooling the less costly assessments of publishers' traits on behalf of authors.[48] The same logic applies to the differential importance of the information to the other side. A publisher loses heavily if a celebrity author's book flops, but the celebrity might be nearly indifferent about which of several mainline trade publishers publishes the book.[49]

Other influences also weigh in. Suppose that it costs the same for a publisher to size up a prospective author as for the author to evaluate a prospective publisher. Even after the gatekeeping agents have swept out the losers, the authors remain more numerous than the publishers. (Think of each house serving as exclusive publisher to a number of authors.) If agents are to pool information on one side of the market only, they should pick the more numerous authors, thereby consolidating more information than if they represented the less numerous publishers. The agent's gatekeeping function, which excludes many authors, is really a special case of this "differential numbers" effect.

The agents' assignment might also be determined in part by functions that they perform along with job-matching. The auditorium sits immobile at the corner of Fourth and Main, while someone must ensure that the band finds its way there; after the concert the band rides off into the night in its limousine, and somebody must check that the venue makes its obligated payment to the artists. Agents will tend to represent the artists, because they place higher value on such auxiliary services. In summary, job-matching agents likely represent the side of the market that has the most clients, is subject to more exclusionary gatekeeping, is less able to reveal credible information about itself, has less need for differential information about the other side, and/or has a greater need for the agent's ancillary services.

How Many Agents?

How many parties will each agent represent, and how many agents serve the market? Suppose that what each seller offers and each buyer seeks could be fully described as quantitative, measurable traits. Suppose also that the best match-up of heterogeneous buyers and sellers can be reduced to a computer algorithm.[50] Then matchmaking, like an automated stock market, would be a "natural monopoly" efficiently run by a single agent. Where the agent's role arises from the costliness and incompleteness of information, however, the virtue of a monopolistic job-matcher breaks down. Wherever the agent's role centers on the costly pooling of heterogeneous information, the agent's capacity to absorb and exchange information is limited, and with it the number of clients each agent can represent. If agencies perform auxiliary services subject to scale economies, the agency firm might become a large partnership of individual agents. But the more idiosyncratic the information and the more often and extensively it changes, the more personalized the agent's role becomes, and the fewer parties he can serve.[51]

The organization of agency relationships is also driven by problems in governing the deal between the agent and the party represented. Take the popular dance bands that toured among ballrooms and theatres in the 1920s through 1940s. Its booking agent might schedule a band at one location for Saturday night, then uncover and accept a better offer for that same night without renegotiating the first—resulting in an enraged presenter and a disgraced bandleader. Or the band might fail to show up due to personal disorganization that could be warded off by a suitably hectoring agent. These problems led to the rise of relatively large booking agencies, notably Music Corporation of America (later MCA). The organizations' sizes were partly due to scale economies in managing the logistics of bands' travels, but the valuable fixed assets of these booking organizations also ensured their diligent and consistent performance to parties on both sides of the market.[52] That is, the victim of a breach of contract could locate the perpetrator and bring suit that could (if successful) allow it to recover its losses from those valuable assets. A fly-by-night operator by definition offers the contracting party no such protection.[53] In the creative industries, large-size firms sometimes owe their prevalence not to conventional scale economies, but to the value of large blocks of exposed assets as collateral for proper performance of obligations. The firm with exposed assets has incentive not to cheat on its obligations; the contracting partner, recognizing this, has more incentive to sign.

While the job-matching agent might formally represent either seller or buyer, there is a reason why he must align with one or the other. Linking seller S and buyer B may be the best deal for both parties, one that would be picked by an agent representing either sellers or buyers. The contract price however, divides the benefit between S and B, and the agent negotiating that price can serve the interest only of one party at the expense of the other. The problem of interest conflict when agents get onto both sides of a transaction recurs throughout the creative industries. MCA fell into the role when it diversified its activities from agency to the production of films, and was forced to divest its agency operations (see Chapter 7).[54] Creative Artists Agency under Michael Ovitz became a successful and innovative packager of scripts and creative talent for TV and cinema films, but also found itself compromised by both hiring and representing its own talent.

Agents in Classical Music

The booking of classical musicians—singers, instrumental soloists, and orchestra conductors—provides a case study of agents' organization. In the United States, booking agents arose in the 1880s as travel became efficient enough for large numbers of musicians to take to the road. The same pattern emerged in Europe of individual agents, usually well-connected people with musical training and often substantial family wealth. The representation role focused on the artists rather than the venues, for several reasons suggested previously.[55] Personal integrity was problematic, for many musicians (then as now) would perform for little pay in order to build their careers; some agents took their money for promotion and did nothing, confident that the artist was going nowhere.[56] Large agencies emerged, such as Ibbs & Tillett in London and Henry Wolfsohn in New York, for the expected reasons. Wolfsohn employed a large staff of road agents to sell his artists to local sponsors in the United States. Ibbs & Tillett carefully built its reputation for integrity in the wake of personal agents who ran into financial trouble and began appropriating funds due to artists; it even took part in bailing out one failing competitor.[57]

The size distribution of agencies' operations has varied over time. Small (personal) scale always yields an advantage in the agent's opportunity to help build the artist's career. For artists of high promise, these services frequently dominate the ones that large agencies can supply efficiently.[58] Large-scale agencies plied different strengths. Arthur Judson's Judson Concert Management arose in the 1920s, becoming Columbia Artists Management Inc. (CAMI). Before blossoming as an agent, Judson had managed both the Philadelphia and New York Philharmonic orchestras. His specialty was representing conductors, and his continuing orchestra-manager job gave him easy access to any promising guest conductor or soloist who appeared with the New York Philharmonic. Conductors are key decisionmakers in recruiting orchestral soloists, so Judson's dominance as an agent for conductors gave leverage for representing soloists. As intermediary in many deals, he could punish any musician who eschewed or dispensed with his services. By 1930 he had bought up the six largest competing agencies in New York. Judson clearly saw himself as the honest broker between music presenters and musicians, and he managed repeatedly to be on both sides of transactions without protest from the contracting parties.[59]

Judson's successor, Ronald Wilford, preserved CAMI's dominance, representing about 100 conductors and 800 musicians overall (mostly singers). Judson's unique advantage of a central position in the information web was sustained, and conductors remain the linchpins for leveraging the placement of other CAMI soloists. CAMI's objective was clearly to maximize benefit for the musicians represented, however. Judson's domain had been the United States, while Wilford became active internationally and began pulling talent away from agents abroad. Wilford pioneered the practice of conductors holding down the job of musical director with several orchestras at once, while topping their incomes with the cream of guest-appearance fees. His success may explain why, from 1960 through 1990, the price of conductors' services was estimated to rise three times as fast as a laborer's average weekly wage.[60] Apparently, either Olympian optimization or outright monopoly over talent can sustain a large-scale agency organization in classical music.

Another success in large-scale organization was the approach to promoting classical music (and its performers) innovated in 1921 by the Redpath-Chicago Lyseum Bureau, particularly its partner Dema Harshbarger. She devised the Civic Music Committee, for which she would identify leading citizens of a town or city and persuade them to organize a concert series, guaranteeing the fees for visiting artists from subscription sales and undertaking local publicity. The Civic Music Committees expanded local demand for concert tickets, reduced the agent's risk of a nonpaying presenter, cut the agent's promotion costs, and usually recruited their soloists from Chicago Lyseum. By 1932 the energetic Ms. Harshbarger had papered 32 states with Civic Music Committees. She was glimpsed on the horizon by Judson, who made haste to defend the east coast with his own Community Concerts Corporation, which mimicked Civic except for requiring that touring artists be taken from his firm's list. Later (1955) this tying arrangement was enjoined under the antitrust laws, but by then declining public interest in the vocal recital, the mainstay of these series, had shriveled its importance.[61]

For ensemble performers, the agent's function in classical music devolves to contractors, who organize orchestras and choral singers for free-lance work. New York's performing groups, except for the New York Philharmonic and Metropolitan Opera Orchestra, are staffed by free-lance musicians assembled for individual concerts by a dozen contractors, who maintain rosters from a pool of about 1,000 free-lancers. The contractor's specialty is knowing exactly the various players' strengths and weaknesses and their compatibility with the conditions of various jobs. They also ensure that the musicians' wages are placed in escrow accounts and payments are subsequently made. The contractors perform a gatekeeping function in admitting new talent to their rosters, but this role was restricted in 1994 by the musicians' union's success in forcing each of the biggest free-lance orchestras to establish its own roster of regular players, whom the contractor is required to contact first. This seniority system obviously impairs the ability of the contractor to assemble the best available group on each occasion.[62]

4

Artists, Starving and Well-Fed

The imperative *art for art's sake* implies that artists will choose low-paid creative work over better-paid humdrum labor. The gatekeeping process further implies that the artist community will include at any one time those who have passed through the gateway and claimed their prizes (great or small), those still clamoring at the gate (earning apprentice wages at most), and those who have relegated their creative urges to hobby status. The mean levels and dispersions of artists' incomes should reflect these processes, as should the split between their earnings from creative and from other work.

Artists' Success: Superstardom

To explain the great dispersion of artists' earnings and the legendary riches of stars, economists have developed a model of the economic position of superstars.[1] Assume that artists (rock performers, say) differ in quality in the eyes of fans, and all who might attend rock concerts agree on who is the best, second best, and so forth (the *A list/B list* property). Assume, too, that we have a way to quantify these quality differences. To attend a rock concert, fans pay the price of the tickets plus the time diverted from other activities. The higher the artist's quality, the more utility fans get, given their time and money costs. In particular, the model assumes that lower-quality performers are poor substitutes for stars. Great and mediocre concerts take up the same time. A strong preference for quality implies that the fan would forgo many concerts by average rock performers in order to hear one by a superstar, even if the superstar's tickets cost more.

The artist incurs a cost of performing. It does not obviously cost the superstar more to perform a concert (she might offer a more glittery light show, but the argument requires only that the cost for artist and light-show together rises less than proportionally to quality). The superstar has an enviable economic choice. If her tickets are priced the same as average artists', she will draw many more fans. Alternatively, she can charge a much higher price and still attract as large a crowd as an average artist. Depending on factors discussed subsequently, the superstar maximizing her profits picks some combination of higher ticket price and larger than average audience. Her revenue (price times audience size) increases more than proportionally to her quality advantage. Graceland Mansion grows affordable.[2]

The superstar effect on performers' incomes depends on the number of close competitors and the quality gap between them and the superstar. Her advantage also depends on special features of concert-going. Suppose that fans' tastes for creative products are in part collectively determined, so the pleasure of revering a superstar increases with the number of other fans who share the enthusiasm.[3] Suppose that rank by itself plays a role: fans dislike saying that they heard a second-ranked performer just to save $5. The gaps between performers near the top of the quality scale can swell, even with little objective basis for higher quality.

Stars and Emerging Artists

The superstar model can be applied to the situations of established (star) performers and emerging artists.[4] Assume that concert-goers distinguish between established performers (known to have put on a good show) and emerging performers (no track record, but might provide a good show). Buying a ticket for the established star need not guarantee a good show, but the chances are substantially higher. Potential ticket-buyers may take different attitudes toward this choice. Discriminating fans who enjoy a good performance much more than a weak one will pay more to hear the star performer. Fans with tin ears who care less about the performance's quality will pay a smaller premium.

Once again, the established star has the advantage over the iffy emerging artist in attracting a bigger audience at the same ticket price, or the same audience at a premium ticket price. The star's revenue exceeds the emerging artist's take more than in proportion to the higher probability that she will give a good concert. The more numerous are the discriminating fans, and the more they value a knock-out concert experience, the greater the star's advantage at the box office. The star's advantage also increases with her own consistency, and with the fans' skepticism that an emerging performer will pull off a good show.

Scope for Superstars

The superstar model supplies a framework for thinking about the consequences of achieving top rank in different creative activities. One factor is the ease of bringing the superstar's performance to ever-larger audiences. The listener's thrill from a rock star's concert appears to suffer little, and perhaps to increase, when it moves from a thousand-seat hall to a hundred-thousand-seat stadium. For a star classical harpsichordist, enlarging the audience would much more sharply impair the quality of the listener's experience. The rock superstar can, of course, be heard on records—at a loss of perceived quality of the listener's experience. Nonetheless, the superstar's compact discs may provide stiff competition for the average performer's live concert, which enhances the superstar effect.

The superstar effect is also limited if the star's cost of performing increases with the audience size or the number of performances. In practice this factor invokes the performer's capacity limit—the number of fans (number of concerts times size of audience) the superstar can manage to thrill in a year. This limit is finite for the pop musician, but not so confining as the number of gourmet meals a superstar chef can supervise in an evening. Many think Jasper Johns paints better than any other contemporary American artist, but he does not paint faster. Auction prices suggest that his canvases might sell for fifty times the price obtained by a merely well-regarded painter who exhibits regularly. Superstar musicians offer their concerts in larger venues, but not at great markups over ordinary musicians, and the superstar's recordings, duplicated in unlimited quantities at tiny marginal costs, usually carry the same price as an unknown's first album.[5]

Another factor affecting the scope for superstardom is its time dimension, which affects the superstar's cumulative wealth beyond the flow of income accruing in a given month or year. Some have creative skills that will fade over time—the opera singer whose voice frays after years of performing, the actor who can play only characters of a given age range. In other creative lines, stardom falters not for loss of skill in execution but from declining creativity in problem-solving, which can set in for the visual artist even as skill in execution is sustained or improved. Another time-related effect on the superstar's supply decision arises from any short-run diminishing returns in satisfaction of the star's audience. Do you want to hear the same great singer every night? Superstars with good technologies for replicating their performances (film and opera stars) need to worry about glutting their market.[6]

Superstars in History

Superstardom's history holds considerable interest. One might suspect that superstars' careers were less starry in the past, if only due to inferior technologies of travel, communication, and the reproduction of creative works. In the nineteenth century neither the performer nor the performer's reputation traveled at today's speeds. The cost to the artist of reaching large audiences was greater, as was the cost to potential audience members of learning about the thrills found in the superstar's charms. Attitudes as well as communication costs may have less welcomed the adulation of stars.

Critics of culture see a tectonic shift toward superstardom in the present day. Daniel Boorstin argued that "celebrity" had shifted from being a state or situation of a person to being a fixed attribute: "the celebrity is a person who is known for his well-knownness."[7] For evidence he drew on Lowenthal's study of biographical articles that appeared in popular magazines. Between 1901 and 1914, 74 percent of the subjects came from business, politics, and the professions. After 1922 well over half came from entertainment, particularly light entertainment and sports.[8] Joshua Gamson associated this shift with the declining workweek and the movement of leisure and amusement activities into the center of American life, a process helped along by technologies that made cheap magazines and newspapers possible and the reproduction of photographs easy.[9] In the early motion-picture industry, film producers chose not to identify the actors appearing in their films, astutely anticipating that the actor who lured the audience to the nickelodeon would lay irresistible claim on the film's profits. Nonetheless, the fans' clamor for information on the "stars" showed that catering to the public's interest in the performers would enlarge greatly the demand for films. By 1914 the actors were identified in all films, and fan magazines that confected lives for the stars beyond the silver screen were the beginning of today's promotion apparatus.[10] Superstardom is increased by the apparatus of promotion, and the apparatus operates because the public is eager to engage with the trappings of superstardom and will spend money to revel in them.

While a good argument can be made that modern technology and the cultural changes that it supports have greased the skids for superstardom, it would clearly be wrong to regard it as a new phenomenon. Frank Mott's history of best-selling books in America shows that the top titles' sales levels, normalized by the U.S. total population, did not systematically increase over the nineteenth and into the early twentieth century. Early or late, most best-sellers depended on the technology of the cheap reprint edition (including paperbacks), and heavy newspaper and periodical advertising was practiced in the late nineteenth century.[11] Promoters of superstar performers have not greatly changed their tactics, as is evident in the similar operations of Phineas T. Barnum in the nineteenth century and Sol Hurok in the twentieth. Hurok's success as a presenter of dancers and musicians owed nothing to any close knowledge of these arts. What he learned early in his career was to appreciate charisma in a performer: "If Hurok had one real talent, it was how to read an audience . . . When a performer made that mysterious emotional connection with the faces and hearts in the hall—when he *projected*—Hurok noticed."[12]

Stardom and Talent

Do economic superstars rise strictly on the basis of talent? Are other attributes essential, in addition to talent? Is any talent needed at all? Auxiliary traits of determination and personal organization have evidently been important for many superstars, past and present. Economics has nothing to say about measuring intrinsic talent, but it does offer a few touchstone points. One ground for doubting the necessity of talent for superstardom lies in the behavior of consumers, specifically the occurrence of fads, fashions, and bandwagon effects. The consumer uncertain about his taste and uninclined to invest in information (through trips to the library, say, or consultation with an expert) may rationally take other people's choices as a cheap indicator of likely quality. Some of those consumers may have better informed tastes, or access to more information (Chapter 11). Alternatively, the consumer may simply get utility from following the crowd and being in style. These processes of choice suggest that superstardom might befall some artist simply from the lucky accident of acquiring some fans, whose choices are observed by other fans, and so forth. Indeed, if buyers one after another pick (say) record albums from those in the store, and each buyer's likelihood of selecting a given record is proportional to the fraction of previous consumers who picked it (a bandwagon effect), then the statistically predicted distribution of sales levels for "hit" records closely matches the distribution of Record Industry Association of America Gold Records over three decades.[13]

Will any test affirm or reject a necessary role for talent? One is the forward-looking evaluation of students' talent level, by teachers or other experts, before they face any market test. One good if rare example is the test of art students' drawing ability done under controlled conditions by Jacob Getzels and Mihaly Csikszentmihalyi, in which teachers' evaluations of the students' drawing ability displayed significant power to predict their subsequent commercial success.[14] Another test of a sort lies in the gamut of piano competitions run by young musicians. In Joseph Horowitz's thoughtful judgment, the competitions do to a degree predict their winners' success without actually causing it (Chapter 1).[15]

Another approach to probing the talent-superstardom link is to devise technical tests for talent that can be applied to superstars. In one study, cumulative sales of records by pop singers and groups (but not present-day rock stars) were related to a technical measure of voice quality based on the richness of the voice's upper harmonics. This quality measure does indeed prove to be a statistically significant indicator of record-sales success, after many other attributes of the artist's career are controlled. The responsiveness of record sales to talent is not as great as predicted by the superstar model, however, which implies that small differences of talent (among the most talented) should produce large differences in success.[16]

Artists' Incomes and Their Distribution

The superstar effect joins with other traits of creative industries to predict features of artists' incomes—their average levels, composition (income from art and other activities), and distribution among artists.

Artists' Labor Supply

The artist's willingness to sacrifice in order to devote herself to creative work *(art for art's sake)* implies several properties of artists' incomes and activity patterns. Given the elastic supply of would-be artists, their competition will depress the average wage earned from creative work below the wage of humdrum labor, by an amount reflecting the strength of their preferences for creative labor. Artists engaged full-time in creative work should then earn lower incomes than persons in humdrum occupations but equipped with the same basic ability and stock of human capital (education, training, and experience). Superstardom does not undermine this prediction about average earnings. If aspiring artists pursue superstardom and its riches as a fair economic gamble, correctly reckoning the odds on success, they should earn the same average pay as other persons with their ability and education. With *art for art's sake* factored in, their pay should average less. And if they make the easy mistake of overestimating the chances for superstardom (Chapter 1), or crave it with an all-consuming passion, their average earnings will be lower still.

Fledgling artists trying to catch the gatekeeper's eye will, we know, accept near-zero artistic wages as an investment in creative success. Still, bread must be kept on the table. If the artist regards basic sustenance as a fixed cost that limits her investment in creative success, she looks for the highest-paying day job she can find, works the fewest hours possible at the humdrum task to meet the fixed living cost, and devotes the rest of her time to creative activities.[17] The higher the humdrum hourly wage, the fewer hours does she work. This is a telling prediction, because it conflicts with another plausible view of the artist's labor-supply decision. Consider an artist who enjoys both pecuniary income (the goods and services that can be consumed with her cash income) and the act of engaging in creative work. She will also earn less per hour from her creative than from her humdrum work-hours. Offered an increased wage on the humdrum job, however, she allots more hours to humdrum work and fewer to making art. Because the joys of consumption now come cheaper, more time is devoted to satisfying consumption wants.

Evidence: Level and Composition

Researchers have used different methods of gathering data on artists' incomes that yield different but complementary empirical conclusions. Data collected by the U.S. census classify individuals to job categories on the basis of their principal source of income. For the census, artists are persons who have achieved enough success in a creative activity that it is their economic mainstay. Also, artistic activities can be defined narrowly or broadly: a broad list includes not only actors and directors, authors, dancers, musicians and composers, painters, sculptors, craft artists, and designers (only those working in theatre, motion pictures, or art museums), but also photographers and postsecondary teachers of art, drama, and music. The last two categories stand some distance away from the core notion of creative artist. In any case, these broadly defined artists on average (in 1979) earned less, but only 6 percent less, than all individuals in the employed population.[18] When the difference is adjusted for the many other factors that influence individuals' incomes (education, experience, health, regional location, demographic properties), the average difference in earnings increases to 10.3 percent. That difference based on incomes in a single year may overstate artists' average poverty, however, because in any one year the arts occupations contain a large inflow of young people, whose low current incomes (if they succeed in and stay on the same career track) can be expected to increase more than average.[19] Many will not succeed, however, and will eventually settle for some other career. Other occupations show this effect less, because smaller proportions of their apprentices throw in the towel.

In terms of revealing the fate of the starving artist, these census-based data suffer one big defect. They depict persons earning their incomes principally from arts occupations, and not those waiting for the gatekeeper to forward their first (or first recent) paycheck. A different research strategy is to start with a sample of persons who have achieved at least some minimal recognition as practicing artists. The incomes they receive from both artistic and humdrum activities then reveal directly what they sacrifice for their art.[20] A survey by Gregory Wassall and Neil Alper of 3,000 artists residing in New England revealed that only 24 percent held no humdrum job (teaching included), and income from artistic work yielded only 46 percent of the artists' total labor income. Median personal income for these artists was indeed only a little (1.6 percent) below the median for the New England labor force generally (although the artists' education, median 16.5 years, exceeded the general labor force's 12.3 years). Median *family* income was 11.3 percent higher than the New England median, which demonstrates artists' dependence on transfer payments from family members.[21] Other surveys of practicing artists confirm these conclusions.[22] Full-time Canadian free-lance writers in 1978 earned median incomes of $12,500 when the all-Canadian median was $14,225. Part-time free-lancers earned only $1,200 (median) from their writing, but their median total income ($17,500) exceeded that of the full-time writers.[23]

A similar 1989 survey of 2,000 visual artists, 13 percent of whom worked in New York City, found that median earnings from art were only about $3,000.[24] This study also gathered information on the artist's direct cost of pursuing her calling: mean art-related costs were $9,625, so that median net income from art was minus $6,000. Eighty percent of sampled artists held humdrum jobs, 40 percent more than one. Yet median total (gross) earnings for various groups in this sample ranged between $10,000 and $20,000. The pattern is clear: the majority of artists support themselves from their own humdrum jobs and/or the earnings of family members. Median net earnings from creative work, for those with some claim for recognition as artists, are very small (perhaps negative). Artists living in New York are making a heavier career investment than those elsewhere. Their net losses from artistic work are $1,000 greater. They spend three more hours a week on art, are younger, better educated, and less likely to be married than artists living elsewhere. They have 30 percent higher non-art incomes, but incur 37 percent higher workspace costs. By contrast, in a regional art center such as New Orleans, 80 percent of artists depend on non-art income (employment or family members). More than a third of their arts-related incomes stem from art-related activities rather than sales or rentals of art, and three-fourths of the sales or rentals come from the local art market.[25]

Artists apparently undertake humdrum employment only as needed to cover the gap between living costs and art income. One indication is the estimated effect of an increase in income on the costs that the artist incurs to make art: an extra dollar of income from art is associated with 11 cents more art cost, but from an extra dollar of non-arts income 21 cents goes to art costs. A similar survey of Australian artists by David Throsby tested the effects of art wages and humdrum wages (average hourly earnings) on hours that artists spent on the two activities. If artists sacrifice all for their art, he reasoned, an increase in their wage from humdrum labor will let them devote more time to art and less to humdrum work. Throsby found that, once humdrum wages reach a certain amount, this effect indeed kicks in.[26]

The study by Gladys and Kurt Lang of nineteenth- and twentieth-century etchers confirms the contemporary evidence. Most artists did achieve middle-class living standards, either from their art or from employment and family support. Those able to sell their etchings regularly produced more works than did other artists; independently wealthy artists produced no fewer etched plates, but they printed fewer impressions (humdrum work).[27]

Every occupation recognizes talents that let persons perform it more or less successfully, but we expect talent to explain more of the differential success of artists than of (say) shoemakers. A testable implication is that education and training should make smaller and less predictable contributions to artists' economic success than to success in humdrum occupations. Randall Filer found the payoff in pecuniary income for the artist of an extra year of education only 70 percent as large as for other persons and less predictable. Work experience, however, has an effect for the artist that is larger and lasts through the first three decades of her working life. In an analysis of full-time art workers in creative activities, Filer confirmed that artists' lifetime income benefits from college education were 37 percent less than managerial, professional, and technical workers. Among types of artists, designers gain 37 percent less; architects 44 percent less; dancers, choreographers, and authors 68 percent less; photographers 81 percent less; and painters and sculptors 87 percent less. Musicians and composers appear on average to get no benefit from a college degree.[28]

Wassall and Alper, with a sample focused more sharply on creative artists, found no systematic positive effect of education on arts income, although it significantly increases the artist's total income. Throsby's Australian artists showed about the same pattern. Ruth Towse's study of the singing profession in Britain documented in detail the high training costs and low returns to education. Because vocal talent is not clearly evident until late adolescence, serious training cannot begin until singers come into what would otherwise be their early employment years, and they reach "young professional" stage only in their mid-twenties (or later, for males). Solo singers need to absorb the cost of learning roles (for which coaches may be needed), lessons, physical conditioning, and, for recitalists, wardrobe investments. From compensation profiles she derived a rough estimate that the median singer earns a private rate of return of 4 percent on her investment in vocal training, while the social rate of return is 1.5 to 2 percent (lower because of public support of educational costs).[29]

Dispersion of Artists' Earnings and Employment

Artists' earnings tend to be uncertain as well as low on average. Several factors predict that the distribution of individual artists' earnings will be widely dispersed. Pooling apprentices with practicing artists by itself widens the range—little if any arts income for the apprentices, larger earnings for those who succeed. (Apprentice wages are commonly low in humdrum occupations, but proportionally higher than for artists.) Among practicing artists, the *A list/B list* property and the superstar effect by themselves imply a wide dispersion. Still another factor emerges in the next part of this book, dealing with creative products that require the inputs of teams of creative and other workers. Deploying a *motley crew* entails close coordination in time *(time flies)*, a situation that requires artists to work on a series of piecemeal jobs. Some downtime almost inevitably occurs between jobs. When dealmakers assemble creative teams, they will prefer A-list personnel unless A-list wages fully offset the skill advantage. B-list talent tend to work only when the A-list artists are all busy. In the manner of the superstar effect, A-list artists likely both earn higher hourly pay and work more of the time. This source of dispersed earnings should turn up in unemployment rates as well as wage dispersions.

There is not much suitable evidence comparing the dispersions of artists' and humdrum workers' incomes. One study of U.S. census data found that visual artists' earned and total incomes were significantly more variable than for other professions.[30] We can compare the dispersions of the creative and humdrum components of artists' incomes. Wassall and Alper calculated a standard measure of dispersion, the coefficient of variation, to measure the spread of total and creative gross incomes for artists with and without humdrum jobs:[31]

	All artists	Art jobs only	Nonart jobs
Total labor income	1.17	1.70	0.92
Creative income	2.48	1.70	2.49

Thus, art income is more unequally distributed than humdrum income, and it is more unequally distributed among artists holding humdrum jobs than among artists able to devote their efforts only to art. Some evidence also suggests that the upper tail of the distribution of artists' incomes is elongated, as the superstar effect implies.[32] The survey by Montgomery and Robinson contributed some information on the upper tail of the distribution of net incomes from visual art: 5 percent of their sample had net art incomes exceeding $20,000, 1 percent exceeding $40,000, and 0.5 percent exceeding $100,000 (1989 income figures).[33]

It is not easy to compare the unemployment of creative workers to that of others in occupations where work is sporadic, but the sheer extent of idleness among performers is suggestive. The relevant data arrive as miscellaneous observations taken at diverse times and places. Around 1990, 572 concert pianists listed themselves in a standard professional directory as available for engagements, but half the opportunities to perform with North American symphony orchestras went to just ten of them.[34] Robert Faulkner and Andy Anderson tabulated the producers and directors who were credited for 2,430 cinema films released in Hollywood during the years 1965–1980. While 22 producers and 24 directors worked on ten or more films, 64 percent of the producers and 57 percent of the directors received credit for only one each.[35] Mark Litwak confirmed that only about 10 percent of the members of the Directors Guild work regularly in that capacity.[36]

Other data show the inequality of earnings among the members of various talent unions. At a time (1985) when the Screen Actors Guild's minimum scale pay was $361 a day, 75 percent of Guild members were earning less than $3,000 a year.[37] Between 1961 and 1978 the fraction of guild members with annual earnings greater than $100,000 varied between 0.4 and 1.0 percent.[38] On December 1, 1952, only 38 percent of Screen Writers Guild members were employed,[39] and the distribution of their weekly earnings during six months of 1945–1946 was the following: over $2,500 a week, 2 percent; $1,000 to $2,500, 23 percent; $500 to $1,000, 30 percent; and less than $500, 45 percent.[40] Of animated film workers, 37 percent reported themselves unemployed in 1981.[41] British Actors' Equity Association reported that about three-fourths of its members classify themselves as unemployed at any given time.[42] One might have expected fuller utilization rates of Hollywood craft guild members under the studio system that prevailed to the 1950s (see Chapter 5), but the picture appears no different. In 1948 only 600 of 8,500 members of the Screen Actors Guild were under contract to studios, and unemployment among cameramen and related crafts was 57 percent.[43] In 1933, at the depth of the Depression, screen actors' annual earnings were distributed as follows: over $50,000, 4 percent; $10,000 to $50,000, 13 percent; $5,000 to $10,000, 13 percent; $1,000 to $5,000, 43 percent; less than $1,000, 28 percent.[44] In the late 1930s a determined collective effort was made to reduce the number of screen extras seeking employment, and the work was divided among 7,007 in 1940, compared to 22,937 in 1936. Nonetheless, the average number of working days per extra rose from 11.7 in 1936 to only 32.6 in 1940.[45] This scattered information leaves a clear impression: seekers of work in creative roles experience high unemployment and highly unequal earnings and activity levels.

II

Supplying Complex Creative Goods

With contracts for single creative inputs understood, we turn to activities that require complex teams of creative and humdrum inputs. These raise the contracting problems already seen, but in acute form due to the more numerous participants. They also lead into the question of whether projects are better contracted one by one, or the inputs hired under long-term contract by a firm—the choice of "firm versus market." Chapter 5 introduces this issue through the dramatic transformation of the U.S. cinema film industry, where most creative inputs were once under long-term contract. In the 1940s and 1950s, this organization was comprehensively transformed into one of mainly casual short-term contracts, with films distributed by the studios largely as before but production taking place through one-shot deals. Chapter 5 exposes the environmental changes that brought the transformation and documents its many dimensions. Chapter 6 explores how deals are assembled and monitored in the face of complete uncertainty about the film's success *(nobody knows)* and intricate problems of temporal sequencing and coordination *(time flies)*. Assembling Broadway stage productions faces similar problems and employs comparable contracts.

Creative artists differ in quality or talent and are subject to constant re-evaluation within their own trade and by others with whom they collaborate *(A list/B list)*. "Pecking orders" might emerge from instinctual behavior, but these can claim economic rationality. Both the artists and those who organize deals are better off (lower transaction and contracting costs) if each creative contributor knows her rank (Chapter 7). Whether to pick from the A list or the B list is an economic decision for the dealmaker, but there is a logic by which A list talents tend to work together on what become A list projects, and B list members similarly. Talent guilds and unions of humdrum inputs both originated in ancient contract failures, and the guilds today mainly function to provide a framework of rules for individual members' contracts and to keep a supply of diverse B list artists available for when their particular talents are needed.

Simple contracting devices and reputation as an effective enforcer make one-shot contracting work well on stage and screen. Nonetheless, *nobody knows,* and disasters do occur. Chapter 8 explains why talented teams of rational individuals can produce costly movies and books that turn out to be ten-ton turkeys. For movies the answer lies in the progressive sinking of costs into a project, which can make it rational to proceed despite ever-deteriorating prospects. For celebrity books the trouble lies with the publisher's efforts to signal a high-profile book's quality to both readers and booksellers.

The relationship between the producers and distributors or exhibitors of complex creative products involves another set of trouble-prone contracts. The parties directly involved are largely humdrum, but the contracts still reflect problems intrinsic to creative goods. A corollary of *nobody knows* is that the creative good's producer cannot inform the prospective consumer about its qualities beyond the weakest of signals. The producer has no less problem with the distributor or exhibitor. The other property that drives these contracts is *infinite variety,* reflected in the many works that reach the marketplace and the large inventories and many small shipments required in the transit from producer to consumer. Chapter 9 addresses these problems in books and records, Chapter 10 in cinema film distribution. Scale economies in these distribution processes account for the high concentration of sellers found in some creative activities.

5

The Hollywood Studios Disintegrate

Some creative activities require not one but many creative inputs. A cinema film needs actors, screenwriters, a director, cinematographer, costumers, a production designer, make-up specialists, special-effects experts, a composer, and an editor. Each brings different creative skills to the work, and with them *art for art's sake* values that find intrinsic merit in the tasks that they undertake and cast up preferences about how these tasks should be performed. Provision of their inputs needs to be arranged in advance and intricately coordinated in time. A stage play demands a similar team of creative skills. Opera and symphonic musical performances require that elaborate teams of musicians all come in on the beat.

Given the creative specialists needed, these teams can be assembled in different ways that range from the one-shot deal to the long-lived organization that hires some or all of the creative inputs as regular employees on long-term contracts. The Boston Symphony Orchestra has existed since 1881 as a continuing group of musicians with low turnover, while the New York Pick-up Orchestra assembles briefly for Peter Schickele's annual desecration of the works of P. D. Q. Bach. Cinema (and now TV) films can be produced by creative inputs under long-term contract to the classic Hollywood studios of the 1930s and 1940s, or by a one-shot team recruited by an entrepreneurial packager. The motion-picture industry provides an especially interesting setting, because it was completely transformed from one organizational regime to another. The studio system emerged after World War I and dominated film production until it was undermined by several developments in the 1940s. The old studio names are still attached to distributors of feature films, but these films are now produced exclusively as one-off deals, and few long-term contracts exist beyond informal alliances.

The Studio System's Heyday

During their years of dominance the studios resembled a stable oligopoly. Six firms—MGM, Paramount, RKO, Twentieth Century–Fox, United Artists, and Warner Bros.—accounted for much of the supply of Hollywood's core product, the feature film. A few other companies, such as Columbia and Universal, specialized in a lower-quality product then known as the B movie, intended for exhibition in a double feature with an A film. Each individual film, then as now, met an uncertain reception in the market. Nonetheless, these companies sustained their positions throughout the studio era through an efficient production system. In the industry's infant stages, short (silent) films were quickly made and sold outright to local distributors, who in turn rented them for exhibition to the nickelodeons of the day. Two changes transformed the industry's organization. The first was the popularity with audiences of the feature-length film, a European innovation that spread to the United States through film imports beginning in 1911. The second was the discovery of the audience appeal of film stars and the subsequent marketing of stars' off-screen lives.

The Studio System and Talent Contracts

By 1913 various companies, notably Adolph Zukor's Famous Players in Famous Plays, were emphasizing stars in feature films. The feature film transformed the promotion and distribution process; films were no longer the nearly homogeneous product that the one-reelers had been. These changes propelled the vertical integration of production with distribution and eventually exhibition, which became a feature of the studio system. Promoting films on the basis of stars both raised movie attendance and made it somewhat more predictable. Bidding among producing organizations quickly raised stars' salaries and uncorked the flood of perks that remains familiar today.[1]

As the studio system matured, many actors, directors, and some writers and other personnel were employed by the studio on the same option contract now used in the pop record industry (Chapter 3). The artist performed exclusively for the studio for seven years, with the studio holding the option (exercisable every six or twelve months) either to renew the contract with an escalating salary or to terminate. The studio could designate roles the actor was to perform, impose a change of name, control the performer's image and likeness in advertising and publicity, and regulate interviews and public appearances. The actor had no reciprocal right to quit, stop work, or renegotiate for higher pay.[2] Legal challenges to these restrictive contracts were usually unsuccessful, but studios varied greatly in how hard-nosed were their enforcement practices. Highly successful performances did lead to voluntary re-negotiation and improved terms. The contract clearly presumed that the studio could and would promote the performer's career, and budding star and studio would benefit together from the studio's strong incentive to make the investment. In the meantime the star received a low-risk and rising income while the studio assumed (and pooled) the uncertainties associated with star potential. When the actor's career flourished, and fans eagerly pressed money on the box office, the star ceded rents to the studio until the seven-year contract ran out.

Besides the studio's temporary interception of rents attributable to popular performers, the actor's inability to select roles provided the other major point of dispute in option contracts. In the prevailing style of filmmaking, the studio sought to develop a persona for the actor that could attract movie-goers to film after film.[3] The studio also had to juggle its personnel under contract among various filmmaking tasks, to keep them fully occupied. Even if both actor and studio had parallel interests in roles that would effectively stretch the performer or build a career, the studio might find that objective overridden by the goal of keeping its contract players busy. Getting some freedom to refuse roles was hence a premier goal when a successful performer renegotiated a new contract. A study of the dealings of actress Bette Davis showed that in later contracts she gained substantial salary jumps, star billing, and a reduced number of films that she was required to make, but she never won control over what roles she played.[4] A practice that helped to reconcile the interests of performer and studio and to increase the studio system's efficiency was loaning out performers to other studios. This was done cautiously, with the lending studio receiving a premium over the star's contract salary and monitoring to protect its investment in the performer's image. In the *Paramount* antitrust case, studios' restriction of loan-outs to the other major studios was attacked as a collusive restraint on new and lesser studios, but the studio's investment in the contract player's image provided a sufficient reason for close control.[5]

Different considerations affected the contract status of screenwriters in studio script departments. From the earliest days, filmmakers received bountiful flows of scripts and film ideas over the transom. They soon learned, though, that considering and rejecting such submissions led to plagiarism suits whenever the studio later made a film that bore some relation to a rejected script. A spot market in script properties proved nonviable, leading the studios to employ writers in-house and to purchase option contracts when filming stories from external sources—novels, plays, magazine stories.[6] The *infinite variety* property pops up elsewhere in the creative industries to hobble a spot market in property rights to closely substitutable creative inputs. Many publishers of popular songs came to employ rigorous procedures for returning over-the-transom submissions unexamined in order to forestall charges of stealing a few bars from rejected melodies. There are only so many likely ways to arrange sequences of musical notes. Music publishers observe that almost every hit song brings an afterwash of threatened suits; court decisions are regarded as a crap-shoot, and the defendants' high win rate comes at a high cost of legal services.[7]

The assets owned or regularly employed by the film studios included all the crafts and physical facilities normally needed to assemble motion pictures. The physical facilities included studio lots with fixed or buildable sets where many films could be made without the expense of travel to distant locations, and with low costs of supervision by the nearby headquarters. Workers with the more technical creative skills and the purely craft skills were under contracts based on collective bargaining; those are discussed in Chapter 7. All of these, along with the actors and directors, were deployed from film to film, and film projects were selected and scheduled so as to keep these contractually tied inputs occupied. Coordinators were employed to mediate between disparate specialists; for example, the studio's musical director could communicate with both the composer and the musically untrained producer, who might fall into disharmony on their own.[8]

The Studios' Assembly Lines

The studio was an efficient system for turning out a regular stream of films with consistent quality of execution (if not always consistent success). Hollywood's legends of excess and indulgence mock any claim for the efficiency of the system, yet the highly conspicuous consumption of rents to talent should be distinguished from the production system that spewed these rents. Studio film production's consistency has been documented from the finished product by film scholars, who identify a vocabulary of techniques and procedures employed in film after film. Innovations were absorbed: sound, for example, and new visual techniques such as those from German films in the 1920s. Standardization, however, facilitated team production of large numbers of commercial films drawing on copious pools of the required skills.[9]

The supervision of a studio film's production was divided between an administrative coordinator (producer) and a creative supervisor (director). The studios once employed a single head of production along with coordinators for individual films, but placed a producer in charge of each film in order to concentrate responsibility. The process commonly began with the purchase of an option to film a novel, play, or other literary source. The option gave the producer a fixed time period to develop a script and make a final decision to proceed; the purchase price of the option was then applied to the pre-negotiated price for the actual use of the property. The option contract minimized the costs associated with the many initially promising stories that resisted translation into an effective screenplay or otherwise failed in the development process.[10] With an optioned property the producer and writer worked closely to turn the story into a suitable script. If a project failed to converge with one writer, it was often passed along to another, and specialized writing skills (gags, dialogue, polishing) might be applied. The quality of the finished script tended to decline with the number of writers whose fingerprints it bore. Natural projects quickly fell in place; the awkward joints of a problematic one survived any number of cosmeticians.[11] The selection of actors heeded the fact that a star's marginal contribution to a film's box-office value (over a capable but cheaper actor's) would be smaller when the script's structure was strongly controlling.[12]

With the so-called continuity script as a blueprint, filming was planned not in the sequence of the story but with scenes ordered to group the work required of one actor or at one location. Bit players were recruited only shortly before they were needed, and extras (persons visible in a scene but with no dialogue) one day ahead. The time budgeted for shooting was an important control variable, as filming costs tended to be closely proportional to the number of days required. The number of pages of script shot per day was a recognized measure of normal progress. Accounting and control systems supported efficiency. The large squadrons of specialist personnel present at filming were due partly to craft-union featherbedding, but they also stood by to deal quickly with equipment failures and other unforeseen problems.[13] Specialists' skills grew more and more finely differentiated. Directors were identified with particular backgrounds and interests. Technical directors emerged who understood the properties of film stocks and lenses in relation to the desired image. Art directors took over some of the director's and camera operator's decisions about lighting and composition. Similar differentiation and systematization took place in costuming, make-up, and the casting of minor parts. Make-up was designed for a particular actor and film and took account of the film stock used.[14]

Throughout the filming process a target quality level was consciously chosen and sustained, despite a continuous tension between creative workers and supervisors: "Do you want it good or do you want it Tuesday?" Standardization was balanced against innovation. Standard practice rested on common repertories of routines and targets of accomplishment, and the various talents applied to a film aimed to blend harmoniously rather than sticking out. Innovation was encouraged but held to a standard of contributing to the bottom line, and successful chance-taking at any level was rewarded with both cash and power.[15] The system conferred increased decisionmaking discretion on successful performers (especially directors and producers)—they were given "muscle" to push their own agendas ahead and resist conflicting preferences.[16] The chosen quality level was central to each studio's planning. The major studios scheduled annually the next year's films, allocating production budgets among A and B films designated by cost.[17] The major studios at times employed separate units to make A and B films, and the B-specialist studios honed their techniques for shooting quickly on standard sets, economizing on story costs by using series formats, remaking old silent films, and the like. The B-specialist studios sought out young and promising talent who would regard their productions as a training ground.[18] A films that had turned out badly, in the eyes of their creators, were sometimes dumped into the B distribution channel, in which films were frequently sold to exhibitors at fixed rentals and were individually much less risky than higher-quality films.[19]

This review of integrated studio film production suggests two reasons for its prevalence. One reason was efficiency: this was simply the most economically effective way to organize the production of Hollywood-style films. The other reason was rent-seeking: the studios succeeded in intercepting some rents imputed to the stars and other filmmaking talent. Because of the market power and entrenchment of the major studios' film distribution and exhibition networks (explained subsequently), a star could not benefit from competitive bidding for her services (at least until her contract expired). The troubled history of United Artists, organized as a joint distribution facility for independent filmmakers, showed the difficulty of organizing an economically viable alternative to the studio system.[20] That the studios thrived on both efficient production and successful monopsony is a hypothesis that can be checked against the performance of the new structure that replaced it.[21]

Transition to Spot Production

Three major disturbances—two growing from public policy, one from the market—accounted for the shift to making films almost entirely under one-shot deals. During World War II, draconian rates of personal income tax created a strong incentive for the highly paid star to form her own production company and thereby reduce her effective marginal tax rate from 90 to 60 percent. The studios accommodated this by signing short-term contracts with independent producers and stars to make limited numbers of films. This tax-avoidance motive did not by itself change the organization of film production. Even if it had, Hollywood's prosperity during the war (when many competing forms of entertainment were unavailable) would have masked any efficiency loss. What had been a tax dodge served as prototype for the industry's new organization.[22]

The second was the *Paramount* antitrust case against seven major studios, decided by the Supreme Court in 1948.[23] The decision, and its various decrees, which took effect between 1946 and 1949, ended the studios' extensive vertical integration into the ownership of theatres and greatly changed the terms under which distributors could market films to exhibitors. The forces that propelled this integration and explained the forbidden distribution practices are described in Chapter 10; here we stick to the consequences of the decision. The studios' extensive ownership of the larger and better-located theatres, whether by intent or not, had created an effective barrier to the entry of new studios or independent producers into the making of quality films. It also let the studio implement a form of price discrimination, to maximize the rents from each film by promoting and exhibiting it initially in first-run theatres (those that were large, centrally located, and charged high admission fees), then after an interval ("clearance") at lower prices in neighborhood theatres. Each studio's films were automatically slotted to its own first-run theatres where those existed, to other studios' first-run theatres elsewhere. This pattern encouraged cooperation among the studios, because each faced the others as a seller in some cities and as a buyer in others, so that any tactic to enhance its position in one local market would on a tit-for-tat basis be used against it elsewhere. Few second-run theatres were under studio ownership, but access to them for any independent or entrant producer-distributor was limited by block booking, which offered the exhibitor a year's package of a studio's films on an all-or-nothing basis. By enjoining these practices and organizational arrangements, the *Paramount* decrees both lowered entry barriers into the industry and undermined the basis for cooperative oligopolistic behavior among the major theatre-owning studios. It also caused the studios to deal with exhibitors so as to maximize the revenue passing through into the distributor's hands. Previously the appearance of profits in the integrated exhibitor's pocket was just as good for, or perhaps even more advantageous to, the integrated studios.[24]

It was less obvious at the time that the decrees also changed the rate of film production and organizational arrangements that promised highest profits to the studios. The major studio no longer geared its production rate to filling the screens of its theatres. The fact that room would open for competing independent filmmakers was no particular threat, because the studios' entrenched distribution systems survived unchanged.

The market disturbance that upset the studio system was the arrival of television as a major new entertainment technology. Coincident with the *Para-*

mount decision and the divestiture of film exhibition, the public could now enjoy B-movie entertainment at home, at no marginal cost and in the comfort of a six-pack and an undershirt. By 1955 two-thirds of United States households had TV sets. The studios' lower-quality films, the newsreels and short cartoons, could now be delivered by a much more cost-effective technology. The studios' production rate was destined to fall, and films' average quality to increase. The studios made major investments in technologies aimed to elevate cinema films above TV fare: three-dimension (3-D) and wide-screen pictures (Cinerama). These unsuccessful efforts had no major residual effect on filmmaking technology.

Because *Paramount* and the tube simultaneously pushed Hollywood toward making fewer films of higher quality, sorting out their respective causal roles is difficult. Film production within the studios did not lose its virtue of efficient regularity, but that virtue was devalued relative to creativity and novelty (in both technique and subject matter), which could compete more strongly against the TV screen. With films fewer and more distinctive, the studio plant no longer warranted high-fixed-cost departments to make properties and costumes, design make-up, and offer other auxiliary skills. Studio sets as film backgrounds had always held the virtue of thrift (no travel costs) rather than visual quality. Independently, changes in camera technology greatly eased shooting on location. The coming of television seems a sufficient explanation for the disintegration of the movie industry, especially since European film industries untouched by *Paramount* apparently underwent similar changes. Whether *Paramount* by itself was sufficient to cause the disintegration is unclear.

The responses to these changed incentives emerged mainly in the 1950s, when the divestitures of the studios' exhibition chains were being completed. The five major studios released only 48 percent as many films in 1956 as in 1940, although expansion by the smaller studios (and United Artists) meant that the largest eight firms' throughput was 66 percent of their 1940 level. The average real negative cost (the fixed cost of producing the film negative) rose by one-third between 1945 and 1955. Much of the increase was associated with tangible quality-enhancing changes, such as the use of color and wide-screen technologies. Films produced by independents and released by studios were only 20 percent of the studios' total releases in 1949, 57 percent in 1957. Around 1950, independent producers' costs were 30 percent lower than the studios. Comparisons of films' costs are hazardous because they include expected rents to talent, but if the studios' advantage lay in intercepting some rents to talent, their efficiency advantage was surely lost. Studio films' profitability was, though, still more predictable than the independents'.[25]

With the wisdom of hindsight, the studios clearly had to narrow their activities to the distribution of movies, their one film-industry function left after *Paramount* that supplied them the protection of an entry barrier.[26] The barrier lay in the fixed cost of a network in the major North American cities of sales offices able to arrange exhibition contracts with large numbers of theatres, manage local sales promotion, and distribute the physical prints for exhibition. The sales offices of the network held the assets of local knowledge and the advantages of repeated dealings with exhibitors, and the system as a whole was capable of coordinating the large-scale simultaneous promotion of a "big" film around the country. Finally, this apparatus was no doubt rendered still less contestable by the difficulty of financing large sales-promotion campaigns from borrowed funds.[27] The existence of this scale-related entry barrier was demonstrated by the high and stable concentration of box office revenue in films distributed by the (six) leading studios in the 1990s, coupled with the considerable variation in their individual market shares from year to year.[28] The studios' profits tempted various new general-release distributors to enter, over the years, but by 1997 only three of them remained, and these had been acquired by the major studios. The others (by and large) were sunk by costly films that failed at the box office, and possibly by the disadvantage of dealing with exhibitors when one has only the occasional film to offer rather than a steady stream (see Chapter 10).[29]

The studios' managements were less than nimble in downsizing their operations. Such economizing commonly came about only with a change in control of the firm: a new owner undertook a bust-up takeover, selling the studio lot or basing a real-estate development on it, licensing the studio's film library for showings on television, and dismantling most of the studio's specialist departments. United Artists, which led the way in 1951, had the simplest task for never having invested in production facilities. It enjoyed a considerable short-term advantage, because its competitors' fixed facilities were uneconomic and constrained filmmakers' creativity.[30] It seized the previously self-denied function of financing independent filmmakers—actors and directors as well as independent producers.[31]

Flexible Specialization

What replaced film production within the dismantled studios was a transformed system sometimes called "flexible specialization," with most inputs required to produce a film coming together only in a one-shot deal. These inputs are selected by an entrepreneurial coordinator (usually the producer) for their suitability to the project's needs and their availability at the right time (the *time flies* issue of temporal coordination). Informally, they may do repeat business with one another. The heterogeneity of film production, however, means that the same ideal list of idiosyncratic talents rarely turns up for two different films *(infinite variety)*. In humdrum industries, pairs of independent sellers and buyers commonly deal with each other repeatedly; to their mutual benefit they become locked in through compatible physical facilities, knowledge of the particulars of each others' needs, and other such uniting factors called "transaction-specific assets." Film production entails no apparent transaction-specific assets: the same cinematographer and set designer work on two films due to their rightness for both films, not because they work harmoniously with each other. Nonetheless, what induces each participant to give each project its best efforts is still the role of reputation. Just as the constant dialogue over *A list/B list* rankings provides a consensual evaluation of quality, it recognizes earnest effort and cooperative behavior. Shirking, hold-ups, and maverick behavior, once observed, are quickly reported through the industry and are duly remembered.

Evidence of Flexible Specialization

While these mechanisms for ensuring best-efforts performance of creative and other inputs in one-shot film deals are hard to document directly, they imply several observable changes in the film industry's structure.[32]

PRODUCTION OUTSIDE OF STUDIOS   While the old studios continued to distribute many films, small competitors did emerge capable of distributing "small" films in limited geographic markets. The major studios also remained important agents for financing film production, but they were not the only vehicle for films with smaller budgets. Between 1960 and 1980 the shares of the films produced by major distributors, other studios, and independents evolved as follows:[33]

	1960	1970	1980
Major distributors	66%	46%	31%
Other distributors	6	9	11
Independents	28	44	58

MORE SPECIALIZED SERVICE FIRMS   The disintegration of the studios meant that functions once performed by their many departments were now carried out by independent services firms. Using business directories, Michael Storper and Susan Christopherson showed that since 1966 (while the industry's total output of cinema films has increased only a little) many types of specialized entertainment-industry service establishments have proliferated:[34]

	1966	1974	1981
Production companies	563	709	1473
Rental studios	13	24	67
Properties firms	66	33	184
Editing	4	31	113
Lighting	2	16	23
Recording/sound	20	33	187
Film processing	43	76	55
Market research	3	5	24
Artists' representatives	242	359	344

SMALLER SPECIALIST FIRMS The spinning off of studios' specialist departments could in principle occur for two reasons: their activities were better carried on in independent firms, or they were subject to scale economies beyond the reach of a single studio. The latter argument implies that they should have grown larger than before. The former, which suggests that they should become smaller and more specialized, clearly agrees with U.S. Bureau of the Census data. Employment per establishment in motion picture production firms behaved erratically between 1958 and 1981, first declining (until 1974), then increasing (to 1981). Specialized service firms were (tellingly) not even identified by the census in 1958, but between 1974 and 1981 those in California declined in average size by 33.1 percent. Those in other states declined, but by less than one-fifth.[35]

AGGLOMERATION ECONOMIES The industry's reorganization entailed many more arm's-length negotiations per film project between firms or economic agents, and it also rewarded casual contact and exchange of information and evaluations of their competence and fealty. These contacts increase the payout to agglomeration. The change should have raised the concentration of entertainment industry service firms in California, even while filmmaking increasingly took place on location outside the state. This concentration is clearly evident in U.S. census data. A study of film animation studios, which employ a specialized but highly mobile labor force, showed that they tend to cluster geographically (for better access to the common labor pool) rather than to disperse (which might make their existing employees harder to poach).[36] For another sort of agglomeration economy, screenwriters find they must be based in Los Angeles to follow the deal-makers' current film interests, which may well have shifted by the time they surface in films released and playing in theatres.[37]

PART-TIME WORK Along with the specialization of service firms should have gone increased specialization of individuals, meaning that a film project employs smaller time inputs of more individuals. Census data on payroll per employee in film industry establishments showed a sharp drop from 1972 to 1982, which strongly suggests that many more people were working part-time for a given employer. Yet the differential between average hourly earnings for craft workers in the film industry and the rest of the economy (nearly 100 percent in 1982) rose substantially from 1977. That is consistent with part-time employment due to increased specialization rather than to slack demand. There was no indication of reduced hours worked per individual, suggesting that full or nearly full-time work commonly involved service to more than one employer.[38]

CRAFT UNION ROSTER Studio craft workers in Hollywood have long been strongly unionized (see Chapter 7) and captured rents by means of high compensation and restrictive rules about work. The disintegration of film production into many small and often transient enterprises posed a major threat to the craft unions' ability to preserve high compensation levels. They were at least able to agree with the major studios in the 1940s to protect seniority by placing members on a job roster according to accrued seniority in the industry overall (regardless of which firm had employed them). The union came to carry out the hiring-hall function for firms using union labor. The overpricing of craft labor services was one factor promoting the disintegration of the industry (and the increase in on-location shooting away from the Los Angeles area)—and one that represented a private saving for the firms. It might not have been a social gain, if the disintegration were due solely to wage savings. The sharp reductions in featherbedding, however, make it clear that overall resource-productivity rose.[39]

INCREASED DEAL-MAKING ENTREPRENEURSHIP When film production was centered in the studios, starstruck newcomers seeking employment had only a few doors on which to knock. Decentralization meant that the quest for work demanded contact with many more potential employers. Agents had long represented actors and directors, but the transformation increased the value of their role in screening the talent seeking employment (like the literary agents discussed in Chapter 3). The large traditional talent agencies such as William Morris functioned by absorbing all available bits of information on the talent needs of nascent film projects and seeking to place the artists whom they represented. They had, however, also been active in assembling projects for TV series and films since the early 1950s, when the TV networks' demands were urgent but the Hollywood studios turned up their noses at the new medium. With entry barriers lowered for the entrepreneur packaging a literary property and appropriate talent (actors, director, writer), talent agents naturally extended their packaging services into cinema films.

The success of Creative Artists Agency, led by Michael Ovitz, rested on seizing just this opportunity.[40]

SOURCES OF STUDIOS' PROFITABILITY The transition shifted the basis of studios' profitability from the talents they had under long-term contract to their prowess in obtaining and promoting commercially successful films. This shift can be tested statistically by means of the proposition that year-to-year variations in studios' profits should have depended during the studio era on stars under contract and theatres under control. After the disintegration, however, profits should have varied mainly with the quality of the films distributed, indicated by outlays on the average film's production and the number of Academy Awards received. Danny Miller and Jamal Shamsie tested this proposition statistically and confirmed this shift in the bases for the studios' profits.[41]

REPEAT BUSINESS We noted previously that a regime of flexible specialization implies few repeats on the teams of inputs for successive films. The more distinctive is each film project, and the more finely subdivided are potentially usable skills, the lower are the chances that any given pair of inputs will work together repeatedly. They would stick together, however, if they shared worked-out routines for cooperation (transaction-specific assets), or if reputations for good (or bad) performance did not travel fast and cheaply. Only anecdotal evidence is available, but it seems to suggest that finding the best package of skills weighs heavily against the advantages of team familiarity. Although many film projects suffer because the principals slated to collaborate on it do not "click," it is not clear that the team that clicked once will repeat reliably.[42]

TRAINING AND FILM SCHOOLS In the studios, directing and other nonacting crafts were learned through on-the-job training on the set. This apprentice method of training was no longer efficient for cinema films after assembly-line production on the studio lot had ceased. The slack was taken up by film schools at several universities and specialized institutions, most located in Los Angeles and New York, where they could interact directly with the film production process. Apprentice directors, rather than receiving apprentice wages, now pay substantial tuition plus the cost of making their student film; as much as $150,000 plus several years' wages forgone in humdrum employment.[43]

FESTIVALS AS FILM MARKETS When the studios dominated film distribution in the United States, film festivals (such as Cannes) served as artistic events and occasions for interchange among creative filmmaking personnel.

With the rise of many independent filmmakers and small-scale distributors in the United States, festivals took on a major market-making role in which distributors around the world could view the available films and make deals for exhibition rights. Beneath its continued glitter, Cannes was transformed into a bustling marketplace, and in the United States the Sundance Festival moved quickly through the same trajectory. The case of Sundance is particularly well documented. Begun from Robert Redford's creative interest in promoting independent films, in the past decade it has proven to possess great if unplanned centripetal power, attracting not only novice filmmakers eager to promote their work and talent but also the distributors, producers, and agents hoping to profit from deploying and promoting new talent.[44] Other festivals function strictly as film markets—American Film Market (Los Angeles) and MIFED in Milan. The many festivals, each scheduled at regular times of year, have diverse rules about whether films shown previously may be entered, whether (costly) subtitles must be attached, and the like. These pose a tricky problem of sequential decisions for the filmmaker. Should she start out low-profile at the Telluride Festival, or risk all to the hazard of negative criticism at the New York Film Festival?[45]

These tangible changes in organization occurred within broader changes in the industry and its product, due partly to flexible specialization, partly to flux throughout the economy and society. Their consistency with flexible specialization bears note, even though measuring causal linkage is hopeless. What has changed is both the mixture of films and the organization of channels for their production and distribution. Independent filmmaking meant not just the disintegration of the studio assembly line but also a broadening of films' subject matter and style. An adjunct of the studio system was the Production Code, which sharply limited the subject matter, style, and content of films. Originally formed to combat film censorship, Code approval became a requirement for showing a film in theatres controlled by the major studios, and hence a potent barrier to entry. In the 1950s the exploration of mature and sophisticated themes became an important port of entry for independent filmmaking.[46] Distribution channels for these films became efficient enough (see Chapter 10) that they could (skill and luck permitting) earn a profit even without reaching a large audience.

The studio distributors, on the other hand, enjoyed a comparative advantage in the mass-market distribution of films that appeal to young and unsophisticated audiences—the action-oriented films packed with special effects that are so familiar today. The innovation probably dates from *Jaws* (1975), which quickly earned a domestic gross box-office revenue of $260 million and set the notion of a blockbuster film oriented not toward character but toward sensations and special effects. It proved profitable to spend heavily on the effects that give such films their novelty and sensation value, and to spend still more promoting them.[47] Marketing these films came to require extensive national sales-promotion (especially television). Because grunts and explosions translate easily into foreign languages, these films tend to sell equally well abroad, where their distribution is similarly a scale-efficient process (see Chapter 10). The major distributors hence settled into producing primarily what are called high-concept films, meaning that their content and style can be conveyed briefly and unambiguously.[48] Each channel sticks to its specialty and enjoys considerable success on its own terms. The studios' product enables them to earn about half of their gross rentals outside the United States. American independent films, meanwhile, have come to compete very successfully for their own audience segment against the "art house" films made abroad, despite the extensive subsidy arrangements that several European countries employ.[49]

The vast differences in scopes of distribution and sizes of budgets between studio and independent films correspond to a disparity between the respective groups of business firms—a disparity that closely parallels the pickers and promoters of Chapter 2. Independent production companies arose that finance but do not distribute films, although they have suffered rapid turnover due to the high variance of films' realized revenues. Martin Dale estimated that independent films, including those picked up for distribution by the major studios, accounted in the 1980s for about one-third of box-office gross revenues, while small-scale independent distributors (a separate group of firms) accounted for less than 15 percent. These distributors also suffer rapid turnover, and both independent production and distribution firms have been displaced by subsidiaries of the major distributors set up to carry on exactly their functions.[50] Whether this displacement reflects risk-spreading advantages, distribution synergies, or the market-power advantages of controlling the full set of differentiated movie products is an interesting question with an unknown answer.

Another policy of the major studios that cuts against the industry's disintegration is the practice of maintaining ongoing relations with key talent, by means of contracts covering series of films or contracts to gain a "first look" at projects that they develop. Each major studio has twenty to thirty of these with directors and actors as well as producers and producing organizations.[51] This policy may arise partly in reaction to the role actively pursued by Creative Artists Agency and other large talent agencies as packagers of film projects designed to use major talents whom they represent.[52]

A final feature of flexible specialization is the avenues that it offers for the entry of talent into the filmmaking business. The studio system's B-movie units were a training ground for actors, directors, and others. That channel remains open, though transformed into TV films and series. Basic filmmaking techniques can be learned at schools, which have replaced the studios' on-the-job training, so the other route of access is simply to raise some money and make one's own film on a micro budget. Would-be actors and directors as well as producers make great personal sacrifices in the starving-artist tradition to get their films made, sometimes to reify their personal artistic or political convictions but also simply to work their way into the industry. Indeed, a lack of reconciliation of career and artistic objectives often marks such beginners' films. Infrastructures can be found to assist them, especially in New York, where there are studio facilities and individual investors willing to take limited partnerships.[53]

Financing for such beginners is decidedly catch-as-catch-can. U.S. and foreign television networks (especially the Public Broadcasting System) have been sympathetic. The life savings of relatives and friends are called into battle. One filmmaker answered every credit-card application he received, maxed out every card to cover the production cost, and sold his film in the nick of time. Many such ventures, however, must go down to defeat. The case studies reported by David Rosen suggest that about one-half of the sampled film projects proved profitable, but their selection doubtless was biased toward successes. Rosen quoted *Variety* that one-third to one-half of completed independent films never succeed in finding a distributor.[54]

Does the new regime of flexible specialization work well? Passably? Very well? Unfortunately, no yardstick comes to hand. The studio system would not be viable today, and there is no way to define an ideal regime of flexible specialization to place beside the actual one. The following chapters nonetheless attempt a partial answer by focusing on aspects of the organization of film industry resources: the contracts that govern individual projects (Chapter 6); the development and use of specialized skills (Chapter 7); the sources of unsuccessful projects (Chapter 8); and the marketing of films to theatrical and other exhibitors (Chapter 10).

6

Contracts for Creative Products: Films and Plays

Cinema films are now financed and made on one-shot deals involving many specialists, as has been longstanding practice on the Broadway stage. This chapter shows how these similar practices are shaped by the quirks and uncertainties intrinsic to creative industries. The complications of two-party contracts swell as the parties grow numerous. They may make their contributions in sequence; each needs to perform up to snuff for a valuable product to result; creative participants each have tastes about the form of their contributions; and expected rents to the project must be divided at a stage when their total amount is deeply uncertain. The chapter shows how contracting processes for cinema films and Broadway plays thread their way through this minefield of problems, including the participation of humdrum lenders in highly risky projects.

The Feature-Film Deal and Its Contract Structure

The production of movies and plays follows similar time lines, with successive creative decisions made and economic costs sunk. A film starts from its story source, either an original screenplay or some external literary form. The entrepreneur who has obtained the literary property then negotiates a deal to secure financing for the project and to recruit the key inputs—director and principal actors. Once these are committed, many other specialists are hired, and planning begins for the actual filming, which is intricately scheduled (Chapter 5). The exposed film then enters post-production processing in which the director, a specialist editor, and perhaps others "cut" the film and assemble it in successive drafts that move toward a completed negative. A composer writes and records a musical score that is added to the soundtrack.

The final version then passes into the hands of the distribution company, which prepares a plan for promoting and exhibiting it. Deals must be ar-

103

ranged with many exhibitors, sometimes by contracts made before the film is completed. After cinema exhibition in North America, the film passes over the next several years into other channels: exhibition abroad, sale on video-cassette, showing on pay TV, then cable and network TV. Most costs are incurred early in the process, when great uncertainty surrounds the revenue that the film will generate. Some costs remain discretionary when production finishes—such as outlays for multiple prints of the film and for sales and promotion. The contracts that carry this economic investment along are drawn under great uncertainty. Little is known about the film's appeal to audiences until it is actually shown in theatrical release to paying audiences. Even test screenings of the finished or nearly finished film yield unreliable results. When the film fails commercially, the weak link in its planning and production often defies identification. When there is no "chemistry" between the leading actors, when audiences fail to grow involved with its story, the fault can seldom be laid at the door of any one participant.

Substantial time elapses before the major cash outflows for a film bring the ensuing cash inflow, making the interest cost important. A day lost when a $40 million film's cost has been sunk incurs perhaps $20,000 in interest expense, while a day at the outset might exact no interest. One consequence of the uncertainty of the cash inflows and their arrival over time is the fundamental importance of the order in which participants get paid.

Contract Structures: The Screenplay

The first step in the process is preparation of the screenplay based on a contract between the dealmaker—usually an independent producer, but sometimes an agent—and the writer. When the story comes from a prior literary source (a novel, story, or stage play), the producer employs the option contract introduced in Chapter 3 to retain access to the copyrighted source while a screenplay is developed. The contract involves an initial payment of around 10 percent of the negotiated purchase price, with provisions for renewal with additional payments. These payments for options credit against the preagreed purchase price. This process does not apply to a best-selling novel or other literary property with obvious potential for conversion into a motion picture, which gives rise to an outright auction. Bids may be conditioned on the success of the literary work in its original form, for example, escalating with the number of weeks that a novel remains on the best-seller list, or the number of copies sold beyond some (high) minimum. The filmmaker's benefit lies in the interest that the novel's acclaim generates in the subsequent film.

The market for film options differs from that for Broadway stage production. On Broadway the Writers Guild Basic Agreement assigns scriptural status to the written text, which cannot be changed without the playwright's consent. Given that the production of a play (not to mention development of a screenplay) inevitably calls for changes in a preconceived text, this provision gives an unrestricted opportunity to the author to hold up the producer and appropriate the option payment. The producer's willingness to pay for the option is consequently depressed, and stage-play options bring little up-front money to their authors.[1]

The optioned literary property or the producer's idea must be turned into a script by a writer, and that transaction poses a severe contracting problem. Literary inspiration does not work steadily nine to five on movie scripts (though it may on TV series and advertising), so time-based compensation invites loafing on the job, haggling over performance, or both. Pay cannot be based on qualitative results. A contract cannot be written that turns on the definition of a "good" script. The writer cannot by right decide what is a finished product, if only for lack of an overview of the other inputs and processes needed to complete the film. The producer, if given decision rights over the script's quality, faces the moral hazard of being able always to demand one more rewrite. The solution reached is to break the scriptwriting process into steps, define (roughly) a contractable output at each stage, and give the purchaser at each step an option to continue for another round. The producer buys a "treatment," or summary of the plot with sample dialogue. If the treatment is accepted, the writer is next paid to provide a complete draft. Subsequent discrete products are rewrites, each with its own price tag. The producer may terminate dealings with one writer and employ another for a "rewrite" or a "polish," or hire specialists in, say, jokes or dialogue.[2] Because the writer is the defining creative input at the outset, discord and dissatisfaction among other (tentative) creative participants tend to be resolved by dropping the writer and starting fresh with another.[3] Chapter 7 provides background on these practices and the disputes that preceded their acceptance.

Original screenplays and ideas for them come from many sources. Movie agents filter screenwriters just as literary agents serve as gatekeepers for the trade-book publishers. An established writer gains access to producers for "pitching" ideas not yet converted into formal scripts (the ability to deliver an articulate and enthusiastic pitch is a valuable skill). The efficient procedure of calibrating enthusiasm for an idea before transforming it into a script, though, is subject to a serious problem of opportunism, because the idea may get divulged to third parties, as when a producer pretests a major distributor's interest in the project.[4] Writing out a treatment and registering it with the Writers Guild is one defense for the writer; another is monitoring by the writer's agent, especially if the agent's firm represents other talents with whom the producer would deal.[5]

A screenwriter working under an option contract can glean large profits from a successful film—depending on the terms of the contract that are enabled if the option is exercised. Nonetheless, during the 1980s the trend was toward the speculative script that could be auctioned in the pursuit of maximum rents to the writer.[6] The auctioning of completed scripts forgoes the advantages of redrafting and manifold input (if advantages they be), but it holds for the writer (and her agent) the advantage of maximum competition among potential acquirers. For a time, at least, agents improved their terms by shortening the time that studios had to review a speculative script to less than a day. By implication, more willingness-to-pay was generated by competitive animal spirits than from cool contemplation of the script's potential.[7]

Assembling the Creative Team

Assembling the key creative inputs to a film amounts to forming a lateral coalition or joint venture. It poses some problems of organization innate to any such deal; other difficulties are marked by distinct "creative" elements. The producer usually has strongly ranked preferences for the director and the major actors (the director may be selected first and inject his own preference for actors). A preference can rest on an actor's suitability or qualities relative to similar actors—horizontal differentiation. It can turn on a performer's *A list/ B list* position, or vertical differentiation: is the top actress worth her asking price? Film projects differ in their commercial prospects' dependence on a star's extant franchise with the film audience relative to original elements in the concept or story. Preference rankings among players give bargaining power to leading candidates. This is not just a matter of the greater audience appeal of the actor best suited for a role. The team making a film has to "click," implying an interactive element: the better suited actor raises the audience's regard for the other elements in the film. The decibels of clicking seem unrelated ex post to the director's coordinating efforts.[8] This interactive aspect (the "O-rings" production function of the Introduction) complicates assembly of the coalition by raising the bargaining power of the last member signing on. Others who are precommitted lose if the last one defects, and hence would sacrifice to keep the optimal coalition from unraveling. The problem of forming such coalitions probably grows more than proportionally to the number of key participants, which is ominous in that each brings his own attitudes and values and exerts interactive effects on the film's quality.[9] The situation grows ever more complex: the film editor, once regarded as a technician rather than an artist, is now seen as a creative force who can help shape a film. This rise in status brought a five- to tenfold increase in compensation.[10]

An artist's interest in joining a film project depends on a number of factors besides promised compensation. The time schedule of the filming requires the player to be available at a specific time. Delaying a project in order to obtain one actor runs the risk that other participants will demand compensation for waiting, or will move on to other projects. The artist's interest also depends on taste and career considerations; she may prefer to work (or not to work) with particular actors and directors. A role may be attractive for its "stretch" of the performer's talent or (alternatively) for its reinforcement of an established persona. Actors and other talent make constant trade-offs between their creative goals (accepting low pay to work on esteemed projects or with artistically respected collaborators) and their economic interests (high-paying roles in high-concept commercial films).[11] Changes to the script, the identities of the other participants, or the "look" of the film sought by the director may affect each one's willingness to join. All of this means a complex bargaining process—due to the interactive element, the many dimensions of candidate talents' reservation prices for joining the coalition, and the difficulty of expressing and contracting some preferences. The writer lacks access to the last-one-in advantage, but even he may hold provision for another rewrite after the director is recruited.[12]

Participants' preferences extend beyond the film's attributes and their pay for taking part to the credit they receive. Screen credits for film participants work exactly as vita entries for research scholars: the bricks from which the structure of career and reputation are built. Any large film advertisement hence contains a block of credits. The type is microscopic, and most names will be unknown to the vast majority of readers, so the "billing block" clearly serves a function other than informing potential viewers about the film. Especially for writers, an urgent issue is who gets formal credit for a script that has passed through several pairs of hands (see Chapter 7). The producer and director, interacting with the writer who prepares the script, have an incentive to meddle in the process enough to claim a writing credit. Also, the principal actors (and possibly the director) compete for the size and position of their names in both screen credits and print and video ads. Does A precede B, in which case B must follow A? Does each get a separate "card" in the screen credits, or do they share?[13]

Descriptive evidence on film deals confirms and extends these patterns. The bargaining instability due to the last-one-in advantage promotes the demand for play-or-pay contracts by many highly ranked participants. Such a contract compels the producer to pay the artist for her role in the film, even if she is replaced or the film not made at all.[14] A producer who has signed a play-or-pay contract with one performer then risks enlarged hold-up threats from others, although play-or-pay commitments can be renegotiated (used on other projects, or traded off). The play-or-pay guarantee to a director is particularly problematic, because the director once hired becomes the artistic coordinator of the film and normally assumes a major role in selecting the other creative inputs. Because a play-or-pay obligation to the director imposes a large risk and hold-up threat for the producer if committed before the rest of the team is assembled, the director may start out on a nonexclusive development deal in which he is paid to assist in assembling the team, but remains free to make other commitments unless a starting date for filming is set by a certain time.[15] Another sensitive issue in the director's contract is what right he obtains to "cut" or edit the film after shooting is completed. Control over editing is important for consolidating the director's vision of how the film will go together. On the other hand, the director might lack the skills or the objectivity of a professional film editor, and the director's taste for retaining creative control may forgo wringing the most value from the editor's bag of tricks.[16] Editing is key to the film's commercial viability and expected profits; hence it is a prime locus for conflict between aesthetic preferences and commercial interests.[17] A common solution is to give the director "first cut" but allow the producer to override the director's choices.

Because of *time flies* and the problem of temporal coordination, deals have a time urgency dependent on the impetus given by the conviction of key participants. If the elements do not come together quickly, the urgency goes out of the negotiating process, and tentative participants move on to other things.[18] On the other hand, key terms of contracts are worked out quite informally among the top participants, and the signing of formal contracts likely postdates the start of work on the project. There is room for negotiating ploys, but reputation effects deter serious cheating. Another factor facilitating contracts is the free circulation within the industry of information on current salaries, which averts protracted negotiations over pay.[19] The effect of conviction and impetus for bringing deals to completion may explain an oddity often noted among Hollywood mores. The dealmaker new to or repositioned in the game first spends money conspicuously though not necessarily wisely: giving "sweet" deals to well-known artists, or simply decorating the office in an extravagantly opulent fashion.[20] In a well-informed competitive marketplace, such a dealmaker would likely put off talent from future dealings, because a fool and his money are soon parted, and one eschews ongoing transactions with a partner unlikely to survive. But one might be attracted to a spendthrift where the outcomes of all deals are highly uncertain, and where the impetus of a deep pocket is important for their initial assembly.

Once the key inputs are committed to a film project, the more routine inputs are assembled. The casting director identifies actors potentially suitable for playing each minor role and available at various rates of pay, so that producer and director can decide on optimal quality. Production managers who recruit crew members face a trade-off between hiring the same people each time (easy coordination, reputation that limits shirking) and seeking the best person for that particular job.[21] The stature of featured players tends to influence the vertical differentiation of the film as a whole; casting an expensive star pulls upward the quality of actors optimally chosen for minor roles, lest the star's performance falter from playing against an inferior foil.[22]

Contingent Compensation in Film Deals

Why can superstars command $10 to $20 million paychecks? And why is this compensation given in the form of fixed payments per film, shares of gross revenue, and/or shares of net profit? Suppose that a film requires a single star, glittering among humdrum inputs. The humdrum inputs work for competitive market wages. The star's charisma determines what the public will pay to see the film. The difference between this sum and the humdrum inputs' cost is the maximum pay the star can command. She may have to settle for less; if a lesser but much cheaper actress could play the part, the star's pay is capped by the extra revenue she attracts over the gross profit (revenue minus lesser actress's pay) that the B-list actress will generate. Superstar salaries thus consist largely of rents. With producers competing to employ her, the star's pay tends to be the expected rent that she can attract. The expectation rests heavily on the box-office performance of her recent films. It indeed likely responds to the "buzz" or expectation concerning any of her films not yet released.[23] If a film's cash flow contains rent attributable to several players, and their individual contributions are difficult to entangle, their maximum combined rent is determined in the same way, but dividing the pie among them depends on bargaining power—and the shared rent's expected erosion if one of them drops out. These considerations incidentally point to the common fallacy of regarding a film's cost as exogenous to its expected revenue.[24] That a wave of successful blockbusters raises stars' paychecks for the next year's films is just the process of rent imputation working itself out when *nobody knows*.[25]

A superstar's pay commonly includes both fixed and variable components, and the aptness of incentive pay is obvious enough when so much is at stake, and when a superstar performing poorly drags down the effectiveness of other talent used in the film. A number of other factors can also affect the mixture of fixed and incentive compensation. Actors who themselves supply impetus to get a film made can show their commitment not only by taking lower total compensation than usual, but also by substituting deferred compensation (that is, pay from the film's revenues) or compensation contingent on profits for up-front pay. Producers should offer incentive pay when an all-out performance, or engagement in a difficult and complex collaboration, is important for the film's success. Darlene Chisholm analyzed a sample of film contracts to isolate factors that explain which stars get some form of revenue participation, and which do not.[26] Her results give some support to the incentive-compensation hypothesis, but are also largely consistent with another hypothesis resting on the effect of large fixed payments to superstars on the risk borne by all other participants. Compare two films, one costing $20 million with no big-name stars, the other $40 million with a superstar. Suppose the superstar's presence indeed increases the second film's expected revenue by just $20 million. Suppose also that the star's presence has no effect on the proportional uncertainty of the film's revenue, in the sense that both films face the same chance of bringing in only half the revenue expected. If the superstar's compensation is a fixed sum, the proportional uncertainty facing the suppliers of all the other inputs (taken together) is twice that faced with the first film. If they are risk averse, any suppliers of other inputs who must absorb this greater risk will demand higher expected compensation for doing to. All parties can benefit from making some of the superstar's compensation contingent, to mitigate the cost penalties of sticking other inputs with all the risk.[27] This hypothesis appears consistent with the historical setting in which gross and net participations emerged.[28] It has not been tested formally, but it implies that stars should share profits in big-budget films when they have established images and can command high pay.

The risk-spreading problem relates to the role of star inputs in film financing, discussed later. Stars are commonly regarded as "bankable" by lenders to the film industry. A star's presence by definition increases the expected gross revenue of a film, but it should not reduce the riskiness of gross profits unless the star takes substantial contingent compensation. The attraction of stars to bankers and other suppliers of debt capital to filmmakers must lie in increasing the likelihood that any given dollar amount of debt can be repaid from the film's gross rentals.

Certain conventions in how films' more humble participants are paid reflect straightforward incentive considerations. Under the Screen Actors Guild Basic Agreement, actors are paid so much a week for a minimum number of weeks' work on a film; actual work during production may be less, but the time required for rehearsal, costuming, rerecording of defective dialogue, and other tasks that come before and after production is not separately metered and compensated.[29] The performer hence minimizes the time spent in these chores. Directors are paid a fixed sum rather than on a weekly basis. The cost of shooting a film rises proportionally to the time elapsed in its production, so any incentive for the director to stretch out the shooting time is to be avoided. Producers' packaging services apparently require no unique entrepreneurial skills and bring them no hefty rents, but some agents have flourished by packaging all major elements of a film from the talents they represent and selling the package on an all-or-nothing basis.[30]

Finance and Distribution Contracts

Financing a film requires a large investment that is sunk and at palpable hazard of loss. The *nobody knows* property implies a high variance of gross profits from film to film. The funds to finance major films ultimately come from humdrum lenders who require a normal profit on average to stay in the game. Who will supply debt capital when the risks are so great, and when the creative talent prefer to risk all for a big win (in this context, debt-equity moral hazard)?[31] Who will supply equity capital at arm's length when the artists gain utility and perhaps professional reputation from cost-increasing perfectionism, resistant to monitoring? The studio system addressed these problems directly. The studio's output pooled numerous risky projects, making their aggregate cash flow reasonably safe for the suppliers of debt, especially since the exhibitors' profits (though sensitive to the business cycle) were relatively immune to the hazards of individual films. Besides, a movie theatre as collateral was comfort food to a banker, but a film negative was not. In the studio era, banks learned that lending some moderate proportion of a studio's production costs was not particularly risky, although specialized and costly monitoring always restricted the business to a few banks who could warrant this fixed cost.[32]

In today's flexible specialization, the major studios retain the two essential functions of financing and distributing films. Each function can be performed outside the major studios, although not for films that aspire to "blockbuster" status. Below that threshold the independent producer can contract with a studio for both functions—a production-finance-distribution (PFD) deal—or finance the project independently. With finance in hand, a distribution contract may be postponed until the film is in production or even completed (a "negative pick-up deal"). Postponing a film's distribution deal holds the advantage of offering a less uncertain product to the studio distributor and thereby eliciting better terms.[33] However financing is done, it becomes entangled with the last-one-in problem already mentioned. The lender wants talent committed to guarantee the project's viability, while the talent prefers to sign only when funds are assured.

The producer's ability to finance a film deal ultimately depends on convincing lenders of the plenitude of the film's expected cash flows. For independent financing the producer can go to foreign exhibition chains, videocassette distributors, and others to presell rights to exhibit the film. These deals bring guaranteed minimum payments, which then can be turned into bank loans, the principal discounted for the elapsed time until the film is available for distribution and the likelihood that the distributor will default on its commitment.[34] A PFD deal with a major studio rests on the distributor's own assessment of the film's prospects—an assessment that may be backed by presales to U.S. domestic exhibitors.

The producer has, or might have, a choice between studio and independent financing. Contracting and governance problems arise either way, as do problems for the financier of adverse selection from the producer's strategic choice of which partner to approach.[35] We start with the studio PFD agreement.[36] The studio agrees to lend the cost of producing the film, manage its distribution to some or all exhibition channels, and share with the producer and perhaps other participants the resulting net profits. A common split is 50 percent to the studio, 50 percent to the producer and others participating in net profits. This term interacts with the producer's quest for an agreement with the major creative participants in ways discussed subsequently. The distributor's services involve acquiring sufficient prints of the film, planning and executing an advertising campaign, and physically distributing the film through its network of branch offices. The distributor's compensation takes two forms. One is an overhead charge deducted from gross rentals (the payments received from exhibitors), which has long been lodged at 30 percent for the major distributors, though 27.5 percent for their smaller competitors and as low as 20 percent for independent distributors that do not operate national branch-office networks (and hence handle specialized films shown only in selected locations).[37] Cash inflow net of the overhead charge is first applied to the distributor's cost of prints and advertising, with the advertising itself subject to a further 10 percent overhead. Interest on funds loaned by the distributor for production costs also has a first claim. The distributor is exposed to significant risk, even when it does not finance the film's production costs: a film that flops miserably does not even cover its advertising and distribution costs. In general, though, the deal gives the distributor a strong incentive to promote the film—possibly too strong, because its compensation increases with both gross revenue and net profit.[38]

The PFD agreement has the familiar option-contract structure. Outlays incurred up to any point in a project's development are sunk, and so the decision to proceed is appropriately given to the party who next must throw good money after what might now appear to be bad. If the studio decides to quit at any such step, the project is said to be in "turnaround." The producer then receives an option (usually for one year) to purchase all rights by paying the studio's cost plus an overhead fee and a profit participation (2.5 to 5 percent) if the film is produced elsewhere. Apparently 25 to 35 percent of films reach completion only after bouts of turnaround, which indicates both the diverse expectations about creative projects and the power of shifting fortunes and events to breathe life into a stranded project.[39] Similarly, the distributor retains full discretion about how and how much to promote the film, and indeed is not obligated to distribute even a completed negative.[40]

Strategic Accounting

The producer's fee for his dealmaking and coordinating services is part of the cost of making the film. With as much as a 50 percent share of net profit, he has a strong incentive to maximize the commercial value of the project. Hollywood PFD deals are notorious, however, for the elusiveness of net profits, even for films that generate enormous box-office gross revenues. The issue arises partly from the studio's rich access to hidden information—it keeps the books.[41] Suspect practices, though, all have roots in the distributor's cost structure. The variable costs of promoting and distributing individual films are charged to those films, although not always recovered. The distribution fee presumably covers fixed costs of the distribution apparatus, although the long-lived conventional 30 percent hardly suggests close alignment.

Finally, the studio distributor incurs general overhead including what is effectively a substantial research and development cost: the development outlays on the many projects that are filtered, explored, but ultimately discarded. A Twentieth Century–Fox executive stated that the company receives 10,000 screenplays, treatments, books, and oral pitches yearly, puts 70 to 100 projects into development, but makes only twelve films. For the viable distributor, gross profits on the twelve must at least cover the cost of reviewing the other 9,988. These costs for the studio are equivalent to about a 10 percent R&D/sales ratio for a manufacturing industry.[42] The PFD agreement loads these and other costs onto the actual production cost of each film. Accordingly the "negative cost" of the film, on the studio's books to be recovered before any net profits appear, is typically two-thirds greater than the production budget of the completed film. That is, the negative cost consists of production budget, 60 percent; overhead, 12 percent; interest cost accrued, 4 percent; "residuals" (expected payments subsequently due to minor talent for revenues from TV and other subsequent exhibitions), 5 percent; "participations" (reserves for payments to star participants who get shares of gross rentals), 15 percent; and 4 percent for other items.[43] Each item embodies a cost appropriately charged against the film's expected revenue stream. The scope for creative accounting is enormous, however, which explains the famous elusiveness of net profits to the producer and other talent whose compensation includes a profit share. For the studio, discretion enters not just in setting the negative cost initially but also in decisions made during the film's commercial exploitation. When positive net profits threaten to appear, the distributor can establish reserves against costs of promoting the film subsequently in other venues, and interest becomes payable on the reserves.[44]

Needless to say, the opportunism in studio accounting impairs the efficiency of filmmaking contracts. It imposes the transaction cost of writing ground rules for the studio's bookkeeping: the definition of net profits in a film contract might run 30 single-spaced pages, and what definition of net profits is selected can be a major issue in negotiating contracts.[45] It also wields an important influence on the terms of participation for major talent. Although both incentive and risk-sharing considerations call for profit-based incentive pay, the elusiveness of net profits induces profit-share candidates to demand up-front fixed compensation, or another solution: "gross participation," or a share of gross rentals received from exhibiting the film (from the "first dollar," like the distribution fee, or perhaps after direct distribution costs are subtracted).[46] When participants' rewards depend on gross revenue, their incentive is to inflate any costs that they control as long as these continue to generate any additional gross revenue. Even if key players did not get gross participations, the signal value of gross rentals for standing in the filmmaking community provides a temptation to maximize revenue rather than profit.[47] Gross participation rates of 10 to 15 percent are apparently not uncommon; combined with the 30 percent distribution fee, they cut sharply into revenue available to cover other costs. The time when net profits appear in the film's exhibition cycle is highly sensitive to the combined percentage rate of gross participations (mainly due to the ever-increasing interest obligation on costs not yet recovered), so that one star's gross participation is decidedly hostile to the producer's and others' prospects for net profits.[48] The contractual inefficiencies that grow from discretionary creative accounting are thus not without cost to the studio, because they likely reduce the expected net cash flows and the studio's share of them, but the proportional size of this offset deterrent is rather small. PFD contracts recognize the studio's interest in accommodating and providing incentives for highly paid net-profit recipients: although such participations come at first from the producer's (normally 50 percent) profit share, as the combined participation rate increases, an increasing part of it comes from the studio's share.[49]

Finance and Efficient Incentives

The problems with studio contracts engender different inefficiencies when they cause the producer to forgo studio finance and rely instead on sales of exhibition rights to foreign exhibitors, TV networks, and others. The studio is potentially efficient at managing the interdependent revenue streams from this series of exhibitors. A film's promotion at each stage likely has spillover benefits of enhancing potential demand at subsequent stages. Analogous to distributors' management of exhibition at first-run and neighborhood theatres before the 1950s, the distributor today can profit from price discrimination by managing the amount and kind of promotion at each stage and the elapsed time between them. The producer who presells rights to several independent exhibitors presumably has difficulty working out bilateral agreements that fully internalize these interdependences between revenue flows from the various exhibition "windows." The studio distributor under a PFD contract should be in a better position.[50] Paradoxically, film directors see a major creative advantage in splintered financing of films, because it means that no one monitor has much leverage for holding the director to artistic choices that will maximize commercial value while limiting the scope for self-expression.[51]

An interesting device in film deals is the completion bond, a service provided by a third party for independently financed films and self-insured by studios for films that they finance. The bond, often required by the financier, commits the third party to take over and finish the shooting of a film if the producer and/or director have allowed it to run some stated amount over budgeted outlay or time spent shooting. The guarantor may invade the contingent compensation (sometimes even the cash compensation) due to producer and director. The guarantor is obligated to complete shooting the script as written. Guarantors charge 6 percent of the production budget, although with 3 percent rebated if the guarantee is not invoked. Although loss of managerial control over the filming process is a serious problem (Chapter 8), who would want to see a film that was completed by a banker? The explanation is that the guarantor rarely steps in, but his looming shadow ensures that a producer and director will resist temptations to throw fiscal rectitude to the winds in pursuit of art. If they do, they lose control of the project.[52]

Finance through the presale of various exhibition rights gives the producer more discretion than the PFD deal about how much risk to keep and how much to lay off. Both subject the producer to monitoring, but he might prefer one monitor to another.[53] An advantage often cited is that each deal on exhibition rights is independent of the others. If one exhibitor suffers a loss, it is not offset against the producer's share of profits from another. That is, it is not "cross-collateralized." This is a dubious advantage, of course, since a lender will offer less when denied the protection of cross-collateralization. Cross-collateralization should depend on the parties' relative willingness to bear risks.

The producer's choices of how much equity to hold and when to contract for distribution (early or late in the film's production) might involve adverse selection. Is the studio offered 50 percent of net profits only for films that the producer regards as commercially shaky? Are presales to exhibitors offered when that producer suspects that the stars and script idea look better at the beginning than will the finished product? Little if any evidence of this can be found: *nobody knows,* and the deal partners must assume that the key creative personnel will always be enthusiastic at the outset. Rather than the insiders having asymmetric information, nobody has any hard information about a project's success.[54] When a film is made under a studio's PFD deal, the filmmakers and studio executives get the same chance to see the "daily rushes," freshly shot and unedited film, so asymmetry of information is not obviously a problem.

Assembling Broadway Plays

Stage plays require a *motley crew* of creative and humdrum inputs similar to the cinema film. The performance once prepared is repeated (audience demand permitting) over and over. The theatre owner replaces the studio distribution network, but otherwise the parallels are strong. The independent producer assembles the deal, starting with the option of a play. Apart from established playwrights, plays worthy of option generally come via agents, who perform the same gatekeeping function as for trade publishers.[55] No one measures the stock of plays put forth for performance, but a characteristic guess spots one successful produced play among 10,000 scripts considered by producers.[56] The option contract gives the producer time to assemble the deal for a small advance against royalties to the author. The inputs include a director, principal actors, a theatre (of the right size, and available at the right time), and financial backers (plus conductor and choreographer for a musical).

The main participants typically take combinations of fixed compensation and a share of gross box-office receipts.[57] In the nineteenth century, playwrights received (if anything) only a fixed up-front payment, a natural choice given the impossibility of monitoring the day's traveling players. Royalty payments arrived along with road companies performing a more formalized repertory to audiences interested in contemporary plays, and with communication technologies more congenial to monitoring.[58] Under a contract standard from the 1920s to 1980s, the author received a maximum 10 percent royalty (for musicals 6 percent shared among book author, composer, and lyricist), the director a fixed fee plus a royalty of 5 percent or less, "name" actors variable shares that usually aggregated to less than 10 percent, and the producer a small (1–2 percent) slice denoted as "office expenses." The theatre owner once received a 25–30 percent share of gross revenue for providing the house, stagehands, ushers, box-office staff, and other such running expenses. In the late 1970s, however, New York theatre owners decided to separate their landlord and risk-bearing roles, converting their charge to a fixed fee calculated to cover variable and fixed costs plus a 5–10 percent share of gross box-office revenues. Investors providing a show's equity capital divide 50 percent of its net profits among themselves; the other 50 percent goes to the producer. If the play runs for 21 performances or more in New York, the producer also claims around a 40 percent share of the author's revenues from subsequent productions (in North America), motion pictures (worldwide), television, and original-cast recording.[59]

The incentive structures of these terms are clear. Subject to risk-sharing with the investors, the producer has a strong inducement both to control costs and to seek maximum profits from the show. In particular he goes for the minimum run of performances necessary to participate in the play's subsidiary income. In general the producer's promotional effort bulks up the playwright's subsidiary income. By granting the producer 40 percent of the royalties on subsequent productions, the playwright could well end up with more total subsidiary income, thanks to the producer's extra effort. Other key participants get small shares of the show's gross revenues, but these can yield large sums. Reviewing the Broadway scene in the late 1960s, William Goldman observed that a top actor's 10 percent gross of a hit play would bring in over a million dollars a year in today's prices, and even the producer's share of box-office revenue would yield $250,000 from a play that ran a year but failed to yield net profits.[60] These incentives push the creative talents to maximize revenues rather than profits, but their efforts likely affect revenues much more than costs, so the deal overall is profit-oriented. Revenue sharing by highly paid participants also aids the acceptable sharing of risks, as for cinema films.

Sticky Terms Unstuck

Major changes in production contracts in the mid-1980s illustrate the opposed forces of convention and change at work on the creative industries' contracts. Many well-established sharing conventions have persisted for decades: the author's 10 percent book royalty, the film studio's 30 percent distribution margin, the playwright's 10 percent share of gross revenue. Economic changes are constantly shifting the net returns that they bring the participants. Why should they hold, when the market equilibrium is in motion and the parties are legally free to jettison them? Several explanations suggest themselves. If a conventional share yields more (or less) than normal profits for some class of participants, the class's membership increases (or falls). Most creative talents, however, are always in excess supply and under-employed, so swings in their number need have little effect on how the participants reach any particular bargain. The exception to this, as we shall see, is a shrinkage of humdrum inputs' supply sufficient to cut into the flow of deals. Another explanation is the very lack of clearly defined marginal costs and revenues to govern most decisions on participating in creative deals. Each party tends to have a wide bargaining range for participation, and hence ample grounds for suspecting bullying tactics when a negotiating partner proposes departing in his favor from a conventionalized share arrangement.

While conventionalized contract terms can resist change, they are not immune. The long-term inflation of live theatre's cost relative to substitute forms of entertainment has reduced New York's number of stage productions (see Chapter 16) and shrunk the average value of rents passing to any of the participants, while still holding out large individual prizes to participants favored by traditional share rules.[61] Anyone receiving more than his opportunity cost, whether playwright or stagehand, might reduce his demands in order to preserve the deal. Or he might do better by sticking fast. When the expected value of the deal declines, the (unionized) stagehands do not necessarily maximize their total earnings by accepting a cut in wages or in featherbedding. The playwright, getting direct utility as well as royalties from stage presentation, and with the script's preparation cost wholly sunk, more likely accepts less generous terms. The decline in plays produced in the 1970s and early 1980s, clearly due to balky investors, rendered the playwright's 10 percent share of gross revenues vulnerable to revision. In fact informal "royalty pool" arrangements were common in which the playwright and perhaps other gross-revenue claimants would accept temporary reductions in their shares to let a play cover its variable running costs.[62] In the mid-1980s this practice was generalized in a new Approved Production Contract that curtailed gross-revenues shares until investors had recouped. It capped the author's royalty at 5 percent of gross weekly box-office revenue unless that revenue sufficiently exceeded running costs.

The point of royalty pool arrangements is to lower conditionally and temporarily the minimum compensation demands of the principal parties. Box office ticket prices are not adjusted much for the success of a production, and so the profitability of a play or musical depends mainly on the length of its run. Even after it opens and the critics' evaluations are known, the ultimate return to a show remains uncertain, dependent on word-of-mouth recommendations. Closing a play seals the fate of its investment; keeping open a play with uncertain prospects preserves the option to continue if fortunes improve. The temporary concessions (perhaps deferrals) in royalty pools help sustain the option.

Financing Plays: Angels and Moguls

Commercial stage productions increase with the willingness of investors to settle for less than normal expected profits on their highly risky investments. This is the role of Broadway "angels," individual investors with a strong interest in the theatre who value personal contact with the creative participants. The fact that part of their profit is subjective implies, especially if new recruits can be easily found, that aggregate pecuniary returns on their investments are below normal. No hard data are available, but on the basis of a careful review of one season (1967–1968) William Goldman offered the "wildly conservative guess" that someone who invested all the money in all the Broadway shows that season would have lost $5 million. Yet one play's investors made a 350 percent profit and another at least 500 percent, so the gambler's attraction to the chance for a big win may also apply.[63] A sample of 948 shows produced in the seasons of 1972–1973 through 1982–1983 disclosed an aggregate loss of $66.6 million on a total investment of $267.5 million; the implied loss rate is overstated, however, because of a lack of public information on a few privately funded shows that were very profitable.[64]

Complex Task, Uncertain Product

Broadway production contracts share with their Hollywood counterparts the central role of an option structure: the party about to sink resources into a project's cumulative investment base always holds the right to cancel.[65] This allocation of decision rights respects the persistence of deep uncertainty reaching from the initial assembly of inputs all the way to opening night and beyond. Observers of the theatre stress the *motley crew* property: a team of diverse talents either does or does not achieve a unified vision of the tone, style, and rhythm of the production.[66] Each participant starts with a vision that informs both his own contribution and his expectation of how other creative participants will shape theirs. As the production develops, decisions are made and become irreversible, promoting factions among the participants if not actual rupture of the coalition. Goldman, for example, argues that a contest occurs over whose vision emerges on stage. A compromise can yield a rudderless production at hazard of failure, but a clear vision imposed by somebody with "muscle" also may turn out clearly wrong.[67] Is the role of muscle a fallout defect of the show's incomplete production contract? Probably not, because nobody knows which of many choices, alone and in combination, will work. Each creative participant seeks to develop and sustain a reputation, and the application of muscle makes the mesomorph's reputation hostage to the rightness of his conviction. Efficient or not, the quest for muscle is a direct corollary of *art for art's sake*, the artist's drive to implement her vision with its clarity and coherence intact. Throughout the creative industries, career lines carry the successful talent into positions conveying more power to control the collaborative product and resist competing conceptions.[68]

The uncertainty of a stage play's success parallels that of its film competitor. Bernard Rosenberg and Ernest Harberg sorted productions into flops (those that did not earn back their investments) and hits over a half-century, finding a 76 percent flop rate for musical comedies and an 80 percent rate for stage plays. Successful producers have flop rates that are lower but not low: David Merrick, 61 percent flops over 1954–1968; Oscar Hammerstein, 65 percent flops before *Showboat,* then 53 percent flops before *Oklahoma!* Directors with excellent track records in musicals stumble badly when they undertake straight plays. The best performance achieved by top producers and producing organizations ran 40 to 50 percent flops.[69] The O-rings property is clearly evident, especially in musicals, which require especially complex teams of creative inputs. So is the intense conflict between the participants' objective assessment of a new show's chances and the sustaining of their effort and enthusiasm in order to maximize whatever chances it does have. As long-time observer Donald Farber remarked, "There are countless show-biz tales of out-of-town flops going on to become theatre history . . ., so producers generally keep their shows alive and bring them in to New York . . . if at all possible."[70]

The production process adapts to this uncertainty as best it can. Creative talents sort themselves out in the vertically differentiated pattern evident in films. Those blessed with past success tend to work with their kind, and can attract financing for projects with large initial investments.[71] Untried talents tend to work with others of a kind, on projects with fewer resources at hazard. (The logic of this pattern appears more fully in Chapter 7.) A strategy increasingly used is to build productions slowly from informal workshop beginnings, often far from Broadway's high costs and perhaps within the sanctum of a nonprofit organization. The gestation period (and the lag between costs and the revenues that it generates) increases, but the opportunity is enhanced to cut losses and reconsider decisions that might otherwise be preclusive.[72]

7

Guilds, Unions, and Faulty Contracts

Both creative and humdrum inputs in creative industries are heavily unionized. The League of American Theatres and Producers bargains with 17 craft unions, guilds, and associations.[1] Although quite different factors cause creative and humdrum labor to rally to the union, incomplete contracts in the organization of creative teams affect both groups. Because each product is unique *(infinite variety)*, the production process cannot be fully specified in advance. Disputes then arise over whether the task requested or action undertaken by the supervisor is consistent with the worker's terms of employment. For creative workers this problem is doubly complex, because their tastes (hence, ideally, their contractual commitment to the project) cover how the creative job is done and not just whether they will work overtime on it *(art for art's sake)*.

These problems are confounded with several others. With diverse inputs all necessarily contributing to the creative product *(motley crew)*, the success of one class of inputs in contractually delineating its tasks (expanding, contracting, or simply codifying them) tends to push the uncertainty of tasks and rewards onto the other participants with incomplete contracts. Because complex creative products need close coordination in time *(time flies)*, the process is deeply vulnerable to hold-ups, with one input able to deny value to the whole coalition by strategically withholding its cooperation. Finally, after the creative task is completed, lumps of rent imputed to durable creative outputs frequently turn up that were not anticipated in the original deal *(ars longa)*. Revenues from old cinema films newly embodied in videocassettes or shown on television are an example. When claimants can invest in pressing claims on unanticipated rents, rent-seeking sets in. The pursuants can spend the whole value of the unanticipated rent trying to lay hands on it.[2]

The collective organizations formed by the creative and humdrum labor differ greatly. Guilds of creative inputs are concerned not just with their terms in the creative deal but also with the rank ordering of vertically differentiated talents *(A list/B list)* and how new talent is recruited and evaluated. Limiting the supply of their craft is seldom a paramount objective. Humdrum inputs, simply in it for the money, are more concerned with rent capture, supply restriction, and seniority.

Origins of Creative Guilds

Actors' Equity

The origins of performers' unions clearly were rooted in exploitation by employers of opportunities supplied by incomplete contracts. The artists sought not higher pay as such, but pay related to effort and insulated from opportunistic management decisions and hazards naturally falling on the entrepreneurial risk-bearer. Alfred Harding's account of the Actors' Equity Association provides evidence.[3] The story began with the touring repertory and stock companies that crossed the United States in the late nineteenth century (and before widespread competition from movies). There was no escrow arrangement by which managers guaranteed the payment of salaries, and in any case the performer paid her own way from the tour's last stop home to the New York base. Stranding thus became a regular problem when a show was failing to cover its running costs. Other creditors such as an unpaid playwright might force a closedown. The stranded actor could sue for redress, but (1) the manager might have incorporated, so that little equity was exposed; (2) when the suit came to trial much later, the actor might be far away; and (3) stagehands and musicians were already organized and able to elbow into the creditors' queue ahead of the actors. Another problem was the "satisfaction clause" in the actor's contract: the manager had total jurisdiction over whether an actor's performance was adequate, and this could support opportunistic discharges done for other reasons.[4]

Other problems arose from incompletely specified costs borne by the actor. Actors were not paid for time spent in rehearsal and incurred some or all of their own costume costs. Conceivably a "full and fair" contract with a producer could impose these costs and risks on the actor, but the room for dispute is obvious when the actor incurs the cost and the manager determines the adequacy of the outlay. When the play fails upon opening after several weeks of rehearsal, the actor's risky investment is lost, yet the producer makes the decisions affecting the likelihood of a flop. That is, even if the actor's expected pay for performances (taking the chance of closing into account) were high enough to compensate fully for rehearsal costs, the contract would still be inefficient, because the producer making the decision to close does not bear all of the risk. The same problem affected costume and other costs borne by the performer.[5]

The commitments that Actors' Equity eventually achieved after its founding in 1913 were directly responsive to these contract failures. A standard contract was established for each class of stage production, with arbitration of contract disputes: two weeks' notice or two weeks' salary for dismissals after a short period of probation; a maximum time limit on unpaid rehearsals; prompt payment of salary and a bond required to cover two weeks of the actors' salary when a play opens; all travel costs paid for road shows, and an Equity-managed fund to cover stranded actors' travel costs; extra pay for performances beyond eight a week; and most costume costs borne by the producer.[6]

This outcome was not easily achieved, and indeed involved a 30-day strike by the actors in 1919. The process shows other problems of efficient contracting in creative activities. It is not clear whether producers as a group stood to gain from the actors' demands. They might have, in the sense that more efficient contracts yield benefits that can potentially be shared between the parties. They probably did not, in that stage-struck actors were likely not the best individual guardians of their economic interests, so Equity annexed net benefits in the course of achieving fairness. In any case the individual producer surely benefited from the opportunity to defect from the Equity contract while other producers adhered. It was necessary to force the producers into a coalition, therefore, in order to bring the contract into widespread use. Up to a point, the organization of producers played to Equity's interest. The efficient scheduling of traveling theatre companies did have an element of natural monopoly, and two chains of theatre owners and managers, the Klaw & Erlanger group and the Shubert interests, came to dominate the market. These two were at each others' throats, however, and Equity apparently had no way short of a strike of forcing all producers into the umbrella Producing Managers Association that could or would make a binding deal. The producers indeed had invested heavily in resistance, sponsoring a competing "company union" of actors, less from objection to Equity's overt demands than from its potential to restrict the supply of performers. Like most creative artists' guilds, Equity did not avow this objective. But it could not foreswear restricting entry once it had become a central contracting agent on the actors' behalf. The Producing Managers Association eventually (1924) did agree to 80 percent Equity casts, at a time when the actual share of actors who were Equity members was around 90 percent.[7]

American Federation of Musicians

An interesting contrast to Actors' Equity appears in the history of the American Federation of Musicians (AFM), a history rooted in the days when many musicians served local markets, playing in theatres, clubs, hotels, at dances, weddings, bar-mitzvahs, and the like. Its origins reflect the same contract failures that bestirred Actors' Equity but also other goals—local fraternal benefits and simple monopolization.[8] AFM locals aimed to curb contract violations by theatre and concert managers, but they also sought to set fees collusively in local markets. Critical for local monopoly was control over musicians traveling through or migrating to the area. Unification of locals into a national union was feasible only with agreement to impose a tax on the travelers, requiring them to charge a premium over local union pay rates that was partly rebated to local musicians and partly retained by the union (and long a major revenue source for it). The union apparently never sought to exclude new local members; more control over the local market could be achieved by including performers rather than leaving them to compete outside the organization. But AFM units in large and growing markets such as Los Angeles and New York resisted transfers of membership by musicians moving from other areas. Considerable tension arose between the craft-union orientation of the local musicians, who served the low-value high-school prom market, and those performing and making recordings in major markets, where much larger rents were accessible. The union sought, without ultimate success, to serve as sole bargaining agent in these high-value markets. These musicians instead took control of their own bargaining with employers. The main union apparatus was left to cope with the long-term decline in the demand for musicians' services—a decline that began with the displacement of movie-theatre musicians by "talking pictures" and continued to the present day's synthesizers and electronic instruments. The AFM's most conspicuous hour came in the 1940s, when a ban on new recordings by union musicians led to a settlement that channeled a small stream of rents directly to the union for the funding of local public concerts by union musicians—a slice of pork for local officials. While the AFM's activities have run to seeking and (especially) preserving rents, it also has dealt with problems of contractual failures. Besides maintaining collectively bargained minimum pay levels, the union ensures that payments promised are in fact made, and requires the recruitment of a contractor for this purpose when a large enough group of musicians is involved.[9]

Major symphony orchestras were unionized through AFM efforts, although the bandleader types who presided over AFM locals ultimately proved unsatisfactory negotiators for symphony musicians, who now manager their affairs independently. The employment terms of symphony musicians certainly allow scope for contract failure and opportunism—in the amount of rehearsal time, touring requirements, and conditions for discharge, for example. But these problems mattered less for union organization of orchestras than for other classes of artists.[10] The symphony musicians instead resemble craft unionists focused on compensation terms, with their negotiations with the orchestra managements marked by acrimony and frequent strikes. The usual explanation invokes the dissonance between the symphony musician's job and the goal of a soloist's career that inspired her long and arduous training. A sense of denied entitlement can certainly explain conventional rent-seeking. In the 1960s, the Ford Foundation bestowed large grants on the nation's orchestras that were mostly absorbed in musicians' wage increases. The rapid rise of real compensation for the major orchestras continued into the 1980s. Factors besides union pressure were at work, though, because many players in major orchestras (in 1974, 47 percent of Cleveland Orchestra players) receive individually negotiated pay in excess of the union scale.[11] These over-scale pay rates move somewhat independent of the union minima, reflecting the willingness of the orchestra board to compete for top-quality players. The role of chronic frustration, however, is also clearly evident in orchestra negotiators' trouble eliciting a consistent set of demands from the members.[12]

Hollywood Talent Unions

The Hollywood talent unions—Screen Writers Guild, Screen Actors Guild, Directors Guild—all emerged or consolidated in the 1930s, reflecting the travails of the time and specifically the film industry's brush with the National Industrial Recovery Act. Their origins lie in contract failures similar to those that bestirred Actors' Equity. For example, in 1939 the Screen Actors Guild moved to protect its members from unscrupulous agents, in particular forbidding agents to produce films and thereby to deal on both sides of the employment table.[13] A different goal fostered the guilds serving crafts with a strong technical as well as creative bent, such as cinematographers and engineers, who sought to share technical information (the creative urge may have contributed to their willingness to share rather than preserve secrets). Their mutual alliances also aided dealing with equipment manufacturers for the improvement of quality, standardization of specifications, and the like. Their interests clearly embraced the creative uses of their technologies, as well as the matter of getting appropriate screen credits.[14] The guilds that represent performing artists have not sought to limit membership; on the contrary, they have pursued inclusiveness. Obtaining membership apparently does not deter the aspiring novice.[15]

The Writers Guild holds particular interest because of the contract-failure problems in its background. Although writers commonly were salaried employees in the studio era, they were generally not on long-term contracts, and their discontents stemmed from spot transactions in screenplays. A writer might provide on request an exploratory treatment of a plot idea, a "free sample" to be considered as a candidate for full development. Her speculative investment soured if the producer clandestinely sought competing submissions from other writers. No writing "on spec" hence became a major goal.[16] A second problem arose from the option structure of complex creative projects, which caused such projects to face termination at any of numerous decision points. The script is developed through a series of stages (Chapter 6), with the writer delivering (and being paid for) each successive approximation to the finished product. These formal if perhaps arbitrarily delimited steps improved on its predecessor, the story conference in which the draft was dissected and subjected to arbitrary and philistine (in the writer's eyes) demands for rewritings. Regularizing the process also formalized the decision points at which the writer might be replaced or saddled with a collaborator.

That producers tend to switch writers on a faltering script probably reflects the idiosyncratic character of the filmmaking process as a whole. If one writer's best shot leaves the collaborators dissatisfied but unable to articulate what is broken and how to fix it, the efficient option is to employ fresh talent. The writer's major objection to this solution concerned screen credits. For writers and other creative talents in filmmaking, the credit for work on a film is the building block of professional capital. When a job such as screenwriting is passed from hand to hand in the project's development, who receives credit? The producer once held discretion in the award of screenwriting credit, which gave him the opportunity to seize personal credit for any rewriting efforts. The screenwriters' critical achievement in a 1941 agreement was an elaborate arbitration procedure, managed by the Screen Writers Guild, in which neutral parties review the successive drafts prepared by contending writers and decide which one or ones (maximum of three names or partnerships) made contributions substantial enough to warrant writing credit.[17] Disputes and arbitrations of screenwriting credits have increased in recent years along with writers' fees (which are commonly tied to the credit they receive). The process consumes resources: writers speak of taking more time to prepare the appeal for credit than they did drafting the script itself. The Writers Guild rules themselves are in contention because they fail to distinguish between original screenplays and adaptations from other literary sources. The first writer who pulls out the key scenes from a novel will likely leave a larger imprint on the film than the revisers who follow, but that selection might represent obvious choices.[18] Equally contentious disputes arise over credit for television writing, because of the riches that can flow from "residuals" (royalties derived from syndication revenues).[19]

Other guilds, notably Directors Guild, pursue credits with equal fervor. A 1939 Directors Guild agreement established the director's right to screen credit, and a 1972 agreement limited the credit to a single director (even if more actually worked on the film). The quest for public recognition in the film credits is a zero-sum game over which the guilds contend. The director gets the last, and thus best, card before the movie begins. In 1995 the writers leap-frogged over the producers to claim the next-to-last position. Producers, who lack rent-gathering prowess, resisted unsuccessfully.[20]

Creative Talents and *A List/B List* Rankings

A regular practice of creative artists of any type is to develop common judgments on how their members rank in perceived skill, reliability, and/or adaptability. These qualities serve the efficient production of commercially successful films and other creative products, but they also represent a judgment on the aesthetic or technical quality of the finished film product, and the process by which it was realized, that is independent of commercial success. The box-office revenue or net profit of a creative worker's films does not exclusively control these rankings. They are constantly tested and reshuffled in conversational interchange not only among members of the group in question but also with other closely collaborating talent groups. These orderings matter both for dealmakers who assemble projects and for other talent groups who work alongside them. The likely success of a project (both creative and commercial), although highly uncertain, is thought to increase with the rank of each talent associated with it. This fact explains why the evolving *A list/B list* rankings for members of a talent group are constantly priced in the reputation market throughout the creative community.[21] Although the ranking process goes on constantly at an informal level, it still leaves room for agents to perform a role of gatekeeper and certifier. One careful study of screenwriters showed that those represented by the strongest talent agencies bring home much higher current earnings, even after controlling for many of their qualifications and their history of past earnings.[22]

Evidence in Chapter 4 indicated that highly ranked talents claim their rents partly in high compensation, partly in fuller and more selective employment. Still another reward to A-list status is control and authority, the utility that a creative worker gains from stamping her distinct imprint onto the finished product. In complex creative products, this quest for "muscle" makes struggles for influence endemic, but it also implies that A-list talents trade pecuniary compensation for control.[23] The large reserves of low-ranked and underemployed talent suggest some market failure: Why do they not either ask lower prices for their services, bringing more business, or turn to other lines of work? To look at it another way, why do the B-list members get paid enough on occasional jobs to keep them in the business? We find two explanations for the "reserve army" of lightly employed B-list talent. One, nicely illustrated by Robert Faulkner's study of Hollywood composers, has to do with recruitment and training.[24] The second (explored in the succeeding section) concerns the value of diversity among the soldiers in the reserve army.

The film score is composed and recorded at the end of the production process, after all other aspects of the film and its sound track are in or near final form. With other costs sunk and interest on a large investment piling up, the composer must start promptly and work fast. The composer is therefore picked on the basis of past track record, stylistic appropriateness, and reliability, given the film's music budget. How high on the rank list to shop is decided initially, taking account of the film's overall budget and the likely importance of the composer's contribution to its success. The algorithm seeks the most stylistically suitable composer in the chosen range of the rank list. Since *time flies,* the choice passes to a less suitable or lower-ranked candidate when the preferred composer is unavailable at the critical time.[25]

Parallel to the rank list of composers is a hierarchy of film projects, ranging from star-studded big-budget films down to the humblest daytime TV series. Each of them commonly seeks newly composed music (sometimes prerecorded music is used in whole or in part). The B-list cinema film composer works on TV programs and modest films. She may indeed have to choose between lucrative steady work in TV and the riskier but more challenging pursuit of jobs in feature films. Producers of low-budget feature films likely put their music needs up for bid, making the composer absorb the risk of any uncertain costs of copying, recording, and the like. Of composers who garnered appreciable numbers of feature-film credits during 1964–1969, 51 percent received no more credits during the next five years, 46 percent stayed at about the same level, and only 3 percent became winners.[26]

TV scoring is a point of entry into the craft for new composers. Faulkner found that Universal Studios, a very large producer of TV programs, was the first job for over half of the inner circle of top-ranked composers in the early 1970s. A larger group of established but lower-rated composers tended to work for both television and the occasional feature film. The quality ladder of film projects not only allows composers the chance to clamber up (or slide down), but also provides an explicit channel for apprenticeship and impetus.

In preparing music for TV shows, there is a hierarchy headed by the composer who scores for the pilot show and sets a style, themes, motifs, and orchestration. This work pays well at the outset, and even better in the royalty income generated by a successful series that goes into syndication. The lead composer's contract allows an exit option, either to subcontract the composing of music for some episodes or to leave the series entirely. Either way, the lead composer has an interest in spotting newcomers capable of taking on these replacement and secondary assignments. Commonly, with the job's time urgency and the inevitable postponements and reschedulings, A-list composers find themselves overcommitted and in need of a "ghost" or a subcontractor. The successful composer thereby captures value from effort spent in identifying and mentoring new talent. The successes and failures of composing efforts, for both new and veteran talent, are just one random component in the successes and failures of the projects that employ them. But the rankings rest on much more information than the degree of success of the person's past projects.[27]

Faulkner argued that this process of ranking and sorting composers applies equally to other creative talents such as directors, cinematographers, and stunt experts. His study of studio musicians playing for film and other recordings in Los Angeles, New York, and Nashville provides an example.[28]

Skill-Ranked Inputs in Complex Creative Projects

The pervasive *A list/B list* rankings and their role in staffing complex creative projects lead to two propositions about how these deals work. One offers a tentative explanation for the high collectively bargained minimum wages of creative talents persisting despite their high unemployment rates. The other explains why A-list talents tend to work with other A-list talents on what thereby become vertically differentiated A-list projects.

Talent Pools and Diversity

Collective bargaining for creative talents commonly sets a base wage for the actor, director, musician, and so on. The base wage is far below what the superstar commands, but it commonly appears high in light of the pool of talent clamoring for opportunities to work.[29] Why do these high minima persist over sustained periods? The individual employer has a clear incentive to deviate and offer lower pay, just as those seeking work and recognition want to accept a below-scale offer. The talent guild cannot easily monitor all contracts, and in the film industry many no-budget independent films escape surveillance. A pure bargaining-power explanation suffices for adherence by the major studio distributors, for whom guild members' sense of fairness is likely a compelling factor. There may be another explanation, however.

Reserve armies of talent such as bit-player actors and session musicians may embody the *infinite variety* property. Their qualities and talents are very similar but not perfectly interchangeable: the casting director or music contractor can frequently find some basis for preferring one to another. A given producer who pays well for the services of such an underemployed talent contributes to keeping that artist in the available pool. The option's value is not captured by that producer, who may never again seek exactly the same qualities. But the enlarged talent pool will (expectationally) benefit the future projects of other producers who occasionally will want just these qualities. The surprise is that many individual employers, each wanting to minimize its own labor costs, should go along with this collective goal. Yet in the 1950s just such an arrangement won agreement for fringe benefits to film workers on limited-duration contracts: a Motion Picture Health and Welfare Fund that received a 12.5 percent override on total wage payments, administered by the unions for their employee members.[30]

This explanation for high minimum compensation levels should not be taken to prove too much. In economic theory, markets for differentiated products do not necessarily sustain too few varieties. They can err in this direction, however. And the explanation comports with the situations of dealmakers willing to overpay to preserve a large talent pool—that is, those dealmakers operating through the studios that are the large-volume contractors for and releasers of films. Another question is why star talent supports guild minimum terms.[31] For the star, above-minimum payments to lesser talents subtract from the maximum rents that her agent could siphon into her own purse, so economic self-interest runs the opposite direction. A "sense of family" perhaps overrides the star's economic interest, but the differentiated-talent story does show why dealmakers acquiesce from sensitivity to the industry's interest.

Vertical Differentiation and Staffing Creative Projects

A commonplace observation is that a creative project is no better than the least capable participant involved.[32] The effects of individual talents' qualities appear to be multiplicative. At worst, let one talent deliver a poor performance, and that cipher makes the whole product valueless. Raise the quality (measured by the wage it can command) of each talent input by 10 percent, and increasing returns may levitate the project's value (consumers' willingness to pay) by more than 10 percent. Replace a B-list participant by one from the A-list in an otherwise A-list project, and its value rises by more than if the replacement had occurred in a B-list project. None of these relationships is inevitable. Some simple mathematical representations of production relationships are consistent with them, others are not.

The hypothesis of multiplicative and increasing returns to talent provides a consistent explanation for behavior patterns that run through all complex creative activities. In principle a successful film could recruit a star (for a star's ransom) and scrimp on the creative elements that will recede into the shade before the star's luster. What seems to knock out this possibility is the interaction of talents whereby each exerts effort proportion to the challenge posed by teammates. Studio executive Jake Eberts described the mechanism: "If you have actors like Al Pacino . . . you do not give them extras to play against. You just don't do it. If you do, they won't play . . . You've got to give them decent actors to play against. Otherwise . . . you won't get any good work from the stars."[33] The highly skilled musician playing in a second-rate orchestra can accomplish little by striving for excellence and may only unbalance the performance. Academic scholars regularly act on the belief that the quantity and quality of one's research increases with the skill (and diligence) of one's colleagues. The process shares the character of rank-order tournaments, commonly used in many organizations where those at a given rank compete for a limited number of promotion opportunities. Individual creative projects seldom offer explicit promotion opportunities, but the continuous flux of *A list/B list* rankings has the same effect. A mid-A-list talent languishing among B-list colleagues probably lacks any immediate opportunity to rise a few places on the A list.

The pattern of collaboration among specialists in cinema film production confirms the complementarity of high-quality inputs in a project. When freelance composers and producers are ranked by the number of film projects on which they have worked, there is a strong and statistically significant tendency for the more active composers and producers to work together. Considering that A-list talents work as much as they wish but lower-ranked ones work only occasionally, this association shows that highly ranked talents tend to work together, while lesser ones find each other for occasional deals. The same pattern holds for producers and directors and for cinematographers and directors. The statistical relationships grow stronger when activity is measured not by number of films but by gross revenue earned by those films. Indeed, one can explain differences in various films' gross rentals by the number of well-known actors in each film and a cumulative measure of the performance (Oscar nominations, awards, and so on) of the various specialists working on it.[34]

Talent Guilds and Craft Unions: The Ongoing Deal

Ongoing relations between guilds and craft unions and the dealmakers who assemble creative projects illustrate other basic forces driving the organization of workers in creative activities.

Hold-Ups

Because of their close temporal coordination *(time flies)*, complex deals are vulnerable to hold-ups. The curtain on Broadway goes up at 7:30. The concert is scheduled for 8 P.M. on Friday. The production cost of a motion picture is largely proportional to the number of days scheduled for filming, and most of the costs continue to be incurred when production is interrupted on short notice. Activities vulnerable to hold-up face a complex problem of contractual commitment and enforcement. Coalition participants able to stage a hold-up possess a valuable asset, because the dealmaker's high unavoidable costs define the size of the bribe that can be demanded to let activity proceed. Once the bribe is collected, the party staging the hold-up has an unchanged incentive to repeat the process. Without a binding commitment to cooperate, the dealmaker's whole expected profit stands vulnerable to capture. No one prudently puts equity capital at risk in the venture, and projects potentially profitable to all parties in the coalition fall through. A contract that can solve the hold-up problem needs to fulfill several conditions. First, the participants who enjoy the hold-up opportunity must be promised enough compensation to make a defection unprofitable. This bounty is a form of "efficiency wage," compensation high enough to make an earnest contribution to the coalition's value more profitable to a party than executing a hold-up. With many skills and talents necessary for the creative product (the multiplicative aspect of production relationships), the ex ante payoffs required to preclude hold-up may be too large to permit the deal. Second, the ex ante deal must be enforceable. Each party with hold-up power must be subject to a "rule of law" or other commitment sufficient to deter cheating on the agreement. Third, all parties with hold-up capacity must be locked firmly into the deal. A no-strike pledge by the stagehands' union must not permit the Alpha Theatre's stagehands to defect from the union and demand their own payoff.

Contractual efforts to suppress hold-ups show up in several patterns. Contracts pervasively contain no-strike provisions. They also embody levels of pay that seem to reflect both the scope for hold-ups and a group's propensity to execute hold-ups: smaller rents to talent guilds (with a taste for the successful pursuit of their creative callings) than to unions of humdrum crafts (focused on pecuniary income). The talent guilds have sought to set only minimum or entry-level rates of pay for the benefit of apprentices and members of routine competence. Craft wages set by collective bargaining both take thicker slices of monopoly rent and reward much larger proportions of the labor group in question. These patterns appear in the weekly wages set under collective bargaining with various groups of New York theatre employees (for the years 1986–1987): press agent, $1,074; company manager, $942; box office treasurer, $756.86; head carpenter or electrician, $743.84; actor, $740; musician, $720; head make-up artist, $580.25; wardrobe supervisor, $559.40; nonplaying musician (several are hired when recorded music is employed in a play), $400.[35] At the time, stage hands in some major New York concert halls were said to earn more than $100,000 annually.[36] The wage premia taken by humdrum crafts have the side effect of disruptive jurisdictional conflicts and restrictive work-rules. If a group's members (when employed) earn a wage generously exceeding their opportunity cost, they can benefit further by rules that increase the time required to accomplish tasks, and by expanding the tasks under their jurisdiction.[37]

Examples abound of the inflated cost of filmmaking associated with union wage differentials and featherbedding. Independent filmmakers estimate they can save 30 to 35 percent of production cost by operating a nonunion project, and one claimed that the optimal size of an on-site crew that might be twelve people is inflated to 120 by union requirements. As many as twenty unions might be present on a movie set. When a cinematographer belonging to the Los Angeles union works in New York, a New York cameraman is hired at $3,850 a week to sit and watch him work. Teamsters Union drivers of wardrobe and equipment trucks stand around all day during shooting, as they may do nothing but drive.[38]

Talent Guilds and Pay Differentials

The talent guilds provide their better paid and more successful members with only a framework for contracts, but they do set minimum wages that affect the demand for modestly talented and apprentice artists. These minimum wages probably have little effect on the demands for creative labor on big-budget film projects, but they do threaten jobs on the industry's impecunious fringe. The talent guilds face the price-discriminator's problem of when to seek to enforce minima and when to look the other way. The guilds' objective is not to deny apprentices entry into creative activities, so the beginning filmmaker's credit-card-financed project is benevolently overlooked. Efficient discrimination may be easier now than when B movies were produced within the major and B-specialist studios. The establishment of Screen Actors Guild minima in 1937 raised the cost of making these films about 15 percent and considerably reduced their output.[39] Settings where tolerating low wages may be attractive to the guild include successful creative enterprises serving low-value parts of the market (for example, children's television) with elastic demands for labor.[40] In the case of stage productions, Actors' Equity pursues price discrimination directly by setting its minima to vary with weekly gross box-office receipts.[41]

The onset of flexible specialization in Hollywood greatly weakened the craft unions while leaving the talent guilds' functions largely intact. The replacement of integrated studio production by casual employers limited the force of reputation as a cheap device for enforcing contracts. The contract-failure problems that had long before brought the talent guilds into existence now worsened, as casual employers came and went, making contacts harder for the talent guilds to monitor. For craft unions, especially those representing skills widely available in the general workforce, the deconcentration of employers and the dispersion of production through on-location shooting cut sharply into their opportunities for either short-run hold-up or long-run monopolization. These predictions match the different consequences of flexible specialization for the two types of employee groups. For craft and technical workers, despite significant concessions by their unions, roughly half of Hollywood employment by 1988 had shifted to nonunion productions. Furthermore, many jobs on nonunion productions are filled by workers who are union members but receive only market rates of pay. The craft unions protected their seniority rents by means of a roster system, in which the studios' craft work forces were pooled and ranked by seniority, with the unions providing the function of hiring hall as well as representation.[42] The talent guilds' organization, however, continued with no substantial changes. As agents expanded their role of matching creative talents and jobs, a new site of potential contract failures opened up for surveillance by the talent guilds. Their membership increased greatly during the 1970s and 1980s as Hollywood took on the function of producing programs, films, and commercials for television.[43]

The most bitter disputes between the motion-picture talent unions and the producers and studios have been over "residuals"—payments of royalties for the exhibition of a feature film subsequent to its theatrical showings. These residual uses have emerged from time to time as innovations made possible by technological advances such as high-quality recording apparatus, television, and videocassettes. These opportunities for profitable recycling were not anticipated in the contracts that covered production of the original material. The producer or studio owning the residuals then enjoyed a windfall, to the dismay of the talent who contributed to the original creative product. A violated sense of fairness sufficiently explains the bitterness of the disputes, but a purely economic consideration also applies. Union members will not spend more time and money striking for, say, higher wages than the increase is worth to them, and one of these factors is the wages they could earn without a strike—the opportunity cost. The residual payment, however, is a pure rent with no opportunity cost, making it worth spending up to the amount of the rent itself. The rights owner, of course, has a parallel incentive to resist the redistribution.

Examples of the problem abound. In 18 of 21 film-industry strikes by creative unions between 1952 and the 1990s, disagreements over residuals were either the main issue or figured prominently. The difficulty of settling them arose not only from rent-seeking incentives but also from the difficulty of writing contracts that quantify payments from unknown future sources of residuals. The size of the payments flow confirms the issue's importance, rising from $1 million in 1954 to $337 million in 1990 (57 percent from TV program reruns, 12 percent from theatrical films on TV, and 32 percent from other supplemental markets).[44]

8

The Nurture of
Ten-Ton Turkeys

While *nobody knows* pervades the creative industries, onlookers still remain baffled by the sums of money sunk in projects that ex post seem piteously inept. Could nobody see the disaster ahead and halt the waste of resources? Was the debacle due to governance problems, with the outcome foretold by parties who were nonetheless contractually induced to carry on? Was it all hubris? And what about the less noticed symmetrical errors—the blockbuster creative products that were previously rejected by everybody in town?

Role of the Option Contract

While there are many ways to squander large investments, the economic conditions that give the option contract its central role are a crucial factor. The end product grows from creative inputs that are combined in sequence. The effort or outlay at each step is sunk and unrecoverable. For an economically rational entrepreneur to set the process in motion, the present value of the revenues expected initially must exceed the project's expected total costs. Suppose that the new project is expected at the outset to break even—worth doing, but no excess profit. The entrepreneur takes the first step, committing (say) 10 percent of the project's total cost. Now some components of the project—a screenplay, set designs, "dailies" (developed but unedited film, freshly shot)—are available for inspection. If they support the initial expectations of a profitable product, or exceed expectations, the decisionmaker happily approves the next production stage. If they fall short, the size of the disappointment is crucial. If expected revenues are now written down by 20 percent, the project is abandoned. If they have shriveled by only 9 percent, however, expected revenues exceed the costs *remaining* to be incurred. The holder of the option chooses to continue, even though the project will appear to have run a loss when the books are ultimately closed. By extension, if expectations about the project's revenues continue to shrink, although no faster than increments of sunk cost are incurred, the last 10 percent of outlay will be authorized even if expected revenues are now only 11 percent of their original level.

This simple reasoning shows how, when costs are sunk progressively and information on the product's quality revealed gradually, rational decision-makers can carry projects to completion that realize enormous ex post losses.[1] It also explains why projects can be abandoned after large investments are made in them. After the negative of a cinema film has been completed, the costs of exhibition prints and sales promotion, which might be 30 percent of the negative cost, remain to be incurred. The completed film might not be released if expected gross rentals fall short of these remaining promotion and distribution costs. Or the disgruntled owner might cast about for a distribution strategy with costs low enough that they might be covered by the desiccated revenue flow that is now expected.

While turkeys can be explained by the uncertainty about creative products interacting with sunk costs and the option structure of decisions about their production, other explanations are at hand. The option steps are, of course, an advantage: it is better to be able to stop a soured project and avert some of its costs than to lose the whole sum budgeted for it at the outset. Nonetheless, the *nobody knows* property poses the stark hazard that no reliable information at all on the project's commercial realization may appear until all costs have been incurred.

Another complication arises because large and complex creative products stem from team efforts. The many choices that the team members make, as the project proceeds, depend on incentives built into their employment contracts, and on the way in which they are monitored or supervised. They may get the bad news about the project's ultimate success (or get it sooner) than those who supervise them. How they act on it depends on their terms of employment. Their personal interest might be better served by continuing, despite evidence calling for a halt. This problem could afflict any risky team project, but the presence of creative participants worsens it. *Art for art's sake* calls for proceeding with creative effort even at adverse personal economic cost, and hence implies that the creative artist might wish to carry on even when an ideally efficient governance system instructs her to halt the project. Apart from the subtleties of contract-based incentives, the leadership of complex creative projects calls for an enthusiastic commitment to continue and triumph over difficulties. Even the most skilled manager will find it difficult to simultaneously fire up the team and ponder dousing it with the cold water of termination. That decisionmaking problem grows tougher when the enthusiasm of the creative team serves as a costly signal to others whose investments (commitments) may favor its success. For the secretly vacillating chief of the creative team, such signals make life still more difficult by widening the variance of outcomes: Hesitate, and a moderate loss is assured. Carry on, and face chances of either a heroic victory or a catastrophic loss.

Failed Motion Pictures

Hollywood has been a bounteous poultry yard for ten-ton turkeys, and the case studies give some feeling for the circumstances that let them flourish.

The Bonfire of the Vanities

One well-documented disaster is the film made by Brian De Palma from Tom Wolfe's novel *The Bonfire of the Vanities*.[2] The governance problems with the project were clear and large. It went into production without a producer actually in place. Peter Guber had been playing this role until he left financier-distributor Warner Bros. He was not replaced, and the role of producer fell by default on director De Palma. That left him with no manager at hand to help keep priorities and objectives in focus, and also with no intermediary between the director and Warner's supervising executive vice president for production, Lucy Fisher. Guber had assembled the main inputs—rights to the book, screenwriter, director, and leading actor Tom Hanks—and promised release of the film for the Christmas season in 1990, leaving De Palma just fourteen months to do the rest.

Filming started in New York with the much-revised script not yet complete, and with De Palma and writer Michael Christofer knowing that major problems remained. Indeed, the film was regarded as a significant risk ex ante, because the novel heaps scorn even-handedly on all groups represented by its characters, which made it difficult to create an element of likeability needed to attract a large film audience. (This problem was never resolved.) Important filming locations had not been nailed down before shooting began; several failed to come through, requiring fast improvisation. Expected total costs kept increasing, but there was no definitive budget because there was no definitive plan.[3]

Monitoring by Warner Bros. executives consisted solely of seeking to keep the cost of the film within a committed budget. For this they had only the bluntest instruments: unannounced visits to New York and threats to shut down the production. De Palma maintained that he needed 78 days to shoot the film; pressed, he agreed to attempt completion in 66 days, but thought he would be fortunate to finish in 75. As shooting neared completion and ran over budget from its original $40 million to $50 million, Warner executives took direct control and sought to dictate what planned scene(s) not yet shot would be eliminated. They finally backed down on the main one in contention, in exchange for a promise to hold the total cost to $75 million. Notably, the studio executives' interventions had nothing to do with the perceived quality of the emerging film, although about half of it was shot at the Warner studio, where they had ample opportunity to assess it.[4]

The project illustrates the costliness of creative inspirations that popped up along the way. A late decision was made to hire Morgan Freeman to play the judge, even though the time when he was available required the rescheduling of shooting, a change in location of a major scene, and renegotiation of contracts with twenty other actors.[5] Many such problems emerged because De Palma tended to work privately and intuitively, so it was not clear to others (if indeed to himself) what would shortly be wanted. Opulence built into the basic plan for the film could not be readily squeezed out as its budget problems grew. The plan called for the construction and furnishing of a luxurious Park Avenue duplex on a Los Angeles sound stage; with cost-cutting missives flying, the production designer responsible for it "ignored the memos and kept working on his masterpiece."[6]

Experienced director De Palma thought all along that he was making a good film, and the possibility of a disaster did not occur to him until the process of previews before invited audiences made apparent this likely outcome. The preview audience's assessments accurately predicted the commercial disaster, but they gave no useful input on possible repairs. Julie Salamon's overall assessment emphasized the overriding momentum of the initial decision to make this a grandly conceived film, one that could accomplish the rare feat of combining intelligence and spectacle. It was "the devil's candy," tempting all participants to work for a big prize that would levitate their future opportunities.[7]

Heaven's Gate

Another example is the film *Heaven's Gate,* made by director Michael Cimino for United Artists (UA), a firm that was sold and dismantled following the movie's disastrous failure.[8] United Artists made a finance and distribution deal for this film with director Cimino in the wake of his successful *The Deer Hunter,* which won five Academy Awards and various other prizes. Well before its release, that film had been at the center of Hollywood "buzz" that carried the sense of an unusual talent. Cimino typically assumed the posture of the uncompromising artist, as UA officials knew from the controversy between Cimino and *The Deer Hunter*'s distributor, Universal. The film ran three hours, due to its internal rhythms and not the needs of its exposition, although Universal wanted the film's running time cut to two hours. UA executives concluded that Cimino's position in this controversy was reasonable and not a pure show of arrogance.[9]

Cimino offered *Heaven's Gate* to UA (and also to Universal, Twentieth Century–Fox, and Warner Bros.) as a package deal that included the script ($250,000), Cimino's services as director ($500,000), his companion Joanne Carelli's as producer ($100,000), and actor Kris Kristofferson as leading actor ($850,000 plus 10 percent of net profits). Kristofferson was regarded as something of a bargain, and casting otherwise encountered no persistent problems. Difficult negotiating issues were resolved in Cimino's favor because of his credible threats to move the project to Warner Bros.[10]

While contracts for the film were being drawn, UA fixed upon having it ready for release for the 1979 Christmas season, when they would have no other ambitious films available. Although meeting this schedule would be a stretch under the best circumstances, it gave Cimino the opportunity to demand that UA be responsible for any cost overruns that occurred, as well as accept various other generous terms (personal expenses, control over promotion, and so on). It evidently did not occur to UA executives that, with this pledge in Cimino's pocket and no independent producer in place, they had lost all financial leverage short of abandoning the film. By the time shooting began, the budget had doubled from its original $7.5 million. Although the film's shooting (on location in Montana) appeared well enough organized, it was falling steadily behind schedule. A Christmas release was clearly out; UA seriously considered abandoning the film, which now seemed likely to cost $35 to $40 million. By this time UA executives had seen some of the exposed film, concluding that its artistic quality was excellent, but that the movie's intrinsic appeal could not justify its current budget. UA began seeking another studio as a partner, but nobody was interested.[11] It also contemplated its substantial exit costs if it abandoned the film, $2 million in play-or-pay contracts and $3 million in other contracts that would have to be renegotiated. UA concentrated on keeping costs from escalating further by installing a financial controller on the set. Cimino replied that he would have nothing to do with this monitor. UA next (August 1979) imposed a take-it-or-leave-it offer of a $25 million maximum final cost for a film lasting less than three hours, with Cimino's control over the cutting of the film removed if the first cut's running time exceeded three hours. This prodded some reform by Cimino, and filming was completed in November. A schedule was set for a final cut of the film in May 1980 for release in November.

In late June, when UA executives were first able to screen Cimino's final cut, it ran five hours and twenty-five minutes and was clearly unreleasable. Should they now fire Cimino? No, because who else could make sense of all that exposed film? As UA continued to seek a shortened and tightened film, Cimino continued with endless reexamination of film footage and mono-maniacal reworking of technical processes. Also in the name of Art he resisted any public testing of the film; he was confident, and that was a question of "mere commerce." At the celebrity preview arranged for November 1980, Bach wrote, the audience was "mesmerized by the spectacle, the enormity of the miscalculation, the perfection that money can buy, the caring that it can't. They were stunned into submission by . . . the luxuriant wastefulness, the overbearing sound, the relentlessness of its self-importance."[12] Should UA quit now, or withdraw the picture and recut it (six months and a million dollars)? The recut was done, and a two and one-half hour version was prepared, leaner and clearer and with all the narrative scenes in place. It was now at least watchable, but when it opened in 810 theatres nationwide, it took in $1.3 million in box-office revenue and quickly flopped. UA's executives were fired by the firm's corporate owner, Transamerica, and the firm was sold to the owner of MGM, who wanted UA's domestic distribution system.

Sources of Disasters

These cases and similar examples rule out none of the explanations for cinematic financial disasters.[13] Deficient budgetary control systems interact treacherously with *art for art's sake*. In the nature of their task, directors constantly seek ways to improve their product, ways that usually increase its cost while having only surmised effects on expected revenue. Indeed, interim evidence on the commercial value of the emerging film seems largely lacking: script flaws and dilemmas that ultimately sank the project were present, but unappreciated, at the outset. The studios show large and systematic differences in their ability to control films' costs (Disney is famously cheap), but the task is never easy.[14] Controllers can intervene on grounds of budgetary overrun, but seemingly not on aesthetic grounds, and (at least in these basket cases) they seem unable to impose take-it-or-leave-it budgetary caps. Their task is not eased by filmmakers who themselves understand the strategic imperative of option contracts and aim for committing or sinking sufficient resources in a project that the distributor regretfully continues rather than folds.[15]

A conjecture suggested by the case studies is that budgetary control over a film suffers from "bounded rationality." The more complex and costly the film, the more difficult is the task of the controller, who must contend with the many collaborators whose interdependent decisions affect the project's realized costs. The larger the total budget, the fewer minutes can the coordinator devote to monitoring the prudence with which any given $100,000 is spent. In that sense, managerial control is subject to diminishing returns as the film's budget grows. This slippage in control likely interacts with another effect. Big-budget films usually involve large pay packets for stars and other top creative performers, and large cash payments tend to be topped off with abundant perks and indulgences as well. Sybaritic life at the top likely promotes a sense of entitlement in less celestial participants, so that decreasingly effective financial control meets an increasing propensity to indulge.[16]

Problems of governance and financial control on the individual film's set have their parallel at the corporate level, where studio executives must make hard choices about troubled film projects. Although distributors do abandon many projects at early stages, executives exhibit extreme reluctance to write off a large sum spent on an out-of-control project. To write off is to concede misjudgment in letting the project get that far, whereas if the project goes to completion and fails, the filmmaker is at fault.[17] Besides, it might still succeed: *nobody knows.*

This interpretation of filmmaking governance—as a crapshoot with weak controls on extravagance and none on quality—is supported by industry assessments of whose reputation suffers from involvement with a turkey. Strikingly, there is seldom any consensus on which creative participant messed up, and the opprobrium gets distributed on other principles.[18] The talent with a good previous record takes a smaller reputational hit than does a newcomer. The artist without close market substitutes (for example, the charismatic male star) loses less than those with good substitutes (female stars). Those with reputations for being responsible and cooperative workers suffer less than uncooperative types, who are now justifiably excluded from future coalitions. And those well integrated into the Hollywood social establishment suffer less.[19]

Mammoth First Printings, Giant Returns

The publishing industry has lately complained about its own type of large-scale flops. Books written (or purportedly written) by celebrities win mammoth advances, appear in huge first printings, then sell abysmally. The publisher of Bill Clinton's *Between Hope and History* saw 70 percent of the copies shipped to bookstores returned unsold. The O. J. Simpson trial proved a negative bonanza: Ballantine paid an advance of $3.5 million for Johnnie Cochrane's *Journey to Justice,* shipping 650,000 copies of which 300,000 were sold. Marcia Clark's *Without a Doubt* earned approximately half of its $4.5 million advance. Other apparent failures were Whoopi Goldberg's *Whoopi* (William Morrow advanced $6 million, with a first printing of 750,000 copies) and Jay Leno's *Leading with My Chin* (a $4.5 million advance by HarperCollins).[20] The pattern afflicts other sorts of books, including novels by well-known authors, but it is particularly important for celebrity books, which in 1996 accounted for nine of the fifteen books on *Publishers Weekly*'s nonfiction best-seller list. Paradoxically, the winner's curse problem probably worsened as the main U.S. trade publishers became business units within large international publishing firms and entertainment conglomerates (Chapter 20). These deep-pocketed owners relaxed liquidity constraints that might have reined in bids for costly book projects, enlarging the curses that could befall winners. The new corporate owners brought little if any capability to second-guess these projects, and the primary decision-makers faced only limited personal penalties for the occasional bad guess.[21]

Why do these huge discrepancies arise between advances and first printings and sales actually realized? Part of the answer is pure uncertainty, which suggests that any class of projects that includes some blockbuster successes will be balanced out with ten-ton turkeys. This pure uncertainty is illustrated by the figures that occasionally surface on the widely differing bids that publishers submit for the same project. For General H. Norman Schwarzkopf's memoir Macmillan bid $1.2 million, Viking Penguin about $3.2 million, and Random House $5 million.[22] Such discrepancies seem to confirm the winner's curse. Economists propose that eager but rational bidders will adjust their bids downward to allow for the possibility of self-deception, but nothing ensures such cool-headedness. In some cases the firm has a plausible (if not persuasive) reason. It may wish to establish itself as a "player" by holding onto or attracting an established writer whose future books are expected to yield positive profits.

But there is more than the winner's curse to explain some of the publishing industry's debacles. Advances for celebrity books are commonly paid on the basis of manuscript samples, so that the finished product may fall far short of its promise. Still, jeweled prose and penetrating insights are not the qualities sought from authors such as these, so manuscripts that palpably fall short of the prospectus can hardly be the main problem. In any case, when the first printing is decided, the manuscript is already in hand, so the publisher knows what product it offers.

Several factors combine to supply an explanation. While sales to readers ultimately matter, the publisher's first problem is to sell the volume to booksellers. They decide what quantities to order on the basis of a jacket design and general information and promotion material from the publisher, but with no more information about readers' ultimate interest. The size of the first printing announced (credibly, it appears) by the publisher therefore serves as an important signal of the publisher's conviction of the book's success.[23] The publisher in turn has a strong incentive to send an optimistic signal, because piles of the book on conspicuous display in bookstores are themselves an effective sales-promotion device.[24] Buyers of celebrity books probably rely little on book reviews, especially as the commercial lifespan of these books (whether successful or not) is quite short. Booksellers have no strong incentive to discount the signal, because they suffer no significant losses if it proves false. By a longstanding policy they may return most unsold books for full credit (although they do pay return shipping costs).[25] The conspicuously announced sizes of first printings cannot be explained by the technology of book production. Apart from the signal value, the extra cost associated with several smaller runs rather than one monster one is trivial. And many copies that return unsold are damaged enough that they cannot be recycled as new stock, even if demand eventually warrants. Giant first printings thus must have a signal value, as indeed do large advances to authors. Proportionally higher returns are therefore expected from books with high (retail) sales than from less conspicuous and more modest-selling books, for which reviews and word-of-mouth matter more to customers and promotional signals are less significant. Data are not available to test this precisely, but casual evidence suggests that recent increases in aggregate return rates for trade books (during 1996 there was an increase of 8.9 percentage points to a level of 35 percent) reflect the volume of celebrity books and similar highly promoted tomes. Also involved is the increasing importance of outlets such as warehouse stores, price clubs, and superstores that stock only books that are jousting for blockbuster status.[26] Another fragmentary indicator is the amounts of advances written off (that is, acknowledged as losses) by major trade publishers: Simon & Schuster about $35 million in one year, and Random House in the range of $50 million to $80 million.[27]

Another factor that contributes to avalanches of returned books is the incentive structure of the author's contract, which bears an advance against royalties. The advance affects the publisher's decisions on printing and promoting the book, because it lowers the marginal cost of a sold copy until sales reach the number of units that earns back the advance. The publisher's incentive to spend on sales promotion is thereby inflated until the advance is recovered (see Chapter 3). If the size of the first printing itself promotes sales, the publisher plunges in on a larger first printing than otherwise (up to a cap given by the number of copies whose sale would recover the advance). Large first printings also seek to energize the publisher's promotion staff. Their effort must be allocated among books on the list, and manic enthusiasm cannot be sustained for every book (publishers' representatives have their own problems of sustaining credibility with booksellers).

In the world of commerce, market distortions tend to generate their own repairs. Because returned books generally cannot be resold as full-price new stock, they must either be pulped or remaindered through bargain outlets. These have become a well-organized market with an annual exhibition (since 1990) and competitive bidding for remaindered books. Chain remainder stores can predict reasonably well what books they can sell, and their increased number has bid up the prices received by publishers. The volume of remaindered books reflects not only the volume of new publications, but also publishers' decisions about inventories of backlist books. Publishers' decreased inclination to sustain books on backlists has fed the remainder market, and the age of the typical remainder book (recently three years) has been creeping down. The average quantity offered per title has been increasing, too, reflecting overruns of (would-be) best-sellers.[28] For the publisher the remainder market serves partly as a way to bury mistakes, but also it achieves price discrimination among a book's potential customers and cheapens the downside risk of the "giant first printing" strategy. For these purposes it matters how often remainder prices exceed the publisher's marginal printing cost per copy—but evidence on this is lacking.

9

Creative Products Go to Market: Books and Records

As complex creative products are assembled and dispatched toward consumers, they usually pass between one or more pairs of independent enterprises: motion-picture studio distributor to exhibitor, publisher to bookstore, record company to music store. The basic properties of creative wares continue to shape these transactions, even though the firms themselves may be humdrum profit-seekers. Because *nobody knows,* both maker and retailer work in great uncertainty about demand for the individual creative product. There is a problem of selecting and dealing in small quantities of the *infinite variety* of close-substitute products. Even with the creative process completed, *time flies* for the costly product's economic value as interest expense accumulates. The finished product's owner has an incentive to reap its cash flows quickly. Pulling against this goal, however, is the fact that consumers' demands for new creative products are time-sensitive in varying degrees, so that it frequently pays the seller to employ price discrimination: higher prices to consumers eager for the latest thing; lower for those who will wait until the novel comes out in paperback, or the movie on videocassette.

The deal between assembler and retailer of creative wares runs into the problems that arise for the organization and governance of transactions between manufacturers and distributors in many markets. The individual producer's goodwill asset, due to consumers' willingness to pay more than his product's cost, is affected by many decisions that its distributors make about how to price and promote it. Because of this interdependence, the deal between producer and distributor is never an anonymous spot-market transaction. Rather, it involves an elaborate set of constraints and conditions imposed by the producer on the distributor's behavior (vertical restraints, in the language of antitrust policy), that may tie manufacturer and distributor together in a franchise relationship, or even lead them to the altar of full vertical integration.

146

This chapter takes up the markets for books and records, in which the *infinite variety* property plays a dominant role. The next chapter on films focuses on timing issues and the problem that *nobody knows*. Both undergird the problem of organizing the distribution of books and records. About 50,000 books are published in the United States each year. Most people do not read the year's best-selling book, and many books sell fewer than 5,000 copies. Every message to a potential reader about a new book's content incurs a fixed cost, yet most will not elicit a purchase. Every shipment of a title to a bookstore incurs another fixed cost that is burdensome because the typical bookstore sells few copies of the typical book. The problem of organizing both the promotion and physical distribution of books centers on minimizing the burden of these many small costs.

At this time the distribution of both books and records threatens to be transformed by electronic commerce. The empirical evidence in this chapter is necessarily retrospective, but it supplies a basis for predicting some aspects of the transformation.

Informing Potential Buyers

Methods of Sales Promotion

While the property of *nobody knows* mainly invokes the uncertain demand for creative goods, it also points to the seller's problem of informing potential buyers about the traits of a new creative product. Publishers long played a passive role. Copies of new books went off to review media in the hope that reviewers would provide, if not a warm endorsement, at least information to let readers match the book to their interests. Publishers confined their direct selling effort (apart from a little print advertising) to retail bookstores rather than readers. Sales representatives called on independent bookstores, conveying the advance information embodied in the book's jacket and blurb and aligning books with any specialty interests of the bookseller. Not every book on a rep's list could be claimed a best-seller; reps implicitly ranked their new titles on commercial merit. The book traveler called repeatedly on the same booksellers, so reputation played its usual important role of encouraging truthful promotions.[1] The efficiency of selling directly to independent bookstores increased somewhat with computerized inventory records, which spared the rep the task of determining what the bookstore already had in stock. On the other hand, the rising value of labor time for both rep and bookseller continuously increases the cost of this method of promotion and has favored the use of intermediary wholesalers.[2]

Book reviewing media made their own accommodations with the fixed-cost problem. Several classes of these certifiers exist. Some serve booksellers and libraries rather than the general public, and they describe the book's likely appeal to readers rather than define its place in the realm of intellect and information. *Publishers Weekly* and *Kirkus Reviews* mainly address booksellers, while the American Library Association's *Booklist* serves librarians. The last supplies a good example of the independent certifier's role.[3] *Booklist* provides about 7,500 advance reviews a year sifted from 30,000 books (galley proofs) received. The publication's influence lies not with books of manifest wide interest (which most libraries would purchase in any case) but in books published in small printings (initially 5,000 or less), for which it opines on both intrinsic merit and likely demand from readers. Its area of greatest influence is children's books, because of the sensitivity of the subject matter; for the librarian a disappointed adult reader and an enraged parent pose problems of wholly different magnitude.

Most book reviews reaching the general reader come packaged in general-interest newspapers and periodicals, which economizes the cost of reaching potential book buyers. Relatively few books get reviewed—the general reader's problem being to select a few likely purchases rather than to exclude the unlikely candidates. A few review media enjoy great influence, notably the *New York Times Book Review,* but it only reviews or notices about one-tenth of new general-interest trade books. Other newspapers devote less space and apparently take their cues from the *New York Times* and the *New York Review of Books.*

The problem of fixed costs of spreading information weighs heaviest on the publisher and book that will interest a small number of readers, but whose readers are not easily distinguished by objective characteristics. Scholarly and specialized professional books pose a simpler distribution problem. Readers seek reviews in specialized publications, and their professional status deposits them on mailing lists that cheapen the publisher's tasks of both promotion and sales. For this reason, and because of both the low wages to authors (small advances) and the high willingness to pay of research libraries and a core of specialized users, commercial publication is viable for books selling few copies.[4] Textbooks, with high fixed costs of production, also are simple to promote, in that the teachers of courses that might use them are easy to identify. That actual selling costs are high reflects the close competition among texts serving secondary-school curricula and popular college courses and the high gross profits won by the publisher (and author) who gain adoptions. Finally, for certain classes of fiction (romance, fantasy), specialized authors and publishers serve dedicated cores of readers, simplifying the problems both of identifying potential readers and signaling content to them.[5]

Companies recording popular music struggle against the same set of fixed costs of promotion and distribution. They enjoy the advantage that established artists are known to record buyers from concerts, radio, and television (cable) airplay. Print reviews have very limited influence, in contrast to book publishing.[6] The recording itself gets played on broadcast media, which provides the main information source for record buyers.[7] Hence, record companies' promotional efforts focus on the broadcasters, with two major consequences. With airplay so influential and broadcast time scarce relative to the flow of new recordings, there is a strong incentive for the broadcaster to auction airplay to the record companies. The resulting "payola" is discussed in Chapter 18. Second, to maximize their listenership, broadcasters plug the songs they expect to be most popular, yet their choices affect record buyers' purchases. This loop is discussed subsequently.

Return Privileges and Resale Price Maintenance

One form of promotion adopted by American publishers in the 1930s has been to allow booksellers unlimited privileges of returning unsold books for full credit. Record companies also allow generous returns for full credit. The policy is costly for publishers, because returned books are frequently no longer in saleable condition (Chapter 8). Full credit for returns reduces risk and increases expected profits for the retailers, however. It also increases net demand for the product, because the physical display of books and records itself is a form of promotion. The practice recognizes the spillover of pecuniary benefit to the publisher from books sold as a result of the bookseller's display. The publisher's gross profit on the typical trade book (after deducting production cost and outbound shipping cost) is about $7 ($9.50 if the author's advance has not yet been earned back), while the publisher's out-of-pocket cost of a book shipped, returned by the bookseller, and pulped is not much more than $3. Hence, an extra book could profitably be shipped on less than a 50 percent probability that it will generate an extra sale. Publishers are divided on free returns, however, and occasionally offer books to sellers at a higher discount (from suggested retail list price) but without return privileges.[8]

The alternative arrangement, followed in the retailing of most economically perishable goods, is for the retailer to absorb the risk of unsold units and employ markdowns and/or hand-offs to specialized resellers to move (what turns out to be) excess inventory. That policy would economize on the bookseller's return shipping costs of copies destined only to be pulped, as well as the marginal production and shipping costs for the publisher. Lower inventories would deprive some readers of the chance to learn about books that would prove a "good read." More to the point for booksellers, markdowns might be less profitable than the returns policy, if readers learn to anticipate eventual markdowns and delay their book purchases until the end-of-season clearance sale.[9]

That many publishers countenance the returns policy need not make it best for publishers, booksellers, and readers taken together. The individual publisher's adherence may stem from the prisoner's dilemma. Each publisher individually would lose by ending free returns, because the promotional advantage of bookstore inventories would pass to competing publishers. Yet cessation by all publishers could lead to smaller retail inventories but lower book prices.[10] The unclear status of the returns policy for economic welfare is related to the issue of resale price maintenance (RPM) for books, a long-standing policy question in several countries. To promote retail stockholding, an alternative to the returns policy is forbidding the retailer to charge less than the publisher's retail price. Higher margins of retail price over cost keep more bookstores in business and encourage the store to hold a larger inventory.[11] Otherwise, competition among bookstores drives down the prices of best-sellers (as it has in the United States) and reduces retail inventories of slender volumes of sensitive poetry.[12] With RPM the John Grisham buyer pays a tax that subsidizes the search costs of browsers seeking more exotic fare.

The returns privilege and RPM have some differing consequences. RPM restricts competition among bookstores and raises readers' prices for popular books. It likely means that fewer books are sold overall, unless the promotional value of retail inventories is strong indeed. It might mean that more unpopular books are published, if readers forgo the latest Grisham at full list price and instead buy more exotic books (but they might instead head for the video store).[13] Compared to return privileges, RPM does not inflate printing and shipping costs, but it does inflate the resources invested in book retailing, as additional stores court buyers willing to pay for expensive best-sellers. The returns privilege directly promotes retail stockholding and display of less popular books, whereas RPM induces retailers to compete for the best-seller customer by whatever strategies (other than low prices) they can devise. The easiest customers to lure, because (by definition) they are so numerous, are those for best-sellers.[14]

Promoting Blockbusters

That leaves the publisher's most conspicuous form of promotion—the costly campaign on behalf of a would-be blockbuster. These many-pronged efforts are aimed at both retailers and readers. They cost as much as $500,000 to

$750,000, even without allowance for costly signaling by means of inflated first printings (Chapter 8).[15] Besides ads in all media, these campaigns include authors' tours of TV and radio talk-show circuits. The broadcasters' need for material and the author's need for exposure create a symbiotic relationship, with the talk less about the book than about its subject. Telegenic authors have an advantage in this game; one publishing house was founded with the explicit goal of publishing authors and books with good potential for TV promotion.[16]

The requisites of sales promotion in book publishing generally, and the promotion of blockbuster books in particular, explain much of the changing sizes and organization structures of the largest publishing firms. Cash spent on promotion is wholly sunk and buys no collateral that the publisher can use to borrow funds. Hence, the ability to finance heavy promotion internally is a valuable asset for the publishing house. Potential blockbuster books then can be signed and promoted for which most other publishers lack the funds, a profitable advantage if the cash-rich publisher can dodge the winner's curse.[17] Promotion techniques also achieve economies from marketing the firm's backlist (books in print published before the current season) along with its current new books. An author's new book tends to bestir an increased demand for her previous works, and this and other opportunities arise for joint promotions of specific new and backlist books.[18]

Promotion techniques do encounter one diseconomy of size. The promotion of additional newly published books (not blockbusters) eventually incurs some disadvantages from congestion in the sales representatives' agendas. While a sales force is a source of scale economies as long as the rep can handily cover more books in a session with the bookseller, lengthening the list eventually wears out the welcome. It also forces some books to the bottom of the heap in the ranking that the credible rep must provide in his repeated dealings with the bookseller. Other scale diseconomies arise because the unit tasks of book publishing (editing, design, advertising) cannot be subdivided and routinized without stifling the creativity of the process.[19]

Promoting a hoped-for blockbuster book requires a large investment that is sunk before readers (or even reviewers) reveal their reactions. The same holds for recordings of leading popular music performers, whose new album may be synchronized with a world concert tour. For lesser authors and musicians the publisher or record company has more discretion to turn on the promotional faucet only after buyers or certifiers have shown some sign of enthusiasm through word-of-mouth, reviews, radio airplay, whatever. This opportunity to postpone outlays until information is in hand invites the profit-maximizing publisher or record company to issue more new titles than otherwise, because some wasted promotional outlays can be avoided ("throw it against the wall and see if it sticks").[20] On the other hand, this flexibility exacerbates contracting with the author or artist, who prefers a firm commitment to heavy sales promotion.

Best-Seller Lists and Top 40 Hits

The information problems of distributing books and records come together in the role of the ubiquitous best-seller lists. These claim to identify the most popular items on the basis of sales of books and sales and airplay of recordings. Yet they also influence what titles are demanded, by affecting both what retailers choose to promote and what buyers select as a cheap way to inform their choices. If best-sellers are what people buy, and people buy what is selling best, where is the fixed point? That question has no general answer, but it leads to others that do.

The best-seller list becomes a type of mechanical but objective certifier. That very facade of objectivity tempts sellers to influence the rankings in favor of their wares. Methods include promotion strategies that exploit the list's method of compilation, or simple bribery of the compiler. Since compilation requires the costly collection of information from some set of distributors, and the list is a public good not easily sold to users, it is a close question how its compiler will both cover the preparation cost and provide a product with credible integrity. How the certifier obtains its revenue is the easy part: such lists usually appear in periodicals popular among market participants, so the list can be bundled with other information for which agents in the market willingly pay. The creation of the list is harder. The listmaker cannot rely on the publisher's or record company's sales figures, which are easily manipulated. Even if shipments to retailers were verifiable, the privilege of free returns allows great slippage between shipments and sales ("gone today, here tomorrow" is a saying in the publishing industry). Only recently has retail sales information become accurately and cheaply collectible from scanner data. Before that, the compiler obtained oral reports from a rotating and confidential sample of retail outlets.

Hit lists for popular records emerged as a casual journalistic exercise that became important only as radio broadcasters started the rotating play of records from the list. Record labels' promotion staffs soon undertook to discover what retail shops were sampled and make heavy purchases of a title targeted for promotion (or simply bribe the staff to rig the report). The cost of buying a place, or a higher rank, near the bottom of such a list was usually low, because the differences in sales rates there were small. Consequently some list compilers reduced the length of their lists in order to improve integrity. In Britain (where the history is well documented), a consortium was put together of the British Broadcasting Company, the phonograph records trade association, and a trade periodical to pay for a well-run survey that elicited accurate reports from carefully sampled stores, sought to keep their identities secret, and carefully checked any suspicious developments. Secrecy was never perfect, however, and the nether reaches of the list remained vulnerable.[21] The U.S. history appears similar. The introduction of scanner data eliminated one point of slippage in the process, but left in place other opportunities for manipulation. Having a new record enter the charts in the No. 1 position is valuable enough to record companies to warrant such practices as subsidizing below-cost sales in reporting record stores and chains, and starting retail sales only after promoting extensive radio airplay.[22]

The vulnerability of U.S. best-seller lists for books was exposed in 1995, when the authors of a business-consulting book purchased some 50,000 copies in order to keep the book on the *New York Times* best-seller lists for fifteen weeks. This costly maneuver was attractive because the best-seller status drew clients to the authors' consulting firm. It turned out that the bookstores sampled by the main compilers of best-seller lists were widely known. They were also rather incomplete, omitting book clubs entirely and skipping some major retail outlets (airports, Christian bookstores).[23]

Another insight into the self-validating realm of best-sellers and top hits lies in the turnover of recordings played by radio stations that employ a top-hits format. While radio stations have lately embraced more diverse methods of setting their playlists, many have relied on playing the Top 40 Hits or some variety of contemporary hit radio. The format's obvious value is to maximize the station's listenership or (more precisely) to attract the young listeners who will elicit advertisers' maximum willingness to pay. Less obviously, other programming methods that involve more independent review and evaluation of new records prove less cost-effective. No disk jockey or programming director can listen to a week's avalanche of new pop records within that week, so casual selection is inevitable. One programming director reported listening to the first few seconds of each new record, discarding it if it lacked a "hook."[24] The leverage for new records' access to the playlist comes from the boredom that ultimately follows heavy airplay and widespread retail purchase of a hit record. Its successor gains leverage from secondary radio stations' willingness to experiment with new records. This experimentation sets off random regional differences in exposure and appeal that cause a record to "break" in some major city or region. These local break-out patterns sometimes accompany the emergence of local music styles into national popularity (Seattle grunge bands, for example). Record-label promoters slant their support of new records to likely break-out cities and quickly carry the news to other cities.[25] In short, the turnover of contemporary pop records resembles a process of innovation and diffusion. In recent years the channels for promoting records have widened appreciably, with cable networks MTV and VH1, college and other nonprofit radio stations, and the internet becoming prominent. A predictable consequence has been a proliferation of small "picker" record labels—but with the high mortality rates and turnover that always plague their kind.

Physical Distribution of Books

The physical distribution of books raises its own organizational problems due to the large number of publishers and retail outlets (which appropriately include libraries) and the small dollar value of the typical wholesale unit transaction. Sound recordings, again, are similar. As with the promotion of books, the pressure of many small fixed costs shapes the choice of organization to distribute them.[26] Their influence takes its most extreme form in the distribution of paperback books through casual outlets such as airports and drug and grocery stores. The venue itself makes no choice of the titles offered, which are packaged by a jobber who frequently adds new titles and removes outdated ones. The return rate is as high as 60 percent, and the leftovers are not even physically returned to the publisher for credit, only their stripped-off covers.

The arrangements for distributing trade books have varied over time, but always with some large-scale firms undertaking to hold inventories and fill orders for a wide range of new and backlist books.[27] Large trade publishers with warehouses and distribution systems service many small publishers. A few wholesalers hold very large inventories from which they serve small bookstores and libraries. A shifting boundary divides direct distribution from publisher to bookseller from distribution through an intermediary wholesaler. The proliferation of small publishing houses spurred by the technology of desktop publishing has led to an accompanying growth of independent wholesalers serving this sector.[28] Wholesalers' ability to provide delivery quicker than publishers has sustained them against the hazard of the uncertainty about demand for individual titles.[29] Chain bookstores have used varying strategies, generally central ordering but not central warehousing and distribution to their stores. In 1989 Waldenbooks switched from ordering directly from publishers to a close collaboration with major wholesalers, profiting from the difference between the discount given by publishers on large direct purchases by retailers (about 46 percent of the suggested retail price) and the discount obtained from publishers by wholesalers (slightly more than 50 percent). Indeed, the apparent persistence (stickiness?) of these conventionalized discounts over time may cause changes in the distribution channels that are economically inefficient, if the discounts fall out of line with costs, subject to continual disturbance from changes in transportation charges and information technologies.[30] Finally, Amazon.com and its electronic kin operate not only without shops but almost without warehouses. In 1997 Amazon.com filled only 5 percent of its orders from its own stock, relying on one of the large wholesalers. (The arrangement is in flux, because the wholesaler is offering to ship books directly to Amazon.com's customers rather than shipping in bulk to Amazon.com for repackaging). Amazon.com is also expanding its own warehouse capability, however.[31] Over the past decade, intermediary wholesalers increased their share in book distribution from 20 to 30 percent, presumably the net result of these various forces.

Decline of Independent Bookstores

Much more in the public eye than these shifts in distributional logistics has been the displacement of the traditional independent bookstore by other retail organizations—chain booksellers and superstores, but also discount stores and warehouse clubs. In the short period 1991 to 1996, these shifts occurred in the shares of books distributed:[32]

	1991	1996
Independent bookstores	32%	18%
Chain bookstores	22	25
Book clubs	17	18
Mail order	5	4
Discount stores	7	9
Warehouse clubs	3	6
Other	15	19

The rise of chain outlets for books rather resembles the transformations that occurred earlier in other lines of retailing. The independent business enterprise requires entrepreneurial supervision and decisionmaking, which is costly human labor. The independent bookseller's selection of books and advice to customers, though cherished by the literati, is a costly use of resources that can be centralized and replicated in bookstore after bookstore. Centralizing entrepreneurial decisions that are largely standard among many business units economizes on this input. It may also confer other economies in the bulk purchase of inputs, efficient performance of specialized services, and the like. Chains such as Waldenbooks and B. Dalton first exploited the economies of chain operation, placing standardized stores in shopping malls, buying books through their central offices, and using computerization to identify early winners and losers among new books. They succeeded most in those parts of the United States where independent bookstores had been few.[33] Just when a debate surged over whether the chains offered less choice of books than had the displaced independent bookstores, the chains were transformed to embrace the superstore, stocking 100,000 titles or more whereas a good bookstore once offered perhaps 30,000.[34] As the superstore innovation diffused, bookstore space in the United States grew much faster than book sales. Superstores in a sense have realized the goal of publishers' free-returns policy beyond their wildest dreams. That is, the 70,000 titles added by the superstore inevitably are those in light demand, so the typical copy in retail inventory is less likely to find a buyer within a given period of time (even if total book sales do increase as a result of bountiful retail display). It is then more likely to be returned for credit, so the chains' return rates are higher than independent bookstores' (apart from their larger piles of ten-ton turkeys).[35] Symmetrically, if publishers cut back their outputs of new titles, given retail bookshelf space, the average title will dwell longer on the shelf, and the returns rate will tend to decrease.

Chains' and superstores' operating methods interact with publishers' ways of promoting books, and in particular with the blockbuster complex. On the one hand, the chains' computerized records and wide overview of the market have enabled them to supply valuable feedback to publishers, especially the smaller ones, before sunk commitments are made in the publishing process. The feedback may bear on jacket design, size of initial printing, or even the decision whether or not to publish a manuscript. Such information comes cheaper and quicker than did its antecedent in book travelers' intelligence, and the reorganized retailing sector decreases the publishers' subsequent regrets. The retailers have reason to provide this information, because better decisions by publishers should reduce the bookstores' own inventory mistakes and increase their profits.[36] On the other hand, the chains and superstores have abetted publishers' heavy direct promotion of potential blockbuster books, with their potential for both large profits and large losses. In order to pay, these strategies require ample stocks on booksellers' front tables at the time when promotion in the media reaches its peak. The fewer retail decisionmakers are involved the easier this coordination.[37] The bulging promotion budgets of publishers and the huge first printings (that invite the frequent development of turkeys, described in Chapter 8) are thus partly consequences of the reorganization of the retailing sector, including not only the chains and superstores but also the general discount chains and warehouse clubs.[38]

The widely lamented decline of independent bookstores has not been strictly a passive and ceaseless retreat. In many local markets a stable ecology prevails of different types of sellers that offer differentiated bundles of services and perhaps serve buyers with different tastes. Independent bookstores once differentiated themselves and obtained about one-fifth of their revenue from special orders, but this niche suffered heavily in the 1970s when the cost of book postage rose much more rapidly than did the prices of books.[39] More recently they have specialized in particular types of books or offered the sorts of readings and events that can be managed only through personal entrepreneurship.[40]

Litigation over Quantity Discounts

Another defensive strategy of the independent booksellers is to pursue a legal attack on the publishers' pricing practices under the Robinson-Patman Act of 1936, which was broadly intended to prevent manufacturers from selling their goods on terms that give some groups of retailers advantage over others. It specifically sought to restrict quantity discounts to the unit cost saving realized by the manufacturer in filling one large order rather than a batch of small ones. A large retailer was not to get a lower price just because of its bargaining power. The U.S. Federal Trade Commission began an investigation of book distribution in 1979 that it terminated in 1996, having negotiated but finally not approved a consent decree to limit the publishers' discounts to chain booksellers. The stumbling block for the FTC's prosecution was the statutory "meeting competition" defense, under which a manufacturer can justify a potentially discriminatory discount by having offered it in good faith in order to meet discounts of competing publishers. Also, the publishers apparently had already amended the questioned practices.[41] The American Booksellers Association, dominated by independent booksellers, had more success in the courts. The practices covered by their complaint overlapped the FTC's—in particular, different schedules of quantity discounts offered to different types of retailers. The other line of the complaint addressed subsidies to the chains' ads that featured the publisher's books; the conditions for the subsidies made them inaccessible to small, independent bookstores. The publishers, without admitting guilt, accepted consent decrees that stipulated the same quantity-discount schedules for all book retailers.[42]

Promotion, Distribution, and Concentration of Producers

Mergers that enlarge the biggest book publishers and record companies have been much in the news, and by merger or otherwise the largest firms have come to account for substantial shares of activity. In 1993 the largest four book publishers received 30 percent of total wholesale book-publishing revenues, and the six largest record companies distributed about 80 percent of all records.[43] While these are not the most concentrated of industries, their concentration is surprisingly high given that all physical production and distribution activities can be contracted out, so that the minimum viable firm is one person with an office and telephone. The scale advantages exploited by the largest firms are clearly those of promotion and distribution, just as in cinema films (Chapters 5, 10). The record industry is the more concentrated, and its largest firms are vertically integrated into wholesale distribution. Large and small firms play different roles in the recruitment of performers and promotion of their albums. The large companies' distinctive competence lies in promotion and record distribution on a large—increasingly, international—scale. The small or independent company performs the gatekeeping function of recruiting new artists and, particularly, identifies and promotes new styles of music and types of performers. The distinction closely parallels that between contemporary art galleries that focus on identifying and developing artists with promise and those devoted to promoting successful artists (Chapter 2). In art galleries the difference between "pickers" and "promoters" appears not so much in scale of operations as in extent and quality of auxiliary promotional services. For record labels the promotional services are subject to substantial economies of scale. These came mainly from the enormous sales of albums by the most popular groups, the associated costs of promoting their tours, and the sizes of the advances that competition among promoter companies elicits for top performers under multi-record contracts.[44]

Several sources of scale economies benefit the major labels, one of which is associated with forward integration into wholesale distribution that occurred in the 1970s. Without regard to economies of physical scale in record distribution, large record companies enjoy a seldom-noticed advantage in dealing with retail outlets. Retailers pay for records only in arrears some time (often 90 days) after receiving them—if then. The cost of legal action to collect these debts is not trivial. The retail outlet commonly has enough local monopoly to deter jettisoning it for a competing local outlet. To combat this chiseling, the record company with a large catalogue has an advantage over the small one, because its threatened embargo of future shipments can deprive the slow-paying retailer of sufficient product to stay in business.[45]

Before the 1970s, record retailers took two forms, stand-alone specialist shops holding extensive stocks and more casual outlets consisting only of racks of top-hit records placed in stores specialized in other merchandise. They depended on different supply channels: the specialists ordered records from wholesalers known as one-stops (because they carried full lines of record companies' products); the racks were served by rack jobbers who selected the titles, stocked the racks, and removed obsolete products. (Bookstores and paperback-book outlets followed the same pattern.) With the soaring popularity of rock music in the 1950s and 1960s, this arm's-length system of distribution grew increasingly unsatisfactory for the major labels, because it frustrated their massive promotions of new albums by major artists—promotions that required the nationwide coordination of record release, touring, and radio airplay. Without integration through the wholesale stage, the labels could not coordinate the levels of retail inventories of individual records with large-scale and time-sensitive promotional campaigns. The situation worsened in the 1960s as the racks increased their share of total retail record sales to around 50 percent; by the early 1970s their share reached 80 percent, as they took over the stocking of the discount stores that sprouted in the nation's shopping malls. Another shortfall of independent distribution stemmed from the high uncertainty about a record's market success. Large record companies, with substantial fixed capacities for obtaining master tapes and making and distributing records, tend to address this uncertainty by maintaining a throughput of releases large enough that their random successes and failures would leave the pipeline full. This practice also calls for close coordination of distribution channels to supply copies of any record that shows signs of popularity.[46] Forward vertical integration hence became the dominant pattern for the major labels in the 1970s. Its relation to successfully integrated promotion is seen in the decline of the rack jobbers and the recovery of record stores' share of retail sales to 69 percent in 1988.[47] This integration no doubt raised entry barriers for any label seeking to mimic the operations of the majors, and it encouraged the integrated firms to expand record production to fill their distribution pipelines. The independent labels did not evidently suffer, however. They had found the independent wholesalers no more satisfactory than did the majors, who agreed (apparently on competitive terms) to undertake distribution for them. (The majors also acquired many picker firms.) Entry probably grew easier for the small labels, whose talent-filtering function may actually augment profits for the promoter firms.[48]

Other scale-related activities favoring the large companies include the ability to finance and manage large-scale promotions for successful performers. At times, advantages have also flowed from integration into the physical production of records. Independent manufacturing firms exist, but distributor-controlled facilities give occasional advantages, such as in meeting market demand for wildly popular records and absorbing the uncertainty associated with new recording technologies.[49] Long ago the technology of recording was complex and costly enough to create barriers to entry; that situation eased after World War II with the arrival of high-quality, low-cost tape recording equipment, which (along with the long-playing record) promoted the entry of more than a thousand new record labels between 1948 and

1954.[50] Pop recording studios lately have become costly technological wonderlands, but they are no longer integrated with recording companies.

Distribution Transformed?

The current buzz over electronic distribution of books and records gives a somewhat antique flavor to the preceding treatment. The fundamental economic problems of conveying information to distributors and ultimate consumers and the structuring of contracts between producers and distributors do not go away, however, and any cogent predictions of the future surely rest on correctly understanding the past. A few suggestions illustrate the process.

First, the physical distribution of both books and records may be transformed with some form of point-of-sale conversion from electronic to physical form. This would not only diminish the cost of holding inventories, but also resolve the contractual problems that have repeatedly affected relations between producers and wholesalers. The different organizational requisites of efficient holding of inventories and efficient promotion of new creative goods might cease to conflict with each other.

Second, electronic commerce is in some ways efficient, in other ways inefficient at transferring information about the books and records available. On-line shopping reduces the buyer's time and travel cost, but arguably gives only a diluted impression of the good considered for purchase. For the indefinite future there seems room for both conventional and electronic retailing.

Third, the potential competitiveness of on-line retailers deserves some thought, especially by the enthusiastic buyers of shares in internet companies. Traditional retailing of books and records is a spatially dispersed activity, and the physical distance between stores itself provides some insulation between them as competitors. The services of internet retailers seem to lack barriers to entry by new firms that replicate incumbents' service programs, and among incumbents the next outlet is just a mouse-click away. Without spatial insulation on-line distributors will likely fall into close competition with each other, affecting both their own profits and their bargaining power with publishers and record labels.

10

Creative Products Go to Market: Films

The newly produced creative good begins a commercial lifespan. Its birth is announced with suitable fanfare to customers and intermediaries serving them. It attracts a stream of purchases that may be large or small, short- or long-lived. For motion pictures, compared to books and records, the process is highly time-sensitive. There is some minimum scale for efficiently promoting and exhibiting a new film, hence a limit on the number that can profitably jostle in the marketplace at one time. The distributor's tactics and the cash flow they generate depend on short-run competition from other freshly released films. Also, they rely on price discrimination over time—showing the film first at a high price to those eager to see it, then at successively lower prices to less eager consumers (or homebodies) on videocassette, pay television, and free network and cable television. The film distributors make complex deals with exhibitors that raise the question whether film distribution and exhibition should be vertically integrated, as at times and in degrees it has been.

Film Distribution and Deals with Exhibitors

The cinema film distributor faces a complicated problem of both dealing with many exhibitors and promoting the movie to customers who might wish to see it. The two tasks are interdependent. The density and duration of theatrical showings influences the number of people who will see it—both now and in its future appearances on other exhibition channels. The decision on how (and how heavily) to promote the film influences the number of theatres in which it is optimally shown. We start with the exhibition contract typically used by the distributor and the individual exhibitor, then deal with these complications.

161

Exhibition Contracts

The long-standing form of the exhibition contract establishes a series of claims on the exhibitor's box-office revenue. The exhibitor's full cost, apparently including a normal profit, stakes the first claim. As usual with contracts in creative activities, the party about to sink resources into a project has either the first right to terminate the venture or the first claim on the revenue that it generates.[1] The exhibitor's cost, the "house nut," is prenegotiated with each distributor. Weekly box-office revenue remaining after the house nut is shared, with as much as 90 percent going to the distributor and 10 percent to the exhibitor at the outset of a film's showing (although an initial split of 70/30 is more common). As the run continues, the percentage shifts in favor of the exhibitor. While the total excess revenue over the house nut is likely declining, the exhibitor's increasing percentage recognizes both the exhibitor's incentive to promote attendance (after the distributor's initial burst of advertising) and the exhibitor's opportunity cost—showing other films that might do heavy business initially. The run automatically continues from week to week if box-office revenue warrants.

Another condition establishes a minimum share of *total* box-office revenue (before the house nut is subtracted) designated for the distributor, starting with 70 percent and falling to 40 percent as the film's run proceeds. This provision loads some of the down-side risk of a turkey on the exhibitor. Exhibitors may commit to making other risk-exposed payments, such as advances and guarantees of gross rentals, in order to obtain exhibition rights for prospective blockbuster films. Because distributors and exhibitors deal with each other in an oft-repeated game, they also rely on routinized forms of equitable relief (discussed subsequently).[2] The forms of these agreements remain stable over time, but the quantitative terms are competitively determined.

The distributor makes several decisions that influence the exhibitor's profit but are not specified in the contract. These hence become a source of haggling and conflict. One is the size of the local market allotted to the exhibitor for showing a film, which can be regulated in two dimensions. In large metropolitan areas a popular film is likely to be shown in several theatres, which thus face some spatial competition from each other to attract customers. Each exhibitor naturally prefers a local monopoly. But the distributor's profit could well increase with the density of exhibitors, which lowers movie-goers' travel costs and makes cinema seats for the film available at the time when its publicity triggers their interest. This source of increased box-office revenue for the distributor trades off, as the number of theatres increases, against the more numerous house nuts to be covered. Even if the exhibitor faces no local competition from other exhibitors showing the newly released film, the distributor may license others to show it at a later time. This form of temporal price discrimination lost most of its importance as suburbanization and the auto killed off the neighborhood theatre, but it is still a salient contract term. One important question not resolved in the exhibition contract is how long the film will play. This decision falls to the exhibitor, but it affects the distributor's profits and so begets a large amount of haggling.[3]

The distributor is legally precluded from specifying the exhibitor's admission price. This raises a contracting problem, because the exhibitor might prefer a lower charge than the distributor. One reason would be spatial competition with other exhibitors showing the same film: left to compete on the ticket price, they might set a price too low to maximize the profit that the distributor can siphon through the revenues shared after the house nut. Another is the large contribution to the exhibitor's profit made by the theatre's refreshment stand. If there are many popcorn lovers only mildly interested in the film, and not too many movie buffs who detest popcorn, the exhibitor maximizes profits by "bundling" a low admissions charge with a high price for refreshments. The distributor, however, shares only in the box-office profits, not the popcorn profits, and so would prefer a higher ticket price.[4]

Bidding, Blind Selling, and Block Booking

Today's exhibition contracts reflect the changes in organization and practice since the *Paramount* decrees reorganized the film industry. That case arose largely from the complaints of independent exhibitors about contracting practices of the studio distributors. First-run films were routinely offered to exhibitors vertically integrated with the producing studio, or with another major studio, so independent theatres had no chance to bid for exhibiting them. Another objected practice was blind selling. The studios have an incentive to minimize the time between the completion of a film and its theatrical exhibition. To cut the lead time needed to arrange exhibition, theatres were pressed to commit to exhibiting a film before it was completed and available for viewing. Second-run or neighborhood theatres were offered major studios' films only in blocks, from which they could not (to the extent they desired) pick and choose. The decrees in the end did not require competitive bidding by the exhibitors, although a distributor would have courted further legal trouble by resisting it flatly. Block booking and blind selling, however, were ruled out.[5]

Economic analysis subsequently raised questions about the prudence of these rulings on block booking and blind selling. Block selling, it is argued, can be efficient when the seller's output unavoidably emerges as an assortment of articles of varying quality.[6] The buyer who has agreed to pay an average price p for an assortment of n films would welcome the opportunity to open the package, keep those worth p or more, and decline the rest. If the average price represents equilibrium terms of trade between competitive sellers and buyers, however, that deal will be unprofitable for the sellers, because they incur (we suppose) the same cost to produce the randomly weak items as the good ones. Unbundling the block must therefore lead to higher individual prices for the good units, lower prices for the weak ones, but (in general) yield the same revenue pn to the seller for the same assortment of n items. If the haggling over each item incurs higher transaction costs than does a deal on the block, it is a pure waste that is avoidable if seller and buyer agree on block trading. This argument is right as far as it goes, but it does not necessarily settle the issue in the context of the studio-era film industry. The neighborhood cinema could then choose among the annual blocks offered by the various studios. It was allowed to reject 10 to 20 percent of the bundle, but that gave the exhibitor only enough wiggle room to decline films of no appeal to his local audience. Transaction costs might have been avoided by taking one studio's output as a block. The chance to pick continuously among all studios' films, however—notably including independents who would thereby have gained market access—might have more than compensated the increased transaction costs.[7]

Blind selling raises the issue that *time flies,* coupled with the unknown commercial appeal of a film until it is shown to paying audiences. If a film is marketed to exhibitors only after its completion, time passes, extra interest costs accrue, and it may prove cheaper to live with the uncertainty of blind selling. How this uncertainty is shared between those making the film (lenders, creative inputs) and potential exhibitors depends partly on their relative risk aversion. Risk-averse exhibitors might nonetheless have reason to countenance blind precommitments, because they need something to show in their theatres. Given that they compete with each other to exhibit the available stream of new films, a decision to avoid blind sales incurs the risk of having to settle for old kung fu pictures. Blind selling remains a live issue.[8] Following the *Paramount* directive, distributors offered advance trade showings, but these apparently have not played an important role in the marketing of films. That blind selling may be a jointly preferred contract is illustrated by the TV networks' dealings with the film distributors. In 1978 the networks found themselves facing fast-rising rental prices for showing completed cinema films on TV, and they shifted to blind purchasing in order to obtain rights when a film was still at an early stage of production. Apparently this absorption of risk succeeded in much reducing the price that TV networks paid to license films for TV showings—until the distributors retrieved the escaped rents by "escalator clauses" tying the film's rental fee to gross rentals that it earned in theatrical exhibition.[9]

Promotion of Films and Ongoing Distributor-Exhibitor Dealings

Is there an organizational alternative that might improve the exhibition contract? The industry's history suggests a possible answer: the vertical integration of distribution and exhibition, terminated in the *Paramount* decrees. Vertical integration indeed increased again in the 1980s, as those decrees lost their force (for reasons explained subsequently). The post-*Paramount* regime—one-shot exhibition contracts for individual films between parties who nonetheless interact repeatedly—must be placed in context of the distributor's general problem: how to promote a film for maximum value of its gross rentals net of promotion costs.

Distributors' Options for Promotion and Exhibition

As cinema films became vertically differentiated from TV fare, the distributors' methods of promoting them changed considerably. The studio's problem is to convey to potential viewers credible information on the type and character of the film and the quality level they may expect of it. As with all creative products, the seller both lacks good ways to convey this information and enjoys a considerable opportunity to "puff" the film's quality. Previews of coming films ("trailers") shown in theatres contain explicit if selective information, as do the similar ads shown on television. Print ads can give only a general impression of the film, apart from hard information on the creative inputs and soft information on reviewers' assessments. Reviews by critics serve as independent (and hence more credible) information sources for prospective viewers, but not all movie-goers bother to read them. Distributors' long-standing reliance on trailers, newspaper ads, and local TV gave way in the 1970s to heavy use of national network TV for major films. TV advertising proved costly but cost-effective for films with large potential audiences. The short-run competition among films currently opening prompted the use of short, intensive bursts of TV advertising, with the advertising augmented by competition to reach potential movie-goers through the congestion.[10] To reap the benefits from nationwide TV promotion, however, the film had to open simultaneously in a large number of theatres. The national-saturation release grew to 2,000 screens in the 1980s. National TV advertising campaigns cost $10 to $15 million, and this method also entails a heavy cost of prints of the film (2,000 at about $1,200 each adds another $2.4 million). Studios thus fell into profit-destroying promotion races with each other when rival major films were released, with escalating wars of national-TV advertising proving especially costly.[11] Furthermore, national-saturation release complicated the contract between distributor and exhibitors. That is because increasing the density of exhibitors required shrinking the geographic span of each theatre's market, previously set by negotiation between exhibitors and distributor. The exhibitors of course drew benefit from the more effective technology of promotion, but the negotiation costs of this adjustment were substantial.[12]

Quite different strategies of promotion and releasing are used for other sorts of films, especially those appealing to specialized and/or more sophisticated audiences and those lacking the high-concept elements congenial to promotion on TV. Distributors then rely on certifiers—favorable reviews and word-of-mouth evaluations. This approach has the advantage of requiring no coordinated and costly national release. The film can be opened in New York (in hope of favorable reviews), and then released gradually in other cities, as support from reviews and word-of-mouth warrants. This low-profile strategy sometimes serves films that become highly profitable, but whose attraction to large audiences can be stirred only by the goodwill of certifiers.[13] It has been somewhat eclipsed, however, by the sheer effectiveness of nationwide TV advertising, and in general the generation of buzz in nationwide video and print media.[14] A strategy of large-scale national release may be chosen by the distributor fearful that a ten-ton turkey is on its hands. The film may "die" after the first weekend, but the box-office revenue from its early viewer-victims plus revenues from abroad and from subsequent exhibition channels may yield at least a positive return on the investment in sales promotion. In 1998, upon realizing the true dreadfulness of its film *Godzilla*, Sony Pictures increased its advertising budget to $50 million and opened the film on a record 7,363 screens. The monster soon died, but Sony will probably not lose money.[15]

A film's content, style, and stars determine the studio's most profitable path for promoting and advertising it. Confirming this, statistical researchers have predicted quite accurately the advertising outlays that distributors select for their various films. Advertising outlays increase with the film's cost of production, the prevalence of stars, and the awards it has won; they also are larger for comedies and action films, in which content is easier to communicate through print ads and short clips on TV.[16] Promotion is also linked to how movie-goers respond to the cascade of information (ads, reviews, word-of-mouth) that assaults them as a new film opens. The initial audience size should depend on the distributor's choice of sales promotion and number of screens for exhibition. Whether the film continues to do brisk business after it opens will depend more on the independent verdict of reviews and word-of-mouth. As Arthur De Vany and David Walls showed, this dependence of movie-goers' choices on previous movie-goers' reactions implies specific statistical properties of the distribution of ticket sales among the films playing at any one time.[17] The distribution is one that would arise if the probability that a customer selects any given film is proportional to the number who have previously chosen to see it. On the day a film opens, however, all possible sequences of attendance patterns are equally likely. A film opened on many screens may either play off quickly or attract blockbuster business. De Vany and Walls found that the distribution of cumulative box-office revenues earned by various films is consistent with this process and inconsistent with other statistical processes by which audiences might distribute themselves among films currently playing. The finding is consistent with the *nobody knows* property: the distributor's release pattern determines the theatre-seat capacity available to patrons for a particular film, but the number of bottoms placed on those seats is determined independently. Word-of-mouth seems to determine a film's audience share after its opening, but the process is consistent with later viewers responding to ads that transmit information about favorable reviews and previous film-goers' positive reactions.

Governance of Distributor-Exhibitor Relationships

The *Paramount*-era issues regarding contracts between distributors and exhibitors live on in the context of these present-day approaches to distributing films. Blind bidding continues to lead a controversial life. Because a film's plot, major stars, and director are useful predictors of a film's box-office revenue (if not its profits), exhibitors competing with one another will guarantee substantial gross rentals for major films. In the early 1970s, Paramount in particular discovered that it could raise one-third and possibly two-thirds of a film's cost in advances and guarantees by exhibitors. The exhibition chains were less successful in economic collusion to resist guarantees than in political collusion to obtain passage of state laws that forbid blind bidding, and by the early 1980s these were in effect in a large minority of states. At least partly due to these laws, the exhibitor who has entered a blind bid commonly has the right to terminate the license agreement before the scheduled opening, after seeing the film.[18] Also, especially when exhibitors have offered guarantees, their deals for the occasional ten-ton turkey appear so inequitable ex post that it is now common practice to take a "look" at such deals and make an ex post adjustment. This might involve the distributor agreeing on a week-to-week basis to give back 10 to 30 percent of the payment contractually due under the exhibition contract.[19] The practice reflects the balancing of equities over time that commonly occurs between partners in repeated transactions—a practice reinforced by the distributor's interest in keeping the exhibitor in the game.[20]

If repeated interactions are smoothed by promises of equitable treatment, they are also policed by threats of termination and the costs of recontracting that follow it. Cinema operators, like other retailers of creative goods, are habitually and strategically slow payers. Exhibitors' guarantees, payable before the film's run begins, may offer advantages in timely collection that exceed their value as sources of working capital for the major distributors. The threat to deny films to slow-paying exhibitors gives the major distributor, with a continuous flow of films to offer, a substantial advantage over the small, independent distributor who deals with a given exhibitor only occasionally.[21]

An important role of repeated dealings in governing distributor-exhibitor relations is to promote negotiation relative to competitive bidding. The *Paramount* decision, which regarded film-by-film competitive bidding as the ideal arrangement, evidently did not reckon with the governance advantages of repeated negotiations. Bidding plays a minor role and offers a backstop to faltering negotiations, as when nearby theatres vie for the same film. When a distributor plans broad release for a film, screenings for exhibitors are followed by bid solicitations (with suggested terms), but the actual deals are still reached by some combination of bidding and negotiation.[22]

While the repeated dealings between the major distributors and local exhibitors help to smooth their interaction, the efficiency of this arm's-length interaction is clearly limited. The distributor does not costlessly observe how much revenue the exhibitor takes in at the box office. Independent checkers are employed to monitor the various ways in which ticket revenues might be skimmed by exhibitors. The promotional outlays on a film in theatrical exhibition and its word-of-mouth reputation increase the demand for it in other exhibition channels—cinema exhibition outside the United States, videocassettes, and various types of TV showings (broadcast network, local, and cable TV). Exhibitors' efforts to promote a film affect the value of this goodwill asset, but they do not share directly in the revenues. Although the distributor has many contractual instruments to align exhibitors' policies to the distributor's profit interest, including cooperative advertising, some slippage no doubt remains. Furthermore, these other channels have grown rapidly in importance as sources of the distributor's gross revenues. In 1983 distributors obtained 39.2 percent of revenues from theatre gross rentals, 13.4 percent from videocassettes, and 47.4 percent from television. By 1993 these figures had become 18.6, 47.7, and 33.7 percent, respectively.[23] The importance of revenues on which distributors and theatre operators have different interests has thus greatly increased. The distributors employ a sophisticated form of price discrimination, with the film shown at steadily decreasing margins of price over cost as it proceeds from one window to the next.[24] Distributors search constantly for ways to refine their price discrimination, recently by offering major video rental chains a discount on prices of videocassettes of popular films in exchange for a share of their income from renting them to viewers.[25]

The newly important channels for the exhibition of cinema films lack the elements of time sensitivity, spillovers, and the like that complicate dealings between distributors and exhibitors. Initially films were licensed to independent operators for videocassette distribution. By 1986, however, the leading studios had taken over the distribution of videocassettes made from their cinema films, and they received 91 percent of the aggregate revenue from cassette distribution. This integration gave them several advantages. For example, it allowed the temporal coordination of a film's distribution through this channel with its distribution and promotion through other channels. Cassette distribution, like cinema film distribution, requires a network of facilities that represent a significant fixed cost, but it also carries the competitive advantage of entrenchment. Finally, videocassette revenues have been integrated into filmmaking contracts in a way that makes them highly profitable for the distributors. In contracting with a film's producer, the studio distributor appropriately takes credit for stirring the public's interest in the cassette through its efforts to promote cinema distribution of the film. On this ground, only 20 percent of the distributor's gross revenues from cassettes are ordinarily counted as part of the film's gross rentals (for purposes of defining net profit). The distributor's cost of the videocassette comes out of the remaining 80 percent, but manufacturing costs are very low, only about 10 percent of the average wholesale selling price.[26] At least in the 1980s, as inventories of videocassettes were first being built up, they supplied a proportionally large stimulus and revenue source for small-scale independent filmmakers. Their cassettes in video stores were side-by-side close substitutes for the studios' major films, whose advantages from heavy sales promotion and access to cinemas were now muted.[27] In the long run, however, the demand for videos is driven by that promotion and the audience that it attracts.

Arm's-Length Deals and Vertical Integration

When contracts between independent firms suffer the problems that afflict distributors and exhibitors, vertical integration poses an alternative for the parties. Costs of pre-contract negotiation and post-contract haggling and monitoring do not vanish when independent businesses unite under a common management, but they may be beneficially transformed into problems of incentive structures and governance within the integrated firm. Such integration is not an option for the artist and the art dealer (Chapter 2) and hardly an attractive one for author and book publisher (Chapter 3). But it prevailed in the heyday of the Hollywood studios until underlying structural changes prompted a complete transformation to a system of one-shot contracts (Chapter 5). Whether film distribution and exhibition work better integrated or independent seems to be a close question. The post-*Paramount* system of arm's-length dealings seems effective, although it owes much to repeated interactions, not the series of auctions contemplated in the antitrust case. In the 1980s the legal constraints on vertical integration derived from *Paramount* were losing effect (literally expiring, or moot due to turnover among the distributors).[28] Parties were again free to choose between arm's-length dealings and vertical integration.[29]

After the *Paramount* decrees, the exhibition chains newly detached from the studios faded rapidly from the scene, because their assets consisted mainly of the old downtown movie palaces that were falling before the advance of TV and the suburbanization of cities. Other chains, however, rose to take their place. Concentration (the share of screens controlled by the largest firms) increased rapidly from mergers during the mid-1980s. The share of the largest four exhibitors rose from about 18 percent in 1983 to 30 percent in 1988, although the increase then greatly abated. Between 1986 and 1988 transactions took place that united five studio distributors with exhibition chains (one transaction involved only a large minority stake, and another was soon reversed). These transactions raised the questions whether the pre-*Paramount* integration was being restored and, if so, what reasons lay behind it. A decade later, it does not appear that distributors and exhibitors have found significant benefits from vertical combinations, while the horizontal combinations of exhibitors have their own causes.

The horizontal integration of theatres (nowadays, multiplexes) reflects the familiar logic of economizing on the cost of managing simple businesses. One chain, Carmike, concentrates on running theatres in small cities, where it faces little or no competition, but also a small enough demand to be profitable only with a highly cost-efficient operation.[30] It and other chains tend to concentrate their operations in particular regions and/or metropolitan areas, also suggesting the role of managerial economies. If the horizontal integration of exhibitors had aimed successfully at monopoly (or monopsony power against the distributors), the number of screens operated by the leading chains should have dropped. In fact the number of screens in the United States increased by 11 percent in the five years after 1988. The explanation is clear: the bigger chains were building ever-larger 20- and 30-screen theatres. While they also closed or sold smaller units, they were setting themselves up to demand more films from the distributors. While part of the multiplex's efficiency lies in juggling blockbuster films among several screens, to adjust seating capacity to demand, the expanding numbers of screens implied an increased demand for films to exhibit, whether blockbusters or small films. Important for an exhibition chain's buying power is the fact that a film's exhibition rights are licensed theatre by theatre and market by market. This was mandated in the *Paramount* decrees, but also flows naturally from local variations in demand characteristics. The exhibition chains appear to decentralize day-to-day operations, including the licensing of films. While the only exhibitor in a small city does have market power against a distributor, it is unclear that an exhibition chain could exert bargaining power across its far-flung screens.[31] The terms of exhibition contracts seem to adjust over time to the balance of distributors' supply of films and exhibitors' screens on which to show them. Various industry observers note that the aggregate ratio of gross rentals to box office revenue shows this movement.[32] Similarly, independent films offer the megaplex an elastic supply of product to be drawn upon as the success of the current studio blockbusters waxes and wanes.[33]

Vertical integration has certainly been increasing between the sources of films and the channels through which they are distributed, but the major combinations with potentially significant consequences have involved not cinema exhibition but broadcast and cable TV. Aspects of those transactions are discussed in Chapter 20.

III

Demand for Creative Goods

Although this book addresses the organization of creative goods' production and distribution, characteristics of consumption play a vital role, just as supply and demand interact to determine a market's size. Consumption of creative goods, like all other goods, depends on "tastes," but for creative goods those tastes emerge from distinctive processes. People invest in developing and refining their tastes for creative goods. They consume them in social contexts, and the "buzz" that circulates among them is important for organizing production. Although *nobody knows* its fate when a new creative good appears, social contacts transmit consumers' appraisals at a very low perceived cost to them, giving "word of mouth" its importance for a creative good's ultimate success. Consumers with some taste for a given line of creative goods may vary greatly in their involvement and extent of their investments in knowledge and experience. The distribution of consumers between "buffs" and "casuals" strongly influences the organization of an art realm—the outcome of the gatekeeping process, and the skills and objectives pursued in the contractual organization of creative production. These traits of creative consumption are treated in Chapter 11.

With infinite variety at least potentially available, how is the consumer to choose? Consumers' investments in refining their tastes for creative goods are costly in time and money. Producers' promotional advice on their own creative goods is puffed. These factors make consumers receptive to recommendations by certifiers—critics and independent advisors of other sorts. These advisory services also have their opportunity cost, and Chapter 12 addresses the economics of certifiers' services—how they are organized and their costs covered. Consumers value these services for their presumed objectivity, which gives producers an incentive to corrupt the certifier. Moral opprobrium attaches to the bribed certifier, but it does not necessarily destroy the signal value of his critical services, and consumers rationally attach some credence to critical opinion even when they expect that the critic's self-interest will be served when they follow his recommendation. Best-seller lists provide a cheap basis for choice among creative goods; reliance on other people's choices can be rational, but previous buyers' choices provide at best a "noisy" signal of quality.

In creative industries, tastes play a role in innovation that seems different from the innovation process in humdrum industries. While making art is always a quest to define and solve new problems, the recognition of a major breakthrough comes in consumers' broad embrace of a novel style. With or without promotion by certifiers, many consumers' willingness to pay for a new style is an essential element of the innovation process. In Chapter 13 case studies of quite diverse sectors (including toys and games) indicate the roles of these interacting elements in the innovation process. The occurrence of innovation feeds back to affect the structure of producing and distributing firms in the creative industry. Promoter firms with entrenched distribution systems can often ride out storms of innovation, even if they play no leading role. Without such entrenchment, however, large and even dominant firms can quickly disappear.

11

Buffs, Buzz, and Educated Tastes

The proposition that it is fruitless to quarrel over tastes *(de gustibus non est disputandum)* is widely accepted and (given its Latin tag) has been long established. Economists have, however, accepted an even stronger proposition: that it is fruitless to try to explain tastes, to understand why people choose to consume what they do. With the sole if notable exception of Thorstein Veblen's work, the economic analysis of consumption has focused on deriving the decision rules that utility-maximizing persons should follow in determining what to consume. Only recently have economists addressed patterns of consumption that seem to defy economic rationality, concluding that they conform to the economic calculus after all. Some of those off-the-street patterns are important for creative industries. Creative goods are consumed in a social context, not by isolated hermits. The pleasure people get from a night on the town depends on the presence of other people at the event itself and the shared residue of memories of the experience. Art collecting never completely escapes the motive of interior decorating, whereby the collector's values and interests are declared to her associates. A book is read in solitude but discussed at the dinner table. Sociologists have given these questions more attention than economists, so this chapter tries to conjoin what the two fields have to say about creative consumption.

Creative Consumption as Rational Addiction

One key feature of creative consumption is the effect of experience and training on one's benefit from consuming creative goods. This effect has been called "rational addiction." We are put off from consuming addictive substances because we know they will impair our future quality of life. On the other hand, we indulge consumption of a creative good, expecting it will raise our capacity to enjoy consuming that good in the future.[1] Our decisions also depend on the fact that consuming creative goods (indeed, just about any good) takes time. What we spend on consumption is limited by our available time as well as pecuniary income. The analysis runs as follows.

Each month we get utility from the amount of (say) music "appreciated"—consumed, and possibly also produced. We also get utility from all the other goods and services consumed that month. The amount of music appreciation increases with the hours of the month devoted to it. The amount also increases with the knowledge of and experience with music (human capital conducive to music appreciation, one form of "cultural consumption capital") that we have built up in the past. Specifically, the stock of music-appreciation capital that we have built up increases the productivity of the time we currently spend on appreciating music—the thrills per hours that we get from it. The stock of music-appreciation capital itself depends on the number of hours devoted to music appreciation in the past. It also depends on the investment we have made in general education (high school and college), which has bundled into it bits of learning and experience that raise our capacity to appreciate music: the required music appreciation course, or simply exposure to people who know and like music. In addition, general education implants the idea of a system of knowledge and prepares us to make comparisons and understand relationships. These "meta" skills raise the efficiency with which we absorb any new body of information, whether a creative realm or some other.

Early piano lessons count: even if a doting parent's hopes for the next Horowitz were frustrated, a reservoir of capacity to appreciate music remains. Family background also matters more broadly for the consumption experiences that are effectively chosen for the young as a spillover of the cultural consumption of older family members. Clearly, initial investments in cultural consumption capital involve a large accidental element. Arts administrators thus recognize the value of subsidizing early exposure in order to start the accumulation of cultural consumption capital. Individual creative producers or organizations, however, can seldom capture the future demands that they have launched, so a free-rider problem exists.[2] This market failure underlines the importance of including cultural exposure in general education.

All of this influences our decision as to how many hours this month to devote to music appreciation. It depends on the cost of music appreciation as well as our income and the prices of other goods. That cost embraces a number of specific prices: concert tickets, compact discs, and the like. The composite cost decreases with the productivity of our time spent on music appreciation: the more experience we have built up, the more thrills per hour we get, and the more hours (other things equal) we devote to music. But we also look into the future when we allocate hours to music appreciation, knowing that this month's experience will buy us still more thrills per hours in the future. So why do young people spend a lot of time listening to music, and is it predicted by this analysis? The answer is not simple, as effects cut against one another. The young tend to earn low wages per hour that they work, because they do not yet have much income-producing education or experience. Because they forgo little purchasing power by not working, they devote more time to music appreciation. One's first experiences contribute a lot to future music-appreciation capital, while that capital stock (and its future benefits) grows less rapidly as additional hours are allotted to music. But heavy listening time logged in youth pays off later in life, when it delivers more thrills per hour and hence encourages more hours spent listening. That is why people might devote more time to music as they age—especially when the opportunity cost of time diminishes in their later years.[3]

This model of cultural consumption capital speaks to a lively issue in the performing arts. Dozens of surveys of performing-arts audiences have found that a person's interest and attendance increase with her income and amount of education: patrons of performing arts are affluent, mature, and well-educated. This unsurprising fact deeply discomforts many enthusiasts. Why do not more people thrill to such cultural offerings? Are these entertainments a playpen for the wealthy, organized and presented so as to keep the underprivileged and impecunious at bay? Could the explanation lie not so much in the discretionary consumption permitted by high incomes, or in the barriers of social class, but in education? People's incomes and educational attainments are positively correlated, of course, which complicates disentangling their influences on attendance at performing arts. Still, the evidence convinces that the effect of education on attendance at performing arts is substantially stronger than the effect of income. Members of the professional classes are the big attenders, with managers (well paid but generally less educated) less numerous. Furthermore, the pattern is not confined to the "high" performing arts—it holds for jazz and folk music and cinema as well.[4] Among the professions, teachers and students prove the leading attenders at cultural events. Four times as many teachers appear in the arts audience as in the general population, three times as many students. The student audience is dominated by those studying this particular creative activity—the serious investors in cultural consumption capital.[5] Surveys in other countries including Australia and Japan closely match the U.S. patterns.[6]

These patterns agree nicely with the "rational addiction" model. Professionals on average probably have more education relative to their cash incomes than do managers and other highly paid groups. The higher one's wage, the more pecuniary income is lost by each hour devoted to arts consumption (and investment in cultural consumption capital). Hence the professionals have two things going for them as arts consumers: a lot of general educational capital, and wages that indulge the odd hour for cultural consumption. And teachers have more educational capital relative to their wages than do other professionals.

Creative Consumption in Its Social Context

The fact that consumption takes place in a social context need not make a big economic difference. Individuals (or households) still reckon about what to buy and how much to spend on various creative goods. What they buy, however, and how they respond to novel opportunities depend on the choices that they observe others making. Bandwagon effects and snob effects are familiar examples.[7] The phenomenon of herd behavior especially pertains to creative goods.[8]

Herd Behavior and Information

Herd behavior might arise from people's ignorance, or cost of informing themselves, about their benefit from some consumption choice. Suppose some novel consumption item costs 50 cents, yet it might turn out to be worth either one dollar or nothing. The consumer cannot ascertain the actual value without making the purchase. From some unspecified source of information, such as examining the article in the store, each of us gets a hunch whether it is valuable or worthless. Every consumer's hunch has better than a 50–50 chance of being correct, but it is no sure thing.

Better than deciding on just her own hunch, the consumer looks to see what everybody else is doing. Specifically, suppose that consumers take turns one by one deciding whether to make the purchase. When her turn comes, each knows what choice her predecessors made (although not what hunches they received, nor whether they are happy ex post with their choices). The first consumer Mary has only her own hunch to go on. If that hunch is good (G), she buys; if bad (B), she passes. If Mary buys, the second consumer Joe infers Mary's G hunch from her decision. If Joe's hunch is also G, he also buys. If Joe's hunch is bad (B), however, the two hunches cancel, and Joe has to flip a coin. If Mary had passed up the purchase, Joe would have used that information in the same way: pass if he gets a B hunch, flip a coin if his hunch is G. The third consumer Ann now is faced with one of three situations. If both Mary and Joe bought, Ann also buys even if her signal is B, because two G's outweigh one B. Likewise, if neither Mary nor Joe bought, Ann passes even if her signal was G. If Mary bought and Joe passed (or vice versa), they cancel out for Ann, who decides on the basis of her own hunch.

The disturbing feature of this process is that the record of observed buy/pass decisions does not accurately cumulate the consumers' hunches. When Joe and Mary both decide to buy, they might have had either two G signals or one G and one B. When Ann buys, following Mary and Joe, they might have had only one G hunch out of three (and the coin tosses drive the selections). Furthermore, successive choosers cannot improve the accuracy of the process by (in effect) pooling data on more and more hunches. The product might indeed be worthless, and consistent with the overall distribution of hunches (fewer G's than B's), yet a wrong-way information cascade could sustain "buy" sequences of decisions. If the individuals could share their hunches and go with the majority's call, they would be better off. Yet a herd outcome results from each consumer's rational decision using all the information at hand (though not the unobservable hunches). This model does not preclude consumers being slavish imitators, but they might appear to be conformists even when they are behaving rationally but are poorly informed.

Herd behavior as a response to consumers' information problems certainly applies to the creative industries. With only a few exceptions (such as the recording heard on the radio), creative industries' products are "experience goods." The buyer cannot accurately assess the qualities of the individual creative good before committing to consume it—read the book, see the play, hear the opera recording. Even products of the visual arts—paintings, sculpture—that are open to casual inspection may yield up their aesthetic quality only when the collector has "lived with them." Other sources of information can be drawn upon pre-purchase. Sellers supply information through advertising—the movie trailer and TV ad, the print ad for a book or recording, the magazine trial subscription. The advertised information helps to align creative goods with the tastes of prospective consumers, but the amount of hard information conveyed is quite limited—usually to the good's general style and content and its key creative participants. Indeed, a sufficient reason for the public's interest in entertainment stars is what the star's persona and performing skills foretell about the next creative product.

Consumers of creative goods rely in varying degrees on critics and certifiers, who hold themselves out as independent and experienced assessors of creative goods. Critics' assessments (see Chapter 12) have the presumed advantage of neutrality and objectivity. The objective critic can help to solve the consumer's information problem in two ways. He can provide a description of the good that would not be credible coming from the good's maker—due to the latter's incentive to "puff" the product. Book reviewers describe and contextualize at length, while the publisher, with no less information about the product and more incentive to broadcast it, settles for a brief jacket blurb. Another strategy for the critic short-circuits most of this transfer of information, and simply internalizes prospective consumers' tastes and attempts to prejudge the creative good's appeal. Critics can fall short of solving the consumer's information problem in several ways. Their tastes may not reliably align to the consumer's. Their independence may be compromised. And the consumer may not vouchsafe the cost in time and money to access the critic's assessment.

These third-party sources of information on creative goods fit into the model of herd behavior. They supply people with hunches, yet without turning these into certainties. Where the herd model really stumbles is in assuming that consumers communicate with each other only through their choices (to buy or not to buy). Not only do people communicate their hunches, but word-of-mouth recommendation is routinely regarded as vitally important to the assessment (and hence commercial success) of creative products such as films (Chapter 10).[9] The reason lies outside the zone of behavior that economics usually covers.

Information in Social Discourse

The missing point is obvious once stated: people like to converse about creative goods.[10] We gain many tangible benefits from our casual communications with others. Individuals' social and economic positions and assets are exposed, enumerated, and evaluated—an exchange of information. The exchange may lead to friendship, itself a source of utility. It may lead to mutually beneficial swaps of innumerable sorts—narrowly economic deals, or broader social links of obligation and reciprocal favor.[11] The exchange may not always benefit all parties, as when social competition is involved, and the party who loses the competition for leadership perforce sinks into follower status. Even the loser in a social rank tournament benefits in a way. There is value in being led by a capable leader, and there are costs of competing for a position or rank that lies beyond one's reach.

If the give and take of social interchange has these valued outcomes, how do we implicitly prepare ourselves for the ritual dance of conversation that exposes these opportunities (or, sometimes, reveals their absence)? We often have no specific deal in mind when we first fall into conversation. Even when we do, the random display of each party's attitudes, interests, values, and skills fruitfully precedes the direct proposition, as connoisseurs of dating ploys are well aware. Here emerges the value of creative goods in interpersonal discourse. One's choice of books, movies, music, and TV shows telegraphs one's interests and attitudes efficiently. The cultural consumption capital that raises one's own benefits from creative goods also lubricates the wheels of conversation.[12] Nothing else that we bring to life's talk show likely yields such easy sharing and reciprocity. One may be able to discourse fluently and at length on the state of the weather, one's career as a dental hygienist, or one's collection of nineteenth-century British colonial postage stamps, but these knowledge stocks may hold little reciprocity value with the randomly drawn conversation partner. Even where a locus of shared interest appears, most vocational and avocational assets provide less efficient channels for transmitting general attitudes and values than do discussions of creative goods.[13]

In short, people value nonpurposive conversation. Creative goods and the cultural consumption capital that surrounds them provide what is likely the most suitable grist. This property has many implications for creative industries. First, word-of-mouth is a far more powerful transmitter of information on creative goods than on goods that lack their cachet as a social catalyst. If I acted on narrow economic self-interest, you could learn my hunch (or my ex post assessment) of a cultural good only upon paying me for my time to inform you. Instead, thanks to the value of conversation, you get my opinion free of charge and perhaps in excruciating detail. No wonder that a "buzz"— a critical mass of favorable, or at least involved, discussion—is treasured among those who promote the sale of creative goods. It is also a check on them, because it mobilizes many involved persons' judgments on the worth of creative works that are the subjects of serious promotional investments.[14] Second, herd behavior has a motive unrelated to eliciting information before a purchase. Reading the best-sellers and watching the most popular films equip one with a stock of conversational resources likely to prove valuable with a randomly drawn partner. This value is independent of the probability that a best-selling book will be an enjoyable read. Third, the superstar effect (Chapter 4) is intensified. Whether or not singing buffs will trade concerts by five ordinary tenors for one by Pavarotti, many people who do not much care about opera will turn out for Pavarotti, partly to enter the discourse on this surefire subject. Superstars' appeal transcends their natural branch of an art realm and attracts those who normally inhabit other branches. Consistent with this, observers of superstardom regularly associate it with ascription and renown, and impresarios from P. T. Barnum to Sol Hurok have sought out charisma rather than extraordinary talent per se (see the subsequent discussion of celebrity).[15] Fourth, the value of less popular (more specialized) creative goods will depend on how easily persons with shared interests make contact with one another. Pity the fan of Chinese opera who dwells in an isolated small town.

Sociologists' empirical evidence on the density of performing-arts organizations bears on the last prediction. It increases more than proportionally with city size. That fact may prove little about consumers' behavior, since the fixed costs of such organizations provide a sufficient explanation (Chapter 14). But they appear also to increase with the diversity of a city's population, indicating the number of subgroups sharing interests. The proportion of a city's workforce classified as artists increases with measures of social inequality.[16] Related sociological analysis that employs the concepts of social mobility and status translates easily enough into economic terms. A consumer of creative goods foresees personal benefit from associating with some group of persons—social prestige, economic deal-making possibilities, whatever. Members of the attractive group are known to share interests in some area of culture and associated creative goods. The astute social climber invests in building his stockpile of conversational knowledge about the area in question, for its value as a gambit in the game of personal interchange.[17]

Fashion: An Application

The social context of creative goods' consumption is nowhere more evident than in the domain of "fashion." Tellingly, we use the word both in the narrow sense of personal attire and more broadly for the style or selection of differentiated (and creative) goods consumed. Fashion suggests competitive emulation, a rank-order tournament in which the prize is social distinction. Rival consumers can pursue it with various resources: taste built upon cultural consumption capital, time spent deploying that capital to search the array of consumption possibilities, or money to recruit advisors or suppliers who can supplement one's own taste and time commitment.[18] Rank-order tournaments have the unattractive feature that, when somebody wins, the others by definition lose. Status competition, however, may overlie an information-sharing process that distributes its prizes more broadly than does a bingo game. In any line of creative goods with the *infinite variety* property, the mixture of varieties available and in use constantly changes, reflecting changes in the technology available for assembling them and the demands or needs that they serve. Put changes in technology aside, and focus on the demand side. Individuals choose among creative goods in a constantly shifting context of the activities that they undertake (both work and leisure) and the terms (prices, qualities) on which they consume all other goods and services—humdrum ones lacking important creative components. Still deeper tectonic changes occur in our values and attitudes[19]—changes that modify the signals about them that we send through our choices of creative goods to consume. The interpersonal interchange process seeks the best match between the available creative goods and people's perceived interests. The needs and desires registered for any one sort of creative good are pushed and hauled by these continual disturbances. The exchange of information and evaluations that shake out judgments on what is fashionable then reflect exactly the process already described, whereby sharing information is valued and rewarded in people's search for better matches of choices to needs or wants. The process distributes prizes to discoverers of the last word, but those prizes are implicitly warranted by the opportunities for better goods-to-wants matches opened up for everybody else.

The process is nicely documented for women's apparel from actions of the gatekeepers who serve the followers of fashion—stores' buyers purchasing women's clothing from designs offered by the major fashion houses. Herbert Blumer observed that the couture house's designers are in the same position as other artists offering creative goods to gatekeepers.[20] The designers know current and past styles, and they cast about among current developments in the fine arts, literature, and social happenings that can be translated into innovative design elements. Although they are competitive and secretive, their independent searches tend to deliver designs that depart in similar directions from the past. Each house offers many designs, knowing that perhaps only 30 percent of these will attract any purchases, and of those perhaps one-fourth will be heavily bought (nobody knows in advance which ones). The buyers for major retailers cannot and do not articulate their reasons for selecting a particular design ("It's stunning!"), yet like the designers they bring a sense of changes occurring in their customers' lifestyles and interests, and in their likely feeling of the relevance and appropriateness of various styling notes and elements. They choose individually, without close communication with each other, although in the context of continuously formed and reformed preferences and choices observed in the style market. Blumer, who called this process "collective selection," stressed that it is strongly driven by the buyers' expectations about retail customers' demands, and that design houses' occasional attempts to unite on some new "look" often fall flat. The process aligns well with the process of choice in a social context for the final buyers.

Fame and Fads: An Application

The collective element in consuming creative goods clarifies the role of fame in superstardom (Chapter 4). The benefit that consumers seemingly gain from the interchange of opinions and attitudes toward cultural goods certainly applies to the consumption of "celebrity." We each value knowing about persons whom we find worthy as moral exemplars; as embodiments of wisdom, virtue, or generosity that we would wish in ourselves; or as possessors of skills or endowments that we covet. The collective element of consumption implies something more—that contemplating such idols pleases us more when others share our admiration. The limiting case is exactly Daniel Boorstin's category of "famous for being famous."[21] The specific basis for distinction may become vanishingly small, if the mechanism for dispensing the aura of fame works well enough.[22]

Celebrity is a flow of adulation that seldom lasts long. That fact matters for the demand for creative goods, because it implies continual turnover in the composition of demand that we associate with fads. People—adults, anyhow—seldom read a book or view a movie twice. They may play a recording varying numbers of times, however, to diminishing pleasure from each repetition. A television series, or a succession of films by an actor, may also encounter diminishing returns, as the variants on the underlying persona or setting are exhausted. Diminishing returns also apply to interchanges with others about cultural goods. Interpersonal contacts enrich our experience with a creative novelty and help us assess its strong and weak points, how it relates to other cultural experiences, and the like, but they also wear out their welcome. Now consider how the density of these experiences might vary between, say, a popular song played continuously on Contemporary Hit Radio and a play seen by only a thousand people a day. Everybody whom we (randomly) encounter has heard the tune, and we can quickly exhaust the joys of discussing it. Only a few people whom we encounter can have seen the play. Discussion opportunities are limited and hence can stretch over an extended time before exhaustion sets in.

Creative goods differ greatly in the technology that determines their speeds of diffusion through the consuming public. That speed controls the maximum pace at which the novelty can be exhausted as a conversational gambit. Hence there is likely a negative correlation between the technical rate of diffusion for a creative good and the time for which it stays in consumers' active stocks. The bigger the fad, the faster the fall. The best evidence appears in the effect of new technologies such as radio, which greatly accelerated the diffusion of new songs and (on one estimate) cut the lifespan of a popular song from eighteen months to three.[23] Leo Braudy argued that renown and superstardom peak more intensely for those artists—actors, musicians—who can be directly observed in an idealized display of their skills. Literary and visual artists, who practice their craft in private, lack the technology to enthrall us so fully.[24] The fad process also depends on the storage technologies available for various creative goods. A great novel of the nineteenth century is physically as easily read as today's summer page-turner, whereas Caruso's primitive recordings compete with difficulty (Chapter 21).

Buffs and Casual Consumers

Almost everybody displays interest in the symbolic expressions conveyed by some creative goods and services, but consumers differ in both the types of expression that attract them and the intensity of their attraction. Some people's tastes run to country and western songs, others to "classical" music, and some to both types. Some consumers display intense involvement, devoting substantial parts of their income and leisure time to a creative activity and building up much cultural consumption capital; casual consumers purchase less and build little capital. The distribution of consumers' preferences for various types of creative goods governs the sizes of the various creative industries but has less to do with the contract structures and niches within them. The distribution of preference intensities matters more for those deal structures and niches and for the filtering of talent.

As Herbert Gans argued, every creative activity attracts audience members with diverse levels of involvement.[25] Most involved are the buffs who cultivate extensive knowledge of the activity and likely possess some training or serious experience in creative activity. Their viewpoint and interests lie close to those of the practicing creative artists, critics, and others professionally involved. They pay close attention to how the cultural product is assembled—the problem-solving effort that the artist exerts; the technique displayed in the execution of the performance; the relationship among form, content, and mood; and the creative product's overt content and covert symbolism. In Gans's words, they "place high value on the careful communication of mood and feeling, on introspection rather than action, and on subtlety, so that much of the culture's content can be perceived and understood on several levels."[26] Innovation and novelty are cherished, especially in form (the outcome of the creative problem-solving process), less in substance. Where both creators and performers are involved, the buff tends to be creator-oriented and less interested in adroit execution by the performer. Where the distinction is relevant, the buff reaches out for the abstract philosophical and social issues raised by the creative effort, leaving for the less involved audience the moral issues raised by the creative work's content.[27]

For no intrinsic reason, buffs tend to be few and pleased with their exclusivity. Compared to their intensive involvement, the larger and more general audience is less engaged—that is, less likely to have had formal training or exposure to the viewpoint of creative talent. Proficient execution attracts the general audience, but its members respond to the effect rather than the technical skill that produces it. Novelty is not always cherished and may be firmly resisted. An important qualification, though, is that the eternal cycle of youthful rebellion supports an interest in novelty and innovation that need not be closely connected to the display of technique or with originality of problem-solving as seen by creative artists themselves.

This skewed distribution of consumers' involvement has many implications for the organization of creative activities. It affects the demand for different types of creative goods or performances within an art realm, whenever buffs' tastes draw them to different goods, rather than just allowing them to see different values in a common set of goods. In country music, for example, a purist audience cherishes traditional songs and performance styles, while the mainstream performance style has gravitated toward the rock concert with its light shows and flashy effects. The "buffness" distribution of the audience will affect the mix of creative activities—the proportion of artists who can viably devote themselves to activities that are cutting-edge as seen by artists and buffs alike, and the degree to which superstars catering to the more general audience can flourish. Buffs may play important roles in bringing economic resources to the would-be cutting-edge performers—either donations from the buffs' own pockets or transfers of resources made by institutions in which the gatekeeping function has passed into the hands of the buffs.

Pop Culture and High Culture

Mention of the social context of the demand for creative goods or "culture" brings to mind the distinction between popular culture and high culture. A long tradition aligns creative activities with social classes and regards the consumption of the goods of high culture as either a defense of upper-class values against the upward mobility of lower-status persons, or a delicate ward to be guarded against the corrupting vigor of popular culture. Because of the social context of creative consumption, if the economist ever acknowledges social classes as economic actors, this should be the setting.[28] But do we need social classes to explain differences in the organization of the art realms of high and pop culture? No, argued sociologist Gans. The same nexus of creators and consumers populates each realm, and the differences between them are second-order.[29] The economic analysis of art realms supports the same conclusion. Artists differ in their training for various realms, but all share the same *art for art's sake* values and the same problem-solving algorithm for achieving innovation and progress. The pattern confutes Clement Greenberg's position that popular culture does not share the problem-solving algorithm of the artist's creativity, which equally characterizes all lines of creativity to some degree. The hypothesis suggests itself that highbrow and lowbrow creative activities differ not in the presence of buffs but in the proportion of the consumers whose involvement crosses the "buff" threshold.[30] Each art realm encounters high fixed costs of training, creation, and/or preparation, which generate organization problems addressed in Chapter 14.

Perhaps the fruitful way to approach the distinction between high and pop culture is to explain differences rather than detect similarities. Differences among art realms in buffness distributions are part of the story. Pierre Bourdieu tested the alignment of culture consumers' buffness with their education and cultural-capital investments. Low-investment types come to creative goods for immediate satisfaction. They judge a photograph, for example, by the attractiveness of its subject, not the formal effectiveness of the photographer's realization of it. The various art realms themselves differ in the degree to which they offer unmediated direct thrills relative to deeper formal content. The more popular arts are longer on unmediated thrills and attract audiences with relatively few buffs. High culture runs to distributions less skewed toward immediate thrills and casual consumers. But this vertical differentiation appears to some degree in every realm of art.[31]

Another difference between high and pop culture realms arises from differences in the size of the total audience (buffs and tyros together). Superficially, this difference fits the social-class formulation of high-culture's difference: opera-goers are elite and few. A purely economic interpretation of the effect of audience size, however, does not need the concept of social class. What matters instead is the fixed cost of preparing and presenting the product of a creative realm, relative to the size of its audience.

Most creative activities incur significant fixed costs: the negative cost of a cinema film or its TV counterpart, rehearsal and staging costs in the performing arts, the cost of preparing a book for printing and distribution (including the author's time in the throes of composition), or the cost of practice and training for the visual or performing artist before she is ready to face the public. The height of fixed costs per consumer, however, varies greatly. The film *Titanic* incurred a fixed cost of $200 million, but its audience turned out to be vast. The most opulent opera production costs only a tiny fraction of that, but its audience is smaller still, and a high cost per patron must somehow be covered. Blockbuster cinema films are a viable art only because they appeal to enormous audiences.

These considerations of audience buffness and cost structures shed light on two other aspects of high versus pop culture. Consumers' demand for elementary instruction in an art supplies resources to the art realm. Any creative skill sets its own training regimen to generate the talent supply that presses upon the gatekeepers. Many children (and nearly all adults) seeking arts instruction, however, are purchasing cultural consumption capital rather than career skills, and their willingness to pay creates a substantial demand for artists' services. The higher the ratio of amateur to "serious" students of a creative skill, the larger is the proportion of the artists' income provided by teaching.[32]

The economic view suggests that each art realm has its natural turf and scale of operation, a balance of demand and supply forces. How does this ecology relate to the long-running charge that pop culture somehow threatens and undermines high culture? The charge is valid at one level: resources used in any economic activity are unavailable for others. Culture critics see pop culture as borrowing from and debasing high culture. But all cultures borrow from one another as a basis for innovation. Such critics attack pop culture as a specific distraction, as "easy listening" that lures consumers from the deeper joys of high culture.[33] The practice that a consumer gains in building one type of cultural consumption capital, however, may well increase the productivity of time and resources (later) spent assembling another type.[34] Also, persons with higher incomes tend to consume more of several types of creative goods, rather than to substitute one for another on an *A list/B list* hierarchy.[35] Is the next Heifetz diverted away to the easy money of rock stardom? Any would-be artist, whether seeking pop or high-culture stardom, makes a heavy investment in training and preparation to gamble on a small chance of success, and many who prepare themselves eventually settle for a humdrum calling. The chance that the next Heifetz will be lost, trampled before the keeper of the gate to rock stardom, seems small indeed.[36]

12

Consumers, Critics, and Certifiers

The *nobody knows* property of creative goods applies to their consumers as well as their producers. The utility that these "experience goods" yield remains uncertain until they are actually bought and experienced. As with any line of goods and services, prospective consumers devote effort (time and money) to gathering any information that helps to improve their choices—raising the chance of spending the evening at a good rather than a bad movie. Information is usually available from several sources. Some emanate from the sellers of the creative goods themselves. The studio and the exhibitor put print and TV ads and trailers conveniently before us; they obviously know the products that they offer and have a motive to provide information relevant to our choice, but we also know that they have an incentive to "puff" (overclaim quality). Other sources of information lack this bias but may be more costly to seek out or (in the case of word-of-mouth) not necessarily expert or accurate.[1]

Important among these third-party sources are independent experts. The consumer can obviously benefit from expert advice on the qualities of various creative goods that she might consume and the match between their attributes and her own tastes. We therefore turn to the physician to suggest remedies for our ills and the interior decorator to suggest styles and objects to create the desired home environment. Compared to our other information sources, they may offer the advantages of both expert status (large stocks of knowledge capital) and absence of bias toward or against the wares of particular suppliers. The amount of authority that critics enjoy depends on how good are consumers' other sources of information. In major urban centers, theatre and dance critics wield nearly life-or-death powers over ticket demand because (word-of-mouth apart) the potential patron can access no other independent evidence before buying the ticket. A work of art, however, is a high-priced purchase that can be viewed at leisure in the gallery, or even behind one's couch, before buying. Theatre and dance critics accordingly exert more influence than art critics.[2]

The services of such certifiers are costly, as their knowledge and taste capital is a humdrum asset that must be compensated. Also, their neutrality is at hazard of corruption by producers. That is, producer and certifier can cut a mutually profitable secret deal whereby the certifier favors the producer's creative goods in advising the consumer, although not so blatantly that the consumer can infer the corruption. Neutrality and corruption, concepts thought to have black-and-white significance both morally and behaviorally, turn out to be not so simple to apply to certifiers in creative industries.

The Market for Critical Opinion

If consumers seek critical opinion in order to get better value from their outlays on creative goods, there is also competition to assume the critical mantle and supply it. Would-be critics face their own gatekeepers. Only wealthy art collectors are likely to employ advisors directly; other purchasers of critical advice have reservation prices too low to warrant much personalized service. Most critical writing and opinion therefore arrives bundled with other information in newspapers, periodicals, and broadcasts. Would-be critics compete for inclusion in these bundles—to be hired (and retained) by editors of periodicals, to get their writings published à la carte, or to win approval from the tenure committees of academe. They compete for credence of their opinions in a loosely defined marketplace. Here the gatekeepers are ultimately consumers receptive to critical opinions. Consumers make these decisions only indirectly, however, by subscribing (or not subscribing) to papers and magazines that include them in their bundles. Proximately the decisions about how much critical writing to bundle are made by editors and other packagers of content. Influence also comes from entrepreneurs and managers involved in assembling and distributing creative goods, and perhaps from artists whose opinions reach the editors and managers.[3]

Malcolm Bradbury traced this competition to criticize through nineteenth- and twentieth-century critical writings in English literature. In the nineteenth century it operated on a broad public frontier during the reign of high-minded but broadly circulated magazines such as *Edinburgh Review,* *Quarterly Review,* and *Blackwood's.* As these withered in the face of innovative mass-circulation magazines, the critical debate receded to the highbrow "little magazines," which themselves published much new writing as well as served an intensely involved but narrow opinion circuit. They were foraged by mass-circulation magazines for the occasional splash of broad interest, but otherwise had no widespread direct influence. The little magazines flourished in the 1910s and 1920s, but Bradbury saw their role as shrinking after World War II, leaving contemporary literature with no "deep" market of certifiers of literary merit.[4] Max Graf traced a similar trajectory of music criticism starting with German-language periodicals in the eighteenth century. The nineteenth century brought the triumph of the romantic artist and spawned the critic's function (his highest function, in Graf's view) of interpreting artistic genius for the public's benefit. Mass-circulation newspapers and periodicals, however, conferred their favor on particularly skilled writers capable of engaging mainstream readers while internalizing their standards and preferences.[5]

One hesitates to call this process an efficient competition that awards pride of place to the critic whose views give best value to ultimate consumers. The process does pull in that direction, although with heavy qualifications dragging behind. One qualification grows from the familiar notion of a "test of time." Critical opinion has a random component, both as expressed by the critic and as absorbed by the recipient. Accurate assessment of the worth of critical opinion hence depends on the precision gained from successive observations over time. Furthermore, critical opinion often entails forecasts: does the excellent work shown by an emerging artist foretell a lustrous career, or is a one-trick pony having a good day? Other qualifications arise from the gap in interests between ultimate consumers of critical opinion and the gatekeepers who proximately filter the critics. The newspaper editor's valuation depends on the group of readers to whom he seeks to appeal and his general strategy for assembling a bundle of information that will attract their readership. The academic tenure committee follows a self-referential standard of the appeal of the critic's writings to those who have previously leapt the hurdle of tenure. Only minimally do they serve as agents for potential consumers of creative goods.

The market for critical opinion has its own *A list/B list* property corresponding to the range of intensities of consumers' chosen levels of investment in cultural consumption capital. At a higher level critics seek to articulate a context in which each creative work is positioned and judge it on explicit criteria. Critics serving a less involved audience tend to internalize the consumers' own likely preferences and simply advise them on whether or not they will like the work in question.[6] The former communicates with consumers presumed ready to make significant investments in cultural capital, the latter with those who settle for a flow of experiences. Indeed, at the more sophisticated end of the spectrum, the critical evaluative function largely falls away. In the romantic tradition, art is whatever artists do, and the critic's obligation to the progress of art is to provide rationale and context and not to impose judgment, although some critics on this frontier choose to instruct artists on how their work should be evolving.[7] At the less sophisticated end of the spectrum, the gratification sought by the audience is indicated by the maker's promotional material (for example, blockbuster "action" films) and depends little on critical evaluation.[8] Nationwide TV advertising prior to the opening of such films in any case forestalls the critical function.[9]

Objectivity and Interest

Thanks to *infinite variety* and the profusion of creative talent entreating the gatekeeper, the issue of payola arises throughout the creative industries (Chapter 18). Costs have been sunk to prepare creative wares for the gatekeeper's gaze. Those whose art passes through will likely receive pecuniary rewards exceeding any additional costs that they will incur. The artist then has a good reason to offer bribes to the gatekeeper. While the gatekeeper has an incentive to choose on economic or aesthetic merit, the choice may be a close one, so the gatekeeper can get more from the bribe than is lost in his clients' goodwill. The issue arises constantly in creative industries, including the visual arts (to be addressed shortly), where, for example, the emerging artist might give one of her paintings to the critic who praises her work. How do such natural acts of gratitude fit in with the critic's modus operandi and the competition among critics in the market for critical reputations?

Consider the involved consumer—the art collector—who ponders whether to ignore the favorable opinion of critic X about artist Jones, upon discovering that X owns works by Jones. She could make the obvious inference that X will push Jones's work not for its merit, but to reap some capital gains when credulous readers take his opinion at face value and bid up Jones's prices. Two factors, however, might encourage a more tempered view. First, the fact that a critic buys the work of an artist he praises, or even receives it as a gift, does not necessarily undermine the collector's valuation of X's views on Jones's quality and prospects. That X chooses to hold some of his wealth in the form of Jones's art (rather than treasury bills or Smith's art) makes X's economic welfare in part a hostage to the probity of X's opinion. While X might indeed want to alter the collector's opinion for the betterment of his wealth, he faces a loss of wealth if the weight of opinion in the critical market writes off Jones as a dud. He also risks his reputation. In that same market for critical authority, X competes with rivals who may render more telling and perceptive judgments if they eschew slanting their views to serve personal interests. Recognizing this, the collector might conceivably take X's holdings as a positive signal about the worth of his favorable opinion of Jones.

Suppose we take the conventional view and call any intrusion of critical self-interest "cheating" on the audience. How much role self-interest plays—alternatively, how viable is the critic as an independent certifier—varies with basic features of the art realm. Consider this hypothetical setting. Although consumers are in the market for a long time, critics' careers are short. Market valuations of artists are volatile, so that a favorable assessment by the market-place produces a quick run-up in the value of the artist's works. Consumers know that critics are open to bribery, but cannot observe who has been bribed, or by which artist. A critic simply offers an opinion on the quality of art and artists without advancing any rationales for his judgment. This is the worst case, in which critics have a strong incentive to take bribes, consumers know that critics are bribe-prone, and hence discount their opinions. No-body values critical opinions, periodical editors therefore eject critical writ-ings from their information bundles, and the critical function atrophies.

Changing any of these conditions opens up room for rational consumers to give credence to critical opinion. If critics' careers are long, they gain access to reputation assets that serve as hostages by suffering costly damage when self-dealing is revealed. If critics provide rationales for their opinions, con-sumers can assess their cogency on the basis of logical coherence and their own experience. If the market is "deep" and prices (reflecting consumers' val-uations) are not much disturbed by critical raves (or pans) and other distur-bances, bribery loses its appeal for the artist (or her dealer). If critics disclose their bribes, consumers can take them into account.[10]

Critics and Dealings in the Art Market

Although the economic significance of critics in the visual arts probably lies near the lower end for creative industries, their well-documented history makes their role particularly clear. In the French art market, Harrison and Cynthia White traced critics' increasingly important role over the nineteenth century. Initially art criticism was a nonspecialized profession with, indeed, little scope left for the interpretive function by the rules of the academy sys-tem, other than to instruct the public's taste in subject matter. Impressionism opened up a new role of mediating communication between the artist and the public, and critics were important for introducing the Impressionists to one another as well as to the art world generally. Style and painting method were open to innovation, and the critic could instruct on how to look at a painting, not just how to interpret its subject matter. This expanded role for critical services coincided in the 1870s with the rise of many small journals, in which favorable mentions of Impressionism were far more common than in general newspapers. Along with group shows, critical support was important for the diffusion of Impressionism despite the vigorous if incomplete resis-tance of the official salons.[11]

This joining of artistic innovation and critical support is a general pattern.

When contemporary work in the visual arts runs on an even keel, with no major innovations, the critical function grows muted, and the critics generally weigh in to evaluate particular artists only after dealers and the involved public have already done the crucial filtering.[12] When innovations occur, however, the market for interpretation opens up, and critics get their shot. Noticeable in the art market of the twentieth century is the positive correlation between critical enthusiasm for a new school or movement and the room that it offers for interpretation. Cubism's facade defied penetration by the average onlooker. The aperture it provided for critical interpretation was eagerly seized by Guillaume Apollinaire, dealer-critic Léonce Rosenberg, and others, but the style still took considerable time to establish itself and achieve a significant volume of sales. Futurism came prepackaged with its own ideology, leaving little room for critical addenda. Surrealism was at first heavily attacked by the ranking critics because of its literary rather than visual inspiration, but that very intellectual program soon revealed copious critical opportunities, and Surrealism diffused rapidly.[13]

The pattern continues with twentieth-century American schools. Abstract Expressionism was a critic's dream for the completeness of its break with established art conventions—and because leading artist Jackson Pollack was withdrawn and inarticulate, critics had a blank slate on which to write. The same was true later with conceptual art, in which the visual component often withered and the intellectual program became the whole show. Conversely, Pop Art and pattern painting left slender opportunities for sophisticated critical strictures, and a realist artist such as Andrew Wyeth, after initial recognition for his technical craft, faced rejection for his accessible subject matter.[14]

Besides demonstrating the scope for the critical function, the visual-art realm exposes the issue of self-interest in critical judgments. The functions of dealer, agent, critic, and publicist often overlap, as shown frequently in the French art market after the dealer-critic system had emerged. Felix Féneon was an enigmatic though highly influential critic who worked for various newspapers before joining a major gallery, Bernheim-Jeune. After becoming a director of the gallery in 1908, he could both select artists for Bernheim-Jeune and promote them in his critical capacity.[15] The noted American critic Clement Greenberg in 1959 agreed to organize a contemporary art department for French and Company, an established New York dealer in traditional art. He showed Barnett Newman and Morris Louis while promoting them in articles under the banner of Postpainterly Abstraction. In general, Greenberg was an aggressive manager of those artists who caught his eye—he instructed them privately on how to paint and what to show, and he was not bashful about accepting gifts of art works from them.[16] Art magazines similarly sometimes fall into linking advertising and editorial coverage. Alice Marquis pointed in particular to *Art International* in the 1970s, when a retrospective show of Mark Rothko's work at Marlborough Gallery was the occasion for extensive advertising by Marlborough and the appearance of two apparently Marlborough-commissioned articles.[17]

The most spectacular instance of critical self-dealing is the partnership between Bernard Berenson, renowned expert on Italian painting, and international Old Master dealer Joseph Duveen.[18] Berenson by the 1890s had established himself as an undisputed master of his subject and in particular as a master of attributions of Italian paintings. Early in the nineteenth century, false attributions had been more rule than exception, and experts who offered certifications were not uncommonly corruptible. Berenson thus certainly improved on both the qualifications and ethical standards of his predecessors. Nonetheless, he engaged in a longstanding partnership with Duveen that gave him at first 10 percent, and later 25 percent, of the profits on all Italian paintings sold by Duveen. For this Berenson provided many services. Initially recruited to catalogue the important collection of Berlin banker Oskar Hainauer that Duveen had purchased, Berenson soon proved useful for the contacts he was building with wealthy American collectors of Old Master art. He succeeded in luring Arabella Huntington to Duveen away from his Paris competitor, Seligmann, and this coup led to the profit-sharing arrangement.

The arrangement, which persisted until the early 1930s, placed Berenson on a slippery slope when making attributions of paintings that affected Duveen's profits. One case documented by Colin Simpson involved a painting purportedly by Giorgione that Berenson had described in print as possibly an early Titian but probably a copy. In 1912 it was in the hands of Italian dealer/restorer Luigi Grassi, who improved it (with Berenson's knowledge) sufficiently that Berenson could recommend it to Duveen for purchase as a Giorgione. A painting described in two of Berenson's books as the work of Marco Basaiti with a faked signature of Bellini metamorphosed into a top-notch Bellini when collector Jules Bache bought it from Duveen. In a switch, another painting sold to Bache as the work of Vicenzo Catena later turned out likely to be a Giorgione worth ten times what Bache had paid, and Berenson was dispatched to suggest to Bache that the painting was not up to the standard of his collection and should be returned to Duveen. The deal between Duveen and Berenson was not without its contractual problems. They quarreled over whether Berenson should share any losses that Duveen incurred on Italian paintings. The carefully concealed terms of the deal gave Duveen the opportunity, apparently used, to cook the books at Berenson's expense.

No stark conclusions can be drawn from these examples, other than that they illustrate both plausible views of critical self-interest. It can amount to a rent-seeking deception, with deluded buyers occasionally making purchases that they would have eschewed with full information. On the other hand, "full information" is a hypothetical construct, and the alternative to a shady deal might be a worse deal still.[19] In any case, critics still praise and certify, and consumers do not perceive themselves to be taken often enough to ignore critical judgments and certifications. Also, the incentive issue in self-dealing is not irrelevant. The deal with Duveen and other such commercial arrangements effectively supported Berenson's research, and Duveen long subsidized the publication of his books.

Prizes and Awards

Aside from the contiguous verdicts of critics, certification also comes from prizes and awards. The Turner Prize, the Booker Prize, Academy Awards, Emmys, Tonys, Obies and their abbreviated kin recognize artistic achievement; they also signal quality to consumers and thereby bring pecuniary gain to producers. Some prizes' sponsors promote the recognition of creative excellence and advancement of the state of the art as charitable *art for art's sake* objectives. Other sponsors have interests in the profitable production of creative goods, and thus in sending positive signals to customers as well as improving the product itself. Consumers face the same problem as they do with critics—the credibility of the received signals. If (say) MGM were to laud a film as MGM Movie of the Month, it would probably have no effect on film-goers' expectations of its quality.

Academy Awards

The Academy Awards, however, sponsored by an industrywide organization—the Academy of Motion Picture Arts and Sciences—present a veneer of objectivity that may or may not be penetrated by interested parties. As a show they command worldwide attention, and with it enormous value as a certification of quality for the films and performers nominated and honored. The Academy was founded in 1927 to advance the art and commercial interest of filmmaking. It sponsored committees of industry insiders to address technical problems, on which it also promoted liaison with equipment manufacturers and other suppliers. It developed contacts with educational institutions to promote film studies. In the 1930s it interacted in complex ways with the emerging talent guilds and with the development of an industry code under the National Industrial Recovery Act. In its early years it played a useful role in arbitrating contract disputes between actors and producers and between writers and producers. Only gradually did the Academy Awards emerge as its principal activity.[20]

The Academy has a membership (now around 5,300) of film industry professionals. While dominated by actors (one-fourth of its membership), it also includes other creative film professionals, executives, and public-relations specialists. Membership is for life and requires a certain amount of screen credits and experience (only about 2 percent of Screen Actors Guild members belong to the Academy). Lifetime membership makes the average Academy member a generation older than most award winners and two generations removed from the industry's median teen-age customer.[21] The process of selecting winners, which has varied over the years, now starts with the Academy's distribution to its members of lists of eligible films. Ballots for nominations are sent out in January, and nomination lists are announced in February. The Academy then arranges screenings of the nominated films for its members, and final ballots are mailed, collected, and counted for the ceremony in March. Nominations for the various talent groups (actors, direction, cinematography, musical score, and so on) are made by Academy members specialized in those activities, but all Academy members may vote on each prize.[22]

Observers of the awards have sought to infer the Academy members' preferences from the nominees and winners selected over the years. Naturally enough, a compromise is struck between art and commerce. A film's box-office success certainly improves its chances of garnering awards, and a best-picture award generally depends on high production values and epic ambitions that can hardly be accomplished with a modest budget. But perceived creative merit does provide the basic platform. An appreciable minority of citations are for the artist's first film, so craft and experience are not dominant factors. Nominations and awards tend to beget further nominations, however, and a lesser performance can bring an award after several respected but unawarded performances and/or unsuccessful nominations. Recognition sometimes goes late in a career to a commercially though not critically successful performer for a routine performance. Repeat nominations for best actor or actress are more common than for supporting roles, for which a sufficient explanation is the superstar phenomenon and the small number of star-status performers relative to the number available for and used in supporting roles. A moderate proportion of acting awards (26 percent) have gone to performances in non-U.S. films, illustrating that the Academy's standard is not entirely commercial. Nonanglophone actors and films, however, have fared much less well than their acclaim by critics would suggest.[23]

Awards clearly increase attendance at films, and acting awards increase performers' expected appeal in future films (and thus their compensation and expected rents). The effect turns up in statistical studies of factors determining films' gross revenues, but more interesting evidence comes from industry-based conjectures on the Oscar's effect on the fortunes of variously situated artists and films.[24] Small-budget films that have not received heavy sales promotion, and films early in their exhibition cycle on awards night, gain the greater benefit. Various casual guesses attribute increments to North American box-office grosses of $5 million to $30 million.[25] Among individual winners, young and new creative talents enjoy the greatest escalation in their asking prices for future projects, whereas established performers whose expected rents (and hence asking prices) are well settled benefit mainly in the widened range of projects available to them. These patterns agree nicely with the substitutability in different types of information that reach filmmakers. The Oscar has its greatest signal value where the film-goer's experience and other information sources hold less information value.

For film distributors the prizes' value clearly warrants efforts to capture them. The major studios are less active than they were in the days of integrated filmmaking (Chapter 5), when the studio had two advantages that it has now lost: it could capture some of the rents due to increased market values of future performances by artists under long-term contract; and the attachment of Academy members to studios yielded a home-team relationship that could be exploited in lobbying for votes.[26] Nowadays studios release their most prestigious and important films in the late fall and early winter, particularly December, to have them fresh in Academy members' minds when Oscar nominations are due; of thirty best-picture nominees during the 1980s, ten were released in December, eleven between September and December, and only four between January and April.[27] Heavy advertising in the Hollywood trade press and the distribution of numerous videocassettes to Academy members (some receive a hundred a year) are common forms of costly promotion, and a tendency has been resisted for the cassettes to arrive in increasingly opulent packages. The studios that invest most actively in cadging votes for their films are not the vendors of blockbusters but the "independent" (but mostly owned by major studios) firms distributing high-quality, modestly budgeted films. Press reports point out Miramax as particularly active in telephone lobbying as well as the devices just mentioned.[28]

Ecology of Prizes

Awards and prizes have proliferated throughout the arts, suggesting that numerous sponsors stand ready to fill the available ecological niches. The interests of these sponsors are evident enough. Associations of artists seek to advance professional standards and leverage their creative preferences against choices driven by the interests of humdrum participants and profit seekers. Independent philanthropists who sponsor and support prizes likely have the same objective. Prizes given by associations of critics serve to advertise and dignify the critics' regular services. Commercial sponsors seek goodwill for their products among the honorees and the public with more than casual interest in the relevant art world. Commercial sponsors therefore naturally tend to be firms based in creative industries (such as publishers) or makers of fashionable and luxurious goods.

The prize-givers' competition to fill niches results in a certain amount of competitive jostling that Richard Todd documented in British prizes for fiction. The Booker Prize got there first, achieving a reputation advantage and devising a format like that of the Academy Awards—the short list announced to the public, with the winner declared only several suspenseful weeks later—that maximizes public attention. Other prizes followed (they now total 40 to 50), each seeking some niche (young authors, for example) to differentiate themselves. Prize money has escalated among the leading contenders, and some leapfrogging has occurred as prize-givers have sought the best position on the calendar.[29]

Sellers Who Certify: Book Clubs

A certifier can offer advice either as a stand-alone service or bundled with the recommended creative goods. The bundling strategy has the attraction of avoiding the market failure associated with the sale of any public good such as information: any purchaser can resell it and become an instant (and low-cost) competitor with the originator. Art critics (we noted) depend on bundling their pronouncements with other editorial content in magazines and newspapers. Some art consultants deal with major collectors one-on-one, and they may bundle their advice with art sold in the capacity of private dealer.

Book clubs provide a classic bundled service for those seeking advice on worthwhile reading to be found in the current outpouring of new books. They began with the Book of the Month Club in 1926, which offered monthly selections of new books made by a board of distinguished literary figures such as Christopher Morley and Heywood Broun—whose reputations presumably were at stake to ensure the taste and perspicacity of their choices. Their advice could be profitably bundled with sales of the recommended books because as the club's membership grew large it could print and distribute its books at relatively low cost and negotiate concessional royalty rates with authors. At the same time the club was structured to avoid cutting into profits of the publishers whose books it selected. Its choices were among soon-to-be-published manuscripts in press at publishers and submitted by them to the club. And its prices did not substantially undercut the retail prices quoted in bookstores (apart from the free books that were the bait for new members). The Book of the Month Club's formula was easy for competitors to replicate, and numerous rivals entered over the years. It also generated a substantial debate in the intellectual periodicals, with its attackers deploring the middlebrow orientation, the suppression of the individual's act of choice, and the authority placed in the hands of the expert selection committees. Because a book is an experience good, one wonders what other counsel the book buyer was supposed to access to inform her choice; as Janice Radway pointed out, attacks coming from independent book reviewers had the flavor of complaints about successfully competing certifiers, a paradox that went unappreciated at the time.[30] In any case, the value assigned by the reading public to book clubs' certification appears in the fact that (in the publishing industry's view) book clubs' choices tend to sell better in the bookstores to nonmember customers.[31]

The viability of the book club's bundle of services suffered in the transformation of book retailing (Chapter 9). Discounting of best-sellers by price clubs and other retailers squeezed the book clubs' margins, and their market share has been declining.[32] Gone are the literary judges, once paid more then $75,000 annually, and the distribution of best-sellers in the general trade-book market has largely displaced critical esteem as a basis for selection. A consistent explanation is that bookbuyers for whatever reason have shifted toward preferring the advice inherent in herd behavior to that offered by whatever panel of experts a book club chooses to recruit.

13

Innovation, Fads, and Fashions

Innovation in creative industries differs importantly from innovation in humdrum industries. The automatic transmission for the family car and the laser printer for the family computer were technical product innovations that improved on established products. They sprang from costly and purposive inventive efforts drawing on underlying scientific and engineering knowledge, and they succeeded because they worked better than preceding products at a cost that many users found attractively low. Nobody suggested that the automatic transmission arose due to an increase in people's aversion to shifting gears, or the laser printer to an outbreak of dot phobia.

Innovation: Character and Consequences

Innovation and Creativity

The analog to product innovation in creative industries seldom rests on such a clear distinction between changes in technology and in the tastes that the product serves. Desktop publishing greatly lowered the cost of publishing books expected to appeal to small numbers of readers, increasing the volume of such books published and the number of publishers offering them. It did not change the physical book, however; to the creative industry of book publishing it was a process innovation, not a product innovation. Compare the innovation of rock 'n' roll. It was not invented out of the blue by Elvis Presley. It had roots deep in rhythm-and-blues music with an established and mainly black audience. Record companies began to seek out white performers when and only when young white record buyers began showing an interest. Was the triumph of rock the result of a shift in tastes or a stylistic innovation? The answer is not clear. Consider an innovation in painting, Abstract Expressionism. The style was certainly a substantial departure from those of

Surrealism and non-objective painting on which it drew. Its widespread acceptance, however, was a story of the acclimatization of tastes—those of critics and venturesome dealers at first, then of an ever-widening general public. An enormous array of varied "raw" creative products or potential products is always at hand *(infinite variety)*. When one of them is swept into popularity, antecedents and forerunners can (with the wisdom of hindsight) usually be found. Popular music innovations involve either the successful popularization of a fringe style or some new synthesis of existing elements.[1] A pathbreaking gatekeeper can achieve an innovation by searching out a new class of artists or presenting them to a previously unserved audience.[2] It is not quite—but almost—appropriate to say that innovation in creative activities need involve nothing more than consumers changing their minds about what they like.[3] For example, an effect of TV's rise was to transform the audience for cinema films from families to teenagers on their own. The effective innovation of the heavily promoted blockbuster "action" film would likely not have succeeded without this shift in demand.[4]

The nature of innovation in creative activities is also blurred by the fact that any creative product that does not just replicate can be defined as an innovation. This is clear from the problem-solving paradigm that seems to capture the essential process of creativity (Chapter 1). Innovation then is the visible tip of the iceberg of everyday creativity—those creative efforts that strike the market as unusually distinctive, satisfying, and/or productive in opening new ground. In the preceding sentence, "the market" is a portmanteau term. Establishing what ranks as an important innovation is a process that involves the flow of information and exchange of views (buzz) as well as the overt economic responses of all the participants—artists, gatekeepers, certifiers, consumers. It is the dialogue about *A list/B list* rankings in its broadest setting. The process of distinguishing significant innovation from everyday creativity varies among creative activities due to the differing porosity of their filters. In a creative activity with tight and clearly articulated standards of performance, critical presumption is loaded against the acceptance of novelty as a valid and desirable innovation. An innovation must either carry the credential of manifest face value, or eke out a slow victory in localized skirmishes between novel and traditionally accepted creative goods. On the other hand, an art realm that welcomes any novelty as a noteworthy innovation necessarily lacks consensus on any critical paradigm. Critical rankings lose their value for consumers to calibrate and rationally order their selections among creative wares. *A list/B list* rankings are impaired for contributing to the efficient organization of complex creative activities (Chapter 7). It is the old issue of liberty versus license. A creative activity that yields the most value for its participants as a group will need a suitable compromise between tight critical standards that resist those innovations that will ultimately overrun the "establishment," and loose standards that yield no stable valuations or points of reference to guide either artists' training or consumers' investments in cultural consumption capital.[5]

Sources and Consequences of Innovation

Whatever their origins in taste changes and creative inspirations, stylistic innovations alter the configuration of humdrum resources employed in creative industries. The intermediary—art gallery, publisher, record company—that latches onto a new style enjoys at least a temporary surge of profits. Depending on the sector's technology of replication, at the least it can command high prices for the wares of the stylistic innovators whom it has under contract. At most it can sell blockbuster numbers of replicated innovative products. Competitors seek to match the innovation and invade its profits, which also are prone to capture by the artist or artists who directly expound or embody the style. Although individual creative goods enjoy copyright protection against piracy or counterfeiting, stylistic innovations freely diffuse to imitators, followers, and knock-offs.

Innovation likely increases the total volume of activity in a creative sector, because it involves more than the restyling of a constant flow of creative goods to consumers. One reason is the superstar mechanism (Chapter 4). Acceptance of a stylistic innovation resembles the appearance of a superstar as a vertically differentiated good. Not only are other styles (or artists) deemed poor substitutes, but also demand is inflated by consumers not ordinarily drawn to that sort of creative ware. The total volume of transactions hence may increase substantially, even while creative goods in older styles are being displaced.[6] The stylistic concentration of a sector's flow of creative goods may well be greater at times when the total number of units purchased is high.

If a successful stylistic innovation elevates the level of activity in its sector, the causation also may run the other direction. The potential market for creative goods has grown greatly in the United States since World War II, not just because the population and national income have grown, but also because many more people have attended college and had occasion to start their investments in cultural consumption capital. More gatekeepers stand ready to admit artists to the marketplace, and more artists struggle for creative success. One component of innovation in creative activities is a lucky or insightful break into a new realm of creative problem-solving. If an innovation is simply a "hit" in the ongoing stream of day-to-day creative effort, and increased demand adduces more effort, it also raises the chances that some artist achieves the innovative hit.[7] That an enlarged market lures more would-be innovators is a proposition upheld by both economic logic and empirical evidence on industrial innovation. Still, art realms offer a possible exception. *Art for art's sake* calls forth creative labor when the expected wage is low or even nonexistent. The committed artist may face a choice between "normal" creative work to serve an extant market and innovative effort to break open an avant-garde frontier. The smaller the pecuniary rewards of normal creativity, the more attractive are the highly uncertain and largely subjective rewards of assaulting the aesthetic frontier. The Abstract Expressionists claimed that their early efforts were spurred by the attitude that nothing they made was likely to sell, so they might as well pursue symbolic rewards on the frontier.[8]

Although pure technology has little to do with most innovations in creative industries, their ease of diffusion does have its technical side. As Howard Becker pointed out, the creative industries—especially those using teams of artistic skills—always depend on a set of conventions to smooth the creative task. All the participants know them, so they require no review, negotiation, or elaborate practice. Popular dance-band musicians who have never played together before can readily collaborate knowing only the tune to be played, the key, and the tempo. If an innovation in creative activity rejects existing conventions and requires that a new set be learned, it suffers from high costs of adoption. Becker cited the musical compositions of Harry Partch, which employ 42 notes to the octave and require novel instruments as well as specially trained musicians to play them. Performances of Partch's music often rested on a year's residency by the composer at some university. In the fall he would recruit a group of interested students, who built the instruments to his designs and under his direction. In the winter they would learn to play the instruments and read the notation that he had devised. In the spring they would rehearse several works and finally give a performance. If n musicians were involved, the audience enjoyed two hours of music from roughly $8n$ person-months of effort.[9] Partch's innovation was ill-designed for widespread diffusion. At the opposite pole, the triumph of Abstract Expressionist painting was smoothed by the fact that it was easy to do passably, if not well.

The technology of creative work may affect artistic innovation in another way. The process of problem-solving at the heart of creative effort feeds on any change that opens up a previously unknown range of problems—or approaches to their solution. Arnold Schoenberg's twelve-tone or serial system of composition provided a rigorous paradigm for the composer that, once learned, revealed a wide range of compositional problems and supplied elegant procedures for solving them. This expanded creative space appealed greatly to composers and to trained musicians with strong interests in musical innovation, and that appeal sufficed to make considerable resources available to support this school. Charitable foundations interested in new music funded composition and performance, and university tenure committees welcomed the composers. The only trouble was that hardly anybody else could stand to listen to the music, and many musicians thought that learning to perform it was at best not worth the cost. Listeners' demand for the performance of music (new music, anyhow) was arguably reduced relative to the hypothetical alternative of a more listener-friendly stylistic innovation, such as the present-day school relying on slowly evolving repetitious patterns (note the success of Steve Reich and Philip Glass).

Innovations that require new techniques or performing conventions of course court failure because they incur high costs for each performance or creative product realized. The various art realms differ systematically in their unit costs of production, and hence in the unit costs of attempted innovations. New styles of opera generally entail very high fixed costs per performance, a sufficient reason for opera being an art realm resistant to innovation. Pop musicians face much smaller costs of pushing their styles in local club dates. In the visual arts, Abstract Expressionism lowered its costs by de-emphasizing technique, and Arte Povera reduced its input costs by making a virtue of the cheap and discarded; earthworks art went the other direction by requiring bulldozers rather than brushes to fabricate the works.[10]

The creative industries are studded with examples of innovation and taste shifts, and selected cases illustrate how stylistic changes that succeed in the market are associated with changes in the creative activity's organization. In popular music the rise of rock 'n' roll blindsided the established record companies and produced considerable turnover in the industry. In toy manufacturing, firms in a large industry live and die by rapidly revolving innovations. In the visual arts the origin and diffusion of Abstract Expressionism show the elements in the diffusion process, and the famous Armory Show of 1913 illustrates how a set of innovations make their way into the market.

Innovation and Organization in Popular Music

Rock 'n' roll surfaced in the 1950s as a transformation of tradition rhythm and blues (R&B) music that attracted a largely black audience into a form that appealed to white teenagers. It also drew on white-oriented country and western (C&W) music. It was a sweeping innovation. Neither R&B nor C&W music had been in close touch with mainstream American popular music, which had devolved mainly from European operetta.[11] It reduced or eliminated the traditional division of labor between songwriter and performer, as songs came to be "composed" in the recording studio. It shifted the accompanying instruments from bowed and brass to plucked. It dumped established song forms and made up its own formal rules. The emphasis went from the accompanied singer to the group. The content was freely vulgar, and lyrics often mattered little. Performing styles changed completely.[12]

A great turnover resulted in the record market because new and small companies uncovered listeners' interest in this innovation largely by accident, while the major record companies that then dominated popular music disdained the innovation until its commercial success was clear. R&B music had been actively recorded in the 1920s and 1930s, paradoxically, by specialist firms that were or soon became subsidiaries of established record companies. The OKeh label, then a U.S. subsidiary of a German firm, was persuaded by a black music-store proprietor in 1920 to record the artist Mamie Smith, and the resulting records sold well and exposed a large market. The established Columbia Records began recording black artists in 1921, and Paramount released a number of blues and gospel records as well as taking over the independent Black Swan label. Columbia acquired OKeh, and two other major record companies, RCA and Brunswick, entered or acquired independent companies. The Great Depression crushed the market for R&B records, and there was little recovery before the musicians union's ban on new recordings during World War II. After the war, tastes shifted away from the "rousing, shouting, throbbing" styles of the early records, and the major record firms allowed these lines of recordings to die out.[13]

Sources of Innovation

At this time low-cost and flexible recording equipment became available for the first time, greatly lowering the barriers to entry into the recording industry.[14] With the major record companies withdrawn from the R&B market, many entrants flooded in, about one-fourth surviving until 1952. The heavy migration of blacks to northern cities during the war led to extensive radio broadcasting of R&B music in the major cities, and this point of contact apparently led to an appreciable market for R&B records among white teenagers in selected major cities and in the South.[15] Several labels picked up this innovative opportunity. Atlantic Records was able to find successful styles for artists such as Ray Charles and Aretha Franklin. Chess Records sought recording artists in the rural South but also found the urban Chuck Berry. Sun Records's manager declared, "If only I could find a white man who had the Negro sound and the Negro feel, I could make a million dollars." He found Elvis Presley, whose contract he sold to RCA Records for $35,000 in 1955, when he badly needed the money. Dot Records employed Pat Boone and other such artists to "cover" (re-record) songs originated by R&B artists.[16] Later, other entrant labels successfully introduced variants on the rock style. Motown developed a homogeneous sound and great skill in selecting and packaging black performers to appeal to a white audience; A&M developed an "easy listening" variant acceptable to older customers.[17] Besides entrepreneurship by small record companies, some artists themselves took an initiative in converting R&B into a commercial form. Bill Haley, who had been playing standard country and western music, began amalgamating elements of R&B into a clear, tight-sound brand of rock 'n' roll that became widely popular when incorporated into several cinema films.[18] In England the Beatles had their roots in a British version of American folk-blues that flourished locally in Liverpool. Apart from their sheer distinctiveness and songwriting talent, the Beatles also innovated by exploiting (with their *Sgt. Pepper* album) the artistic possibilities of the record album as an integrated production, rather than a collection of songs.[19] Another source of supplemental innovation in the 1960s was modern sound-editing equipment. Independent record producers skilled with such equipment could produce a distinctive "sound" by recording each sound source separately and combining them with multitrack dubbing.[20]

The major record companies (despite the historic R&B material in their vaults) were slow to respond to the new style. The pop music market that they served was dominated by singers who came from the "big band" era of the 1930s and 1940s, when works by independent songwriters were performed. The label's in-house producer selected the songs to be performed, and the artist showed up and sang them. In particular, Columbia Records's Mitch Miller was regarded as an infallible judge of pre-rock songs and singers. He deplored the wildly successful new artists such as Presley and Buddy Holly, considering them a passing fad. Apart from short-sightedness, Columbia and its leading competitors may have had an economic reason for complacency. If successful, rock 'n' roll would siphon profits away from traditional pop music. Profits made from rock by these labels would cut into their profits from traditional pop, whereas the independent companies faced no such drag on the up-side of their rock investments. The major companies did use covers of rock songs as a form of containment.[21]

Turnover among Record Companies

The initial success of rock 'n' roll speeded the turnover of performers, a change sustained to this day. What proves interesting is to follow the consequences for the record industry as this succession of performers waxed and waned, by drawing on the quantitative analysis of sociologists Richard A. Peterson and David G. Berger.[22] They employed the weekly Top Ten listings of record sales appearing in the trade press, starting in 1948. For each year they totaled the number of record companies represented in the weekly Top Ten and the concentration of hits (share of Top Ten entries accounted for by the largest four firms). They calculated measures of turnover: the number of records and also the number of performers making the weekly Top Ten during the year; the shares of performers who were new, established, or fading stars. They also observed the proportional change in record sales (at constant prices) from year to year. With 1955 the year when rock burst onto the scene, they first compared the base period 1948–1955 with 1956–1959, years of gale-force change. The share of Top Ten hits due to the largest four companies, around 75 to 80 percent in the first period, fell to around 35 percent in the second. The number of companies with Top Ten hits (initially ten to thirteen) tripled. The proportion of Top Ten performers who were new began around 25 percent, rose to 50 percent in 1953–1955, and exceeded 70 percent in 1956–1959. The share of established hit performers, initially around 40 percent, fell below 20 percent in 1955 and down to 10 percent in the following years. Unit sales of records, rising slowly at first, grew at 15 percent annually during 1956–1959. The major stylistic innovation thus massively dislodged established artists and companies and brought many new customers into the record market.

The analysis was carried forward by Paul D. Lopes over successive periods down to 1990. In 1960–1963 the number of record companies with hits stabilized, and the concentration of the largest four settled around 25 percent. The share of Top Ten hits due to new performers declined slightly to around 60 percent, but still they turned over much faster than before the rock revolution. The growth rate of sales fell off, while measures of diversity (the number of records making the Top Ten in a year, or the number reaching the number-one position), remained very high. When sales growth again reached 15 percent annually in 1964–1969, these diversity measures remained at high levels. The turnover of companies declined, however, as the major labels devised strategies for dealing with the new turbulence. They sought to develop their own rock artists or (more commonly) acquire the contracts of those successfully launched by the new record firms. They also began proliferating the number of record labels (analogous to brands) that they issued. That change reflected a structural shift in the industry like the one that struck the major Hollywood studios in the 1950s. In both cases, what kept the major firms "major"—the entry barrier sustaining their position—was a large-scale promotion and distribution apparatus, supplemented by a library of past titles that could be efficiently marketed along with new ones. New competitors could replicate the distribution system, but they could not use it efficiently without a backlist and a painstaking build-up of new titles. Indeed, forward integration into wholesale distribution increased during the 1970s, serving to augment the record firms' capability for large-scale promotion of hits (Chapter 9). While this apparatus cemented an oligopoly of successful firms as "promoters," these firms did not perform the "picker" function well. Hence they resorted to buying up established artists and investing in subsidiary labels run by successful pickers. Thus, in the late 1960s and early 1970s the number of record companies with top hits remained high, but the number of Top Ten labels per Top Ten firm increased, as did the concentration of the promoter firms (the largest four companies accounted for about 40 percent of unit sales during 1964–1969, about 50 percent during 1970–1973).

When the pattern is followed to 1990, the diversity (total number) of performers with hit records remained high, but the concentration of records shipped by the promoters increased to over 80 percent. The volume of total record sales fluctuated in harmony with the number of successfully established new styles, with a recession in 1979–1983 when disco fell from popularity and nothing immediately replaced it.[23] The number of new artists with hits fell during that recession period, as labels chose to promote fewer new artists. The promoter companies' successful reconciliation of the quest for new talent with the maintenance of a fixed, large-scale promotion and distribution structure was shown in their immediate capture of new styles either directly, or on independent labels with which they had distribution agreements. While the sales of records fluctuated with the supply of successfully innovative artists, record-company executives also believe that congestion occurs. That is, the presence of a large stock of mature artists currently before the public raises the threshold of promotional resources and public attention needed for a new artist to "break" successfully.[24]

The major record companies may have made their business innovation-proof because their flexible access to new talent is coupled with a fixed production and distribution apparatus. That conclusion is consistent with the recent stability of their combined market share. But the *nobody knows* property lives on and condemns them (like the Hollywood distributors) to wide year-to-year swings in individual shares and profits. These swings are propelled by luck in developing or acquiring new performers, by the varying successes of individual recordings by established top stars, and by commercial life cycles of stars who fade and groups who break up. Stars switch companies as a result of competitive renegotiations of contracts, and companies lay down different bets on the chances of reviving a fading career. A company with a number of current top groups under contract has both the cash and the aura to attract others. Artists speak of "hot" and "cold" labels, assuming (plausibly, given the lack of other information) that promotional skills successful for other artists will also work for them. Yet a label also grows vulnerable to broad shifts in taste and to the ability of "hungrier" companies to promise performers their undivided promotional attention.[25]

The rise of rock reveals all the processes involved in innovation in creative industries—the creative breakthrough of a major reconfiguration of stylistic elements that opens a wealth of new opportunities, a distributor industry in which humdrum entrepreneurship advances the innovation commercially, and a potential audience ready and willing to invest in the cultural consumption capital to welcome and reward the innovation. A contrasting episode in country and western music shows that the innovation can come in the presentation of the creative good rather than in its substance: the shift from an unpolished, simple performance style to elaborate presentations suited to large audiences (copied from the top rock performers).

Country Music Goes to Town

The evolution toward pop styles of singing, use of orchestra arrangements, and the like took place roughly during 1972–1977, but it had roots in the earlier growth of and change in the radio broadcast of C&W music and the associated expansion of its audience.[26] Although rock music, triumphant in the 1950s, competed for listeners' attention with the concerts and records of C&W, it also increased interest in country music outside of its traditional audience. A threefold expansion of radio stations broadcasting a C&W format occurred between 1961 and 1965. By 1974 the 81 stations on the air in 1961 had grown to 1,016. Few disk jockeys knowledgeable about C&W were available to tend all these turntables. To cover that shortage, stations resorted to a Top 40–type of repetition of the most popular recordings, which greatly reduced the number of artists and styles receiving airplay. What began from necessity in the 1960s, however, was continued for a more positive reason in the 1970s: this format attracted listeners who were younger, female, and valued much more by advertisers than the traditional C&W audience, which bought chewing tobacco and work pants. Advertising revenues strongly supported the expansion of C&W radio.

This newfound popularity scrambled the ranks of C&W performers, rewarding the top names and the rock-slanted new performers who appealed to this newly broadened audience. Country gospel, folk, crooners, and bluegrass music were frozen out, as were second-string mainline performers whose recordings failed to win promotion on the hits-oriented C&W radio stations. For companies recording C&W music, the payout increased for large-scale promotion of top-ranked artists, or those who might have a shot at stardom. Albums that were produced for $20,000 gave way to those with production budgets five times as large. Superstars emerged such as Garth Brooks, whose music and performing style were developed for stadium shows, and total album sales by 1996 had reached 60 million. Shania Twain's recordings were produced by a former rock producer at a cost reaching $500,000, with the vocals elaborately reworked and layered with all sorts of instrumental bits; although she traveled extensively to promote her records, she could not do concert tours, because the sound on the recording could not be reproduced at a concert. Reba McEntire, based in the more traditionalist wing of C&W, became highly successful with a touring show "worthy of a small circus." Her enterprise marketed her recordings, a book, her concerts, and the T-shirts and keepsakes that went with them; "everything in her professional life sold something else."[27] In short, the innovation in C&W did not change the basic song material so much as it did the package of sensations that it provided to listeners on recordings and at concerts. It uncovered a willingness to accumulate C&W consumption capital in an audience that had previously ignored it.

Innovation in Toys and Games

Innovation in the toys and games industry resembles that in popular music—major eruptions in style or technology that transform a continuous quest for everyday novelty. It offers an interesting contrast, however, because the larger companies appear to enjoy little of the insulation of fixed promotion and distribution systems that protect the leading record (and movie) distributors. In those industries, the large-scale fixed (and sunk) distribution systems leave no room for entry by head-to-head competitors and force product innovators to deal with the incumbent gatekeepers. Scale economies in toy production do not matter; it is mostly contracted out. Leading toymakers such as Mattel and Hasbro enjoy a different advantage, and perhaps a more precarious one: the ability to finance the large-scale promotion of would-be innovations from the firm's existing cash flows.[28]

Innovation and Turnover

Many new toys appear yearly on the U.S. market (6,000 is a representative guess), most of which achieve few sales and disappear before the next season.[29] Similar innovations commonly appear for the same reasons as in couture (Chapter 11), and knock-offs of successful designs are common. A few new designs become wildly popular, causing competitors to lay low and forgo innovations in that line.[30] They may enjoy long commercial lives (Barbie, G. I. Joe), or they may wear out their welcome and disappear after a few years (Cabbage Patch Kids), although revivals occur. About 60 percent of retail toy sales take place in the last quarter of each year. Designs for the holiday season are prepared more than a year in advance for vetting by the major retailers, then presented to retailers at large in an annual fair in February. Orders taken then govern decisions made about quantities to be manufactured (mostly outside the United States). The orders and production decisions rest on little information beyond buyers' and manufacturers' hunches. The market's reaction is not fully known until into the fourth quarter. There is then no time to reorder popular designs. *Nobody knows* what three-year-olds will want next year, and experimental testing with groups of children (though extensively performed) is believed to have no value for predicting success, although some for predicting failure. Whatever herd behavior marks adults' choices of creative goods is multiplied in their offspring, widening the gap for the average design between the units produced and units demanded. So it is common for production to fall far short of demand for the year's "hot" toy, which then sells out before the Christmas holidays.[31] Conversely, the production costs for large runs of "cold" toys are incurred before the bad news arrives. The inventory's salvage value is minimal, and these reverses can inflict large and even fatal losses on quite big companies.

As with other creative goods (books, films, records), the distribution of successes seems to have grown more skewed in recent decades with the rise of media (television) that allow the massive promotion campaigns that spur the herd into motion (if they work), while likely shortening the life spans of blockbuster successes.[32] Toys were long promoted mainly through retail channels (department stores and specialty toy retailers), with the message aimed at adult buyers. The toy designs themselves encouraged children's play along the lines of rehearsal for the adult roles to come (motherhood and housekeeping for girls, manual work and combat for boys). Television brought a sweeping change not just to the scale of promotion, but also to its substance. The toy could be presented directly to the child, and not just depicted but shown in action. Furthermore, when made the centerpiece of a children's TV program, it could be packaged with its own surround of fantasy—a four-year-old's consumption capital coming direct from the tube. Also, TV programs and cinema films came to provide their own stock of toy designs through licensed characters (starting with Disney in the 1920s); the toy manufacturer pays a royalty for license to use of the copyright character, but obtains as a spillover the promotion and the complementary fantasy.[33]

While some of the risk of licensed toys is handed off to the licensor, the toy manufacturers carry much of both the risk and the profit potential of toy innovations. Where large rents flow to copyright holders, the manufacturers' positions depend crucially on whether they own the rights or (in the manner of book publishers) license them from authors. Sources of toy innovations (other than licensed characters) are diverse. Some originate within toy companies—designers or other employees. Some come from independent professional designers or from amateurs.[34] Like song publishers, the toy manufacturers avoid dealing with amateur designers in order to ward off infringement suits on successful designs. (Such problems arise even in dealings with professional designers; toymakers' in-house designers keep dated logs of their work.)[35] The traditional royalty rate received by independent toy designers has been a modest 5 percent of net wholesale revenue.[36] That figure reflects both the large development and promotion investments made for toys with the potential of broad success in the market and the high risk involved. With electronic games the hardware manufacturers are forced to give up more of the profits—and also the risk—to game designers who produce the software. That is because a strong complement of games is essential for customers to demand the hardware. Hardware makers' competition for top game designers hands over to them ownership interests or royalties of up to 40 percent of wholesale revenues from the games.[37]

Innovation and Toymakers' Concentration

The changing techniques for promoting toys with the potential for widespread popularity have increased greatly the toy industry's concentration. In the 1950s the four largest firms accounted for only one-eighth of the toy industry's shipments.[38] By 1996, when Mattel sought to acquire Hasbro, the combined shares of these two leading firms were estimated to be between 28 and 40 percent (depending on market definition).[39] More variable success with new toys by itself raises the concentration of the industry: the biggest firms are simply those that were very lucky once, or quite lucky several times. But the changing process of promoting toy innovations itself suffices to explain increased concentration. Promoting a new design by means of a TV show incurs a high fixed cost. In the mid-1980s a full TV launch required financing 65 half-hour episodes costing $250,000 each; these would last for thirteen weeks and then go into reruns. To meet the costs of this and other forms of promotion, the two leading firms were by then spending $200 million yearly, nearly three times the annual sales of a representative midsize toymaker.[40] Since firms cannot readily borrow from the bank to finance sales promotion, companies making these plunges had to draw on cash flows from their previous innovative successes. The leading firms not only possessed these "cash cows." They also learned to preserve and extend their franchises by bringing out annual new models of the toy or new sets of accessories, or by deriving families of "collectables" that had the incidental advantage of hooking some adults as well as their offspring.[41]

If not developed internally, this cushion of cash flows could be bought by acquiring smaller toymakers that owned classics (for example, board games such as Monopoly). While acquisition offers risk-spreading advantages, it comes with a major drawback. The target firm's market value already represents the financial market's valuation of its cash flow. Acquiring control requires paying a premium over this market value that is rarely less than 20 percent and often much more. A cash-flow cushion stitched together by mergers thus can easily cost more than the value that it accesses—the opportunity to undertake risky, large-scale promotional investments.[42]

Another promotion technique that fostered the concentration of toy companies is the licensing deal for marketing toys that represent characters in a cinema film or TV program. A license that carries only a modest royalty rate need not yield any advantage to the large over the small toy firm as licensee. Competitive bidding among toymakers for licenses, however, not only escalates the royalty rate but also adduces guarantees that are credible only from licensees with cushy cash flows. This was apparent when Lucasfilm Ltd., owner of *Star Wars,* renegotiated the expiring licenses held by Hasbro and Galoob Toys. Mattel, drawn into the competition, offered not only to raise the current 12 and 14 percent royalty rates to 20 percent, but also to include stock options and minimum guarantees as high as $300 million.[43] Such competitive bidding of course hands the fruits of the large toy companies' promotional advantages over to George Lucas. At the same time, it explains why big toymakers enjoy an advantage over small firms in striking such deals: If Lucas accepted a $300 million guarantee from a firm with few existing assets, he would in effect be making a $300 million equity investment in that firm.

Leading toymakers were also enlarged by their dealings with increasingly concentrated retailers, such as specialist Toys "R" Us and general merchandise discounters such as Wal-Mart. The increased advantage of size for the toymakers stems from both bargaining power and the ability to accommodate the large chains' logistical requirements. The obverse of this tendency for big to deal with big is the continuous flow of new toy designs from small or start-up manufacturers that are marketed mainly through small or specialty toy stores. The latter emphasize classic and/or high-quality toys, designs from small manufacturers who cannot profitably undertake massive promotional investments, and complex toys or toys with specialty appeals that need to be demonstrated to the buyer in the store. One independent toy store manager reported buying from 250 manufacturers.[44] Thus, the leading toymakers not only face a competing fringe of small firms with substantial innovative capacity, but also continue to contend with large risks to their own profit flows.[45] Losses as large as 20 percent of annual sales are common. Coleco's Cabbage Patch Kids had sales of $540 million in 1984, $600 million in 1985, and $230 million in 1986, when Coleco had predicted $450 million, and as a result lost $111 million. The next year it sold $126 million and lost $105 million. The failed video game maker Atari sold $2 billion in 1982 and $1.1 billion in 1983, when it lost $539 million.[46] Thus, catastrophic losses can result not just from failed innovations but also from successful innovations that play out unexpectedly.

Video Games

Video games were a different sort of innovation, one relying on electronics technology. Several established U.S. toymakers sought unsuccessfully to enter this market, which has been dominated by new or entering Japanese firms (such as Sega, Nintendo, and Sony). The product relevant to the consumer is the combination of the hardware console and the software games that can be played on it. Rivalry has shown a leapfrog pattern, with each firm in succession developing a console that uses a more advanced basic technology, permitting faster action and better graphics than its predecessor. To succeed, each console innovation has to be accompanied by a roster of attractive games. In 1998 the U.S. market was dominated by Sony (a cumulative 51 percent share of hardware sold) and Nintendo (41 percent). They appealed to different age groups (Nintendo the 10-to-14 age bracket, Sony to older players) by offering different hardware-software packages. Nintendo's games come in cartridges (expensive to manufacture, but fast in play), Sony's on compact discs (CDs—cheap to make, with enormous storage capacity, but slower in play). Sega launched a new design in 1999, as observers wondered whether imitators might strike too soon for it to be profitable.[47]

The games companies employ a form of price discrimination that is common where hardware and software complement each other. Consoles are sold at prices yielding very thin profit margins, whereas the games are sold at very high mark-ups over variable cost. This practice brings marginally enthusiastic customers to the store for the bargain machine while extracting the surplus from enthusiasts who purchase numerous games. Sony offers large numbers of CD-based games sold for moderate prices, Nintendo a smaller number of highly popular games at higher prices. Many games come from outside firms and developers; the hardware firms, in the "promoter" role, choose not to manage the creative task in-house.[48]

Thus, the turnover of the makers of electronic games, like the precarious persistence of the largest makers of conventional toys (amidst many small competitors), reflects the underlying technology of creating and promoting innovations in this realm.

Innovation in the Visual Arts

In the visual arts, innovation also involves a broadly based process in which the creative inspiration of an artist or group is a necessary condition, yet its ultimate consequences depend on much else—the circumstances of the buyers who purchase it and the certifiers and dealers who serve as intermediaries. In the long run, the prevailing styles of visual art appear to be consistent with the economic and social positions of those who buy art and the physical settings in which they display it. Furthermore, innovative styles seldom appear to spring exclusively from discrete innovations by particular artists. Had the leading figures in most schools not existed, there were capable if lesser talents working the same vein whose efforts likely would have affixed the style in its place and time.[49] That pattern certainly holds for Dutch seventeenth-century art, where the rise of a substantial middle-class market drew forth the styles of landscape and portraiture that clearly reflected the domesticity of the purchasers. It also reorganized the art market, downgrading the role of the patron and raising that of entrepreneurial production of art to be held in stock with no specific purchaser in mind. After the Industrial Revolution created a prosperous middle class in nineteenth-century Europe, the innovations of France's Barbizon school and Impressionism responded to this new element of demand, as did the English landscape and anecdotal genre artists.[50] These patterns suggest a particularly close relation in the visual arts between artistic inspiration as the source of innovation, on the one hand, and the state of collectors' demands and the gatekeepers' selection process, on the other.

Abstract Expressionism

The triumph of Abstract Expressionism during the 1940s provides a useful case study of how these elements come together in the innovation process. Its best-known artists—Jackson Pollock, Robert Motherwell, Barnett Newman, Clyfford Still, Ad Reinhardt, Adolph Gottlieb, and Mark Rothko—presented very different stylistic personalities but shared an interest in gesture and plumbing the subconscious. These they inherited from Surrealism, thanks to extensive contacts with the major Surrealists who sat out World War II in the United States. Chance procedures, and even the process of dripping paint onto a canvas, were there to be absorbed, even as the Abstract Expressionists rejected Surrealism's subject matter.[51] A secondary interest lay in primitive imagery, which they saw as insulation from "historical reality." Their program emphasized art as an adventure into the unknown, with the artist as a guide to seeing the world in a new way. Technique was regarded as unimportant. They had developed their work during the 1930s undistracted by commercial success. The artists knew each other and interacted extensively in the New York art community (one-third of the first-generation Abstract Expressionists were born in New York, another one-third in Europe). That community had been split into two camps during the intellectual radicalism of the 1930s. The American Artists Congress (with Stalinist leanings) was affiliated with regional and genre painting and representational art related to social issues. The Federation of Modern Painters and Sculptors (with Trotskyite leanings), which included the Abstract Expressionists, was much more apolitical and concerned with artistic quality. Other important factors affecting the values and objectives that the artists brought to their work included the influence of European modernist styles, brought home by Alfred Barr's highly influential survey exhibitions at the Museum of Modern Art and by the influx to New York of some of these very artists at the beginning of World War II.

On the demand side, New York experienced an art boom during World War II, presumably the result of personal wealth flowing from the fully recovered economy and the unavailability of other baubles that money usually buys. Auction sales were active, and the number of art galleries in New York increased from 40 at the beginning of the war to 150 in 1946. The new collectors showed an affinity for American art; American works were plentiful and cheaper than European modernism, and patriotism called to some buyers. Nor was the demand for art narrowly based in an elite; in 1942 William Randolph Hearst sold a large collection of art objects through Gimbel's department store, and Macy's offered old-master paintings in response.[52]

The role of dealers in seeking out artists and emergent schools was described in Chapter 2. Peggy Guggenheim opened Art of This Century in 1942 as a cross between gallery and museum, giving shows to Motherwell, Pollock, Reinhardt, and William Baziotes, later to Still, Willem de Kooning, Gottlieb, and others. After the war she returned to Europe at the first opportunity, but successor galleries were opened by Charles Egan, Sam Kootz, and Betty Parsons.[53] Critical reception was mixed. Clement Greenberg came to the fore to provide a rationale for the movement, but more traditional critics, such as Edward Alden Jewell of the *New York Times,* wanted artists to be more engaged with the external world in general and the war effort in particular.[54] Pollock, discovered and widely accepted in 1943–1944, immediately appealed to sophisticated critics and curators for his work's exuberance and openness and (not least) the wide latitude that it offered for critical interpretation. A significant channel for the diffusion of modern art styles to the general public is industrial design and illustrations in fashion-oriented periodicals. In 1944 *Harper's Bazaar* was presenting high fashion against backgrounds of Leger and Mondrian, and soon the Abstract Expressionists had their turn.[55] Commercial art generally pursues the objective of attracting attention, and fine-art innovations can serve that goal even for persons not attuned to the style.[56]

Immediately after World War II, the Abstract Expressionists were in close competition with other styles. Contemporary survey exhibitions such as the Whitney Museum's showed great stylistic diversity, including some artists who followed Picasso and other Parisian styles, as well as others attracted to U.S. regionalism or the constructivist abstraction of Gabo and Pevsner. By 1948 Abstract Expressionism had clearly won. Although these artists' prices remained low until the beginning of the 1950s, the innovative galleries were prospering, Pollock had shown in the prestigious Venice Biennale, and prizes were raining down.[57] As with any art style, however, Abstraction Expressionism faced the hazard of exhausting its realm of opportunities. The very dominance that the style achieved perhaps contributed to the heaviness with which a sense of depleted possibilities hung over it by the end of the 1950s. The artists themselves kept forming and reforming groups, but the aesthetic goals of the movement became less challenging, and the artists' community disintegrated. Young artists could find no further room to maneuver within the style, and a vacuum was created for the Pop Art that followed.[58]

In summary, Abstract Expressionism illustrates many of the features of innovation special to creative activities: the core breakthrough to an enlarged realm of aesthetic problem-solving; the entrepreneurial role of dealers, critics, and other intermediaries; the contributing factor of an affluent potential market; and the fade-out associated with both the exhaustion of aesthetic opportunities for the artists and sated experience in consumption among the collectors.

The Armory Show

The vast survey of modern art from Goya to Cubism shown in New York in 1913 was not an artistic innovation, but rather a spectacular diffusion of European modernism to America's virgin aesthetic soil. Its influence shows how aesthetic innovation interacts with the responses of art-world intermediaries and the general public. It suggests a sort of superstar effect, an event of critical mass that brings a creative innovation forcibly before a large public, effectively advertising a previously unknown line of cultural consumption and affecting many people's operative tastes over a long period of time.[59]

Before 1913 only a few American artists worked in modernist styles, and they largely lacked commercial outlets. The main venue for distributing art was the National Academy of Design's annual exhibitions, which were conservative in the extreme. Max Weber, an important early modernist, submitted work once to the National Academy, was rejected, and never tried again. The only significant exposure for modern art was given by Alfred Stieglitz, who began showing work of many pioneer modernists in his Photo-Secession Gallery (founded 1908) and publicizing them through his quarterly publication *Camera Work*. A few venturesome small museums also displayed modernist works. Only a few newspaper critics showed any warmth or understanding in writing about new art.[60]

The Armory Show was the work of group of sixteen distinguished artists who had exhibited at the National Academy of Design but were not happy with its standards. On the other hand, these were not the artists who came to be known as the American avant-garde (Weber, John Marin, Marsden Hartley, and so on)—that is, those already committed to modernism in their own work. The organizers' coup depended on their aesthetic middle position; they were open to modernism but were not partisan. The initial intent of the new Association of American Painters and Sculptors was to stage its own invitational exhibitions. Although it fell accidentally into sponsoring the Armory Show, it was exceptionally well qualified in two ways. First, the artist Arthur B. Davies emerged as president of the group; although he appeared as passive and ephemeral as the figures in his paintings, he turned out to be a fireball administrator. Second, Davies and several others were well connected to patrons who proved willing to provide funding, and attorney John Quinn (who later became an important collector) assisted greatly with legal and publicity work.[61]

The show owed its genesis to a large, varied, and inclusive exhibition mounted in Cologne in 1912. Davies sailed to Europe in late September 1912 with the objective of obtaining the core of the German show for exhibition in New York. A commitment was successfully obtained. Davies then hastened to Paris, where he was also able to add a great deal of French material, with the aid mainly of Ambroise Vollard and Galerie Emile Druet. With a speed that now seems breathtaking, given that day's technologies of transportation and communication, by the opening on February 13, 1913, 399 paintings and 21 sculptures had been shipped to New York, installed as an exhibition, and photographed for the exhibit catalogue. The exhibition included as well a large number of American works selected by the organizing committee.

The exhibition drew 70,000 viewers in New York, 189,000 subsequently in Chicago, and 12,000 in a truncated Boston showing. It attracted abundant publicity. Much of it was ridicule, but the New York press and especially the professional critics reviewed it in a serious and conscientious manner, although mostly without using the largely unknown aesthetic arguments for Fauvism, Cubism, and Futurism. The freaks-and-clowns atmosphere was especially marked in Chicago, where the large attendance apparently owed much to wildly optimistic expectations of erotic thrills. Many of the works were for sale, and purchases were quite numerous. The important buyers were not the established great collectors but those whose collecting careers began at this time—Quinn, Albert Barnes, Walter Arensberg, and others. In current publicity and sales the American works came off somewhat better than the European ones, because on average they were less advanced aesthetically. The artists who attracted the most attention at the show were indeed those whose fame long survived it, although a few then-conspicuous names disappeared without a trace.

The long-run effect of the show is evident from the collections launched from it and the New York dealers who opened in its wake. Eight significant new galleries were counted within the next several years. Books began to appear on contemporary art. Several large, recurring exhibitions receptive to modernist art opened in the next several years in New York and other cities, although none of them was long-lived. The most important was Katherine S. Dreier's Société Anonyme, which was effectively a traveling museum of modern art that made its rounds accompanied by lectures from Ms. Dreier or occasionally some of the artists.[62] Department stores had emerged since the late nineteenth century as upscale emporia that included cultural uplift among their portfolio of quality signals. Showing advanced art was part of the packaging. In the 1930s exhibitions of the Museum of Modern Art sometimes traveled to department stores in the Midwest. Some commercial illustrations after the Armory Show began reaching for a higher level of sophistication by adapting elements of modern art.[63]

Overall, the Armory Show illustrates several features of innovation and its diffusion. It achieved a critical-mass breakthrough to superstar status. It illustrated the force of certification among artists themselves, for governing the diffusion of new styles. And it affirmed the dominant role of modification of tastes in the diffusion of innovations in art realms.

The preceding cases of innovation are highly diverse, but they do illustrate important links between the responsiveness of tastes and the organization of creative activities. The Armory Show exposes the taste-change process itself: how novel styles of creative goods attract buffs and certifiers who can, when they command sufficient resources, set off herd behavior that cumulates to a major change in operative tastes. The triumphs of Abstract Expressionism and rock 'n' roll broadly shared this diffusion process, which spreads outward from a core of buffs and certifiers. With toys and games the launch mechanism is completely different—large-scale promotion by the innovating firm— but it aims for a similar (but more intense) herd behavior.

How innovation affects the organization of supply varies greatly among these cases. We generally expect successful innovating firms to flourish, failed innovators and non-innovators to fade. The art realms show this process, but also reveal much more. Firms with entrenched distribution systems or other such capacities can preserve their positions if they can cut their losses on faltering styles and open their facilities to innovation (the record companies). On the other hand, without entrenchment, and with no way to avoid large losses on failing styles, innovation can cause enormous turnover among large firms (the toy industry). The turnover process is more natural and continuous when gatekeeping firms are small and without sunk or committed resources—like art galleries or small toymakers.

IV

Cost Conundrums

Potential *infinite variety* goes unrealized in some creative-good markets because an activity's fixed cost is high relative to customers' combined willingness to pay. Nonprofit organization offers a vehicle for getting these fixed costs covered efficiently. In addition, it performs the vital task of facilitating a deal between customers and manager about the nature and quality of the product. Chapter 14 develops these relationships and examines how they shape what goals nonprofit organizations in the performing arts actually pursue. The ongoing organization likely has no master contract with its customers, but their continuing interaction implicitly sets and adjusts its terms, as the manager selects and implements policies and the customers' donations wax or wane in response. Evidence on where nonprofit organizations prevail and how they behave in the performing arts seems to support this model.

In creative industries, fixed costs do not emerge as some mandate of technology. They grow from and depend sensitively on the quality or elaborateness of the creative product that is offered. Quality of the creative product, fixed cost, and nonprofit status thus are all bound up with creative choices and consumers' responses to them. The history of symphony orchestras' organization (Chapter 15) illustrates clearly how ambitions for improved performance quality relentlessly pushed their organization toward the donor-supported nonprofit form (or its European counterpart, state subsidy). This organization—a self-perpetuating board of directors with residual responsibility for covering costs—works surprisingly well, thanks to the network of personal opportunities and obligations that surround it. Board members hold something like equity shares in the organization—shares that pay dividends of esteem when it performs well. The empirical evidence on charitable work and donations by wealthy families shows how this governance mechanism works.

The roles of fixed costs and nonprofit organizations lead to a problem of public concern in the performing arts. These are labor-intensive activities with no direct access to productivity gains, and so their real production costs tend to increase steadily (the "cost disease"). Creative goods can be consumed in forms that do benefit from technological advance—movies, recordings rather than live performances—so one adjustment is to shift the form of consumption. The cost disease has led to a number of adjustments within the performing arts (Chapter 16). The number of plays staged on Broadway has declined, and the hits run longer (as they must, to cover the increasing real fixed costs). Theatre organizations shift toward nonprofit status, especially in regional theatre. Bucking the trend is the recent wave of blockbuster musicals that have found new ways to cover their enormous fixed costs.

14

Covering High Fixed Costs

Many of the costs incurred in creative activities are both fixed and sunk. Fixed costs do not vary with the quantity of output produced. If some costs are fixed, then the average total unit cost of an activity declines as the quantity produced increases.[1] Sunk costs are those necessary for an activity that cannot be recovered or reversed if that activity ceases. The two concepts are independent of each other. A sunk cost might vary with the scale at which production is carried out (that is, not be fixed). A fixed cost might be recoverable when the activity is suspended (that is, not be sunk). We fall into the habit of expecting fixed costs to be mainly sunk, and sunk costs mainly fixed, because they usually are. In the creative sectors, while both properties are important, they are sometimes independent. When the sculptor carves a series of twenty statues of President Millard Fillmore, the costs of her time and (probably) materials are sunk, yet they likely vary in proportion to the number of Fillmores in the series. The performing-arts organization that rents a theatre on a long-term lease incurs a cost that is fixed, but not necessarily sunk if it may sublet. The sunkenness of many costs of creative activities has been emphasized so far, accounting for the option contract's central place. Fixed costs' implications are different but no less central to creative activities' organization.

Fixed Costs in Creative Activities

Fixed costs are pervasive in creative activities. The cost of a film negative is the same, whether it is seen by a thousand or a million people. So is the cost of recording an album or of staging and rehearsing a play or an opera. Every work by the visual artist demands a fresh burst of creative effort, and the musician incurs a cost to perform each concert—variable costs. For both visual artist and musician, however, the large cost of training and apprenticeship is fixed (and sunk). Fixed costs pose a fundamental problem for economic organization.[2] First and foremost, there may be no ticket price that a performing-arts organization (for example) can charge and still cover its average unit cost (fixed plus variable). Suppose that a play's variable running cost is $15 per seat for each performance. If it charges that price, it could sell out a substantial number of performances. It must charge more, however, to cover its fixed costs. As it raises the price above $15, each ticket sold contributes more and more to cover the fixed cost, but also more and more play-goers choose to stay home. There might be no ticket price for which total revenue will cover total fixed plus variable cost. Roughly speaking, fixed costs "bite" when they are large relative to customers' combined willingness to pay.

We generally shed no tears over products that go unproduced because they cost more than their worth to customers, but with high fixed costs, the missing product may involve a market failure. Suppose that demand for admissions to a play is such that a $30 ticket price maximizes gross profit—makes the maximum contribution to covering fixed cost. Yet this maximum contribution still falls just short of covering the fixed cost. This frustrates the theatre company, because many play-goers who buy $30 tickets would pay more. If part of their consumers' surplus could be collected, the show could go on. Another lump of potential revenue lurks in the pockets of play-goers who pass up $30 tickets but would pay more than $15, the average variable cost of an extra performance. Suppose that, at the end of the run, a ticket-price cut to $20 will sell out some additional performances. The $5-per-seat gross profit nudges total revenue toward covering fixed cost.

Many a seller of creative goods pursues these lumps of consumers' surplus by means of price discrimination. The best seats in the house go for $50 to people with a high willingness to pay, while the less eager climb to the second balcony for $20. The cinema buff pays $7.75 when the film opens, while the casual customer sees it a year later on broadcast TV for the "price" of watching the soft-drink commercials. Many other forms of price discrimination turn up: higher admission charges on weekends than weekdays, lower charges per admission for season tickets than for singles. Price discrimination generally can raise the gross profit from a differentiated product, and is pursued by profit-seekers whether or not it is necessary to cover fixed cost and produce a positive net profit.

Fixed costs have profound effects on the structures of markets for creative goods. Make them large enough relative to the market's size, and no set of price-discrimination gimmicks will generate enough revenue to cover fixed costs. Enlarge the market just enough, though, and a monopoly seller can turn a handsome profit without attracting entry by a competitor. (The competitor's arrival would push down prices and each firm's demand until neither entrant nor incumbent was profitable, but the incumbent's misery makes the situation no better for the entrant.) Enlarge the market further, and it can support a few firms (oligopoly), likely earning positive profits. *Infinite variety* is only potential.

Consider the Hollywood studios that dominate the exhibition of large-budget films by virtue of their distribution systems (Chapter 10). Those organizations incur a large annual fixed cost to operate. With the distribution system in place, a studio can promote and distribute a certain number of films each year at no additional cost except for the prints and advertising of each individual film. Only a handful of studios perform this function, and on average they earn ample profits. New competitors do not enter (or grow into the role), because a newcomer could not expect to earn positive profits from North American distribution, once its distribution capacity is added to that of the existing studios. Perhaps for this reason, the new studio Dreamworks, founded with much fanfare by three super-rich entertainment executives, chose to arrange for distribution of its films through Universal rather than to build its own distribution network. The same pattern appears among the "promoter" firms found in the record industry, book publishing, and toys and games. Their prices exceed the marginal costs of their outputs, and they earn on average more than enough profit to keep them in the game, even while would-be competitors cannot expect to find sufficient room to prosper if they enter and mimic the incumbents.

In short, a high enough incidence of fixed costs makes even a monopoly opera company strain for enough revenue to cover its costs, while a moderate relaxation of the fixed-cost constraint allows a profitable oligopoly to prevail.[3] Enlarge the market greatly, holding the fixed costs constant, and many rivals find room, though the typical one earns little excess profit. The U.S. magazine industry and New York art galleries are examples among the creative industries.

Nonprofit Organizations and the Fixed-Cost Problem

Nonprofit organizations are very common in creative-good markets where the fixed-cost problem is severe. It seems logical that nonprofits take over where profit-seeking enterprises cannot cover their fixed costs. Yet that explanation in its simplest form is wrong. Costs have to include a normal profit on the capital and managerial services, regardless of who incurs them. The profit-seeking enterprise will stay in the game if it can cover those costs, although it would *like* an extra profit. The nonprofit, unless it enjoys some special advantages, cannot survive without covering these same costs. Neither has an advantage over the other.

In creative markets with fixed-cost problems, however, nonprofit organizations (NPOs) do enjoy several advantages that explain their prevalence. Consider a valuable device for covering high fixed costs—the two-part charge by which customers pay a fixed or membership fee plus a unit charge for each ticket or use of the facility. However the enterprise is organized, this device offers a major efficiency advantage. The per-use fee can be set equal to marginal cost. The fixed charge collects enough of the consumers' surplus to cover the organization's fixed cost. If necessary and feasible, the fixed charge itself can be differentiated to pick off more surplus from the consumers who value the creative good highly. The gold-card member's enthusiasm wins her an invitation to a party after the opening-night performance, while the less keen tin-card member gets only the privilege of buying tickets at marginal cost.

Contract Failures and Nonprofit Organizations

On its face the two-part charge is equally attractive to profit-seeking and nonprofit organizations facing high fixed costs. The former uses the fixed charge (if possible) to skim some excess profit, while the nonprofit uses it only to the extent needed to cover fixed costs. Of course, consumers are not indifferent, and would prefer the NPO for its lower fixed or membership fee. That still leaves the door open for the profit-seeker willing to match the NPO's membership fee and settle for normal profits. But there are more subtle advantages that the NPO enjoys in running a two-part pricing system in a creative activity with high fixed costs. It is easy enough to describe two ways to organize the arts enterprise centered on two-part prices. The profit-seeking manager organizes the firm, offers a contract, and signs up members upon their payment of the fixed fee. Or consumers form a club in which each member agrees to pay the fixed fee, and they contract with a hired manager to supply the desired creative service.[4] Why might the two organizations perform differently?

The answer is that the two contracts will both prove imperfect, but the NPO in a creative activity might well work better.[5] We normally welcome the power of profit incentives to promote the efficient operation of an enterprise, expecting the profit-motivated manager to beat out the salaried management of a NPO. This advantage crumbles, though, if the contract cannot effectively specify just what product the manager will supply, for the profit-seeking manager may have both incentive and opportunity to cheat on the quality or variety of product offered, while a hired-hand nonprofit manager would not. Creative goods with all their noncontractable properties invite this problem, though it also turns up elsewhere. When her toddler is sent to a day-care center, the parent cannot practically observe the quality of the lunch that is served. Would she prefer that the decision be made by a manager who minimizes costs, or by a manager who loves children? When a hospital stay is required, and the quality and thoroughness of the treatment cannot be contracted in advance, does one prefer a manager who minimizes costs or one who wants the best for humankind?

As these examples show, the profit-seeking organization may have a double disadvantage. The quest for profit promotes forms of opportunism such as giving customers a product inferior to what they expected when they paid their fixed charges. Furthermore, the NPO may be able to contract with a manager who gets positive utility from supplying a product with just the attributes sought by the customers who form the NPO club. The manager of the concert series or the repertory company cannot feasibly write a contract with audience members specifying the thoroughness of preparation or the prowess of the artists. Will a manager who minimizes costs deliver as much audience satisfaction as a manager who loves good theatre or music? The audience rationally trades off the incentive for efficiency against the incentive to seek high quality; some *art for art's sake* in the manager's tastes is better than none. As often happens with contract failures, repeated transactions between audience members and a profit-seeking manager might get around the problems of writing a satisfactory contract for the one-shot provision of creative wares. The infrequency with which performing-arts "seasons" come around, and the difficulty in determining ex post why a creative product was unsatisfactory (Chapter 6), deflate the value of repetition and reputation for solving the problem of contracting with the profit-seeking arts manager.

Club membership as a way to cover high fixed costs does face a problem of forming the club at the outset. One reason why people buy club memberships is that nonmembers can be excluded from consuming the good or made to pay more for a ticket. If nonpaying audience members cannot practicably be excluded from performances (concerts in the park, for example), forming the club becomes problematic in the first place, as prospective consumers dodge the membership drive hoping to become free-riders at actual performances. All we can say is that, at the outset, either enough people make irrevocable pledges for costs to be covered, or there is no club and no performance. This problem of free-riding carries over to the ongoing performing-arts organization that seeks recurring contributions but chooses (as most do) not to restrict ticket purchases to whose who make donations. Then the lapsed member has little reason not to free-ride on others' donations, as dodging the solicitor is unlikely to deal the fatal blow to the organization's ability to cover its costs. To keep the donations flowing without excluding nondonors from the performances, it clearly helps if people take an altruistic view of the support that they donate to an arts organization. The feeling that built-up cultural consumption capital has improved the quality of one's life easily brings a warm glow upon making a donation likely to trigger this improvement in others' lives.[6] Altruism suffices to explain why performing-arts clubs welcome (indeed, pursue) nonmember ticket buyers and new audiences. Nonaltruistic club members benefit, however, when more wallets can be pried open to cover fixed costs.

Contract Failures with Creative Inputs

These contracting problems that favor nonprofit enterprise have been presented from the viewpoint of consumers of creative goods. Because of the *art for art's sake* attitudes of artists, parallel problems arise for their services in providing creative inputs. Their reservation wages are low, but their eagerness to perform with an organization depends as well on the particular creative tasks assigned to them, the degree to which those tasks challenge and develop their skills, and the match between their values and those of the director or coordinator who sets the organization's aesthetic program. Nothing about the profit-seeking status makes a manager intrinsically callous about these creative objectives. But in the for-profit arts enterprise, they can fall prey to the pursuit of profit. The creative performer faces exactly the same problem of contracting with the manager as does the club of consumers. The creative coordinator cannot articulate and thereby commit to a contractually enforceable set of policies.[7] Still worse, the role of inner necessity in creative activities causes the artist to resist precommitment in principle. The artist's best chance lies with a manager who not only espouses values compatible with her creative objectives, but also does not trade them against profit goals. The nonprofit manager can hence hope to attract capable and ambitious creative talent on better pecuniary terms than can a profit-seeker under suspicion of compromising aesthetic goals. The longer the time period for which artists attach themselves to a performance organization, the more do they hold aesthetic shares in the creative goals that it pursues, and the more important should this consideration be. Of course, the creative urge of performing artists likely interacts with altruism of donors, favorably for the NPO, because the knowledge that one's donation lessens the dedicated artist's privation is a likely source of a warm glow.

In summary, the fixed-cost problem yields a number of predictions about the economic organization of creative activities. It explains some of the pricing schemes that are in common use. In light of the problems of writing contracts for creative activities, it predicts where NPOs will undertake the production of creative goods and something about the tastes of managers that commend them to astute coalitions of arts consumers. The contracting problem of course exists independent of the fixed-cost problem. Profit-seeking investors in Broadway shows or Hollywood movies face their own contracting problem of motivating the producer and director to pursue their profit goal. Two things simplify their task. First, "profit" is easier to define contractually than "artistic excellence," and profit shares to the creative participants help align their choices with the investors' goal. Second, the fixed-cost problem does not "bite" so severely on Broadway or in Hollywood, large markets in which many competing projects are viable. The pressure of competitors leaves decisionmakers in creative ventures less room for pursuing quixotic courses of action, simplifying the investors' problems of channeling their objectives.

The "Cost Disease"

One more element intersects with the contracting and fixed-cost problems: the "cost disease" flagged by William J. Baumol and William G. Bowen in their celebrated book on the performing arts.[8] In the long run people's real incomes rise because of innovations that raise the quality of goods and services, and productivity gains that decrease the costs of producing them. The corollary of higher real incomes is rising real wages. These tend to increase producers' costs of production, cutting against the cost savings that come from technical progress. Because productivity advances at uneven rates in different industries, this process alters the relative prices of goods, cheapening those with the greater opportunities for productivity advance. The performing arts, goes the argument, are the losers in this game, as the labor hours required to perform a Beethoven string quartet remain exactly what they were when Beethoven wrote it. Over the long run the cost of producing performances rises without limit relative to other things on which people spend their incomes. Other consumption goods and services will be substituted for the increasingly expensive performing arts until they disappear from the marketplace, their fixed costs squeezing relentlessly against the public's willingness to pay. This analysis has been put forth as an argument for public subsidy to the performing arts.

The cost-disease proposition calls for a number of qualifying comments. If the cost disease has made some forms of cultural consumption more costly, it has certainly cheapened those delivered by new media technologies—television, compact discs, videocassettes. Some arts producers and consumers, the ones not favored by new technologies, are worse off. Others (the superstars whose performances are favored by new replication technologies, and consumers who thrill to them) are better off.[9] Another qualification concerns the effects of rising incomes on how people divide their spending among types of consumption: the "income effect" of advancing prosperity, as distinguished from the "substitution effect" spotlighted by the cost-disease hypothesis. Suppose that we can sort the goods and services that people consume into "necessities" and "luxuries," and that increases in incomes are spent entirely on luxuries, once the necessities are in hand. Performing arts and other luxuries, if their relative prices were held constant, would then attract increasing shares of consumers' incomes.[10] This seems especially likely in view of the bias in consumers of the performing arts toward those with high education levels and incomes—households not wanting for necessities (Chapter 11). The cost-disease effect of course fights against this income effect, but rising incomes could lift arts spending enough to offset the impact of rising costs on the quantity of performances. A particular form of this income effect on cultural consumption might be a taste for improved quality in the cultural experiences consumed. That is an important possibility, because attending higher-quality performances increases the efficiency with which scarce time is used, making it indeed likely that the willingness to pay for higher quality should increase. That change favors the real thing in the performing arts over the second-hand experience of a reproduced performance.[11]

Nonprofit Organization in the Performing Arts

The fixed-cost problem hangs pervasively over the performing arts, which also show an abundance of NPOs. The profit seekers of the Broadway stage are an exception, and even they are seldom profit finders (Chapter 6). We can probe nonprofits' role in two ways—by examining the habitats and behavior of nonprofit performing-arts firms, and by digging into their origins for insight on what profit-seeking rivals they might have faced, and what strategies they used to outlast those competitors (investigated in Chapter 15).

Incidence of Nonprofit Firms

The incidence of NPOs varies greatly among creative sectors.[12] In performing arts NPOs are widespread, and they completely dominate what people call the high-culture sector. Theatre is split, with New York theatre and its traveling-show outposts in other cities for-profit, regional theatre and repertory companies nonprofit. Book publishing is largely commercial but includes a substantial fringe of university presses and other publishing adjuncts to nonprofit research organizations. In the 1980s, the nonprofit share was about 12 percent in book publishing, higher (22 percent) in magazines. In radio and television broadcasting about one-fifth of stations are nonprofit, although this share reflects an explicit public-policy decision. NPOs and public-sector firms dominate "cultural storage," that is, museums and libraries.

The list seems to support the hypotheses stemming from the fixed-cost and contract-failure explanations for NPOs. The performing arts incur high variable costs for each audience member served; high variable costs plus the need to cover high fixed costs imply high admission charges, which restrict audience size. Also, the audience pays travel costs as well as ticket costs, which narrows the organization's market geographically. The New York theatre sector remains commercial because its large size makes room for a substantial number of productions playing at one time. That does not hold for theatre organizations in other cities. The contrast between repertory companies (nonprofit) and single-play productions suggests an additional element. The repertory company both incurs the fixed costs of a number of productions and employs its personnel on a sustained basis. Such a coalition likely is viable only with shared artistic goals among the creative personnel, and with access to donations to support coverage of the recurring fixed cost. Dance companies especially rely on a pact among the creative personnel that sustains the pursuit of shared artistic goals despite paltry pecuniary reward.

In the publishing industry, nonprofit firms turn out scholarly books that find relatively few buyers but (it is hoped) generate value in the knowledge they convey that exceeds what buyers pay. The university presses conform to the fixed-cost explanation, but also to the fact that knowledge is a pure public good that is hard to deny to nonpaying consumers. Of course, universities and research organizations themselves are organized mainly on a nonprofit basis, partly for the fixed-cost reason, but more from the difficulty for a profit-seeking firm to write a precise and enforceable contract to provide a good general education. (For-profit organizations commonly provide training in specific skills that are observable and contractable.)

The affinity of NPOs for high culture is a puzzle, because high culture as such does not imply any particular cost structures or contract problems. If high culture is defined as a rejection of broad-based taste standards, then the fixed-cost constraint applies. A better explanation may lie in the role of quality in creative activities, with the artists having an unbounded and continuing interest in the frontier of creative attainment. The individual artist pursues quality and distinctiveness using all available resources—essentially acting as a one-person NPO—in cinema film, the recording of popular music, and other largely commercial creative activities.[13] It is a short step from this to the nonprofit coalition of artists.

The fixed-cost explanation for NPOs gets a lift from evidence on the ecology of cultural activities. Only a few nonprofit cultural organizations of each type—operas, dance companies, theatre groups, or museums—operate even in large cities. Their numbers face limits imposed by their cost structures and the sizes of the audiences on whom they draw. Judith Blau explored this relation statistically, obtaining counts of cultural organizations in 110 U.S. cities and relating them to the city's size, wealth, social diversity, and other factors.[14] She found that city size (population) strongly regulates the numbers of these organizations, especially the museums, ballet companies, and symphony orchestras that are pinched the tightest between high fixed costs and the extent of the market. Her statistical findings from measures of economic and social inequality and diversity generally imply that demand for the arts is favored by a large class of affluent households that are well and similarly educated. Only as the city becomes very large do the counts of cultural organizations increase with measures of diversity, implying that social and ethnic groups' differing styles and tastes give rise to distinct cultural institutions only where the fixed-cost burden does not press too hard. As city size grows, the count of cultural activities increases less than proportionally. This pattern implies that cultural activities of a given type compete with one another for audience and resources. If a city must grow to size n before it can support one dance company, it must reach some size larger than $2n$ before it can support a second.[15] A bigger city likely supports bigger and better-quality museums, not just more museums. Supporting evidence comes in Philip Hart's observations on cities' varying levels of generosity in donations to support symphony orchestras. Positive factors are competition for social position and a history of German settlement. Negative factors are a blue-collar population and lack of a local industrial base of corporate headquarters.[16]

This U.S.-based evidence is not readily extended to other countries, but Japan does make an interesting case. Tokyo's numerous symphony orchestras fill various ecological niches. The major ones depend heavily (53 percent) on donations from governments, broadcasters, and other corporations; they provide permanent employment to most of their musicians. A second group receives little donations and depends heavily on box-office revenue (fortified by presenting more soloists than the majors) and "concerts upon request" (hiring the orchestra out for operas and other uses); they rely more on freelance personnel. Provincial orchestras, lodged between these two patterns, receive 36 percent of their income from donations and lean heavily on school concerts for earned income.[17] While Tokyo's large market for classical music makes room for some commercial operation, theatre (both Japanese, or *kabuki,* and western-style) rests (except for a ragtag avant-garde) on continuing organizations of performers. Western-style theatre *(shigeki)* depends on numerous permanent production companies with large memberships of actors and crew, who not only present full seasons from a fixed base but also tour extensively. Their actors, paid a pittance, mostly take sideline jobs; audiences support them with subscriptions but not donations. Commercial theatre is in the hands of two large companies that offer both *kabuki* and Broadway-style theatre, especially musicals in translation. They earn most of their income from cinema films and TV, and their actors are under contracts covering these other media as well.[18] Thus, organizational patterns in Japan bear a resemblance to those in the United States, but there is ample room for institutional differences.

Nonprofits' Policies and Motives

The ecology of NPOs agrees well with the implications of the fixed-cost problem, but there remains another testable implication. Nonprofit managers should pursue goals that help to avert the contracting problems described previously. Empiricism on motives does not come cheaply, as people seldom verbalize them candidly to interviewers, and indirect tests are tricky. It helps to think abstractly about what coherent motives the nonprofit manager might pursue. Nonprofit status means that total revenues are supposed to equal total costs. If a profit-maximizing firm could turn a positive profit, the nonprofit manager in the same situation has room for choices that raise costs or lower revenue, thus bringing them into equality. One solution is simply to charge lower prices. That serves the *art for art's sake* motive of encouraging more people to taste the joys of creative activities, an interest that both artists and potential donors might share. Another solution is to offer performances of higher quality. A profit-seeking manager makes a conscious decision about the performance's quality, of course, selecting whatever quality has the most favorable effect on the margin between cost and the public's willingness to pay. If a nonprofit manager goes for a higher quality, costs will rise by more than potential revenue, pushing total revenue toward equality with total cost. High quality of performance serves *art for art's sake* tastes, and it likely appeals as well to the most involved audience members, those enjoying the largest surplus and hence with the greatest potential willingness to donate.[19] Bringing in new audiences and raising the quality of performance are only two goals that nonprofit managers might plausibly pursue. They could stage challenging new work, thereby serving their artists' careers while risking that many customers will feel overly challenged and stay home. They could increase the pecuniary or other benefits of artists. Whatever the goal, its economic result is pinned down by identifying how it affects the organization's revenue-cost relationship and pushes the two sides toward balance.

These motives suggested for nonprofit managers agree nicely with the contract-failure model suggested for NPOs: audience members hand over their fixed payments to a manager who convincingly asserts a taste for serving their desired objective. What we see in practice, though, is not a foundation-stone contract but interaction over time in an ongoing nonprofit firm that operates without much contractual precommitment.[20] The manager (with a board's budgetary approval) selects a set of policies for the season's presentations. The club-member audience observes the results and second-guesses the manager when it contributes to the annual appeal, likely increasing donations when the policies align with the donors' preferences and cutting back when they diverge. The nonprofit manager hence gets more scope to pursue his policies when the donors approve, but faces a financial squeeze when they do not. The squeeze compels the manager to change course: shift either toward policies that raise box-office revenue relative to costs, or toward policies more pleasing to the donors. Thus, the nonprofit manager's policy choices affect the organization's revenue-cost balance both directly and through the induced change in donations.[21] Patrons' donations may adjust in another way that is important. If the organization receives a government subsidy or major support from a foundation, its patron-donors may see their funds making a smaller incremental contribution to its performance and cut back (a free-rider problem). This sketch of mutually adjusting revenues, costs, and donations omits one important factor—the uncertainty associated with each of these flows. Revenues (including donations) that were expected ex ante to cover costs can fall short ex post. In profit-seeking enterprises, this risk is borne by equity capital. In nonprofits, however, nobody has the right to carry off any unanticipated profit, and nobody is formally obligated to make up a loss. Alarmed appeals may go out to donors, but they are normally not committed to serve as guarantors (although members of the board of directors may assume this function).[22] Consequently, the debts of a besieged NPO likely fall on the unwary creditor.

This perspective on the performing-arts organization departs sharply from the view heard in performing-arts circles: The performing arts cannot cover their costs, and donors (or government subsidies) must come to the rescue and close the (exogenous) gap between revenue and costs. In fact, the gap is not exogenous; it depends on the supply of donations. If some change (a stock-market crash) shrinks the donations called forth by any given set of performing-arts policies, the NPO takes action to cut its costs and increase its revenues. Of course, if a big enough shrinkage of donations occurs, there might be no set of policies yielding enough revenue (box office plus donations) to cover the organization's costs, and it shuts down.

This sketch of the nonprofit arts organization has leaned heavily on deductive reasoning, because empirical evidence is hard to find and organize. What does exist, though, suggests that the treatment is on the right track. NPOs' managers, as predicted, do bring different preferences and attitudes to their job. One survey of a business school's graduates going into profit and non-profit organizations found no difference between the two groups in problem-solving ability, intelligence, or creativity, but the nonprofit group differed greatly in personality, values, and behavior (scoring higher on personal relations, dominance, capacity for status, social presence, and flexibility; lower on need for power and for security, as well as importance of pecuniary rewards).[23] A survey of managers of Australian theatres receiving public subsidy reported their preoccupation with performance quality and with the total size of the audience attracted and their indifference to detailed issues of ticket pricing.[24]

Casual evidence is abundant on the reality of the trade-offs involved for nonprofit managers. A report on Britain's Royal Opera House concluded that the most popular operas commanded a 10 to 20 percent premium in opera-goers' willingness to pay. Forgoing new productions would reduce a season's costs by 14 percent; forgoing superstar singers would lower costs by 21 percent, but likely lower by even more the willingness to pay. Also observed were the British opera companies' responses to reductions of public subsidy during the 1980s. Scheduling fewer new productions and coproductions effected much of the adjustment, reducing not only the fixed cost but also the costs of singers, whose fees (per performance) decline with the number of performances of a given opera and increase with the amount of rehearsal required.[25] A statistical study concluded that U.S. nonprofit performing-arts organizations expand their operations beyond the scale that a profit-maximizer would select.[26] During the 1960s, when the Ford Foundation made major supporting grants to a number of symphony orchestras in the United States, the principal effect observed was an increase in the wages and yearly weeks of employment of the musicians.[27] One might read this transfer as a managerial concern for artists' welfare, though the unionized and chronically discontented musicians provide explanation enough.

Studies of American opera companies expose their operating objectives in several ways. Opera companies compete primarily on quality, mainly the vocal prowess (or at least renown) of their principal singers. The share of opera-house budgets devoted to personnel expenses accordingly increases with their size—53 percent for the smallest group, 70 percent for the largest.[28] The conservatism of an opera company's repertory increases with the conservatism and income per capita of the city it serves; repertory choices are also more conservative when the company has full-year contracts with its artists, which implies heavier fixed costs and reliance on donations. Conversely, opera companies with slender budgets are more venturesome in repertory.[29] In terms of managers' and patrons' preferences, the dominant pattern for a coalition seems to favor maximum quality in conservative repertory, while an alternative coalition structure with parsimonious productions but venturesome programming (and casting) may be viable in some settings.

An ideal test for what motivates a nonprofit arts organization would be experimental: give its management an unrestricted donation and observe how the largesse is used. One statistical study tried to mimic this experiment by comparing the situations of symphony orchestras that are members of the American Symphony Orchestra League, which includes a wide range of "major," "metropolitan," and "community" orchestras.[30] The variables conjectured to depend on grant income were ticket prices, audience size, and compensation per musician (taken as a measure of quality, given that higher salaries usually attract better players). The study found strong evidence that more grant income is associated with better compensation of players. This relationship could reflect either a preference for maximum attainable quality or the musicians' bargaining power. No evidence was found that fiscal ease leads orchestras to lower ticket prices—on the contrary, more grant income was associated with higher ticket prices. Audience attendance is if anything increased, no thanks to higher ticket prices, but perhaps because higher-quality performances are offered.[31] Another such experiment occurs when an NPO suffers an unexpected shrinkage of its donations. In response, it commonly raises the price of its product, which of course would only hurt it if the price were already set to maximize its profits.[32]

The tradeoffs made by nonprofit arts organizations seem to be diverse and often improvised. Indeed, skeptics wonder whether they typically sustain commitment to any specific goal or clear set of goals, or if arts managers are even prone to think in terms of a committed set of abstract objectives.[33] Ill-defined objectives may rest on a more fundamental cause: that the arts organization's policies reflect not one manager's objectives but a set of goals negotiated among its various members. This view emerges from studies of the development of successful organizations, which often start from loose alliances of artists investing the equity of their own time and gaining a voice in decisions in lieu of pecuniary compensation. The successful organization takes on an expanded set of activities and likely adds creative personnel with increasingly diverse policy preferences. It also comes to need the coordinating efforts of humdrum administrators. The growth of bureaucracy in an arts organization stems from not just its enlarged size but also the need for donations, which requires the organization of fund-raising and the bureaucratic display of orderly procedure and accountability. Furthermore, governmental and private foundation donors prefer supporting new projects and initiatives to the boring task of covering ongoing fixed costs, and the arts organization needs administrators to service the donors' taste for novelty.[34] The organization commonly starts with a small number of patrons who provide most of the financial support and exert corresponding influence on policies. Growth, however, brings dependence on more numerous purses and on institutional donors. Tension inevitably arises between administrators and artists over the organization's goals.[35] Various case studies of successful organizations show both the easy consensus on pursuit of creative excellence during their early lives and their bureaucratization as they expand and mature.[36]

Whether an arts organization pursues a manager's or a coalition's goals, it is subject to monitoring by a board of directors. Evidence suggests that directors in for-profit corporations have a significant if qualified role in aligning managers' interests with those of the shareholders. The governing board of a well-established nonprofit arts organization is likely picked not to give vigorous monitoring of policies by its club of patrons but to provide feel-good rewards to those important in fund-raising. In the realm of publicly traded profit-seeking corporations, the performance of the governing group—the board of directors and top managers—is subject to the discipline of takeovers in the market for corporate control. Nonprofits, lacking tradable ownership shares, are immune to this threat. This insulation expands the space for the arts organization to pursue internally generated goals. We pursue the role of nonprofit boards in Chapter 15, where the evidence warrants a somewhat brighter view of their influence.

15

Donor-Supported Nonprofit Organizations in the Performing Arts

Nonprofit organizations in the arts plausibly flourish where high fixed costs and contract failures would bedevil profit-seekers. The origins of nonprofit organizations in the performing arts provide confirming evidence. Symphony orchestras and opera companies these days cling exclusively to the nonprofit form. During the nineteenth century, however, there was considerable diversity. Music performance and museums once were chiefly profit-seeking ventures, and the forces that pushed them to change are apparent. The clubs formed to implement nonprofit status invariably sought higher performance quality than what other organizational forms delivered. Why the effort to upgrade quality led so decisively to donor-backed nonprofit organizations proves an interesting question.

Organization of Music Performance

The American Scene

Organized music performance in nineteenth-century America had its roots in two organizational forms.[1] One-shot for-profit ventures offered potpourri programs of various types of music performed by orchestra and soloists. Amateur choral societies (Boston's Handel and Haydn Society, founded in 1815, was one of many) were members' cooperatives, insofar as they had any formal economic structure at all. The choral societies benefited from the relatively small amount of training and practice needed to achieve competent performance. Traveling European virtuosi sought their fortunes in the hinterlands along with British actors. Some for-profit orchestras did enjoy extended lives. The immigrant Germania Orchestra, washed up on American shores by Germany's upheaval in 1848, toured the United States impecuniously between 1848 and 1854, giving a total of 900 concerts and backing touring virtuosi

238

such as Jenny Lind and Ole Bull. When it disbanded, its members settled and became prominent musicians in various U.S. cities. Louis Jullien brought a large orchestra to the United States in 1853–1854; despite a flashy facade (jeweled baton, white gloves), he was a capable musician who achieved a high level of performance. The most important entrepreneurial orchestra was that organized by Theodore Thomas, which gave its first New York concert in 1862. Thomas possessed personal force, organizational skill, and musicianship, and he scheduled programs of higher quality and greater cohesion (whole symphonies, not scattered movements) than was then customary. Between 1862 and 1869 Thomas developed an increasingly stable (though not full-time) group of players, which offered various program series in and around New York and later on tour. By the 1880s the economic viability of Thomas's touring operation was slipping, due to higher railroad passenger fares (thanks to the onset of government regulation in 1880) and stiff competition in the eastern United States from the touring Boston Symphony.[2] In 1891 Thomas resettled his orchestra in Chicago as the foundation of the Chicago Symphony Orchestra. His 62 players were expanded to 85, and two concerts a week were offered for 20 weeks a year. This was a "club" operation with a well-constructed plan for local financial backing, although tours of the Midwest and South remained necessary for the organization's viability.[3]

The symphony orchestra as a permanent organization was a European innovation (discussed subsequently) dating from the foundation of the London Philharmonic Society in 1813 and the Société des Concerts du Conservatoire de Paris in 1828. After two earlier failed attempts, the New York Philharmonic was organized as a musicians' cooperative in 1842. Not an entrepreneurial organization, it for years elected its conductor from its membership. Responding to the vaulting ambition of composers of the romantic symphony from Beethoven on, it was larger than the theatre and pick-up orchestras in which its players also worked. It also sought and achieved a higher level of performance, and in its early years paid its members better than the going wage for pick-up performances. The New York Philharmonic quickly discovered the joys of price discrimination: "Associates" were allowed to attend Friday afternoon rehearsals, which grew into a series of concerts for ladies' at that hour. The Philharmonic faced appreciable competition from Jullien's orchestra, and later from Theodore Thomas. The Philharmonic's cooperative organization lacked strong leadership, while Thomas recruited his musicians carefully, paid them well, and gave them opportunities for solo work. By the 1870s the pool of first-rank orchestral musicians around New York was large enough for the Philharmonic to withstand Thomas's competition to recruit musicians. Where it suffered was in the quality of its product. Thomas's programs were not only more serious and balanced, but also surpassed the Philharmonic's in quality of performance. The Philharmonic could not upgrade by replacing its existing members, because its cooperative status gave members a property right. It could not require its members to attend rehearsals regularly and to pass up profitable outside jobs as they arose. Thomas at times served as conductor of the Philharmonic, and by the late 1870s the two orchestras' personnel overlapped appreciably. But the cooperative organization form showed its intrinsic limits for sustaining high levels of performance.

The Philharmonic also faced new competition. Leopold Damrosch had briefly conducted the Philharmonic in 1876–1877, but fell before rivalry from Theodore Thomas. Damrosch proceeded to found his own Symphony Society of the City of New York, differentiating his programs from the Philharmonic's through an adjunct chorus, the Oratorio Society. This orchestra (an entrepreneurial venture, but one that benefited financially from Damrosch's social connections) was taken over by Walter Damrosch on his father's death. In the space vacated by Thomas's departure for Chicago, the Symphony Society competed successfully with the Philharmonic, thanks to top players imported from Europe, as well as to Damrosch's venturesome programming (French repertory added to the German musical diet) and showy choices of visiting musicians (such as Tchaikovsky in 1891).

The upgrading of orchestras' quality in the nineteenth century had numerous causes, some exogenous to any city's local scene. The introduction of the romantic symphony raised the optimal size of the performing orchestra and the virtuosity required of musicians. Improvements in brass and woodwind instruments made more virtuosic playing possible. Improvements in transportation made soloists of international repute available (although with their fees bid up accordingly). These changes also speeded the rise of the virtuoso conductor, a scarce talent able to command substantial rents.[4] An important goad for improving performance quality in any one city was visits by high-quality orchestras, which for New York included Theodore Thomas's Chicago Symphony and Victor Herbert's Pittsburgh Symphony. The greatest challenge to the Philharmonic's level of performance quality came from annual visits to New York of the Boston Symphony, the prototype of what was to be the dominant form of donor-supported nonprofit organization.

The Entrepreneurial Nonprofit Organization

The Boston orchestra had been founded in 1881. It long thrived on one donor, Henry Lee Higginson, who hired top players and conductors and insisted on both regular attendance by the players and strict priority over any outside engagements. A Pops season was invented and added in 1885 to extend the musicians' employment. The rate of pay and length of season were unmatched by any other U.S. orchestra. Whatever deficit resulted (never less than $20,000 a year) was made up by Higginson, who had both wealth and musical training, and who over 33 years picked up cumulative annual deficits of $900,000. Higginson leveraged his charitable outlays by recruiting a club of other wealthy Bostonians to fund the construction of Symphony Hall in 1900, on the tacit understanding that he would continue to fund the flow deficit.[5]

In New York the Philharmonic did not lack for potential wealthy backers, but the cooperative organizational structure resisted major upgrade. It was marked for abandonment in 1908, when a wealthy donor group ("the Guarantors") not only proposed to cover any deficits for three years and to seek an endowment, but also brandished the (credible) threat to form a new orchestra if the Philharmonic did not open to an infusion of new players. The orchestra's membership was overhauled substantially, and Gustav Mahler was brought in as conductor.[6] A large bequest by Joseph Pulitzer in 1912 contained provisions that triggered the formal abandonment of the cooperative organization in favor of a donor-supported nonprofit form. The reformed Philharmonic continued to benefit from rivalry for social position between its own backers and those of the Symphony Society. Nonetheless, competition between donor-supported New York orchestras did not long prove viable. Several hostile factors emerged at the beginning of the 1920s. A third competitor surfaced, the New Symphony Orchestra (subsequently the National Symphony), with its own coalition of wealthy backers and the remarkably talented composer Edgard Varèse as conductor. Varèse's good looks did not long offset the backers' distress at the new music that he programmed, but he was replaced by the able Willem Mengelberg. The Philharmonic and the other orchestras all faced a problem of increasing costs of players and soloists, as competing bids for this talent came from newly energized orchestras in a number of U.S. cities. Finally, the conductor recruited for the Philharmonic after Mahler's death, Josef Stransky, was popular with audiences and a good administrator—but he was a relative lightweight in the competition to upgrade performance and hence by 1920 a source of stalemating controversy in the Philharmonic's board. From the latter nineteenth century, as the conductor became a dominant administrator, orchestra boards faced a constant tension between picking crowd-pleaser conductors who sold tickets and solid types who appealed to critics and sophisticated music lovers. As a result, the two tended to alternate.[7] The board chairmen of the Philharmonic and National orchestras finally worked out a merger that made Mengelberg the dominant musical force, with Stransky eased out and more than 50 Philharmonic players losing their jobs.[8]

After the consolidation of the Philharmonic and National orchestras, and of their respective wealthy boards, the amplitude of funds led to a considerable expansion of the orchestra's activities to summer concerts, young people's and college concerts, broadcasts and recordings, and a program to encourage American music. The orchestra was enlarged to 111 players, and top conductors such as Arturo Toscanini and Wilhelm Furtwängler were brought in. These expenses outran the orchestra's earned revenue, however, and the deficit made up by the donor group ballooned from $100,000 to $150,000 at the start of the decade to $700,000 by the 1927–1928 season. This led to a merger with the remaining competitor, the Symphony Society, in 1928. The merger pushed the donor clubs together and forced a sharing of titles, but that solution apparently appealed more than the alternatives of lesser performance quality and donations sustained at rates needed to cover two orchestras' fixed costs.[9] The subsequent adjustment permitted a reduction in donations (from the total for the two orchestras together), as well as an increase in the activities of the combined orchestra (tours, education programs, and pension benefits for players).[10] The Depression forced further mutual adaptation of donations, earned income, and expenditures in such an organization. Conductor Toscanini proved a strong draw, but earned income still declined by 30 percent from 1929–1930 to 1934–1935, while total expenses were reduced by 20 percent through cuts in the orchestra's size, the length of the season, and the salaries of conductors and performers. The annually financed deficit rose 66 percent but was still only 26 percent of total outlays. After World War II the regularly financed deficit settled at a level around 20 percent of the budget.[11]

The outcome in New York was essentially the same as in all other U.S. cities: a dominant symphony orchestra organized on a nonprofit basis and dependent on a club of donors for a substantial share of annual revenue. In some cities such as Cleveland and Los Angeles, the organization sprang from the efforts and wealth of a single individual in the mold of Higginson. In other cities (Chicago, Cincinnati, Philadelphia, and San Francisco) a club consisting of numerous guarantors came together to launch the organization. As with New York, the competitive effect of a superior visiting orchestra was a common catalyst (for example, the Boston Symphony in San Francisco in 1915).[12] A coalition successful at the outset need not stay together. The initial compact cannot prevent free-riding, and coalitions were severely tested by the Great Depression. Finally, one interesting exception is Washington, D.C., where an orchestra did not attain a firm footing until 1948; this one-industry town lacked the local commerce and moneyed society needed to form the requisite club.[13]

European Patterns

The rivalry of institutional forms also played itself out in major European cities. They provide a comparison to New York, especially as both faced the same enhanced opportunity created by new styles of composition and improved instruments. Musical performance in Europe had traditionally enjoyed aristocratic patronage for private consumption, but the rising middle-class audience for public performance was a new development that posed no less of an institutional-building challenge than it did in New York. During the period 1830–1848, the number of announced public concerts per year about tripled in London and Paris, growing less rapidly in Vienna only because of an earlier start there.[14] The cities' populations were growing, but the number of concerts per capita more than doubled. Their sponsorship was diverse: individual musicians, formal and informal groups of performers, cultural societies, music periodicals and music publishers, charity organizations, theatres, and fledgling impresarios. Demand for concerts was sustained by the popularity of music-making and amateur musical skills in the bourgeois household, which was also associated with the profusion of inexpensive printed musical scores, including arrangements suited to household performing forces and skills. Demand for music teachers was correspondingly enlarged.

In the 1840s the bulk (45 to 66 percent) of the concerts in these three cities were "benefit concerts," meaning that they were presented for the benefit of the principal performing musician or musicians, who might be touring virtuosi or the local player making a regular annual splash. Local musicians performed in each others' benefit concerts, and these also served to consolidate client groups who employed the musicians as teachers and performers in private salons. For local performers, benefit concerts were sufficiently competitive that they probably depended on an indirect payoff from promoting the musician's teaching and other services.[15] Other concert styles included permanent groups of professional musicians that were predecessors of the great symphony orchestras, organized as loose cooperatives in the manner of the early New York Philharmonic. Novelty and virtuosity were the reigning virtues of music performance. The division of labor between composer and performer was just emerging, along with musical scores calling for the large, modern symphony orchestra proficient in performing them. The idea of an established canon of classic compositions was a revolution yet to come (see Chapter 22).

Each city enjoyed an ascending quality of classical-music concerts that involved, as in New York, consolidation and tendencies toward one dominant organization. Whereas the benefit concerts were intrinsically one-shot affairs, the new model required some kind of ongoing "club" relationship for members of the audience, a development facilitated by the construction of larger concert halls with reserved seating and price discrimination among ticket buyers. Audience involvement was necessary for upgrading, although not sufficient. At least in London, the losers were ingrown organizations with closed audience memberships and modest musical standards. They had started out with substantial amateur contingents of performers (players and audience overlapping), employing the practices shown to limit performance quality in New York: rotating leadership and a continual flux of substitute performers—the deputy system under which regular players could send substitutes to rehearsals and even performances when they found better-paying engagements. The deputy system was efficient given that all musicians' jobs were casual and part-time, but it clearly capped the level of performance that a group could achieve.[16] Their musician members enjoyed parity in the organizations, and no one had the authority to weed out weak players.[17] The successful performance societies that became dominant were studded with members from the liberal professions, elite civil servants, and some leftover aristocrats. In contrast to New York, the businessmen-patrons tended to be happy with the antique model of the traveling virtuoso's concert of bonbons.[18] The really important contrast to America, however, was the failure of the donor-supported, self-perpetuating nonprofit organization to emerge, although the European orchestras eventually found a substitute in ongoing government support.

The process of upgrading performance in London benefited from various musical entrepreneurs of Theodore Thomas's variety. Michael Costa became the regular conductor of the Philharmonic Society in 1846. He was a strong technician and drill master whose organizational skills at eliciting high-quality performances from large forces were displayed in oratorio performances at the time of the Crystal Palace Exhibition (1851). Louis Jullien resided in London from 1838 to 1859, purveying his polished pops-oriented programs. Charles Hallé, when invited to Manchester to take over a moribund "Gentlemen's Concerts" series, insisted on having the authority to hire and fire and on regular membership by his musicians; like Theodore Thomas, he took his group on extensive tours through northern England to cover the fixed costs of full-time employment. Henry J. Wood, director of the Queen's Hall Promenade Orchestra, was one of the major upgraders (although not until 1904 did he manage to end the deputy system).[19] Entrepreneurial efforts provided cheap concert seats in ever-larger arenas such as the Crystal Palace, where the resident orchestra, conducted by August Manns, provided a mainstay supply of music from 1855 to 1901.[20] Seaside resorts, notably Bournmouth, ventured into public subsidy of an ambitious orchestra as a tourist attraction.[21] Music publishers stepped in as entrepreneurs to organize orchestra concerts, or to offer regular but temporary support.[22] Individual concerts enjoyed subventions from wealthy patrons, often in the name of some charitable cause. But England never achieved either European-style sustained government support or the American-style permanent donor-supported organization. The country lacked not only performing organizations but also music schools, which developed on a hand-to-mouth basis to generate an ample supply of provincial music teachers, but few musicians of high aspiration or achievement.[23] The supply of music depended on the public's willingness to pay by subscription, and this willingness never sufficed to support the upgraded quality that required long-term employment contracts and an end to the deputy system.

The pattern continued into the twentieth century, as shown by the history of the London Symphony Orchestra. Formed in 1904, it continued the tradition of a players' cooperative that accepted the deputy system, but it aspired to (and sometimes achieved) high standards of performance. It suffered a good deal of internal tension as it periodically sought to remove underperforming players.[24] It also sought now and again to deal with the adverse effects of the deputy system, which grew more problematic during the Depression as the musicians chased whatever paying engagements they could find. One unsuccessful approach was to establish a nuclear "permanent orchestra" surrounded by a fringe of "associates."[25] External pressure to improve performance quality came not so much from the box office, which could be placated by conservatizing and popularizing the repertory, but from outside employers such as record companies and film studios commissioning soundtrack recordings.[26] The London Symphony also faced competitive pressure from other orchestras bidding for musicians, especially the British Broadcasting Company orchestra, organized in 1930, which offered full-time employment. Pressure also came when Sir Thomas Beecham organized the London Philharmonic in 1932, subsidizing it from his considerable personal fortune.[27] Personal and corporate patronage were continually sought. But those who paid the pipers invariably wished to call the tune, and conflict ensued.[28]

John Mueller noted that upgrading moved less rapidly in Europe than in the United States. He speculated that the difference might be due to an interesting interaction of elements. The United States had ample immigrant musicians whose baggage contained the new romantic ideal of the composer as a revered creator. As for the audience, the United States lacked a musically sophisticated middle class, but placed great bundles of wealth in the hands of persons interested in cultural consumption of the highest quality. Some of the newly rich knew enough about music to give resources and authority to conductors and other musicians able to reach the ascending heights of musical performance. Competition to make successful cultural investments clearly helped.[29]

Fixed Costs and Upgraded Quality

This evidence clearly shows the motive of upgrading musical performance to be the force that brought the donor-supported nonprofit organization to dominance in the United States. Changes in music composition styles and innovations in musical instruments created the room for upgrading, and this form of organization seized the opportunity in a process of Darwinian survival. This conclusion needs alignment with Chapter 14's analysis of high fixed costs (along with contract failures) as a propellant for nonprofit organizational status. If improving performance quality requires a rise in the fixed-cost component of the total costs of performance, the case is closed.

The answer is clearly affirmative. All of the upgraders saw the core of their task as establishing a regularly and exclusively employed body of musicians. To compete with free-lance commercial opportunities for musicians required higher pay arriving more dependably. The cost of musicians was converted from a variable to a fixed cost. Placing the power to hire and fire in the hands of a musical director imposed a risk that the musician did not face in the early cooperative organizations, one that required a compensating benefit in higher and more secure pay while employment continued. The positive association between quality and fixed cost should not be over-generalized, however. Chapter 5 showed that the film industry's disintegration improved the quality of cinema films by allowing the right bundle of specialized inputs to be assembled for each project. The studios sloughed off considerable fixed cost. Opinions differ on whether the one-shot Broadway team or the repertory company is the best way to achieve quality in staging plays. While the relation between quality and fixed cost is important, it depends closely on the technology for improving quality in the art realm.

Creating and Sustaining Nonprofit Organizations

The major symphony orchestras offer some insight on the rise of donor-supported nonprofit organizations (NPOs) in the performing arts. Their case suggests that the free-riding problem, to economists the scourge of this organizational form, is somehow brought to heel. The empirical evidence on what happens when people actually face the problem needs to confront economists' theoretical expectations. The reasoning proceeds along the following path: In situations commonly found in the performing arts, conventional profit-seeking firms might not generate maximum social benefits. They might charge too much, settle for inferior quality, or fail to produce some creative goods at all. (These points were explained in Chapter 14.) Donor-supported NPOs can in principle repair the deficiencies. Conceptually we could add up the benefits to consumers of each ameliorative NPO, along with the economic cost of the inputs that it employs, and determine how many NPOs should exist. The difference between this ideal population and the actual body count of NPOs then identifies the cost to society when clubs are not founded when they should be, or when free-riding shrivels the flow of continuing donation support. This hypothetical shortfall cannot be pinned down empirically, so we approach actual behavior from the other end, by asking how NPOs are created and sustained *at all*. If people make little headway against the pitfalls of forming and sustaining NPOs, the missing part of the NPO population is likely to be large. If society turns out clever at beating these problems, the shortfall may be small.

Motives of Potential Donors

Economic theory bets no chips on intrinsic human goodness and assumes, as a first approximation, that each family acts selfishly to maximize its own benefit. With that presumption laid down, it then hears appeals from alternative views of people's preferences. People may get utility from altruism, from feeling better when they know their neighbors can hear the performances of an excellent symphony orchestra (that is, a pleasure beyond any net benefit they themselves get from attending). People may get utility from the warm glow that they enjoy upon making their donations (and upon seeing their names in the program booklet). Incidentally, the altruism and warm-glow motives sound the same, but have quite different implications. If the government steps in to subsidize a performing-arts organization and expand its activities, the altruist finds his donations less needed and cuts back. Public funding need not diminish the donor's warm glow, however, so private donations might not be displaced.[30]

Altruistic motives tell us little about the organizational problems of NPOs, because they explain only why rational and self-interested individuals will write checks for good causes. NPO clubs get formed in social contexts, however, which focuses attention on how potential donors might behave as groups. Suppose the community includes N households, each wishing that the town had a good symphony orchestra. Specifically, for the privilege of buying tickets (priced at their marginal cost) over the coming years, each household would be willing to contribute an endowment of at least x. If some number of the households n ($n < N$) each contributes x, creating an endowment of nx, the orchestra is feasible; without the endowed coverage of fixed costs, however, no ticket price will bring in enough revenue to cover costs, so no orchestra is formed. A civic leader now proposes to collect pledges of x that become legally binding commitments to contribute to the endowment, once n households have pledged. Some households might hold back, hoping that enough others will contribute to bring in nx. But then there is no orchestra. Since each gains more than x benefit by coughing up x for the endowment, it is irrational to hold out. So forming the club initially should be feasible, and it gets easier if a contribution generates esteem from others who have already signed their pledges.

This story focused on donations for endowment, because it makes the formal assumptions of the argument quite plausible. Everybody knows the total sum needed, and everybody can observe how many pledges are already in hand. The same analysis applies if the problem is raising donations annually to cover the year's fixed cost, although it might differ in empirically important details. Many costs are discretionary for an ongoing performing-arts organization, and the total contribution needed is not a hard number. Nor can other people's willingness to contribute be observed. Nonetheless, the same "principle of reciprocity" can potentially work: we will contribute x if $n - 1$ other households do the same.[31] It should matter for the viability of the NPO whether social linkages among donors can ease these tasks of lining up pledges and monitoring the reciprocity process.

Donations in Social Context: Nineteenth-Century Boston

The upgrading of symphony orchestras through the creation of NPOs rested, as we saw, on clubs formed among wealthy individuals. Paul DiMaggio's study of nineteenth-century Boston demonstrated how that process can beget and sustain NPOs in a string of arts organizations, each subject to the common hazards of free riding and contractual failures.[32] By mid-century the Boston Brahmins had developed a taste for quality in creative products: the "nobility of art and vulgarity of mere entertainment." Also in place was a tradition of sending their young to be "finished" among the cultural treasures of Europe. Furthermore, they had a head start over other major U.S. cities in founding and sustaining NPOs for just such purposes. Foundation and support of earlier organizations—such as Harvard University, the Boston Atheneum, the Handel and Haydn Society, and Massachusetts General Hospital—had not been broadly based in the community, but it had established the institution of the nonprofit corporation with a self-perpetuating board of directors. Board membership both recognized past contributions of money and effort and imposed a contingent obligation to contribute funds as cur-

rently needed. Self-perpetuation contains the threat of inbreeding and ossification, but it also imposes an obligation on the member to see long-run
projects through to completion—as if board members held social equity
shares that would fall in value if the institution's level of performance were to
erode.[33] Finally, this governance structure was able to deal with diffuse and
changing goals, because it was surrounded by a continuous implicit negotiation over just these matters in the interested community.

The financial base favored institution-building in the latter nineteenth century, as Boston's count of millionaires rose from "a handful" in 1840 to
around 400 in 1890. DiMaggio also argued that the Brahmins' loss of political control of the city intensified the incentive to rely on high-culture NPOs
as the means to achieving shared objectives. The Museum of Fine Arts and
the Boston Symphony Orchestra, the main progeny, centralized cultural and
artistic activities in institutions that could define artistic quality. The museum
sprang partly from a number of individual collections of objects looking for
permanent homes.[34] Its charter (1870) followed from a desire of the trustees
of the Atheneum, who were negotiating with other decisionmakers, to set
a mainly educational role for that institution. Boston collections avowedly
lacked highly important works of art in quantity, so the consensus on the museum foresaw its use as a fulcrum for their acquisition. The orchestra long was
Higginson's personal fief, but his success with its development rested on a
deeper social contract. In Boston as in New York, less able orchestras initially
provided competition. Higginson made a peace treaty with the Handel and
Haydn Society. Two others—the Philharmonic Society and the Harvard Musical Association—both had their supporters, but Higginson's own position
and dedication enabled him to tough out their complaints of predation.

Similar scenarios played out for many other American orchestras. They
found generous supporters, guarantors, or other individuals whose support
was substantial but irregular. But such people can lose interest, go broke, or
die. The organization then sought to regularize a "friends" group, and was
on its way to donor-supported NPO status.[35] The donor-supported NPO
does not guarantee permanence, although its track record is good; Kate
Mueller studied 27 U.S. symphony orchestras from their founding (or 1890,
whichever was later) to 1970, finding only eight episodes of shutdown (from
one to seventeen years) among seven orchestras.[36] Such boards may be short
on influence over the organization's policies, with power resting de facto in
the managers or an insider subgroup. Yet the boards of larger and more complex organizations have typically included larger proportions of members
with business and law backgrounds, and smaller proportions of artists and
educators.[37] While self-perpetuation of these boards has its well-known hazards, the service motive that impels financial support also promotes the selec-

tion of new directors to maximize the NPO's long-run value. That incentive seems to dominate among the larger and more successful NPOs, and it is abetted by the value that some corporations perceive in placing their executives on prominent boards.[38]

An interesting case study is the Los Angeles series of "Monday Evening Concerts" of contemporary music, which flourished with a highly informal organization. It drew on a large pool of free-lance musicians, who enjoyed ample well-paid performing opportunities and would accept engagements with this group for a pittance. Donations were elicited, apparently with ease, from a tight-knit audience group.[39]

Charity and Implicit Contracts

The historical cases clearly indicate that NPOs emerge from clubs formed in a social context of continuing interchange and (perhaps) competition for rank and esteem among potential donors and beneficiaries. The context provides for the punishment of free riders and the balancing of favors over time (reciprocity) needed to sustain private support of collective or group benefits and to deter one-shot selfish actions by holding out the continuing benefits of cooperation. This benevolent pattern seems obvious enough, once stated, but some of its working mechanisms are subtle. This is shown by studies of philanthropy involving both arts organizations and other charities.[40]

The evidence starts with the observation that the wealthy do behave altruistically and feel an obligation to make gifts. Francie Ostrower compiled a roster of large donors to 48 institutions in New York City, finding that she had picked up no less than 82 percent of the New Yorkers on the *Forbes* list of the wealthiest Americans residing in New York. If the altruistic motive is strong, there remains the question how donations get allocated among competing organizations. The crucial point is that large donors do not simply sign checks. They are themselves active fund-raisers and members of NPOs' boards of directors. Of Ostrower's large donors, 75 percent (of the random sample interviewed) serve on an NPO's board, 60 percent on more than one. Seventy-eight percent raise money for one or more organizations.[41] The NPOs benefit from the tradition of the nonworking wife, because giving by women is strongly associated with "volunteer work." For cultural and other NPOs the tradition has generated a large supply of skilled white-collar labor that lacked any other socially accepted outlet. Although present-day employment patterns undermine that tradition, the female proportions of NPOs' board members are increasing strongly, so that women's human resources available to NPOs may be transformed rather than reduced.[42]

The altruism of these large donors is not abstract and generalized. They regard the recipient social and cultural institutions not only as providers of merit goods, but particularly as a social infrastructure serving themselves and people of similar situations and interests. The organizations' outputs generally are not strictly public goods, but the network of institutions provides a set of options and opportunities that are public goods in the sense that the exact benefits they will provide and the identities of future beneficiaries are unknown.[43] The altruism of wealthy donors is clearly slanted toward the needs and interests of people like themselves, but for Ostrower's interviewees any taste for exclusiveness was strongly tempered by a welcome for donations of "new money."[44]

Board memberships reward large donations by conveying both prestige and decision rights. While board members who are appointed to reward donations need not prove the most effective monitors, they do sustain (as DiMaggio noted) an interest in the organization's long-run value as a social asset. That long-run outlook is evident in the way dynastic families socialize their offspring in the role of charity.[45] Because of the board's residual responsibility for the flow of donations (both steady-state and to make up random shortfalls), the membership system also motivates donors as fund-raisers and promoters. Their governance and fund-raising services leverage the effect of their own donations and increase the utility gained therefrom. This linkage among decision rights, social equity in the organization, and fund-raising responsibility affects the allocation of donations among the competing NPOs through a process of reciprocity: you contribute to my favorite charity, and I shall remember yours. Wealthy donors not only allocate their own dollars, but also through impetus and conviction affect the distribution of other donors' funds as well.[46] An obvious but subtly relevant fact is that cultural NPOs and their donor clientele are geographically localized, so that reciprocity and rank-order tournaments for social contribution tend to increase total donations and raise all the NPO boats in a metropolitan area, not just reallocate fixed pools of resources among them.[47] Ostrower found that most donors focus their funds on a small number of institutions, except for tit-for-tat contributions.[48]

Corporate Charitable Contributions

The preceding analysis of individuals' donations to cultural organizations and other NPOs suggests that the problem of forming and sustaining clubs of donors is solved through reciprocity and impetus working through a network of social obligations and competition. What about corporations' charitable contributions? The profit-seeking corporation has no interest in its social esteem per se. A purely profit-seeking business enterprise will contribute to cultural and other charitable NPOs to the extent that its own expected profits are enhanced.[49] A donation that raises profits must either lower its cost of production or increase the demand for its product. The obvious source of lower costs is a reduced reservation wage for the employees it hopes to recruit and retain. Living and working in a particular city grows more attractive as the infrastructure of cultural and other NPOs improves. More people choose to locate there, or fewer to move away to other cities. People's choices depend on both the prevailing wages and the living conditions as affected by the NPO infrastructure. A better infrastructure hence lowers what a firm must pay to recruit any given number of workers. The higher the skill and education levels that a firm needs in its employees, the stronger are workers' tastes for NPO-supplied cultural and other services. The high-skill firm gets a higher payout and makes larger donations.[50]

The demand for a firm's products might expand when knowledge of its good works enhances customers' goodwill toward its products. The consumer who benefits from a cultural NPO and finds herself otherwise indifferent between two brands of gasoline rationally buys from the firm that donates to the NPO. Less plausibly, the consumer, if uncertain about the quality of a firm's product and unable to evaluate it perfectly even after purchase, might infer that a soulful corporation that gives to charity would not wittingly offer a poor-quality product. If the firm's charity also gives utility to its managerial decisionmakers, additional factors affect donations. Personal tastes of the firm's managers for cultural or other charities (whether altruistic or not) can be gratified using the stockholders' money.

Peter Navarro's statistical test confirmed that most of these factors help explain the rates of charitable spending by a sample of large corporations. Firms' contributions clearly serve their profits by reducing costs, enhancing demand, or both. Firms for which labor accounts for large shares of their total costs make larger contributions, although they cut back if located in a large city where many other firms share in the support of cultural and other NPOs. Firms that court public goodwill through advertising also seek it through charitable contributions.[51] Companies whose managers likely can use corporate funds to warm their own charitable glows, however, do not contribute more. Finally, in some cities clubs have been formed to encourage contributions by corporations domiciled there, and these clubs in fact significantly enlarge donations. Thus, the club-membership mechanism that matters so much for personal donations seems to work in corporate society as well.[52]

16

Cost Disease and Its Analgesics

The economic features of creative industries on display in this part of the book are easily confused. The problem is not that arts organizations incur fixed costs, but the size of these costs relative to the public's willingness to pay. Donor-supported arts organizations run into free-rider problems, not because nondonors' exclusion is infeasible, but because their exclusion via a closed-membership policy hampers other creative objectives. The "cost disease" addressed in this chapter—consequences of the performing arts' lack of access to productivity gains—also needs a label warning about confusion. Performing-arts organizations' operating deficits are often blamed on their ineluctably rising relative costs. As Chapter 15 showed, that view misunderstands the donor-supported NPO, which really addresses the problem of high fixed costs by means of a sort of two-part pricing system. Yet the cost-disease problem does have an indirect relationship to the fixed-cost problem: given that much of the typical performing-arts project's cost is fixed, the cost disease pushes it relentlessly in the direction of facing problems of covering fixed costs.

Effects on Real Costs and Quantities of Creative Product

The main question is whether the cost disease will shrink the creative sector. As Chapter 14 showed, it might, if the negative effect of rising relative costs and prices is not offset by positive effects from rising incomes and income-elastic preferences. There are also questions about how activities in creative sectors get reorganized in response to sustained cost-disease pressures. Although the cost-disease vise closes relentlessly, at a rate driven by the average rate of labor productivity in the rest of the economy, it bestirs many sorts of adaptations and adjustments as artists and organizers in creative industries try to evade the problem. However welcome their analgesic efforts may be, they complicate quantifying the cost disease. We cannot just measure the increasing real cost of the average play produced, if producers dodge their dilemma by selecting plays that require fewer sets and actors. The change in average cost per symphony orchestra concert is ambiguous if orchestras have been reducing the time players spend in rehearsals and increasing that spent in public performances.

With that problem in mind, we can review some data that document the cost disease. For a group of regional theatre organizations, real cost per performance rose 1 percent annually during 1974–1983, while real cost per audience member rose 2.2 percent. During that same period symphony orchestras' real cost per performance rose by 0.9 percent, while cost per attendee rose 2.2 percent. The difference between the two cost-inflation measures reflects the fact that both groups of organizations increased the numbers of performances that they offered, attempting to spread their fixed costs but lowering the proportion of seats sold at each performance. Major symphony orchestras were then implementing a commitment to year-around employment for their players that involved increasing the number of performances, and during 1974–1979 real costs per performance actually fell. These organizations take the form of donor-supported NPOs analyzed in Chapter 15, in which the fraction of costs covered by donations (apart from unexpected shocks in the short run) rests on a conscious policy decision. We would hence not expect the fraction to show a trend, and for the theatres it indeed fluctuated without trend.[1] Symphony orchestras did show a steady increase in donations' share of revenue in the 1960s and 1970s. It is reasonably interpreted as an exogenous increase in the supply of donations, although major donors (notably the Ford Foundation) were influenced by the plight of symphony musicians suffering from declining real incomes.[2] An analysis of 25 major symphony orchestras (fiscal years 1972 to 1992) showed a small increase of income earned from performances as a share of total revenue (64.0 to 65.5 percent), while the short-run deficit (after subtracting grants and donations) fell from 5.4 percent to 5.0 percent. Real average ticket prices rose 143.4 percent overall, 95.8 percent for multi-concert subscriptions.[3] Since statistical evidence indicates that rising prices depress attendance, and people's spending on tickets rises only a little faster than their incomes, these data suggest that the typical arts organization had decreasing economic room for covering its fixed costs.[4]

To an economist accustomed to humdrum industries, analysis of the effect of cost disease on a creative sector seems straightforward. Potential customers will buy certain amounts of creative product at any given price. Each firm (actual or potential) incurs a certain structure of costs (fixed and variable). Depending on how the firms compete with one another, some number will "fit" into the market. If one more enters, it (and the rest, for that matter) will fail to cover its costs. The cost-disease problem implies that, with market size held constant, the number of viable firms will decline over time. This generally useful way to study viable firm and market size unfortunately breaks down in creative activities, because of the pervasive vertical differentiation of creative goods. Does a count of books published include the one printed at the author's expense and given away to friends and neighbors? Does the minimum public concert include two amateurs playing a piano duet? For any one time period, drawing a line to define a population of credible creative products is tricky enough. Determining whether such an arbitrary count has risen or fallen over time is near hopeless.[5] The most insight comes from informal evidence on how creative activities adjust in the face of cost-squeeze pressures.

Broadway and Regional Theatre

The New York stage play makes a choice case to study, partly for Broadway's reputation as a "fabulous invalid," but even more because it defines a type and quality of creative product that stays comparable over time. A decline has certainly occurred in the number of new productions per season—for musicals, from a maximum around 48 in the late 1920s to around 15 in the 1960s and 9 in the 1980s. New straight plays numbered around 35 in the 1950s and 1960s, half of that in the 1980s.[6] The information available on whether or not shows recoup their investments ("hit" or "flop") points directly to the cost disease's site of infection. A stage play has a relatively simple cost structure—a fixed cost to mount and rehearse, followed by a stable running cost from week to week.[7] The cost disease increases both components, without an equal increase in the public's willingness to pay for tickets. Fewer plays can cover their fixed costs, and fewer are produced. Play-goers have fewer choices, which means that more of them seek tickets for the average play that does light the marquee, and longer runs are feasible that recoup fixed costs and yield profits for some plays. A direct indicator of the squeeze therefore is the number of performances needed to recoup. What matters for revenue is tickets sold rather than number of performances, but a play that in its early weeks does not run close to capacity (taking account of the exogenous variation in demand between weekend and most weekday shows) will not recoup in any case. The long-run increase in the recoupment period is clear. Around the time of the Civil War, a run of two to three weeks was a smash hit. By the latter 1920s, when the annual total number of Broadway productions peaked, the average play ran 70 performances (115 for musicals). Recoupment then was achieved in five-and-one-half to eight weeks. By the 1960s the average run had increased to 150 for plays (over 300 for musicals), while the number of productions had declined. Even though recoupment times in these various periods cannot be compared directly, they clearly must have increased for the longer average run to be consistent with a smaller number of productions.[8] Had recoupment periods stayed constant, profits from longer average runs should have induced more productions. The change over time implies that the average fixed costs of mounting shows increased more rapidly than the weekly operating surplus, which was confirmed by direct evidence. In the 1920s that relationship took an upward jump when actors first came to be paid for rehearsals as well as performances, shifting the risk toward producer and investors. Over the long run, though, the increase of fixed costs was concentrated in costumes and sets, which suggests an upgrading of production standards.[9]

Adjustment to the cost disease could in principle have followed two complementary courses. Suppose that producers (individually and as a group) could with some accuracy rank unproduced plays by their likely commercial success. They would select for production those more likely to succeed. When the cost squeeze tightened, they would pass up the less likely chances, and the proportion of plays that flop would decline. Alternatively, suppose that they can only sort unproduced manuscripts roughly into those with some chance and those with no chance of success. Plays that get produced are drawn randomly from the former group *(nobody knows)*. The squeeze causes fewer productions of plays with some chance of success. As previously explained, play-goers have fewer choices; more of them see the average play that opens. Suppose that they divide their visits between hits and flops in the same proportions as before. Suppose that the recoupment period doubles. Then the number of performances of the average flop (by definition, less than the recoupment number) will also double, as will the number of performances of the average hit. Suppose, instead, that flops are known immediately after opening night, when the critics voice their opinions. Then the average flop's business increases less than the recoupment period. The average hit's run has to increase proportionally more than the recoupment period, in order for investors on average to get the same rate of return.[10]

These cases yield an important empirical prediction. With the cost squeeze in progress, either the flop ratio falls, the average length of run rises for hits (proportionally more than the run length for flops), or both changes occur in complementary amounts. The pattern is clear. Between 1945 and 1990 the flop rate fluctuated around its average value (80 percent) with no discernible trend. The flop rate for musicals fluctuated around its average value (76 percent) with no trend, except possibly for an increase in the 1980s.[11] The increase contradicts the predicted change, though it is easy enough to explain, if investors needed some time to convince themselves that musicals' expected returns had fallen as low as they had. The prediction of a reduced flop rate of course defies the adage that *nobody knows*, and the prediction's failure reaffirms its doleful truth.[12] The predicted increase in run length can be tested indirectly. Between the 1920s and 1960s the number of theatre-weeks (number of theatres lighted each week, summed over weeks of the season) fell by about one-half, but the number of productions declined about three-fourths, so run lengths on average increased substantially.[13] Between 1920 and 1990 only 63 Broadway shows (all types) ran more than a thousand performances, and all but six of them opened after 1940.[14] For musicals that opened between 1945 and 1990 we can separate run lengths for hits and flops using data collected by Bernard Rosenberg and Ernest Harburg. Averages were calculated for the first ten seasons, 1945–1946 through 1954–1955, and the last ten, 1980–1981 through 1989–1990. The average run for flops was 102 performances in the former period, 120 in the latter. The average runs for hits were 633 and 870. Thus, the flops' run length increased by 18 percent, the hits' by 37 percent. The pattern is consistent with producers selecting their plays with little ability to predict success, while flop status is typically known early in the run.[15] An incidental confirmation of this trend lies in the increased importance of the general manager who supervises day to day operation of a continuing show, and the incentive compensation that now goes with the job.[16]

Substitute Creative Products

The cost disease is usually portrayed as a race to claim economic resources, in which the creative sector with no access to productivity gains loses out to the humdrum sectors with scope for steady improvement of productivity. Of course, productivity has risen enormously in the creative sector, if we define its output as consumption experiences per consumer of its goods. Motion pictures deliver entertainment much more cheaply than did vaudeville, and television and videocassettes eliminate the cost of travel to the site of consumption. Compact discs and contemporary phonographic reproduction equipment not only reduce the resource cost of hearing a given musical performance, but also make available, in passable sound, performances by musicians long deceased. Cheap reproductions of paintings by Picasso and Matisse brighten many a dorm room. Even within a given performance technology, innovation has helped. The powerful sonority of the iron-framed, cross-strung piano, developed in the latter nineteenth century, much enlarged the concert hall in which a keyboard performance could be heard and enjoyed. Performers and consumers who have invested heavily in the refinement of their tastes may bristle at any paean to these indirect experiences of creative consumption. But just as vertical differentiation allows some to choose a better experience at a higher price, in these cases technical change offers a lesser experience at a much lower price. Those terms have appealed to many consumers. Hence, the apparent cost-disease problem in practice is due largely to the substitution of cheaper forms of creative consumption that have benefited from productivity gains, rather than the substitution of cheapened humdrum goods for creative goods overall.

The distinction is important for thinking about the fate of creative activities (stage plays, live concerts of classical music) that lose out in these substitution processes. A squeeze afflicts the noninnovating sector because, at any given price for a creative product, some (perhaps many) consumers will prefer the cheaper version. There is a possible offset, in that the cheaper technology for creative consumption assists people's early investments in creative consumption, which they may choose later to upgrade to the high-priced venue (Chapter 11). Another form of substitution, however, also gnaws at the creative sector on the losing end of such technical innovations. The revenue productivity of its creative personnel is greater when they collaborate with high-productivity technology for delivering creative consumption; that sector can pay them more and bid them away from live performances. The creative activity that wants productivity gains gets squeezed on both the supply (cost) and demand (price) sides.

This guise of the cost-disease problem appears throughout the long interaction between live and filmed performances. The first encounter occurred not in the New York center but in local entertainment markets around the United States. Before 1870 the dominant theatrical unit was the resident stock company, whose manager owned or leased the theatre, employed a company of actors, and directed the plays (insofar as they were directed). Occasionally traveling stars—English actors such as Edmund Kean—might be employed, with ticket prices elevated accordingly. The extension of the railroad network, which allowed much faster and cheaper travel, led to a quality-improving innovation—the traveling "combination company" that took a single play from city to city. Local stock companies gave way, declining from fifty in 1871 to seven or eight in 1880, and New York served as the site for organizing combination companies.[17] Before 1900 there were at least 2,000 theatres in the United States outside of New York. Live theatre then encountered the innovation of motion pictures, a technical novelty available at perhaps one-fifth the price of a stage-play ticket. Vaudeville's variety shows were particularly at risk, since its skits and routines were close substitutes for the entertainment offered by early one-reel films. Furthermore, theatre buildings were easily converted from stage to screen entertainment. The number of theatres in the United States shrank 56 percent between 1910 and 1925, and the average number of productions on the road fell to about 70 in the early 1920s.[18]

The concentrated Broadway theatre did not find its customers and venues snatched away, but it did face substantial competition for its actors and other creative talent. By the time feature-length films replaced one-reelers (the 1910s), stage actors were being offered (depending on stardom) $1,000 to $5,000 a week at a time when Broadway salaries could at most have been $500 to $600 weekly; furthermore, Hollywood's paychecks arrived regularly, but Broadway's came only when the actor was performing (stage actors were not yet paid for rehearsals). Film work could be done in summers and thus complement stage acting, but there was a clear net drain of talent and increase in reservation wages.[19] In 1929 the arrival of talking films brought a new surge of demand for Broadway talent, because many stars of the silent screen lost their glitter when they became audible. The average differential between Broadway and Hollywood pay had not diminished, and in 1934 the head of Actors' Equity estimated that 70 percent of all film actors came from the stage. Directors and playwrights were also attracted. Network radio by this time also exerted a pull on acting and writing talent.[20] Skepticism initially prevailed among playwrights as to whether Hollywood was friend or foe to their interests in stage production (see Chapter 6), but it became clear that stage production increases the value of scripts for subsequent film production. The goodwill won by the play promotes the film, and even those who had seen the play might well also view the film.

Sound movies stepped up the demand for literate scripts, and from 1928–1929 on, about one-fifth of each season's new plays were sold for screenplays. That demand rose again during World War II, when the loss of star actors to the military raised Hollywood's willingness to pay for strong story material; between 1941 and 1945, 27 percent of Broadway plays were sold.[21] The large rents to the playwright from film production indeed led to a bargaining down of the producer's share of the author's subsidiary-rights income to 40 percent from the 50 percent that had once prevailed.[22] In the 1920s Hollywood's average payment for a script was about large enough to cover the cost of producing a modest play, and small and unpopular theatres were sometimes rented for the purpose of stretching out the stage run to enough performances for the producer to share in subsidiary income.[23] This complementarity between stage play and film only mitigated Hollywood's squeeze on the stage's demand and costs, but stage production long retained its value as a primer for sale to Hollywood. In 1965 an estimated $15 million was invested in Broadway and Off-Broadway plays, $2.3 million in losses were incurred from the stage productions, but $11.5 million was received for film rights.[24] The puzzle is why the stage production should yield an increase in the story's value for film production enough to offset its own expected loss. A veteran filmmaker viewed the reduced risk as worthwhile, but of course the stage production's losses fall at least partly on the producer and his financial backers.[25]

One response of the Broadway stage to the rising popularity of cinema films was to upgrade the quality of the product that it offered. In the mid-1920s Broadway saw many shoestring productions casually assembled, partly to fill the excess capacity of stages that followed a building boom in theatres. The flop rate surged briefly when talking pictures arrived, and these productions disappeared. A substantial turnover occurred in the leading Broadway producers as a different group, specializing in shows of higher quality, entered.[26] The mechanism parallels the process by which Hollywood later upgraded its own output to differentiate it vertically from televised entertainment.[27]

Other Adjustments on Broadway

Whether the disease comes from inaccessible productivity gains or the rise of cheap substitutes, the performing arts have ways to fend off the consequences. One is in the selection of plays for production. Hilda Baumol and William Baumol reported that the average cast sizes of Broadway plays declined 50 percent between 1946 and the 1980s, and they conjectured an increase in single-set plays that require no stagehands for shifting scenes.[28] A surprising innovation of recent years, however, is the high-cost blockbuster musical that attracts enormous audiences and can be taken by touring companies around the nation, and indeed around the world. The surprise comes because a cost-squeezed sector producing differentiated products likely turns to varieties with lower fixed costs. When an activity with high fixed costs grows unprofitable in its current configuration, however, a possible response is to escalate the product's fixed costs greatly, on the chance that demand will shift outward so much that the activity becomes profitable. Technically, that means uncovering a range of outlays on improving and promoting the product that are subject to previously unknown increasing returns. The profits from the successful experiment depend not just on uncovering these increasing returns in the form of hoards of willing customers, but also on being able to serve them effectively at variable costs less than their willingness to pay.[29]

Just such a strategy lies behind the run of blockbuster musicals associated with composer Andrew Lloyd-Webber, producer Cameron Mackintosh, Livent Inc., and Disney Studios (for example, *Cats*, *Les Misérables*, *Ragtime*, and *The Lion King*). These ventures depart in numerous ways from the fragmented system of one-off deals that has long prevailed in stage plays (and

since the 1960s in cinema films). The most obvious element lurks in their resemblance to blockbuster films—the high fixed costs expended on sets and
exotic special effects. *Cats* required a $2 million renovation of its Broadway
theatre, and *Ragtime* cost Livent $2 million to stage in New York even fol-
lowing a Toronto production. This splurge on production costs is coupled
with levels of sales promotion far beyond Broadway custom. For *Ragtime*, $2
million was spent prior to the New York opening. The advertising for *Cats*
emphasizes its logo and never quotes critics' evaluations.

A second element in the strategy for blockbuster musicals is the revival of
touring companies. Modern technology makes these shows' special effects
portable, and a touring company incurs a lower fixed cost than the original—
for *Ragtime*, $8 million rather than $12 million.[30] The source of increasing
returns to heavy sales promotion is obviously its national and international
reach to a huge potential audience. This saturation comes from both the direct diffusion of messages and the news coverage won via the "buzz" that
these theatrical events generate. To ensure large flows of net revenue from
touring companies, the enterprises have resorted either to owning selected
large theatres in major cities or to negotiating partnership arrangements with
chains of independent theatres. Either form of vertical integration can prevent hold-ups by theatre owners, and the purchase strategy might yield some
rents that would otherwise go to independent theatre owners. Livent followed the purchase strategy (perilously, it appears). Pace Entertainment employs the partnership, combining it with the sale to theatre-goers of season
subscriptions to a series of musicals. This arrangement requires it to keep
enough shows aloft to satisfy its subscription commitments in the 31 or so
cities where it operates.[31] Both arrangements depend on transactions internalized to a degree quite outside Broadway's traditional mode of organization. They do, however, recall the natural-monopoly element in the coordinated booking of a series of performers to a series of venues (see Chapter 3).

The third element lies in the nature of the shows themselves. They depend
mainly on concept and special effects, and not on the charisma of individual
star performers. This property facilitates setting up road companies that replicate the initial show, and it also eases the adaptation of the shows for
nonanglophone audiences around the world. International road companies
multiply manifold the revenue directly generated by the initial successful production. By mid-1997 *Cats* had taken in $329 million on Broadway, but its
worldwide box-office gross was $2.2 billion.[32] Finally, because the show is
not star-dependent, its rents stick to the entrepreneurial producer or creative
team and do not pass to the performers. Disney's approach varies this formula by recycling the creative elements that have already been successful as
cinema films *(Beauty and the Beast, The Lion King)*.

The profits of these ventures have been impressive for a cost-squeezed industry; Lloyd-Webber, for example, has achieved a worth of $600 million. Nonetheless, their long-run success remains to be seen. Lloyd-Webber's production company sustains its own high fixed cost (at one time, a staff of 60 employees) for the very specialized task of producing his musicals. His *Sunset Boulevard* ran for two and one-half years in New York before closing, but it lost money because both its fixed and its running expenses were so high. Worldwide, it lost $20 million.[33] Despite pooling risks over several shows and relying on revivals such as *Showboat* (arguably less risky than new musicals), Livent suffered a financial crisis, a change in control, and eventually bankruptcy.[34] A veteran of the old Broadway system providentially observed that New York producers have learned to live with an 80 percent flop rate, whereas Livent's strategy required a 20 percent rate to succeed.[35]

Cost Squeeze in the Theatre

While the Broadway stage has retreated and adapted to the cost squeeze in expected ways, performing groups organized as donor-supported NPOs have to some degree defied it and expanded. Accurate counts of their activity levels over time are unavailable, but signs of life are clearly evident in Off- and Off-Off-Broadway theatre, regional and community theatre, and also symphony orchestras in smaller cities. Only part of the Off-Broadway theatre sector is formally organized as NPOs, but projects undertaken effectively as artists' cooperatives and/or with vanishingly small expectations of economic profit lie close to the NPO model. To suggest that NPOs have somewhat defied the cost squeeze is not to assign them magic-bullet status. NPOs provide a way for consumers to contribute to covering fixed costs, and artists to donate or subsidize creative work on terms acceptable to them. The cost disease proceeds without limit, however; starving artists eventually do either starve or depart for the humdrum labor market, and donors to NPOs have their own reservation prices for the efficacy of their contributions.

Regional and Noncommercial Theatres

Regional and community theatres went through at least two surges in the twentieth century. They blossomed from 50 groups in 1917 to 500 by 1925 and over 1,000 by 1929, only to fade during the Great Depression. Most were started by entrepreneurs with creative objectives, who were inspired by the grand European state-supported theatres and put off by the featherweight fare of the touring combination companies. They sought to perform unusual plays. They usually employed a repertory format, to improve acting standards and also because their distance from New York's centralized market discouraged casting different actors for each play produced. Other noncommercial motives included bringing theatre to the workers and giving voice to leftist causes. Actors and managers settled for submarket earnings in exchange for artistic freedom—the artists' cooperative mode of nonprofit organization (Chapter 14). Jack Poggi noted the high mortality and turnover of these organizations.[36] Generally lacking the continuity of donor-supported NPOs, they could be wiped out by one production that flopped. On the other hand, success was also a hazard. It unleashed a drive to improve quality and build an institution. That elevated fixed costs and vulnerability to future negative shocks. It also opened the way for disputes among the cooperating talent, each having suffered through lean times and holding strong views about the proper uses of prosperity *(motley crew)*.

Another cycle of regional theatre organization followed World War II, with the number of companies soaring from a handful in the 1940s to 226 in 1992.[37] Some of them had achieved long life as NPOs supported by donors and foundation grants. In Joseph Zeigler's study these fell roughly into two groups.[38] One group sprang from local theatre visionaries (not New York fugitives) eager to direct plays. They began on a shoestring and worked mostly or wholly with unpaid volunteer actors. Talent and energy were devoted to directing and not to administering, but the survivors were those leaders who knuckled down to the administrative role and built a local operations base of patrons and supporters. When the Ford Foundation was actively assisting such groups in the 1960s, it correctly spotted the importance of supporting individual leaders, rather than theatre companies as such, and encouraging them to travel and learn tricks from each other; some grants were discontinued when the energizing individuals left or were ousted from their companies.[39] Again, success posed the hazard of having to choose among creative preferences—undertaking more challenging plays, obtaining more skilled (and costly) performers, bestowing Actors' Equity wages on those who had toiled for no pay. Those companies that did build supportive boards of directors had to choose between members who believed in the entrepreneur-director's creative work and those with greater potential for raising resources. Again, several collapses occurred when audiences deserted theatres that offered increasingly esoteric repertory. Most people go to the theatre to be entertained, while society's sufferers, cherished by many directors, do not attend.[40] This trade-off was demonstrated in a study that measured the conformity of each theatre's choice of plays to those most commonly chosen by the other regional theatres in the sample. The less conforming ones were more likely to fail during the ten-year period of observation. Among the survivors, the more conforming were able to increase the shares of their expenses covered by earned income; the less conforming flourished only if they successfully attracted donation support (so their earned-income coverage could fall while their budgets still grew).[41]

The other group of regional theatres identified by Zeigler managed to start with contractual arrangements that guaranteed some access to resources. In the best cases, the theatre gained a dowry of donor-supported NPO status and a good chance for a long lifespan. The founding contract that guaranteed resources also tended, however, to install an "establishment" board that might lack strong sympathy with the director's aesthetic objectives. The director either managed the board sensitively, or conflicts and turnover of directors occurred. For both groups of theatres Zeigler noted a geographic pattern, with the pioneers located away from New York in the Midwest, West, and South. Diffusion to the East Coast cities, with their stronger cultural traditions, actually came later. This pattern prevailed despite the advantage that proximity to New York held for recruiting actors, so the dominant spatial influence must have been theatre-goers' (and theatre buffs') lack of easy access to New York's theatre agglomeration.[42]

Regional theatres have had an ambivalent attitude toward doing new plays. Against the cachet of novelty stands the hazard of the flop rate, and the NPO does not readily collect the rents to a successful experiment with a new play that goes on to profitable productions elsewhere.[43] Nonetheless, regional theatres gain at least esteem and pride from mounting a play that transfers to Broadway.[44] The arrangement has a clear option value against the traditional method of trying out Broadway plays in their full professional stagings before opening them in New York. The regional theatre production provides the option of continuing to Broadway while sinking a lower cost.

Off- and Off-Off-Broadway

With local monopolies, and the sometimes-astute use of the donor-supported NPO, many regional theatre companies have proved viable if not necessarily stable in the face of the encroaching cost disease and cheaper forms of entertainment. New York's stratified theatre market differs in how it faces intense competition from other theatrical offerings. It displays a three-tier vertically differentiated structure that rests legally on talent-guild and craft-union agreements that implement price discrimination on behalf of the employee groups: higher minimum or contract wages where the theatre's revenue-productivity is greater. The stratification is based, naturally enough, on the theatres' seating capacities. This explanation for the stratified structure is sufficient, but probably not necessary. Smaller theatres permit proportionally lower fixed costs. They make viable productions with specialized appeal and/or esoteric and experimental fare that attracts theatre professionals and buffs. As with the regional theatres, they have no ultimate solution to the cost-disease problem, but they have evaded the erosion of the commercial branch.

The Off-Broadway sector grew rapidly in the late 1940s with an influx of would-be actors from school and military service eager for theatrical work and experience. They involved themselves in projects at little or no pay and with skimped production values. Some experiments were highly successful, often with good plays that had been mangled on Broadway or intimate musicals that benefited from smaller houses. The press began to take notice. Eventually a large share of serious drama relocated to Off-Broadway, where it had no less access to Hollywood's market for potential film scripts.[45] The productions' formal organization was typically for-profit, but in hope more than expectation. In the early 1960s three-fourths of the aggregate investment in Off-Broadway productions was being lost, and eleven of twelve plays failed to return their investments.[46] Apart from *art for art's sake,* it was economically efficient to perform the more risky experiments Off-Broadway, where fixed and sunk costs were low, because the option of a transfer to a larger Broadway theatre in a more opulent production usually lay open. The apprentice element in the wages of Off-Broadway actors is recognized in their contracts, which allow them to quit with two weeks' notice if something better comes along (on Broadway, contracts are normally for the run of the play).[47] For ongoing groups the usual dynamic of creative success was evident: increases in cost due to elevated quality and the selection of more challenging plays, leading to increased chances of flops, followed by the company's disappearance or reversion to more commercial material.

Off-Off-Broadway catered largely to the theatre professionals and buffs. It served as the strictly experimental wing, motivated by figures such as Peter Brook and Jerzy Grotowski. In 1972–1973 the median total outlay of a sample of Off-Off groups was only $23,000 ($85,000 in present-day purchasing power). Forty-two percent of the companies did not pay their actors, and about 70 percent of Off-Off actors went unpaid. Box-office receipts covered only one-third of Off-Off budgets, with government and foundation grants important in the balance. The work was largely unknown in the United States outside of theatre circles, but was internationally recognized among the professionals.[48] This vertically differentiated theatrical sector has an intrinsic logic that is independent of the cost disease (to which Off-Broadway ultimately is just as susceptible), but the diversion of activity away from Broadway to venues that are nonprofit in either intent or result is a consistent adjustment to it.[49]

Cost Squeeze and the Symphony Orchestra

Symphony orchestras in the United States have long employed the NPO form, ranging from stable donor-supported boards for the major orchestras to cooperatives of largely amateur musicians in local community orchestras. Organizations in the smaller cities have by no means been in steady retreat.

Consistent long-run counts are not available, but a large number were formed in the prosperous decades after World War II.[50] By 1971 the American Symphony Orchestra League counted 291 orchestras with some regular annual budget (college-based orchestras omitted). Among the league's budget-delineated categories, the number of "regional" orchestras (bracketed between "major" and "metropolitan" or city orchestras) grew from 16 in 1975 to 39 in 1987. This group is vulnerable because it spans the transition from "night services" to "day services" by its members: that is, from amateurs and part-timers who play in the orchestra outside their regular jobs to professionals working mainly as symphony musicians, though perhaps with part-time side jobs. A regional orchestra grown from a lesser organization hence experiences a large increase in pecuniary fixed costs. Its donors do not always prove up to the task, with macroeconomic conditions posing hazards and the cost squeeze continuing. At least two have expired, and several others have been at the edge.[51]

Among major symphony orchestras, the squeeze has had many consequences. The musicians who make up these orchestras are anything but contented artists (for reasons noted in Chapter 1), which has led to repeated strikes and aggressive demands for better terms of employment.[52] These terms have taken the form of increased rates of base pay (many players receive negotiated pay rates higher than these bases) and of commitments to pay for the whole 52-week year and not just for a shorter concert season.[53] The latter change increased both the orchestra's total budget and its fixed proportion. Additional performances that can occupy the orchestra through the year (minus paid vacation) incur lowered marginal costs, so managements in search of the needed increment of revenue sought to add additional season performances, summer programs, tours, "run-outs" (day trips) to nearby cities, and private concerts for commercial sponsors.[54] Other orchestras have used the increase in players' services to invest in goodwill by dispatching individual players on outreach programs in local schools, churches, and other organizations.[55]

Recording contracts have at times been important sources of revenue for U.S. symphony orchestras, but a declining demand for classical records and the accumulation of past performances on good-sounding compact discs have constricted this flow. Although the differential has shrunk over the years, American orchestras cost 40 to 50 percent more to record than their European competitors. They have priced themselves out of the market, since the orchestra itself does not contribute much to the differentiation or distinctiveness of the resulting record. The conductor and soloist (where applicable) do, but those talents jet around the world and can be backed by whatever orchestra of suitable competence offers the best deal. The American Federation of Musicians has not seen fit to allow a price cut, although at one time the Utah Symphony had an arrangement for members to receive most of their recording-session pay as it was earned from royalties on the records.[56] The Philadelphia Orchestra's loss of a recording contract with EMI that backed a guarantee of $6,000 annual income for each musician led to a bitter strike in 1996, and in the settlement the "guarantee" came to depend on the orchestra's earnings from records.[57] Another entrepreneurial venture was the Louisville Orchestra's distinguished program to record new or previously unrecorded contemporary compositions. For a number of years this series broke even after factoring in the substantial foundation grants that the program attracted. The musicians were paid the standard union fee for the recording sessions, which substantially supplemented their incomes. There was, however, a negative effect on the orchestra's local audience, which had its ears stuffed with music that was not only contemporary but also sometimes of less than the highest quality (which perhaps explains why it had gone unrecorded?).[58]

Orchestras have increasingly organized the pursuit of donations, but their supply is ultimately limited. The coalition of donors that averts free-riding and sustains the social equity of fund-raising board members (Chapter 15) depends on an integrated network of "society," whose members once bought season subscriptions to the orchestra's concerts and made it a focal point of their activities. Nowadays, lessened interest or more diversified activities have fractured this network. Orchestras have responded rather successfully by selling menus of short subscription series at some cost in the complication of their program-building. Their sustained flow of donations is threatened, however, because organized but impersonal appeals for donations to more casual audience members will likely prove less revenue-productive than did the social network.[59] Orchestras' long-run fate will depend on several interacting trends. Will rising incomes favor or deter concert attendance as a substitute for cheaper but lower quality music consumption? Will NPOs grow more skilled at extracting donations? Will musicians' collectively bargained wages resist compression in real terms?

V

The Test of Time

Creative goods typically contain some durable and reusable core—if not the creative good itself, then the template from which it is made or distributed (*ars longa*). Keeping the work for future users incurs storage costs, but the full cost of reproduction need not be repeated. The template can travel to permit consumption in far-flung locations, perhaps incurring transport costs but (again) not the full cost of reproduction. Chapter 17 lays out many implications of these durability properties, and the remainder of Part V develops some of them in detail.

The intangible artistic element of a creative good incurs a fixed cost for the artist—it does not vary with the number of copies produced from it. The creative good's asking price hence tends to exceed its marginal cost. Any use or performance of a creative good tends to spill promotion benefits on its owner by enlarging demand. These two propositions together explain many practices that receive the label of payola (Chapter 18). The same pair of propositions explain something very different—the corporate ownership links (vertical integration) that arise between firms that produce creative goods (TV programs, for example) and those that provide distribution channels for them (broadcast networks and cable systems). Rather than buy a presentation of a creative good, its owner buys the presenter and makes it a regular conduit for distributing its creative output (Chapter 20).

Consider the composer who holds copyright in her song and can legally demand compensation whenever it is played in public, recorded, or otherwise performed. More than other artists, she faces the problem that many listeners will value her creation, though each in only a small monetary amount. Efficient collection of these many small lumps of rent poses an organizational problem. Copyright collectives have arisen around the world to pursue these rent streams for the artists and their publishers. As Chapter 19 shows, these collectives pose a dilemma for public policy, because they increase the efficiency of royalty collection yet act to some extent as joint monopolists for the artists. Efficient collection of rents is also a declared objective of conglomerate media firms that assemble humdrum businesses engaged in making successive uses of creative templates. These organizations carry a tough burden of proving their value, because each template's independent owner has an excellent alternative—to auction off use of the template in each market or venue to the highest bidder (Chapter 20). An auction is a very efficient way to extract maximum value, so the conglomerate is hard-pressed to squeeze more from it.

Durable creative goods (which include most of the visual arts) pose two economic problems—covering their storage costs, and arranging trades (or rentals) to put them in the hands of their most eager owners (users). The efficient performance of these tasks depends on numerous market participants and institutions. In the visual arts they include collectors, secondary dealers, auction houses, and museums. Here the gatekeeper function for contemporary art continues as a diffuse filtering process—what to keep, what to throw out—that determines the accumulated stock of recognized art objects and its distribution. To understand these processes we can regard them in two ways: how they work, and thus what biases or distortions might creep into the filtering and allocating process (Chapter 21); and how they respond to major disturbances that change the stock of durables or shuffle many of them into different hands (Chapter 22). New creative works compete with the accumulated stock for consumers' attention. Some art realms have evolved canons of recognized masterpieces that threaten to close off access to new contenders, while in others contemporary creations enjoy advantages over their predecessors.

17

Durable Creative Goods: Rents Pursued through Time and Space

Economists take the typical market to resemble that for freshly baked bread. The product is not durable, so the market repeats and adjusts to a new equilibrium each day. Bread is a private good: my consumption leaves no crumbs for you. Creative goods commonly differ somewhat in both properties. The *ars longa* property flags the durability of creative elements—the visual artist's painting, the author's book, the film or recording of the artist's performance. The owner of a durable creative good can store and retrieve it periodically, to beguile new consumers or refresh the golden memories of others. That access to reuse over time parallels the creative product's status as a proprietary public good at any point in time. The owner can—more or less simultaneously—pursue its rents among a number of distinct markets. Those markets may be fenced off by national or other boundaries, or separated by transforming or repackaging the product in a way that differentiates it from the core creative good or its other embodiments. To put it pretentiously, this section of the book addresses the pursuit of creative goods' rents through time and space.

Durability of Creative Goods and Its Implications

Physical Preservation

To yield value or satisfaction over time, some core component of a creative good must be durable, and people's taste for it must persist. Both conditions are necessary for economic durability. A sculpture in stone or bronze can be viewed by only so many art lovers at one time, but with appropriate protection it will last indefinitely. Those who enjoy viewing it today impose no opportunity cost on those who wish to view it tomorrow, or in one hundred years, beyond the cost of the physical storage site. The sculpture contrasts to a work of visual art on paper, such as a drawing or watercolor, that suffers

271

some degradation from each exposure to light. It has a limited lifespan in public exhibition, so that those who view it today do impose some opportunity cost (beyond the storage cost) on future viewers.

The preservation of creative goods faces an economic test: the cost is warranted only if benefits to future viewers or consumers are sufficient. Who does the "thinking" about those costs and benefits is a close question. On the *nobody knows* principle, consumers are ill-equipped to value experiencing some durable creative good, even as they cross the threshold for that purpose. A creative durable's owner can hardly foretell consumers' interest in experiencing this good in the future. Whoever incurs the cost of preserving creative goods must risk their value to future consumers. Not only is the investment risky, but also the public-good problem complicates collecting from future consumers, even if each enjoys a real benefit. Two solutions prevail. One is altruistic or public-sector investment in storage (museums, libraries), undertaken out of regard for the interests of future consumers, but with no assumption that they will pay up to cover the accumulated storage costs. The other is commercial speculation by the owner of a durable creative good (who might or might not be its original fabricator), who incurs storage costs hoping to recoup its accumulated value from future consumers. Film libraries and master recordings generally rely on commercial investors, but part of the job falls to nonprofit organizations. The physical preservation of old cinema films has exacting requirements, and the Museum of Modern Art has (with the aid of donor organizations) made extensive investments in preserving film archives whose copyrights had expired or whose rights holders expected no positive return from preservation investments. Museums and private collectors both preserve works of visual art. The revival of interest in an artist or school that has been out of fashion regularly draws large quantities of the objects onto the market.[1]

Many creative wares pass through stages of fabrication on their way to consumers, opening an economic choice of the best stage in which to store them. A book might be preserved in its original manuscript form or (nowadays) in machine-readable storage, or printed copies may be held in a library. It costs more to store the book than the diskette containing its text, but producing a fresh copy from the diskette is also costly. Musical scores are preserved either in their original form or embodied in the recording of a particular performance. The dollar that it might cost a library to store a book for a year may someday exceed the cost of preserving it electronically and producing a copy on demand. Sometimes the opportunities of the creative durable's owner are limited by competitive storage. The textbook's publisher hopes to profit from selling it to successive generations of students. The book is durable, as is the copyrighted manuscript. What the publisher can charge next year's students depends on the storage supplied by those who buy used texts from lighthearted students who have just completed their final examinations. To circumvent competitive storage, the publisher might rent rather than sell the book—not a common choice in practice. More usually, the publisher sets a price that recognizes each book's prospect of reuse; the student then regards his textbook cost as the purchase price minus the (discounted) expected recovery from the secondhand sale. And, of course, the publisher prods the author to undertake frequent revisions to capture the subject's latest nuances and to speed the depreciation of the stock previously sold.

Cheap reproduction and storage are not necessarily in the artist's economic interest, because rarity can increase collectors' willingness to pay. Original prints are published in editions of sizes that may reflect technical limits, but more commonly signal an economic choice of the number of impressions that will maximize value for artist and publisher. Video art has posed a problem because most artists have conceived video works as unique, but the collector pondering the unique work's price tag reflects on the ease with which videocassettes are duplicated.[2]

The future revenues of the investor in storage also depend on the additional inputs needed to bring durables to life for the consumer. Storing works of fine and decorative art is costly to the museum, but such works need only dusting when they again go on view. Music manuscripts and published scores cost little to store, but they serve the listener only after musicians have devoted rehearsal and performance time. The chances of a newly produced creative good successfully surviving in the world's recognized stock depends, besides its intrinsic quality, on the size of these transformation costs relative to the enjoyment value for the consumers who are served. The visual artist should worry about art museums' operating costs, while the composer's hopes rest on the future wages of musicians (see Chapter 22).

Storable templates allow easier and more accurate replication for some creative goods than for others. The manuscript of a book is definitive. A modern-day musical score leaves the trained musician in little doubt about the composer's instructions, although pre-nineteenth-century scores provide decreasingly complete instruction as they recede into the past. Composers once assumed that all music held only contemporary interest and hence saw no need to write out instructions of the day's performing tradition. Performances of early music therefore rely heavily on imaginative reconstruction. Finally, choreographic compositions can be recorded in dance notation, but the resulting instructions at best leave much to be determined when they are revived.[3] Before the advent of videotape, the survival of choreography depended heavily on performers' memories. Before the phonograph became popular, jazz had nothing but its performance tradition.[4]

Taste and Value of Durability

The economic storage of creative goods depends on the values that people assign at different times to their consumption or enjoyment. How customers value old or classical and contemporary works differs greatly among creative industries. The regularly performed body of classical music has hardened over time, as the concept of a masterpiece took hold and the core of accepted classics became more and more incontestable for new compositions (Chapter 22). Older stage plays, perhaps because they frame human relationships in forms tied to particular times and places, compete less successfully with their contemporary counterparts; the main competition for *Cats* does not come from *Twelfth Night*. One study of Broadway theatre in the seasons 1920–1921 to 1930–1931 found that almost all of the ten longest-running plays of each year were sentimental fluff that could never be taken seriously today. Among plays that ran for 100 or more performances, however, were the best-known works of Eugene O'Neill, Philip Barry, Sidney Howard, Maxwell Anderson, Elmer Rice, and Robert E. Sherwood—the authors whose works still excite interest in competition with present-day plays.[5]

That pattern leads to the question of how much time and exposure the market needs to arrive at a consensus view of the quality of currently produced creative goods. Part of the myth of the romantic artist holds that creative geniuses are ignored and rejected in their own time, only to win honor from posterity. If everyone agreed that this were true, it would pose a nasty problem of cultural storage. Everything must be saved until time's rivulets leach out the masterpieces. High costs would be incurred to store much dross, in order to keep the masterpieces' options alive, or high costs of resuscitation and performance would be lavished on the screening process. How these predictable costs should be shared, when they offer only very small probabilities of large payoffs (because so few masterpieces ultimately emerge), is hard to imagine. Fortunately, given *infinite variety*, the bulk of evidence suggests that contemporary gatekeepers do a fairly good job. Artists and their durable works that ultimately enter into the canon are usually popular or at least recognized in their own time. Vermeer did slip from sight, but van Gogh's works became popular within a decade of his early death, and Beethoven's popularity came immediately.

Trade in Durable Creative Goods

The values of durable creative goods depend on their rates of physical and economic depreciation. As with the world's stock of automobiles, as a first approximation the culture stock's economic value does not depend on exactly who owns which piece of it. Purchases and sales of individual items obviously leave the total stock unchanged. Yet they matter a great deal to the individual owner, who benefits in two ways from the opportunity to trade her holdings. She can adjust her stocks of durable creative goods, as part of the process of managing the size and composition of her portfolio of humdrum and creative assets (a source of current income and also a buffer of disturbances affecting income and consumption). A common adage among art auctioneers is that the supply of works on the block is driven by death, debt, and divorce. A more subtle benefit from trade in creative durables lies in the opportunity to speculate on changes in the value of components of the stock. An English pre-Rafaelite painting passes from collector A, who expects its value to remain low, to collector (or museum) B, who expects the school to rise in value and esteem. Even though the two expectations cannot both prove correct, the two parties are subjectively better off from the opportunity to trade and increase the expected values of their wealth.

Although the opportunity to trade is valuable to the market's participants, trade in durable creative goods is limited by high transaction costs. These stem from *infinite variety*. Each unit is distinctive, and determining a work's current value requires cumbersome and subjective comparisons to other articles in its class. Even works that have identical siblings, such as original prints issued in editions (of, say, 50 examples), command different values, due to variations in condition and provenance as well as random factors. A study of auction prices for prints found that examples of a given work traded within 30 days of one another show a spread of values on the order of 30 percent.[6] This spread cannot be apportioned between real differences in condition or provenance and random factors, but each no doubt weighs in substantially.

One reason why it matters who owns the stock of creative durables is the owners' differential abilities to collect the rents that these stocks can continually generate. This factor is evident in some mergers that occur in the book publishing industry. A publishing house is a rather odd bundle of assets for a corporate merger transaction. It has no factory. Its key personnel are highly mobile and likely to walk out the door in the ensuing reorganization. The backlist of previously published books appears the main tangible and specific asset that influences the occurrence and pricing of such mergers. Publishers enjoy economies in promoting backlists and current publications jointly, which could support changes in control that center on the redistribution of backlists. The ratio of in-print backlist titles to the year's frontlist might be fifteen to one,[7] and so the efficient physical distribution of books is strongly affected by the handling of the backlist, even if most promotional effort goes to the current season's titles (see Chapter 9). The recent reorganizations of the assets of the Hollywood film studios have been strongly influenced by trade in film libraries (Chapter 20).

Scale economies arise in managing a backlist. Their source lies in *infinite variety,* the large number of creative goods (popular songs, books), and the small economic scale of individuals' one-by-one decisions to draw upon individual creative goods. The singer selects one song at a time, the disk jockey one record, the reader one book. The economic rents to creative durables come (if at all) in many small lumps. The organization problem is to pool storage and/or to standardize the collection of these rents because many of them are too small to merit individual negotiation. Given the efficiency of standardized terms, economies of scale arise in applying the same system of pricing and collecting rents to similar small transactions in multitudes of creative goods. Chapter 19 addresses these economies in the collection of performance royalties for popular songs.

Wherever they are important, scale economies keep numbers of transactors small, and with few transactors prices are unlikely to be competitive. Creative industries suffer from another disease that distorts prices and extracts its welfare costs: contract failure, which causes parties to resort to conventionalized prices that are "sticky" and usually out of equilibrium. These conventionalized prices likely fall out of line with agents' marginal costs, and they generate their own variety of smelly deals. When the performer of a popular song has been pressed to pay a performance royalty that exceeds the marginal cost to the song's copyright holder (zero, the song being a proprietary public good), the individual copyright holder grows willing to bribe the performer to warble his song rather than somebody else's. The bribe grows if the performance spills other benefits to the copyright holder, such as stimulating the purchase or recordings or sheet music. Chapter 18 traces some of the consequences.

Durability and Creative Inspiration

The durability of goods is partly an economic choice. An automobile can be designed to run trouble-free for a longer period of time, but at higher cost. The extra service it can provide must be balanced against the increased cost, especially since the cost is incurred now while the benefits come later. Freely reproducible creative goods pose no such problem of physical durability, although the artist willing to stake a bet on future aesthetic standards might take steps to increase the stylistic durability of her work. Physical durability does matter for the fate of visual artists' work, forcing its consideration upon the artist.

Some art writers have argued that the scale and configuration of contemporary art objects are not independent of the architecture of the contemporary museums where the artist hopes her works will dwell. Their expanses of white wall space with neutral lighting invite sprawling works that lack the self-contained property of the traditional representational painting in its beaux-arts frame. Expansive works are integral to the space around them and call out for an exclusive visual turf. The standard gallery of contemporary art, now a "white cube" rather than the simulacrum of an opulent home, abets this creative strategy.[8] The traditional framed picture was a window onto a scene, and such pictures could be stacked and packed in salon exhibitions without the works violating each other's visual integrity.

Spatial Markets for Creative Goods: The Trip through the Galaxy

Explaining the Sequence

Just as rents to creative durables can be pursued down the corridors of time, so can they be sought in one market neighborhood after another. That *ars longa* has its counterpart in spatially or otherwise differentiated markets is illustrated by cinema film distribution (Chapter 10). The core creative element that can survive unimpaired from decade to decade similarly can be exploited in successive markets without draining its life's blood. For proprietary public goods, the cost of achieving and embodying the original conception need not be repeated when the creative good is taken to new markets. Better yet, it is often self-promoting. The producer's advertising generates a stream of messages aimed at potential customers. These messages are targeted to particular groups (in location or demographics). The promotional arrows, however, fly off in somewhat random directions. Many strike consumers uninterested in the current embodiment of the creative good (a cinema film, say), but who may remember it when some other window of presentation is opened for the good (cable TV, videocassette). Promotional spillovers bestow a second blessing on the producer of a successful creative durable. Indeed, the creative good's owner enjoys yet a third blessing via the mechanism of buzz. People like to talk about creative goods (Chapter 11). Members of the community of personnel (both creative and humdrum) directly involved in their production constantly review creative goods' competing merits. The *A list/B list* mechanism provides a sufficient explanation for this use of their time and conversational resources. The buffs talk about them to update their large stocks of cultural consumption capital. Because consumers (buffs or not) welcome information on creative goods, the media present stories and information about them that function as free advertising for the creative good's owner. In short, creative outputs with elements of proprietary public goods enjoy a built-in advantage for arbitrage from one market to another.

For the creative good's owner who pursues rents to remote venues, the mechanism of buzz has several implications. The dynamic of collective cultural consumption (Chapter 11) implies that only a few creative goods at a time bask in the limelight of buzz, and they turn over with a frequency that reflects the pace of cultural digestion as well as the arrival rate of newly buzz-worthy cultural goods. There is thus a superstar mechanism at work in the leverage of buzz, whereby the merely intriguing falls before the truly sensational. The creative durable's owner has only modest leverage for elevating its buzz level among consumers—his sales-promotion outlays and his choice of timing in relation to buzz-worthy competing creative goods. The mechanisms of spillover and buzz hence bestow a blessing, although a highly unpredictable one.[9] After all, negative buzz can accompany the ten-ton turkey on its way to slaughter.

The mechanisms of promotion spillover and buzz clearly imply some sequence that is most profitable for the creative good's owner—succession of venues, time elapsed between each opening. The venue that generates the greatest spillover benefits has a strong case for coming first, with the others trailing behind it. This influence is independent of another sequence-determining factor indicated in Chapter 10—price discrimination, which posits serving the most eager consumers first and the more patient ones with more price-elastic demand later, but for a lower price. The price-discrimination and promotion-spillover mechanisms probably run together in practice. What distinguishes buffs from ordinary consumers is the buffs' eagerness to consume the latest creative good, and their lesser willingness to substitute one such good for another. Their demands tend to be price-inelastic. They are also active buzzers. For the humdrum consumer, however, one TV movie may be about as good as the next. The spillover mechanism might explain some features of the sequence that the price-discrimination story cannot, such as the time elapsed between when a U.S. film opens in North America and when it opens in other countries. If the United States exports buzz as successfully as it exports movies themselves, the sequence makes sense.

Licensing Spinoffs

Complex creative goods such as cinema films and television series not only require a *motley crew* of inputs, but also can deliver a stream of outputs separable from the main product and able to yield rents elsewhere. An example is the toys based upon characters or devices shown in cartoons and live-action films. Because the creative elements are often carried to an industry or market very different from the one for the primary creative good, the transfer usually involves some licensing arrangement between independent firms. These rents ride on the goodwill asset built up with the viewer of the original creative product. Entertainment experience delivers utility not just at the time of viewing but also in the pleasant haze of subsequent recollection. In the manner of a souvenir, a licensing arrangement ties the stimulation of fond memory to some independent consumption good and raises the consumer's willingness to pay for the souvenir good. The tie may be obvious, such as a toy replica of a film's action figure. Or it may involve an unrelated good, as when purchase of meals from a fast-food chain gives access to free or discounted toys or videocassettes. With the souvenir value, the toymaker sells more units (or gets a higher price) than without it. The burger chain sells more burgers than if it had not offered the tied souvenir. The owner of one creative intangible can write a franchise contract to extract some of the extra revenue pulled in by the toymaker and/or the burger chain.

The holder of the copyright to a licensable character, if perfectly informed about the rents it can earn for a licensee, will proceed as follows. Calculate the present value of the extra revenue that the licensee can earn by incorporating the licensed element or concept. Calculate the present value of any extra costs incurred to incorporate the element, and subtract from the present value of the extra revenue. Make an all-or-nothing offer to grant the license in exchange for that sum (minus ten cents, to make it just worthwhile). In practice this lump-sum approach is never used, for several reasons. The expected revenue usually is highly uncertain. The licensee paying a lump sum has a powerful incentive to exert maximum effort (he keeps all of any extra net revenue), but with revenue uncertain he faces a forbidding risk that shrivels the lump sum he will pay. The best feasible licensing deal, given these problems, is usually to charge the licensee a percentage royalty on sales of goods incorporating the licensed element (5 percent, but sometimes much more). This arrangement shares risk between the two parties; its incentive structure resembles those of book and recording contracts (Chapter 3).

Merchandise licensing has long been an important revenue source for film studios. Walt Disney himself until 1937 was associated with United Artists; he received about 60 percent of gross rentals on his films as well as royalties from 80 or so manufacturers licensing Disney characters. He presciently left when studio head Samuel Goldwyn refused to let him keep rights to license his cartoons to newly invented TV.[10] Present-day blockbuster films unleash floods of license revenue. The film *Batman* took in $250 million at the box office, probably half that in gross rentals for the distributor, who also received $50 million in license fees. The film *Jurassic Park* was accompanied by over a thousand products identified as official merchandise.[11]

The governance and coordination problems of licensing arrangements reveal much about the forces determining the scope of firms in the creative industries (Chapter 20). A merger between Disney and McDonald's would probably not yield an efficient integrated enterprise and is not in the cards, but the two still may choose how closely to coordinate their independent activities in sharing creative intangibles. Motion pictures' dates of theatrical release are often uncertain, due to delays in production or the competitive short-term juggling of release dates for completed films (Chapter 10). But production plans for tied-in merchandise must be set a year in advance, and media promotion campaigns also require advance commitments to specific dates. If licensee and licensor do not coordinate continuously, one party can inflict serious incidental losses on the other.[12] Communication between licensor and licensee while the film is being scripted and its characters defined can potentially increase the licensee's willingness to pay and the two parties' joint profits. One-shot licenses on single films or other products have a certain advantage in not requiring resource-absorbing communication between the parties, and it is the only feasible approach for television series given that success is unpredictable until the series has been aired for a time.[13] Furthermore, if licensees' complaints are believed, the licensors can extract most of the available rents.[14]

Nonetheless, licensing has shifted toward long-term collaborations. In 1996 Disney and McDonald's signed a ten-year agreement involving an annual payment by McDonald's of $100 million for an exclusive relationship. This will absolve McDonald's of bidding competitively for each Disney film, although it will likely commit it to take weak projects as well. A principal motive for the deal is both firms' extensive international operations. Disney's fare is readily licensed for theatrical exhibition around the world, and McDonald's international operations are far more extensive than those of competing fast-food systems.[15] In a manner common in oligopolistic markets, this preemptive agreement led competitors immediately to seek parallel links. Lucasfilm reached a similar three- to five-year agreement with PepsiCo., owner of three fast-food chains.[16] The studios and the major toy manufacturers staged a parallel race to form long-term agreements.[17]

Rights to Visual Artists' Works

The visual artist (or her dealer) can sell her works outright, with all rights to future use and exhibition passing to the purchaser. Or she can subdivide those rights for separate sale, or sell some while retaining others. Most art works are sold unconditionally, but public policy has intervened to impose some conditions. Since 1957 France has had a law *(droit de suite)* giving the artist title to a 3 percent share of the price received in any subsequent sale. Italy imposes a tax of up to 10 percent on the capital gain from resale. California's Resale Royalties Act of 1976 (amended 1982) levied a 5 percent royalty on gains resulting from sales valued at more than $1,000 (lasting to 25 years after the artist's death). Under the common law artists may enjoin the alteration of their works. The effect of the resale laws has been mainly to divert sales to markets in other jurisdictions.[18]

There have been some instances of art sale transactions involving separation of rights. Before photography and photographic reproduction came into widespread use, paintings were commonly reproduced by means of wood engravings. The production and duplication of these engravings could be profitable, and in nineteenth-century England was sometimes separated from ownership of the painting. Victorian painter William Powell Frith exhibited his gigantic *Life at the Seaside (Ramsgate Sands)* at the 1854 Royal Academy show, selling it to a dealer for £1,050. Queen Victoria herself took a fancy to it. The dealer sold it to her at cost but retained engraving rights, which were then sold separately for £3,000. Frith himself sold his next major painting, *Derby Day,* for £1,500 to a purchaser for postponed delivery, while the right of temporary exhibition after the Royal Academy show went to a dealer for £750 and engraving rights to another dealer for £1,500. Frith's *Railway Station* was sold to a dealer for £5,250, including £750 for exclusive exhibition rights (it would not be included in the Royal Academy show).[19] More recently, American realist Andrew Wyeth completed a series of images referred to as the Helga paintings, which received much attention for having been done in secret and carrying the spice of an alleged affair between artist and model. An entrepreneur purchased the whole series for $6 million, including all reproduction rights. His promotion efforts generated three museum shows, a book-length exhibition catalogue that sold 400,000 copies, and resale of the paintings (plus some related material) in Japan for a price believed to be $40 to $45 million.[20]

While artists' use of subdivided rights has been sporadic, the practice has been urged upon them. In 1971 New York attorney Robert Projansky drafted a model contract that an artist could use to retain these rights: 15 percent of the capital gain upon each sale; notice of exhibitions; right to borrow the work for exhibition; right to be consulted on repairs; a 50 percent share of any income the owner receives from renting the work; and all reproduction rights. This contract has seen some use, but apparently most artists do not employ it.[21]

Copyright law is of course important as a baseline for establishing what rights regarding duplicating and imitation intrinsically belong to the artist. European law recognizes the artist's right to restrict reproduction of a work that has been exhibited and sold. Until twenty years ago an American artist could regulate copying of a work once it was exhibited or sold only by attaching the copyright (©) symbol, often an unattractive aesthetic option.[22] Artists and their heirs often seem more concerned with regulating the form and context of reproduction than with collecting royalties. For the artist's emblems to appear on coffee cups and beach towels is seen not as free publicity but an impairment of the aesthetic (if not the economic?) value of the artist's corpus of work. As with patent law, the boundaries of the copyright privilege retained by the artist are sometimes problematic. The estate of Alexander Calder has restricted the sale in museum gift shops of mobiles employing the artist's creative strategy, although not his specific images. Did Calder hold the right to control the use of this strategy for making art, or only the right to prohibit reproduction of specific mobiles that he created?[23]

Because artists have complained vigorously of getting no cut from collectors' capital gains, one wonders why they do not unilaterally impose the restraint. One reason is surely the difficulty of monitoring a work's commercial migration once it leaves the hands of the artist's dealer. More subtly, the collector who first purchases a work subject to rebated capital gains is willing to pay less than for the same work with an unrestricted title. For the starving young artist, extra dollars from that first sale probably trade at a premium against the small chance of sharing capital gains years hence. Besides, artists have a likely superior way to lay claim on future capital gains (one that they commonly employ): retaining ownership of some of their best works, or trading for works of admired peers whose prospects for capital gains are likely correlated with their own.[24] The legislative enactment of *droit de suite* is a different matter, because it overrides sale contracts already written between artist and collector, imposing an unanticipated tax on the collector and transferring income from collector to artist. The benefit of course goes to successful artists, who also gain at the expense of emerging artists whose works (once the capital-gains tax is mandated) now fetch lower prices.

International Movement of Creative Goods

Creative goods are consumed in cultural contexts that vary from country to country. The good inevitably bears marks of the cultural ambience in which it was created. It therefore tends to appeal more to consumers steeped in the same or similar cultural ambience. Although most creative outputs (visual arts excepted) do not incur such large transportation costs as coal or steel, the nationally localized patterns of consumption look as if they did. With regard to *infinite variety*, novels in French are for most readers a poor substitute for novels in English. Where this property holds, independent organizations produce and distribute creative goods in different countries, dealing with each other only in isolated one-shot transactions. Conversely, where the imprint of cultural context is light—star classical musicians, or Hollywood action and special-effects films—the distribution process at worst incurs small extra costs at the national border. The production and distribution organizations tend to operate worldwide.

Dealmakers who plan creative projects such as cinema films should reckon on the basis of expected rentals in all markets. About 50 percent of gross cinema rentals for Hollywood films on average come from outside the United States, and for a film such as *Titanic* the international share may reach two-thirds.[25] The expected share will vary greatly by subject matter—films about American football have little market abroad—so the mix of films made will be affected.[26] More subtle factors determining U.S. films' international appeal surface when we extract, from a list of films with highest all-time box-office revenue, those obtaining more than two-thirds of their revenue in the United States and those obtaining more than two-thirds abroad. Those with strong appeal abroad are mostly action films and/or films with well-known stars, with a few exceptions for films with stories more relevant to audiences abroad (such as *Schindler's List*). Films earning mainly domestic revenues are mostly comedies, which appear to have a higher content of national culture than other films, and movies lacking well-known stars.[27] A current trend is for U.S. independent film producers, invigorated by the disintegration of Hollywood studio production (Chapter 5), to draw more of their revenues from abroad either by renting U.S.-made films through independent distributors or actually making films abroad intended for local audiences.[28] Opportunities to obtain rents from foreign markets can obviously affect the number of films made, as well as their types and styles. An enlarged market for a proprietary public good, such as a cinema film or TV series, also has a more subtle effect of inducing the production of higher quality films—"quality" in the sense of a larger fixed cost incurred in order to attract more viewers. If a $1 million increase in a film's production cost attracts 10 percent more customers, a larger production cost will be warranted when the film can reach a foreign audience as well as its domestic one.[29]

The cultural specificity of creative products implies that the typical creative good attracts more demand per capita in its homeland than elsewhere, less and less in foreign markets as the product travels to those with little cultural and linguistic affinity. To the great annoyance of creative producers in other countries, those based in America enjoy access to large domestic and linguistic markets, and their appeal abroad is topped off by the manifest exportability of the whole U.S. cultural context. The Hollywood studios hence find it profitable to maintain their own distribution networks outside the United States. Japan and India have large domestic markets but low levels of cultural affinity outside their borders. Germany and Italy have relatively small domestic markets and little linguistic turf externally. An implication of this pattern, confirmed by the evidence, is that the locally produced share of films exhibited in a country increases with its competitive advantage in the world market. That proposition is confirmed for several measures of competitive advantage, such as the number of foreign countries in which its films are regularly distributed and the number of countries in which this nation is the leading supplier of films.[30] The United States has the greatest competitive advantage of any nation on each of these measures.

This situation leads to the emotive but economically empty complaint that U.S. creative goods are "subsidized" abroad by the large domestic market. Like everyone else's creative goods, they are exported if and only if they are profitably sold or exhibited abroad. The advantage conveyed by the large domestic market is to increase the number of films produced and the production cost worth lavishing on each film. Furthermore, the large U.S. market is to some degree an advantage to foreign filmmakers as well, because the competitive distribution apparatus provides points of entry for films that will appeal only to small U.S. audiences (Chapter 10). Indeed, about 20 percent of films released in the United States are imported, although the rentals that they earn per film are clustered at the low end of the distribution.[31] The emotive value of the charge of subsidy no doubt lies in its power to push national governments abroad into subsidizing local film production. These funds commonly subsidize domestic filmmakers' costs of production rather than rewarding them for the ticket revenue that their films attract. That choice responds to the budding filmmaker's lack of cash. Commercial success thus is not promoted, however, as it would be if the government matched box-office revenue. Whether artistry and creativity are fostered is a judgmental question.[32]

Book publishing provides a contrast because of the height of linguistic barriers. Where these are minimal, in medical texts and science and technology, publishing activity falls mainly to multinational specialists such as Elsevier. For novels and other books that require translation, that fixed cost is high enough to deter international publication except for books expected to achieve either a long commercial lifespan or large immediate sales.[33] Blockbuster U.S. authors and the apparatus that promotes them, for example, have proved able to leap linguistic barriers successfully (John Grisham's annual foreign earnings are said to exceed $10 million). No comparable flow exists for imports to the United States, except for a few English writers of mysteries and thrillers.[34] The best-seller lists in the various European countries show little correlation with each other.[35] The entertainment conglomerates that have acquired book publishers in different countries apparently do not coordinate their activities closely, although they claim the ability to make deals with authors covering hardback and paperback publishing in several countries.[36]

A major issue of international diffusion of creative goods is the regulation of piracy and counterfeiting. It will not be pursued here beyond noting that it raises the same issue of conflicting national interests as does the patent system. A country maximizing the welfare of its own citizens will try to help them to extract rents from foreign users of their intangible assets, while letting them practice piracy on foreign rights holders. Given that copyrighted creative intangibles (like new industrial knowledge) will be underprovided worldwide in the absence of intellectual property rights, countries that both export and import knowledge can generally agree to respect and help enforce the rights of each other's citizens. The more a country's interest lies in appropriating intangibles from other countries, and the less exportable are the intangibles devised by its own citizens, the greater is its incentive to withhold cooperation in the international enforcement of copyright.

Even where intellectual property rights have long been respected, however, private contracts have not always been complete enough to collect and allocate the international rents imputed to creative goods. In contracts for exhibition of cinema films, careful allocation of territories evolved only gradually.[37] The recent boom in reissues of older recorded music on compact discs has exposed the incompleteness of the original contracts for dividing international royalty income between artist and record company, causing some large companies to make payments on the basis only of fairness (R&B artists were particularly affected). Another problem appears with contracts that are incomplete and thus leave room for multiple claimants to the same rights. When an artist has recorded several versions of a given song, sometimes only the artist (if still among us) can tell which source was employed for an anthologized reissue.[38] While present-day contractual arrangements often accord well with the economic analysis of fully specified contracts, it is hard to explain why completeness was achieved at a gradual pace rather than emerging full-grown.

18

Payola

"Payola" is a bribe paid in order to influence a gatekeeper's choice among competing creative products. In the United States broadcasting stations are legally restricted from taking pay for airplay. In fact payola occurs in markets for differentiated goods of all sorts, but it does have a special affinity for creative goods. That is because *infinite variety* tends to ensure a large number of creative goods clamoring at the gate, *nobody knows* which the ultimate consumer will prefer, and the creative good's cost is mostly fixed and sunk.

Logic of Payola

Some simple economic considerations point to the likely settings for payola. In a purely competitive market, many sellers provide a homogeneous product to many buyers at a single prevailing price. Each seller, if seeking maximum profits, offers the quantity of its good such that the last unit's marginal cost equals the market price. Since the last unit sold earns the seller zero profit, there is no gain from offering the buyer a price cut to purchase one more unit. Payola would not pay. In other market conditions payola is profitable for the seller, either as a selective bribe or as a regular rebate. They all involve the seller's "regular" price exceeding its marginal cost, creating a standing incentive to cadge an extra sale by a selective price cut, rebate, or bribe. The seller can sometimes identify reluctant customers who value the product less than the standard price but more than its marginal cost. A special price, which could take the form of a selective rebate or bribe, then makes a sale while bringing the seller some profit. The conventionalized prices commonly found in creative industries, when they exceed sellers' marginal costs, create the same incentive.

Two features that promote payola are common in creative activities. The first is the prevalence of costs that are fixed (do not vary with the seller's output) and sunk (irrecoverable). These increase the gap between a price that covers the seller's average cost and marginal cost of another unit, thereby inflating the value of an extra sale and intensifying the incentive to "deal" or bribe. Conventionalized prices and price competition muffled by product differentiation (*infinite variety*) also weigh in.

The second feature appears when the buyer's purchase yields a spillover benefit to the seller without affecting the buyer's willingness to pay. When a radio station plays a pop record, it attracts listeners, who in turn bring the station profit from advertising revenue. Airplay causes some of these listeners to buy their own copies; the record label profits from those purchases, but the radio station gets no benefit. The spillover inflates the effective net price that the label gets without raising its marginal cost. Even if the station pays no explicit price for the individual record or the right to play it, the publicity spillover can still make a bribe profitable for the label.

The situation of the buyer (and bribe recipient) needs a closer look. The legal concept of bribery focuses on the employee (disk jockey—DJ) who accepts payment for playing (say) a record that is not the first choice of the station's listeners, and hence cuts into the station's profits. Payola could, however, be a profitable deal for the station. With records differentiated, in principle there exists one best playlist to maximize net revenue for the station, and any deviation lowers profits. *Infinite variety*, however, tends to make the loss of ratings and profit small, easily offset by a modest bribe.[1] The station is the loser, however, if the DJ employee pockets the bribe, unknown to the station owner who suffers the associated loss of profit. How bribe-prone is the DJ, and whether payola cheats the station, depends on the DJ's employment terms. Paid a straight salary and not monitored, he would take any bribe that came along. Dependent on the station's audience ratings, he would require a big enough payment to offset the likely drag of a weak record on the ratings. If he owns the station and receives all of its profits, the bribe must fully offset the station's expected profit loss. If taking payola is potentially profitable to the station, the payment might well be not a clandestine bribe but a factor rolled into the DJ's compensation package. In the former case the station owner shuns payola; in the latter he quietly welcomes it.

Payola and the Sound of Music

Payola's long history in the popular music industry began with publishers of sheet music in the nineteenth century and continues with record labels to the present day. The mechanism at work is clear. Many songs compete to be sung, or records to be played, and for the gatekeeper many are often close substitutes. The 1920s singer who popularized a song increased sales of its

sheet music, just as the station's airplay causes some listeners to purchase a record today.[2]

Music Publishing

The competing music publishers on New York's Tin Pan Alley (28th Street)
employed "song pluggers" whose job was to make the nocturnal rounds of
the city's bars, dives, and theaters to get the publisher's songs played or sung
by whatever means worked. Petty bribery was the standard procedure: a
round of drinks for the band, a small payment to the singer.[3] Hiring claques
to applaud the publisher's songs was another practice. The rise of ballroom
bands and of radio stations to broadcast them increased and formalized the
payments. Bandleaders wanted arrangements suited to their styles, and publishers could be induced to hire expensive arrangers to supply them gratis.
Leading singers could command a formal share of royalties for a period of
years on songs that they introduced. Plugging an unknown song in the
1900s was said to cost around $1,300 for a cash advance and ongoing royalty
payments, with the singer's picture on the cover of the sheet music as part of
the deal. Some deals gave the singer a period of exclusive use of a song, providing a strong incentive to perform it.[4] Rent was extracted from the publishers fully enough to send some of them to deal with lesser singers, who might
ask a fixed sum for a few performances.

The publishers could gain by colluding to restrict the transfer of rents to
singers, and in 1917 the Music Publishers Protective Association (MPPA)
was formed for this purpose. Interestingly, it was promoted by the trade publication *Variety,* whose advertising services competed with payola for getting
a song played. Among the publishers, its support came mainly from those
having trouble getting through to the top singers. It was no more successful
than most cartels that are unable to detect and punish cheating, but it did
manage to convince some vaudeville executives that payola distorted the
choices of songs used in vaudeville acts enough to impair their profits significantly.[5] In 1934 the song pluggers themselves formed a union called Professional Music Men. Ostensibly founded as a mutual-benefit association, one
of its main objectives was to deter payola, which the pluggers correctly saw as
substituting for their own direct song-promoting services and reducing their
employment.[6]

Payola and Radio Airplay

As phonograph records became more and more popular, the song publisher's
efforts to maximize the value of its copyrights focused increasingly on getting

the firm's songs recorded. That made the labels' A&R (artist and repertory) personnel the natural targets for payola. The practice's best-known appearance comes, however, one step farther along in the production process as the label seeks airplay for the records it has released. The central role of airplay in a record's success was shown in Chapter 9. The best documented pattern of broadcasting payola came in the 1950s and led to Congressional hearings followed in 1960 by legislation that made payola under certain circumstances a crime.

A true entrepreneur of payola was broadcaster Dick Clark, who began his career by taking over the program *Bandstand* on a Philadelphia TV station. Records were played as teenagers danced to them, and recording artists occasionally appeared to lip-synch their songs. The popular program generated substantial local sales of the records that were played. Viewers got a chance to see the recording artists, and for the artists a *Bandstand* appearance substituted for numerous local promotional visits. Philadelphia was an excellent base for the program. A large metropolitan area with a number of local record-distribution companies, it was also a "break-out city" in which popular records were commonly tested before national distribution. The program's local success led the ABC network to pick it up for national distribution as *American Bandstand*.[7] It was a huge success on ABC, and it began to drive the playlists of local DJs around the country, as listeners would request local play of songs heard on *American Bandstand*.

Clark's predecessor *Bandstand* host had joined with partners to start his own record label to "cover" (re-record a song with a different singer from its originator) national rhythm and blues hits, and these records sold well in Philadelphia thanks to *Bandstand* exposure. Even before the program received national distribution, a local record company offered Clark 25 percent of the publisher's royalties to a promising song in exchange for a major promotional "hype," a practice that was already common among Philadelphia DJs.[8] Clark built up this practice by organizing a dummy company to hold the rights and receive payments, and it came out in the Congressional hearings that 145 of the 162 song copyright interests Clark then owned had been given to him.[9] Clark's empire expanded to soak up other rents generated by *American Bandstand*'s promotional prowess. Performers appearing on the program received union-scale wages for their appearance, but they were expected to sign these back to Clark's corporation, or have their record company pay for the performance directly. The ABC network had its own label, Am-Par Records, and Am-Par assigned Clark substantial publishing royalties for songs promoted on the program.[10] The program's practice of not playing songs on labels that lacked national distribution opened the way for package deals that brought artists onto Clark's program and to Am-Par Records.[11]

The several record companies that Clark himself owned joined with other Philadelphia record-company interests to form a distribution company, which extended Clark's rent-interception apparatus one step forward in the production chain.[12] It was also extended one step backward through Clark's ownership of a record-pressing plant, as record companies discovered that using this plant increased their chances of getting songs on *American Bandstand*.[13] Finally, Clark was partner in an artist-management company, which steered the promising rock 'n' roll guitarist Duane Eddy to one of Clark's record companies, where he apparently received a substantially lower royalty rate than competitive bidding would have supported. Eddy appeared many times on Clark's shows, and many of his releases made top-hit lists.[14]

The story of *American Bandstand* illustrates the situation of the payola recipient. Clark could not arbitrarily make a hit out of a weak song (some records that he played repeatedly never landed on the "top hit" lists), but he had discretionary influence and checked carefully on the degree to which the market was following his choices.[15] Evidence that emerged in the Congressional hearings of the late 1950s showed the widespread use of payola by record-label sales personnel with the DJs who were the gatekeepers of radio stations' airplay lists. The low ratio of new records played to records received by a station (see Chapter 9) ensured that many choices were made casually based on little consideration, which favored payola. The practice had greater value for small, independent labels than it did for the major ones. The majors' representatives dealt with the DJs on a regular basis and could offer their reputations as leverage to get airplay for records that the label thought would benefit the most. Independents lacked this asset but could deploy payola as a substitute. Also, independents worried less about loss of corporate reputation if payola should become a scandal.[16] The supply of payola was selectively enhanced by the concentration of radio stations on Top 40 Hits. For a song with a shot at the national list, the value to the record company of airplay on an additional station could be quite high, for the number of relevant stations was said to be only 42.[17]

Consequences of Payola and Its Regulation

If the Top 40 format encouraged the use of payola to break into the winners' circle, the format was itself encouraged by the public revelation of payola practices. Radio stations responded to the public scandal by taking their airplay lists out of the hands of DJs and placing them in the station's program director. By implication, payola had bribed the DJs against the interest of the station's profits. Station managers, however, could hardly have been ignorant of the apparently widespread practice. If DJs received compensation in the form of payola, the station could get their services for less straight pay.[18] Payola reforms may have served the public's sense of morality more than the stations' economic interests. They may also have had some unintended consequences. Program directors live and die by the station's audience ratings, while most DJs have substantive interests in new music and performers and can capture some reputation benefits by making astute if risky selections among new records. This R&D or innovative function was cut back.[19]

The payola scandals and their aftermath also illustrate the efficiency advantage that bribe-based promotion may enjoy against "respectable" forms that cost more in economic resources. The case was vividly put by independent record-label executive Hy Weiss: "Payola is the greatest thing in the world because it means that you don't have to spend time with some schmuck you don't like, eat dinner and all that, you pay him off . . . Instead of having an army of promotion men spending your money . . . , living off your expense account, you give it all to one guy and save yourself a million dollars."[20] When payola was restricted by the Federal Bribery Act of 1960, the major record companies augmented their staffs of professional pluggers to persuade program directors to playlist their wares. The fixed cost of promotion staffs put the smaller independent labels at a disadvantage, and the disappearance of a number of independent R&B labels may have been due partly to the suppression of payola.[21]

The saga of payola and its restriction took a striking turn during the late 1970s and 1980s. The practice never died out after the 1960 legislation, if only because of generous loopholes in the statute. It addressed the payment of money or "valuable considerations," but it left untouched phony contests that DJs could win and no-work consulting assignments or master-of-ceremonies jobs for which they could be hired. Payola continued at a low level, though executives of major record companies remained studiously uninvolved, from fear less of the little-enforced bribery statute than the Racketeering Influenced and Corrupt Organizations Act.[22] During the 1980s payment by the record companies for airplay again escalated greatly, and in a way that resulted from the legislative restrictions.[23] Promoters of records to broadcasting stations could be either independents or employees of one company. Stations preferred the independents, whose prioritized recommendations among the gaggle of new records would at least be neutral among labels. So, at this time, did major labels, if only because any payola that passed from independent promoters to the stations could not be traced back to implicate the label's executives.

Beginning in 1980 most of the large record companies instituted a pay-for-play policy with the independent promoters, paying a set fee each time a radio station added a record to its playlist. Competition among the labels quickly escalated the fee to the range of $500 to $3,000, raising the cost of promoting a hit single record to about $150,000. Eventually, the fee reached $10,000.[24] This form of incentive compensation proved all too powerful. It attracted to the independent-promotion business a group of men (large and accompanied by bodyguards) who were willing and able to gain control of radio stations' playlists. Their reliance on bribes and threats for this purpose is not well documented, but Mafia connections seem very likely. Worse yet, the independent promoters managed to collude with one another in their dealings with the record labels. They divided stations among themselves, so that each had a chain of stations whose playlists were his property. The labels dealt not with (say) one promoter per song, but with the promoter who controlled access to a particular station. The labels could not avoid what had turned into extortionate payments for independent promotion. In the early 1980s, CBS was spending $8 million to $10 million annually on independent promotion, and the industry as a whole was spending probably $40 million. By 1985 the industry was spending $60 million to $80 million at a (prosperous) time when its pretax profits were at most $200 million.[25]

Neither individually nor collectively could the major record companies resist effectively. In 1980 the Warner label initiated a halt to independent promotion. CBS followed, but other labels dragged their feet. The independents' network retaliated by knocking off the charts one promising song of each company that bowed out.[26] Prevented by the antitrust laws from colluding formally to restrict promotion, in 1985 the companies sought to have the independents investigated for payola through their trade association, Record Industry Association of America, but that plan also crumbled. One reason is that the recording artists and their managers had nothing to lose from the transfer of profits from labels to promoters (and possibly stations). The labels were bailed out exogenously by a TV journalist's report on the promoters' Mafia connections, which allowed the record companies to express shock and indignation and swear they would stop using independent promoters. The stations also reaffirmed their anti-payola policies, and the practice went into retreat.[27] One consequence is that independent promotion once again became an economical policy for small, independent labels. The major labels' thralldom to the independent promoters had had the incidental advantage of raising their smaller rivals' promotion costs.[28]

The evidence supports a simple interpretation of the economics of payola in broadcasting. Promotion benefits to the label cannot be captured directly by the broadcaster, who lives by advertising revenue that generally will not reflect this benefit. Payola compensates for valuable promotion, and leaves us wondering why it is stigmatized as bribery rather than recognized as payment for services rendered. The broadcasters evidently assume that their goodwill asset with the listening public depends on the apparent exercise of independent judgment in the music to be played. This assumption might be accurate, or it might just internalize the regulatory constraint that U.S. broadcast licenses are held on a public-trust basis. Payola then looks like a compromise, invading this goodwill asset to an extent just offset by the net profit increase from the payment. But then why does the transfer so often seem to benefit station personnel rather than the profit of the broadcast enterprise? This paradox lends interest to a recent trend toward overt payments for airplay in broadcasting, analogous to the "infomercials" that are a staple of television.[29]

Recent interest in pay-for-play arises from the rapid reorganization of the U.S. radio broadcasting industry. Removal of Federal Communications Commission restrictions on stations' common ownership has led to a great turnover of ownership, with more than one-quarter of the nation's 10,000 or so stations having changed hands in two years. Ownership has become concentrated in groups such as Jacor Communications, Inc., with 192 stations. The logic of this consolidation, as with movie theatres and fast-food restaurants, lies in economizing on entrepreneurial or managerial input into relatively simple and similar business units. Any new owner naturally seeks additional profit opportunities, and radio chains pursue economies of centralized dealings with suppliers such as record companies. Jacor and CBS Radio both floated the idea of pay-for-play in country music, which might take the form of an hour-long showcase program broadcast over the firm's stations nationwide. Another idea was à la carte purchase of several plays for a single song. Country music is a natural site for the experiment, because sales of country albums have been declining, and labels' promotion budgets are smaller for country music than for rock records. The proposal left some record labels and broadcasters looking nervously at ghosts of payola past, and it was not obvious how the fact of commercial sponsorship could be conveyed in the broadcast with sufficient candor to satisfy the Federal Communications Commission.

Other examples have surfaced, such as a deal between an independent station and a label to play an emerging artist's song 50 times in five weeks in exchange for $5,000. A new artist's success is always highly risky, and the deal was seen as a sharing of risk between label and station. A music-video TV channel in 1994 adopted a program (called Playola) of showing a record company's video 42 times during two weeks in exchange for $27,000. These developments have met the standard objections about compromised independence and deception of listeners. Could compilers of Top Hits lists distinguish between autonomous and purchased play? The potential efficiency gains from pay-for-play, however, were also noted. It could replace under-the-counter contracts by which airplay depended on conventional ads on the station purchased by a label. Artists are sometimes pressed to play concerts sponsored by radio stations in order to gain airplay or retain a place on a station's playlist.

Payola in Other Settings

The broadcasting sector illustrates one factor—spillovers—that promotes payola. Other creative activities also harbor payola driven by promotional benefits. In popular entertainment, fan magazines commonly trade mentions in their news columns for advertising purchases, free trips for writers, and the like. Reviewers are paid little but may receive records and other freebies, free travel, or possibly job opportunities from the companies whose records they review.[30] Television broadcasts and cable channels whose program content deals with cinema films commonly demand advertising from studios whose new films they feature, atop contributions to the cost of preparing the program material.[31] Some clubs and venues hold particular value for promoting artists beyond the listeners whom they attract directly. To obtain bookings there, a label may pick up part of its group's regular fee, or buy large numbers of tickets and pay charges for numerous invited guests.[32] A New York club of moderate size was viewed by promoters as a particularly attractive rung on a ladder of venues for successful groups, and in competitive bidding by presenters it obtained an arrangement to share profits on subsequent local appearances by groups that had performed there.[33]

Another spillover promotion benefit generates payment for the placement of a manufacturer's product in a cinema or TV film. The cornflakes box visible in the breakfast-table scene must be one brand or another, or perhaps a contrived one. Filmmakers once resisted giving incidental plugs to existing brands, on grounds of creative autonomy. But the cereal maker will pay for the exposure of its trademark. Because of the huge audiences attracted by popular films, the promotional benefits to products can be very large. When a child fed Reese's Pieces to a friendly alien in the film *E.T.*, the candy's sales rose 65 percent.[34] Filmmakers must obtain releases for the conspicuous exposure of any trademark, but rather than paying for the privilege, the game is to extract maximum rents from the trademark's holder. The product's placement can be more or less conspicuous or favorable in the film. The extra product sales can yield large or small profits to its maker. Hence, payments can vary from free provision of the product up to very large sums. Daimler-Benz reportedly paid $1 million for its M-Class sports utility vehicle to appear in *The Lost World*. Fees in the range of $20,000 to $100,000 are common; since a film might offer twenty to fifty potential placement opportunities, it can easily realize $1 million in additional revenue.[35] This market for product-placement opportunities has attracted its own brokerage industry, with fifteen to thirty independent companies seeking placements for their manufacturer-clients and negotiating terms.[36] It has been an area of significant litigation, because studio and product-maker find it difficult to contract before the film is completed on the positiveness of the product's use.[37]

The other explanation for payola, sticky prices, has its own domain in the creative industries. It seems to apply to deals offered by chain bookstores and superstores to book publishers. Bookstores can selectively promote particular books by placing large quantities on display at the front of the store, giving publishers a special space for newly published works, including certain books in catalogues, and the like. The superstores and chains best able to offer these services are also the ones that commonly discount books from their retail list prices (so the buyer swayed by a book's promotion in one store gets no benefit from buying it at another). With special displays and promotions proximately benefiting the retailer's own sales, spillovers do not explain why publishers might pay extra for these services. The book chain does pick one book over others for special promotion, however, and the publisher is vulnerable to demands for payment to get his onto the front table. Publishers' prices to retailers are expressed as discounts from the trade book's suggested retail price; these do not vary from book to book, and so constitute the requisite sticky price. The chains can efficiently coordinate such promotions among their many stores, offering the publisher various promotional packages that cost little per book but do add substantially to the stores' profits. Barnes and Noble's "Discover Great New Writers" program assures that a book appears face-out in every store for two or three months and gets a review in a special brochure, for $1,700 per title. To have a book featured for a month on a special stand at the front of each store costs $10,000. End-of-aisle displays go for $3,000 a book or $10,000 for the whole display. Borders charges $15,000 for a package that includes a month of front-of-store display and advertisement of the book discounted by 30 percent in a special issue of *USA Today*.[38] Amazon.com briefly joined the party by charging publishers for putting titles on its recommended list.[39] These practices have entered into the controversy between publishers and the traditional independent booksellers over promotional allowances and other terms that disproportionately benefit chains and superstores. The problem in part is one of transaction costs: the deal that is worthwhile when it covers a chain's hundreds of stores does not repay the negotiating costs and paperwork for a single store.

The bookstores' practices resemble those of grocery chains, which also find their stores' shelf capacity inadequate to display all the products that manufacturers would offer. The solution is not simply to make the stores bigger, because (among other reasons) diminishing returns set in for the shopper as the cart-miles needed to fill the grocery list increase. Given grocers' mark-ups, the store's shelf space comes to acquire a positive shadow price. New products come to require "slotting allowances" to get stocked, and end-of-aisle positions can command a premium.[40]

Vertical Corporate Mergers: Capitalized Payola

The essentials of payola transactions appear in a seemingly different setting—the mergers and acquisitions that have been common among large entertainment firms. A small number of major studios distribute films that, after their round of exhibition in cinemas, become available for showing on television. A small number of television networks and cable channels provide outlets for showing these films. The films' negative costs and the costs of their promotion to cinema audiences are fully sunk. Although the marginal cost of making the film available for broadcast exhibition is negligible, the studios are able to extract substantial rents from the broadcasters. A broadcaster might be nearly indifferent among several available films. Clearly, in a spot transaction a studio would willingly offer payola to get its film selected. Now allow a studio (Disney) to acquire control of a broadcast network (Capital Cities–ABC). The ABC network can be instructed to pick Disney films over those offered by other studios. ABC's payment to Disney is an internal transfer that leaves the firm's profits unaffected, while the same payment to another studio is a direct cost. The Disney film might draw fewer viewers than another studio's, but the in-house selection remains a good deal until the lost profit approaches the size of the license fee to another studio.

19

Organizing to Collect Rents: Music Copyrights

One rides the elevator in a modern high-rise building soothed by a bland re-corded arrangement of "Tea for Two." This respite from silence might be worth, say, $0.0025. Can the composer collect that sum? What about the re-cording artists? Creative goods enjoy legal copyright protection, but the holder of the copyright must enforce it and collect payments for use of the copyrighted good. Many legal and economic issues of intellectual property rights are not specific to creative industries and apply to patents and trade-marks as well. One exception, localized to the music industry, is flagged by the elevator rider's benefit: the lumps of rent are very small, very numerous, and hence feasible to collect only through some cooperative organization.

Intellectual Property Rights in Creative Activities

Copyrights to music compositions make the same compromise between eco-nomic costs and benefits as other legal rights to intangible intellectual prop-erty. Songs are public goods. Once written down, recorded, or even just per-formed in public, they come available to persons other than the songwriter at no (or little) marginal cost. If the song is free for the taking, the songwriter reaps no reward for her creative labors. Valuing *art for art's sake,* she may still bestow her lyrical gifts on the world; but she must earn a living somehow, so supplies even of creative goods shrivel when no economic rewards can be claimed. Giving the songwriter a property right, however, leads to another social cost. If the resource cost of the song's passage to another listener is zero, yet the songwriter charges each listener a positive price, a market distor-tion results (price exceeds marginal cost). The best compromise solution to this problem is the one that public policy actually embraces: give the song-writer her monopoly and let her collect her tribute, but limit the monopoly in time (in the United States, the creator's life plus 50 years). After that the song reverts to the public domain.

Several other issues entwine the copyright. Even the artist ready to donate her lyrical gift still needs the collaboration of humdrum inputs. The firm that publishes the song or issues its recording holds out for a normal return on its investment. Although humdrum inputs demand their paychecks, they may be clever about obtaining them in other ways, if intellectual property rights are not available. A book publisher, for example, might print initially enough copies of an uncopyrighted manuscript to serve its expected demand. Once this fixed cost is incurred and sunk, any pirate faces the authorized publisher as a competitor with a zero marginal cost, hence willing to meet any low price the pirate quotes and preclude the pirate's covering his fixed costs. A drawback of the intellectual property right is the rent-seeking that it induces. Successful creative goods regularly attract lawsuits from parties who claim that the work was stolen from them. Songs are particularly vulnerable, because notes can be arranged in only so many ways, so similar (short) sequences can easily occur by chance.

Songwriters and Royalty Sources

Some historical background sheds light on the royalty streams earned by songs and the institutions that collect them. Popular songwriters (composers and lyricists) once were typically not performers, only authors who took their creations to publishers, who in turn printed sheet music for sale to professional and amateur performers. Their song-plugging efforts (Chapter 18) sought to promote the sheet-music sales that were the source of royalties to the songwriter and profits to the publisher. Time brought new technologies for delivering professional performance to the music-loving public: recordings, radio, sound motion pictures, broadcast and cable television. The parlor piano fell into disuse, sheet-music sales plummeted, and the royalty and profit streams for songwriter and publisher increasingly depended on public performance.

The role of the publisher was transformed to the point where the term is now a misnomer. First, the publisher's best strategy for maximizing the rent stream to himself and the songwriter abruptly shifted from subsidizing public performance to taxing it (Chapter 18). U.S. legislation in 1909 both provided for compulsory royalties on music reproduced mechanically (then, record cylinders and piano rolls) and permitted copyright holders to collect royalties for public performances undertaken for profit. This law launched an effort to organize institutions to collect the newly authorized royalties. Second, the seismic shift in popular-music styles since the 1950s and the rise of the songwriter-performer made the physical printing of songs increasingly irrelevant. Since 1976 copyright no longer requires a song to be fixed in printed form (a recording will do), and many copyrighted songs are not printed. The publisher still promotes songs to performers and filmmakers who might use them, but he is mainly a collector of rents.

Mechanical Royalties

Under U.S. law, songwriters nowadays obtain royalty income from two major and several minor sources.[1] Mechanical royalties (the name harks back to the mechanical reproduction of sound) are paid by record companies for each copy of a song that they record. The complex job of negotiating and collecting royalties of a few cents per record was resolved mainly by legislation. The 1909 act set a statutory royalty rate of two cents per song per recording. That rate persisted until 1976 legislation created a Copyright Royalty Tribunal to set an inflation-adjusted rate, now 6.95 cents per song of standard length. A nonprofit organization, the Harry Fox Agency, emerged that gathers royalty revenues, audits recording company records, and disburses the revenues received minus its expenses.[2] In 1994 mechanical royalties made up 31 percent of music royalty income.[3]

Mechanical royalties stem from a compulsory licensing requirement. After a song's first recording, anyone else may record it, subject to the payment of mechanical royalties. When songwriter and performer were different artists, this practice was unexceptional. The interest of the songwriter and publisher lay in the song's widest possible dissemination—the most performers recording it, and the most records sold. The marginal cost to the copyright's owner was zero unless a singer somehow devalued a song's appeal to others. The singer picking a song to perform could hardly search the world's songwriters for one willing to knock off a penny per record. The terms for mechanical royalties resemble the other conventionalized or (in this case) statutorily fixed prices, around which most parties find no net benefit in negotiating. The correspondence is not quite complete, however. That is because the compulsory rate carries rather onerous record-keeping requirements, so record label and publisher often settle on a negotiated rate below (but apparently related to) the statutory rate.[4] Also, when the songwriter is also the performer, record-company contracts normally truncate what the artist receives for so-called controlled compositions at 75 percent of the statutory rate.

The singer-songwriter may well have reason to resist compulsory licensing. As a songwriter, she benefits from the maximum number of singers attracted to her sing. As a singer, however, she recognizes other singers as competitors whose records compete with her own. If allowed to set royalty rates for other singers, she could select the right set of singers and charge each a royalty rate that would maximize the joint profits from all versions of her song, and require other singers to remit the profit shares falling into their hands.[5] She is not allowed to set such a rate, however. The force of this limit was evident in the diffusion of rock 'n' roll in the 1950s, with "cover" versions of blacks' R&B songs, cleaned up for white audiences, taking the dominant share of the record market.[6]

Performance Royalties

Any public performance of music (with a few exceptions) incurs an obligation to pay performance royalties: live entertainment, recorded songs performed on radio or television, juke boxes, background music. A (near-) duopoly of copyright collectives, ASCAP (American Society of Composers, Authors, and Publishers) and BMI (Broadcast Music, Inc.), arose to negotiate royalty payments with these users. ASCAP is also responsible for another conventionalized price: the equal division of performance royalties between songwriter and publisher. The copyright collectives and the reorganization of the publishing industry that resulted from this fixed division of rents are treated subsequently. Performance royalties in 1994 accounted for 44 percent of total royalty income.

The benefits to music presenters from public performance of recorded music depend on the score devised and presented by songwriter and publisher, but also on the solo performer, background musician, recording engineer, record producer, the label's support personnel, and others. How many of these participants get performance royalties? A successful recording depends on at least competent performance by each of the participants (by the *motley crew* property). Market data cannot expose even roughly the values of individual contributions by most of these participants. That leaves their entitlements a matter of public policy and private rent-seeking efforts. U.S. public policy has cut off participants other than songwriter and publisher by means of the doctrine of first sale, meaning that their claims do not reach beyond the record buyer's purchase into the buyer's use of the recording. The American Federation of Musicians in the 1940s tried to capture performance rents by the indirect method of curtailing the production of new recordings in order to force public presenters to employ more "live" musicians. This campaign did succeed in imposing a tax on sales of recordings, with the revenue passing to the union and not to the particular musicians who made them. That choice caused trouble within the union by creating a conflict between musicians (especially in New York and Los Angeles) who were the sidemen on the recordings and other musicians who were the main beneficiaries of the tax. The former were allowed to bargain separately for higher recording-session wages, and eventually captured revenue from a tax on payments for the reuse of filmed TV programs.[7]

Other Sources

When a copyrighted song is included in the soundtrack of a cinema film or TV program, the producer obtains a so-called synchronization license from the publisher. Unlike the mechanical and performance royalties, individual transactions are sufficiently heterogeneous and important to warrant case-by-case negotiations. While the rent that any one song can command is limited by terms quoted by the publishers of competing songs, the prices and terms vary mainly with the value of the song's use to both the filmmaker and the publisher. License fees for using a single song in a cinema film were quoted (in the early 1990s) between $12,000 and $35,000 for the life of the song's copyright. The conspicuousness of the song's use (for example, is it sung by a character in the film?) is one determining factor. For TV use the fee may vary with the particular channel(s) involved—free, cable, or pay TV. The price drops if the filmmaker commits to a nationally distributed soundtrack album—in this case the publisher reaps mechanical royalties as well, and the filmmaker can press for a co-ownership share of the copyright or share of the mechanical royalties to capture the film's contribution.[8] Synchronization license fees for TV are quite low ($3,000 to $8,000), because the publisher also receives performance royalties from TV showings. For the producer of a continuing TV series, price-shopping and quantity discounts may affect the license fee. TV synchronization income for the producer may have the advantage of depending little on the program's success, in contrast to feature films' highly variable box-office outcomes.[9] When songs are licensed for TV commercials, publishers tend to hold out for a high fee ($100,000 to $300,000 for a year's use), because of the likely negative impact on the song's potential for future mechanical and syndication licensing.[10]

Publishers' income from synchronization royalties in 1994 was 8 percent of their total royalty income. Royalties from printed music were similar (9 percent), based on a conventional 20 percent royalty rate on the retail price of single-song sheet music and about half of that on folios or collections of songs. The remaining 8 percent of royalty income stems from still other sources, such as "grand" rights for the performance of a whole musical-comedy score. These are negotiated individually.[11] The boundary line between grand rights and those for single songs cleared routinely through the performing-rights organizations is wobbly and litigious because the parties may differ as to which approach yields them the better terms.[12]

Copyright Collectives

This review of sources of royalties for publishers and songwriters indicates that performance royalties pose the most difficult problem for organizing the collection process. Hundreds of thousands of songs might be performed over vast numbers of radio and television outlets, hotels, clubs, ballrooms, juke joints, college campuses, and the like. For the holder of copyright in a single song, the transaction cost of authorizing or detecting performance and collecting payment would be prohibitive except for the most conspicuous and accessible users. Even a collective organization faces a daunting task of identifying all users legally obligated to pay, negotiating terms, monitoring their use of music, collecting the royalties and remitting them to the appropriate rights holders. The history of ASCAP and its main competitor, BMI, illustrates the many analytical and organizational problems posed by these tasks.[13]

Assembling the Coalition

In 1909 U.S. legislation first authorized the collection of royalties when copyrighted music was performed in public for profit. Organization to collect these royalties from venue owners coincided with efforts by the Tin Pan Alley song publishers (that is, the mainstream publishers of popular songs) to collude on limiting payola to performers for promoting a song's performance.[14] After World War I the sheet-music business underwent a meltdown, with many stores closing their music departments and sheet-music sales of reasonably popular songs falling from 500,000 in the 1920s to 50,000 in the 1930s. The publishers, recognizing that demand had grown less elastic as it contracted, tripled the price in 1919.[15] The receding importance of sheet music and the possibility of capturing royalties from public performance both reduced the spillover value of public performance and created a legal basis for collecting tribute. The publishers who joined the Music Publishers Protective Association (Chapter 18)—that is, the bulk of major publishers of contemporary popular music—were the same ones who shortly after climbed aboard ASCAP. The main problem of assembling the coalition of publishers was thus solved at the outset by their common interest in trying to reverse the stream of payments between publishers and the parties involved in public performance. Publishers could take different views of how to deal with their key revenue sources, however, and there were numerous withdrawals and rejoinings among the smaller publishers. The organization's feasibility was not confirmed until the U.S. Supreme Court resolved the meaning of "public performance for profit" (explained subsequently).

Collective organizations face the hazard of their membership unraveling, when their core policies leave some members with better options outside and the defection of these members impairs the scale economies that benefit the still-loyal. Once ASCAP was established as a copyright collective, it was fairly well insulated against defection. The service it provided was not a public good, because nonmembers could be excluded from its benefits. Even a large independent publisher doing its own licensing could not touch its scale economies. The only holdout would be a publisher whose special situation made performance royalties easy to collect.[16] When ASCAP came to face competition from BMI (discussed subsequently), its problem was its own exclusion of publishers of popular music in styles other than Tin Pan Alley's, until it was forbidden to do so by the 1941 consent decree that followed an antitrust intervention. The ASCAP members may have sought to weaken or exclude competitors, or they may simply have acted from snobbery.[17]

Negotiating Royalty Payment

Rent-seeking is always highly litigious. The pot of gold need not be mined, only captured. Not picks and shovels but lawsuits and political campaigns are the tools of choice for either annexing or retaining property rights in streams of rents. The collection of performance royalties illustrates the point well: no substantial group of payers ever gave in without litigation, and skirmishes continue eight decades after ASCAP's founding. Hotels and clubs or cabarets were pressed at the outset. Both sought exclusion on the ground that they provided music as a bundled service and, while operating for profit, did not charge their patrons for music as such. This argument prevailed through the U.S. district and appellate courts, but the Supreme Court saw these music users' bundled services for what they are. Motion pictures were silent in ASCAP's early years, but film exhibitors did employ the piano accompanist to heighten the visual effect with whatever melodies seemed appropriate. The motion picture exhibitors were targeted by ASCAP for licenses. In response they raised a war chest, sought Congressional action, and instituted a lawsuit on grounds similar to the hotels' and cabarets'. ASCAP prevailed with its own infringement suit, with the district court rejecting the first of many claims that ASCAP violated the Sherman Antitrust Act. The theatre owners then proceeded with another two-pronged attack. They sought to enlist the film studios in a general boycott of music represented by ASCAP, and to develop non-ASCAP sources of music by promising the exhibitors' promotional assistance to any publisher supplying music outside of ASCAP. Neither maneuver worked, and by 1924 the majority of theatres were licensed.[18] ASCAP's cumulative total legal expenses then exceeded the royalty income it had received.

One puzzling feature of ASCAP's early operations is its failure to seek royalties from the vaudeville theatres that were then the nation's main form of musical entertainment. Like the touring theatre troupes, vaudeville was then manifestly declining in the face of motion-picture competition, and many theatres were converting in part to showing films ("pic-vaude houses"). ASCAP may have skipped a fight with the vaudeville interests for that reason alone, but the decision was apparently more complicated. Vaudeville theatres and the booking of talent were then largely controlled by the Albee-Keith organization. It apparently had significant monopsony power with performers, and was deemed capable of capturing some payola rents they had received for plugging Tin Pan Alley's songs. The Albee-dominated vaudeville managers' association proposed to ASCAP that it subcontract the collection of performance royalties from the pic-vaude houses and from non-Albee theatres, in exchange for a 50 percent cut of what it collected and exemption of Albee's own theatres from performance royalties.[19] This smelly deal never took effect.

New Music-Distribution Technologies

In the 1920s and 1930s, ASCAP dealt with two important new technologies for disseminating musical entertainment—sound motion pictures and radio broadcasting. Warner Bros.'s first sound film, *The Jazz Singer* (1927), was hugely profitable and made it clear that music would be embodied in films and not just played as accompaniment. As noted previously, the importance and heterogeneity of music's use in cinema films from the start warranted direct negotiations over licensing with the publisher rather than clearance through ASCAP. Nonetheless, the studios' switchover to sound films did affect ASCAP's core membership. In the late 1920s the studios bought controlling interests in several of the major music publishers. The reason for these acquisitions is clear. Music embodied in films would add greatly to the studios' profits, and exhibition of sound films would strongly promote their songs in other embodiments (recordings, sheet music). These spillovers would bring profit windfalls (performance and other royalties) to the music publishers, windfalls that would accrue to the studios if they could buy publishing firms at market values that did not fully anticipate these rents. The studios' fast action likely captured much of this prize. The studios may also have sought insurance against an ASCAP-mounted squeeze on music sources.[20] This development affected ASCAP's governance in that the studios now controlled a substantial bloc of its voting members. The studios had reason to welcome ASCAP's efficient mechanism for collecting performance royalties, however, and the captive publishers' relations with ASCAP continued unchanged. ASCAP was in any case somewhat insulated from the defection of publishers (even if it had been in their interest to defect). That is because publishers and songwriters were admitted to ASCAP separately and on different bases, making it tricky for a publisher to exit without harming the interests of the songwriters it had published.[21]

The early radio industry relied heavily on broadcasting music, recorded or live, and became a key target for ASCAP in 1922. The broadcasters, not yet profitable and facing a property-right claim on their lifeblood, were understandably concerned. The major companies then involved in radio (RCA, AT&T, General Electric, Westinghouse) indicated a willingness to discuss reasonable royalties, but ASCAP made the tactical error of declaring that it expected radio to be a major revenue source. The stations rejected wholesale the temporary licenses that ASCAP offered, while long-run royalty rates remained unresolved. The National Association of Broadcasters (NAB), the independent stations' trade association, sought to develop non-ASCAP sources of music. Publishers with backlists of more traditional music indeed were not well represented in ASCAP in 1922, which provided an opening for the NAB, but ASCAP vigorously recruited them during the next two years. Several legal challenges from the NAB were defeated in the courts, and attempts to obtain an exemption from Congress or federal regulation of ASCAP's rates were unsuccessful. By 1932 all the major broadcasters were licensed.[22] Furthermore, ASCAP's publisher-members were congruent with the trade group that negotiated mechanical licenses for the broadcast networks' "electrical transcriptions," special recordings of music and programming for the use of network's member stations.[23]

Structure of ASCAP's Charges and Disbursements

ASCAP faced problems of both how to collect from users and how to divide the revenues among its members so as to keep the coalition together. The most efficient way to extract rents enjoyed by (say) a radio station is to identify the increment of profit associated with the use of ASCAP songs and demand it as payment in an all-or-nothing offer. The profit increment might be identified either as specific to each individual song played, or as an aggregate due to the station's selections from the whole ASCAP catalogue.[24] The latter, blanket-license approach had the great advantage of simplicity, but it also clearly placed ASCAP in the position of a cartel pricing the use of its members' songs collectively. If, instead, each ASCAP member priced its own songs' use separately, with ASCAP serving only as collecting agent and bookkeeper, the organization's subsequent vulnerability to antitrust charges would have been much lessened. But it was long accepted that individual pricing of ASCAP's many songs, with each price conditional on user and use, was infeasible.[25]

ASCAP settled early on the blanket license for all ASCAP songs, with a royalty tied to the theatre's number of seats or the broadcaster's gross revenue (after deductions).[26] Besides keeping transaction costs low, this system could claim economic efficiency. The costs incurred to write and publish ASCAP's songs were all sunk. The marginal cost of using a song is zero. Therefore, it was efficient for ASCAP's charges to impose no tax on the use of an additional ASCAP song, on the replacement of a non-ASCAP song by an ASCAP-represented one, or on the use of one song rather than another.[27] Furthermore, the music user's costs typically did not vary with the number of ASCAP songs used, so that the songs' contribution to the user's profit was the same as their contribution to its total revenue.

While blanket licenses efficiently targeted the royalties for collection, the disbursement of the proceeds to members did require ASCAP (and later BMI) to identify what songs were actually used. This was done by requiring major users to keep logs of the music performed, while minor users were sampled.[28] A projection of the extent and nature of use of each song assigned it a certain number of "points," and the payment made per point was simply ASCAP's total receipts less operating costs divided by the total number of points awarded. Again, subject to sampling error, the system induced no biases among members by under- or overrewarding particular songs or types of songs.

Two features of the distribution of royalties that ASCAP collected, however, did have important effects. One was the convention of dividing royalties equally between publisher and songwriter(s), which to this day applies to mechanical and synchronization royalties as well as performance royalties. Its effects are discussed subsequently. The other is ASCAP's practice of rewarding songwriters and publishers not just on the basis of points allocated for current use of their music. The songwriter may choose between this plan and an alternative that favors cumulative play of the writer's songs and also benefits the classical composers who are ASCAP members. BMI adopted a similar system, without as much seniority bias but also including a feature that escalated the rewards to the most successful songwriters. Both collectives paid publishers on the basis of current performance.[29] This seniority bias in ASCAP's allocation became important when it faced competition from BMI, because it disfavored the currently "hot" songs and songwriters and pushed them to seek BMI membership. The problem with ASCAP's publisher members was similar. Due apparently to ASCAP's founders and its original governance structure, publishers were divided into several groups with the effect of multiplying or discounting the royalties due them in relation to the play that their songs received. In 1935 Warner Bros.'s song publishers, on the losing end of this hierarchy, withdrew and sought to create their own licensing organization, but the scale-economy advantages of sticking with ASCAP proved overwhelming.[30]

ASCAP Faces Competition

By the late 1930s ASCAP had brought all major classes of music users under license for performance royalties. Its licensees were sullen but not mutinous. ASCAP then began maneuvering to impose an increase that would double its royalty stream from radio, with the change structured to load the burden on the broadcast networks and ease it on individual small stations.[31] With existing licenses expiring at the end of 1940, ASCAP furthermore was coy about exactly what terms it would demand, so the odor of a hold-up reached the networks' nostrils. In 1939 the National Association of Broadcasters set to work establishing BMI as a competitor to ASCAP. This did not prove a difficult task, because the radio industry (the principal source of performance royalties) stood ready to welcome new songs and songwriters. Only one major publisher was attracted from ASCAP, because of the problem of relocating a publisher and his songwriters all at once.[32] A substantial clientele of songwriters and publishers was receptive to the invitation, however, because the organization had never welcomed other music styles—such as rhythm and blues, country and western, and Latin.[33] Furthermore, in 1940 the admission of any publisher or songwriter to ASCAP was subject to rather stringent conditions of prior activity and success. Restrictiveness obviously benefited current members, who could divide the blanket-license revenue among fewer recipients, but it opened the door to a competing coalition.[34] In April 1940 NBC and CBS instructed their music departments to avoid use of ASCAP songs whenever possible, and a progressively imposed boycott eliminated ASCAP songs from radio play by the beginning of 1941. Between BMI's holdings and public-domain music, the boycott brought only a minor jolt to the nation's radio audience.[35] In the settlement finally reached with ASCAP in late 1941, royalty obligations were indeed focused on the networks (a function of their numbers of affiliates and gross revenues), with simple blanket licenses for individual stations, but the charges represented a cut rather than the increase that ASCAP had sought. One estimate held that, had ASCAP's 1941 contract been in effect during 1935, ASCAP would have collected $3.1 million rather than the nearly $5 million that it actually collected.[36]

Important changes in ASCAP's internal policies sprang from this competition, when it led the Department of Justice to intervene in 1940. Probably intending to force an ASCAP-radio settlement, the Justice Department brought broad charges of illegal pooling, price-fixing, and discrimination against ASCAP, BMI, NBC, and CBS. BMI soon signed a consent decree permitting its members to license songs directly when they wished (that is, membership did not entail exclusive licensing) and requiring that per-piece or per-program as well as blanket licenses be offered. ASCAP came under similar restrictions. That organization was also forced to ease its entry restrictions and reform its old-boy governance structure. The reformed payment system placed increased weight on performance and decreased weight on seniority in payments to songwriters. In 1950 the consent decrees were modified to impose arbitration by a U.S. district court when ASCAP and licensees could not agree on terms. ASCAP became in principle a regulated monopoly, although there has been little resort to arbitration.[37]

This episode not only introduced competition in royalty collection but also affected the songwriting and music publishing industries substantially. The number of active music publishers and the turnover in their success with top-hits songs increased, and the copyright registrations of songs increased more than the nation's economic recovery seems able to explain.[38]

Ongoing Negotiation and Rivalry

ASCAP and BMI settled into a pattern of rivalry with each other and continual conflict with licensees and potential licensees involving a morass of negotiations, lawsuits, threatened lawsuits, and contests for political influence. The blanket licenses favored by both ASCAP and BMI have been under continuous attack despite their previously noted efficiency, and despite the fact that licenses on a per-program basis had to be offered since 1941. Licensees' attacks usually rested on this sort of reasoning: The licensee pays ASCAP (or BMI) X for use of any or all of the many thousands of songs it represents, but it only wants to use a small fraction $1/n$ of these, so instead it should be allowed to pay (X/n) for just the songs that it wants. Given ASCAP's legal power to extract the value added by performance of copyrighted songs, the argument is spurious. The licensee has in fact already made his choice of the $1/n$ songs that he actually uses, and pays a license fee reflecting (presumably) the value added by this ad-libed selection of songs. The tactical purpose of the position is to force ASCAP to quote license fees on specific songs; because the copyright collective may not prevent the publisher from making his own deal, that would allow the licensee to start a bidding war between ASCAP and its member publisher. The outcome would leave ASCAP serving only as a collection agency.[39] One version or another of this attack on blanket licenses was pursued first by the broadcast networks (led by CBS), then in a class-action suit by local TV stations, and most recently by cable program suppliers and cable system operators. In each round, the courts declined in the end to find blanket licenses illegal.[40]

What one makes of blanket licensing as a matter of economic policy depends on the level of the license fees set. If transaction costs were magically swept away, and holders of song copyrights could compete freely to line up licensees and collect from them, the licensees would get the benefit of lowered prices due to rivalry among these differentiated products. If ASCAP's blanket licenses represented a pure monopolization of songwriters' services, they would create an economic distortion. ASCAP does compete with BMI, however. Also, it operates under supervisory court decrees that hold out arbitration as a cap on license fees. Although the effect on license fees cannot be quantified, ASCAP and BMI have certainly competed in setting terms with the main groups of licensees. Licensee groups do not typically seek bids and take one or the other collective's bundle of songs. Both are bought, but their bundles of songs (though different considerably in composition because they still reflect their respective origins) are comparable in overall size, so that one collective cannot generally hold out for a blanket license fee much higher than the other's.[41] The collectives appear to be unable to price their blanket licenses monopolistically, although the amount of shortfall is unclear.

Rivalry between ASCAP and BMI has also affected the terms that they offer to publishers and songwriters. ASCAP's favoritism of its old boys has been a point of vulnerability. If some members get more than the royalties imputable to their songs, others must get less, and the competing collective can perhaps offer them a better deal. Although each organization's rules impose some lock-in, they are active rivals in recruiting members, and this has squeezed out some of the redistribution implicit in their disbursement methods.[42] The favorable effects of rivalry between ASCAP and BMI in setting license fees and attracting members should be weighed against the element of natural monopoly that brought ASCAP into being in the first place. Each maintains an administrative apparatus that represents a separate fixed cost.[43] Combining them into a single entity would save one fixed cost, plus the cost of their continual legal skirmishes with each other, but the benefits of their competition would be lost.[44]

The struggle to bring public music users into licensee status continues. Jukebox operators succeeded for two decades in preserving a Congressional exemption from royalty payments, but finally lost it in the copyright legislation of 1976. Cable television also became liable for licensing at that time. The act removed the "for profit" condition on public performance subject to license, pushing the Public Broadcasting System into licensee status. Religious broadcasters were put under license, although they have lately followed the course of seeking exemption or rate regulation from Congress.[45] ASCAP, with perhaps more legal propriety than political savvy, sought to license the Girl Scouts and other campfire singers of copyrighted songs.[46]

Songwriters' and Publishers' 50–50 Split

The equal division of all types of music royalties (except sheet-music sales) between songwriter and publisher is another puzzling conventionalized price. ASCAP adopted this rule early in its history, and songwriters and publishers hold equal numbers of seats on its board of directors. The rule cannot claim to be an equilibrium price, clearing the market for services of songwriters and publishers. Since publishers serve as gatekeepers, and many songs go unpublished (and unsung), the amount of music published will depend on this rule. Increase the songwriters' share, and fewer songs will be published, although each will earn more revenue. Over the twentieth century the publisher's contribution to a song's success has greatly diminished. The crumbled market for sheet music and the dominance of the singer-performer as recording artist removed most of the music publisher's promotional function (although the pursuit of mechanical and synchronization royalties remains) and left him with mainly bookkeeping tasks.

If the 50–50 split represented a market equilibrium when it was adopted in the 1920s, it evidently moved toward overvaluing the publisher's contribution. This could lead to a number of adjustments, such as underemployed publishers pursuing a diminished supply of songwriters and seeking kernels among the chaff of unpublished songs. In fact the publisher's role has contracted to the point where anybody can be a music publisher. The only essential task is the administration of the copyright, and that can be subcontracted to other firms. The movie studios first responded to this incentive with the coming of sound, which put them in need of access to music catalogues. It also generated opportunities to publish (and collect royalties for) music written for use in films, notably "work for hire" whose copyright benefit flowed to the employer rather than the salaried composer. By the early 1930s Warner Bros. controlled no less than 20 percent of ASCAP-assigned music.[47]

With the arrival of rock and the singer-songwriter, music royalties came to yield immense wealth to publishers as well as songwriters, incidental to the process of making and promoting recordings. By 1990 Paul McCartney's "Yesterday" had been recorded by 1,600 other artists worldwide, all yielding mechanical royalties to the songwriter.[48] The record labels moved vigorously to start or acquire their own music publishers, especially in Britain, land of the Beatles.[49] If the label could become a music publisher, so could the songwriter, and in the 1970s successful songwriters began owning their own publishing companies.[50] A publishing firm can dwell in a file drawer, owned by the songwriter but administered by one of the major (conventional) music publishers. As a consequence, ASCAP recently represented 29,400 songwriters but also 12,000 publishers, while BMI counted 65,000 and 37,000, respectively.[51]

Music publishers' royalties become a contention in contracts between songwriter-performers and labels because both wished to claim the publisher royalties. Labels tend to demand publishing rights for a new and untried artist because of the high probability that the advance will not be fully recouped. That is because mechanical royalties to the artist's publishing company are not recoupable by the label, while those due to its own publisher flow directly to its pocket. When the artist does retain the publishing function, the label caps the rate of mechanical royalties to 75 percent of the Copyright Royalty Tribunal rate.[52]

The publisher's share of music royalties has turned into a freely traded cash flow.[53] The copyright administrator still performs bookkeeping and perhaps promotional tasks, but the administrator may be the assignee rather than the owner of publishing rights, so nothing impedes trading them like any other speculative asset. In 1985 Michael Jackson bought the ATV catalogue, including some 250 Beatles songs and numerous others, for less than $50 million.[54] In 1988 the copyright on "Happy Birthday to You," with 22 years of life remaining, was bought by Warner Communications for $28 million.[55] Bargains have no doubt been available in this market when estate sales and corporate reorganizations put song catalogues on the market, but rivalry among international entertainment and publishing conglomerates has pushed up prices, to the benefit of owners of song catalogues.[56]

Creative Work without Copyright: British Novelists in Nineteenth-Century America

Copyright and other intellectual property rights are largely settled in the laws of the industrial countries, but they raise an international conflict with other countries that deny protection to foreigners' intellectual property and then do a brisk business in pirated and counterfeit editions. Economists are curious about how people adjust to different systems of property rights. In the field of copyright, history offers an adroit controlled experiment. The United States did not extend the copyright privilege to books by foreign authors until 1891, and so Britain's Victorian novelists and their publishers had to cope with a thriving band of piratical U.S. publishers.

Lacking a legal property right, parties seek a preemptive substitute.[57] Before 1891 British books were regularly pirated in the United States, but subject to considerable honor among thieves. A published book imported from Britain could be copied without payment to author or publisher, but it could be copied earlier if the British author were paid to provide proof sheets of the London edition. The U.S. publisher with a known head start had a decisive advantage, unless the book was so popular that it made a second American version profitable. That mechanism let British writers command substantial honoraria from the pirates. Typesetting technologies in the early nineteenth century caused the author to receive proofs in small batches over relatively long periods of time, and so the author's duplicate proofs often (without benefit of author's corrections) made their way across the Atlantic.[58]

This preemptive strategy was supported by a practice of "trade courtesy" among the U.S. publishers. When an ad was placed in *Commercial Advertiser* announcing the publication of a foreign author, it was accepted as fixing priority among a quite large number of reputable U.S. publishers (whether or not the British author got paid). Coordination problems were not absent, however, because U.S. publishers had no way to know whether the British author or the publisher held the right to publish abroad, so conflicting negotiations could take place.[59]

The lack of copyright did not necessarily preclude mutually agreeable repeated dealings between U.S. publishers and British authors, a practice well illustrated by the experience of novelist William Makepeace Thackeray. His first "book" was a pirated U.S. edition of a serial that had appeared in *Fraser's Magazine* in 1837, and it and subsequent piracies gained him a substantial reputation in the United States that later created an eager demand for his lecture tours (which Thackeray considered easy money). Harper and Brothers became his regular pirate, thanks to trade courtesy, and made substantial voluntary payments for all his books beginning with *Henry Esmond*. Only one duplicating pirate edition appeared, for *The Virginians*, which was expected to be his most profitable book in the United States. Appleton did issue Thackeray's works extensively in a paperback series, and they also offered compensation of 100 pounds sterling for editing volumes out of his contributions to *Punch*; these Thackeray could later use in a series of collections put out by his British publisher.[60]

Before 1891 American authors had long supported U.S. copyright privileges for their British colleagues, perhaps from professional courtesy, but certainly because their royalty-free volumes were low-cost competitors. Wendy Griswold sampled novels published in America between 1876 and 1910, divided about equally between U.S. and foreign authors. Before 1891, she found, books by American authors carried higher list prices ($1.04 versus $0.64 during 1876–1884); after 1891, American books were cheaper ($1.22 versus $1.38 during 1905–1910). The proportion of authors in her sample who were Americans rose from 48 percent to 67 percent, as the obligation to pay royalties cut into the profitability of British authors' U.S. editions. She also found some evidence that, before 1891, American authors had differentiated their subject matter and themes some distance away from the British novelists. That divergence declined after the change in copyright policy.[61]

Copyright in Perspective

This chapter has focused on a few issues of the many that arise with intellectual property rights and the behavior that they promote. Composers of songs, symphonies, dances, and plays all require the collaboration of performing artists, and they all hold the right to collect royalties when their creations get public performance. Only song composers face a dire problem of efficient collection. The educational use of brief passages of published text, however, is quickly sending their copyright holders to watch over the photocopy machine and the website, hoping to scoop up increasingly similar streams consisting of many small particles of benefit. Collective collection seems inevitable in this area as well.

For other artists, rent streams are easier to capture, because public presentation of their works involves a large and conspicuous transaction—a new production of a play or opera, a new edition of a novel. Still others find themselves at a disadvantage, cut off from access to the small rents that could flow from their creations. The novelist collects every time her book is sold, but not every time it is read. She might price discriminate between libraries (many prospective readers) and sales to individuals (one or a few readers), as do many scholarly journals. The composer is fenced off by practicality from collecting each time a music-lover plays her recording. The legal doctrine of first sale here codifies practicality. The visual artist neither legally nor practically can collect from each viewer who enjoys her work on the museum wall—although she can now generally collect each time her work is photographically reproduced.

Similar margins of practicality affect other artists who might lay claim to rents. For complex goods assembled by a *motley crew* of artists, feasible collection falters because the proportional contribution of each to the finished work defies definition or negotiation. That has not precluded the bitter disputes over unexpected rents from cinema films, with the copyright owners repeated and vigorously pressed by creative participants to hand over some of the bounty (Chapter 7).

20

Entertainment Conglomerates and the Quest for Rents

Diversified firms carry out activities in different product and geographic markets. The media and entertainment conglomerates are wrapped up with the pursuit of rents from creative goods because these families of companies link markets wherein creative goods materialize with those through which final consumers receive them.[1] The causes and consequences of large, diversified firms and their merger transactions form a huge subject, and this chapter is highly selective. It is not about the sources of synergistic gains to conglomerates in general. It is not about whether large mergers create value for the participants, or whether the heads of such firms maximize benefits for their shareholders or for themselves. And it is not about conglomerates' effects on the structures of the markets in which they operate. Instead, this chapter explores how the distinct properties of creative industries interact with the activities of conglomerates.

An enterprise can operate in several markets without being big or well-known, but the giants stand out conspicuously in the creative industries. Time Warner carries out magazine and book publishing, makes and distributes cinema and TV films, distributes sound recordings, and operates cable TV networks and systems. Viacom, Disney, and News Corporation show similar spans. Germany's Bertelsmann and Britain's Pearson undertake publishing activities in numerous countries. The creative industries have seen waves of expansionist urges that struck several competitors at the same time. In the 1960s American firms sought to link "hardware" and "software" activities. In the 1970s hardcover and paperback books were combined. Then linkages between media content and media distribution channels became the fashion of the day, followed in turn by the expansion of international conglomerates centered in book and magazine publishing.

Creativity and Bureaucracy

A large enterprise must be bureaucratic and rule-based to coordinate its team members in pursuit of a common set of objectives. Carrying out related tasks in several markets only deepens the need. One expects that the inner-driven and nonconforming artistic temperament and the rational and rule-bound bureaucratic organization will not mix. That is true, and nicely illustrated by Judith Adler's chronicle of California Institute for the Arts, but their immiscibility does have subtle implications about the limits of applying orderly bureaucratic procedures to creative activities.[2] However capable conglomerate organizations are at pursuing streams of rents, they are limited by their infelicity for organizing creative work.

When it comes to organizing economic activity, "bureaucracy" is a mechanism, not a put-down. A business firm or nearly any purposive organization adopts a hierarchical decision structure in which a top coordinator sets tasks and incentives, gathers and analyzes information on activities and performance, and distributes rewards. Such an organization is rational in the sense that it can explain why it did what it did. Its chosen action might prove disastrous, but it is seldom capricious. Its actions generally appear fair if one accepts the axioms on which its rules are based. It can make plans, and it can filter from the chaff the important bits of information on which the top coordinators must concentrate. Yet many tales (like those in Chapter 8 on failed films) record the woes of fitting creative activities within a benign bureaucracy.

The first problem is that *nobody knows,* and yet business planning requires multiyear cash-flow projections. A book publisher is acquired by a large, bureaucratic firm, and its editors and other personnel are asked for medium-term projections of how many books they will publish and how many copies of each will be sold. Estimates are duly written down, but there is no place to record the wide bands of uncertainty that surround them. The problem is not the editor's accountability per se: after signing a series of turkeys, any editor expects to be seeking new opportunities. The trouble is that costly resources are used to contrive and justify forecasts that convey little reliable information.[3] More costly still, low-precision estimates become grist for the planning process with their uncertainty suppressed, so that planners focus on adapting to the predicted outcome rather than adapting to the width of the range of plausible outcomes. Consider how the problem bears on particular investment decisions. Building a warehouse and issuing a new rap album are both capital outlays that a firm might make. The former should be capable of reasoned justification on the basis of its construction cost and its operating value for reducing shipping costs, serving customers more rapidly, and so on.

For the album the talent scout can meaningfully say only that he likes it and that it falls within recognized and salable genres ("A crossed with Z" is a shorthand form commonly used to classify creative goods). The vagueness of the justification is not a remediable problem, simply a given. The problem is the resources used in contriving and reviewing the justification. In 1998 the international record company PolyGram NV found itself with a chief executive widely regarded as a strong strategic planner, yet who got into repeated friction with the creative heads of independent record labels purchased by PolyGram.[4] Cases seem fairly common in which an entrepreneurial firm in a creative activity is bought by a bureaucratic enterprise, only to see the departure en masse of the leaders who provided much of whatever rent-yielding assets the acquired business possessed. For example, the United Artists studio in 1967, owned by Arthur Krim and Robert Benjamin, prospered from having anticipated the reorganization of filmmaking from the integrated studio to the one-off deal (see Chapter 5). It was acquired by Transamerica, a large insurance company, which sought to impose its managerial systems on United Artists. After a decade of internal warfare Krim, Benjamin, and three other executives departed to form a new company (Orion).[5]

Columbia Pictures was rocked by an embezzlement by its head of production, David Begelman. In most other lines of business, the crime would be reported (by law) to the U.S. Securities and Exchange Commission and the embezzler discharged. But Begelman's success as a filmmaker and his place in the network of Hollywood dealmaking ultimately caused the board instead to fire the CEO who sought to discharge him.[6]

One reason for the skewed size distributions of firms found in most creative industries is the distinction between pickers and promoters (Chapter 2), a distinction rooted in the problematic interface between artists and bureaucracies. The promoter can provide extensive distribution and advertising services, while the picker can offer personalized attention unfettered by bureaucratic rules. The promoter pays a cost for rule-based resistance to the free swings of creative inspiration, and separating the functions minimizes the strained contacts between artist and bureaucrat. Another source of the conglomerate's problems with artists is pressures to provide comparable treatment to artists who view themselves as comparable. Consider the problem in the abstract. Recording stars A and B, self-perceived close competitors, are under contract to different companies, each having taken the best deal offered. If A feels that B has the better deal, there may be anguish, but there is no recourse in A's contract. Now put A and B under contract to the same company. The terms of A's contract renewal become the floor of B's demands the next time around, and grounds for discontent and departure if B's wish is not satisfied. The attitude should not be written off to pettiness or self-regard on the artists' part. Bureaucratic enterprises constantly face the problem of comparable treatment with their humdrum employees, who might rationally suspect opportunism on behalf of the firm: for example, that the firm is taking advantage of knowledge that A's spouse's job precludes easy movement to a new employer. In Clive Davis's account of his dealings with artists at Columbia Records, the problem surfaces repeatedly. Despite Columbia's efforts to obfuscate the comparability issue, the firm found itself losing artists or failing to gain new ones because of the implied costs lurking in perceived comparability.[7]

The bureaucratic firm in creative industries may fumble not because it is large, but because it is dealing in an unfamiliar market. Its bureaucratic apparatus may be attuned to humdrum activities, so that it misperceives causes and effects in the market at hand. The British film studio Goldcrest was undermined by an inexperienced CEO and board of directors. The board chose to set a target rate of return, then discuss the number of films to make—an approach by no means folly in a predictable, humdrum business. The unappreciated fundamental constraint was the supply of good projects.[8] Similarly, when Columbia Pictures was owned by Coca-Cola, Columbia's own veteran producers were well aware of the haste-makes-waste problem in assembling film projects—raising the number of film deals lowers the chances of assembling the optimal crew for each. Top management, however, demanded a larger output. They knew that film deals are risky, but thought they would grow no riskier as the number was increased.[9] Another familiar type of control-system failure occurs when management misperceives a short-term run of luck as a heaven-sent sign of its prowess rather than a random event, and acts to increase creative output.[10] A survey of editors who work for publishing houses with large corporate owners elicited a list of disadvantages that all turn on the controlling enterprise's lack of understanding of the publishing business. They did benefit, however, from higher salaries, access to funding for large projects, and improved technical services.[11]

Bureaucratic budgetary and financial control over creative projects poses a particularly severe problem, as Chapter 8 showed. Humdrum investment projects sometimes incur cost overruns, but in a predictable environment blame can be traced to specific exogenous shocks or to somebody's error. Thanks to *infinite variety* no two creative projects have identical input-output technologies, so the sources of cost overrun are difficult to pin down. With *art for art's sake* the creative worker tends to face limitless opportunities to incur costs for possible aesthetic gains. The bureaucracy that monitors the artist tries to regulate costs that are uncertain at the start, and in the hands of a decisionmaker with a strong incentive to increase them.

Some horror stories from Hollywood suggest that this problem of financial monitoring extends to the creative firm or subsidiary overall—studio heads and not just film directors. The economic logic (which also pertains to the music industry) is tricky to explain. Randomly successful films bestow large lumps of rent on the creative participants, and their conspicuous consumption is a ripe tradition. If success brings excess in activities where the outcomes of today's efforts are so unpredictable, can excess not have some value for signaling success? Examples recur of large enterprises—especially those based outside the United States—taking control of successful creative firms in the hope of injecting capital to let them expand on their past successes. When Sony acquired Columbia Pictures, it not only paid richly for the firm itself but spent an extra billion dollars obtaining the management services of successful filmmakers Peter Guber and Jon Peters (buying out their current contracts, acquiring their own business assets). Although neither man had previously run a major enterprise, their taste and talent for on-the-job consumption were immediately put to use. Financial controllers soon discovered that the studio's overhead was running $50 million to $75 million a year higher than those of competing studios.[12]

A similar example in the music industry involves Casablanca Records, which quickly rose and fell in the 1970s along with the disco fad. Started in 1973 and initially financed by Warner Bros., the label was highly successful with some of its artists. In 1977 PolyGram bought a half-interest in the firm and made funds freely available to expand its output. PolyGram also acquired several other U.S. record companies and a large, automated distribution system, with the intent to establish itself as a major competitor in the U.S. popular record industry. Casablanca satisfied PolyGram's eagerness for a large volume of output by shipping huge volumes of records to retail stores that had full return privileges. The soundtrack album from the film based on "Sgt. Pepper's Lonely Hearts Club Band" sold 3 million copies and would have been highly profitable, except that 8 million copies were shipped and 5 million returned. While the disco market was collapsing in 1979, Casablanca was still signing new artists for six-figure advances plus promotion expenses. PolyGram, which had similar problems with another U.S. record subsidiary, by 1985 had lost $220 million in the United States.[13] Any multiactivity firm faces a difficult task in motivating its various divisional managers to pursue a common objective (presumably, maximizing the parent firm's profits). Where loose-jointed creativity and on-the-job consumption of perquisites are hard for the outsider to distinguish, the control problem burgeons.

Rents, Auctions, and Media Conglomerates

If media conglomerates emerge despite these difficulties, the decisionmakers who assemble them must expect some offsetting benefits. The benefits are seldom articulated clearly to the public when the firm assembles its portfolio of businesses. They may be difficult to detect after the deal is completed. That is not only because within-the-firm adjustments are hard to observe and obscured by other disturbances that are always occurring, but also because the benefits may be contingent, and the circumstances that would trigger them may never arrive. The benefits may simply prove illusory, as is suggested by the frequent reverses of merger transactions and reshufflings of acquired assets.[14]

Conglomerates versus Arm's-Length Auctions

One benefit ("synergy") regularly sought by media conglomerates has been the pursuit of rents to the creative good over time and among the niches of various markets. Consider the full-fledged media conglomerate whose trade-publisher branch signs what turns out to be a successful and popular novel. The firm's paperback publisher can later bring out the cheap edition. The firm's film studio can contract for and distribute the motion picture in the United States and abroad. The studio later shows the film on the conglomerate's TV broadcasting network and over its cable systems. The film's screenplay is "novelized"—reconverted to a novel, illustrated with stills from the film—and published as another book by the paperback division. The conglomerate's music division issues the film's sound track on compact disc, and the firm's TV film division builds a dramatic series around its characters. All these cash flows contain excess profits, because the underlying literary property is a sunk cost, an asset that can be endlessly recycled at only the cost of restyling or transforming it.

This vision of the media conglomerate's inexhaustible cash machine has a fundamental defect. Who owns the property right in the underlying literary work, and what role does ownership play in this sequence of transactions? The novel's author holds the right. Her agent will maximize the value of her asset (and thereby the agent's commission) by staging an auction, not just for the whole bundle of uses of the property but for each one individually, or for bundles of them where they are interdependent.[15] Trade publishers bid for the initial hardback publication. Paperback publishers bid for paperback publication rights. Filmmakers bid for the right to convert the novel to a film; the winning film studio will reckon in the profits that it subsequently expects to reap by auctioning the film for subsidiary showings after its initial round on the exhibition circuit. If the author's agent can manage each auction capably, and if the bidders in each auction have the same capability for squeezing revenue out of the rights that they seek, all the rent attributable to the underlying novel in each of these uses will flow to the author, who has the primary unique, rent-yielding asset in this chain of activities.[16] A media conglomerate could offer the agent a package deal covering the whole bundle of uses, but unless the conglomerate enjoys some *other* efficiency advantage over independent trade publishers, film studios, and the like, it cannot profitably bid more than the aggregate value that the agent can extract in various separate auctions. The conglomerate might benefit opportunistically by manipulating transfer prices in its various internal transactions so as to divert revenue away from the artist's royalties. This is hardly a long-run winning game, as artists are all too ready to expect it.[17] The media conglomerate's vision of rents from in-house exploitation of the literary property may be an illusion.[18]

In only one plausible set of circumstances can the conglomerate squeeze more revenue from an underlying creative input. Consider a concept for a major motion picture that promises profits from successive windows of theatrical and TV exhibition, soundtrack album, figurines distributed through fast-food restaurants, toys, and keepsakes. The independent studio gifted with the concept can make and distribute its film, auctioning each subsidiary use to the highest bidder. If it were an integrated conglomerate enterprise, however, it might be able to raise the value of the whole stream of rents, in the following way. Suppose that the value generated in each subsidiary use depends on initial creative decisions about how to make and promote the underlying film. Suppose also that the film studio, whether independent or part of a conglomerate, cannot itself identify all the ways in which its decisions about the cinema film might be bent toward increasing rents in subsidiary uses, but business units active in the subsidiary-use markets do have this information. The conglomerate perhaps can raise the value of the whole stream of rents by bringing its business-unit siblings into the project at the beginning. The idea is to optimize the first embodiment of the concept (the cinema film) not just for maximum revenue from the cinema-exhibition market, but from this and the series of subsidiary markets taken together. With this input incorporated, the conglomerate's profit can exceed what an independent owner of the concept could exact through auctioning exhibition rights.[19]

Conglomerates' Role in Practice

The trade publishing industry is a good site for studying conglomerates' role in pursuing rents. The ownership of many large publishing houses has passed among diverse buyers over the years. The publishing industry also offers a feature affined to creative activities—a tradition of publishers who value the promotion of good books as a worthy activity, implying that some profits on commercially successful books get diverted to cover losses run by meritorious volumes. One role of the proverbially heartless large enterprise—or of *any* enterprise closely monitored by equity holders interested only in humdrum profits—is to halt such diversions of profit. The evidence leaves several impressions about the major changes and conglomerates' roles in them.

PREDOMINANCE OF AUCTION VALUES   Among books that reasonably aspire to large sales, the auction of rights has become the regnant allocation mechanism, whether it is the agent's invitational auction of a manuscript among selected publishers (an event designed to tease out complex, multiterm offers) or an open auction of paperback or film rights (where the only issue is the cash offer). Auctions extract value in a straightforward fashion. The auction is timed with respect to the hardback's publication schedule, after the publisher has committed some of its own promotional outlays, a maximum buzz has been set off, and certifications such as book-club selections are in hand. A round of sealed bids may precede an open auction, allowing the auctioneer a flexible approach to exposing the maximum willingness to pay. The winning bidder seems unlikely to hang onto much of its expected profit, and indeed it is at hazard of the winner's curse (the victor is the bidder who most overestimates the property's value).[20]

COMPETITION AMONG PUBLISHERS   The predominance of auction values (helped by the entry of "unsentimental" value maximizers) has tied the major publishers' policies more tightly to maximizing economic value. An important implication of the one-time "gentlemanly" publisher is that losses on good but noncommercial books had to be covered somehow, likely by excess profits on commercially successful books. Cheney's survey of the 1920s industry suggests that publishers indeed then did not compete in royalty rates and advances for highly promising books, thus generating the necessary surplus.[21] Growing competition for these winners pushed publishers' policies toward those that maximize economic value. For example, the publishing-house editor's work once centered on assisting the author with the manuscript's final shaping and polishing, but has shifted toward entrepreneurial shepherding of the book through the publishing house and, in particular, managing its promotion.[22]

CONGLOMERATES' PUBLISHING OPERATIONS   Publishing arms of media conglomerates have not been able to halt the auction's capture of maximum value for the author and had to work within it. The experience of paying top dollar at auction no doubt led paperback publishers to form their own hardback divisions.[23] The integrating firms probably thought that their internal communications links would give them an advantage in an auction-dominated environment, but observers find little evidence of that.[24] A hardback publisher's favorable treatment of its corporate sibling's paperback publisher of course invites a legal challenge from the author for self-dealing. The efficient scale (titles per year) for a paperback publisher is far larger than for a hardback publisher, so that self-supply would be awkward for a paperback house to organize, even if it worked well. Paperback licenses are not open-ended but are for short fixed terms, such as five years. Paperback publishers who acquired or started their own hardback publishers learned that the sales-promotion processes at the two stages are quite different.[25]

One test of the auction's role draws on the policies of conglomerates that control several publishers who might compete against one another in a given auction. The enterprise of course has reason not to let its houses bid outright against one another. If auctions usefully flush out independent viewpoints on the value and development potential of a literary property, however, the parent enterprise might well let them compete as long as other (independent) houses remain in the auction. The conglomerates appear to follow just this policy, halting the internal competition only when the last independent drops out.[26]

The presence of free-spending conglomerates in trade publishing probably enriched the authors of blockbuster books more than it did the conglomerates themselves. If incumbent publishing houses are constrained for cash to offer big advances to such authors, the well-heeled outside firm sees the opportunity to get into the game by outbidding the incumbents and still making a profit. It takes only two big spenders in an auction, however, to transfer much of the surplus to the lucky author.

CONGLOMERATES' LONGEVITY A survival test seems appropriate for the economic productivity of conglomerate businesses in the publishing industry.[27] The technology-based firms that acquired publishers in the 1960s later exited from the industry. General Electric and Litton Industries sold their publishing branches; Xerox sold its college publishing division to John Wiley; RCA sold the Random House group of publishers to the Newhouse newspaper interests.[28] Later, the entertainment conglomerates mostly lost faith in their publishing acquisitions. Newhouse sold Random House to the German book and magazine publisher Bertelsmann. MCA (Universal), upon its purchase by Seagram, sold Putnam Berkeley to British publisher Pearson. Viacom has placed Simon & Schuster on offer. Only Time Warner clings to part of Little, Brown. The gains from international diversification within the publishing industry are now under test, as firms bet that they can exploit their copyright material internationally better through integrated operations than by licensing.[29]

The better do markets function (the more smoothly, more predictably, lower transaction costs), the less scope remains for improving on them through transactions within diversified companies. Auctioning the paperback version of a trade book is an easy case. The article to be auctioned is down in black and white (or its electronic equivalent). The paperback house merely prints it on cheap paper and has little scope for either improving it or spoiling it. In the deal between agent or hardback publisher and the paperback houses, only the money matters. When the best sequence for pursuing rents among successive venues is unclear, when each venue's styling of the core creative product might affect (favorably or unfavorably) the rents collectible in other venues, internalization within the firm might offer greater advantages.

Evidence on this point is only suggestive. To confirm a synergy, one must not only pin down the cash flow that it contributes, but also show that it would elude arm's-length transactions. The Disney Corporation and its theme parks pose an example. Disney's core assets are its copyrighted cartoon characters and a reputation for providing wholesome family entertainment. These could hardly have been licensed at arm's length to an independent operator of theme parks, as no such industry existed. Furthermore, the real possibility exists that a licensee might use Disney's assets in ways (say, an adult-entertainment corner of the theme park) that would be profitable for the licensee while reducing the value of Disney's intangible assets. The licensing contract's terms would seek to prevent that, of course, but a major reason for internalization within the firm is exactly the difficulty of writing contracts that anticipate all the disparities of interest that may arise between independent (self-interested) parties who share a common asset.[30] The same may apply to Disney's recent venture into the production of Broadway musicals based on its animated films. An independent producer could have been licensed, but the uncertain technology of producing a musical show and the difficulty of contracting on further uses (traveling companies, show-tune albums, and the like) certainly argued against it.

Another condition favoring synergy in the integrated firm is uncertainty about the initial styling of the core intangible product or about the sequence in which its rents should be pursued. The success of Michael Ovitz's firm Creative Artists Agency was attributed to the packaging of creative elements (script or literary property, actors, directors, and so on) without any form preconceived for its initial embodiment in a finished creative good (a cinema film? TV series? novel?).[31] If such fungible opportunities exist to style and combine creative inputs, they give value to the opportunity for screening the "raw" creative inputs at the earliest possible stage. One reason for an entertainment conglomerate's integration into book or magazine publishing lies in the volume and variety of elemental creative inputs seen at that stage.

Great value might be found not in the polished book or article that may then be auctioned for subsequent use, but in the idea or concept turning up on an acquisition editor's desk but better developed for another embodiment, or for a whole sequence of uses. An investment seeking just this benefit was Disney's decision to hire *New Yorker*'s former editor Tina Brown to start a new magazine that might screen material useful to Disney. The expected rate of return to magazine start-ups would hardly be a directly promising investment of Disney's funds, a fact that underlines the central role of synergistic benefits in the deal.[32] Such trade in creative seedlings does have its counterpart in transactions between firms, in the symmetrical exchanges of information that occur among editors employed by different publishing houses or engineers from different high-tech firms, but for these exchanges to be mutually productive the parties must bring roughly comparable endowments of information to the swap.[33]

Vertical Integration: Rent-Seeking or Trap-Avoiding?

Many conglomerates in creative industries become vertically integrated, following the tracks that take creative goods from their fabrication through the distribution channels to consumers. Vertical integration is commonplace in the economy and usually solves a clear-cut problem. The actions taken by the parties "upstream" (U) and "downstream" (D) affect each other's profits. U's car part is more valuable to D when designed specifically to work in D's auto. When U skimps on the part's fabrication cost, it may cause related components in D's car to fail more often. When U encounters a production or shipping problem, and the parts arrive late, D incurs costs from disrupted production. The merger of U and D "internalizes" these problems—addresses them to maximize U's and D's profit together—and aids their efficient resolution.

Merging with a Gatekeeper

This explanation seldom has much force for vertically integrated media conglomerates—the film distributor that acquires the broadcast TV network, the cinema chain, the cable TV network, or the cable system operator. U is more in the position of the artist seeking or ensuring selection by the gatekeeper, while gatekeeper D is concerned for the adequacy or continuity of supply from U and its competitors.[34] Over time U offers a stream of creative goods that vary unpredictably in their appeal to ultimate customers: *nobody knows*. D shops for a portfolio of creative goods to provide its customers *(infinite variety)*; it may shift the portfolio's composition from time to time, but it can post notice of this for all program suppliers. It occurs to U, why not acquire control of D as a regular channel for the distribution of U's output? U might benefit in two ways. First, however U and D go about sharing the fluctuating and uncertain profits that individual creative goods elicit from consumers, U will face less uncertainty if D gives an equally warm reception to U's blockbusters and turkeys. Second, the higher the price D firms pay for the program inputs they select, the more value does U realize by controlling D's choices and diverting them from competing suppliers to its own outputs. Vertical integration then becomes the capitalized payola mentioned in Chapter 18.

The trouble with this plan is that if an independent D occasionally recognizes one of U's products as a turkey and rejects it, D's profits will be dragged down (and their uncertainty increased) when it becomes U's captive outlet. U may pick up some profit when a captive D takes a turkey that an independent D would decline, but D's profits suffer as a result, and U tends to lose on its investment in D what it gains when D accepts its turkey. A market with many U's and D's and with uncertain quality of individual products would work well enough without any vertical integration. Indeed, if the D's have some ability to spot turkeys among their suppliers' offerings, U's investment in D will not pay: the captive D will waste resources on a turkey that independent D's would let expire. Independence of the D and U firms will lead to better performance. If the D's are all controlled by U's, and each takes only its partner's creative goods, the performance of the D's suffers in two ways. Each D offers consumers a weaker package when it is limited to just one U's goods than when it can pick among all of them. And consumers suffer through some turkeys that no D would present without lock-in to a partner U.[35]

So far, the argument has assumed that both the U's and D's are numerous. If they are few in number, and each fears strategic attacks by its rivals, vertical integration is more likely to spring up and persist. Suppose that one U buys control of one D, gaining the power (if it chooses) to decline to take the creative goods of other U's. Even if such foreclosure does not pay, other U's may nonetheless fear that the integrated firm may choose self-supply. The remaining independents have fewer transaction partners. Other U and D firms march to the altar, with the incentive growing stronger as the marriage partners become fewer. Fears of predatory exclusion are laid to rest by integration, but this profit consumed as untroubled sleep has no pecuniary benefit to the combined firms; indeed, if customers enjoy a better selection among creative goods in a nonintegrated market, realized profits will decline. These circumstances imply that such business combinations likely occur in waves. They might also be undone in waves: the more unintegrated U's and D's, the less the incentive for others to remain hitched.[36]

Vertical Mergers in Media Industries

The combinations and deals that have occurred among the large media firms seem to match this defensive interpretation. The evidence comes in the pattern of the mergers (who hitches up with whom), the reasons given or conjectured by observers, and the presence of the predicted herd behavior when candidate parties are few. The *Paramount* case (Chapter 10) provided one instance, but with the twist that the symmetrical structures of the studios' distribution and exhibition assets apparently helped them to limit their competition at the distribution stage, and thus made integration pay by delivering some monopoly profits. The integrated theatre chains were detached by court order, and vertical integration has not been revived in anything approaching its 1940s form. Nonetheless, mergers and acquisitions linking media content and distribution channels have been numerous.

In one cluster of cases the major broadcast networks sought to integrate back into cinema film production. The first such moves sprang from something that resembled preemption: the market price to a network for showing a cinema film rose considerably from around $100,000 in 1961 to $800,000 in 1967. Another jump took place in the mid-1970s. The price surges likely reflected a simple rebalancing of demand and supply for films suited to TV exhibition, so we cannot judge whether the networks saw a threat of preemption from the movie studios, or simply thought that they could supply themselves with films at a net cost below the prevailing market prices. In 1966 and 1967 both ABC and CBS entered into cinema film production, turning out some 80 films between 1967 and 1971, between 40 and 50 percent of what they required for TV showings. The networks' entry led to litigation, because it arguably conflicted with both the *Paramount* decision and the financial interest and syndication rules that the Federal Communications Commission had imposed on the networks. Whatever the litigation outcome, the networks' lack of economic success in their film ventures led to their exit in 1972. The cycle repeated itself in the late 1970s and early 1980s, when all three networks entered, but with no more success than before.[37]

In the 1980s the cinema film studios restored some of the integration into exhibition that had once existed. In 1986 MCA (Universal) acquired a 50 percent interest in Cineplex-Odeon, then the second largest theatre chain in North America, and Cannon bought the ninth-ranked circuit. In 1987 Columbia acquired full control of Tri-Star, including the former Loew's theatre circuit, and the next year it added another chain to control the sixth largest theatre circuit in North America. Viacom, Paramount's corporate parent, had extensive theatre holdings before it absorbed Paramount, part of them held jointly with Time Warner. Other media-content firms later chose integration with television channels. When Time acquired Warner Bros., the studio became linked to Time's cable TV networks, and several more networks were added when Time Warner acquired Turner Broadcasting. Twentieth Century–Fox preferred to acquire TV stations and establish the Fox broadcasting network, while Disney acquired the TV stations and broadcast network of Capital Cities–ABC.[38] A different but related acquisition was Sony's purchase of Columbia; consumer-electronics manufacturer Sony was obsessed by a previous episode that found it excluded from access to entertainment software, and the consumer electronics firm was bent on ensuring that its videocassette recorders and other apparatus would not be starved for lack of films.[39] Statements by the companies voicing defensive motives for these mergers are abundant.[40] They commonly involve some disturbance that leaves sellers or buyers feeling rationed out of a market when prices do not adjust fully in the short run.[41]

Some reintegration of film distribution with exhibition took place in a cluster of transactions in the 1980s, which suggests a strategic concern with foreclosure. So does the increase in the concentration of theatre ownership that occurred in the mid-1980s, with the largest four exhibition circuits accounting for about 18 percent in 1983 and 29 percent in 1988. Guaranteeing exhibition outlets was apparently a major objective, underlined by a coincident sharp increase in the number of films being offered for exhibition.[42] Although most of those vertical links between distribution and exhibition remain, observers have seen little consequence. The increase of concentration in the exhibition sector reversed in the 1990s, with some mergers dismantled and a great many theatres bought and sold among the cinema circuits. Exhibitors' capacity increased with the construction of large multiscreen cinemas, and their day-to-day dealings with film distributors if anything grew more decentralized.[43] True, it seems odd to attribute a group of mergers to fears of preemption when none was ever observed, but perhaps the mergers served to ward it off.

Observers of the media conglomerates' post-merger behavior generally detect no significant synergies. Disney and ABC have engaged in only a limited amount of cross-promotion of each other's wares, and these resources could have been used (just as well?) for other promotional purposes. No organizational integration has occurred.[44] U.S. executives of Sony could identify only piddling synergies between the software and hardware operations.[45] A decision by Warner Communications to make a profitable sale of film exhibition licenses to CBS was stopped by Ted Turner, Time Warner's largest shareholder, who demanded that they go instead to Time Warner's own cable networks that were part of his former Turner Broadcasting.[46] The demand suggests that a costly self-supply is now in place.[47]

On the other hand, the major acquisitions that assembled these firms conveyed numerous hints of foreclosure. The Time Warner combination occurred when the film studios were seeking ways to curb the near-monopoly over pay television held by Time's HBO and Cinemax cable networks (a move that suggests the value of a captive supply of films). The combination of Viacom and Paramount was assigned a similar motive. In the 1990s Disney, Warner, and Paramount all integrated into broadcast network operations, Disney by acquiring ABC, Warner and Paramount by starting their own networks. The three studios accounted for about one-third of the leading four networks' prime-time programming, and the abolition of the Federal Communications Commission's financial interest and syndication rules restored a strong incentive for the networks to supply themselves with programming.[48] Both Time Warner and Disney have in fact announced moves toward self-supply of programming to their networks.[49]

In sum, the basic traits of creative industries cast a pall of skepticism over the growth of entertainment conglomerates. The synergies they pursue are probably illusory when they seek to improve on the rent-extracting power of auctions. They at best offer defensive value when they unite media content with distribution channels. To create greater value from their integration of functions demands complex collaboration in the development of creative inputs, which requires a water-and-oil mixture of creative talents with bureaucratic planners.

21

Filtering and Storing Durable Creative Goods: Visual Arts

The joys of consuming visual arts swell from direct contact with the objects themselves. Most are physically durable, and some can retain a place in our stocks of aesthetic capital, so we devote resources to storing and preserving them. Still, this storage is costly, and so we preserve only a small proportion of the art that is currently being produced—even of what achieves commercial sale as contemporary art. Collectors (personal and institutional) provide the first filter, abetted by the auction houses and secondary dealers who mediate trades in the stock. Works circulate among collectors until they land in a museum, which usually serves as a permanent resting place. The remnant saved by these actors' choices becomes our visual arts heritage. The modus operandi of each actor—collector, secondary dealer, auctioneer, museum—influences what art works survive and where they repose at any given time.

Collectors as Gatekeepers

The term "collector" itself points to the point for understanding this process. Many people who buy art regard themselves as decorators concerned not with the stylistic heritage or critical esteem of a work of art, but only its harmony with the home or office environment in which they wish to present it (the "swatch people"). The collector plays a fundamentally different game. The Linnaean idea of collection itself devolves from the concept of classification, drawn from biology, that upgraded the one-time cabinet of curiosities to a body of objects sharing familial affinities. The objects in a collection can be located within a comprehensive set of categories that seek to be mutually exclusive and collectively exhaustive. Not every box need be filled for objects to comprise a collection, but it gains from populating enough of them, or enough within some patch of classificatory space, to give body to the classification scheme.

Given the pleasure of filling out a set of categories, the collector's gleanings become a special case of forming and drawing upon cultural consumption capital (Chapter 11). Rational addiction warrants an early investment in taking courses, visiting galleries and museums, training one's eye, learning to place art works in context, and honing the practice of connoisseurship—of plucking out the features of heterogeneous art objects that can support a reasoned judgment as to why one excels another. We think of connoisseurship sometimes as unqualified—it is a beautiful object compared to all other objects. Often it is conditional—C is a beautiful object to juxtapose with A and B. The utility yielded by the emerging collection lets purchases easily escape the law of diminishing returns. Each added object stretches and extends the collector's knowledge and connoisseurship experience, and thus the capacity to appreciate the next object viewed or collected. Each filled box in the classification scheme brings the collector, like a bingo player, one step closer to spanning some classificatory terrain.

While other investments in cultural capital mostly cost time, collecting absorbs purchasing power. An art object has a market value at any given time. Viewed coldly as an investment, it offers the prospect of some rate of return, measured by the expected capital gain (net of any incremental costs of storing and protecting it, and transaction costs in selling it). Whatever her motives for collecting, the purchaser cannot avoid deciding what proportion of her wealth to hold in art objects, because each art purchase precludes some conventional investment. The alternative, say a stock or bond, will have its own expected rate of return (net of storage and transaction costs). Implicitly or explicitly, the collector values the subjective enjoyment from possessing the art work by the difference between the pecuniary return expected on the art object and that anticipated on the conventional investment. The riskiness of the two types of investments also influences the collector's choice. Future values of contemporary art works are highly risky, like the newly issued stocks of young companies (Initial Public Offerings, or IPOs). The modal rate of return on IPOs is minus 100 percent, although a few prove very profitable. Similarly, one dealer guessed that only 0.5 percent of painting and sculpture made and sold today will retain any market value in 30 years.[1] Risk aversion provides a strong incentive to curb one's collecting instincts in favor of more conventional investment vehicles. What matters for overall risk, though, is the correlation among the risky returns to one's various investments, not just their risk levels, and art works may hedge against certain risks (notably inflation). This model of collectors' behavior implies that collectors' pecuniary rates of return on their art should on average be less than returns on portfolios of conventional investments. This prediction is confirmed by a large body of research.[2] The difference measures the joys from living with the art, along with any slippage between the rates of return that collectors expected and what actually transpired.

Another implication is that aggregate rates of return to investments in art and in stocks should be positively correlated. Collectors who are also investors are sensitive to differences in the two assets' rates of return; if the return on stocks is high, people desert art and depress current art prices until the expected rate of return is raised. Capital gains realized on financial assets also increase the wealth that people have available to buy art. William N. Goetzmann's study covering 1850 to 1986 found the returns to art and financial instruments highly correlated.[3] Furthermore, average returns to art and stocks were about equal over this period. Returns to art were a good deal more volatile, so one can conclude that art investments were as profitable as stocks only for risk-neutral collectors—that is, collectors who are neither risk-seeking nor risk-averse.[4]

Behavior Patterns of Collectors

Major collectors have drawn extensive attention from biographers, so plenty of evidence survives on their motives and behavior.[5] These are of course the successful collectors whose achievements gained public renown; no record survives of those whose prized possessions suffered the indignity of a garage sale. This literature lays heavy emphasis on the motives of pursuing social esteem and leaving an enduring monument. (The role of wealthy collectors in funding museums is discussed subsequently.) Clearly art as an investment (successful speculation) carries little weight; collectors revel instead in high aesthetic valuations assigned to their choices by other buffs and certifiers. There are exceptions, however, such as collectors of contemporary art who stray into the role of dealer in the secondary market.[6] The desire to leave a monument becomes a factor once the collection process is successfully under way, but one wonders whether bequest-type motives provide much insight into the initial launch.

At the very beginning a somewhat different set of forces emerges. Major collectors are always described as highly entrepreneurial and purposive individuals for whom the rounded and distinguished collection represents a challenge.[7] Malcolm Gee's study of French collectors emphasized that the prevalence of businessmen and financiers was due not just to their wealth but also to their familiarity and comfort with large, risky investment decisions.[8] They compete vigorously with one another, in particular when their gazes fall on the same prize, behavior that opens strategic opportunities for dealers and museum directors. Competition for contemporary art challenges the collector to scramble to the head of the queue for "hot" new work, and explains collectors' silent-partner investments in art galleries.[9] If not competing personally, they compete against "the market" for gains in reputational capital for the objects that they select relative to those that they pass up.[10] A psychiatrist writing on collectors strongly confirmed the attraction of comprehensiveness and a spanning of some space of classification.[11] Other evidence of the importance of classification in collection comes from the historical association between collecting art objects and scholarly writing about them. The causation may run either direction, and a distinguished collection may help to shape the perceived organization of a field.[12] The other strongly apparent feature is that satisfaction comes not so much from the stock that has been collected as from the specimens currently added. Metaphors of sport and chase abound; bringing down the pheasant matters more than the resulting dish.[13] One might ascribe this to genetic selection during our many long centuries of hunter-gatherer existence, but it is equally consistent with the increasing returns to investments in cultural consumption capital.

By definition successful collectors applied good taste and connoisseurship to their tasks, but these qualities themselves are forms of human capital accumulated through either personal investments in training the eye or reliance on astute counselors. Aline Saarinen's study of American collectors found such an advisor in nearly every case. Mrs. Potter Palmer relied heavily on the American artist Mary Cassatt, who topped off her own distinguished career with vigorous promotion of her French Impressionist colleagues. Isabella Stewart Gardner early latched onto Bernard Berenson and helped fund his travels around Europe, training his eye. Dr. Albert Barnes was saved from acquiring a correct collection of French Barbizon School paintings by the artist William Glackens, his boyhood friend, and Katherine S. Dreier relied on expatriate artist Marcel Duchamp.[14] Museum directors and curators commonly assume this role, at hazard of conflict of interest unless the collector is already committed to a gift or bequest to the museum in question. In the presence of such a commitment, though, the collector enjoys the advantage of advice that is both disinterested and costless.[15] In general the successful collectors latched onto cheap and objective counsel.[16] Some major collectors such as J. P. Morgan did rely on dealers for advice and wound up with flawed collections unless their own connoisseurship was strong. Some self-taught collectors have weeded out many early mistakes before placing their collections on public view.[17]

The attributes of successful collectors vary with the sort of art collected. The evidence just cited bears mainly on collectors of Old Master paintings and recent but well-reputed works. Collecting closer to the contemporary frontier requires more engagement with the intellectual ferment of artists' problem-solving efforts. It is also riskier, but it demands less financial resources. Major collectors of then-contemporary art early in the twentieth century were members of the professional classes and persons with substantial art training, unlike the captains of industry who collected Old Masters. On the other hand, contemporary art has gained greatly in social acceptance and consistency with contemporary design and architecture, so that contrast may not hold today.[18]

Corporate Collections

The industrial corporation is a relatively new but active collector. Over 1,000 U.S. companies were collecting art in the 1980s, accounting for as much as 50 percent of contemporary art sales in some regional markets. Nearly all of the collections were started after World War II, most during or after the culture-conscious 1960s.[19] Like corporate charity, corporate art collecting can serve two broad interests. It might enhance the profits of the firm by advertising its policies or reputation to customers or lowering the cost of attracting desired sorts of employees. Or it might benefit top decisionmakers who can divert the shareholders' wealth to indulge their own on-the-job consumption. When companies are closely controlled, ownership and management come to coincide, along with the motives of personal and corporate collectors. Both scenarios help explain the observed patterns of corporate collecting. More than 70 percent of companies report that their collecting stems from the chief executive's personal interest; this does not prove that a consumption motive is dominant, but many such executives serve on boards of donor-supported nonprofit cultural organizations, and blue-ribbon collections of "difficult" art usually are the achievement of such executives.[20] Corporate collections commonly are started in years when the firm's profits are high and free cash flows are available for such consumption (perhaps in conjunction with a new flagship corporate headquarters);[21] they are sold off when hard times return or a change in control occurs.[22]

Most corporate art, however, is displayed in public and employee spaces and aims to improve the firm's relations with customers and workers. Difficult art is avoided, and acquisitions run to accessible styles.[23] Relatively inexpensive works are commonly included, with the nether reaches (prints, posters) approaching the realm of interior decorating. Smaller companies lean toward local artists for their locational identity and likely lower prices.[24] Collecting seems more common among services and financial firms that seek highly educated employees, and also among firms short on goodwill with the public due to their involvement with carcinogens, environmental degradation, and the like. The type of art collected is often aligned with the image that the firm wishes to present.[25] During the 1970s, at least, some companies regarded art as a valuable hedge against inflation. Collections are sometimes sold to realize capital gains.

Intermediaries: Auctions and Secondary Dealers

Ownership of the stock of recognized art objects churns continually as collectors arrive on and depart from the scene. High-quality art disappears into museums (seldom ever to return to the market). Some new art gains a level of acceptance that preserves or raises its market value. Auction houses and secondary dealers mainly perform the market-making function that prices and reallocates this evolving stock.

Auction houses are among the few natural monopolies in creative industries. A basic proposition of economics holds that market participants as a group benefit from doing all their trading in one unified marketplace. Anybody who is artificially fenced off from buying or selling in a central market would pay to get in the door. Correspondingly, auctions benefit by consolidating, so that buyers and sellers can contemplate many choices at one time. Art auction houses also gain scale economies in performing specialized tasks, such as appraising and valuing classes of art objects. Auctioneers face many problems of credibly maintaining fair dealing; while these might be solved in several ways, one possibility is to be a monopolist market-maker (perhaps among a small number of firms) offering his or her reputation as collateral insuring continued scrupulous behavior. An auctioneer's natural monopoly does face a spatial limit; most people will not travel far to bid on a cookie jar (but compare the current fad of internet auctions). The natural market structure for auctioneers hence tends to be worldwide for highly valuable and well-known objects, and more localized for lesser objects that slide into the categories of decorative arts and household goods. The principal art auction houses clearly fit this pattern, with Christie's and Sotheby's sharing a world duopoly of high-value works that attract far-flung interest, while a few other houses handle important art of particular national markets and a larger number conduct auctions of lower-value decorative objects. While the natural-monopoly element in bringing together sellers and buyers may be limited by distance and travel costs, the expertise and administrative functions are footloose and can deliver their services anywhere at modest travel cost. It is thus expected that leading auction houses should tend to operate worldwide, conducting individual sales at focal sites.[26]

Christie's and Sotheby's, both centuries-old London-based firms, have recently extended and consolidated their international positions. Their rivalry takes place in this context of natural-monopoly structure and is wrapped up with modern developments in the secondary art market, including its sharing between auction houses and dealers. Both houses are investor-owned commercial firms, but they face some of the problems of moral hazard and opportunism that push performing-arts organizations toward nonprofit status (Chapter 14).[27] These problems stem from advantages of asymmetrical information that the auctioneer might enjoy against individual sellers and buyers. Advantage could be taken by overclaiming quality or authenticity of auctioned lots, various forms of self-dealing, and the like. The point is that reputation built up in repeated dealings becomes an important asset for an auction house, especially in its competition with secondary dealers, who have their own need and opportunities to establish a good reputation. Pursuing pecuniary profit while both avoiding the appearance of sharp dealing and taking strategic advantage involves a delicate trade-off. Consistent with this dilemma, until after World War II both houses operated in a decorous manner that cherished amateurism and traditionalism, traits that scanted efficiency while sustaining reputation and, incidentally, curbed duopolistic rivalry between the firms.[28]

We pick up the story with the London auctioneers' entry into the New York market, which was dominated around 1960 by Parke-Bernet.[29] Sotheby's had maintained representatives there to attract consignments, and the two competed actively for sellers. While Sotheby's did not conduct auctions in New York, its standard London commission rate was lower than Parke-Bernet's, and it published auction catalogues that were more scholarly although less showy. Rivalry to obtain major collections sometimes left the winner with very thin profits.[30] Parke-Bernet came on the block in 1963 following its president's death, and also due to ill-chosen terms in the lease on its showcase Madison Avenue building—terms that imposed a crippling tax on its gross income (but would be renegotiable following a change in control). Facing an asking price of $2 million, Sotheby's issued a press release in London announcing that it would establish its own auction gallery in New York if the acquisition did not succeed. The announcement was apparently credible, as the asking price fell to $1.5 million. Christie's stayed out, believing it could not finance a competitive bid. Sotheby's acquisition quickly proved quite profitable.[31] Sotheby's reputation assets (with museums, in particular) apparently excelled Parke-Bernet's, and it brought this advantage to New York along with its innovations of auctioning large volumes of small-value lots of decorative arts and collectibles.[32] Christie's did not match Sotheby's New York strategy until 1977 (when a lesser London competitor, Phillips, also entered). The effect of Christie's entry on the value of Sotheby's New York investment was not entirely negative, because it established New York as a focal point in the world's secondary art market.[33] The two houses came to hold back-to-back auctions of each class of art objects, essentially achieving a natural monopolist's advantage of agglomeration for the sellers and buyers.

Charges to Sellers and Buyers

With the great expansion of the art auctioneers' activities and their transformation from wholesale to retail activities, the cataloguing and promotional services supplied per lot auctioned have no doubt increased over recent decades.[34] Accordingly, the premiums—the prices charged by the auctioneers for their services—have if anything increased. The London houses once subsisted on a 10 to 15 percent cut of the hammer price, payable by the seller. Parke-Bernet employed a 20 percent seller's premium. In 1975 a 10 percent buyer's premium was added in London, and New York's 20 percent was restated as a 10 percent premium charged to each party.[35] More recently the buyer's premium was increased to 15 percent on small-value lots (the first $50,000 of the hammer price on any lot). These surcharges have been the source of some confusion. The buyer's and seller's premiums together represent a wedge between the seller's reservation price and the buyer's willingness to pay: a lot will sell only when the seller's and some bidder's reservation prices differ by more than the sum of the premia. As a first approximation, it does not matter whether the premium is levied on buyer or seller. That choice fixes the hammer price's position between the seller's and buyer's respective reservation prices, and one must know how it is divided to infer what those reservation prices actually are. Nonetheless, the nominal allocation of the premium between seller and buyer does matter in two ways.

First, when the percentage is not "small," a charge to the seller based on the hammer price inclusive of the charge has a higher incidence than a buyer's premium of the same percentage levied on the hammer price before the premium is added. Thus, if the seller nets $100 and the buyer pays $125, the auctioneer's take could equivalently be specified as a 20 percent seller's premium or a 25 percent buyer's premium. The choice should make no difference to buyer and seller, for whom it is only the $25 size of the wedge that matters. Nonetheless, the conversion in the 1970s of New York's 20 percent seller's premium to a 10 percent charge on each party, which was actually a small price cut by the auctioneers, was widely seen as a benefit to sellers and a penalty on buyers. A significant amount of illusion may prevail; at least, people acted as if it did.

A second consideration, one more fundamental, may explain the shift toward employment of a buyer's premium. The seller can stage her own auction by seeking bids of the two houses for terms under which they will sell a substantial collection or estate. The special treatments that they may offer range widely, but the terms may well involve the auction house's giving up part or all of the seller's premium and a guaranteed minimum net revenue from the sale. Any charge levied on the seller is at risk of being bid away; indeed, the seller offering a large and choice collection might be able to demand part of the buyer's premium. By the rules of the auction itself, however, the buyer can only make (or decline to make) cash offers in fixed increments for each lot. There is no opportunity to haggle over the buyer's premium. The upshot is that, if the full buyer's premium provides a sticking point at which the house can resist further transfers of revenue to the seller, imposing its charge as a buyer's premium offers a strategic advantage.[36]

Rivalry for Major Collections

The auctioneers' role has turned into a retail operation sweeping through a wide range of fine and decorative arts and collectibles. Although auctioneers seem to have better profit opportunities now, they have been pressed into competition for major collections and estates that may leave the winner with little surplus. Large guarantees are offered: while auction houses used to offer sellers of high-profile art 50 to 80 percent of the art's estimated auction value, now they sometimes advance nearly 100 percent or buy pieces outright.[37] A vast range of promotional efforts can be contracted by major consigners—international tours of key art works, opulent catalogues, special treatment of potential buyers for major lots, even the services of top auctioneers. With estates from prominent celebrities such as Jacqueline Kennedy Onassis and Andy Warhol, promotional outlays can unleash a superstar effect that draws in potential buyers ordinarily uninterested in art or auctions.[38] Success in acquiring such business has indirect effects as well, pulling in lesser consigners who rationally expect to benefit from the attraction of numerous potential buyers. The intensity of competition for choice collections or estates is heightened by the auction houses' commitment to a regular schedule of sales, which creates a pressure to sustain a timely inflow of appropriate major art works.

Christie's sale in 1997 of the collection of Victor and Sally Ganz illustrates these pressures and their outcomes. Christie's spent more on promoting the sale than on any other in its history: it published both a hardback book and an opulent sale catalogue, rented a townhouse in which to install the Ganz paintings, and showed them to potential buyers at many dinners and receptions. Christie's negotiated a separate deal with each of the four heirs that involved cash advances and commitments valued at more than $120 million. Made eight months before the auctions, this commitment exposed the firm to a huge downside risk from a stock-market crash, war, or other event that might temporarily squash buyers' reservation prices and inflict huge carrying costs to hold the works in inventory for years.[39] Once Christie's had beaten out Sotheby's for the Ganz sale, Sotheby's was left to scramble for what it could find, which was the Evelyn Sharp estate containing "a nice, rather treacly collection of French pictures." Christie's exploited the situation, offering to buy the Sharp collection outright and hold it for a time, to avoid a traffic jam with the Ganz sale. Failing that, Christie's bid the desperate Sotheby's up on the Sharp collection to a guarantee said to be $60 million. Sotheby's had to place aggressive estimated prices on the paintings and hope for the best.[40] The best was not forthcoming; the sale realized $41.2 million (plus the revenue that might later be realized on unsold works).[41] Christie's took in $206.5 million for the Ganz paintings.

Auctions and Secondary Dealers

Many art galleries and private dealers also provide intermediation for the existing stock of art works. The auctioneers have encroached on the dealer market, but a natural division of labor prevails between them. The dealer can offer advice and present choices styled to the potential buyer's interests, which the auction house cannot do. The auction house instead offers a strictly competitive price to those who know what they want. The dealers' and auctioneers' market shares thus depend on the extent of buyers' demands for the dealer's bundled services. The division of the market can be regarded more generally, however, in terms of the service of matching buyers and sellers that both auctioneers and secondary dealers provide. The auction has two key properties. First, for the seller it ensures a market outcome at a particular time, although the outcome may be that potential buyers' reservation prices fall short of the owner's. Second, the auction incurs a large fixed cost for each item, in preparing and illustrating its page in the catalogue, and in occupying the time of a large number of persons (bidders and auction-house personnel alike) during the moments when that lot is auctioned. The auction's advantage therefore lies in relatively well-known art that might on a particular day appeal to many potential bidders. The secondary dealer, on the other hand, holds an advantage for art works that are more idiosyncratic or less widely known. That means only a few potential buyers will be interested and have well-established reservation prices for them. The secondary dealer faces little temporal urgency for matching work to buyer, especially if the work is consigned so that most of the holding cost falls on its owner. Thus, each intermediary has its natural domain. Nonetheless, the auction houses continue to encroach on the dealers' function by engaging in "private treaty sales" (essentially the same as the private dealer's market-making activity), acquiring retail galleries to offer the consigner a choice of market conduit, and making explicit guarantees of authenticity that long were implicit but not explicit terms of the auction house's services.[42] Auction-price guarantees also encroach on the dealer's function: they reassure in much the same way as does a dealer's offer of outright purchase.[43] Private sales, however, also pull some big-deal transactions away from the auction room. When a valuable work is auctioned and fails to sell, potential buyers learn something about the distribution of other people's reservation prices that may well cause them to lower their own. The auction consigner thus faces the risk that a work may get "burned." Although offering it by private sale lessens this hazard, doing so also increases the cost of contacting potential buyers.[44]

The structure of secondary dealer markets intertwines with that of primary (contemporary) dealers described in Chapter 2. Many private dealers and galleries specialize in some type of art or group of artists, both to exploit the dealer's knowledge stock and to develop continuing relationships with collectors sharing these interests. The *A list/B list* property of the stocks of art works generates a corresponding distribution in the operating scales of secondary dealers.[45] This link is best seen in the leading Old Master galleries, which have long been few and which each serve an international clientele of affluent collectors. Their fewness reflects their large capital investments in inventories of high-value works of art. For example, in 1959 Wildenstein in New York held over 2,000 paintings by famous masters.[46] They may hold currently unfashionable works for long periods, chancing shifts in buyers' interests, and their large carrying costs imply that the firms command prices that are high relative to current auction results.[47] The more subtle reason for their fewness and the consequent barriers to new entrants is the credence asset of attribution and authenticity. The opulent premises and glittering inventories offer the dealer's reputation as insurance against inflated claims. While dealers may be able to sustain such reputations while still engaged in selective cheating, they do make major investments to establish reputations for being both knowledgeable and truthful.[48] When J. P. Morgan expressed doubt about an eighteenth-century German porcelain that he was offered, dealer Jacques Seligmann elicited written opinions on its genuineness and importance from several experts, lugged the piece to New York, and donated it to the Metropolitan Museum (which received it happily), thereby capturing Morgan's trust.[49] The example of Old Master dealers seems to generalize across the price range of art objects in the world's stock. The higher an art work's market price, the larger the pecuniary risk to the buyer, and the greater the dealer's outlay on opulent premises and scholarly exhibitions required to suppress the motive to misrepresent and overclaim.

The resulting distribution of secondary dealers—in numbers, degrees of specialization, vertical differentiation of their premises, and exhibitions—somewhat resembles the distribution in the market for contemporary art, where it is driven by the distinction between the pickers and promoters. The mechanism in the secondary market is different, however. As new art works become seasoned in the market, a general-consensus valuation emerges for each school, artist, and individual work. All dealers need the "picker" skill, derived from close knowledge of this consensus, for works in their area of specialization. They differ in where along the *A list/B list* continuum they pick. The dealers who operate at "promoter" scale do so because of the necessary large investment in both inventory and credence assets, rather than because of economies of scale in the promoter function.[50]

Museums and Their Policies

Museums as Donor-Supported Nonprofit Organizations

The art museum is the absorbing storehouse of visual artworks; it receives or purchases works but rarely sells them. In the United States, most museums take the organizational form of the donor-supported nonprofit organization (NPO; see Chapter 15). While some receive government support, it does not come as residual funding to fill deficits (or absorb surpluses). In other countries, the decision rights and residual funding much more commonly lie in governmental hands. The museum's task of preserving and displaying valuable works of art fits comfortably into the model of the NPO. The marginal cost of accommodating another visitor is very small (save for congestion) relative to the average cost, so that setting prices with the goal of maximizing profits would likely exclude many visitors willing to pay their marginal cost. Correspondingly, museums widely employ the annual membership, a two-part price with usually a variable charge of zero per visit. It provides an efficient form of so-called second-degree price discrimination, by letting visitors select themselves into two categories: the occasional user who pays the single admission fee, and the heavy user who benefits by purchasing a membership. The museum enjoys economies of scale, the second condition for NPOs, because the fixed costs of the building and its operating costs seem to increase less than proportionally to the number of objects possessed or displayed.[51] Museum visitors also enjoy scope economies in the chance to view an array of related objects—that is, they can participate briefly in the collector's Linnaean pleasures of comparing and contrasting related works.

The founding of U.S. museums provides insight into their status as NPOs. Some sprang up to house individual major collections, so that the building, principal holdings, operating endowment, and governance policies stem directly or indirectly from a single wealthy collector. These include the Gardner in Boston; Frick, Guggenheim, and Morgan Library in New York; Barnes in Philadelphia; Corcoran, Freer, Hirshhorn, and Phillips in Washington; and Norton Simon and Getty in Los Angeles. The largest U.S. museums, however, emerged during 1870 to 1920 as something of an innovation that diffused through all the major cities in the nation. New York's Metropolitan Museum of Art, Chicago's Art Institute, Boston's Museum of Fine Arts, and others did not spring from any single collection but from large coalitions of individuals willing both to share the responsibility for initially funding the institution and to serve on the board with residual responsibility for its operations. The Metropolitan grew from a Committee of Fifty, formed in 1869, which was composed of individuals who were mainly associated through two clubs, the Century (which had arts-related interests) and the Union League (whose focus was political reform). Early fund-raising was broadly based and did not come easily. Its initially announced objectives spanned the whole range of roles that U.S. museums have since pursued: encouraging the collection of art and its donation to the public for both aesthetic and educational purposes, organizing special loan exhibitions, encouraging development of the decorative arts, providing educational services, and enriching the lives of the poor. It began with no major collections in hand. In 1870 a leading trustee was in Europe at the outbreak of the Franco-Prussian War and was able to purchase several Old Master collections quite cheaply, and the first director stacked the museum with the fruits of his own archeological work in Cyprus. Major collections and endowments of purchase funds came only later. Boston's Museum of Fine Arts similarly began as a "club" organization, although one with roots in existing donor-supported organizations. The established Boston Atheneum, serving the broader objectives of a library and cultural center, faced the question of whether to take on seriously the role of an art museum at a time when several collections were seeking homes. A broad-based fund-raising group (like New York's) obtained land from the City of Boston but raised its initial $260,000 from a thousand donors. Key oriental and Egyptian collections were soon obtained from scholarly collectors who could draw on family wealth and had educated themselves on their subject. Similar patterns apply to other cities such as Philadelphia.[52]

Some entrepreneurial strategies for founding museums were notably successful. Washington's National Gallery began as a single-collection museum based on Andrew Mellon's holdings. Rather than attach his own name to the entity, Mellon wanted to keep its collection open-ended to receive other worthy collections. The Kress, Dale, and Bruce collections duly arrived to create a combined collection of great quality and depth. New York's Museum of Modern Art (1929) sprang from the concept of three wealthy collectors of modern paintings who were interested somewhat in a destination for their personal collections but much more in an institution to codify and proselytize for the modern styles to which they were committed. They were fortunate in their initial choices for leaders of the administrative and curatorial branches: A. Conger Goodyear and Alfred Barr, respectively. During the 1930s Barr mounted a series of defining shows that forcefully put the case for modern styles. Furthermore, once the Modern had been installed in its West 53rd Street building, it led a transformation of the function of museums everywhere by promoting a modern style of design and decorative arts, and by abandoning the atmosphere of the traditional Beaux-Arts temple to become a clubhouse where art-lovers and intellectuals might view art, see films, shop, and dine.[53] A glance at major museums outside the United States (both art and other types) underlines the role of an entrepreneurial person, frequently either a collector or a state collector's agent. The entrepreneur in several cases had experience with world's fairs or major industrial exhibitions, whose combination of didactic exhibits and mass attendance and hoopla would have suggested that a museum might operate on a large scale and high-profile manner. Innovative ideas about material to collect and exhibit were common: for example, peasant ethnology in Arthur Hazelius's open-air Skansen in Sweden, and plants in William Jackson Hooker's Royal Botanical Gardens at Kew, England. Other innovations involved methods of display.[54]

Museums' Choice of Policies

The NPO arts organization is generally launched without any single well-defined objective. In principle at least, a profit-seeking enterprise can devise one coherent set of policies intended to best serve its goal. The arts NPO commonly chooses among noncommensurable policies, and the trade-offs among them are bargained out among its decisionmakers. In the performing arts the goal of upgrading performance quality commonly lay behind the NPO's rise (Chapter 15). Founders of U.S. museums in the nineteenth century likewise sought to displace the gaggles of curiosities presented by P. T. Barnum and lesser entrepreneurs by more systematic collections of high-quality material honestly presented.[55]

But quality is a more diffuse concept for a museum than for a symphony orchestra. American museums have long struggled with two, possibly three objectives that pull their policies for acquiring and presenting material in quite different directions. One of these is didactic. Early in the nineteenth century that meant training artists using a method based on drawing from plaster casts of classical sculpture and, generally, close contemplation of the works of previous masters. That training regimen is long departed, although what museums display and how they display contemporary art continues to influence strongly artists' art-making strategies.[56] There remained the task of educating the general public and, particularly, of encouraging design and craftsmanship in industry. This pedagogical role was promoted especially by John Cotton Dana, the first director of the Newark Museum (1909). Counterpoised to Dana's didactic approach was a fundamental loyalty to unique art objects and to the task of bringing scholarly order to their display and presentation. This sacralization of the art object implied that the museum should function as a church rather than a school. It implicitly downplayed the educational role and regarded the splendid art object as directly communicating a fundamental aesthetic truth without the aid of historical context, wall labels, or acoustical guides.[57] Reverence for unique art objects also points to a tension between displaying versus preserving them. Most art objects are subject to some physical degradation over time (inherent vice, in the language of insurance policies). Their preservation consumes resources, and modern climate control and restoration techniques have expanded the envelope for preservation while enlarging the opportunities to spend money for this purpose. Just as display and pedagogical use of objects expose them to preservation hazards, so do the costs of preservation compete with the costs of organizing shows, acquiring yet more objects, and the like.[58]

Observers commonly suggest that the contest between museums' educational and sacramental roles has been won by the latter. The training of curators orients them toward the study of the unique art object in its context, not toward the docent role (which museums commonly farm out to volunteers). The director gains utility from announcing the acquisition of an object or collection of great distinction or rarity.[59] Sufficiently great distinction brings on the superstar effect, and the awe-struck public arrives in droves.[60]

This classic dichotomy in art museums' roles opens onto a more complex set of choices among the museum's activities and means of financing them, with each choice of activity affecting the funding options and each funding source exerting its own pressure on the set of policies chosen.[61] The museum's function as storehouse and sanctuary appeals to collectors who donate their objects for safekeeping and veneration. Those functions themselves provide no strong lures for noncollectors to donate, with one important exception. Museum buildings give rise to "naming opportunities" that can attract large pecuniary contributions, and the interest of major architects in museum commissions raises the perceived payout of expansionism.[62] Enlarged capital stocks of art and buildings, however, swell the operating expenses (which lack naming opportunities). Organizations trawling for large donations for projects that beget increased operating costs should rationally hold out for an endowment to cover the increment to operating costs, but at the bargaining table the museum director will usually chance finding funds for the operating costs elsewhere rather than lose the substantial capital contribution.[63] Similarly, foundations and governmental suppliers of funds prefer to support particular projects (exhibitions or performances). Their donations cover one-shot outlays that would not be required for the museum's normal operations, but they do not cover the continuing flow cost of facilities and administrative apparatus capable of mounting the special attraction.

Museums, affected like other NPOs by trends in the distribution of household wealth and their own operating costs, have shifted toward soliciting small contributions from large numbers of people rather than large gifts from a few. These contending strategies of donor support align with choices between two potentially viable sets of operating scales and exhibition policies. The museum can operate at a small scale—preserving objects of great distinction, displaying them for sophisticates well equipped with cultural consumption capital, and living on funds from a few wealthy and sympathetic donors. Or it can operate on a larger scale, attracting a larger though less sophisticated clientele with shows that presume less knowledge, and financing the work from many smaller donations (and from sympathetic institutional donors). When push comes to shove, museum directors and boards tend to choose the large-scale course.[64]

The actual choices about what to display are continuous rather than dichotomized. Special exhibitions that a museum might mount range between "blockbuster" presentations of material that is relatively well known in art circles (hence adding little to the knowledge frontier of specialists) and esoteric shows that extend the scholarly frontier while offering few visual treats to the nonspecialist. Highbrows disapproving of the blockbuster seldom recognize that its favorable effect on the museum's net revenue may well be what finances the scholarly exhibition. Shows with broad appeal frequently (if not always) contribute net revenue to the museum, and the associated increases in permanent memberships suggest that they have value for encouraging investments in cultural consumption capital.[65] The same debate circles around the clubhouse function embraced by the designs of recently constructed museum buildings and expansions, which devote high-profile space to shops, restaurants, and promenades.[66] Museum-goers have registered their approval through their willingness to pay for these additional activities, a financial support that is applied to fixed overheads and other activities. The effect of these changes on the supply of small donations is not known, but it would be surprising if small donations did not increase along with the number of people visiting museums and the sums they are willing to spend on admissions charges and for various discretionary purchases.[67]

Among NPOs, museums struggle with an internal governance problem present in all creative activities—the *art for art's sake* preferences of each creative participant that call for exercising her own specialty. Once a performing-arts organization has decided to do *Hamlet* or *Aida,* there remains a struggle over the many choices to be made about the production. A museum typically designates a particular curator to mount an exhibition, but the contest still arises because curators charged with the responsibility for acquiring, preserving, and displaying particular classes of art objects naturally contend for the interests of their specialties. This contention has its counterpart on the museum's board, which commonly includes persons with collecting or other interests in particular classes of art. Alliances between curators and trustees are therefore prone to politicize important choices of policies—what shows to mount, and which workspaces and exhibition galleries to allot to each curatorial department.[68] In regional museums, local artists' demands for opportunities to exhibit clash with the curators' desire to engage with bigger creative fish.[69] Perhaps more than most arts-related NPOs, the museum's objective is negotiated within the organization rather than selected by the director and key board members.[70] The problem is made worse by the propensity of dissatisfied boards to fire the director rather than to wrestle with articulating a consistent choice among the museum's noncommensurable policy options.[71] The professionalization of museum directors probably fostered contests with trustees—formerly over the trustees' resistance to modern art styles, recently with the roles reversed and directors sometimes opposing trendiness.[72] And the burgeoning scale of museums' operations and reliance on continual fund-raising has made the director's job a hard-to-fill combination of aesthete and bagman.[73]

Competition among Museums

Museums, like other NPOs, generally face little direct competition from closely similar organizations, but they do interact as rivals in several ways.[74] One is in the pursuit of collections for donation (or, occasionally, for cut-rate purchase). The significant collector commonly can choose among competing recipients and has the outside option of selling or specifying sale by the estate. Museums seek to obtain collections with minimum restrictions, while donors like to specify that the collection be kept together in dedicated gallery space, not sold, perhaps not loaned, and so on. Collusion among museums to resist such requests seldom succeeds, as shown by the Metropolitan Museum's several wings extending into Central Park.[75] Competition also frames the problem of the museum director who is offered a mixed-bag collection on a take-it-or-leave-it basis. The donor holds the bargaining power, and the director with a capacious storage basement can always consign the weak items to a dark corner.[76] Museums also compete in and around the organizing and presenting of blockbuster shows. These extravaganzas usually involve assembling loans from far-flung sources and settling which museums will show the exhibit during the time the donors will allow their treasures to be on the road. A museum's permanent collection is important trading stock in this game of coalitions.[77] One's chances of securing a major show are increased by the ownership of important potential loans. The Metropolitan was recently unable to obtain major retrospectives of Cezanne and Vermeer; Philadelphia and Washington's National Gallery, respectively, had the marbles in the form of essential loans and could command the only U.S. stops. Small museums with choice works to lend may not make the exhibition itinerary, but they can demand reciprocal loans to dress up their collections in the interim.[78] The perambulations of loan shows also reflect the parochial interests of directors and curators; some major museums resist taking traveling shows in which they lack organizational equity.

Economists are prone to berate museum directors for their disinclination to focus on the market value of the works they own or to engage in trade to maximize the values of their portfolios (in the manner of an astute mutual-fund manager).[79] The point has both its merits and its limits. The objects that a museum houses incur both storage and holding costs, and storage occupied by one work is unavailable for another. Insofar as a museum seeks to display objects in the fabric of their historical context, there is a clear argument for deaccessioning (the standard euphemism for selling or swapping) duplicates or near-duplicates in order to fill palpable gaps. On the other hand, a consensual goal of the museum as a NPO is the preservation of a heritage of human achievement conceived as a continuous fabric. The perceived salience of particular threads (reflected in their market prices) may vary greatly from time to time. The museum's preservation function implies a positive option value for works now unfashionable but capable of resuscitation. That such works should be stored *somewhere* of course does not argue against sale by a hard-pressed museum that will otherwise forgo more valuable options. But collectors collect in part because they believe that the value of their hoards is immune to the ravages of the discount rate and temporary swings in taste. A museum that shares their assessment of aesthetic value in turn benefits from a reputation for being a sanctuary for the long run, one that will not lightly deaccession. Such a commitment relies on a tight firewall between the museum's operating budget and its funds for acquisition and deaccession of art, funds that are supplemented by the NPO status that blocks the appropriation of incoming funds as profit.[80] Furthermore, the active exchange of loans for special shows is a good substitute for turnover in the ownership of works. Museums are also making better use of their entrenched holdings. The Guggenheim rotates its treasures among far-flung branches, and the Museum of Fine Arts in Boston has established a long-term partnership of assistance and loans to the Nagoya Museum.[81]

For the effect of economic organization on our available heritage of visual arts, the whole is the sum of its parts. The efficiency of the secondary market affects the information people have about art objects and the likelihood that such objects repose in the hands of those who value them most. The tastes of collectors, the competition among them, and their shrewdness in arranging the disposition of their collections influence the concentration and coherence of art stocks subsequently available to the public. Museums' policies and the efficacy of their donor-support governance mechanisms determine the presentation of the art heritage to the public, affecting the next generation's cultural consumption capital and even the problem-solving strategies chosen by its visual artists. Chapter 22 continues the story by showing how art holdings and their values change in response to disturbances and reevaluations.

22

New versus Old Art: Boulez Meets Beethoven

The longevity of durable works of visual art depends on resources devoted by collectors and museums to their protection and preservation. A painting that has languished for 50 years in museum storage plays only a tenuous role in our visual capital stock. Nonetheless, it could be dusted off and exhibited at trivial incremental cost. The same goes for disused books on library shelves. It costs much more to bring other durable creative goods to life. The musically trained can read a score, but for most of us the score must be rehearsed, performed, perhaps recorded by skilled musicians. The effective heritage is not the scores stacked in the music library but the pieces that find their way onto concert programs and compact discs.

Stocks and Flows of Visual Artworks: Some Relationships

The effective stock of past creative works competes with newly made flows. The gatekeeper's welcome to today's artist depends on the stock of art made previously and the valuations placed on old and new art by the collectors and other holders. Suppose that collecting older art grows more popular. Its existing stock cannot be increased (forgery excepted), so its prices must be bid up until collectors are again just satisfied with holding that stock. For collectors, contemporary art is a substitute that now is relatively cheaper. With her deceased competitors carrying higher prices, the contemporary artist sells more paintings and gets higher prices for them; only she can actually increase the stock available to hold, and so more contemporary art evades the fate of the garage sale and makes its way into the recognized stock. When a period of vigorous innovation in contemporary art attracts collectors, they seek to sell off their holdings of older art in order to catch the new wave. When demand shifts away from a fixed stock of durable goods, however, the physical stock stays unchanged. The prices of older art works must sink to leave collectors and others willing to hold them. The same process applies to shifts in fashion toward or away from some part of the stock. Prices of the hot stuff rise, those

348

of yesterday's fancy fall, until collectors, dealers, and museums as a group are again willing to hold the fixed stocks (Chapter 21). Without writing the history of the world's art prices, we can spot some of the changes that reflect these stock/flow relationships.

Art Stocks, Fashion, and Relative Prices

If a collector cherishes several classes of art equally, a rise in the price of one class induces her to sell off that class and make new purchases in the others. If enough collectors have such flexible tastes, and if they spread their combined interests broadly enough among schools of art, then the prices of all schools will move more or less in parallel. The differences in these price movements then suggest how unwilling collectors are to shift their holdings. Geraldine Keen's study of the components of the Times-Sotheby index of art prices shows how disparate these movements have been. For Old Master prints the index's value in 1969 was 37 times its value in 1951. The increase was 29-fold for modern paintings, 24 for Chinese ceramics, 22 for Old Master drawings, 18 for Impressionist paintings, 13 for antiquarian books, 10 for English pictures, 8 for English silver, 7 for Old Master paintings, and 5 for French furniture.[1] The low substitutability implied by these diverse rates of increase is no surprise given the collector's economic decisions. Serious collecting (or dealing) in a given field requires a substantial initial and continuing investment in knowledge of that field. The investment is a sunk and unrecoverable cost, and the collector does not lightly hop onto a new bandwagon should her chosen collecting field turn out to yield disappointing returns in market and critical value. That is, the stubborn collector of decreasingly popular art perseveres, not just from conviction about her taste, but also because collecting her chosen line can continue without sinking an investment in a new line of cultural consumption capital. Impairment of her wealth by capital losses on her collection itself deters incurring the fixed cost of a new stock of such capital. Keen observed that collecting in newly fashionable areas spreads rapidly once interest has been stirred up by an important exhibition, publication of a new book, or other event. New collectors make the knowledge investment and hop on the bandwagon. On the other hand, established collecting areas decline slowly in the face of faltering general interest and/or the removal from the market of the best examples of the genre.[2] This asymmetry follows from the sunk investments that collectors make in particular segments of the heritage.

Histories of collecting and taste confirm these patterns.[3] In highly stylized fashion, the story begins in the eighteenth century with Italian Renaissance art occupying a pinnacle of esteem and everything else attracting only parochial interest. Only the declining availability of that material and the increasing recognition of the risk of forgery turned French collecting interests to Dutch and Flemish cabinet pictures. During the Napoleonic plunder of Italian art (discussed subsequently), the less successful pillagers of Renaissance art turned their attention to early Italian painting. An important English collector, Edward Solly, living in Berlin during the Napoleonic period, grew interested in early German artists under the influence of budding German art historians. German collectors grew interested in Northern art, and that interest diffused to England. Major art museums emerged in the nineteenth century, and influential temporary exhibitions were taking place (for example, in Manchester during 1857). These made people widely aware of art works that had been known only locally, and opened the way for widespread collecting and increases in market prices. The old technology for reproducing paintings (wood engravings and mezzotints) was displaced by photographic reproduction. That invention, in addition to cheapened book publishing, further spread the knowledge of the available heritage of art, simultaneously transforming some holdings from local and parochial to international and raising market values.[4]

The pattern continues with the build-up of the great American collections of Old Masters during the first half of the twentieth century. In 1927–1929 imported art works were 1 percent of all U.S. imports. These works disappeared into museums, thereby radically reducing the stocks on the market in a comparatively short period of time, and leaving for collectors of Old Masters mainly lesser works and those of dubious provenance. The great American collecting boom did levitate one previously parochial genre, English portraiture, thanks to Joseph Duveen and other dealers who sagely guessed the appeal to newly rich Americans of surrogate titled ancestors.[5] This flow of art genres into international esteem underlines the point that stocks of established art do not change, but some of them languish (or *have* languished) in obscurity. Low-value, little-appreciated art has a low holding cost for its possessor, with not much downside risk and the possibility of discovery (or rediscovery) followed by a boom. This option value explains the virtue of patience emphasized by Old Master dealers (Chapter 21). It also explains a pattern observed in newly active areas of collecting. Whereas little work of the newly fashionable genre has been evident and on view, suddenly it "comes out of the woodwork" where it has quietly nursed its option value.

Art Market and Boundaries of Collecting

We conceptualize our heritage of art works as a fixed stock that gets swapped among collectors and museums, but in practice the effective stock is expansible. That is because a work of collectible art need not have been branded "art" at the moment of its creation. There is a long history of utilitarian articles such as armor and timepieces being absorbed into the domain of art. Whatever decoration or styling was supplied by their original makers, even if usually incidental to the object's functional role, can become the dominant attribute for a collector, whose classification scheme then subverts one based on the object's function. Joseph Alsop argued that the stock of objects perceived as collectible on the basis of their aesthetic properties—those that become art objects—has expanded regularly and substantially over time.[6] In recent decades the auction houses have accelerated this process by holding regular sales of new classes of collectible objects. They thereby augment the common stock of knowledge about the class of objects: dispersing that knowledge by sending experts on the road to inspect people's possessions, encouraging collectors, and providing them liquidity in the form of reasonably predictable market prices.[7] Not every potential collector will regard, say, Andy Warhol's cookie jars as a good substitute collectible for medieval English ivories, but the existence of some such substitutability among classic art, decorative objects, and collectible functional objects makes the stock of art objects essentially flexible and adaptable to changes in demand. As medieval ivories outside museums grow rarer and more costly, some frustrated or new collectors *will* take an interest in cookie jars.[8]

Museums abet this process when they are willing to store and display functional objects. Their didactic role and the traditional goal of encouraging improvements in industrial design, though later subordinated by the culture of the wondrous unique art object, was formerly a major influence on their policies. Particularly influential was London's South Kensington Museum (now Victoria and Albert), a direct outgrowth of the 1851 Crystal Palace Exhibition. Early in its career the Museum of Modern Art (MoMA) seized this role with its design collection of contemporary manufactured articles, which received widespread attention and had manufacturers clamoring for inclusion. Annual good-design shows were held, though they were eventually dropped as too much of a shoppers' service and a basis for overclaiming by the included producers.[9]

Museums' interest in the design of currently produced functional objects contributes a feedback loop by promoting the fabrication of objects that can have both functional and decorative roles. This is an eddy in the larger stream on which contemporary styles of fine art diffuse into the consciousness of industrial designers and influence the appearance of clothing and household articles.[10]

Museums, Old Art, and New Art

Along a moving frontier, contemporary art clamors to become part of the sanctified stock of recognized art. Museums strike a delicate balance. As a storehouse of unassailable treasures, the museum holds out the rigor of its standard of acceptance as a signal to the current successful collector, who hopes to maximize the future contribution of her hoard to the stock of human aesthetic achievement. The credibility of the museum's signal is at risk when the museum shows and collects contemporary art, because consensus may be lacking on what is most valuable. Today's consensus among sophisticated certifiers might give way when the next artistic innovation changes perceptions of what immediately preceded it. On the other hand, the public's interest in current styles in visual art is high nowadays, and so carefully selected activity in contemporary art improves the museum's ability to generate donations. Furthermore, museum curators of contemporary art advance their careers by assuming the role of critic and certifier, a role in which they formulate an interpretation of and a case for current developments in art.[11] The conflict with the museum's sanctification role becomes acute when curators accept the popular critical posture that art is whatever artists make, and by extension that the certifier's role is to interpret but not to judge. The dilemma extends to the museum's purchases of contemporary art. Heeding pressure to avoid the role of a forefront certifier, the museum finds itself pulled along by the current of opinion and as a result gets in at the top of the market.[12]

The filtering of contemporary art might seem to be the province of commercial dealers, but room remains for donor-supported nonprofit museum-type organizations that display art but do not collect it, in the spirit of the European *Kunsthalle*. Organizations such as the Dia Center for the Arts and P.S. 1 in New York display contemporary art without poaching on dealers' activities, by embracing "difficult" art that defies both physical exhibition in gallery spaces and commercial sale to collectors.[13] They enjoy an advantage over collecting museums of being able to move quickly, which is important if an institution is to enter the dialogue among artists on current creative problems and solutions (Chapter 2). Indeed, earthworks, installation art, and conceptual art seem to attract artists partly for their very defiance of possession by collectors. Whatever ideological attraction this posture holds, it walls off the artist from commercial sales. She depends for support on agents who accept the view that display opportunities for contemporary art are commercially underprovided and will advance resources to remedy the perceived shortfall.

A quip attributed to Gertrude Stein captures the problem: you can be modern, or you can be a museum, but not both. The MoMA has struggled mightily with this dilemma. MoMA, founded to broadcast the message of European modernism, was intended to be a museum of contemporary art. Its collection would turn over and always be weighted strongly by the contemporary. Up to World War II its official policy was that MoMA's older art would be periodically transferred, perhaps to the Metropolitan Museum of Art, to make room for the new. After the war, rapidly rising prices for modern art pointed up the folly of MoMA's simply handing over its golden oldies. Furthermore, the museum's very success accorded to its collection a world-wide canonical status. It metamorphosed ineluctably into a storehouse of treasures. After a few limited sales, including one to the Metropolitan, the turnover policy expired.[14] In 1947 the Metropolitan, Whitney Museum, and MoMA drew up an agreement that assigned each a nonoverlapping sphere of collecting, but it quickly came apart, and each went its own way.[15] Within MoMA's governance circle there was serious support for the idea of closing out its interest in contemporary art and assuming the status of a museum of the modernist movement.[16] MoMA decided to have it both ways, however: it retained its domain back to 1880, but expanded its exhibition space and continues to collect at the contemporary frontier.

Museums as Absorbers of Art

The process by which art disappears from the revolving circuit of collectors into the vaults of museums has interesting properties, not least for competition among the museums as acquisitors. One possible view of the process is that, as museums are founded from time to time, a first-mover advantage accrues to the oldest. With a filtered stock of Old Master art in existence, the first museum gets to skim off the cream of established masterpieces, leaving mainly works of lower fat content for museums that come later. Peter Temin tested this hypothesis by relating museum attendance figures to controls such as building size, number of employees, and total revenue, and to the museum's age. No relationship to age appeared.[17] The failure is not too surprising. New museums are continually organized, and new art continues to add to the heritage. The world's stock of works regarded as masterpieces continues to grow, perhaps rapidly upon the arrival of a highly popular style such as Impressionism. The masterpiece stock is a moving target for the acquisitive museum, and the first comer has no perpetual advantage.[18] An interesting case is the late-coming but enormously wealthy Getty Museum. Its strategy is to pay top prices for any classic masterpieces that do come on the market, while otherwise focusing its collecting on art genres such as photography and Old Master drawings, for which top-quality examples still repose in private collections.[19]

With many art museums willing and perhaps eager to acquire recent art, their patterns of absorption tell something about the motives and constraints involved. Diana Crane studied the diffusion of six recent styles starting with Abstract Expressionism, then Pop, Minimalism, Figurative, Photorealism, and Pattern. She identified the artists associated with each and determined the proportions of them represented in museum collections (or given museum shows) five and ten years after each style's origin. These varying rates of diffusion were tested on the acquisition patterns for the New York museums (MoMA, Whitney, Guggenheim, Metropolitan, and Brooklyn), and also for a group of eighteen regional museums. The New York museums were quick to embrace the first three styles, much slower to warm to the latter three. She thinks that a pattern of curatorial commitment was involved, with the first three styles enjoying more intellectual cachet and posing a more vigorous challenge to the general art-viewing public. The regional museums were much more active in acquiring works of the three more accessible styles. Crane attributes this mainly to the greater conservatism of their trustees and their art publics, although later arrival to the active collecting and exhibiting of contemporary art may also be involved (that is, some regional museums may have missed out on the earlier styles and enjoyed the opportunity to participate only with the later ones). Other hypotheses that she tested are progressive ossification of museums' tastes and interests over time (which she rejected) and a diversion of their energies in the 1970s to outreach and expanding the range of their activities (to which she gives some support).[20]

Plunder

As a sweeping generalization, stocks of visual art have long tended to move toward the newly prosperous and aggressive and away from the impoverished and militarily weak. Wars have redistributed art, not only through vast campaigns of plunder but also from distress sales made under threat of plunder and expropriation. Wilhelm Treue's study of plunder throughout history traced it from pure malice and destruction in early times to the calculated transfer of artistic wealth that it became in the Napoleonic wars.[21] While earlier royal conquerors simply sought to furnish their own palaces, Napoleon's goal was to stuff the Louvre with looted treasure for the greater national glory. In addition to this official goal of the military campaign, especially in Italy, Napoleon's army was unpaid and expected to support itself from more readily saleable plunder.

The Napoleonic wars drove down the prices of works of art, especially in France and Spain, as owners sought to realize what value they could against the threat of total loss. The British in particular benefited from these distress sales. Even though Spain was cleaned out much less fully than Italy, English collectors' attention was for the first time drawn to such artists as El Greco, Cano, and Zurbarán. Even earlier the French Revolution had induced large sales of art from French royal hands, and much of this also made its way to Britain, where important French dealers continued to do business through the wars. The material that they displayed tipped off the English gentry that they could indeed decorate their homes in the style they had seen on their Italian Grand Tours. After Napoleon's defeat, much of what went to the Louvre was returned to its owners, but Britain's bargains continued to decorate stately homes.[22]

It was the Americans' turn to benefit from the Franco-Prussian War and related disturbances.[23] In 1870 the Metropolitan Museum was freshly founded and as yet without any significant dowry of great art. One of its leading trustees was in Europe that year and able to buy very cheaply several Old Master collections, mostly seventeenth-century Dutch and Flemish paintings.[24] The National Gallery became the indirect beneficiary of the Russian Revolution when the Soviet government decided to sell a large block of paintings from the Hermitage Museum in St. Petersburg. These were bought by the National Gallery's founding donor, Paul Mellon, through a consortium of galleries, with the galleries taking a commission and Mellon getting first pick before the material was put on the open market. Mellon decided to keep the whole lot.[25]

During World War II, first Germany and then the USSR followed Napoleon's tradition by devoting awesome effort and resources to the plunder of art at a time when purely military concerns would have seemed the highest priority. Hector Feliciano recently revealed the story of the Germans' successful effort to uncover and commandeer the great riches of French Jewish collections.[26] Hitler planned to create an immense museum at Linz, Austria, and several of his key lieutenants were bent on stealing for themselves. Upon the fall of France, Hitler set three separate agencies to the task of running down the French art treasures, inventorying them, and shipping them to Germany. The collectors had enough warning to hide most of their art, mainly in France outside of Paris. German thoroughness left little uncovered, however, and between 1941 and 1944, 120 railway cars of art objects made their way from Paris to Germany. The Nazis notoriously had their own ideas of what was proper in art, but they were happy to take anything valuable. Disapproved works such as Impressionist paintings were sold mostly in Switzerland, where the law giving a good-faith buyer clear title after five years assuaged concerns that purchasers might otherwise have had. Swiss dealers also handled "degenerate art" snatched by the Nazis from Germany's own museums. Austria was another busy outlet for German plunder, with the Dorotheum auction house one of the most important fences in Europe. Occupied France lost art through ordinary commercial transactions as well. The Paris secondary art market boomed as French collectors who had not been raided needed liquid funds and a favorable exchange rate drew prosperous buyers from Germany, Switzerland, and the Low Countries.

At the war's end the USSR took whatever art it could find from the part of

Germany that it occupied. The victorious Western allies wanted to return all works they had recovered to the dispossessed owners. Indeed, a lot of material warehoused in Germany was recovered and returned. Feliciano guesses that half or more of the French Jewish collections were recovered. Nonetheless, as is well known, a great many works stolen during the war remain in other hands, and proceedings to test the legal validity of their holders' titles will continue for some time.[27] The political redistribution of art stocks continues to this day, as Hong Kong collectors facing the territory's return to Chinese Communist rule sent great quantities of Chinese art and antiques into storage and some onto the market abroad. Their concern was not so much expropriation as restrictions on the export of art more than 50 years old.[28]

Musical Masterpieces and the Hardening Repertory

The heritage of human achievement in the visual arts is fruitfully regarded as a stock augmented by successful new creations and the aesthetic transformation of once-utilitarian objects. The accumulated scores of "serious" music also make up a fixed stock, but one replicated cheaply at the nearest photocopy machine and with only minor storage cost. Performance, however, is decidedly costly in the skilled labor of musicians, the time required for rehearsal, and the physical venue. The consumer also incurs a time cost, and perhaps a cost of consumption capital necessary to gain maximum value from the experience (Chapter 11). A flow of performances takes place that depends on the costs of musicians' services and listeners' willingness to devote time and money (I omit the role of recordings). Actively performed compositions—the only part of the stock with any current economic significance—are those scores that can meet the opportunity cost of other music that might appear instead on the concert program.

Elbowing into this flow of performances is a daunting task for the contemporary composer. A hearing for a new composition "costs" a rehearing of one that is already familiar. Besides her own fixed cost of composing a work, musicians must learn and rehearse it, and the audience must accept it in expectation as meeting the opportunity-cost test for musical consumption.[29] Beethoven's scores, showing no wear and tear of depreciation, stand always available for performance. Familiar to musicians, they need less rehearsal. It helps that listeners get diminishing utility from rehearing a familiar piece too frequently, but the newly crafted score remains frozen out if the stock of masterpieces is large enough to keep the pieces sounding somewhat fresh. In this competition for positions in the repertory, one should distinguish known compositions that are (or are not) played with some frequency from new scores that are (or are not) premiered. A premiere holds out a chance of discovering a major masterpiece, an achievement that offers career value for the participating musicians. Ordinary listeners (not buffs) get no such value, and are more likely risk-averse about investing their time in untested innovations. Hence, musicians' tastes are important for the amount of experimentation, but subject to a tightening constraint from performing-arts organizations' ability to cover their costs in the face of the cost disease (Chapter 16).[30]

Entry to the Music Repertory

Consider how this competition between new and familiar compositions plays out over time. If we begin with Orpheus and no accumulated music stock, new compositions easily enter the actively performed repertory. Some of these gain masterpiece status and invite repetition, raising the barrier for new entrants into active performance. Nonetheless, new masterpieces do come along and enlarge the stock of actively performed works. Even if more accumulated masterpieces lure listeners to more concerts, the undepreciating stock of compositions keeps raising the threshold quality required of new scores to gain entry to the repertory. The performed repertory should grow more and more slowly over time. Nothing precludes an equilibrium in which audiences give unheard compositions no significant chance to beat out a rehearing of a familiar work and the repertory becomes closed.[31]

Observers have seen just this process in the realm of symphony compositions and operas. We can date the beginning of an accessible heritage stock of performable music in the late eighteenth and early nineteenth centuries. Up to that time, organized composition and performance (impromptu public entertainment aside) was the province of church and royal court. Secular music was composed on order for particular occasions and often with specific performers in mind. There was apparently little reuse of compositions or circulation of scores from the initial venue to others. A public audience for music performance emerged with the industrial revolution and rise of the middle class, and was encouraged by the development of keyboard instruments effective in large halls. Also important was the development of low-cost music publishing, which allowed scores to circulate widely. Given these preconditions, the general cheapness of labor at that time favored a large flow of public musical performance. A taste for new music at first prevailed as fully in public performance as in the courts, to the benefit of composers such as Haydn, who went from the modest compensation of his years at the Esterházy castle to spectacular earnings in London.[32] Nonetheless, the preconditions were set for the idea of an accumulated heritage of musical masterpieces.

London was a major site for this development. In 1776 a group of noble-men founded a "Concert of Antient Music" to perform a repertory drawn chiefly from the early decades of the eighteenth century. In 1784 a grand fes-tival was staged in honor of Handel, then 25 years in his grave. The Concert's performances continued for a half-century, adhering to the rule of perform-ing nothing less than 20 years old. A still-older Academy of Ancient Music had focused on madrigals, but it shifted to imitate the Concert's style of pro-grams and made a successful transition from private club to public concert se-ries. Other imitators appeared in the English provinces. The Concert actually withered away, as it stuck to its 20-year rule while its imitators picked up the music of Haydn, Mozart, and Beethoven as they emerged. By the 1810s the term "classical" for a canon of music was in general use. The first domi-nant orchestral "classic" in England was clearly Arcangelo Corelli's Concerti Op. 6, which appealed enormously to the English music public as fully real-ized artistic creations of impeccable taste and satisfying completeness. Be-sides, they were fairly easy to play. By 1800, 42 editions of Op. 6 had been published. Purcell's major sacred works also flourished in revival, although he later fell before the Handel juggernaut, as the festival market for oratorio per-formances got rolling.[33] The new music of the time, what we now call the classical core of Haydn through Beethoven, then quickly pushed into the masterpiece stock, bringing England into its second generation of canon for-mation. The same process was occurring in Paris, Vienna, and Berlin, but in a slower and more diffuse fashion than in England.[34]

In the United States the increased dominance of the symphonic concert repertory by established masterpieces has been traced from concert programs dating back to the 1840s.[35] Beethoven entered the repertory immediately and by the end of the nineteenth century had commanded a stable share of 12 percent of duration-weighted performances by 27 American orchestras. Mendelssohn, Wagner, Liszt, Brahms, Dvořák, Tchaikovsky, and Richard Strauss all caught on promptly. Over the period 1890 to 1970 some compos-ers in the established canon lost shares of performance time: Schubert, Men-delssohn, and Weber. Others gained: Bach, Bruckner, Haydn, Mahler, and Mozart. New contenders kept getting trials, with some establishing posi-tions, others disappearing. Several—Sibelius, Rachmaninov, Debussy, Franck, and Rimsky-Korsakov—rose to appreciable shares (around 2 percent) in the interwar period, then fell off in the face of both older and newer competition. The performance of American composers showed a strong regional pattern, with orchestras picking up the local champion, whose works then diffused to other orchestras if they found an audience. The crucial test for a congestion effect is the number of new composers establishing a threshold share (1 per-cent) over time. This clearly declined: seven between 1890 and 1920, three between 1920 and 1940, three between 1940 and 1970. Although in the 1960s American composers' percentage of music played averaged around 7 percent, it was splintered among many composers, and nobody reached the threshold.

The same congestion problem has recently thrust itself upon the music recording industry, with the build-up of modern recorded performances in listenable sound and available on durable compact discs. This stock poses formidable competition for any new recording of a well-known masterpiece that seeks to cover its costs, and only with a splashy new performer are such investments likely to pay. The current flow of classical recordings runs heavily to lesser-known composers of the present or past, played by B-list performing forces whose compensation demands are no doubt modest. With a worldwide market to serve and competing records unlikely to arrive, large numbers of such releases can expect to cover their costs. As for the major record labels that specialize in recording A-list performers in familiar music (once again, the distinction between promoters and pickers), a repertory executive recently marveled: "I haven't a clue what there will be left for me to do in five years' time."[36]

Composer's Plight

Among creative workers the serious composer faces a particularly adverse situation. Besides the *art for art's sake* oversupply common to all creative workers, she faces Beethoven as a formidable and undepreciating competitor who benefits from lower performance-preparation costs and asks no royalties. Pecuniary incomes reflect this directly. In 1974, as part of the only broadly based direct survey to date, 494 American composers reported obtaining 25.8 percent of their composing income from performing-rights fees, 34.4 percent from royalties, 36.2 percent from commissions, and 3.6 percent from prizes and awards.[37] Their median gross family income was $20,000, comfortably above the median for all U.S. families then, although probably not above the median for families with comparable education. Net income from composing, however, was negative, with gross median earnings of $168 and gross median expenses of $380. Composer William Schuman remarked that "the copyist of your music often makes more money than you do composing it."[38]

In order to reach listeners, composers depend on performers who must somehow cover their costs. Here the composer gains some benefit from the interest in performance of contemporary music of some professional musicians, some music buffs, and charitable donors. First performances in particular involve creative challenge and prestige for the performers and are not so hard to obtain. The 1974 survey concluded that most new scores do enjoy premiere performances within six months of completion, although the audience is typically small and local. The problem is that the first performance does little to induce a second performance or establish the work in the canon. Critics' reactions on first hearing a new work, without studying the score, are regarded as random. Limited rehearsal for a complex contemporary piece likely means a rough-edged performance. Finally, fixed costs of music publication are high, and composers and performers complain of blights of printing errors.[39] The problem seems particularly acute for would-be opera composers, because the fixed costs of first performance are enormously high and the competition from Puccini fearsome. A striking example is John Adams's operas *Nixon in China* and *The Death of Klinghoffer*. The innovative subject matter and accessible style made their first performances highly successful, yet no significant revivals have occurred.[40]

High fixed cost limits the publishing of new scores. Composers responding to the 1974 survey indicated that over 70 percent of their scores are never published and survive only in manuscript. The photocopy machine is always at hand, of course, but publishers promote performances as well as circulate the physical scores. Publishers are few worldwide (the fixed-cost problem again). The circulation in published form of the music of Arnold Schoenberg and his followers depended essentially on one man, Emil Hertzka of Universal Edition (Vienna).[41]

The paucity of performances for contemporary composers not only limits their incomes but also impairs the effectiveness of their compositional labors. Like most creative activities, composing enjoys agglomeration benefits from the opportunity to hear one's own music performed and also to learn what other composers are doing. Cities with large populations of free-lance musicians, such as New York and Los Angeles, enjoy the easier organization of new-music concerts. Oral histories by Deena and Bernard Rosenberg document the importance in Los Angeles of a longstanding Monday evening concert series that drew on a pool of 100 to 125 musicians (paid a pittance) and a stable audience of new-music buffs (themselves mostly musicians), all financed by assorted grants and personal donations.[42] Some charitable foundations that support contemporary composers have emphasized the provision of performance opportunities.[43] Composers holding university appointments benefit, among other ways, in having a supply of student performers at hand.

The adverse economic conditions faced by contemporary composers obviously frame the much-discussed issue of new music's unpopularity with general concert audiences. During the years when Schoenberg's school dominated the interests of composers and sophisticated certifiers, the charge was often made that new music was excluded from concert programs because composers were writing nothing that listeners wished to hear.[44] A chicken-egg problem was obviously present. Composers frozen out by the incontestable classical repertory might well follow the solipsistic course of writing only for fellow composers, or for their own pleasure in creative problem-solving.[45] Their artistic choices do still make an economic difference, however. Composers employing minimalist and repetitive techniques (Glass, Reich, Pärt) are achieving more success, and those who write for more modest performing forces than opera companies and large symphony orchestras get a better shot at performances.[46] The accumulating stock of cherished masterpieces and the cost disease's threat to the volume of current performance (Chapter 16) do load the dice against contemporary composers, but the process leaves open a small chance that an innovator will break through.

In rueful contrast to the contemporary serious composer is the success of popular music composers in nearly extinguishing the performance of the classic popular song. That body of work emerged from the nineteenth-century operetta tradition. Its top examples display great melodic and lyrical skill, written within tight conventions of a 32-bar AABA form, with a story told in 75 to 100 words sharply constrained by rhyme and vowel-sound requirements. Although many were written for Broadway musicals, their self-contained character made them highly flexible for performance. But the songs and much of their performance context were swept away by rock songs that commonly follow their own conventions (or none at all) and that often are capable of effective performance only by their composers.[47]

Epilogue

The theory of contracts and industrial organization focuses a useful array of searchlights on the organization of creative industries, picking out pattern after pattern that prevails across them. Creative work pursues goals just beyond its reach, with the performing arts striving for higher levels of quality and proficiency and the fabricating arts seeking novel problems and new strategies for solving them. These goals of the creative process strain against the economic resources available for the task, bringing the artist into anguished contact with the gatekeepers who select among the creative works and talents on offer. Ecological forces in the market determine the organization of gatekeepers themselves. There may be few or many gatekeepers; the artist may face them in succession, welcomed through one gate but stopped at the next (higher) gate; and gatekeeping may be combined with other functions—an agent can represent successful artists in deals with humdrum enterprises, and a manager may select artistic inputs and supervise their collaboration with humdrum inputs. The many would-be creative workers who suffer rejection either toil in dedicated poverty or settle for humdrum work, while those who experience creative success reap adulation and wealth in what tend to be winner-take-all contests.

The contracts that govern the cooperation of creative and humdrum inputs regularly employ an option structure. Costs are sunk progressively into complex creative products. At each fabrication stage, decision rights get assigned to the party whose fungible resources are next in line for commitment to the project. That party has the incentive to make fullest use of current news about the project's ultimate success. While uncertainty remains high until the moment of the premiere or the unveiling, the option contract makes best use of what omens are available mid-course. Yet paradoxically, that contract and the forces supporting it also explain why large commercial disasters can occur, possibly (if not necessarily) as a result of informed decisions by rational people. A project goes ahead as long as expected revenues cover its remaining costs, even if costs already sunk are clearly lost. Option contracts in creative industries reek of unfairness to the artist, who loses decision rights over her creation, yet the artist's plight really results from the primacy of her contribution to the final creative product and the excess supply of would-be artists. The artist can demand decision rights over subsequent stages, but at great cost in what the next-stage fabricator will pay for her work.

Artists idealize their creative process as arising out of inner necessity. The muse whispers erratically, and rarely on demand. This unpredictable and uncommittable character of creative inspiration hamstrings formal contracts between artists and gatekeepers or organizers of creative products. This problem principally affects the artist's commercial dealings at arm's length, but it also shapes commercial organizations in which artists collaborate with humdrum resources. Organizational arrangements strive, one might say, to keep the creative and humdrum inputs out of each other's hair. In the clearest evidence of this, firms in creative industries are commonly bifurcated into the small-scale pickers that concentrate on the selection and development of creative talents and the large-scale promoters that undertake the packaging and widespread distribution of creative goods in pursuit of winner-take-all successes. The pickers are immersed in artists' activities and devote themselves to realizing the potential of the creative process. The promoters tend to work with developed and tested creative inputs. The creative industries that display stable oligopoly structures owe it to entry barriers that grow from the promoters' large-scale distribution systems.

Finally, creative industries' organizational patterns reflect the large proportions of cost that are fixed and independent of output levels. These first-copy costs (in newspaper-industry parlance) occur in all creative activities, but give rise to perceived problems only when they become large relative to the market (that is, to customers' combined willingness to pay). Nonetheless, these costs govern everywhere the degree to which potential *infinite variety* (differentiation) can be realized. Fixed costs affect both day-to-day competition and basic structures in creative industries. They affect the everyday pricing of creative wares because they require prices to exceed marginal costs, if average costs are to be covered. Close competition, however, can beat prices down to marginal costs. If it does, unprofitable competitors must get out until competition softens enough to sustain prices that cover average costs. Here *infinite variety* tends to save the day (and the competitors), by sustaining prices in excess of marginal costs. The abundance of payola and price discrimination in creative industries testifies to ubiquitous gaps between prices and marginal costs. Fixed costs that are large relative to market demand drive the activity's organization toward the "club" of customers or the donor-supported nonprofit organization. The prevalence of nonprofit arts organizations is well explained by the pressure of high fixed costs, whose effect is amplified by the cost-disease problem. But nonprofits also result from the shared quest of artists and art buffs for higher quality creative outputs. For most visual artists this quest involves only solitary striving. For the filmmaker it calls for the one-shot contract that seeks to assemble the ideal set of creative inputs for each project. For performing arts and for cultural storage, however, the nonprofit organization supplies an essential device for elevating creative quality by means of a high fixed-cost operation.

This book has sought to widen the perspective on what economics can contribute to understanding "art worlds."[1] Economics has more to offer than just the doleful message that costs (of humdrum inputs, of the artist's sustenance) must be covered for a creative work to be viable. It can supply an understanding of why art worlds are organized the way they are. It draws on the logic of contracts (and their enforcement) and industrial organization, supplemented by some propositions about how consumers behave in markets for creative goods. The explanatory power of this apparatus demonstrates that art worlds, while not all organized alike, are all ordered according to the same coherent process. Each art world has its audience of buffs and casual consumers. These consumers, in varying degree and number, invest in training their eye, ear, or palate, and their demand for training is itself important for an art world's supply side. Consumers rely on critics and certifiers for expert second-guessing of the gatekeepers' choices, when such advice is relevant and cost-effective. On the supply side, budding artists in each art world undergo an apprenticeship to prepare for encounters with gatekeepers. The contracts linking creative and humdrum inputs respond to the same underlying problems of uncertain outcomes and the progressive sinking of costs. The scales, activity patterns, and longevity of firms producing and distributing creative outputs can be explained as the outcome of a contest (sometimes historical, sometimes a thought experiment) between competing sets of contractual arrangements aimed at the same creative objective. A good test of the force of this economic logic lies in the distinction between high culture and popular or mass culture. It is hard to distinguish between them on the basis of aesthetic philosophy.[2] The logic of organization, however, explains the clear differences that appear among them even while it employs the same paradigm for explicating all art worlds. Although both high and popular cultures serve both buffs and casual consumers, the scale of investment in cultural consumption capital is on average much higher than for high culture. Regular customers are less numerous (apart from the mob that will turn out for a superstar), and the fixed costs more pressing. Simple and complex creative goods differ in their organizational arrangements, and the ecologies of firms operating within them, yet both simple and complex creative goods turn up on the shelves of both high culture and pop culture.

Another explicable set of differences among art worlds arises in the nature and extent of innovation. Why grand opera's active repertory stops with *Turandot* while Broadway theatre and the visual arts slaver for the day's new sensation is a question with no entirely economic response, but the answer certainly contains economic elements. The fixed cost of realizing an innovation is an obvious factor. For a new opera (or an old score with no performance tradition), singers and musicians must learn and rehearse roles, sets must be built, costumes designed and made, and so on. For a visual artist or a jazz musician, however, an attempted innovation is just one more riff. Another distinguishing factor lies in the subjective tastes of artists taking part in the innovative process, especially when performers are distinguished from creators. The performing artist's quest for excellence in noninnovative performance fights against demands to hone new skills that can serve only to bankroll innovative performances of uncertain success (and slim prospect of repetition), so innovation may depend partly on the supply of "downtown" performers with a taste for the new. Sometimes, too, the creative innovator devises successful innovations in performing technologies as well as in the substance performed, thus lining up performers to proselytize for their stylistic innovation; think of choreographers Martha Graham and Twyla Tharp. Finally, innovation depends on the insulation that the established canon enjoys from changes in the social and physical context that surrounds consumers' demands for creative goods. Contemporary plays, locked into current modes of expression and issues of social concern, are vulnerable to cultural changes that can undermine their creative force. On the other hand, paintings of seventeenth-century Dutch domestic scenes do not palpably suffer from the lack of modern home appliances on view, nor is the popularity of Brahms's music evidently impaired by his neglect to write for electronic instruments.

The approach supports other compare-and-contrast patterns of this type. Teams producing complex creative goods are stable and long-lasting in some art worlds, transient in others. The shift of filmmaking regimes away from the classic Hollywood studio illustrates the determining process, which serves equally well to explain contrasts between art worlds. The more strongly does effective performance depend on the close cooperation of different artists, the stronger the case for organizing long-lived teams. Excellence in the performance of symphonic and chamber music has long been pursued through long-lived coalitions of players. Furthermore, most works in the standard repertory require about the same team of performers, so no inefficiency arises from large numbers of team members sitting out some performances. The cast of a Broadway play tends to stick together through its run; whether performance quality gains in a repertory company that sticks together from play to play is, however, a closely debated question. The same principal oboe player is equally effective in Beethoven and Stravinsky, but that generally does not hold for the male lead playing Falstaff and Stanley Kowalski. Jazz musicians seek new performance partners as a way of exchanging new ideas through improvisation.

The patterns of organization and behavior uncovered in the creative industries seem relatively distinctive. They do have apparent counterparts elsewhere in the economy, however. The contracting problems of professional sports leagues overlap considerably with those of complex creative activities. Specialized individual talents must be assembled into teams. Many skilled players can lay claims to rents (some small, some vast), and the team organizer also pursues rents attributable to his packaging activities. The resulting struggles over a team's cash flow resemble those of the one-time Hollywood studios, in which the organizer advances the cost of the talent's early development, then seeks to intercept rents to fulfilled talents until the initial contract runs out. Indeed, sports leagues face a more vexing problem than do the movie-makers in getting the *motley crew* under contract, because the outside option of shifting to one-shot deals (pick-up teams, in the sports context) undermines the product's quality, while this shift enhanced it for the movie-makers. (In this regard, sports teams more closely resemble symphony orchestras.)

In complex creative industries, a great deal of information flows within and among firms—the *A list/B list* ranking process and the jostling over nascent projects that might or might not prove successful. This process also operates in other industries in which flows of new information hold comparable importance. Economists usually assume that the competitive firm's primary concern is to protect its proprietary knowledge from appropriation by would-be raiders. Yet the firm's better strategy may be to tolerate extensive leakage of knowledge from its corridors and conference rooms, in exchange for keeping its own receptors tuned to knowledge seeping from competing firms. Extensive swapping of information between employees of competing firms takes place in many high-tech activities, as indeed does job-hopping from firm to firm. Academic researchers in the social and natural sciences conceive of the research process essentially the same way as do creative artists—as a way of identifying new problems of substantial importance and devising compelling solutions to them. Scholarly researchers assign high value to an open culture with unfettered exchange of information.

Finally, the *A list/B list* ranking process goes on in many settings where vertically differentiated inputs contend for high-ranked positions and superstar status. The higher-education sector provides an example. Positions in the rankings are a continuous preoccupation of faculty members and university administrators, who take great interest in indicators such as the frequency with which competing scholars' writings are cited by other authors. Equally accepted as the natural order is a ranking by quality of research universities, or of university departments in a particular field. That birds of finest feather should flock together in the top department is accepted as the natural arrangement, and few seem to wonder what mechanism may cause it to dominate. Perhaps the answer lies in the multiplicative production function: the total research product of a field is maximized if its personnel are assembled into vertically ranked teams rather than into *A list/B list* portfolios each of equal average talent. Perhaps it lies in the murky objectives and diffuse decisionmaking power of nonprofit university organizations, which serve tenured faculty and moneyed alumni, while catering to student customers ill-equipped to evaluate the university's expensive product before purchasing it.

Notes

The following abbreviations are used for the titles of frequently cited newspapers and periodicals:

BG	*Boston Globe*
BW	*Business Week*
JCE	*Journal of Cultural Economics*
NYT	*New York Times*
NYTNE	*New York Times* New England Edition
PW	*Publishers Weekly*
WSJ	*Wall Street Journal*

Introduction

1. William D. Grampp, *Pricing the Priceless: Art, Artists, and Economics* (New York: Basic Books, 1989).
2. When the CBS network was approached with the idea of a puppet show with various animal characters, the network responded that its research division had established that there was no demand for a program hosted by a frog. Kermit thus sprang directly into independent syndication. See David F. Prindle, *Risky Business: The Political Economy of Hollywood* (Boulder, Colo.: Westview Press, 1993), p. 34.
3. I give it this name in honor of William Goldman's much-quoted observation about the motion picture industry: "Nobody Knows Anything." See William Goldman, *Adventures in the Screen Trade: A Personal View of Hollywood and Screenwriting* (New York: Warner Books, 1984), p. 39. That is, producers and executives know a great deal about what has succeeded commercially in the past and constantly seek to extrapolate that knowledge to new projects. But their ability to predict at an early stage the commercial success of a new film project is almost nonexistent.
4. William T. Bielby and Denise D. Bielby, "'All Hits Are Flukes': Institutionalized Decision Making and the Rhetoric of Network Prime Time Program Development," *American Journal of Sociology* 99 (March 1994): 1287–1313.
5. For a theoretical demonstration of the efficiency of option contracts, see Georg Nöldeke and Klaus M. Schmidt, "Sequential Investments and Options to Own," *RAND Journal of Economics* 29 (Winter 1998): 633–653.

See Albert Guérard, *Art for Art's Sake* (Boston: Lothrop, Lee, and Shephard, 1936), especially pp. 34–35; Raymond Williams, *Culture and Society, 1780–1950* (New York: Columbia University Press, 1958), ch. 2.

7. Howard S. Becker, *Art Worlds* (Berkeley: University of California Press, 1982), pp. 199–200.

8. This theory was so named in reference to the ill-fated *Challenger* space shuttle. See Michael Kremer, "The O-Rings Theory of Economic Development," *Quarterly Journal of Economics* 108 (August 1993): 551–575.

9. The concepts of fixed and sunk costs surface repeatedly in this book, so their definitions must be clear. A fixed cost of producing some article is one that does not vary with the number of units produced. A sunk cost is one that cannot be recovered if production ceases. Fixed costs are frequently sunk and vice versa—the specialized chemical plant that has no other use, if the market for its product disappears—but they may diverge. The "first-copy cost" of producing a newspaper is fixed, regardless of how many copies are printed, but avoidable when the newspaper ceases publication. The visual artist's costs increase in proportion to the number of canvases she paints (are not fixed), but they are sunk and cannot be recovered if nobody likes her paintings.

10. Becker, *Art Worlds,* pp. 352–353, 362.

11. Rent is an economic concept that recurs throughout this book. For the artist it is the difference between earnings in a successful creative role and in the next-best occupation: Arnold Schwarznegger in *Terminator* films versus, say, running a gym. What revenue is available for capture as rent depends on the revenue that the successful artist's film brings in minus the cost of other inputs. The artist's pay (including the rent) is often negotiated before that revenue is known, which means simply that the entrepreneur making the film has to guess the expected revenue while bidding for the artist's services.

12. Rent here takes on a slightly different sense from that explained in note 11. Once the fixed costs of a successful creative product (a book, say) are incurred, the publisher can supply it to many consumers, each willing to pay more than the *incremental* cost of another copy. That net revenue is a rent to the owner of the copyright, one that the author tried to capture (in anticipation) under the original contract. For the publisher the rent in part recoups the humdrum component of his fixed cost; what goes to the author is a rent to talent, once it exceeds the humdrum wages forgone while she wrote the book.

13. Herbert J. Gans, *Popular Culture and High Culture: An Analysis and Evaluation of Taste* (New York: Basic Books, 1974).

14. Clement Greenberg, *Art and Culture: Critical Essays* (Boston: Beacon Press, 1961), especially pp. 4–12.

15. For a good, simple account see Paul Milgrom and John Roberts, *Economics, Organization and Management* (Englewood Cliffs, N.J.: Prentice Hall, 1992), chs. 5–7.

16. Theoretically, parties can write a contract so that their expected profit shares add up to more than 100 percent, by injecting cash contributions at the start that allow more than the whole profit "pie" to be divided at the end.

17. It is important that performance under contracts can be observed by persons not party to that contract. Otherwise, "he said, she said" problems arise, and addi-

tional hold-up possibilities appear in the form of false charges that a contract partner has misbehaved and incurred a penalty.

1. Artists as Apprentices

1. Jacob W. Getzels and Mihaly Csikszentmihalyi, *The Creative Vision: A Longitudinal Study of Problem Finding in Art* (New York: Wiley Interscience, 1976). Also see Anselm Strauss, "The Art School and Its Students," in Milton C. Albrecht, James H. Barnett, and Mason Griff, eds., *The Sociology of Art and Literature* (New York: Praeger, 1970), pp. 159–177.
2. Getzels and Csikszentmihalyi, *Creative Vision*, p. 19; also Bernard Rosenberg and Norris Fliegel, *The Vanguard Artist: Portrait and Self-Portrait* (Chicago: Quadrangle Books, 1965), p. 238.
3. Getzels and Csikszentmihalyi, *Creative Vision*, pp. 38, 50, 69–72, 77; Charles R. Simpson, *SoHo: The Artist in the City* (Chicago: University of Chicago Press, 1981), pp. 53–57. Rosenberg and Fliegel, *Vanguard Artist*, p. 70, summarized other research that supports these patterns.
4. Getzels and Csikszentmihalyi, *Creative Vision*, pp. 112–113.
5. Ibid., pp. 167–168, 177–178.
6. Henry Kingsbury, *Music, Talent, and Performance: A Conservatory Cultural System* (Philadelphia: Temple University Press, 1988). Towse's study of the singing profession in Great Britain reached many similar conclusions. Music college teachers tend to be oriented toward the solo voice and develop the student in ways that are dysfunctional for choral singing: their voices may not blend, and they may lack sight-singing ability. See Ruth Towse, *Singers in the Marketplace: The Economics of the Singing Profession* (Oxford: Clarendon Press, 1993), p. 39. For recent trends in conservatory education see James R. Oestreich, "Julliard Tries to Nurture Well-Tempered Artists," *NYTNE,* May 23, 1999, sec. 2, pp. 1, 27.
7. Towse, *Singers,* p. 41, noted that training institutions for British singers are numerous, and most operate at small scales. Thus the ranking that could occur early in a more concentrated setting to distinguish the talented from the richly talented does not take place, and the hopeful, doomed mostly to frustration, are encouraged to make further large career investments. For an argument that people generally overestimate small probabilities of very large prizes, see Robert H. Frank and Philip J. Cooke, *The Winner-Take-All Society* (New York: Free Press, 1995), ch. 6.
8. Towse, *Singers,* pp. 177–178.
9. Howard S. Becker, "Arts and Crafts," *American Journal of Sociology* 83 (January 1978): 862–889; Barbara Rosenblum, "Style as Social Process," *American Sociological Review* 43 (June 1978): 422–438.
10. Getzels and Csikszentmihalyi, *Creative Vision*, p. 191; Rosenberg and Fliegel, *Vanguard Artist*, pp. 16–17; Simpson, *SoHo*, chs. 4–6; Sally Ridgeway, "Artist Groups: Patrons and Gatekeepers," in Arnold W. Foster and Judith R. Blau, eds., *Art and Society: Readings in the Sociology of the Arts* (Buffalo: State University of New York Press, 1989), p. 208. Ridgeway's survey suggests that more successful artists actively promote newcomers whose work they value by drawing them into group shows, purchasing their works, and the like.

11. Simpson, *SoHo*, pp. 3–9, 19–21; Raymonde Moulin, *The French Art Market: A Sociological View*, trans. Arthur Goldhammer (New Brunswick, N.J.: Rutgers University Press, 1987), pp. 91, 95.

12. Alice Goldfarb Marquis, *The Art Biz: The Covert World of Collectors, Dealers, Auction Houses, Museums and Critics* (Chicago: Contemporary Books, 1991), pp. 34, 39–40, 65, 67; Glenn O'Brien, "Andy Warhol's Nocturnal Exposures," *NYTNE*, Nov. 2, 1997, sec. 9, pp. 1, 6.

13. JoAnn Wypijewski, ed., *Painting by Numbers: Komar and Melamid's Scientific Guide to Art* (New York: Farrar Straus Giroux, 1997).

14. Simpson, *SoHo*, pp. 22–24; Lawrence Alloway, "When Artists Start Their Own Galleries," *NYT*, Apr. 3, 1983, sec. 2, pp. 29–30.

15. Rosenberg and Fliegel, *Vanguard Artist*, pp. 249–250.

16. Simpson, *SoHo*, ch. 3, especially p. 48.

17. Ibid., p. 85, cited evidence that of 20 out of 30 galleries surveyed, none in a given year had taken on a new artist not referred by other artists. Also John Russell Taylor and Brian Brooke, *The Art Dealers* (New York: Scribner's, 1969), p. 174; Laura de Coppet and Alan Jones, eds., *The Art Dealers* (New York: Clarkson N. Potter, 1984), pp. 300, 304.

18. Moulin, *French Art Market*, pp. 55, 124; Liah Greenfeld, *Different Worlds: A Sociological Study of Tastes, Choice, and Success in Art* (Cambridge: Cambridge University Press, 1989), p. 126. The Langs' massive study of etchers' careers concluded that recognition by peers was the crucial first step in long-run success, followed by dealers' and certifiers' promotion; Gladys Engel Lang and Kurt Lang, *Etched in Memory: The Building and Survival of Artistic Reputation* (Chapel Hill: University of North Carolina Press, 1990), especially p. 247.

19. Ridgeway, "Artist Groups," pp. 212–215. She quoted one artist: "Artists run the art world and sooner or later the artists win out. A good artist can show anywhere and other artists know a good artist when they see one."

20. De Coppet and Jones, *Art Dealers*, pp. 203, 240, 293–295; Rosenberg and Fliegel, *Vanguard Artist*, pp. 70–74; Barbaralee Diamonstein, *Inside the Art World: Conversations with Barbaralee Diamonstein* (New York: Rizzoli, 1994), p. 243.

21. Rhona Hoffman, "Dealing from Chicago," in Lee Evan Caplin, ed., *The Business of Art* (Englewood Cliffs, N.J.: Prentice-Hall, 1982), pp. 291–297; de Coppet and Jones, *Art Dealers*, pp. 278–279.

22. Rosenberg and Fliegel, *Vanguard Artist*, pp. 153–158. Despite the widespread acceptance of this position, one notes the number of successful artists who once survived as window dressers and sign painters. Moulin, in *French Art Market*, pp. 122–123, noted that avant-garde artists tend to subsist on jobs unrelated to art while other artists take related work in teaching and commercial art.

23. Simpson, *SoHo*, pp. 57–67.

24. Getzels and Csikszentmihalyi, *Creative Vision*, pp. 191–193.

25. Stuart Plattner, *High Art Down Home: An Economic Ethnography of a Local Art Market* (Chicago: University of Chicago Press, 1996), pp. 88–92, 122–123.

26. Rosenberg and Fliegel, *Vanguard Artist*, pp. 44–45.

27. Plunging rail travel costs and journey times were necessary for London's emergence as a dominant literary and publishing center in the mid-nineteenth century.

See J. A. Sutherland, *Victorian Novelists and Publishers* (Chicago: University of Chicago Press, 1976), pp. 62–67.

28. Howard S. Becker, *Art Worlds* (Berkeley: University of California Press, 1982), p. 53.

29. Simpson, *SoHo*, ch. 1.

30. Anne E. Bowler and Blaine McBurney, "Gentrification and the Avant-Garde in New York's East Village" in Judith Huggins Balfe, ed., *Paying the Piper: Causes and Consequences of Art Patronage* (Urbana: University of Illinois Press, 1993), pp. 161–182; Peter Plagens, "There Goes the Neighborhood," *Newsweek*, Sept. 9, 1996, pp. 78–79; Lynda Richardson, "Painted into a Corner in Brooklyn's Dumbo," *NYT*, July 24, 1995, pp. B1, B2; Evelyn Nieves, "Artists Paint a Failing City in a New Light," *NYT*, Jan. 16, 1997, p. B1; Michael Janofsky, "Providence Is Reviving, Using Arts as a Fuel," *NYT*, Feb. 18, 1997, p. C12; Peter Marks, "As It Turns Artistic, A Noirish Enclave Steps into the Light," *NYTNE*, Oct. 10, 1997, pp. B1, B26.

31. New York, Chicago, and Los Angeles combined had 26 percent of the United States's self-reported visual artists in 1970, 21 percent in 1980, and 16 percent in 1990. See Plattner, *High Art*, p. 76.

32. Ibid. In Appendix 5, Plattner plotted these data but did not note or formally test the nonlinearity hypothesis. Inspection of his plots suggests that it holds, but the convexity depends on only a few large cities.

33. Simpson, *SoHo*, pp. 118–119. On recent developments see Roberta Smith, "The New York Artist Is Now from Everywhere," *NYTNE*, Apr. 18, 1999, sec. 2, p. 36.

34. Rosenberg and Fliegel, *Vanguard Artist*, ch. 3; David W. Galenson, "The Careers of Modern Artists: Evidence from Auctions of Contemporary Paintings," working paper 6331, National Bureau of Economic Research (1997).

35. Richard Fine, *West of Eden: Writers in Hollywood, 1928–1940* (Washington: Smithsonian Institute Press, 1993), p. 38 (ch. 1 generally).

36. Helmut K. Anheier and Jürgen Gerhards, "Literary Myths and Social Structure," *Social Forces* 69 (March 1991): 811–830; Helmut K. Anheier, Jürgen Gerhards, and Frank P. Romo, "Forms of Capital and Social Structure in Cultural Fields," *American Journal of Sociology* 100 (January 1995): 859–903.

37. Malcolm Bradbury, *The Social Context of Modern English Literature* (Oxford: Blackwell, 1971).

38. Ibid., pp. 148–152.

39. Cristina Bodinger-deUriate, "Status Judgments among Free-lance Musicians," in Judith H. Balfe and Margaret Jane Wyszomirski, eds., *Art, Ideology, and Politics* (New York: Praeger, 1985), pp. 80–99.

40. R. Serge Denisoff, *Tarnished Gold: The Record Industry Revisited* (New Brunswick, N.J.: Transaction Books, 1986), ch. 2. Two particularly useful studies deal with the ecology of music groups in English cities. On rock groups in Liverpool, see Sara Cohen, *Rock Culture in Liverpool: Popular Music in the Making* (Oxford: Clarendon Press, 1991); on all types of performing groups in Milton Keynes, see Ruth Finnegan, *The Hidden Musicians: Music-Making in an English Town* (Cambridge: Cambridge University Press, 1989).

41. Gwendolyn Freed, "Young Musicians Orchestrate Careers in Florida," *WSJ*, Oct. 27, 1998, p. A20.

42. Joseph Horowitz, *The Ivory Trade: Music and the Business of Music at the Van Cliburn International Piano Competition* (New York: Summit Books, 1990), pp. 14–15.

43. Private auditions and behind-the-scene networking do not test public performance skills, and the traditional New York debut recital has lost its usefulness now that press reviewers seldom show up. See ibid., p. 148.

44. Allan Kozinn, "Pianists Battle for a Shot at Obscurity," *NYTNE*, May 29, 1997, pp. B1, B6.

2. Artists, Dealers, and Deals

1. Laura de Coppet and Alan Jones, eds., *The Art Dealers* (New York: Clarkson N. Potter, 1984), p. 296; John Russell Taylor and Brian Brooke, *The Art Dealers* (New York: Charles Scribner's Sons, 1969), p. 193; Lee Evan Caplin, ed., *The Business of Art* (Englewood Cliffs, N.J.: Prentice-Hall, 1982), pp. 269–270. For a test of the effects of these promotional steps on the ultimate viability of the artist's work in the secondary auction market, see Leslie P. Singer, "The Utility of Art versus Fair Bets in the Investment Market," *JCE* 14 (December 1990): 1–13.

2. This problem for the artist and dealer appears in the economics literature on "vertical restraints" between a manufacturer and the firms that distribute his product.

3. See Peter Watson, *From Manet to Manhattan: The Rise of the Modern Art Market* (New York: Random House, 1992), p. 83; Richard Meryman, *Andrew Wyeth: A Secret Life* (New York: HarperCollins, 1996), pp. 247–251.

4. The dealer incurs a cost in his time and resources for each type of promotional effort he undertakes for the artist. Each should be pursued to the point where the expected extra revenue that it produces just covers its cost in time and effort. The opportunity cost of a dealer's services to one artist may be the services not provided to the gallery's other artists, which worsens the dealer's already complicated problem of demonstrating to the artist the plenitude of his promotional efforts.

5. The artist has (we assume) some intrinsic facility at devising new problems and solutions. Within this envelope of capacity, however, the artist chooses an optimal pace of production and sale. Her output should be large enough that the art world becomes fully acquainted with the artist, but not so large that it presses down the collector's willingness to pay—now or, in anticipation, in the future. That is, the price that collectors will pay for the artist's work currently in the gallery depends not only on the number of pieces on hand but also on the number of works that the artist is expected to offer in the future, which will compete with today's work offered for resale and depress its expected future value.

6. This objective itself is clearly defined only if both parties' preferences can be reduced to a pecuniary common denominator. Artists sometimes have preferences about who purchases their works—collectors who will cherish them for the right reasons—that will not matter to the dealer. See Bernard Rosenberg and Norris Fliegel, "The Artist and His Publics: the Ambiguity of Success," in Milton C. Albrecht, James H. Barnett, and Mason Griff, eds., *The Sociology of Art and Literature* (New York: Praeger, 1970), pp. 499–517.

7. The parties do have some theoretical room to improve their profit-sharing deal. Suppose, for example, that the dealer is motivated by expected profits, while the

artist creates solely from inner necessity. The artist could improve her economic lot by giving the dealer a larger share of sales revenues in exchange for an up-front "signing bonus." In general, the value of such contracts can be increased by moving the marginal profit share in favor of the party with more discretion about actions that affect the deal's joint value. By means of up-front fixed payments, the marginal incentive can be adjusted independent of the expected average distribution of the parties' joint profit.

8. Taylor and Brooke, *Art Dealers,* pp. 179–182, 208–212.
9. Stuart Plattner, *High Art Down Home: An Economic Ethnography of a Local Art Market* (Chicago: University of Chicago Press, 1996), pp. 137–144.
10. Ibid., pp. 150–154.
11. Making astute commercial decisions, even if this talent is in the artist's repertory, seems to impugn her seriousness as a creator. See ibid., pp. 22–23, 79.
12. Caplin, *Business of Art,* pp. 259, 285; Charles R. Simpson, *SoHo: The Artist in the City* (Chicago: University of Chicago Press, 1981), pp. 47, 78; de Coppet and Jones, *Art Dealers,* p. 145.
13. Taylor and Brooke, *Art Dealers,* pp. 176–177; Calvin Tomkins, *Post- to Neo-: The Art World of the 1980s* (New York: Henry Holt, 1988), p. 34; John E. Dowell, Jr., "Promoting Yourself and Your Art," in Caplin, *Business of Art,* pp. 181–208. The artist may be asked to give up a somewhat larger share of revenue from discounted sales to a "certifier" such as a consultant or decorator.
14. Suppose that the extra dollar brings in $1.20 additional revenue (clearly desirable for the dealer and artist together). With a 50 percent commission rate the dealer reaps $0.60 additional revenue, and hence loses $0.40. If the dealer took instead a 50 percent share of net profit, he would get credit for the dollar and receive (net) $0.10 of the $0.20 increase in total net profit.
15. In the preceding note's numerical example, the extra dollar spent by the dealer gives the artist $0.60 under revenue sharing, only $0.10 under profit-sharing.
16. Raymonde Moulin, *The French Art Market: A Sociological View,* trans. Arthur Goldhammer (New Brunswick, N.J.: Rutgers University Press, 1987), pp. 53–55.
17. In an ideal contract with accurate expectations about the artist's future success, artist and dealer would share the optimal speculative stash between them. If they do not pool, each has an incentive to overinvest, because each gets all the capital gain from his or her successful speculative holdback, while the loss of promotional value from the forgone current sale is split between them. This incentive problem would not arise if they split the eventual speculative profits between them. The artist's holdback problem (but not the artist-dealer relationship) is analyzed by Leslie P. Singer in "Supply Decisions of Professional Artists," *American Economic Review* 71 (May 1981): 341–346; also see Walter Santagata, "Rights Allocation in the Contemporary Art Market: Copyright, 'Droit de Suite,' 'Right to Exhibit,'" in Alan Peacock and Ilde Rizzo, eds., *Cultural Economics and Cultural Policies* (Dordrecht: Kluwer Academic, 1994), pp. 111–124.
18. Pierre Assouline, *An Artful Life: A Biography of D. H. Kahnweiler, 1884–1979,* trans. Charles Ruas (New York: Grove Weidenfeld, 1990), pp. 29, 32–34, 96; Watson, *From Manet to Manhattan,* pp. 157–158. Kahnweiler regarded contracts as only a reassurance that rested on a more fundamental commitment of personal word and honor.

19. Alice Goldfarb Marquis, *The Art Biz: The Covert World of Collectors, Dealers, Auction Houses, Museums, and Critics* (Chicago: Contemporary Books, 1991), p. 239.

20. Tomkins, *Post- to Neo-*, pp. 12, 159–161.

21. Caplin, *Business of Art*, pp. 259–260. In general the experience of the present-day French art market with artist-dealer relationships parallels that in the United States. See Moulin, *French Art Market*, pp. 113–116, 120, 129.

22. The sale after expenses realized 63,207 francs on an original investment of 27,500. Storage and management costs are not deducted, but it is reasonable to assume that those were offset by the pleasure yielded to those who held the works. If the initial investment had all been made in 1903, an internal rate of return of 7.9 percent would have been realized; the investment was in fact made over several years, shortening the holding period, and so this figure is biased downward. See Michael C. Fitzgerald, *Making Modernism: Picasso and the Creation of the Market for Twentieth-Century Art* (New York: Farrar, Straus, and Giroux, 1995), pp. 38–40.

23. Fitzgerald (ibid.) provided extensive details on Picasso's relationships with his dealers.

24. Simpson, *SoHo*, pp. 44–45.

25. Fascinating collateral evidence appears in the nineteenth-century emergence of the modern art market based on dealers and critics. See Harrison C. White and Cynthia A. White, *Canvases and Careers* (Chicago: University of Chicago Press, 1993); Peter Paret, *The Berlin Secession: Modernism and Its Enemies in Imperial Germany* (Cambridge, Mass.: Harvard University Press, 1980).

26. It sounds—and is—paradoxical that more firms can fit into the market the less competitively they behave, because we generally expect that increasing the number of market rivals will make them price more competitively. Nonetheless, the two relationships can exist independently because of factors other than the number of firms that affect competitiveness in pricing. Pervasive product differentiation in the art market (*infinite variety*) curbs price competition.

27. The qualifying "probably" recognizes that *art for art's sake* tastes might also embrace selling art at lower prices than humdrum sellers would charge, thereby making it harder for galleries to cover their fixed costs and thinning their number. In the "boutique" end of the California wine market, however, firms likely to be motivated by love of wine set higher mark-ups of price over costs; see Fiona M. Scott Morton and Joel M. Podolny, "Love or Money? The Effect of Owner Motivation in the California Wine Industry," working paper, University of Chicago, 1998.

28. Watson, *From Manet to Manhattan*, pp. 275–279, 285–286; Marcia Bystryn, "Art Galleries as Gatekeepers: The Case of the Abstract Expressionists," *Social Research* 45 (Summer 1978): 390–408.

29. Barbaralee Diamonstein, *Inside the Art World: Conversations with Barbaralee Diamonstein* (New York: Rizzoli, 1994), pp. 71–85; John Bernard Myers, *Tracking the Marvelous: A Life in the New York Art World* (New York: Random House, 1983); Caplin, *Business of Art*, p. 269; Tomkins, *Post- to Neo-*, pp. 11, 22–23; de Coppet and Jones, *Art Dealers*, p. 243.

30. Ivan Karp, "Dealing from New York," in Caplin, *Business of Art*, pp. 267–272; Plattner, *High Art Down Home*, pp. 125–127.

31. Alix M. Freedman, "For Art Dealers Outside New York, City's Dominance Poses Problems," *WSJ*, Oct. 8, 1985, p. 33; Myers, *Tracking the Marvelous*, pp. 163, 185.

32. Diana Crane, *The Transformation of the Avant-Garde: The New York Art World, 1920–1985* (Chicago: University of Chicago Press, 1987), p. 4.

33. De Coppet and Jones, *Art Dealers*, pp. 44, 126; Plattner, *High Art Down Home*, p. 201. Aware of the hazards of a single backer—one fight, and you're done—Patricia Hamilton recruited a group of them while keeping 51 percent control of her gallery (de Coppet and Jones, *Art Dealers*, pp. 260–263).

34. De Coppet and Jones, *Art Dealers*, pp. 143–144.

35. Fitzgerald, *Making Modernism*, p. 195.

36. At the onset of Pop Art, the Castelli Gallery apparently acquiesced in the movement to other galleries of two artists who were promising but similar to others in Castelli's stable. Their coordinated shows would supply impetus to the new style. Martin Elkoff, "The American Painter as a Blue Chip," in Albrecht, Barnett, and Griff, *Sociology of Art and Literature*, pp. 321–322.

37. Simpson, in *SoHo*, (pp. 34–39), called attention to Louis K. Meisel, who in 1973 collaborated with a collector on an elaborate catalogue and show of Photorealist works in his new SoHo gallery. The works shown were indeed not for sale, but the art-magazine publicity and subsequent tour to galleries and museums in smaller cities made the promotional investment pay off.

38. Watson, *From Manet to Manhattan*, pp. 365–366.

39. Assouline, *Artful Life*, pp. 101–110.

40. Tomkins, *Post- to Neo-*, pp. 46–48; de Coppet and Jones, *Art Dealers*, pp. 198–200.

41. Assouline, *Artful Life*, pp. 155–158, 160, 165, 184; Tomkins, *Post- to Neo-*, pp. 25, 31.

42. Plattner, *High Art Down Home*, pp. 127–137.

43. Galleries at the lower end of the price spectrum may not be clearly distinguished from the artist's loft or the collector's living room. Carol Kino, "Living-Room Galleries," *Atlantic Monthly*, July 1996, pp. 99–102; Ellen Pall, "The Do-It-Yourself Dealers," *New York Times Magazine*, Sept. 1, 1996, pp. 29–65.

44. See Bystryn, "Art Galleries as Gatekeepers." In Diamonstein, *Inside the Art World* (pp. 78–85), Arne Glimcher described the extensive services provided to high-profile artists and the heavy fixed costs incurred by a gallery that supplies them. Such a gallery, he observed, could be "very destructive for young emerging artists to be made so self-conscious of everything they do."

45. Cynthia Salzman, "Meet Arnold Glimcher, Who Links the Worlds of Art and Commerce," *WSJ*, July 31, 1981, pp. 1, 8; Allan Schwartzman, "Can I Interest You in a Schnabel, Mr. Ovitz?" *New York Times Magazine*, Oct. 3, 1993, pp. 31–50.

46. Meryman, *Andrew Wyeth*, pp. 247–252.

47. Carol Vogel, "The Art Market," *NYT*, June 11, 1993, p. C18; Ralph E. Lerner, "Agreements for the Visual Artist," *Entertainment and Sports Lawyer* 16 (Fall 1998): 19–21.

48. Taylor and Brooke, *Art Dealers*, p. 46. Marquis, in her *Art Biz* (p. 267), described the Dintenfass Gallery's decision to stick with figurative artists during the boom of Abstract Expressionism. It did survive, thanks to a loyal if small group of collectors and to its control of the estates of several important American modernist pioneers who stayed in favor.

49. Bystryn, "Art Galleries as Gatekeepers"; de Coppet and Jones, *Art Dealers*, pp. 246, 274–278.

50. Bystryn "Art Galleries as Gatekeepers"; Lee Seldes, *The Legacy of Mark Rothko* (New York: Holt, Rinehart, and Winston, 1978), pp. 56–60; Marquis, *Art Biz*, pp. 241–245; Watson, *From Manet to Manhattan*, pp. 286–289. Guggenheim in 1947 closed her gallery and left New York to dwell in Venice, and several other of her artists migrated to Kootz or Parsons.

51. Watson, *From Manet to Manhattan*, pp. 326–327.

52. Crane, *Transformation of the Avant-Garde*, Appendix A.

53. Liah Greenfeld, *Different Worlds: A Sociological Study of Taste, Choice, and Success in Art* (Cambridge: Cambridge University Press, 1989).

54. Crane, *Transformation of the Avant-Garde*, pp. 37–41; Tomkins, *Post- to Neo-*, pp. 115–116.

55. Compare V. Ginsburgh and A.-F. Penders, "Land Artists and Art Markets," *JCE* 21, no. 3 (1997): 219–228.

56. Plattner, *High Art Down Home*, pp. 127–137, on St. Louis; Moulin, *French Art Market*, pp. 32–33, on the French art market; and Greenfeld, *Different Worlds*, ch.1 and pp. 30–32, on Israel.

57. Freedman, "For Art Dealers," p. 33; Charles Giuliano, "Surveying Forty Years of Dealing Art with Boston's Barbara Krakow," *Art New England* (February/March 1999): 86.

3. Artist and Gatekeeper

1. Malcolm Bradbury, *The Social Context of Modern English Literature* (Oxford: Blackwell, 1971), ch. 9.

2. Lewis A. Coser, Charles Kadushin, and Walter W. Powell, *Books: The Culture and Commerce of Publishing* (New York: Basic Books, 1982), pp. 130–132.

3. Publishers Weekly, *The Business of Publishing: A PW Anthology* (New York: R. R. Bowker, 1976), especially pp. 52, 60–61.

4. Publishers Weekly, *Business of Publishing*, pp. 54–57, 61.

5. James Hepburn, *The Author's Empty Purse and the Rise of the Literary Agent* (London: Oxford University Press, 1968), pp. 53–64; Coser, Kadushin, and Powell, *Books*, pp. 286–287.

6. Martin Arnold, "The Agency Has Many Faces," *NYTNE*, Jan. 8, 1998, p. B3; "Is the Agent Really Needed?" *NYTNE*, Jan. 15, 1998, p. B3.

7. Lavonne Neff, "The Rise of Agents in Christian Publishing," *PW*, Nov. 11, 1996, pp. 36–37.

8. Coser, Kadushin, and Powell, *Books*, pp. 133–135; Walter W. Powell, *Getting into Print: The Decision-Making Process in Scholarly Publishing* (Chicago: University of Chicago Press, 1985), pp. 48–50, 101.

9. Powell, *Getting into Print*, p. 88.

10. G. Bruce Knecht, "HarperCollins Reverses Get-Tough Plan to Recover Advances for Canceled Books," *WSJ*, Aug. 22, 1997, p. B13; Richard Brookhiser, "Pop Authoress Seduces Jury, Keeps Advance," *WSJ*, Feb. 15, 1996, p. A12; Roger Cohen, "For Authors, the Key Words Are in the Book Contracts," *NYT*, Aug. 27, 1990, pp. D1, D8.

11. No systematic data are available, so we rely on recent anecdotal information from Ken Auletta, "The Impossible Business," *New Yorker,* Oct. 6, 1997, pp. 50–63. On a trade book with a $25 retail list price, the publisher receives wholesale revenue of about $12.25 and incurs marginal costs of about $6.25 ($2.50 printing and binding, $2.00 distribution, $1.75 marketing, which here is appropriately treated as a marginal cost of "buying" sales). The author who receives a standard royalty of 10 percent of the list price takes $2.50, leaving $3.50 gross profit for the publisher. With a highly successful book a higher royalty rate will apply, but at least some of the publisher's variable unit costs decline, so the profit split probably does not change much.

12. The advance can also deter a publisher from opportunistically declining the completed manuscript. He might do that when the manuscript on receipt likely will profit author and publisher together, but the contract terms award the whole profit (or more) to the author. See Henry Hansmann and Reinier Kraakman, "Hands-Tying Contracts: Book Publishing, Venture Capital Financing, and Secured Debt," *Journal of Law, Economics, and Organization* 8 (October 1992): 628–655.

13. That is, publishing appears to be an industry with easy entry of new firms, so that average profits in the long run are normal or competitive.

14. This argument applies with much less force to academic publishing, where the low-reward publication of a quality specialized monograph carries no opprobrium.

15. Coser, Kadushin, and Powell, *Books,* pp. 240–243.

16. Hepburn, *Author's Empty Purse,* pp. 12–14; Allan C. Dooley, *Author and Printer in Victorian England* (Charlottesville: University of Virginia Press, 1992), pp. 59, 101, 119–120; Donald Sheehan, *This Was Publishing: A Chronicle of the Book Trade in the Gilded Age* (Bloomington: Indiana University Press, 1952), pp. 80, 88–97.

17. J. A. Sutherland, *Victorian Novelists and Publishers* (Chicago: University of Chicago Press, 1976), pp. 87–92, 139, 218–219.

18. Publishers Weekly, *Business of Publishing,* pp. 70–72; Powell, *Getting into Print,* pp. 76–81.

19. Publishers Weekly, *Business of Publishing,* pp. 69–72.

20. In *Getting into Print,* Powell (pp. 129–33) reported that editors are subject to little if any formal evaluation or held accountable for the performance of books that they have signed. Poor sellers can always be rationalized as bad guesses, but editors do know that sponsoring a string of failures will result in discharge (p. 142).

21. Michael Norman, "A Book in Search of a Buzz," *New York Times Book Review,* Jan. 30, 1994, p. 22.

22. Coser, Kadushin, and Powell, *Books,* ch. 4; Publishers Weekly, *Business of Publishing,* p. 69. On the property-right problems with editors' mobility, see Laura Mansnerus, "Not the Usual Farewell: Editors Quit and Are Sued," *NYT,* Nov. 25, 1996, p. D7.

23. Powell, *Getting into Print,* p. 133.

24. Powell (especially in ibid., ch. 6) studied the network process among editors; also see Coser, Kadushin, and Powell, *Books,* ch. 3; Martin Arnold, "Art of Foreplay at the Table," *NYTNE,* June 11, 1998, p. B3. On the parallel phenomenon in the

semiconductor industry, see Everett M. Rogers and Judith K. Larsen, *Silicon Valley Fever: Growth of High-Technology Culture* (New York: Basic Books, 1984).

25. Donald S. Passman, *All You Need to Know about the Music Business* (New York: Simon & Schuster, 1994), pp. 48–54. There is obvious scope for disputes arising from the fact that the manager's claim on the group's income may persist after his capacity to contribute to its development is exhausted.

26. Richard A. Peterson and David G. Berger, "Entrepreneurship in Organizations: Evidence from the Popular Music Industry," *Administrative Science Quarterly* 16 (March 1971): 97–106.

27. Passman, *All You Need to Know*, pp. 34–35.

28. R. Serge Denisoff, *Tarnished Gold: The Record Industry Revisited* (New Brunswick, N.J.: Transaction Books, 1986), p. 4; Simon Frith, *Sound Effects: Youth, Leisure, and the Politics of Rock* (London: Constable, 1983), pp. 101–102.

29. The phenomenon is studied in computer software by Thomas J. Prusa and James A. Schmitz, Jr., "Can Companies Maintain Their Initial Innovative Thrust? A Study of the PC Software Industry," *Review of Economics and Statistics* 76 (August 1994): 523–540.

30. The Beatles reached a figure of 25 percent. In the late 1980s Michael Jackson's royalty rate was 41 percent of the wholesale price (which corresponds to a rate of approximately half that on the retail list price), while Bruce Springsteen's was 38 percent. Both Jackson and Springsteen also received large nonrecoupable advances (up to $3 million), transferring a good deal of risk to the label. See Passman, *All You Need to Know*, p. 109; Fredric Dannen, *Hit Men: Power Brokers and Fast Money inside the Music Business* (New York: Vintage, 1991), p. 339. Minimum royalty rates quoted in earlier sources for the 1970s were lower, 7 to 9 percent, suggesting an upward trend in the floor.

31. Passman, *All You Need to Know*, pp. 88–98. He suggested that these devious terms dominate a straightforward lower royalty rate by giving the artist bragging rights on the nominal rate. Royalty payments are also adjusted for records returned unsold by retailers (Chapter 9).

32. Another option step may be interposed at the outset. Before the artist is signed to produce a full-fledged album tape, the company pays for a high-quality demo, holding the option to commit the advance to fund the album itself after reviewing the demo. See ibid., pp. 117–118, 146–147.

33. Once contracts were written in terms of calendar time, but the growing technical complexity of pop recording techniques made calendar-based deadlines impractical. Contracts could not be based exclusively on a total number of albums obligated for delivery, either, because a performer who delays long in delivering the next album may be forgotten by the audience. See ibid., pp. 121–122.

34. For additional details on record contracts in practice, see Sidney Shemel and M. William Krasilovsky, *This Business of Music*, 6th ed. (New York: Billboard Books, 1990), pp. 3–17; Jeffrey Brabec and Todd Brabec, *Music, Money, and Success: The Insider's Guide to the Music Industry* (New York: Schirmer Books, 1994); and R. Serge Denisoff, *Solid Gold: The Popular Record Industry* (New Brunswick, N.J.: Transaction Books, 1975), pp. 68–70.

35. Passman, *All You Need to Know*, pp. 125–126.

36. Steve Chapple and Reebee Garofalo, *Rock 'n' Roll Is Here to Pay: The History and*

Politics of the Music Industry (Chicago: Nelson-Hall, 1977), p. 184. Artists have resorted to such drastic expedients as bankruptcy filings to break contracts. See Katharine Q. Seelye, "Bankruptcies by Musicians Inspire a Bill," *NYTNE*, May 15, 1998, p. A18.

37. Marc Eliot, *Rockonomics: The Money behind the Music* (New York: Franklin Watts, 1989), pp. 171–175.

38. In the 1980s good recording studios rented for around $20,000 a week. Skilled producers and engineers are expensive inputs; the total compensation to an independent producer might amount to 5 to 10 percent of an album's gross revenue. See Denisoff, *Tarnished Gold*, pp. 169–173, and his *Solid Gold*, pp. 152–164.

39. In standard economic terms this phenomenon is called debt-equity moral hazard.

40. Eliot, *Rockonomics*, pp. 200–221.

41. Shemel and Krasilovsky, *This Business*, pp. 75–81. For a case study, see Geoffrey Stokes, *Star-Making Machinery: Inside the Business of Rock and Roll* (New York: Vintage Books, 1976).

42. Neil Strauss, "A Chance to Break the Pop Stranglehold," *NYTNE*, May 9, 1999, sec. 2, pp. 1, 51.

43. Denisoff, *Solid Gold*, pp. 72–79, and his *Tarnished Gold*, pp. 57–58, 67. In his *All You Need to Know*, Passman (p. 334) offered another example: clubs with well-established "showcase" reputations may charge new artists to perform there.

44. George Tremlett, *Rock Gold: The Music Millionaires* (London: Unwin Hyman, 1990), p. 47.

45. Frith, *Sound Effects*, pp. 136–137; Tremlett, *Rock Gold*, pp. 112–115; Passman, *All You Need to Know*, pp. 336–339.

46. Michael Cable, *The Pop Industry Inside Out* (London: W. H. Allen, 1977), pp. 131–135; Chapple and Garofalo, *Rock 'n' Roll*, pp. 124–131, 152; Robert Stephen Spitz, *The Making of Superstars: Artists and Executives of the Rock Music Business* (Garden City, N.Y.: Anchor Press/Doubleday, 1978), pp. 121–132, 159–164, 167.

47. The transfer of the digested information need not be costless; it is only necessary that digestion yields sufficient economies to compensate for the opportunity cost of the agent's services.

48. Although a good reason will emerge why an agent represents only one party in a matching transaction, a different platoon of agents might represent each side. Our concern here is with the two sides' differential pull.

49. This reasoning might seem to neglect an obvious point—that the agent functions as the artist's salesperson—but it really does not. A salesperson provides information to the recipient of his "pitch." If the information is puffed, or puffed beyond the conventions for displaying enthusiasm in this particular market, the salesperson will make no second sale.

50. That best match-up is what the sellers and buyers would achieve on their own if they could costlessly investigate all possible hook-ups, and all deals remain provisional until no two parties can beneficially ditch their present partners and link with each other.

51. Natural-monopoly tendencies were evident long ago in the booking of variety and vaudeville acts into local theaters. See Jack Poggi, *Theater in America: The Impact of Economic Forces, 1870–1967* (Ithaca, N.Y.: Cornell University Press,

1968), pp. 11–26; Russell Sanjek and David Sanjek, *American Popular Music Business in the Twentieth Century* (New York: Oxford University Press, 1991), chs. 2, 3.

52. Leo Walker, *The Wonderful Era of the Great Dance Bands* (Berkeley, Calif.: Howell-North Books, 1964), sec. 2, ch. 5; David W. Stowe, *Swing Changes: Big-Band Jazz in New Deal America* (Cambridge, Mass.: Harvard University Press, 1994), pp. 103–106.

53. MCA's success also relied on the market power exercised by requiring large ball-rooms to employ only MCA's bands if they used any of them. Dennis McDougal, *The Last Mogul: Lew Wasserman, MCA, and the Hidden History of Hollywood* (New York: Crown, 1998), pp. 108, 123, 224.

54. David F. Prindle, *The Politics of Glamour: Ideology and Democracy in the Screen Actors Guild* (Madison: University of Wisconsin Press, 1988), pp. 78–80, 88–90.

55. The gatekeeper function is clearly relevant. Also, the orchestra recruiting a soloist or singer will need quite intricate evidence and quality assurance of the per-former's ability, while the musician is relatively indifferent between performing in (say) Cleveland or Cincinnati.

56. Milton Goldin, *The Music Merchants* (New York: Macmillan, 1969), ch. 7; Nor-man Lebrecht, *Who Killed Classical Music? Maestros, Managers, and Corporate Politics* (Secaucus, N.J.: Birch Lane Press, 1997), especially pp. 66, 78, 90.

57. Goldin, *Music Merchants,* pp. 162–163; Lebrecht, *Who Killed Classical Music?* pp. 80–84. The integrity problem arose partly because of opportunism, partly be-cause financial acumen and diligence did not necessarily accompany the other skills needed for agenting.

58. Goldin, *Music Merchants,* pp. 161–162; Lebrecht, *Who Killed Classical Music?* pp. 62–69, 92–93; Joseph Horowitz, *The Ivory Trade: Music and the Business of Music at the Van Cliburn International Piano Competition* (New York: Summit Books, 1990), pp. 114, 118; Barbara Jepson, "How Musicians and Managers Co-exist," *NYT,* July 18, 1982, sec. 2, pp. 17, 20.

59. But see Lebrecht, *Who Killed Classical Music?* p. 130.

60. Norman Lebrecht, *The Maestro Myth: Great Conductors in Pursuit of Power* (Lon-don: Simon & Schuster, 1991), p. 321 and ch. 16 generally; Lebrecht, *Who Killed Classical Music?* ch. 7 (especially pp. 172–173, 199–200); Ralph Blumenthal, "Gray Eminence of Classical Music's Stars," *NYT,* May 23, 1995, pp. C13, C16.

61. Goldin, *Music Merchants,* ch. 7; Lebrecht, *Who Killed Classical Music?* pp. 108–110; James F. Richardson, "Vocal Recitals in Smaller Cities: Changes in Supply, Demand and Content since the 1920s," *JCE* 5 (June 1981): 21–35.

62. Allan Kozinn, "Who Makes Music with Whom Is the Work of Hidden Hands," *NYT,* Jan. 2, 1995, pp. 11, 17. A similar market for choral singers in Britain is de-scribed by Ruth Towse, *Singers in the Marketplace: The Economics of the Singing Profession* (Oxford: Clarendon Press, 1993), pp. 13–15, 98.

4. Artists, Starving and Well-Fed

1. Sherwin Rosen, "The Economics of Superstars," *American Economic Review* 71 (December 1981): 845–858.

2. In their *The Winner-Take-All Society* (New York: Free Press, 1995), Robert H. Frank and Philip J. Cook argued that rank-order tournaments generating superstar winners are pervasive in our economy. They also explained clearly (pp. 106–109) why the process involves a market failure. Society benefits from another artist joining the quest for superstardom by the marginal increase in quality of the superstar expected to emerge. The artist's incentive to join the race is greater than this social gain, however: an average chance (at the outset) of winning the big prize. Too many artists pursue superstardom.

3. The basis for a collective element in fans' preferences is discussed in Chapter 11.

4. Glenn M. MacDonald, "The Economics of Rising Stars," *American Economic Review* 78 (March 1988): 155–166.

5. Despite some fans' high reservation prices for the superstar's record, it is not obvious that aggregate market demand is less elastic than for an ordinary artist. That is because the superstar attracts many purchasers who do not ordinarily make such purchases, and whose reservation prices may be modest.

6. On film superstars' balancing decisions, see "Now You See Them . . . Now You See Them Again," *NYTNE,* Nov. 16, 1997, sec. 2, pp. 1, 28.

7. Daniel Boorstin, *The Image, or What Happened to the American Dream* (New York: Atheneum, 1962), p. 57.

8. Leo Lowenthal, *Literature, Popular Culture, and Society* (Englewood Cliffs, N.J.: Prentice-Hall, 1961), ch. 4.

9. Joshua Gamson, *Claims to Fame: Celebrity in Contemporary America* (Berkeley: University of California Press, 1994), pp. 17–23.

10. Ibid., pp. 22–28; Richard daCordova, *Picture Personalities: The Emergence of the Star System in America* (Urbana: University of Illinois Press, 1990).

11. Frank Luther Mott, *Golden Multitudes: The Story of Best Sellers in the United States* (New York: Macmillan, 1947), especially pp. 197, 297.

12. Harlow Robinson, *The Last Impresario: The Life, Times, and Legacy of Sol Hurok* (New York: Viking, 1994), p. 28.

13. Kee H. Chung and Raymond A. K. Cox, "A Stochastic Model of Superstardom: An Application of the Yule Distribution," *Review of Economics and Statistics* 76 (November 1994): 771–775.

14. Jacob W. Getzels and Mihaly Csikszentmihalyi, *The Creative Vision: A Longitudinal Study of Problem Finding in Art* (New York: Wiley Interscience, 1976).

15. Joseph Horowitz, *The Ivory Trade: Music and the Business of Music at the Van Cliburn International Piano Competition* (New York: Summit Books, 1990), especially p. 141.

16. William A. Hamlen, Jr., "Superstardom in Popular Music: Empirical Evidence," *Review of Economics and Statistics* 73 (November 1991): 729–733.

17. Evidence in Chapter 1, and David Throsby, "A Work-Preference Model of Artist Behaviour," in Alan Peacock and Ilde Rizzo, eds., *Cultural Economics and Cultural Policies* (Dordrecht: Kluwer Academic, 1994), pp. 69–80.

18. Randall K. Filer, "The 'Starving Artist'—Myth or Reality? Earnings of Artists in the United States," *Journal of Political Economy* 94 (February 1986): 56–75.

19. Specifically, Filer (ibid.) calculated present discounted values of predicted future earnings for all individuals in his sample using the data on earnings of their older occupational colleagues in 1979. The mean present value of lifetime incomes for

those in arts occupations was only 2.9 percent less than for persons in other occupations.

20. Filer's Table 3 (ibid.) provides one tip-off to this issue's importance. While self-employed persons in the general population in 1979 earned $4,725 a year more than otherwise similar members of the general labor force, self-employed artists earned $2,046 less than otherwise similar artists on payrolls.

21. Gregory H. Wassall and Neil O. Alper, "Toward a Unified Theory of the Determinants of Earnings of Artists," in Ruth Towse and Abdul Khakee, eds., *Cultural Economics* (Berlin: Springer Verlag, 1992), pp. 187–200. A study of visual artists in Australia reported the same fraction of income due directly to art work (including grants received); see G. D. Snooks, "Determinants of Earnings Inequality amongst Australian Artists," *Australian Economic Papers* 22 (December 1983): 322–333.

22. Of applicants for New York State Foundation for the Arts fellowships, only 26 percent earned their major living from art, 25 percent as arts instructors, and 39 percent in non-arts related work; 53 percent earned less than $2,000 from art in 1987. Joan Jeffri and Robert Greenblatt, "Between Extremities: The Artist Described," *Journal of Arts Management and Law* 19 (Spring 1989): 5–14.

23. Brian R. Harrison and John T. Thera, "Economic Status of Canadian Freelance Writers," in William S. Hendon and James L. Shanahan, eds., *Economics of Cultural Decisions* (Cambridge, Mass.: Abt Books, 1983), pp. 143–153.

24. Sarah S. Montgomery and Michael D. Robinson, "Visual Artists in New York: What's Special about Person and Place?" *JCE* 17 (December 1993): 17–39.

25. James J. McLain, "The Income of Visual Artists in New Orleans," *JCE* 2 (June 1978): 63–76.

26. David Throsby, "Artists as Workers," in Towse and Khakee, *Cultural Economics,* pp. 201–208. He also found that arts income increases in proportion (unit elasticity) to time allocated to arts work, whereas non-arts income increases with respect to hours of humdrum work with an elasticity of only 0.4. The difference is consistent with artists spending at humdrum labor only enough hours to bring in an adequate income.

27. Gladys Engel Lang and Kurt Lang, *Etched in Memory: The Building and Survival of Artistic Reputation* (Chapel Hill: University of North Carolina Press, 1990), ch. 8.

28. Randall K. Filer, "Arts and Academe: The Effect of Education on Earnings of Artists," *JCE* 14 (December 1990): 15–38. Consistent with this, artists who hold non-arts jobs possess more educational capital than those who do not. See Gregory H. Wassall and Neil O. Alper, "Occupational Characteristics of Artists: A Statistical Analysis," *JCE* 9 (June 1985): 13–34.

29. Ruth Towse, *Singers in the Marketplace: The Economics of the Singing Profession* (Oxford: Clarendon Press, 1993), pp. 11–12, 17, 26, and ch. 6; Towse, "Economics of Training Artists," in Victor A. Ginsburgh and Pierre-Michel Menger, eds., *Economics of the Arts: Selected Essays* (Amsterdam: North-Holland, 1996), pp. 303–329; James F. Richardson, "Career Patterns of American Opera Singers," in William S. Hendon, James L. Shanahan, and Alice J. MacDonald, eds., *Economic Policy for the Arts* (Cambridge, Mass.: Abt Books, 1980), pp. 176–183.

30. The coefficient of variation for artists' earned incomes was 1.20, while the highest coefficient of variations for the other professions was 0.79. See C. Richard Waits and Edward M. McNertney, "Uncertainty and Investment in Human Capital in the Arts," in Hendon, Shanahan, and MacDonald, *Economic Policy for the Arts,* pp. 200–207.

31. The coefficient of variation is the standard deviation divided by the mean.

32. Snooks found that the skewness of the distribution of Australian visual artists' earnings was 2.4 times as great as the distribution for all workers. G. D. Snooks, "Determinants of Earnings Inequality," pp. 322–332.

33. Montgomery and Robinson, "Visual Artists."

34. Horowitz, *Ivory Trade,* p. 15.

35. Robert R. Faulkner and Andy B. Anderson, "Short-Term Projects and Emergent Careers," *American Journal of Sociology* 92 (January 1987): 879–909.

36. Mark Litwak, *Reel Power: The Struggle for Influence and Success in the New Hollywood* (New York: William Morrow, 1986), p. 204.

37. Ibid., p. 139. In 1984, 85 percent of Screen Actors Guild members were not employed as actors (this union includes many members whose acting experience was transitory, but who retain guild membership); see David F. Prindle, *The Politics of Glamour: Ideology and Democracy in the Screen Actors Guild* (Madison: University of Wisconsin Press, 1988), p. 11.

38. Harold Horowitz, "Work and Earnings of Artists in the Media Fields," *JCE* 7, no. 2 (1983): 69–89.

39. Hugh Lovell and Tasile Carter, *Collective Bargaining in the Motion Picture Industry* (Berkeley: Institute of Industrial Relations, University of California, 1955), p. 38.

40. Hortense Powdermaker, *Hollywood: The Dream Factory* (Boston: Little, Brown, 1950), p. 132.

41. A. J. Scott, "Territorial Reproduction and Transformation in a Local Labor Market: The Animated Film Workers of Los Angeles," *Environment and Planning D: Society and Space* 2 (September 1984): 277–307.

42. John Pick, *Arts Administration* (London: E. & F. N. Spon, 1980), p. 31.

43. Anthony A. P. Dawson, "Hollywood's Labor Troubles," *Industrial and Labor Relations Review* 1 (July 1948): 638–647.

44. Murray Ross, *Stars and Strikes: Unionization in Hollywood* (New York: Columbia University Press, 1941), p. 108.

45. Ibid., pp. 163–165, 169.

5. The Hollywood Studios Disintegrate

1. For example, Tino Balio, "Struggles for Control, 1908–1930," in Tino Balio, ed., *The American Film Industry,* rev. ed. (Madison: University of Wisconsin Press, 1985), especially pp. 110–115; Thomas Schatz, *The Genius of the System* (New York: Pantheon, 1988).

2. For example, Tino Balio, *Grand Design: Hollywood as a Modern Business Enterprise, 1930–1939* (New York: Charles Scribner's Sons, 1993), pp. 144–146; Horence Powdermaker, *Hollywood: The Dream Factory* (Boston: Little, Brown, 1950), pp. 84–85.

3. Darlene Chisholm argued that this asset was an important basis for the studios' long-term contracts, and that it raised a significant problem of asset-specificity because the persona did not travel well from one studio's typical films to those of a different studio. See her "Asset Specificity and Long-Term Contracts: The Case of the Motion-Pictures Industry," *Eastern Economic Review* 19 (Spring 1993): 143–155.

4. Cathy Klaprat, "The Star as Market Strategy: Bette Davis in Another Light," in Balio, *American Film Industry*, pp. 351–376.

5. Balio, *Grand Design*, pp. 157–159; Powdermaker, *Hollywood*, pp. 210–215; Mae D. Huettig, *Economic Control of the Motion Picture Industry: A Study in Industrial Organization* (Philadelphia: University of Pennsylvania Press, 1944), pp. 92–95.

6. Janet Staiger, "The Hollywood Mode of Production to 1930," in David Bordwell, Janet Staiger, and Kristin Thompson, *The Classical Hollywood Cinema: Film Style and Mode of Production to 1960* (New York: Columbia University Press, 1985), p. 146.

7. Hazel Meyer, *The Gold in Tin Pan Alley* (Philadelphia: Lippincott, 1958), ch. 11; Christine Lepera and Michael Manuelian, "Music Plagiarism: A Framework for Litigation," *Entertainment and Sports Lawyer* 15 (Summer 1997): 3–12.

8. Robert R. Faulkner, *Music on Demand: Composers and Careers in the Hollywood Film Industry* (New Brunswick, N.J.: Transaction Books, 1983), ch. 6.

9. David Bordwell based such an analysis on a sample of 100 films. See David Bordwell, "The Classical Hollywood Style, 1917–60," in Bordwell, Staiger, and Thompson, *Classical Hollywood Cinema*, pt. 1.

10. Powdermaker, *Hollywood*, pp. 91–92.

11. Ibid., pp. 152–159; Janet Staiger, "The Hollywood Mode of Production to 1930," in Bordwell, Staiger, and Thompson, *Classical Hollywood Cinema*, pp. 93–94.

12. Dore Schary (as told to Charles Palmer), *Case History of a Movie* (New York: Random House, 1950), pp. 42–43.

13. Staiger, "Hollywood Mode of Production," pp. 125–127, 143–145; Schary, *Case History*, pp. 46, 56–62, 66. Schary observed that union seniority rules had their bright side: with film production technique so idiosyncratic, older craft workers had an advantage of experience with how unusual problems had been solved in previous films (p. 93).

14. Staiger, "Hollywood Mode of Production," pp. 325–329.

15. Ibid., pp. 110–112.

16. Powdermaker, *Hollywood*, pp. 192–204, 218–226.

17. Douglas Gomery, *The Hollywood Studio System* (New York: St. Martin's Press, 1986), p. 15; Schatz, *Genius of the System*.

18. Roger Corman with Jim Jerome, *How I Made a Hundred Movies in Hollywood and Never Lost a Dime* (New York: Random House, 1990). Corman, "king of the B's," is particularly amusing on the cheap but ingenious methods used to get tawdry special effects.

19. Film budgets fluctuated with the general level of demand for movie tickets, the average falling off 50–70 percent in the Great Depression from the 1920s level, and diving again when film attendance slumped after World War II. It is unclear

how much of these fluctuations was due to shriveled rents in stars' and others' salary costs. See Audrey Solomon, *Twentieth Century–Fox: A Corporate and Financial History* (Metuchen, N.J.: Scarecrow Press, 1988), pp. 14, 68–69.

20. Tino Balio, *United Artists: The Company Built by the Stars* (Madison: University of Wisconsin Press, 1976).

21. The term monopsony refers to a single buyer, just as monopoly indicates a single seller.

22. Robert H. Stanley, *The Celluloid Empire: A History of the American Movie Industry* (New York: Hastings House, 1978), pp. 140–143.

23. *United States v. Paramount Pictures,* 334 U.S. 131 (1948). See Michael Conant, *Antitrust in the Motion Picture Industry: Economic and Legal Analysis* (Berkeley: University of California Press, 1960).

24. The studios dealt with each other on both sides of the distribution-exhibition market. Exhibition contracts that roughly split the profits between these sectors dampened the incentive of any studio to shift its assets toward or away from the exhibition sector and in that way tended to stabilize the oligopoly. (In the late 1930s the studios did, however, differ substantially in their numbers of affiliated theatres.) For any one studio, profits realized in exhibition would be a good deal more stable from year to year than those from distribution (and production), due to films' random variations in success. Gathering substantial profits at the exhibition level was therefore a form of profit-sharing among the studios that should have stabilized their oligopoly. See Solomon, *Twentieth Century–Fox,* pp. 49–53, 56. In the 1940s, once the studios began distributing films made by independent producers, another compelling reason emerged for taking profits at the exhibition level. The net profits commonly split between distributor and producer were those based on gross rentals received from exhibitors, so profits realized at the exhibition level escaped the knife in this melon-cutting exercise.

25. Conant, *Antitrust,* pp. 112–125; James A. Robins, "Organization as Strategy: Restructuring Production in the Film Industry," *Strategic Management Journal* 14 (Summer 1993): 103–118. No systematic data have been assembled on whether the studios' disintegration brought more rents into the stars' hands, but casual evidence suggests that it did. See Dennis McDougal, *The Last Mogul: Lew Wasserman, MCA, and The Hidden History of Hollywood* (New York: Crown, 1998), pp. 156–157, 205.

26. An entry barrier is some structural economy of scale or first-mover advantage that permits the incumbent seller to earn excess profits without attracting new competitors.

27. Paul A. Baumgarten, Donald C. Farber, and Mark Fleischer, *Producing, Financing, and Distributing Film: A Comprehensive Legal and Business Guide,* 2d ed. (New York: Limelight, 1995), pp. 113–114.

28. See Barry R. Litman, *The Motion Picture Mega-Industry* (Needham Heights, Mass.: Allyn and Bacon, 1998), pp. 24–25.

29. Andrew Hindes, "Distrib Debs Take Walk on the Wide Side," *Variety,* Jan. 20, 1997, pp. 1, 57.

30. Steven Bach, *Final Cut: Dreams and Disasters in the Making of "Heaven's Gate"* (New York: William Morrow, 1985), pp. 46–53.

31. United Artists was immediately lucky. Stanley Kramer left the firm for Columbia

Pictures owing United Artists one film under his contract. He next made the hit-to-be *High Noon,* and Columbia chose to pass and let it go to United Artists. Directors such as Otto Preminger, Billy Wilder, Joseph Mankiewicz, and William Wyler soon were releasing films through United Artists. See Robert H. Stanley, *The Celluloid Empire: A History of the American Movie Industry* (New York: Hastings House, 1985), pp. 137–139; Jason E. Squire, ed., *The Movie Business Book,* 2d ed. (New York: Simon & Schuster, 1992), pp. 187–188.

32. Much of this evidence comes from the research of Susan Christopherson and Michael Storper. See Michael Storper and Susan Christopherson, "Flexible Specialization and Regional Industrial Agglomeration: The Case of the U.S. Motion Picture Industry," *Annals of the Association of American Geographers* 77 (March 1987): 104–117; Susan Christopherson and Michael Storper, "The Effects of Flexible Specialization on Industrial Politics and the Labor Market: The Motion Picture Industry," *Industrial and Labor Relations Review* 42 (April 1989): 333–347; Michael Storper, "The Transition to Flexible Specialisation in the U.S. Film Industry: External Economies, the Division of Labour, and the Crossing of Industrial Divides," *Cambridge Journal of Economics* 13 (June 1989): 273–305; Susan Christopherson, "The Origins of Fragmented Bargaining Power in Entertainment Media Industries," *Proceedings of the Forty-Fourth Annual Meeting, Industrial Relations Research Association,* 1992, pp. 10–17.

33. Storper, "Transition to Flexible Specialisation," Table 6.

34. Storper and Christopherson, "Flexible Specialization."

35. Storper, "Transition to Flexible Specialisation," Tables 10, 11.

36. A. J. Scott, "Territorial Reproduction and Transformation in a Local Labor Market: The Animated Film Workers of Los Angeles," *Environment and Planning D: Society and Space* 2 (September 1984): 277–307.

37. Squire, *Movie Business Book,* p. 110.

38. Christopherson and Storper, "Effects of Flexible Specialization."

39. Ibid.; Mark Litwak, *Reel Power: The Struggle for Influence and Success in the New Hollywood* (New York: William Morrow, 1986), pp. 275–276.

40. Richard Slater, *Ovitz: The Inside Story of Hollywood's Most Controversial Power Broker* (New York: McGraw-Hill, 1997).

41. Danny Miller and Jamal Shamsie, "The Resource-Based View of the Firm in Two Environments: The Hollywood Film Studios from 1936 to 1965," *Academy of Management Journal* 39 (June 1996): 519–543.

42. Paul N. Lazarus III, *The Movie Producer: A Handbook for Producing and Picture-Making* (New York: Barnes and Noble, 1985), pp. 94–95.

43. Margalit Fox, "Where Auteurs Learn the ABCs," *NYTNE,* May 6, 1999, sec. 2, pp. 29, 30.

44. Bernard Weinraub, "At Sundance Festival, Films Take Diversity to Another Frontier," *NYT,* Jan. 20, 1997, pp. C11, C15; Peter M. Nichols, "A Showcase for Works by Fledgling Directors," *NYTNE,* Sept. 22, 1997, pp. B1, B6; Bernard Weinraub, "Anything Can Still Happen at Sundance Festival," *NYTNE,* Jan. 19, 1998, pp. B1, B14.

45. Suzanne Mary Donahue, *American Film Distribution: The Changing Marketplace* (Ann Arbor, Mich.: UMI Research Press, 1987), ch. 4; Janet Maslin, "Beyond the Upstart Image," *NYTNE,* Feb. 1, 1998, sec. 2, p. 21.

46. Conant, *Antitrust,* pp. 40–43, 112–114; Martin Dale, *The Movie Game: The Film Business in Britain, Europe, and America* (London: Cassell, 1997), p. 55.

47. Neal Gabler, "The End of the Middle," *New York Times Magazine,* Nov. 16, 1997, pp. 76–78.

48. "*Lethal Weapon:* black/white buddy police story, Mel Gibson, Danny Glover, drugs ring, boom." See Jake Eberts and Terry Ilott, *My Indecision Is Final: The Rise and Fall of Goldcrest Films* (New York: Atlantic Monthly Press, 1990), p. 32.

49. Dale, *Movie Game,* ch. 7, offered an interesting analysis of the subsidy regimes and the reasons for their limited aesthetic and even more limited commercial success.

50. Ibid., pp. 15–20, 55–56, 60; Ira Deutchman, "Independent Distribution and Marketing," in Squire, *Movie Business Book,* pp. 320–327. Dale and Deutchman identified several factors that have explained the fluctuating fortunes of independent production and distribution companies, including the U.S. investment tax credit that prevailed from 1976 to 1986 and the video market boom that peaked in the late 1980s (p. 93).

51. Mark Litwak, *Dealmaking in the Film and Television Industry: From Negotiations to Final Contracts* (Los Angeles: Silman-James, 1994), pp. 14–16; Dale, *Movie Game,* pp. 46–47. European studios employ the same practice.

52. The agents' role is discussed in Chapter 6. See Litwak, *Reel Power,* pp. 51–52.

53. Dale, *Movie Game,* pp. 110–115; David Rosen, with Peter Hamilton, *Off-Hollywood: The Making and Marketing of Independent Films* (New York: Grove Weidenfeld, 1989).

54. Rosen, *Off-Hollywood,* pp. 274–275, 304–305.

6. Contracts for Creative Products

1. Paul A. Baumgarten, Donald C. Farber, and Mark Fleischer, *Producing, Financing, and Distributing Film: A Comprehensive Legal and Business Guide,* 2d ed. (New York: Limelight, 1995), pp. 22, 34.

2. Mark Litwak, *Dealmaking in the Film and Television Industry: From Negotiations to Final Contracts* (Los Angeles: Silman-James, 1994), pp. 25–26.

3. Jason E. Squire, ed., *The Movie Business Book,* 2d ed. (New York: Simon & Schuster, 1992), p. 35.

4. Writer-director Frank Pierson asserted that 90 percent of the scripts submitted to studios by producers have not been optioned or bought, although the writer may have consented. See Litwak, *Dealmaking,* p. 184.

5. Ibid., pp. 168–171.

6. Julie Salamon, *The Devil's Candy: "The Bonfire of the Vanities" Goes to Hollywood* (Boston: Houghton Mifflin, 1991), pp. 297–298.

7. John Brodie, "Tales from the Script," *Variety,* Mar. 25, 1996, pp. 1, 21.

8. Writer-director Paul Schrader: "There is absolutely no way to individuate the elements of a film. The people involved can't separate the work of the director and the writer and the art director and the cinematographer and the actors and the producer." See Mark Litwak, *Reel Power: The Struggle for Influence and Success in the New Hollywood* (New York: William Morrow, 1986), pp. 177–178; Donald

Chase, *Filmmaking: The Collaborative Art* (Boston: Little, Brown, 1975), pp. 103–107.

9. Squire, *Movie Business Book,* pp. 38, 87; Chase, *Filmmaking,* p. 210. Giving one person multiple tasks (director and screenwriter, say) is one way to reduce discord. See Wayne E. Baker and Robert R. Faulkner, "Role as Resource in the Hollywood Film Industry," *American Journal of Sociology* 97 (September 1991): 279–309.

10. Paul N. Lazarus III, *The Movie Producer: A Handbook for Producing and Picture-Making* (New York: Barnes and Noble, 1985), p. 129.

11. See, for example, Rebecca Johnson, "Her Brilliant Career," *New York Times Magazine,* Nov. 16, 1997, pp. 108–109. Salamon (pp. 85–87) wrote of the "doomed uncompromisers" who hang around Hollywood getting nowhere because they will not accept the necessity that the product be commercially viable.

12. Litwak, *Dealmaking,* p. 166; Baumgarten, Farber, and Fleischer, *Producing, Financing, and Distributing Film,* pp. 37–38; Chase, *Filmmaking,* pp. 48–57. For specific examples, see William Goldman, *Adventures in the Screen Trade: A Personal View of Hollywood and Screenwriting* (New York: Warner Books, 1984), pp. 200–201, 257–279.

13. Baumgarten, Farber, and Fleischer, *Producing, Financing, and Distributing Film,* pp. 174–175; Squire, *Movie Business Book,* p. 213.

14. Litwak, *Dealmaking,* pp. 12–14; Squire, *Movie Business Book,* p. 199.

15. Baumgarten, Farber, and Fleischer, *Producing, Financing, and Distributing Film,* pp. 182–188; Litwak, *Dealmaking,* p. 187.

16. Ralph Rosenblum and Robert Karen, *When the Shooting Stops . . . the Cutting Begins: A Film Editor's Story* (New York: Viking, 1979), especially ch. 16.

17. Squire, *Movie Business Book,* p. 200; Litwak, *Dealmaking,* pp. 124, 189.

18. Litwak, *Reel Power,* pp. 75–77; Jake Eberts and Terry Ilott, *My Indecision Is Final: The Spectacular Rise and Fall of Goldcrest Films* (New York: Atlantic Monthly Press, 1990), pp. 28–30.

19. Litwak, *Reel Power,* pp. 161–164.

20. After United Artists lost an outstanding management team, the replacements immediately paid $2,500,000 for screen rights to Gay Talese's *Thy Neighbor's Wife;* there were no competing bids for the property, and no film ever emerged (Goldman, *Adventures in the Screen Trade,* pp. 44–45). When Peter Guber took charge of Sony Pictures, to attract successful writer-director James L. Brooks he outbid the competition by $20 million, and several other talents followed on very sweet terms; see Nancy Griffin and Kim Masters, *Hit and Run: How Jon Peters and Peter Guber Took Sony for a Ride in Hollywood* (New York: Simon & Schuster, 1996), pp. 276–277.

21. Lazarus, *Movie Producer,* p. 93.

22. Eberts and Ilott, *My Indecision Is Final,* p. 420.

23. John Brodie and Anita M. Busch, "Stars Breaking Bank While Megapix Tank," *Variety,* Mar. 4, 1996, pp. 1, 90.

24. In the 1980s films with complex physical productions and elaborate special effects brought in huge rents imputable to these talents and to actors suited to such films. See Squire, *Movie Business Book,* pp. 128–130, for a correct account of how their popularity inflated the costs of subsequent films of the type, and the strate-

gies used by studios (Disney, in particular) to assemble film projects so that some rents stuck to the studio, rather than passing to the talent.

25. A study that supports this interpretation (somewhat inadvertently) is W. Timothy Wallace, Alan Seigerman, and Morris B. Holbrook, "The Role of Actors and Actresses in the Success of Films: How Much Is a Movie Star Worth?" *JCE* 17 (June 1993): 1–27. In essence they removed from the U.S. gross rentals (earned by each film in a large sample) the factors affecting audience demand other than the presence of any of a group of stars. They also subtracted the total cost of the film's inputs (which includes the stars' salaries, although not any participation in net profits). For about one-fifth of the stars they could then find statistically significant effects of their presence on residual profit—some positive, some negative. While they emphasized their discovery of significant rent components for 22 percent of their stars, they passed over the implication that for the other 78 percent compensation was about equal to the star's expected revenue-generating potential. This study is thus consistent with the stylized model in the text, which predicts that random lumps of net profit (loss) remain after the star gets paid. The negotiated paycheck anticipates the expected rent but predicts it inaccurately.

26. Darlene C. Chisholm, "Profit-Sharing versus Fixed-Payment Contracts: Evidence from the Motion-Pictures Industry," *Journal of Law, Economics and Organization* 13 (April 1997): 169–201.

27. Mark Weinstein, "Profit-Sharing Contracts in Hollywood: Evolution and Analysis," *Journal of Legal Studies* 27 (January 1998): 67–112.

28. See ibid. and Audrey Solomon, *Twentieth Century–Fox: A Corporate and Financial History* (Metuchen, N.J.: Scarecrow Press, 1988), pp. 146–147.

29. Baumgarten, Farber, and Fleischer, *Producing, Financing, and Distributing Film,* pp. 157–164.

30. Litwak, *Reel Power,* pp. 144–147; Litwak, *Dealmaking,* pp. 154–155; Dennis McDougal, *The Last Mogul: Lew Wasserman, MCA, and the Hidden History of Hollywood* (New York: Crown, 1998), pp. 109, 227, 236; Robert Slater, *Ovitz: The Inside Story of Hollywood's Most Controversial Power Broker* (New York: McGraw-Hill, 1997), pp. 66–68, 87–90, 93–95.

31. Consider the entrepreneur who borrows $9 from a bank for a project expected to generate $10 gross profit. The entrepreneur can follow two plans, one yielding the $10 as a sure thing, one with equal chances of yielding $8 and $12. If financing the project himself, the (risk-averse) entrepreneur would pick the safe plan. With the bank in the picture, he likely takes the risky one. If the project brings in only $8, the entrepreneur makes nothing (the bank loses $1). If it succeeds, he makes $3. The risky approach thus yields him an expected profit of $1.50, the safe one only $1. The bank understands this, of course, and demands collateral and/ or limits its loan accordingly.

32. Janet Wasko, *Movies and Money: Financing the American Film Industry* (Norwood, N.J.: Ablex Publishing, 1982), ch. 2, p. 127.

33. Squire, *Movie Business Book,* p. 142. That could mean more certainty about poor prospects, of course.

34. Martin Dale, *The Movie Game: The Film Business in Britain, Europe, and America* (London: Cassell, 1997), p. 98.

35. The problem of adverse selection arises in contracts when party A offers a deal

(health insurance, for example) that partners B, C, and so on may freely choose to accept. If the partners have private knowledge about their benefits under the contract that A cannot observe, A tends to be the loser when the contract is accepted only by partners who know they can benefit most (at greatest cost in payouts to A).

36. There are many published descriptions of film contracts but apparently no systematic tabulations or summaries of their provisions. The descriptive accounts differ in details, perhaps due to sampling variations in the authors' experiences, perhaps due to changes in typical practice between times when observations were made. The account given here is concerned with the logic of contracts rather than with providing a guide to practice.

37. The basic overhead figure of 30 percent applies to exhibition revenue (gross rentals) from United States and Canada; A rate of 35 to 37.5 percent applies to the United Kingdom, 40 percent to the rest of the world, and 25 percent to gross receipts from U.S. television networks and cable TV systems. The distributor keeps 80 percent of wholesale sales revenue from videocassettes (a considerable benefit, because their gross margin is very high) and 50 percent of music publishing and sound-track recording revenues (see Chapter 9 on music royalty streams). The high rates of capture of videocassette and music revenues implicitly assign to the studio's promotion efforts a large share of the value created in these channels. See Baumgarten, Farber, and Fleischer, *Producing, Financing, and Distributing Film,* pp. 53–55.

38. Suppose the distributor had already identified and incurred outlays for prints and advertising that would maximize net profit from the film. Now, as an experiment, the distributor spends an extra dollar. Net profit falls, because (with profit already maximized) it takes more than another dollar of advertising to buy the extra dollar of net revenue. The distributor suffers half the loss in net profit. It recovers as an expense, however, not only the cost of the extra advertising but also its overhead charge. When the distributor both finances the film and has a net profit participation, this distortion of incentives might be eliminated or reversed.

39. Squire, *Movie Business Book,* pp. 209–211; Baumgarten, Farber, and Fleischer, *Producing, Financing, and Distributing Film,* pp. 81–82; Litwak, *Reel Power,* p. 100.

40. Baumgarten, Farber, and Fleischer, *Producing, Financing, and Distributing Film,* pp. 115–116.

41. When two studios co-finance a costly film, they commonly divide the revenue sources between themselves. Agreeing on a plan to maximize net profits and divide them would in principle yield a much more efficient contract, so the practice illustrates the lengths that studios will go to avoid being on the losing end of strategic accounting. See Martin Peers, "Risk-Ridden H'wood Is Costing for Cash," *Variety,* Jan. 9, 1995, p. 1, 83.

42. Litwak, *Reel Power,* pp. 68, 157; Dale, *Movie Game,* p. 29.

43. Dale, *Movie Game,* p. 36.

44. Adam Sander, "New Recipes Cooking for Net Profit Pie," *Variety,* June 5, 1995, pp. 7, 15.

45. Baumgarten, Farber, and Fleischer, *Producing, Financing, and Distributing Film,*

p. 3; John W. Cones, *The Feature Film Distribution Deal: A Critical Analysis of the Single Most Important Film Industry Agreement* (Carbondale: Southern Illinois University Press, 1997), p. 26 and ch. 6; Hillary Bibicoff, "Net Profit Participation in the Motion Picture Industry," *Loyola Entertainment Law Journal* 11, no. 1 (1991): 223–253.

46. See Cones, *Feature Film Distribution*, pp. 66–70.

47. Ibid., pp. 16–17.

48. Ibid., pp. 81–82; Baumgarten, Farber, and Fleischer, *Producing, Financing, and Distributing Film*, pp. 72–73; Squire, *Movie Business Book*, p. 148. For an example from one successful film, see Nina Munk, "Now You See It, Now You Don't," *Forbes*, June 5, 1995, pp. 42–43.

49. The producer is said to bear the whole sacrifice down to a "soft floor" of 20 percent of net profits due to him. Then producer and distributor split the sacrifice down to a "hard floor" of 15 percent, beyond which the studio takes the entire hit. Baumgarten, Farber, and Fleischer, *Producing, Financing, and Distributing Film*, pp. 194–196.

50. Ibid., pp. 150–151.

51. John Brodie, "Directors' Deals in 'Crisis' Mode," *Variety*, Sept. 19, 1994, pp. 1, 90.

52. Squire, *Movie Business Book*, pp. 145, 212–213, 216–229; Baumgarten, Farber, and Fleischer, *Producing, Financing, and Distributing Film*, pp. 86–87, 138–139; Eberts and Ilott, *My Indecision Is Final*, pp. 26–27.

53. Wasko, *Movies and Money*.

54. Baumgarten, Farber, and Fleischer, *Producing, Financing, and Distributing Film*, p. 146. As Chapter 5 indicated, films are differentiated in their natural choice of distribution channel, and that factor itself strongly determines the dealmaker's choice of financing and contracting strategy.

55. Mel Gussow, "Theatrical Den Mother Nurtures Her Lions," *NYTNE*, June 9, 1998, pp. B1, B8; Colin Chambers, *Peggy: The Life of Margaret Ramsey, Play Agent* (London: Hern, 1966).

56. Bernard Rosenberg and Ernest Harberg, *The Broadway Musical: Collaboration in Commerce and Art* (New York: New York University Press, 1993), p. 87.

57. For texts of and commentary on standard contracts, see Donald C. Farber, *Producing Theatre: A Comprehensive Legal and Business Guide*, rev. ed. (New York: Limelight Editions, 1987); for an economic analysis, see William J. Baumol and William G. Bowen, *Performing Arts: The Economic Dilemma* (New York: Twentieth Century Fund, 1966), pp. 18–24.

58. Jack Poggi, *Theater in America: The Impact of Economic Forces, 1870–1967* (Ithaca, N.Y.: Cornell University Press, 1968), pp. 245–250, ch. 10.

59. Sidney Shemel and M. William Krasilovsky, *This Business of Music*, 6th ed. (New York: Billboard Books, 1990), pp. 291–294.

60. William Goldman, *The Season: A Candid Look at Broadway* (New York: Harcourt, Brace, 1969), pp. 106, 190.

61. Rosenberg and Harberg, *Broadway Musical* (p. 23), quoting producer Gerald Schoenfeld.

62. In the 1970s established authors of plays produced Off-Broadway were observed

to pass up a 10 percent royalty for the 5 or 6 percent that was more common for novice playwrights. See Donald C. Farber, *From Option to Opening*, 3d ed. (New York: Drama Book Specialists, 1977), p. 10.

63. Goldman, *The Season*, pp. 391–393.

64. Harold L. Vogel, *Entertainment Industry Economics: A Guide for Financial Analysis*, 3d ed. (Cambridge: Cambridge University Press, 1994), pp. 266, 345 n. 9. Sporadic investments in Broadway productions by film and record companies have a curious history. The investors apparently saw some rents for the taking, and the Dramatist Guild's hostility implied the same. Yet the investments gained nothing more than first-refusal on rights auctioned for subsequent production. See Robert McLaughlin, *Broadway and Hollywood: A History of Economic Interaction* (New York: Arno Press, 1974).

65. Farber, *Producing Theatre*, p. 82.

66. Rosenberg and Harberg, *Broadway Musical*, pp. 125, 168. They argued (pp. 112–113) that few musicals start rehearsal with "a well-conceived theme and a story that goes from a beginning to an end"—a situation that leaves ample room for confusion to befall the creative process.

67. Goldman, *The Season*, pp. 285–298; Rosenberg and Harberg, *Broadway Musical*, pp. 88–89, 226, and ch. 7 generally. For a case study, see William Gibson, *The Seesaw Log* (New York: Knopf, 1959).

68. Note, for example, the transit of TV writers into the status of writer-producers. See Horace Newcomb and Robert S. Alley, *The Producer's Medium: Conversations with Creators of American TV* (New York: Oxford University Press, 1983), pp. 130, 150.

69. Rosenberg and Harberg, *Broadway Musical*, pp. 16, 71, 92, 137, 265, Appendix 6; Goldman, *The Season*, pp. 272–273.

70. Farber, *Producing Theatre*, pp. 214–215; Rosenberg and Harberg, *Broadway Musical*, p. 78.

71. Thomas Gale Moore, *The Economics of the American Theater* (Durham, N.C.: Duke University Press, 1968), p. 24.

72. Rosenberg and Harburg, *Broadway Musical*, p. 168.

7. Guilds, Unions, and Faulty Contracts

1. Bernard Rosenberg and Ernest Harburg, *The Broadway Musical: Collaboration in Commerce and Art* (New York: New York University Press, 1993), p. 81.

2. If two people believe that each has a 50 percent chance of proving ownership of a stray dollar bill, each will rationally spend up to fifty cents in the effort.

3. Alfred Harding, *The Revolt of the Actors* (New York: William Morrow, 1929).

4. These dissatisfactions bore in on the actors especially when theatre road companies were contracting from around 300 a week during 1900–1910 to around 60 a week in the 1920s, so declining business no doubt inflated the closings and strandings. Also, the film industry provided substantial employment opportunities for actors, improving Equity's bargaining power. See Robert McLaughlin, *Broadway and Hollywood: A History of Economic Interaction* (New York: Arno Press, 1974), pp. 3, 41–42.

5. Harding, *Revolt of the Actors*, pp. 3–20.

6. Ibid., pp. 501–503.

7. Ibid., pp. 456–462. Producers' resistance to Equity varied between those members who were theatre owners, with a strong interest that the show should go on, and others who faced no major unavoidable costs. On the recent state of Equity's supply restriction, see Mark D. Meredith, "From Dancing Halls to Hiring Halls: Actors' Equity and the Closed Shop Dilemma," *Columbia Law Review* 96 (January 1996): 178–236.

8. Robert D. Leiter, *The Musicians and Petrillo* (New York: Bookman Associates, 1953); George Seltzer, *Music Matters: The Performer and the American Federation of Musicians* (Metuchen, N.J.: Scarecrow Press, 1989), ch. 2.

9. Sidney Shemel and William Krasilovsky, *This Business of Music*, 6th ed. (New York: Billboard Books, 1990), pp. 64–66. The origins and policies of England's British Actors' Equity Association and Incorporated Society of Musicians seem similar. See Ruth Towse, *Singers in the Marketplace: The Economics of the Singing Profession* (Oxford: Clarendon Press, 1993), pp. 9–10, 93–94, 98, 133–134.

10. John H. Mueller, *The American Symphony Orchestra: A Social History of Musical Taste* (Bloomington: Indiana University Press, 1951), pp. 328–352; Edward Arian, *Bach, Beethoven, and Bureaucracy: The Case of the Philadelphia Orchestra* (University: University of Alabama Press, 1971), ch. 4; Philip Hart, *Orpheus in the New World: The Symphony Orchestra as an American Cultural Institution* (New York: Norton, 1973), ch. 5, pp. 156–163.

11. Seltzer, *Music Matters,* p. 189. Larger fractions of overscale compensation in the 1970s were casually mentioned—two-thirds for the Boston Symphony, 88 percent for the New York Philharmonic. See George Seltzer, ed., *The Professional Symphony Orchestra in the United States* (Metuchen, N.J.: Scarecrow Press, 1975).

12. Consider the chronicles of the Philadelphia Orchestra in the 1960s by Arian *(Bach, Beethoven, and Bureaucracy)* and Hart *(Orpheus).*

13. David F. Prindle, *The Politics of Glamour: Ideology and Democracy in the Screen Actors Guild* (Madison: University of Wisconsin Press, 1988), pp. 78–80, 88–90. MCA, then the largest talent agency in Hollywood, bought a waiver from the Guild in 1952 by promising to pay residual royalties on films licensed for exhibition on television, but the U.S. Department of Justice intervened and forced MCA to separate its filmmaking and agent businesses.

14. David Bordwell, Janet Staiger, and Kristin Thompson, *The Classical Hollywood Cinema: Film Style and Mode of Production to 1960* (New York: Columbia University Press, 1985), pp. 106–108, 254–260.

15. Anne K. Peters and Muriel G. Cantor, "Screen Acting as Work," in James S. Ettema and D. Charles Whitney, eds., *Individuals in Mass Media Organizations: Creativity and Constraint* (Beverly Hills, Calif.: Sage, 1982), pp. 53–68.

16. For a present-day recurrence of this same contract failure, see Brett Atwood, "Music Clip Creators Seek Protection," *Billboard,* June 7, 1997, pp. 6, 89.

17. The resolution of contract and credit issues in screenwriting was a complex process that extended from the 1920s to the 1940s, and it was tangled with political conflicts and demands for royalty income as well. See Murray Ross, *Stars and Strikes: Unionization of Hollywood* (New York: Columbia University Press, 1941), pp. 56–63, 175–183, 188–189; Richard Fine, *West of Eden: Writers in Hollywood,*

1928–1940 (Washington, D.C.: Smithsonian Institute Press, 1993), pp. 91–92, ch. 4; Hugh Lovell and Tasile Carter, *Collective Bargaining in the Motion Picture Industry* (Berkeley: Institute of Industrial Relations, University of California, 1955), pp. 35, 41–42; Nancy Lynn Schwartz, *The Hollywood Writers' Wars* (New York: Knopf, 1982).

18. Michelle Willens, "How Many Writers Does It Take . . . ?" *NYTNE*, May 17, 1998, sec. 2, pp. 17, 27.

19. Muriel G. Cantor, *The Hollywood TV Producer: His Work and His Audience* (New Brunswick, N.J.: Transaction Books, 1988), pp. 99–103.

20. Virginia Wright Wexman, "Success Has 1,000 Faces (So Do Films)," *NYT,* May 28, 1995, sec. 2, p. 16.

21. Aspects of *A list/B list* in the setting where *nobody knows* were discussed by Keith Acheson and Christopher J. Maule in their "Understanding Hollywood's Organization and Continuing Success," *JCE* 18, no. 4 (1994–1995): 271–300.

22. William T. Bielby and Denise D. Bielby, "Organizational Mediation of Project-Based Labor Markets: Talent Agencies and the Careers of Screenwriters," *American Sociological Review* 64 (February 1999): 64–85.

23. Lewis Coser, in his *Men of Ideas: A Sociologist's View* (New York: Free Fress, 1965), pp. 325–331, astutely flagged Hollywood writers as a hard case of artists who are conditioned to place the highest value on control but are dropped into a collaborative process that could not efficiently accommodate it.

24. Robert R. Faulkner, *Music on Demand: Composers and Careers in the Hollywood Film Industry* (New Brunswick, N.J.: Transaction Books, 1983).

25. Ibid., pp. 36–39.

26. Ibid., pp. 101–105, 108.

27. Ibid., chs. 2–3. Faulkner (p. 73) quoted one composer: "You're gambling all the time: will this series make it, what about this pilot, maybe this will take off, you see? Nobody knows whether it's going to make it or not. You just work for this musical director at the studio . . . the producer on this project, and they learn over time that they can depend on you."

28. Ibid., ch. 10; Robert R. Faulkner, *Hollywood Studio Musicians: Their Work and Careers in the Recording Industry* (Chicago: Aldine Atherton, 1971). Also see Richard A. Peterson and Howard G. White, "The Simplex Located in Art Worlds," in Arnold W. Foster and Judith R. Blau, eds., *Art and Society: Readings in the Sociology of the Arts* (Buffalo: State University of New York Press, 1989), pp. 243–259.

29. On cartoonists see A. J. Scott, "Territorial Reproduction and Transformation in a Local Labor Market: The Animated Film Workers of Los Angeles," *Environment and Planning D: Society and Space* 2 (September 1984): 277–307; on screen extras, Prindle, *Politics of Glamour,* p. 125; on screen actors, Anne K. Peters and Muriel G. Cantor, "Screen Acting as Work," in James S. Ettema and D. Charles Whitney, eds., *Individuals in Mass Media Organizations: Creativity and Constraint* (Beverly Hills, Calif: Sage, 1982), pp. 53–68.

30. Susan Christopherson, "The Origins of Fragmented Bargaining Power in Entertainment Media Industries," *Proceedings of the Forty-Fourth Annual Meeting, Industrial Relations Research Association,* 1992, pp. 16–17.

31. Michael H. Moskow, *Labor Relations in the Performing Arts: An Introductory Survey* (New York: Associated Councils of the Arts, 1969), p. 39.

32. For examples see Fine, *West of Eden*, p. 67, quoting Ben Hecht; William Goldman, *Adventures in the Screen Trade: A Personal View of Hollywood and Screenwriting* (New York: Warner Books, 1984), pp. 100–103.

33. Jake Eberts and Terry Ilott, *My Indecision Is Final: The Spectacular Rise and Fall of Goldcrest Films* (New York: Atlantic Monthly Press, 1990), p. 457 (also p. 431).

34. Faulkner, *Music on Demand*, Table 1.2; Robert R. Faulkner and Andy B. Anderson, "Short-Term Projects and Emergent Careers," *American Journal of Sociology* 92 (January 1987): 879–909.

35. Figures taken from Donald C. Farber, *Producing Theatre: A Comprehensive Legal and Business Guide*, rev. ed. (New York: Limelight Editions, 1987).

36. Bernard Holland, "Making the Deals behind the Music," *NYT*, Oct. 12, 1986, sec. 2, pp. 1, 34.

37. Lovell and Carter, *Collective Bargaining*, pp. 1–6.

38. Mark Litwak, *Reel Power: The Struggle for Influence and Success in the New Hollywood* (New York: William Morrow, 1986), pp. 275–276; Julie Salamon, *The Devil's Candy: "The Bonfire of the Vanities" Goes to Hollywood* (Boston: Little, Brown, 1991), pp. 114, 172; Donald F. Prindle, *Risky Business: The Political Economy of Hollywood* (Boulder Colo.: Westview Press, 1993), pp. 129–131.

39. Brian Taves, "The B Film: Hollywood's Other Half," in Tino Balio, *Grand Design: Hollywood as a Modern Business Enterprise, 1930–1939* (New York: Scribner's, 1993), ch. 8, especially p. 326.

40. John Lippman, "Screen Actors Guild Orders Its Members to Refuse to Work on Any Saban Show," *WSJ*, Jan. 30, 1998, p. B8.

41. Donald C. Farber, *From Option to Opening*, 3d ed. (New York: Drama Book Specialists, 1977), pp. 98–99.

42. The roster system compromised an awkward dilemma for the craft unions. If they continued highly restrictive membership policies, they would only speed the exit of film production from the studio system. If they sought more inclusive membership, the roster system with its seniority-oriented benefits would sooner or later be voted down.

43. Alan Paul and Archie Kleingartner, "Flexible Production and the Transformation of Industrial Relations in the Motion Picture and Television Industry," *Industrial and Labor Relations Review* 47 (July 1994): 663–678.

44. See Prindle, *Risky Business*, pp. 133–136; Prindle, *Politics of Glamour*, pp. 84–86, 126–132; Paul and Kleingartner, "Flexible Production"; Robert F. Stanley, *The Celluloid Empire: A History of the American Movie Industry* (New York: Hastings House, 1978), pp. 154–156; Jay Greene, "Rights Squabble Begins over New Media Explosion," *Variety*, Jan. 2, 1995, pp. 4, 5.

8. The Nurture of Ten-Ton Turkeys

1. Industry observers have noticed this mechanism. See Hortence Powdermaker, *Hollywood: The Dream Factory* (Boston: Little, Brown, 1950), pp. 113–114;

Mark Litwak, *Dealmaking in the Film and Television Industry: From Negotiations to Final Contracts* (Los Angeles: Silman-James, 1994), p. 14.

2. Julie Salamon, *The Devil's Candy: "The Bonfire of the Vanities" Goes to Hollywood* (Boston: Houghton Mifflin, 1991).

3. Ibid., pp. 38, 120–122.

4. Ibid., chs. 10, 13.

5. The major scene that was relocated took place in a courtroom. A half-built studio set in Los Angeles was abandoned for an actual one in the New York area. See ibid., pp. 112–113.

6. Ibid., p. 298.

7. Ibid., p. 126.

8. Steven Bach, *Final Cut: Dreams and Disaster in the Making of "Heaven's Gate"* (New York: William Morrow, 1985).

9. Ibid., pp. 117–120.

10. Ibid., pp. 121–125, 183–196.

11. UA's motive was not only to lay off some of its risk but also to curb the credibility of Cimino's continual threats to take the film to another studio.

12. Bach, *Final Cut,* p. 361.

13. On *Apocalypse Now* see ibid., pp. 123–127; on *Rhinestone,* Mark Litwak, *Reel Power: The Struggle for Influence and Success in the New Hollywood* (New York: William Morrow, 1986), pp. 21–31; on *Water World,* Terence Rafferty, "Lost at Sea," *New Yorker,* Aug. 7, 1995, pp. 83–85; on *Last Action Hero,* Nancy Griffin and Kim Masters, *Hit and Run: How Jon Peters and Peter Guber Took Sony for a Ride in Hollywood* (New York: Simon & Schuster, 1996), pp. 364–373, 382, 384, 430; on *Revolution,* Jake Eberts and Terry Ilott, *My Indecision Is Final: The Spectacular Rise and Fall of Goldcrest Films* (New York: Atlantic Monthly Press, 1990), pp. 352, 420, 456, 462–464.

14. Griffin and Masters, *Hit and Run,* pp. 348–349.

15. Filmmaker John Boorman: "You must inch the financiers toward the brink. You continue to spend more and more of their money, edge them into commitments until they find they have spent so much it is cheaper to make the film than abandon it." John Boorman, *The Emerald Forest Diary* (New York: Farrar Straus, & Giroux, 1985), p. 74.

16. See Harold L. Vogel, *Entertainment Industry Economics: A Guide for Financial Analysis,* 3d ed. (Cambridge: Cambridge University Press, 1994), pp. 68–69.

17. Peter Bart, *Fade Out: The Calamitous Final Days of MGM* (New York: William Morrow, 1990), p. 149.

18. The same conclusion holds for sound recordings. See R. Serge Denisoff, *Solid Gold: The Popular Record Industry* (New Brunswick, N.J.: Transaction Books, 1975), pp. 144–153.

19. Bernard Weinraub, "Feeling the Pain When a Film Fails," *NYTNE,* Nov. 24, 1997, pp. B1, B4.

20. Daisy Maryles, "How High Can You Go?" *PW,* Apr. 7, 1997, pp. 42–47; Judy Quinn, "They Shall Return," *PW,* Apr. 7, 1997, pp. 48–51; Judy Quinn, "Celebrity Book Roulette," *PW,* Aug. 4, 1997, pp. 30–34.

21. Meg Cox, "Book Publishers Face a Painful Austerity after Lavish Spending,"

WSJ, Nov. 21, 1989, pp. A1, A11. The winner's curse is the proposition that the party willing to bid most for a property may be the one who most overestimates its value.

22. Roger Cohen, "Big Gamble on Schwarzkopf Book," *NYT*, July 15, 1991, pp. D1, D8.

23. The effect operates even more strongly in phonograph records. Their well-known certifications of popularity, "gold" and "platinum," are based on numbers of copies shipped rather than numbers of copies sold at retail. What appears to be an objective popularity index is thus within the producer's strategic reach. See William Knoedelseder, *Stiffed: A True Story of MCA, the Music Business, and the Mafia* (New York: HarperCollins, 1993).

24. Those large storefront tables in chain bookstores are themselves a scarce resource for which publishers compete, a fact that enlarges the signaling incentive for gigantic first printings.

25. Sources of subsidiary-rights income may in some cases also respond to the first-printing signal.

26. Quinn, "They Shall Return."

27. Ken Auletta, "The Impossible Business," *New Yorker*, Oct. 6, 1997, pp. 50–63. Auletta reported that the first-printing signal—along with other information including the publisher's advertising budget and the "buzz" that editors try to generate—works with large chains such as Barnes and Noble as well as with independent booksellers.

28. Bridget Kinsella, "Bargain Books: A Stronger, More Competitive Market," *PW*, Sept. 16, 1996, pp. 42–44.

9. Creative Products Go to Market: Books and Records

1. Bruce Bliven, Jr., *Book Traveler* (New York: Dodd, Mead, 1975).

2. Judith Rosen, "On the Road: A New World for Sales Reps," *PW*, July 1997 anniversary issue, pp. 92–98; Edwin McDowell, "The Book Industry's Best-Selling Middleman," *NYT*, July 8, 1984, sec. 3, pp. 8, 9.

3. Susan DeGrane, "Librarians Seeking a Good Book Turn to Him," *NYTNE*, Feb. 24, 1997, p. B9. Also see Martin Arnold, "A Critique of the Critics," *NYTNE*, Apr. 23, 1998, p. B3.

4. Walter W. Powell, *Getting into Print: The Decision-Making Process in Scholarly Publishing* (Chicago: University of Chicago Press, 1985), especially pp. 19–20, 31, 51. One of Powell's two case studies is a commercial publisher of scientific monographs, for which authors, series editors, and readers make up a relatively self-contained community.

5. Robert K. J. Killheffer, "Fantasy Charts New Realms," *PW*, June 16, 1997, pp. 34–40; Ann M. Eike, "An Investigation of the Market for Paperback Romance Novels," *JCE* 10 (June 1986): 25–36.

6. R. Serge Denisoff, *Solid Gold: The Popular Record Industry* (New Brunswick, N.J.: Transaction Books, 1975), ch. 6.

7. Of respondents to one survey, 43 percent learned about a record's availability from videos, 41 percent from radio play, 36 percent from retail stores' displays, 36

percent from word-of-mouth, 15 percent from print ads, and 15 percent from reviews. (Respondents could check more than one information source.) *Billboard*, May 5, 1997, p. 66.

8. Data taken from Ken Auletta, "The Impossible Business," *New Yorker*, Oct. 6, 1997, pp. 50–63. Also see Lewis A. Coser, Charles Kadushin, and Walter W. Powell, *Books: The Culture and Commerce of Publishing* (New York: Basic Books, 1982), pp. 358–360. Harper Canada analyzed returns from their direct-sale accounts, finding that 2 percent of them had return rates exceeding 40 percent while the remaining 98 percent averaged only 23 percent. Harper stopped shipping direct to most of the offending group and referred them to wholesalers, who do not accept returns for full credit (*PW*, Apr. 14, 1997, p. 13).

9. Clearance sales potentially achieve price discrimination between eager readers willing to pay list price and patient ones willing to wait for the discount. Paperback versions of hardcover books pursue just this objective, but their issuance lags substantially after the hardcover original, and their physical quality often is substantially degraded. The Barnes and Noble chain urged publishers to share retail markdowns as an alternative to the returns policy (G. Bruce Knecht, "Book Superstores Bring Hollywood-Like Risks to Publishing Business," *WSJ*, May 29, 1997, pp. A1, A6), but their resistance suggests that the change might not pay. A returned and pulped book's incremental cost to the publisher is around $3, to the publisher and bookseller together perhaps $4. Markdowns would on average need to be smaller than these figures to be unambiguously preferred by the booksellers.

10. The prediction of lower book prices comes from the competitive or free entry structure of both publishers and bookstores. Lowering the average cost of book production and distribution then implies some combination of more books published and lower prices per book.

11. Record companies responded to declining demand for records and bankruptcies among retailers by pressing a policy of minimum advertised prices that constrains discounting, enforcing the policy by the withdrawal of funds for cooperative manufacturer-retailer advertising. Don Jeffrey, "Labels Took Steps to Ease Retailers' Woes," *Billboard*, December 1996–January 1997 special issue, pp. 53, 55.

12. George Bittlingmayer, "Resale Price Maintenance in the Book Trade with an Application to Germany," *Journal of Institutional and Theoretical Economics* 144, no. 5 (1988): 789–812.

13. In Britain, where a century-old voluntary RPM policy known as the Net Book Agreement recently crumbled, some publishers voiced this view. See Sarah Lyall, "Book-Pricing Pact in Britain near Collapse," *NYT*, Sept. 29, 1995, p. D4.

14. The German publishing industry has long maintained RPM, but doing so has not obviously slowed the displacement of small, independent bookstores by large chains. See Christian Baumgaertel, "Fearful German Booksellers Will Fight Push against Price-Fixing," *NYTNE*, Nov. 11, 1997, p. D9.

15. Meg Cox, "To Make Their Big Books Even Bigger, Firms Are Spending the Biggest Bucks," *WSJ*, June 19, 1991, pp. B1, B3; Gayle Feldman, "'Intensity' Plan Shows Publishing's Big Profit Hunt," *NYT*, Jan. 22, 1996, p. D7.

16. Thomas Whiteside, *The Blockbuster Complex: Conglomerates, Show Business, and Book Publishing* (Middletown, Conn.: Wesleyan University Press, 1981), pp. 17–38.

17. The industry's reorganization (Chapter 20) suggests some statistical tests of best-seller sales figures (from *PW*) over the last 50 years, to see whether book sales are concentrating more and more on the top items. For fiction, but not nonfiction, I found that total sales of the year's top few best-sellers have risen disproportionately in the past two decades.

18. Esther B. Fein, "Publishers' Best Seller: The Backlist," *NYT*, June 8, 1992, p. D6; John Mutter, "Random Puts Backlist Front and Center," *PW*, Jan. 23, 1995, pp. 21–22.

19. Esther B. Fein, "Book Lists Dwindling as Publishers Cut Fat," *NYT*, Mar. 30, 1992, pp. D1, D8; Winthrop Knowlton, "Competition in Book Publishing," in U.S. Federal Trade Commission, Bureau of Competition, *Proceedings of the Symposium on Media Concentration* (Washington: Government Printing Office, 1978), pp. 565–572.

20. Denisoff, *Solid Gold*, ch. 3.

21. Michael Cable, *The Pop Industry Inside Out* (London: W. H. Allen, 1977), pp. 94–103.

22. Clive Davis, with James Willwerth, *Clive: Inside the Record Business* (New York: William Morrow, 1975), p. 200; Fredric Dannen, *Hit Men: Power Brokers and Fast Money inside the Music Business* (New York: Vintage, 1991), p. 88–90; Neil Strauss, "Are Pop Charts Manipulated?" *NYT*, Jan. 25, 1996, pp. C15, C20.

23. Willy Stern, "Did Dirty Tricks Create a Best-Seller?" *BW*, Aug. 7, 1995, pp. 22–24; also *BW*, Aug. 14, 1995, p. 41; Patrick M. Reilly, "How a Book Makes the Bestseller Lists, and How the Bestseller Lists Make a Book," *WSJ*, Sept. 7, 1995, pp. B1, B10.

24. A hook is what Beethoven's Symphony No. 5 famously possesses.

25. Steve Chapple and Reebee Garofalo, *Rock 'n' Roll Is Here to Pay: The History and Politics of the Music Industry* (Chicago: Nelson-Hall, 1977), p. 183; Robert Stephen Spitz, *The Making of Superstars: Artists and Executives of the Rock Music Business* (Garden City, N.Y.: Anchor Press/Doubleday, 1978), pp. 246–247; Denisoff, *Solid Gold*, pp. 233–250; Davis, *Clive*, p. 198.

26. For an account of failed experiments at dealing with the problem, see John Tebbel, *A History of Book Publishing in the United States*, vol. 3, *The Golden Age between Two Wars, 1920–1940* (New York: R. R. Bowker, 1978), p. 445; Benjamin M. Compaine, *The Book Industry in Transition: An Economic Study of Book Distribution and Marketing* (White Plains, N.Y.: Knowledge Industry Publications, 1978), pp. 138–141.

27. For a full description see Coser, Kadushin, and Powell, *Books*, ch. 13. On the historical evolution of bookselling's organization, see Donald Sheehan, *This Was Publishing: A Chronicle of the Book Trade in the Gilded Age* (Bloomington: Indiana University Press, 1952), ch. 7.

28. Doreen Carvajal, "For Smaller Publishers, Sales Are Rising as Returns Dwindle," *NYTNE*, Dec. 1, 1997, pp. D1, D8.

29. John Mutter and Jim Milliot, "Wholesale Change," *PW*, Jan. 1, 1996, pp. 44–46.

30. Edwin McDowell, "Two Giant Booksellers Find Themselves at Odds with Publishers," *NYT*, July 24, 1989, p. D9. Too little information is available on the regularity (at a point in time) or stability (over time) of these trade discounts to know whether substantial inflexibility exists.

31. Anthony Bianco, "Virtual Bookstores Start to Get Real," *BW*, Oct. 27, 1997, pp. 146–148. Barnes and Noble's announced acquisition of the largest wholesaler adds to the flux. Doreen Carvajal, "Book Industry in Big Shift Focused on Product Delivery," *NYTNE*, Nov. 18, 1998, pp. C1, C10.

32. *PW*, July 1997 anniversary issue, p. 100.

33. Coser, Kadushin, and Powell, *Books*, pp. 349–353.

34. The superstore evidently followed "category killers" in other lines of retailing, and depended for its effectiveness on low-cost intensive computerized record-keeping. See Patrick M. Reilly, "Where Borders Group and Barnes & Noble Compete, It's a War," *WSJ*, Sept. 3, 1996, pp. A1, A8; Mark Feeney, "Pumping Up the Volumes," *BG*, Dec. 11, 1997, pp. C1, C8.

35. Hardy Green, "Superstores, Megabooks—and Humongous Headaches," *BW*, Apr. 14, 1997, pp. 92–94.

36. Doreen Carvajal, "Book Chains' New Role: Soothsayers for Publishers," *NYTNE*, Aug. 12, 1997, pp. A1, D5.

37. Patrick M. Reilly, "Bertelsmann's Bantam to Punish Stores That Sell Its Books before Release Date," *WSJ*, Aug. 14, 1995, p. B8.

38. That the chain booksellers' high return rates result largely from their involvement in the promotion of blockbusters is confirmed indirectly by the still-higher return rates (around 40 percent) of these other mass merchandisers, who handle only best-sellers. See Knecht, "Book Superstores," p. A6.

39. Coser, Kadushin, and Powell, *Books*, pp. 353–354.

40. See William Grimes, "Book War: Shops vs. Superstores," *NYT*, Aug. 3, 1995, pp. B1, B2; Anne Roiphe, "Frail Species, Endangered but Surviving," *NYTNE*, May 30, 1997, pp. B1, B16; Jeffrey A. Tannenbaum, "Small Bookseller Beats the Giants at Their Own Game," *WSJ*, Nov. l4, 1997, pp. B1, B2.

41. *PW*, Sept. 30, 1996, pp. 10, 22; Albert R. Karr, "FTC Dismisses Its Pricing Complaint against Publishers, Ending Long Probe," *WSJ*, Sept. 23, 1996, p. B9.

42. Meg Cox, "Booksellers Say Five Publishers Play Favorites," *WSJ*, May 27, 1994, pp. B1, B5; Doreen Carvajal, "St. Martin's Settles Suit with Booksellers," *NYTNE*, Aug. 12, 1996, p. D7; *PW*, Nov. 25, 1996, p. 10.

43. *Book Industry Trends 1995*, quoted by Albert N. Greco, *The Book Publishing Industry* (Needham Heights, Mass.: Allyn and Bacon, 1997), p. 58; *Billboard*, Jan. 21, 1995, p. 42.

44. Simon Frith, *Sound Effects: Youth, Leisure, and the Politics of Rock* (London: Constable, 1983), pp. 148–149.

45. Marc Eliot, *Rockonomics: The Money behind the Music* (New York: Franklin Watts, 1989), pp. 240–241. The same pattern applies to film distributors and exhibitors (Chapter 10).

46. Dannen, *Hit Men*, p. 64; Harold L. Vogel, *Entertainment Industry Economics: A*

Guide for Financial Analysis, 3d ed. (Cambridge: Cambridge University Press, 1994), p. 144.

47. Denisoff, *Solid Gold*, ch. 3; Chapple and Garofalo, *Rock 'n' Roll*, pp. 83–84, 89–91; R. Serge Denisoff, *Tarnished Gold: The Record Industry Revisited* (New Brunswick, N.J.: Transaction Books, 1986), pp. 213–224; Paul D. Lopes, "Innovation and Diversity in the Popular Music Industry, 1969 to 1990," *American Sociological Review* 57 (February 1992): 56–71.

48. Dannen, *Hit Men*, p. 112; Denisoff, *Tarnished Gold*, pp. 213–224; Alexander Belinfante and Richard L. Johnson, "Competition, Pricing and Concentration in the U.S. Recorded Music Industry," *JCE* 6 (December 1982): 11–24.

49. Frith, *Sound Effects*, p. 138; Anita M. McGahan, "The Incentive Not to Invest: Capacity Commitments in the Compact Disc Introduction," *Research on Technological Innovation, Management and Policy* 5 (1993): 177–197.

50. Eliot, *Rockonomics*, pp. 37–38; Peter J. Alexander, "New Technology and Market Structure: Evidence from the Music Recording Industry," *JCE* 18, no. 2 (1994): 113–123.

10. Creative Products Go to Market: Films

1. The exhibitor's capital is sunk when the theatre is leased, but the deal with the distributor concerns whether *this week* it will be committed to one film or another. Other sharing arrangements had been used earlier in the industry's history, notably flat charges. These put the exhibitors heavily at risk, however, and distributors found that they could capture more revenue by absorbing some of the box-office risk. Michael Conant, *Antitrust in the Motion Picture Industry: Economic and Legal Analysis* (Berkeley: University of California Press, 1960), pp. 70–71.

2. For descriptions and assessments of the exhibition contract, see Arthur De Vany and W. David Walls, "Bose-Einstein Dynamics and Adaptive Contracting in the Motion Picture Industry," *Economic Journal* 106 (November 1996): 1493–1514; Jason E. Squire, ed., *The Movie Business Book*, 2d ed. (New York: Simon & Schuster, 1992), especially pp. 277–278, 314; Harold L. Vogel, *Entertainment Industry Economics: A Guide for Financial Analysis*, 2d ed. (Cambridge: Cambridge University Press, 1994), ch. 3.

3. Andrew Hindes, "Pic Jam Leads to Hit and Run," *Variety*, Apr. 7, 1997, pp. 1, 40.

4. Arthur De Vany and Ross D. Eckert, "Motion Picture Antitrust: The *Paramount* Case Revisited," *Research in Law and Economics* 14 (1991): 51–112.

5. Conant, *Antitrust*, ch. 5.

6. Roy W. Kenney and Benjamin Klein, "The Economics of Block Booking," *Journal of Law and Economics* 26 (October 1983): 497–540.

7. Conant, *Antitrust*, especially pp. 78–79. If blind selling did indeed economize on transaction costs, sellers and buyers together could have improved their lot by allowing the exhibitor to opt out of showing particular films of the distributor at a penalty, when something better came along. For a model explaining this mechanism, see Philippe Aghion and Patrick Bolton, "Contracts as a Barrier to Entry," *American Economic Review* 77 (June 1987): 388–401.

8. A statistical study suggests that exhibitors suspect opportunism when they must make blind bids and thus hold back on the terms they offer. Marsha A. Blumenthal, "Auctions with Constrained Information: Blind Bidding for Motion Pictures," *Review of Economics and Statistics* 70 (May 1988): 191–198.

9. Barry R. Litman, *The Motion Picture Mega-Industry* (Needham Heights, Mass.: Allyn and Bacon, 1998), p. 81.

10. Peter Passell, "Hollywood Bets Its All on Openings," *NYTNE*, Dec. 13, 1997, pp. B1, B3.

11. Leonard Klady, "Hollywood Suffers Severe Sell Shock," *Variety*, Mar. 11, 1996, pp. 1, 12; Andrew Hindes, "Prints and the Paupers," *Variety*, Apr. 8, 1996, pp. 1, 74; Kenneth S. Corts, "The Strategic Effect of Vertical Market Structure: Competitive Crowding in the U.S. Motion Picture Industry," working paper, Harvard Business School, 1998.

12. Squire, *Movie Business Book*, pp. 25, 133, 184, 292, 297; Paul A. Baumgarten, Donald C. Farber, and Mark Fleischer, *Producing, Financing, and Distributing Film: A Comprehensive Legal and Business Guide*, 2d ed. (New York: Limelight, 1995), pp. 234–236.

13. An example is Goldcrest Films's *Gandhi*, which opened in only four cities in North America but was extensively screened before invited audiences of opinion leaders; had it opened on a large scale, "the figures on the first weekend would probably have been so bad that the cinema-owners would have dropped it long before its audience had a chance to build." See Jake Eberts and Terry Ilott, *My Indecision Is Final: The Spectacular Rise and Fall of Goldcrest Films* (New York: Atlantic Monthly Press, 1990), pp. 135–136.

14. Leonard Klady, "Studios Ponder Perils, Payoffs of Platforming," *Variety*, Jan. 16, 1995, pp. 11, 15.

15. Corie Brown, "The Lizard Was a Turkey," *Newsweek*, June 15, 1998, p. 71; also Bernard Weinraub, "*Avengers* Gets a Stealth Opening," *NYTNE*, Aug. 12, 1998, pp. B1, B8.

16. Jay Prag and James Casavant, "An Empirical Study of the Determinants of Revenues and Marketing Expenditures in the Motion Picture Industry," *JCE* 18, no. 3 (1994): 217–235.

17. De Vany and Walls, "Bose-Einstein Dynamics."

18. Gary R. Edgerton, *American Film Distribution and an Analysis of the Motion Picture Industry's Market Structure, 1963–1980* (New York: Garland, 1983), pp. 78–80; Squire, *Movie Business Book*, pp. 237–238.

19. John W. Cones, *The Feature Film Distribution Deal: A Critical Analysis of the Single Most Important Film Industry Agreement* (Carbondale: Southern Illinois University Press, 1997), pp. 42–43; Lee Beaupre, "How to Distribute a Film," in Paul Kerr, ed., *The Hollywood Film Industry: A Reader* (London: Routledge & Kegan Paul, 1986), p. 192.

20. We get so used to the efficacy of repeated market interactions in everyday life that it takes imagination to see how much they accomplish. Consider the distributor who has sunk the cost of a single film and who now seeks to license it to exhibitors, each of whom monopolizes its local cinema market. The exhibitor can demand rental terms that leave the distributor no more than enough revenue to cover marginal costs of distribution and promotion. The fixed costs of making the

film are not covered. The distributor runs a loss and will sink the costs of no more films. See David Waterman, "The Structural Development of the Motion Picture Industry," *American Economist* 26 (Spring 1982): 16–27. Repeated interactions (and competition among exhibitors) prevent this hypothetical unraveling of the market.

21. Beaupre, "How to Distribute a Film," pp. 202–203; Cones, *Feature Film Distribution Deal,* pp. 44–45; Edgerton, *American Film Distribution,* p. 80; Squire, *Movie Business Book,* p. 326; Baumgarten, Farber, and Fleischer, *Producing, Financing, and Distributing Film,* p. 148. Producer Martin Ransohoff observed that the independent "is told to wait four months or take 25% [reduction]"; see Litwak, *Reel Power,* p. 257.

22. Baumgarten, Farber, and Fleischer, *Producing, Financing, and Distributing Film,* pp. 234–236; Squire, *Movie Business Book,* pp. 313, 343–344.

23. Litman, *Motion Picture Mega-Industry,* pp. 98–100. A 1995 report by Goldman, Sachs (see *Variety,* Apr. 15, 1996, p. 1) put the share of Hollywood's worldwide revenues from home video at 53 percent.

24. This has been shown in a study by David Waterman, summarized in Bruce M. Owen and Steven S. Wildman, *Video Economics* (Cambridge, Mass.: Harvard University Press, 1992), pp. 36–37.

25. Peter M. Nichols, "Why Shelves Empty Faster," *NYTNE,* July 3, 1998, p. B27.

26. Janet Wasko, *Hollywood in the Information Age: Beyond the Silver Screen* (Austin: University of Texas Press, 1995), pp. 40–43; Baumgarten, Farber, and Fleischer, *Producing, Financing, and Distributing Film,* pp. 53, 150–151. Videocassette prices vary greatly from film to film, reflecting the fact that the typical household's reservation price is much lower than the video rental outlet's. A film appealing to a large number of collectors yields a small profit per unit on many units, making it profitable for the distributor to forgo the much larger profit per unit on a cassette priced to the rental outlet's willingness to pay. If household demand is small, the cassette is priced to extract the surplus from the rental outlets, at the cost of minimal sales to households.

27. Squire, *Movie Business Book,* p. 80.

28. Gerald F. Phillips, "The Recent Acquisition of Theatre Circuits by Major Distributors," *Entertainment and Sports Lawyer* 5 (Winter 1987): 1–2.

29. The initial rise of distributor-exhibitor integration in the 1920s was a vivid experiment in organizational change driven by two strong factors. Severe governance problems with arm's-length exhibition contracts cost the distributors 35–40 percent of gross rentals due them, and horizontal integration of exhibitors provoked defensive integration to avoid foreclosure.

30. Anita Sharpe, "Small-Town Audience Is Ticket to Success of Movie-House Chain," *WSJ,* July 12, 1995, pp. A1, A8.

31. Litman, *Motion Picture Mega-Industry,* ch. 7; Bruce Orwall, "Theater Consolidation Jolts Hollywood Power Structure," *WSJ,* Jan. 21, 1998, pp. B1, B8.

32. David J. Londoner, "The Changing Economics of Entertainment," in Tina Balio, *The American Film Industry,* rev. ed. (Madison: University of Wisconsin Press, 1985), pp. 603–630; Leonard Klady, "Screen Squeeze Sows Exhib-Distrib Discord," *Variety,* Oct. 3, 1994, pp. 13, 16.

33. Leonard Klady, "Megapix Crash Arty Party," *Variety,* June 12, 1995, pp. 1, 90.

11. Buffs, Buzz, and Educated Tastes

1. The following analysis comes from George J. Stigler and Gary S. Becker, "De Gustibus Non Est Disputandum," *American Economic Review* 67 (March 1977): 76–90. See also Roger A. McCain, "Cultivation of Taste, Catastrophe Theory, and the Demand for Works of Art," *American Economic Review* 71 (May 1981): 332–334.

2. Concentrated sectors (opera, symphony orchestras) have an advantage here. See Anthony Tommasini, "Opera as Something to Try," *NYTNE,* June 22, 1998, pp. B1, B3.

3. Stigler and Becker ("De Gustibus") suggested that the "thrills per hour" effect will dominate, so that hours spent listening to music increase with age, partly because the music-appreciation capital built up in one's early years is assumed (like all sorts of capital) to depreciate over time. Also, when one is age 18, the benefit of the music-appreciation capital on which one expects to draw at age 70 is probably subject to a very large discount factor.

4. Paul DiMaggio and Michael Useem, "Cultural Democracy in a Period of Culture Expansion," in Arnold W. Foster and Judith R. Blau, eds., *Art and Society: Readings in the Sociology of the Arts* (Buffalo: State University of New York Press, 1989), pp. 141–171. The effect has been long established; compare the early surveys: William J. Baumol and William G. Bowen, *Performing Arts: The Economic Dilemma* (Cambridge, Mass.: MIT Press, 1968), ch. 4; Alvin Toffler, *The Cultural Consumers: A Study of Art and Affluence in America* (New York: St. Martin's Press, 1964), ch. 3.

5. Howard S. Becker, *Art Worlds* (Berkeley: University of California Press, 1982), pp. 52–54.

6. C. D. Throsby and G. A. Withers, *The Economics of the Performing Arts* (New York: St. Martin's Press, 1979), pp. 99–101; Yoshimasa Kurabayashi and Yoshiro Matsuda, *Economic and Social Aspects of the Performing Arts in Japan* (Tokyo: Kinokuniya, 1988), pp. 178–195.

7. Harvey Leibenstein, "Bandwagon, Snob, and Veblen Effects in the Theory of Consumers' Demand," *Quarterly Journal of Economics* 64 (May 1950): 183–207.

8. Abhijit Banerjee, "A Simple Model of Herd Behavior," *Quarterly Journal of Economics* 107 (August 1992): 797–812; Sushil Bikhchandani, David Hirshleifer, and Ivo Welch, "A Theory of Fads, Fashion, Custom and Cultural Change as Information Cascades," *Journal of Political Economy* 100 (October 1992): 992–1026. The text follows the latter paper's exposition.

9. Arthur De Vany and W. David Walls tested a model that closely resembles herd behavior to explain the distribution of attendance levels at cinema films, finding that it outperforms other models of attendance patterns that lack the herd aspect. See their "Bose-Einstein Dynamics and Adaptive Contracting in the Motion Picture Industry," *Economic Journal* 106 (November 1996): 1443–1514.

10. The following analysis draws on Paul DiMaggio, "Classification in Art," *American Sociological Review* 52 (August 1987): 440–455. See also Randall Collins, *The Credential Society: An Historical Sociology of Education and Stratification* (New York: Academic Press, 1979), pp. 58–60.

11. The economic value of such exchanges among workers in creative industries was discussed in Chapter 7.

12. "Listening to rock and roll was learning a secret language. There was something conveyed by the attitude of the bands and their records that stood apart from the music, and the way you spoke that language told people how you felt about the world. When you first met someone, the conversation turned immediately to music because once you knew which bands a person listened to, you knew if you were going to get along." Fred Goodman, *The Mansion on the Hill* (New York: Times Books, 1997), pp. ix–x.

13. See Simon Frith, *Performing Rights: On the Value of Popular Music* (Cambridge, Mass.: Harvard University Press, 1996), pp. 4–5.

14. Art critic Harold Rosenberg judged it an effective filter for the promotions launched by dealers, museum curators, and collectors. See his "The Art Establishment," in Milton C. Albrecht, James H. Barnett, and Mason Griff, eds., *The Sociology of Art and Literature* (New York: Praeger, 1970), pp. 388–395.

15. Frith, *Performing Rights,* pp. 30–33. For an interesting discussion of the utility that people get from contemplating the famous, see Leo Braudy, *The Frenzy of Renown: Fame and Its History* (New York: Oxford University Press, 1986).

16. Judith R. Blau, "The Elite Arts, More or Less *de rigueur:* A Comparative Analysis of Metropolitan Culture," *Social Forces* 64 (June 1986): 875–906.

17. In his "Classification in Art," Paul DiMaggio cited evidence of "high culture" interests pursued intensively by upwardly mobile groups that lack other types of grease for their skids. For evidence of people's rationality in selecting "opinion leaders" to follow, see Elihu Katz and Paul F. Lazarsfeld, *Personal Influence* (Glencoe, Ill.: Free Press, 1955), part 1 and ch. 13.

18. Stigler and Becker, "De Gustibus," pp. 87–89. Their main objective is to argue that occasional shifts in tastes for fashionable goods and services need reflect no instability in people's underlying preferences (for warmth, comfort, personal attractiveness, etc.).

19. This unavoidably vague phrase provides cover for our sense that some fashions from the past appear irrational and bizarre, even with all the conditions of their own times taken into account. The adaptive process by which fashions change carries no implication that the "fit" of creative goods to wants and desires gets better over time.

20. Herbert Blumer, "Fashion: From Class Differentiation to Collective Selection," *Sociological Quarterly* 10 (Summer 1969): 275–291.

21. Daniel Boorstin, *The Image, or What Happened to the American Dream* (New York: Atheneum, 1962), p. 57.

22. Joshua Gamson, *Claims to Fame: Celebrity in Contemporary America* (Berkeley: University of California Press, 1994), chs. 7, 8.

23. John Ryan, *The Production of Culture in the Music Industry: The ASCAP-BMI Controversy* (Lanham, Md.: University Press of America, 1985), p. 36. Also see Hazel Meyer, *The Gold in Tin Pan Alley* (Philadelphia: Lippincott, 1958), pp. 54–55, 71. For similar effects in children's toys, see Gary Cross, *Kids' Stuff: Toys and the Changing World of American Childhood* (Cambridge, Mass.: Harvard University Press, 1997), pp. 216–217.

24. Braudy, *Frenzy of Renown,* pp. 524, 550.

25. Herbert J. Gans, *Popular Culture and High Culture: An Analysis and Evaluation of Taste* (New York: Basic Books, 1974), p. 12–14.

26. Ibid., p. 77.

27. Buffs are sought out by gatekeepers in pursuit of tips on likely artists to select. See Robert M. W. Dixon and John Godrich, *Recording the Blues* (New York: Stein and Day, 1970), pp. 58, 77; Stephen Singular, *The Rise and Rise of David Geffen* (Secaucas, N.J.: Carroll Publishing, 1997), p. 124.

28. One adroit experiment confirmed this by showing that listeners' tastes for recorded music in various styles are correlated with socioeconomic class, with their levels of music training controlled. Karl F. Schuessler, *Musical Taste and Socio-Economic Background* (New York: Arno Press, 1980).

29. Gans, *Popular Culture and High Culture,* pp. 17–64.

30. Gans, who sketched varying degrees of audience involvement in creative activities (ibid., pp. 76–93), aligned them with a descending scale of socioeconomic classes. His remarks elsewhere suggest, however, that popular-culture and high-culture activities lack fundamental qualitative distinctions in their organization, and specifically share this dispersion of audience involvement. Frith in *Performing Rights* extensively developed Gans's hypothesis that the mechanisms of high and pop cultures do not differ fundamentally.

31. Pierre Bourdieu, *Distinction: A Social Critique of the Judgment of Taste,* trans. Richard Nice (Cambridge, Mass.: Harvard University Press, 1984). Writing and reading poetry might count as the art realm with the highest ratio of buffs to total consumers. See Holland Carter, "A Louder Voice for Poetry," *NYTNE,* July 14, 1998, pp. B1, B8.

32. The traditional "high" performing arts in Japan and dance in the United States seem to provide examples. See Thomas R. H. Havens, *Artist and Patron in Postwar Japan: Dance, Music, Theater, and the Visual Arts, 1955–1980* (Princeton, N.J.: Princeton University Press, 1982); Sasha Anawalt, *The Joffrey Ballet and the Making of an American Dance Company* (Chicago: University of Chicago Press, 1996), p. 124.

33. This seems the essence of Clement Greenberg's famous complaint about kitsch as a danger to high art. See his *Art and Culture: Critical Essays* (Boston: Beacon Press, 1961).

34. For precise evidence of substitution in cultural capital, see Louis Levy-Garboua and Claude Montmarquette, "A Microeconomic Study of Theatre Demand," *JCE* 20, no. 1 (1996): 25–50.

35. Gans, *Popular Culture and High Culture,* pp. 109–110.

36. Virginia Lee Owen, "The Effects of Mass Markets on Artistic Quality," *JCE* 3 (December 1979): 23–39.

12. Consumers, Critics, and Certifiers

1. Richard E. Caves, "Information Structures of Product Markets," *Economic Inquiry* 24 (April 1985): 195–212.

2. Laura de Coppet and Alan Jones, eds., *The Art Dealers* (New York: Clarkson N. Potter, 1984), pp. 61, 148. For an interesting attempt to taxonomize critics' con-

trol over symbolic and pecuniary rewards to artists in various realms, see Diana Crane, "Reward Systems in Art, Science, and Religion," in Richard A. Peterson, ed., *The Production of Culture* (Beverly Hills, Calif.: Sage, 1976), pp. 57–72.

3. Some elements of this process are discussed in Raymonde Moulin, *The French Art Market: A Sociological View* (New Brunswick, N.J.: Rutgers University Press, 1987), pp. 76–78; and Howard S. Becker, *Art Worlds* (Berkeley: University of California Press, 1982), ch. 5. On the ecology of book reviewing, see Lewis A. Coser, Charles Kadushin, and Walter W. Powell, *Books: The Culture and Commerce of Publishing* (New York: Basic Books, 1982), ch. 12.

4. Malcolm Bradbury, *The Social Context of Modern English Literature* (Oxford: Blackwell, 1971), ch. 9.

5. Max Graf, *Composer and Critic: Two Hundred Years of Musical Criticism* (New York: Norton, 1946).

6. These patterns were traced in low- and highbrow newspapers and magazines by Kurt Lang, "Mass, Class, and the Reviewer," in Arnold W. Foster and Judith R. Blau, eds., *Art and Society: Readings in the Sociology of the Arts* (Buffalo: State University of New York Press, 1989), pp. 191–204.

7. Liah Greenfeld, *Different Worlds: A Sociological Study of Taste, Choice and Success in Art* (Cambridge: Cambridge University Press, 1989), ch. 4; Harold Rosenberg, *Art on the Edge: Creators and Situations* (New York: Macmillan, 1975), pp. 248–249.

8. This probably explains the finding of a study that correlated the favorableness of reviews of films and their numbers of awards with box office receipts. These correlations proved negative. Since no controls were employed for the costliness of inputs (stars, special effects), the result probably shows that reviewers tend to judge films on the effective use of whatever inputs they employ, not on the opulence of those inputs. See Elizabeth C. Hirschman and Andrew Pieros, Jr., "Relationships among Indicators of Success in Broadway Plays and Motion Pictures," *JCE* 9 (June 1985): 35–63.

9. Janny Scott, "A Steady Critical Eye on Film's Shifting Currents," *NYTNE,* June 28, 1998, sec. 2, pp. 1, 16.

10. Some fine points can be made about the technology of bribery. The reason for economists' intellectual tolerance of bribery is its element of efficiency: the producer who expects to reap the most value from passage through the gate is willing to pay the highest bribe; if this value reflects social benefit (the producer really does offer good value or enjoy low costs), this outcome is desirable. That proposition is less help in creative industries, however, because *nobody knows.* A bribe will most likely align the critic's incentives with his collector-client's interests if the bribe's value is related to the general market's assessment of the artist's work. A gift of the artist's work on that ground is a more constructive transfer than, say, a bundle of cash delivered in exchange for a meretricious one-shot rave. The reasoning is the same as for the incentive value of the dealer's ownership of his artist's work (Chapter 2), where its credence value to the collector is obvious.

11. Harrison C. White and Cynthia A. White, *Canvases and Careers: Institutional Change in the French Painting World* (Chicago: University of Chicago Press, 1993), pp. 10, 95–96, 117–124, 150–152.

12. Malcolm Gee, *Dealers, Critics, and Collectors of Modern Painting: Aspects of the Parisian Art Market between 1910 and 1930* (New York: Garland, 1981), pp. 268–269.

13. Ibid., pp. 279–281.

14. Alice Goldfarb Marquis, *The Art Biz: The Covert World of Collectors, Dealers, Auction Houses, Museums, and Critics* (Chicago: Contemporary Books, 1991), pp. 32–33; Greenfeld, *Different Worlds,* ch. 4; Richard Meryman, *Andrew Wyeth: A Secret Life* (New York: HarperCollins, 1996), ch. 22.

15. Pierre Assouline, *An Artful Life: A Biography of D. H. Kahnweiler,* trans. Charles Ruas (New York: Grove Weidenfeld, 1990), pp. 59, 106–107.

16. Marquis, *Art Biz,* pp. 98–100, 132.

17. Ibid., pp. 112–113, 130. For other alleged ties between advertising and editorial coverage, see de Coppet and Jones, *Art Dealers,* p. 238.

18. Colin Simpson, *The Partnership: The Secret Association between Bernard Berenson and Joseph Duveen* (London: Bodley Head, 1987); Peter Watson, *From Manet to Manhattan: The Rise of the Modern Art Market* (New York: Random House, 1992), pp. 139–141, 167.

19. For an example, see Simpson, *Partnership,* pp. 212–213.

20. Pierre Norman Sands, *A Historical Study of the Academy of Motion Picture Arts and Sciences* (New York: Arno Press, 1973); Murray Ross, *Stars and Strikes: Unionization in Hollywood* (New York: Columbia University Press, 1941), ch. 5.

21. Emmanuel Levy, *And the Winner Is . . . : The History and Politics of the Oscar Awards* (New York: Ungar, 1987), pp. 5–8.

22. Ibid., pp. 8–13, 42–43.

23. In ibid., ch. 3, Levy reported finding these patterns. With all Academy members voting in every category, Levy (p. 214) pointed out that popularity tends to outweigh talent.

24. Jay Prag and James Casavant provided a statistical study in their "An Empirical Study of the Determinants of Revenues and Marketing Expenditures in the Motion Picture Industry," *JCE* 18, no. 3 (1994): 217–235. The authors controlled for the film's negative cost, its evaluation by critics, and other variables. Also see Lisa Bannon, "Nods from Oscar May Help Small Films Win Audiences," *WSJ,* Feb. 14, 1996, pp. B1, B8; Peter Gumbel et al., "What's an Oscar Worth?" *WSJ,* March 20, 1998, pp. W1, W4.

25. Levy, *And the Winner Is,* pp. 259–264. Similarly, Grammy awards to recordings make the most difference in sales for those in esoteric or obscure genres. See Kris Goodfellow, "What Is a Grammy Worth?" *NYTNE,* Feb. 24, 1997, p. B9.

26. Levy, *And the Winner Is,* pp. 289–290.

27. Ibid., p. 329.

28. Mark Landler, "How Miramax Sets Its Sights on Oscar," *NYTNE,* Mar. 23, 1997, sec. 2, pp. 17, 28; Bernard Weinraub, "The Oscar Chase: Power and Dollars," *NYTNE,* Mar. 6, 1998, pp. B1, B8; also *NYTNE,* Jan. 9, 1998, p. B14.

29. Richard Todd, *Consuming Fictions: The Booker Prize and Fiction in Britain Today* (London: Bloomsbury Press, 1996), pp. 57, 87–91.

30. Janice Radway, "The Scandal of the Middlebrow: The Book-of-the-Month Club, Class Fracture, and Cultural Authority," *South Atlantic Quarterly* 89 (Fall 1990):

703–736; Benjamin M. Compaine, *The Book Industry in Transition: An Economic Study of Book Distribution and Marketing* (White Plains, N.Y.: Knowledge Industry Publications, 1978), pp. 100–107.

31. N. R. Kleinfield, "Book-of-The-Month Club(s)," *NYT,* Feb. 3, 1980, sec. 5, p. 1, 11.
32. Doreen Carvajal, "Triumph of the Bottom Line," *NYT,* Jan. 1, 1996, pp. D1, D5.

13. Innovation, Fads, and Fashions

1. Marc Eliot, *Rockonomics: The Money behind the Music* (New York: Franklin Watts, 1989), pp. 57–65, 185–186; Paul Hirsch, *The Structure of the Popular Music Industry* (Ann Arbor: Institute for Social Research, University of Michigan, 1969), p. 12.
2. Publisher Horace Liveright, a Jewish outsider in the inbred U.S. publishing industry, drew upon important European writers and U.S. radicals; he also devised the Modern Library series. See Tom Dardis, *Firebrand: The Life of Horace Liveright* (New York: Random House, 1995), pp. 51–52.
3. For reflections on the character of innovations in several art realms, see Howard S. Becker, *Art Worlds* (Berkeley: University of California Press, 1982), ch. 10.
4. Audrey Solomon, *Twentieth Century–Fox: A Corporate and Financial History* (Metuchen, N.J.: Scarecrow Press, 1988), p. 161; Robert H. Stanley, *The Celluloid Empire: A History of the American Movie Industry* (New York: Hastings House, 1978), pp. 242–246. The median age of movie-goers in 1984 was about 23, in a survey quoted by Mark Litwak.
5. See Mihaly Csikszentmihalyi, *Creativity: Flow and the Psychology of Discovery and Innovation* (New York: HarperCollins, 1996).
6. The empirical hypothesis behind this statement is that the *infinite variety* property tends to hold not just for one sort of creative good but also for the various competing forms of leisure, entertainment, and cultural consumption. For consumers without strongly committed interests (heavy investment in one form of cultural consumption capital), they are good substitutes. One realm of creative goods will attract demand from others if the cost of consuming it falls—a standard economic proposition. And such a realm may attract even more strongly from others when it is abuzz with innovation.
7. William D. Grampp, *Pricing the Priceless: Art, Artists, and Economics* (New York: Basic Books, 1989), pp. 61–66.
8. Martica Sawin, *Surrealism in Exile and the Beginning of the New York School* (Cambridge, Mass.: M.I.T. Press, 1995), p. 95.
9. Becker, *Art Worlds,* especially pp. 31–33.
10. D. Sagot-Duvaroux, S. Pflieger, and B. Rouget, "Factors Affecting Price on the Contemporary Art Market," in Ruth Towse and Abdul Khakee, eds., *Cultural Economics* (Berlin: Springer-Verlag, 1992), pp. 92–102.
11. The story of country music is more interestingly complex than this statement recognizes. See Richard A. Peterson, *Creating Country Music: Fabricating Authenticity* (Chicago: University of Chicago Press, 1997).

12. Arnold Shaw, *The Rock Revolution* (New York: Crowell-Collier, 1969).

13. Robert M. W. Dixon and John Godrich, *Recording the Blues* (New York: Stein and Day, 1970).

14. Effects of this technical innovation were studied by A. Franklin Murph in his "The Classical Record Industry in the United States," *JCE* 8 (June 1984): 81–89.

15. Steve Chapple and Reebee Garofalo, *Rock 'n' Roll Is Here to Pay: The History and Politics of the Music Industry* (Chicago: Nelson-Hall, 1977), pp. 29–31.

16. Ibid., pp. 32–52.

17. Ibid., pp. 87–89. A significant aid to record companies' entry was the willingness of record-pressing plants to finance their inventories. If pressing services were priced above their marginal cost, and if in a pinch the pressers could dispose of loan-collateral records more effectively than could a bank, such deals are easily explained. See Eliot, *Rockonomics,* pp. 107–108.

18. Chapple and Garofalo, *Rock 'n' Roll,* pp. 36–37.

19. Michael Cable, *The Pop Industry Inside Out* (London: W. H. Allen, 1977), pp. 9–11; Simon Frith, *Sound Effects: Youth, Leisure, and the Politics of Rock* (London: Constable, 1983), p. 96.

20. Chapple and Garofalo, *Rock 'n' Roll,* pp. 78–80.

21. Ibid., pp. 34–36, 45–46; R. Serge Denisoff, *Solid Gold: The Popular Record Industry* (New Brunswick, N.J.: Transaction Books, 1975), pp. 113–121.

22. Richard A. Peterson and David G. Berger, "Cycles in Symbol Production: The Case of Popular Music," *American Sociological Review* 40 (April 1975): 158–173; and Paul D. Lopes, "Innovation and Diversity in the Popular Music Industry, 1969 to 1990," *American Sociological Review* 57 (February 1992): 56–71.

23. Recent reports continue to suggest that total record sales fluctuate mainly with the number of individual records achieving very large sales. See Patrick M. Reily, "Music Business Can't Find a New Beat," *WSJ,* Jan. 3, 1997, pp. B1, B2; Jon Pareles, "All That Music, and Nothing to Listen To," *NYT,* Jan. 5, 1997, sec. 2, pp. 34, 44.

24. Clive Davis with James Willwerth, *Clive: Inside the Record Business* (New York: William Morrow, 1975), p. 276.

25. See Denisoff, *Solid Gold,* pp. 113–139; Frith, *Sound Effects,* pp. 97–98; Cable, *Pop Industry,* pp. 67–77; R. Serge Denisoff, *Tarnished Gold: The Record Industry Revisited* (New Brunswick, N.J.: Transaction Books, 1986), pp. 93–105; Davis, *Clive,* especially pp. 139, 160.

26. This section draws upon Richard A. Peterson, "The Production of Cultural Change: The Case of Contemporary Country Music," *Social Forces* 45 (Summer 1978): 292–314; John Ryan and Richard A. Peterson, "The Product Image: The Fate of Creativity in Country Music Songwriting," in James S. Ettema and D. Charles Whitney, eds., *Individuals in Mass Media Organizations: Creativity and Constraint* (Beverly Hills, Calif.: Sage, 1982), pp. 11–32.

27. Laurence Leamer, *Three Chords and the Truth: Hope, Heartbreak, and Changing Fortunes in Nashville* (New York: HarperCollins, 1997), especially pp. 145, 155–156.

28. Two good studies of the toy industry's organization and development are Sydney

Ladensohn Stern and Ted Schoenhaus, *Toyland: The High-Stakes Game of the Toy Industry* (Chicago: Contemporary Books, 1990); and Gary Cross, *Kids' Stuff: Toys and the Changing World of American Childhood* (Cambridge, Mass.: Harvard University Press, 1997).

29. Nikhil Deogun, "An Inventor Finds Toys a Tricky Game," *WSJ*, Dec. 19, 1995, pp. B1, B2.

30. Stern and Schoenhaus, *Toyland*, pp. 9, 77, 94, 156, 241–242.

31. Joseph Pereira, "If You Can't Locate That Special Plaything, Call, or Blame, a Scalper," *WSJ*, June 24, 1996, pp. A1, A6.

32. Joseph Pereira and William M. Bulkeley, "Toy-Buying Patterns Are Changing and That Is Shaking the Industry," *WSJ*, June 16, 1998, pp. A1, A8.

33. Cross, *Kids' Stuff*, ch. 6, and especially pp. 104, 108, 164, 197.

34. Richard C. Levy and Ronald O. Weingartner, *From Workshop to Toystore* (New York: Simon & Schuster, 1992).

35. Stern and Schoenhaus, *Toyland*, pp. 231–233. Amateur designers either start their own companies or deal with small toy manufacturers that do no systematic design work in-house.

36. Ibid., p. 113.

37. Dean Takahashi, "Electronic Arts Battles Defection of Star Game Designers," *WSJ*, Aug. 7, 1998, pp. B1, B4.

38. In 1958, the figures were 12 percent for dolls and 13 percent for the rest of the toys and games industry. U.S. Federal Trade Commission, *Industry Classification and Concentration* (Washington, D.C.: Bureau of Economics, Federal Trade Commission, 1967).

39. Geraldine Fabrikant, "Mattel Seeks Hasbro But Is Rebuffed," *NYT*, Jan. 25, 1996, pp. D1, D2.

40. Stern and Schoenhaus, *Toyland*, pp. 46, 55, 174.

41. Joseph Pereira, "Hasbro Enjoys Life Off the Toy-Market Roller Coaster," *WSJ*, May 5, 1992, p. B4; Joseph Pereira, "Toy Business Focuses More on Marketing and Less on New Ideas," *WSJ*, Feb. 29, 1996, pp. A1, A8; Joseph Pereira, "Galaxy of *Star Wars* Products Has New Glow," *WSJ*, Dec. 10, 1996, pp. B1, B5; ibid., pp. 116–117.

42. Elizabeth Lesly, "Will Tyco End Up in a Rival's Toybox?" *BW*, Feb. 28, 1994, pp. 78–79; Linda M. Watkins, "Coleco Aims to Broaden Its Product Base," *WSJ*, Oct. 28, 1986, p. 6; Dana Canedy, "Takeovers Are Part of the Game," *NYTNE*, Feb. 9, 1999, pp. C1, C11.

43. Lisa Bannon and Joseph Pereira, "Toy Makers Offer the Moon for New *Star Wars* Licenses," *WSJ*, Aug. 19, 1997, pp. B1, B5.

44. Stern and Schoenhaus, *Toyland*, pp. 12, 26; Joseph Pereira, "Toys 'R' Them: Mom-and-Pop Stores Put Playthings Like Thomas on Fast Track," *WSJ*, Jan. 14, 1993, pp. B1, B7; Stephanie Strom, "A Palace of Toys Looks for a Profit," *NYT*, Dec. 23, 1993, pp. D1, D4. A small manufacturer's successful innovation tends to pull its distribution away from these stores and toward the chains; see Dana Canedy, "Growing Pains for a Little Toy Maker," *NYTNE*, Mar. 29, 1997, pp. 25, 28.

45. The toy industry does not exactly match the distinction between promoters and

pickers, found in other creative realms, but size is clearly associated with one mode of promotion.

46. Stern and Schoenhaus, *Toyland,* pp. 14, 28, 109, 171. The firm that picked up the game Trivial Pursuit saw its sales rise from $20 million to $350 million in two years (p. 125).

47. Kris Goodfellow, "Sony Comes on Strong in Video-Game War," *NYTNE,* May 25, 1998, p. D5; Irene M. Kunii, "Sega's Dream Machine," *BW,* Sept. 13, 1999, p. 60.

48. Seanna Browder et al., "Nintendo: At the Top of Its Game," *BW,* June 9, 1997, pp. 72–73. The bulk of games successful on personal computers and game players have come from small "picker" firms.

49. Geraldine Pelles, *Art, Artists and Society: Origins of a Modern Dilemma* (Englewood Cliffs, N.J.: Prentice-Hall, 1963), pp. 147–151.

50. See Chapter 2; also Harrison C. White and Cynthia A. White, *Canvases and Careers: Institutional Change in the French Painting World* (Chicago: University of Chicago Press, 1993), and Paula Gillett, *Worlds of Art: Painters in Victorian Society* (New Brunswick, N.J.: Rutgers University Press, 1990).

51. Principal sources of information are Serge Guilbaut, *How New York Stole the Idea of Modern Art: Abstract Expressionism, Freedom, and the Cold War,* trans. Arthur Goldhammer (Chicago: University of Chicago Press, 1983); Peter Watson, *From Manet to Manhattan: The Rise of the Modern Art Market* (New York: Random House, 1992); Diana Crane, *The Transformation of the Avant-Garde: The New York Art World, 1940–1985* (Chicago: University of Chicago Press, 1987); and Sawin, *Surrealism in Exile.*

52. Guilbaut, *How New York Stole,* pp. 91–94.

53. Ibid., pp. 67–68; Aline B. Saarinen, *The Proud Possessors: The Lives, Times, and Tastes of Some Adventurous American Art Collectors* (New York: Random House, 1958), pp. 329–332; Watson, *From Manet to Manhattan,* pp. 275–279, 285–289.

54. Guilbaut, *How New York Stole,* pp. 75–80, 82, 86.

55. Ibid., p. 95; Saarinen, *Proud Possessors,* p. 335.

56. Ken Johnson, "A Hard-Edged Zeal in Images of Avant-Garde," *NYTNE,* Sept. 4, 1998, p. B28.

57. Watson, *From Manet to Manhattan,* pp. 289–290, 305, 308; Guilbaut, *How New York Stole,* pp. 114–115, 180.

58. Crane, *Transformation,* pp. 25, 27.

59. A similar effect flowed from the famous Ballets Russes productions in Paris designed by Picasso and other prominent contemporary artists. See Raymonde Moulin, *The French Art Market: A Sociological View,* trans. Arthur Goldhammer (New Brunswick, N.J.: Rutgers University Press, 1987), p. 17.

60. John I. H. Baur, *Revolution and Tradition in Modern American Art* (Cambridge, Mass.: Harvard University Press, 1951), pp. 124–126; Robert Doty, *Photo-Secession: Photography as Fine Art* (Rochester, N.Y.: George Eastman House, 1960), pp. 58–60.

61. For a comprehensive account of the Armory Show, see Milton W. Brown, *The*

Story of the Armory Show (New York: New York Graphic Society for Joseph H. Hirshhorn Foundation, 1963).

62. Baur, *Revolution and Tradition*, pp. 127–129; Saarinen, *Proud Possessors*, pp. 215–217, 243–249. Dreier's collection eventually settled at Yale University.

63. Michael Kimmelman, "Art in Aisle 3, by Lingerie, and Feel Free to Browse," *NYT*, Mar. 19, 1995, sec. 2, pp. 43, 46.

14. Covering High Fixed Costs

1. This is true until and unless production hits diminishing returns, so that its average variable costs rise with output.

2. The text summarizes a standard analysis that is spelled out in James Heilbrun and Charles M. Gray, *The Economics of Art and Culture: An American Perspective* (Cambridge: Cambridge University Press, 1993), chs. 6, 7; and C. D. Throsby and G. A. Withers, *The Economics of the Performing Arts* (New York: St. Martin's Press, 1979).

3. The text omits other important factors influencing the number of oligopolists that can coexist in equilibrium. Given fixed costs, higher variable costs reduce their number. Given all costs and the size of the market, the more vigorously the rivals compete, the fewer of them (paradoxically) are viable. Also, the fixed cost of an activity is to some degree a decision variable and can perhaps be reduced by (for example) settling for a lower-quality product. What matters for this chapter is that, among art realms, fixed costs unavoidably vary relative to market size.

4. The concept of a club should not be taken too literally. Individuals with sufficient combined willingness to pay need to contract with an agent to provide the creative product. It does not matter how this deal comes into existence.

5. As with fixed costs, the analysis of nonprofit enterprise is standard in the literature of economics and summarized briefly here. See Susan Rose-Ackerman, ed., *The Economics of Nonprofit Institutions: Studies in Structure and Policy* (New York: Oxford University Press, 1986); Burton A. Weisbrod, *The Nonprofit Economy* (Cambridge, Mass.: Harvard University Press, 1988); Susan Rose-Ackerman, "Altruism, Nonprofits, and Economic Theory," *Journal of Economic Literature* 34 (June 1996): 701–728. For a broad treatment of ownership issues, see Henry Hansmann, *The Ownership of Enterprise* (Cambridge, Mass.: Harvard University Press, 1996), especially ch. 12.

6. One statistical study analyzed nonprofit organizations' expenditures to persuade potential donors to contribute. Specifically, it tested whether organizations' promotion outlays are optimal, on the criterion of spending up to the point where the last dollar bags just one more dollar of donations. Nonprofits apparently do maximize net donations in that sense. Donors to nonprofits in the arts are more responsive to promotional outlays than are donors to other sectors. See Burton A. Weisbrod and Nester D. Dominguez, "Demand for Collective Goods in Private Nonprofit Markets: Can Fundraising Expenditures Help Overcome Free-Riding Behavior?" *Journal of Public Economics* 30 (June 1986): 83–95.

7. Manifestos and statements of principles are in good supply among creative orga-

nizations; the issue here is whether parties can agree on their translation into specific actions and obligations.

8. William J. Baumol and William G. Bowen, *Performing Arts: The Economic Dilemma* (Cambridge, Mass.: MIT Press, 1968).

9. For a case study, see Carl M. Colonna, Patricia M. Kearns, and John E. Anderson, "Electronically Produced Music and Its Economic Effects on the Performing Musician and the Music Industry," *JCE* 17 (December 1993): 69–75.

10. Some empirical evidence supports the implication that income elasticities of demand for arts are greater than one. See Throsby and Withers, *Economics of the Performing Arts*, pp. 103–118.

11. The time cost of consumption does have an adverse effect on the consumption of original performances, however: the fixed time-cost of transporting oneself to and from the performance exceeds the time cost of setting up the reproduced performance.

12. The discussion relies on Paul DiMaggio, "Nonprofit Organizations in the Production and Distribution of Culture," in Walter W. Powell, ed., *The Nonprofit Sector: A Research Handbook* (New Haven, Conn.: Yale University Press, 1987), pp. 195–220.

13. See, for example, filmmaker John Boorman, *The Emerald Forest Diary* (New York: Farrar, Straus, Giroux, 1985), pp. 125–126.

14. Judith R. Blau, "The Elite Arts, More or Less de Rigueur: A Comparative Analysis of Metropolitan Culture," *Social Forces* 64 (June 1986): 875–905.

15. The economic reasoning behind this observation is that the first organization becomes viable when the market lets it just break even while selling as a monopoly. For a *2n* city to suffice for attracting a second organization, the two must behave as if they shared the monopoly between them—not competing on admission prices, quality, or other things. If competition did break out, the two could not both cover their costs unless the market were enlarged further. This line of analysis was applied to counts of service businesses in isolated small towns by Timothy F. Bresnahan and Peter C. Reiss, "Entry and Competition in Concentrated Markets," *Journal of Political Economy* 99 (October 1991): 977–1009.

16. Philip Hart, *Orpheus in the New World: The Symphony Orchestra as an American Cultural Institution* (New York: W. W. Norton, 1973), pp. 180–181, 213, 265, ch. 12.

17. Yoshimasa Kurabayashi and Yoshiro Matsuda, *Economic and Social Aspects of the Performing Arts in Japan: Symphony Orchestras and Opera* (Tokyo: Kinokuniya, 1988), pp. 59–79.

18. Thomas R. H. Havens, *Artist and Patron in Postwar Japan: Dance, Music, Theater, and the Visual Arts, 1955–1980* (Princeton, N.J.: Princeton University Press, 1982), ch. 6.

19. There is a subtle economic problem for any enterprise in determining what quality to offer. The profit-seeking enterprise performs the experiment of raising quality a little, then observing how much demand increases at the going price for tickets. What this reveals is the interest in quality of those audience members willing to pay only the going ticket price. It fails to expose the attitude toward quality of enthusiasts with a higher willingness to pay, who will buy tickets in any case. In

this setting enthusiasts are likely to value increments of quality higher than the marginal customers (in other markets they might value it less). The nonprofit enterprise that both sells tickets and asks its customers for donations has a chance to pick a quality level closer to what is socially optimal.

20. The club-membership model treats the patron-donors as a collective principal contracting with the manager as an agent. For an ongoing arts organization, however, such treaties of constitutional force are devoid of commitments of either party's future actions and too general to carry much weight. The founding patrons give way to a board of directors that can hire and fire the manager. Short of that form of discipline, however, it becomes useful to think of the arts management and the organization's donor clientele interacting as independent decision-makers: the donors present a supply function of donations, the manager chooses policies that determine how much donations actually arrive. See Throsby and Withers, *Economics of the Performing Arts*, pp. 14–25.

21. For a theoretical model constructed along these lines, see Henry Hansmann, "Nonprofit Enterprise in the Performing Arts," *Bell Journal of Economics* 12 (Autumn 1981): 341–361. On the average importance of donations in nonprofits' income, see Heilbrun and Gray, *Economics of Art and Culture*, p. 119.

22. For case studies of long-lived organizations that rely on donors as guarantors, see Roland Kushner and Arthur E. King, "Performing Arts as a Club Good: Evidence from a Nonprofit Organization," *JCE* 18, no. 1 (1994): 15–28; John O'Hagan and Mark Purdy, "The Theory of Non-Profit Organisations: An Application to a Performing Arts Enterprise," *Economic and Social Review* 24 (January 1993): 155–167.

23. James R. Rawls, Robert A. Ullrich, and Oscar T. Nelson, Jr., "A Comparison of Managers Entering or Reentering the Profit and Nonprofit Sectors," *Academy of Management Journal* 18 (September 1975): 616–623.

24. Throsby and Withers, *Economics of the Performing Arts*, pp. 128–129.

25. Ruth Towse, *Singers in the Marketplace: The Economics of the Singing Profession* (Oxford: Clarendon Press, 1993), pp. 112–113, 118–119.

26. James H. Gapinski, "A Layperson's Guide to Production Structures of Nonprofit Performing Arts," in William S. Hendon, James L. Shanahan, and Alice J. MacDonald, eds., *Economic Policy for the Arts* (Cambridge, Mass.: Abt Books, 1980), pp. 261–269. The volume also contains papers on subsidized theatres in England and Sweden suggesting that variations in public subsidy mainly affect the number and opulence of productions and the length of runs; effects on ticket prices appear minor.

27. Samuel Schwarz, "The Economics of the Performing Arts: A Case Study of the Major Orchestras," in Jack B. Kamerman and Rosanne Martorella, eds., *Performers and Performances: The Social Organization of Artistic Work* (New York: Praeger, 1983), pp. 269–279.

28. Rosanne Martorella, *The Sociology of Opera* (New York: Praeger), p. 54.

29. Ibid., pp. 97–109; J. Lamar Pierce, "Programmatic Risk-Taking by American Opera Companies: An Econometric Study of Money, Music, and Culture," senior honors thesis, University of Puget Sound, 1997.

30. Mark Lange, William Luksetich, and Philip Jacobs, "Managerial Objectives of

Symphony Orchestras," *Managerial and Decision Economics* 7 (December 1986): 273–278.

31. The conclusions of this study (ibid.), like many of the creative industries, require some discount. That is because variables such as grant income are taken as exogenous, although they may well be tangled in two-way causation. The Lange study's purported findings might arise because bigger grants go to the better and more prestigious orchestras that employ better players and charge higher ticket prices.

32. Judith Dobrzynski, "Passing on the Pain at the Met," *NYTNE,* Apr. 14, 1999, pp. B1, B4.

33. DiMaggio, "Nonprofit Organizations"; Philip Kotler and Joanne Scheff, *Standing Room Only: Strategies for Marketing the Performing Arts* (Boston: Harvard Business School Press, 1997), p. 48. With regard to museum directors, Frey and Pommerehne argued that personal goals (prestige, excellence of working conditions) are advanced by an intentional vagueness of general goals. See Bruno Frey and Werner W. Pommerehne, *Muses and Markets: Explorations in the Economics of the Arts* (Oxford: Blackwell, 1989), p. 71.

34. Heilbrun and Gray, *Economics of Art and Culture,* p. 191.

35. For a good sketch of this process, see Richard A. Peterson, "From Impresario to Arts Administrator: Formal Accountability in Nonprofit Cultural Organizations," in Paul J. DiMaggio, ed., *Nonprofit Enterprise in the Arts: Studies in Mission and Constraint* (New York: Oxford University Press, 1986), pp. 162–183; also Frey and Pommerehne, *Muses and Markets,* pp. 33–35. Throsby and Withers, in their *Economics of the Performing Arts* (135–136), tested but failed to confirm the hypothesis that the share of administrative costs in arts organizations' total expenditures increases with their size and dependence on grant income.

36. Sondra Forsyth and Pauline M. Kolenda, "Competition, Cooperation, and Group Cohesion in the Ballet Company," in Milton C. Albrecht, James H. Barnett, and Mason Griff, eds., *The Sociology of Art and Literature* (New York: Praeger, 1970), pp. 221–255; on Chicago's Steppenwolf Theatre, see Kotler and Scheff, *Standing Room Only,* especially pp. 242–245, 432–433; Sasha Anawalt, *The Joffrey Ballet: Robert Joffrey and the Making of an American Dance Company* (Chicago: University of Chicago Press, 1996).

15. Donor-Supported Nonprofit Organizations in the Performing Arts

1. Principal sources of information are John H. Mueller, *The American Symphony Orchestra: A Social History of Musical Taste* (Bloomington: Indiana University Press, 1951); Philip Hart, *Orpheus in the New World: The Symphony Orchestra as an American Cultural Institution* (New York: W. W. Norton, 1973); and Howard Shanet, *Philharmonic: A History of New York's Orchestra* (Garden City, N.Y.: Doubleday, 1975).

2. On Thomas's orchestra, see Hart, *Orpheus,* pp. 10–31.

3. Ibid., pp. 31–44. In the 1870s Thomas had sought to settle his orchestra in Philadelphia. That effort floundered when local backers failed to meet their promises and a work commissioned at high cost from Richard Wagner arrived as decidedly shoddy goods.

4. Shanet, *Philharmonic*, p. 192. For extensive background on cultural upgrading, see Lawrence Levine, *Highbrow/Lowbrow: The Emergence of Cultural Hierarchy in America* (Cambridge, Mass.: Harvard University Press, 1988).

5. See Hart, *Orpheus*, ch. 3. In Hart's judgment (p. 70), no one of Higginson's ideas was new, but he had the unique combination of breadth of vision, social position, and business acumen to create a viable organization capable of the highest quality of performance.

6. The club that effected this change aimed to raise enough money "to rebuild the Philharmonic into an orchestra of the first rank, paying sufficient salaries to the players and to the conductor to enable them to give their full time" during the concert season. See Shanet, *Philharmonic*, pp. 207–210, 220, 224–225.

7. Ibid., pp. 231–232. A similar pattern was noted for the Philadelphia Orchestra. Conductor Leopold Stokowski's flamboyance and inventive programming made him a commercial success, despite the anguish for conservative ears of the modern music that he had programmed. Stokowski collected a salary that apparently captured most of the rent from his commercial effectiveness, however, and his resignation was accepted in a dispute over that salary. He was replaced by the stodgy but comforting Eugene Ormandy. See Edward Arian, *Bach, Beethoven, and Bureaucracy: The Case of the Philadelphia Orchestra* (University: University of Alabama Press, 1971).

8. Shanet, *Philharmonic*, pp. 232–234, 245–247.

9. Ibid., pp. 235–245, 252–253.

10. Ibid., pp. 255–260.

11. Ibid., pp. 272–278, 287, 316–317, 455.

12. Mueller, *American Symphony Orchestra*, p. 154.

13. Ibid., pp. 101–105, 115–117, 125, 156, 163, 166–168, 179–181.

14. William Weber, *Music and the Middle Class: The Social Structure of Concert Life in London* (New York: Holmes & Meier, 1975), pp. 16–18.

15. Weber (*Music and the Middle Class*, p. 43) documented the frequency with which musicians distributed free tickets to fill the house for their benefit concerts—first to those whose attendance would be prestigious, then to anybody likely to attend.

16. In this context of casual employment, its efficiency arose from the incentive for the player sending a deputy to select one with adequate capability; a bumbler would sully the regular player's own reputation and reduce future opportunities.

17. On the continent these organizations were successors to the musical establishments of aristocratic houses, where professional and amateur performers mingled (Weber, *Music and the Middle Class*, p. 37). See also Reginald Nettel, *The Orchestra in England: A Social History*, revised ed. (London: Jonathan Cape, 1956), pp. 87–99.

18. Weber, *Music and the Middle Class*, pp. 40–42 and ch. 4.

19. Ibid., ch. 5; Nettel, *Orchestra in England*, pp. 161–170, 176–180, 210–212.

20. Cyril Ehrlich, *The Music Profession in Britain since the Eighteenth Century* (Oxford: Clarendon Press, 1985), p. 61.

21. Ibid., p. 65.

22. Ibid., pp. 61, 74; David Cox, *The Henry Wood Proms* (London: British Broadcasting Corporation, 1980), pp. 42–43, 64, 66, 82.

23. Ehrlich, *Music Profession in Britain*, ch. 4.

24. Maurice Pearton, *The LSO at 70: A History of the Orchestra* (London: Victor Gollancz, 1974), pp. 30, 45, 49, 72, 80, 93, 176. Several other London orchestras later fell into cooperative status when they lost governmental or other patronage; see pp. 29, 99, 170.

25. Ibid., pp. 78, 107, 142–143.

26. Ibid., pp. 113, 139.

27. Ibid., pp. 75, 95–97, 109; Nicholas Kenyon, *The BBC Symphony Orchestra: The First Fifty Years, 1930–1980* (London: British Broadcasting Corporation, 1981), p. 42, 79.

28. Pearton, *LSO,* pp. 61, 82, 92, 100–102, 163.

29. Mueller, *American Symphony Orchestra,* pp. 290–296.

30. James Andreoni, "Impure Altruism and Donations to Public Goods: A Theory of Warm-Glow Giving," *Economic Journal* 100 (June 1990): 464–477.

31. Robert Sugden, "Reciprocity: The Supply of Public Goods through Voluntary Contributions," *Economic Journal* 94 (December 1984): 772–787.

32. Paul DiMaggio, "Cultural Entrepreneurship in Nineteenth-Century Boston: The Creation of an Organizational Base for High Culture in America," *Media, Culture, and Society* 4 (January 1982): 33–50.

33. The distinction is between a governance structure that aligns donations to short-run needs—covering this year's deficit, say—and one that recognizes an arts organization's many expenditures that amount to investments in its long-run performance and viability.

34. The behavior of collectors and the role of museums will be discussed in Chapter 21.

35. Mueller, *American Symphony Orchestra,* pp. 334–339.

36. Kate Hevner Mueller, *Twenty-seven Major American Symphony Orchestras: A History and Analysis of Their Repertoires* (Bloomington: Indiana University Press, 1973), pp. xviii–xx. Orchestras below this top group had more checkered histories.

37. Russell Lynes, *Good Old Modern: An Intimate Portrait of the Museum of Modern Art* (New York: Atheneum, 1975), pp. 213, 281, 434–435; Rosanne Martorella, *The Sociology of Opera* (New York: Praeger, 1979), pp. 128, 141–144.

38. Monica Langley, "Even CEOs Sweat Out Carnegie Hall Tryouts; For the Board, That Is," *WSJ,* July 30, 1998, pp. A1, A12; Lisa Gubernick, "Buying Your Way On to a Board," *WSJ,* May 7, 1999, pp. W1, W4; Monica Langley, "Nonprofit Broker Puts Corporate Hotshots onto Charitable Boards," *WSJ,* Sept. 17, 1999, pp. A1, A10.

39. Deena Rosenberg and Bernard Rosenberg, *The Music Makers* (New York: Columbia University Press, 1979), pp. 14–15, 120, 245–246, 401–402.

40. The following discussion draws upon Teresa Odendahl, *Charity Begins at Home: Generosity and Self-Interest among the Philanthropic Elite* (New York: Basic Books, 1990), and especially Francie Ostrower, *Why the Wealthy Give: The Culture of Elite Philanthropy* (Princeton, N.J.: Princeton University Press, 1996).

41. Ostrower, *Why the Wealthy Give,* p. 29. See James Andreoni, "Toward a Theory of Charitable Fund-Raising," *Journal of Political Economy* 106 (December 1998): 1186–1213.

42. Ostrower, *Why the Wealthy Give,* ch. 3 and p. 81. Of the women interviewed by Ostrower, 69 percent did not work, while 24 percent worked in a cultural or human service profession (7 percent were managers in such organizations) (p. 70). Also see Odendahl, *Charity Begins at Home,* p. 32.

43. "Nonprofit organizations are focal points around which upper-class life revolves. Through their philanthropy, wealthy donors come together with one another and sustain a series of organizations that contribute to the social and cultural coherence of upper-class life." Ostrower, *Why the Wealthy Give,* p. 36. See also Odendahl, *Charity Begins at Home,* pp. 4–5.

44. Also Odendahl, *Charity Begins at Home,* p. 35.

45. Ibid., ch. 5.

46. Ibid., pp. 37–42.

47. Julian Wolpert and Thomas Reiner, "The Philanthropy Marketplace," *Economic Geography* 60 (July 1984): 197–209.

48. Ostrower, *Why the Wealthy Give,* p. 31.

49. This analysis draws on Peter Navarro, "Why Do Corporations Give to Charity?" *Journal of Business* 61 (January 1988): 65–93.

50. The preceding analysis of individual donations suggested that social competition gives rise to positively sloped reaction functions for donations to all NPOs taken together: an increase in one donor's outlay tends to spur others on. This model of corporate donations suggests negatively sloped reactions among enterprises in the same city: the enhanced infrastructure due to one firm's donation reduced the marginal value (for lowering labor costs) of the next firm's donation.

51. One notices among the heavy corporate contributors many firms producing petroleum, cigarettes, and other commodities for which many consumers have negative images. Similar motives operate in other countries; see Rosanne Martorella, ed., *Art and Business: An International Perspective on Sponsorship* (Westport, Conn.: Praeger, 1996).

52. Joseph Galaskiewicz, "An Urban Grants Economy Revisited: Corporate Charitable Contributions in the Twin Cities, 1979–81, 1987–91," *Administrative Science Quarterly* 42 (September 1997): 445–471.

16. Cost Disease and Its Analgesics

1. Hilda Baumol and W. J. Baumol, "The Future of the Theater and the Cost Disease of the Arts," *JCE* 9 (Supplement, 1985): 7–31.

2. Samuel Schwarz, "The Economics of the Performing Arts: A Case Study of the Major Orchestras," in Jack B. Kamerman and Rosanne Martorella, eds., *Performers and Performances: The Social Organization of Artistic Work* (New York: Praeger, 1983), pp. 269–279.

3. Marianne Victorius Felton, "Evidence of the Existence of the Cost Disease in the Performing Arts," *JCE* 18, no. 4 (1994–1995): 301–312; and her "Historical Funding Patterns in Symphony Orchestras, Dance, and Opera Companies," *Journal of Arts Law and Management* 24 (Spring 1994): 8–31.

4. Many other data of this sort can be found. In their 1966 book, William J. Baumol and William G. Bowen argued that over the preceding three decades the perform-

ing arts had not increased their claim on personal disposable income, thereby debunking the notion that a "culture boom" was under way. See Baumol and Bowen, *Performing Arts: The Economic Dilemma* (New York: Twentieth Century Fund, 1966), ch. 3.

5. Different but related problems arise in studying changes in the population of artists. The share of performing and visual artists in the U.S. labor force increased from 0.28 percent in 1970 to 0.39 percent in 1990, seemingly defying the cost disease. Employment of some artists however, benefits from new media technologies. See David Throsby, "Economic Circumstances of the Performing Artist: Baumol and Bowen Thirty Years On," *JCE* 20, no. 3 (1996): 225–240; James Heilbrun, "Growth, Accessibility, and the Distribution of Arts Activity in the United States," *JCE* 20, no. 4 (1996): 283–296.

6. Bernard Rosenberg and Ernest Harburg, *The Broadway Musical: Collaboration in Commerce and Art* (New York: New York University Press, 1993), appendix 4, tables 1, 3.

7. Chapter 6 indicated this proposition's main qualifications. Costs as commonly measured include some rents that are compressible in a pinch. Also, the Broadway production raises the expected value of subsidiary rights to the author and producer, with possible effects on the recoupment track record.

8. Thomas Gale Moore, *The Economics of the American Theater* (Durham, N.C.: Duke University Press, 1968), pp. 10–13. In renaissance London a play could be profitable after a two-week run. See Mary I. Oates and William J. Baumol, "On the Economics of the Theater in Renaissance London," *Swedish Journal of Economics* 74 (March 1972): 136–160.

9. Moore, *Economics of the American Theater*, pp. 46–51.

10. In principle, raising ticket prices for hits and lowering them for flops could be part of the adjustment process. In practice, ticket prices are omitted in recognition of their small role. Special prices are sometimes offered for weak shows and/or for performances on weekdays when demand is light, but prices are not raised to maximize the value of a hit. The reason for this pattern, found throughout the performing arts, is unclear. Moore (pp. 30–31) offered the Broadway-specific explanation that members of talent guilds and unions benefit from long runs of plays but not from high ticket prices, and so oppose ticket premia in preference for excess demand and prolonged runs. Also see William J. Baumol, "On Two Experiments in the Pricing of Theater Tickets," in Michael J. Boskin, ed., *Economics and Human Welfare: Essays in Honor of Tibor Scitovsky* (New York: Academic Press, 1979), pp. 41–57.

11. Rosenberg and Harburg, *Broadway Musical*, appendix 4, tables 1, 3.

12. Rosenberg and Harburg stressed that the more successful producers and producer groups have average flop rates that are lower than others, but still not low—40 to 50 percent (pp. 92, 265). Successful producers have limited capacities, and they sometimes lose their touch. Apparently there is not much room, when the cost disease presses, for an adjustment that squeezes out neophyte producers and raises the share of productions due to producers with good track records, thereby lowering the aggregate flop rate.

13. Jack Poggi, *Theater in America: The Impact of Economic Forces, 1870–1967* (Ithaca, N.Y.: Cornell University Press, 1968), pp. 60–61.

14. Rosenberg and Harburg, *Broadway Musical*, p. 53.

15. Data from ibid., appendix 6.

16. Richard Hummler, "Legit Managers Now B'way Stars," *Variety*, Apr. 2, 1980, pp. 1, 86.

17. Poggi, *Theater in America*, pp. 3–8, 250–253.

18. Ibid., pp. 28–35; Moore, *Economics of the American Theater*, ch. 7; Robert McLaughlin, *Broadway and Hollywood: A History of Economic Interaction* (New York: Arno Press, 1974), ch. 1.

19. McLaughlin, *Broadway and Hollywood*, pp. 37–39.

20. Ibid., pp. 105–110.

21. Ibid., pp. 112–116, 144–145. In the talking-films era Hollywood first relied heavily on filmed plays, but cinematic values reasserted themselves as the sound innovation was digested (pp. 103–105).

22. That is, with the film-royalty pie enlarged, competition among producers for promising plays made them willing to settle for smaller shares (though no smaller expected dollar royalties).

23. McLaughlin, *Broadway and Hollywood*, pp. 58–59, 122, 159–161, 252–253.

24. Ibid., p. 252.

25. McLaughlin (ibid., p. 257), quoting Ray Stark: "It is important to us to be able to judge potential movie audience reaction before we make the movies. The reaction of a Broadway audience is a good guide. Broadway, for us, is a sort of tryout town."

26. Ibid., pp. 95–98, 102–103. One study assigns an earlier start to the upgrading of stage plays, on the basis of evidence that the flop rate was higher in the 1920s than it had been in the 1910s. See Poggi, *Theater in America*, pp. 74–77.

27. Moore (*Economics of the American Theater*, p. 15) observed that between the 1926–1927 and 1934–1935 seasons the total number of tickets sold to Broadway plays declined 60 percent while real ticket prices climbed 21 percent.

28. Baumol and Baumol, "Future of the Theater," p. 16.

29. The economic mechanism is at heart the one discovered by John Sutton in his study of the concentration of certain food-product markets in the hands of a few sellers. See his *Sunk Costs and Market Structure* (Cambridge, Mass.: MIT Press, 1991).

30. Jack Kroll and Maggie Malone, "Broadway Bonanza," *Newsweek*, June 15, 1998, pp. 64–65.

31. Eben Shapiro, "From the Hinterlands, an Upstart Producer Barrels Up Broadway," *WSJ*, Apr. 28, 1998, pp. A1, A10. In order to provide a predictable stream of shows for its touring operation, Pace developed an alliance with a New York theatre owner and producing organization, Jujamcyn, to set up "housekeeping" arrangements with independent producers in the manner of present-day Hollywood studios. See Rick Lyman, "Two Theatrical Giants Melding Broadway and Road Shows," *NYTNE*, June 9, 1997, pp. A1, A25; Peter Marks, "Broadway's New Corporate Playmakers," *NYTNE*, June 10, 1997, pp. B1, B2.

32. William Grimes, "With 6,138 Lives, *Cats* Sets Broadway Mark," *NYTNE*, June 19, 1997, pp. A1, A32.

33. Robert Frank, "Lloyd-Webber Takes Center Stage at Production House," *WSJ*, June 16, 1997, pp. B1, B5.

34. Livent has employed other strategies for reducing risks, such as developing its productions gradually through workshops and low-profile tryouts that give it the option to abandon a faltering project without having sunk much cost. Livent also concentrated its developmental work in Canada, where costs are lower. John Lahr, "The High Roller," *New Yorker*, June 2, 1997, pp. 70–77.

35. Eben Shapiro, "Ovitz Team Takes Control of Livent from Drabinsky," *WSJ*, Apr. 14, 1998, pp. B1, B4. Livent's troubles illustrate the difficulty of organizing a highly risky activity through a publicly traded corporation. The economic rate of return to the investment in a stage production is never fully known until the last drop of rent has been squeezed from it and a discounted-cash-flow rate of return can be calculated. Judging its profit from current book profits is particularly hazardous, because there is no objective way to allocate the depreciation of the original cost to particular periods of time when the cash flows are being realized. Livent openly employed the procedure of assuming that each show would run for five years, but then charging off any and all remaining costs when a company closed. The former procedure squares poorly with the Broadway theatre's long-run 80 percent flop rate, yet the resulting write-offs still came as an unexpected shock to the investors. See Bruce Weber, "Gambling on a Trip from 'Ragtime' to Riches," *NYTNE*, Feb. 19, 1998, pp. A1, A18; Bruce Weber, "Big Losses to Confront Livent's New Leader," *NYTNE*, June 2, 1998, B1, B4.

36. Poggi, *Theater in America*, chs. 6, 7, especially p. 145.

37. James Heilbrun and Charles M. Gray, *The Economics of Art and Culture: An American Perspective* (Cambridge: Cambridge University Press, 1993), p. 24.

38. Joseph Wesley Zeigler, *Regional Theater: The Revolutionary Stage* (Minneapolis: University of Minnesota Press, 1973).

39. Even the foundation's benevolent effort crossed the directors' *art-for-art's-sake* preferences in some ways. Concerned with the regional theatres' survival, Ford pressed them to converge on a set of policies likely to produce viable organizations. But that conflicted with tastes for local distinctiveness and for complete autonomy in creative choices. See ibid., pp. 184–187.

40. Ibid., especially pp. 175–179.

41. Paul DiMaggio and Kristen Stenberg, "Conformity and Diversity in American Resident Theaters," in Judith H. Balfe and Margaret Jane Wyszomirski, eds., *Art, Ideology, and Politics* (New York: Praeger, 1985), pp. 116–139. A study of British provincial repertory theatres similarly associated the venturesomeness of the plays chosen with the amount of subsidy that the theatre received. See David Austin-Smith, "On the Impact of Revenue Subsidies on Repertory Theatre Policy," *JCE* 4 (June 1980): 9–17.

42. Zeigler, *Regional Theater*, pp. 110–111.

43. For a case study, see Poggi, *Theater in America*, pp. 193–195.

44. Zeigler, *Regional Theater*, ch. 12.

45. William Goldman, *The Season: A Candid Look at Broadway* (New York: Harcourt, Brace, 1969), p. 413.

46. Poggi, *Theater in America*, pp. 193–194.

47. Baumol and Bowen, *Performing Arts*, pp. 121–122.

48. Baumol, "On Two Experiments."

49. Hilda Baumol and William J. Baumol, "On the Finances of Off-Off Broadway

and Other Small Theaters," in Hilda Baumol and William J. Baumol, eds., *Inflation and the Performing Arts* (New York: New York University Press, 1984), pp. 43–55.

50. Opera companies have also proliferated. More than half of Opera America's member companies entered the organization since 1970, more than two-thirds since 1960. James R. Ostreich, "Opera Enjoys Its Charmed Life," *NYTNE*, Apr. 28, 1997, pp. B1, B5.

51. Philip Hart, *Orpheus in the New World: The Symphony Orchestra as an American Cultural Institution* (New York: W. W. Norton, 1973), ch. 6; John Rockwell, "Many Orchestras in Financial Straits," *NYT*, Jan. 19, 1987, p. C11.

52. For an extensive study see Edward Arian, *Bach, Beethoven, and Bureaucracy: The Case of the Philadelphia Orchestra* (University: University of Alabama Press, 1971), ch. 4.

53. At the end of its current contract (2004) the New York Philharmonic's members will receive a minimum of $2,000 a week for a 52-week year. Compensation patterns are similar for the handful of top orchestras. With performing-skill differentials involved, it is hard to reach firm judgment on the point, but the pay rate seems to include substantial rent. See Ralph Blumenthal, "Philharmonic Reaches Pact for 6 Years," *NYTNE*, Dec. 12, 1997, p. A35.

54. Judith H. Dobrzynski, "Orchestras Welcome Corporate Overtures," *NYTNE*, Oct. 16, 1997, pp. B1, B6. A related development in Europe is the proliferation of music festivals that come in the summer holiday period and can fill out musicians' employment. They can be assembled from coalitions of commercial advertisers and local interests that enjoy pecuniary spillovers from the attending tourists. They can differentiate themselves by offering specialized repertory or types of performance, and they may avoid union and governmental restrictions that constrain music performance in the regular season. See Bruno S. Frey, "The Economics of Music Festivals," *JCE* 18, no. 1 (1994): 29–39.

55. Greg Sandow, "Mozart at the Big Muddy: Inner City Symphony," *WSJ*, June 25, 1998, p. A20.

56. Will Crutchfield, "Why Today's Orchestras Are Adrift," *NYT*, Dec. 22, 1985, sec. 2, pp. 1, 24; Hart, *Orpheus*, pp. 184–185.

57. Allan Kozinn, "Strike in Philadelphia: What Stopped the Music," *NYT*, Sept. 17, 1996, pp. C11, C16; Allan Kozinn, "Philadelphia Strike Settled, But Musicians Are Wary," *NYT*, Nov. 20, 1996, pp. C17, C24. When Riccardo Muti was its director, he loyally insisted on making all of his recordings with the Philadelphia Orchestra. With jet-set conductors nowadays serving several orchestras at once, such loyalty cannot normally be expected.

58. Hart, *Orpheus*, ch. 9.

59. Crutchfield, "Why Today's Orchestras Are Adrift," p. 24.

17. Durable Creative Goods

1. John Russell Taylor and Brian Brooke, *The Art Dealers* (New York: Scribner's, 1969), p. 91.

2. Marina Isola, "An Uncertain Market in Video Art," *NYTNE*, Feb. 15, 1998, sec. 2, p. 38.

3. Jennifer Dunning, "How to Tell the Computer from the Dance," *NYTNE*, Feb. 23, 1999, pp. B1, B3.

4. For further discussion and examples, see Joseph Bensman, "The Phenomenology and Sociology of the Performing Arts," in Jack B. Kamerman and Rosanne Martorella, eds., *Performers and Performances: The Social Organization of Artistic Work* (New York: Praeger, 1983), pp. 1–37.

5. Jack Poggi, *Theater in America: The Impact of Economic Forces, 1870–1967* (Ithaca, N.Y.: Cornell University Press, 1968), pp. 270–272.

6. James E. Pesando, "Art as an Investment: The Market for Modern Prints," *American Economic Review* 83 (December 1993): 1075–1089.

7. Michael Lane, *Books and Publishers: Commerce against Culture in Postwar Britain* (Lexington, Mass.: Lexington Books, 1980), p. 30.

8. Brian O'Doherty, *Inside the White Cube: The Ideology of the Gallery Space* (Santa Monica, Calif.: Lapis Press, 1986).

9. Something that increases the potential profitability of creative goods by lowering cost or augmenting demand need not raise realized profits, because it also invites the production of still larger numbers of public goods.

10. Robert H. Stanley, *The Celluloid Empire: A History of the American Movie Industry* (New York: Hastings House, 1978), p. 103.

11. Janet Wasko, *Hollywood in the Information Age: Beyond the Silver Screen* (Austin: University of Texas Press, 1995, pp. 196–209.

12. Anita M. Busch, "Tie-ins Alter 'Jungle' Code," *Variety*, Dec. 2, 1996, pp. 1, 83.

13. Gary Levin, "Series Toy with Merchandising," *Variety*, Aug. 21, 1995, pp. 17–18; Gary Levin, "Merchandising R Us: Studios Play with Toy Biz," *Variety*, Feb. 19, 1996, pp. 5, 27.

14. Carol Diuguid, "Marketeers Armed with License to Sell," *Variety*, June 9, 1997, pp. 9, 14.

15. Anita M. Busch and Gary Levin, "Mouse Marches to Arches," *Variety*, Apr. 15, 1996, pp. 1, 42.

16. Anita M. Busch, "PepsiCo Wins 'Wars,'" *Variety*, May 20, 1996, pp. 5, 12.

17. Gary Levin, "Disney, Mattel Ink Three-Year Deal," *Variety*, Apr. 8, 1996, p. 28.

18. Walter Santagata, "Rights Allocation in the Contemporary Art Market: Copyright, 'Droit de Suite,' 'Right to Exhibit,'" in Alan Peacock and Ilde Rizzo, eds., *Cultural Economics and Cultural Policies* (Dordrecht: Kluwer Academic, 1994), pp. 111–124; Randall K. Filer, "A Theoretical Analysis of the Economic Impact of Artists' Resale Royalties Legislation," *JCE* 8 (June 1984): 1–28.

19. Paula Gillett, *Worlds of Art: Painters in Victorian Society* (New Brunswick, N.J.: Rutgers University Press, 1990), pp. 83–85, 91; Gerald Reitlinger, *The Economics of Taste: The Rise and Fall of Picture Prices, 1760–1960* (London: Barrie and Rockliff, 1961), pp. 86, 98, 148–150.

20. Richard Meryman, *Andrew Wyeth: A Secret Life* (New York: HarperCollins, 1996), chs. 18–21.

21. Summarized in Filer, "Theoretical Analysis."

22. Grace Glueck, "For Artists, a Way to Stop Ripoffs?" *NYT*, Aug. 3, 1977, p. C4.

23. David Colman, "Picassos Reclaim Their Patrimony," *NYT*, Apr. 17, 1996,

pp. 39, 42; Winnie Hu, "Store Wars: When a Mobile Is Not a Calder," *NYTNE,* Aug. 6, 1998, pp. B1, B3.

24. Nobody suggests that artists should compensate collectors for any subsequent capital losses. See Filer, "Theoretical Analysis"; William D. Grampp, *Pricing the Priceless: Art, Artists, and Economics* (New York: Basic Books, 1989), pp. 142–147; also Roger A. McCain, "Artists' Resale Dividends: Some Economic-Theoretic Considerations," *JCE* 13, no. 1 (1989): 35–51, who bases a case for *droit de suite* on the inability of both artist and collector to anticipate future "masterpiece" status at the time of first sale.

25. The film industry was more fully internationalized in the days before "talkies" than after, because the international transfer of silent films required only translated title cards. In the era of sound films, U.S. distributors' foreign revenues fell to around 15 percent of total. Film industries in small countries such as Sweden were extinguished. See Thomas H. Guback, *The International Film Industry: Western Europe and America since 1945* (Bloomington: Indiana University Press, 1969), pp. 3, 8–9.

26. Linda Lee, "U.S. Theme Can Make a Film a Tough Sell Abroad," *NYTNE,* Apr. 26, 1998, p. D10.

27. I am grateful to Professor Hideki Yamawaki for providing this unpublished analysis. See also Leonard Klady, "Foreign B. O. Beckons," *Variety,* Aug. 28, 1995, pp. 1, 79.

28. Cacilie Rohwedder, "Ein Popcorn, Bitte: Hollywood Studios Invade Europe," *WSJ,* Nov. 5, 1997, pp. B1, B11.

29. Steven S. Wildman and Stephen E. Siwek, *International Trade in Films and Television Programs* (Cambridge, Mass.: Ballinger, 1988), ch. 4.

30. Ibid., pp. 14–18.

31. Ibid., pp. 22–24.

32. Martin Dale, *The Movie Game: The Film Business in Britain, Europe, and America* (London: Cassell, 1997), especially ch. 7. Dale also pointed out (ch. 8) that European filmmaking is in the hands of media conglomerates similar to those in the United States, so financing constraints are not a likely source of market failure.

33. One major U.S. trade publisher, Simon & Schuster, reported that 13 percent of its annual revenue came from the export of books. See Mary B. W. Tabor, "Book Deals: Losing Nothing in Translation," *NYT,* Oct. 16, 1995, pp. D1, D8.

34. Herbert R. Lottman, "How American Books Conquered the World," *PW,* July 1997 anniversary issue, pp. 110–114; Martin Arnold, "When Volumes Cross the Sea," *NYTNE,* June 18, 1998, p. B3.

35. Craig R. Whitney, "No Common Market in Book Publishing," *NYT,* March 28, 1989, pp. C15, C19.

36. Tabor, "Book Deals," p. D8; Meg Cox, "Murdoch Puts Global Imprint on Books," *WSJ,* May 4, 1990, pp. B1, B4; Doreen Carvajal, "Book Publishers Seek Global Reach and Grand Scale," *NYTNE,* Oct, 19, 1998, pp. C1, C9.

37. Kristin Thompson, *Exporting Entertainment: America in the World Film Market, 1907–34* (London: British Film Institute, 1985), especially pp. 31–32, 41.

38. Dominic Prid, "The Thorny Issue of the International Royalties," *Billboard,* June 10, 1995, pp. 1, 79–80.

18. Payola

1. On the theory of bribery, see R. H. Coase, "Payola in Radio and Television Broadcasting," *Journal of Law and Economics* 22 (October 1979): 269–328.

2. Sidney Shemel and M. William Krasilovsky, *This Business of Music,* 6th ed. (New York: Billboard Books, 1990), pp. 121–123.

3. For evidence, see Coase, "Payola"; Hazel Meyer, *The Gold in Tin Pan Alley* (Philadelphia: Lippincott, 1958), especially ch. 4; Nicholas E. Tawa, *The Way to Tin Pan Alley: American Popular Song, 1866–1910* (New York: Schirmer Books, 1990), especially ch. 3; and Kerry Segrave, *Payola in the Music Industry: A History, 1880–1991* (Jefferson, N.C.: McFarland, 1994).

4. Marc Eliot, *Rockonomics: The Money behind the Music* (New York: Franklin Watts, 1989), pp. 70–71. Some sources quote much higher promotion costs.

5. In 1933 a successor organization to the MPPA sought to develop a code under the National Recovery Administration that had stopping payola as a main feature.

6. The song publishers also provide an example of a creative good whose sellers' reservation price is negative, so that in equilibrium either buyer might pay seller or seller might pay buyer. The article in question was the "song slide" that publishers produced with lyrics of songs that cinema operators could project for singalongs with the theatre's piano or organ. These were at first given away to support the song plugger's local efforts, but the publishers discovered they could obtain payments of $5 a set (Meyer, *Gold in Tin Pan Alley,* pp. 54–55).

7. John A. Jackson, *American Bandstand: Dick Clark and the Making of a Rock 'n' Roll Empire* (New York: Oxford University Press, 1997). This transaction put Clark for once in the position of being relieved of some rents. His Philadelphia radio station was owned by Triangle Publications, the publisher of *TV Guide.* Clark retained a property right when the show went to ABC, but Clark supplied the show to Triangle for $2,000 a week, and Triangle resold it to ABC for $3,175 while launching a major promotion for it on *TV Guide* (p. 68).

8. The record company (Cameo) gained leverage for signing recording artists who faced competition from covers of their songs. If the group signed with Cameo, Clark would play their version; if not, he would play the cover (ibid., p. 76).

9. Ibid., p. 184.

10. Ibid., pp. 90–91.

11. Ibid., p. 179.

12. Ibid., pp. 87, 96.

13. Ibid., p. 130.

14. Ibid., pp. 118–121, 193. Still other rent-seeking ventures of Clark's shows are described by Robert Stephen Spitz, *The Making of Superstars: Artists and Executives of the Rock Music Business* (Garden City, N.Y.: Anchor Press/Doubleday, 1978), pp. 125, 129.

15. Jackson, *American Bandstand,* p. 150.

16. R. Serge Denisoff, *Solid Gold: The Popular Record Industry* (New Brunswick, N.J.: Transaction Books, 1975), p. 231; Steve Chapple and Reebee Garofalo, *Rock 'n' Roll Is Here to Pay: The History and Politics of the Music Industry* (Chicago: Nelson-Hall, 1977), pp. 45, 60–62.

17. Ibid., pp. 216–223, 267, 271–272.
18. Segrave presented mixed evidence on the respective interests in payola of performers and managers in the days of vaudeville and song pluggers as well as the radio era. Vaudeville managers resisted the degrading of song selection due to payola (*Payola*, pp. 13, 16–17, 32), but there was evidence of performers' fees being lowered to offset access to payola (pp. 35, 48, 86, 102) and managers seeking to channel enhanced payola into advertising revenue (pp. 83, 92, 93).
19. Denisoff, *Solid Gold*, pp. 256–257.
20. Quoted by Simon Frith, *Sound Effects: Youth, Leisure, and the Politics of Rock* (London: Constable, 1983), p. 119.
21. Ibid., pp. 119–120; Eliot, *Rockonomics*, pp. 86–87. Eliot noted the paradox that Dick Clark and others survived the payola scandals to promote a style shift in R&B toward a sanitized version suited to white audiences (pp. 87, 96–97).
22. Also at hazard were the licenses of the radio stations belonging to the major record companies, which might have been forfeited if payola were traced back to the labels. See William Knoedelseder, *Stiffed: A True Story of MCA, the Music Business, and the Mafia* (New York: HarperCollins, 1993), pp. 191–192.
23. These developments were reported in ibid., ch. 23, and by Fredric Dannen, *Hit Men: Power Brokers and Fast Money inside the Music Business* (New York: Vintage Books, 1991).
24. Knoedelseder, *Stiffed*, pp. 179–185.
25. Dannen, *Hit Men*, pp. 7–17.
26. Ibid., pp. 207–215.
27. Michael Cieply, "A Few Promoters Dominate Record Business," *WSJ*, Apr. 18, 1986, p. 6. Paradoxically, information that surfaced in subsequent racketeering prosecutions suggests that the independent promoters indeed depended on carrot rather than stick; they simply paid large bribes to radio station personnel. See Larry Rohter, "At Payola Trial, Primer on Forms and Mechanics," *NYT*, Aug. 25, 1990, p. 11.
28. Knoedelseder, *Stiffed*, pp. 188–190.
29. Patrick M. Reilly, "Radio's New Spin on an Oldie: Pay-for-Play," *WSJ*, Mar. 16, 1998, pp. B1, B8; Neil Strauss, "Pay-for-Play Back on the Air But This Rendition Is Legal," *NYTNE*, Mar. 31, 1998, pp. A1, A21.
30. Denisoff, *Solid Gold*, ch. 6; Geoffrey Stokes, *Star-Making Machinery: Inside the Business of Rock and Roll* (New York: Vintage books, 1976), pp. 167, 209–210.
31. Eben Shapiro, "On MTV, There Aren't Many Free Plugs," *WSJ*, May 29, 1998, pp. B1, B8.
32. Stokes, *Star-Making Machinery*, p. 200.
33. Neil Strauss, "Concert Rivals to Run Irving Plaza," *NYTNE*, Nov. 24, 1997, p. B3.
34. Mark Litwak, *Dealmaking in the Film and Television Industry: From Negotiations to Final Contracts* (Los Angeles: Silman-James, 1994), p. 27.
35. A reviewer of the James Bond film *Tomorrow Never Dies* called it a "dramatized trade show," with whole sequences constructed for the camera to linger on conspicuously identified merchandise.

36. Litwak, *Dealmaking,* pp. 26–28; Janet Wasko, *Hollywood in the Information Age: Beyond the Silver Screen* (Austin: University of Texas Press, 1995), pp. 188–193.

37. Stuart Elliott, "The Spot on the Cutting-Room Floor," *NYT,* Feb. 7, 1997, pp. D1, D2.

38. Mary B. W. Tabor, "In Bookstore Chains, Display Space Is for Sale," *NYT,* Jan. 15, 1996, pp. A1, D8.

39. Doreen Carvajal, "For Sale: On-Line Bookstore's Recommendations," *NYTNE,* Feb. 8, 1999, pp. A1, A21; George Anders, "Amazon.com Reverses Course on Fee Decision," *WSJ,* Feb. 10, 1999, p. B8.

40. Greg Shaffer, "Capturing Strategic Rent: Full-Line Forcing, Brand Discounts, Aggregate Rebates, and Maximum Resale Price Maintenance," *Journal of Industrial Economics* 39 (September 1991): 557–575.

19. Organizing to Collect Rents

1. Sidney Shemel and M. William Krasilovsky, *This Business of Music,* 6th ed. (New York: Billboard Books, 1990), pp. 179–183.

2. The agency undertakes audits of company records at a cost of $10,000 to $20,000 each, too costly for most individual publishers; its transaction costs are 4.5 to 5.5 percent of its revenues. See Donald S. Passman, *All You Need to Know about the Music Business* (New York: Simon & Schuster, 1994), p. 222.

3. Industry data sources quoted in *BMG Music Publishing,* Harvard Business School, Case N9-797-002 (1997), exhibit 3.

4. Passman, *All You Need to Know,* p. 213.

5. That is, she must devise licensing terms that will cause her licensees to select the price that maximizes joint monopoly profits and then to remit those profits to her (minus the pittance needed to keep them in the game). Britain chose a policy giving the songwriter more control. See Alan Peacock and Ronald Weir, *The Composer in the Market Place* (London: Faber Music, 1975), pp. 50–51. Their book provides interesting comparisons to many U.S. patterns discussed in this chapter.

6. John A. Jackson, *American Bandstand: Dick Clark and the Making of a Rock 'n' Roll Empire* (New York: Oxford University Press, 1997), p. 87.

7. George Seltzer, *Music Matters: The Performer and the American Federation of Musicians* (Metuchen, N.J.: Scarecrow Press, 1989), especially pp. 31–32, 41–45, 57–66, 79–80, 91.

8. Jeffrey Brabec and Todd Brabec, *Music, Money, and Success: The Insider's Guide to the Music Industry* (New York: Schirmer Books, 1994), pp. 176–178. On p. 196 they quote one example of a synchronization license that yielded a $25,000 fee but over $1 million in other royalties from radio and TV performance royalties, mechanical royalties, and sheet-music royalties both in the United States and abroad.

9. Ibid., pp. 151, 153, 219.

10. Ibid., p. 228.

11. A breakdown is available of royalties received over twelve recent years on "Heartbreak Hotel," a song introduced by Elvis Presley in 1956. Mechanical royalties accounted for 41 percent of revenues, synchronization royalties for 27 percent,

performance royalties 19 percent, non-U.S. royalties (all types) 11 percent, and sheet-music royalties 2 percent. Kris Goodfellow, "One Inspiration, Years of Pay-off," *NYT,* June 24, 1996, p. D7. On the marketing of grand rights, see Lisa Gubernick, "Coming to a Theater Near You," *WSJ,* June 5, 1998, pp. W1, W5.

12. "Rts. Issue in *Gershwin* Suit vs. 'Let's Call,'" *Variety,* Mar. 12, 1980, pp. 1, 108.

13. Principal sources of information are John Ryan, *The Production of Culture in the Music Industry: The ASCAP–BMI Controversy* (Lanham, Md.: University Press of America, 1985), and Russell Sanjek and David Sanjek, *American Popular Music Business in the 20th Century* (New York: Oxford University Press, 1991). The latter book is a condensation of Russell Sanjek, updated by David Sanjek, *Pennies from Heaven: The American Popular Music Business in the Twentieth Century* (New York: Da Capo Press, 1996), which contains additional information on some points.

14. According to Kerry Segrave, as late as 1930 the radio industry was still receiving more in payola than it was paying in performance royalties. See Segrave, *Payola in the Music Industry: A History, 1880–1991* (Jefferson, N.C.: McFarland, 1994), p. 37.

15. Ryan, *Production of Culture,* pp. 27–29, 36.

16. The economic theory of natural monopolies makes much of another exception: scale economies might be substantial but exhausted short of ASCAP's actual scale of operation. That scale economies are exhausted in ASCAP's functions seems quite unlikely.

17. Ryan, *Production of Culture,* ch. 4.

18. Ibid., pp. 16–24.

19. Sanjek and Sanjek, *American Popular Music,* pp. 8, 10, 19.

20. Ibid., pp. 35, 38.

21. Ryan, *Production of Culture,* pp. 24–26.

22. Ibid., pp. 31–36.

23. Ibid., pp. 40–43.

24. ASCAP, when first bringing radio stations under license, made it strategically inconvenient for stations to ascertain what songs were and were not under ASCAP control; the station's knowledge that the number is "large" but hard to pin down would deter resistance to taking an ASCAP license (ibid., p. 38).

25. Paradoxically, computerized handling of such complex schedules is probably feasible nowadays, long after the issue was litigated. For further treatment of the economics of copyright collectives, see Stanley M. Besen and Sheila Nataraj Kirby, *Compensating Creators of Intellectual Property: Collectives That Collect,* report R–3751–MF (Santa Monica, Calif.: RAND Corporation, 1989).

26. Ryan, *Production of Culture,* p. 37; Sanjek and Sanjek, *American Popular Music,* pp. 18, 26–29, 191.

27. At the outset, ASCAP's licenses to broadcasters based payments on the hours of ASCAP music broadcast (Ryan, *Production of Culture,* p. 37).

28. Present-day procedures were described by Shemel and Krasilovsky, *This Business* pp. 200–201.

29. For current practice, see ibid., pp. 206–210.

30. Ryan, *Production of Culture,* pp. 79–81; Sanjek and Sanjek, *American Popular Music,* pp. 67, 72, 74.

31. On ASCAP's tactics see Hazel Meyer, *The Gold in Tin Pan Alley* (Philadelphia: Lippincott, 1958), pp. 89–99.

32. Ryan, *Production of Culture,* pp. 83–85; Sanjek and Sanjek, *American Popular Music,* pp. 63–64, 92.

33. Ryan, *Production of Culture,* pp. 56–75.

34. Ibid., pp. 53–54.

35. Advertisers did observe a small reduction in seasonally adjusted listenership ratings, while the music publishers' sheet-music sales were down 60 percent (Ryan, *Production of Culture,* p. 89).

36. Ibid., pp. 87–93.

37. Ibid., pp. 93–99; Sanjek and Sanjek, *American Popular Music,* p. 97; Besen and Kirby, *Compensating Creators;* and Paul C. Weiler, *Entertainment, Media, and the Law: Text, Cases, Problems* (St. Paul, Minn: West, 1997), pp. 810–811, 830–832.

38. Ryan, *Production of Culture,* ch. 6.

39. See Sanjek and Sanjek, *American Popular Music,* pp. 199–200, 202, 226–228, 242.

40. Weiler, *Entertainment, Media, and the Law,* pp. 811–830.

41. See Sanjek and Sanjek, *American Popular Music,* pp. 199, 202, and 226 for examples.

42. Ibid., pp. 201, 225–226. In 1997 a complaint was festering from jingle writers, whose airplay time is considerably discounted for purposes of determining their royalty receipts. See Ralph Blumenthal, "King of the Jingle Hunts Royalties," *NYTNE,* Apr. 29, 1997, pp. B1, B2.

43. In 1996 ASCAP distributed to members 84 percent of the revenue that it received. See Blumenthal, "King of the Jingle," p. B2.

44. Also relevant to this welfare calculation is the fact that a cooperative organization with open membership is a self-extinguishing monopoly. Suppose that ASCAP starts with an arbitrary number of members and succeeds in extracting monopoly profits from licensees. The generous flow of performance royalties to the writers attracts more songwriters—and songs. The licensees can find themselves paying the same price, but with more songs to choose from, while the average songwriter earns less. See Stanley M. Besen, Sheila N. Kirby, and Steven C. Salop, "An Economic Analysis of Copyright Collectives," *Virginia Law Review* 78 (February 1992): 383–411. Britain's Performing Rights Society at one time tried to raise its performance royalties, to compensate its old members for the dilution resulting from new members (Peacock and Weir, *Composer in the Market Place,* pp. 77–80).

45. Dan Carney, "Odd Battle over Song Royalties," *NYT,* July 15, 1996, p. D4.

46. Lisa Bannon, "The Birds May Sing, But Campers Can't Unless They Pay Up," *WSJ,* Aug. 21, 1996, pp. A1, A8; Elisabeth Bumiller, "Battle Hymns around Campfires," *NYT,* Dec. 17, 1996, pp. B1, B5.

47. Meyer, *Gold in Tin Pan Alley,* pp. 87–88.

48. George Tremlett, *Rock Gold: The Music Millionaires* (London: Unwin Hyman, 1990), pp. 18, 76–77.

49. Simon Frith, *Sound Effects: Youth, Leisure, and the Politics of Rock* (London: Constable, 1983), pp. 140–141.
50. Sanjek and Sanjek, *American Popular Music*, p. 213.
51. Shemel and Krasilovsky, *This Business*, pp. 197–198.
52. Passman, *All You Need to Know*, pp. 224–226. On pp. 264–265, Passman advises artists to try to retain the publishing function, or at least hold the record company's publisher to only mechanical royalties on the artist's songs.
53. Shemel and Krasilovsky, *This Business*, pp. 305–316.
54. *BMG Music Publishing*, p. 6.
55. Marc Eliot, *Rockonomics: The Money behind the Music* (New York: Franklin Watts, 1989), p. 20.
56. Johnnie L. Roberts, "'How Sweet It Is . . .,'" *BW*, Jan. 26, 1998, p. 70; *BMG Music Publishing*, p. 6.
57. Before musical compositions enjoyed the copyright privilege, the composer often would publish simultaneously in each major musical city, leaving the pirate with too small a market to cover his fixed costs. See Reginald Nuttel, *The Orchestra in England: A Social History*, rev. ed. (London: Jonathan Cape, 1956), pp. 102–103.
58. Donald Sheehan, *This Was Publishing: A Chronicle of the Book Trade in the Gilded Age* (Bloomington: Indiana University Press, 1952), p. 61; Allan C. Dooley, *Author and Printer in Victorian England* (Charlottesville: University of Virginia Press, 1992), pp. 50–52, 98.
59. Sheehan, *This Was Publishing*, pp. 64–66, 71.
60. Peter L. Shillingsburg, *Pegasus in Harness: Victorian Publishing and W. M. Thackeray* (Charlottesville: University of Virginia Press, 1992), pp. 123–145.
61. Wendy Griswold, "American Character and the American Novel: An Expansion of Reflection Theory in the Sociology of Literature," *American Journal of Sociology* 86 (January 1981): 740–765.

20. Entertainment Conglomerates and the Quest for Rents

1. The term "conglomerate," sometimes a pejorative, is here used solely as a label.
2. Judith Adler, *Artists in Offices: An Ethnography of an Academic Art Scene* (New Brunswick, N.J.: Transaction Books, 1979).
3. Thomas Whiteside, *The Blockbuster Complex: Conglomerates, Show Business, and Book Publishing* (Middletown, Conn.: Wesleyan University Press, 1981), pp. 90, 145, 148.
4. Patrick M. Reilly, "At PolyGram, Imperfect Harmony," *WSJ*, May 18, 1998, pp. B1, B6.
5. Steven Bach, *Final Cut: Dreams and Disaster in the Making of "Heaven's Gate"* (New York: William Morrow, 1985), pp. 53–60.
6. David McClintock, *Indecent Exposure: A True Story of Hollywood and Wall Street* (New York: William Morrow, 1982).
7. Clive Davis with James Willwerth, *Clive: Inside the Record Business* (New York: William Morrow, 1975), pp. 50–58, 110–111, 152–153.

8. Jake Eberts and Terry Ilott, *My Indecision Is Final: The Spectacular Rise and Fall of Goldcrest Films* (New York: Atlantic Monthly Press, 1990), especially p. 395.

9. Nancy Griffin and Kim Masters, *Hit and Run: How Jon Peters and Peter Guber Took Sony for a Ride in Hollywood* (New York: Simon & Schuster, 1996), p. 207.

10. Jason E. Squire, ed., *The Movie Business Book,* 2d ed. (New York: Simon & Schuster, 1992), pp. 184–185.

11. Walter W. Powell, "From Craft to Corporation: The Impact of Outside Ownership on Book Publishing," in James S. Ettema and D. Charles Whitney, eds., *Individuals in Mass Media Organizations: Creativity and Constraint* (Beverly Hills, Calif.: Sage, 1982), p. 40.

12. Griffin and Masters, *Hit and Run,* especially pp. 276–277, 284, 424–427, 429.

13. Fredric Dannen, *Hit Men: Power Brokers and Fast Money inside the Music Business* (New York: Vintage Books, 1991), ch. 9. Conspicuous managerial consumption was also evident. Everybody got a Mercedes convertible, and "at 3 o'clock in the afternoon, an adorable little girl would come up and take your order for the following day's drug supply" (p. 170).

14. Passing economic judgment on the ex post consequences of a change in corporate control requires a great deal of caution. For example, when firm A purchases business unit B and then subsequently sells it off, that does not prove that the initial purchase was a mistake. A might have injected some asset into B that increases the unit's value, or extracted some asset from B that is more valuable to itself. Or A's purchase may represent an astute speculation—that of buying B at a time when the market's valuation of B is about to rise.

15. Subsidiary rights income was once conventionally divided 50–50 between author and publisher, but the publisher's share was competed away in the 1980s. Edwin McDowell, "Doubleday's Decline: What Went Awry?" *NYT,* Oct. 2, 1986, p. C17.

16. Other rent-gaining assets such as star actors may also come aboard, but they must be paid their expected rents, too.

17. On integrated Disney's problems with independent filmmakers, see Joe Flint, "Disney Disses 'Home' Rule," *Variety,* Mar. 3, 1997, pp. 1, 84.

18. True, the author likely needs an established reputation for blockbusters in order to manage this process. For a novice the trade publisher will hold out for a slice of subsidiary-rights income, because its selection and promotion of the work's first incarnation will contribute to its value in subsidiary uses. Whether a conglomerate-owned publisher might have an advantage will be addressed subsequently.

19. This argument has a possible weak spot. Why can the independent film studio not hire advice on a consulting basis from independent experts in the subsidiary markets? That strategy might work, but markets for vaguely defined information (distinguished from a copyrighted novel manuscript or film treatment) are prone to fail in various ways.

20. For descriptions of such auctions, see Whiteside, *Blockbuster Complex,* pp. 155–183, and Trip Gabriel, "Call My Agent," *New York Times Magazine,* Feb. 19, 1989, p. 45–59.

21. O. H. Cheney, *Economic Survey of the Book Industry, 1930–1931: Final Report*

(New York: National Association of Book Publishers, 1931). Cheney did find some evidence that authors switching publishers got better terms, (p. 149), but discovered that publishing houses generally did not compete on terms, and few authors switched publishers (pp. 148, 158).

22. Whiteside, *Blockbuster Complex,* pp. 92–93, 149.
23. Ibid., pp. 82–83.
24. For example, ibid., p. 189.
25. Publishers Weekly, *The Business of Publishing: A PW Anthology* (New York: Bowker, 1976), pp. 210–213.
26. Martin Arnold, "Nervous Twitch in the Wallet," *NYTNE,* July 2, 1998, p. B3.
27. Recall the qualification stated in note 14, this chapter.
28. Powell, "From Craft to Corporation," p. 37.
29. Doreen Carvajal, "Book Publishers Seek Global Reach and Grand Scale," *NYTNE,* Oct. 19, 1998, pp. C1, C7.
30. Illustrations of negative goodwill effects are not hard to find. Time Warner retreated in mortification from its ownership of Interscope Records when the lyrics of the firm's gangsta rap records became controversial. Coca-Cola gave up its ownership of Columbia Pictures partly from concern that envelope-pushing behavior condoned in Hollywood might repel the mainstream customers it sought (Griffin and Masters, *Hit and Run,* p. 210).
31. Whiteside, *Blockbuster Complex,* pp. 70–74 (and pp. 76–79 for an example of such a deal that was not fully internalized within one firm); also Richard Slater, *Ovitz: The Inside Story of Hollywood's Most Controversial Power Broker* (New York: McGraw-Hill, 1997), for example, pp. 66–68, 169.
32. Bernard Weinraub, "A Match Made in Hollywood: The Marriage of Razzle and Dazzle," *NYTNE,* July 9, 1998, p. D4; Martin Arnold, "Does Synergy Really Work?" *NYTNE,* July 16, 1998, p. B3.
33. Walter W. Powell, *Getting into Print: The Decision-Making Process in Scholarly Publishing* (Chicago: University of Chicago Press, 1985), pp. 93–103; Everett M. Rogers and Judith K. Larsen, *Silicon Valley Fever: Growth of High-Tech Culture* (New York: Basic Books, 1984).
34. That is, the gatekeeper benefits from a reliably large supply of creative inputs, while the creative inputs starve for lack of an open gate.
35. This argument was anticipated in Paul Hirsch's pioneering *The Structure of the Popular Music Industry* (Ann Arbor: Institute for Social Research, University of Michigan, 1969).
36. A common advantage of vertical integration in differentiated or monopolized sectors is avoiding "double marginalization"—when independent, successive monopolies mark up their selling prices over already swollen input costs. The creative industries price some transactions so that they avoid this problem, but not all.
37. Barry R. Litman, *The Motion Picture Mega-Industry* (Needham Heights, Mass.: Allyn and Bacon, 1998), pp. 80–81.
38. Ibid., pp. 28–30.
39. The victim was Sony's Betamax standard for videocassettes, which was technically superior to rival VHS but lost out due to Sony's inability to make more film titles

available. Sony's acquisition of CBS Records was a way to secure a library of audio material in reserve for when digital audio tape and players appeared. See Dannen, *Hit Men,* pp. 309–310.

40. On Disney's acquisition of ABC, see "Michael Eisner Defends the Kingdom," *BW,* Aug. 4, 1997, pp. 73–75; on Turner Broadcasting's sale to Time Warner and Warner's decision to launch a broadcast TV network, see Eben Shapiro, "Brash as Ever, Turner Is Giving Time Warner Dose of Culture Shock," *WSJ,* Mar. 24, 1997, pp. A1, A10.

41. The capacity limits of cable channels provide a recent example. Leslie Cauley, "Scripps Quickly Proves an Outsider Can Start a Cable-TV Network," *WSJ,* Nov. 13, 1998, pp. A1, A9. For a statistical study of self-supply between premium cable networks and operators, see David Waterman and Andrew A. Weiss, "The Effects of Vertical Integration between Cable Television Systems and Pay Cable Networks," *Journal of Econometrics* 72 (May 1996): 357–395.

42. Litman, *Motion Picture Mega-Industry,* 101–104; Thomas Guback, "The Evolution of the Motion Picture Theater Business in the 1980s," *Journal of Communication* 37 (Spring 1987): 60–77.

43. Litman, *Motion Picture Mega-Industry,* pp. 106–118.

44. Bruce Orwall and Kyle Pope, "Disney, ABC Promised 'Synergy' in Merger; So, What Happened?" *WSJ,* May 16, 1997, pp. A1, A9.

45. Griffin and Masters, *Hit and Run,* pp. 306, 330.

46. Shapiro, "Brash as Ever," pp. A1, A10.

47. One synergy that is vigorously asserted but hard to test is that diversifying mergers enlarge the enterprise and spread the risks of individual large projects that it might undertake. Economists are chronically skeptical about how the firm can create value for its owners by behaving in risk-averse fashion, when the owners themselves can easily diversify their financial portfolios and spread risks. Diversification moves to spread risks or fill out a portfolio can be directly unprofitable when the investment does not perform well; see Bruce Orwall, "Walt Disney Reorganizes Its Music Unit, Naming Robert Cavallo as the Chairman," *NYTNE,* Jan. 12, 1998, p. B8. Or they may distract managerial resources from the effective operation of existing businesses; see Eben Shapiro and John Lippman, "Film Flops, Dated Tunes Bedevil Warner Co-Chairmen," *WSJ,* Dec. 4, 1997, pp. B1, B10.

48. Litman, *Motion Picture Mega-Industry,* pp. 125, 127, 132–133.

49. Geraldine Fabrikant, "Time Warner Is Licensing Twelve Films to Its Cable Outlets," *NYT,* Jan. 16, 1997, p. D10.

21. Filtering and Storing Durable Creative Goods

1. James Corcoran, "Dealing from Los Angeles," in Lee Evan Caplin, ed., *The Business of Art* (Englewood Cliffs, N.J.: Prentice-Hall, 1982), p. 274. For statistical evidence that contemporary art is riskier than older art, see Leslie Singer and Gary Lynch, "Public Choice in Tertiary Art Markets," *JCE* 18, no. 3 (1994): 199–216.

2. William J. Baumol, "Unnatural Value, or Art Investment as a Floating Crap

Game," *American Economic Review* 76 (May 1986): 10–14, and references cited therein.

3. William N. Goetzmann, "Accounting for Taste: Art and the Financial Markets over Three Centuries," *American Economic Review* 83 (December 1993): 1370–1376.

4. For parallel conclusions drawn from a shorter time period but with more price observations, see James E. Pesando, "Art as an Investment: The Market for Modern Prints," *American Economic Review* 83 (December 1993): 1075–1089.

5. For example, Aline B. Saarinen, *The Proud Possessors: The Lives, Times, and Tastes of Some Adventurous American Art Collectors* (New York: Random House, 1958); Frank Herrmann, *The English as Collectors: A Documentary Chrestomathy* (London: Chatto & Windus, 1972); John Walker, *Self-Portrait with Donors: Confessions of an Art Collector* (Boston: Atlantic–Little, Brown, 1974); Francis Haskell, *Rediscoveries in Art: Some Aspects of Taste, Fashion, and Collecting in England and France* (Ithaca, N.Y.: Cornell University Press, 1980); Joseph Alsop, *The Rare Art Tradition: The History of Art Collecting and Its Linked Phenomena Wherever These Have Appeared* (London: Thames and Hudson, 1982).

6. See Walker, *Self-Portrait with Donors*, ch. 10, on Armand Hammer. Art-world opinion marked Charles Saatchi as a collector evolved to dealer—one who showed artists in his private museum, supported the shows with sophisticated publications, then reaped capital gains from the enhanced reputations. See Barbaralee Diamonstein, *Inside the Art World: Conversations with Barbaralee Diamonstein* (New York: Rizzoli, 1994), p. 82. In countries with less stable political-economic conditions, art collecting may serve the economic motives of hedging against inflation and converting wealth into a portable form. See Nicholas Faith, *Sold: The Revolution in the Art Market* (London: Hamish Hamilton, 1985), pp. 74, 80–81.

7. Saarinen, *Proud Possessors*, p. xx.

8. Malcolm Gee, *Dealers, Critics, and Collectors of Modern Painting: Aspects of the Parisian Art Market between 1910 and 1930* (New York: Garland, 1981), pp. 180–182, 208–209.

9. See evidence cited in Chapter 2 and Alice Goldfarb Marquis, *The Art Biz: The Covert World of Collectors, Dealers, Auction Houses, Museums, and Critics* (Chicago: Contemporary, 1991), pp. 186, 192–193.

10. Stuart Plattner, *High Art Down Home: An Economic Ethnography of a Local Art Market* (Chicago: University of Chicago Press, 1996), ch. 6.

11. Werner Muensterberger, *Collecting, an Unruly Passion: Psychological Perspectives* (Princeton, N.J.: Princeton University Press, 1994), especially ch. 11. He also linked the appeal of a collection's controlled and dominated universe to traumas, insecurities, and childhood sorrows whose residues of self-doubt and unassimilated memories could be screened off by involvement in collecting (p. 13).

12. See Hilton Als, "Wagstaff's Eye," *New Yorker,* Jan. 13, 1997, pp. 36–43; Alsop, *Rare Art Tradition*, ch. 5; Herrmann, *English as Collectors*, pp. 15–16.

13. A vivid example surfaced as Sotheby's representatives assembled the copious collections of the late artist Andy Warhol for auction. They could find no jewelry, although they knew Warhol had bought a great deal. Finally, they discovered what

turned out to be $3 million worth that had been tossed up onto the top of a canopy bed. See Robert Woolley, *Going Once: A Memoir of Art, Society, and Charity* (New York: Simon & Schuster, 1995), pp. 163, 165.

14. Saarinen, *Proud Possessors*, pp. 19, 219–220, 241.

15. Walker, *Self-Portrait with Donors*, especially pp. 258, 261, 268.

16. Berenson's disinterestedness, however, was in question. See Colin Simpson, *The Partnership: The Secret Association of Bernard Berenson and Joseph Duveen* (London: Bodley Head, 1987).

17. See Walker, *Self-Portrait with Donors*, on the Kress (pp. 134–140) and Mellon collections (p. 104); Saarinen, *Proud Possessors*, on Joseph H. Hirshhorn.

18. Geraldine Keen, *Money and Art: A Study Based on the Times-Sotheby Index* (New York: Putnam, 1971), pp. 220–221, 229; Gee, *Dealers, Critics, and Collectors*, pp. 208–209, on French collectors.

19. Rosanne Martorella, *Corporate Art* (New Brunswick, N.J.: Rutgers University Press, 1990), pp. 14, 22, 53–54.

20. Ibid., p. 29.

21. Ibid., pp. 63–64.

22. Lee Rosenbaum, "Downsizing Corporate Art Collections," *WSJ*, May 23, 1995, p. A20.

23. In Martorella's survey (*Corporate Art*, p. 72), representational art accounted for 45.9 percent, abstract (color-field and post-painterly abstraction) for 20.7 percent, and traditional figurative art for 14.4 percent.

24. Ibid., p. 65.

25. Ibid., pp. 32, 36–39.

26. Correspondingly, lower-profile auction houses in New York (Doyle) and London (Bonhams) recently formed an alliance to permit auctioning particular lots or collections at the more advantageous place. Carol Vogel, "Inside Art: Auction Houses Align" *NYTNE*, Jan. 9, 1998, p. B34.

27. Christie's and Sotheby's are profit-seeking firms that have been at various times closely held and publicly traded. Some of the European auction houses (Drouot in Paris, Dorotheum in Vienna) are government-controlled.

28. Principal studies of these firms' histories include Frank Herrmann, *Sotheby's: Portrait of an Auction House* (London: Chatto & Windus, 1980); Nicholas Faith, *Sold: The Revolution in the Art Market* (London: Hamish Hamilton, 1985); and John Herbert, *Inside Christie's* (London: Hodder & Stoughton, 1990).

29. Parke-Bernet's local monopoly emerged from a series of predecessor firms, with one successively displacing another in a manner consistent with a natural-monopoly market. See Wesley Towner, *The Elegant Auctioneers* (New York: Hill & Wang, 1970).

30. Herrmann, *Sotheby's*, pp. 349, 376–377, 384, 387, 389.

31. Ibid., ch. 34, especially pp. 387, 393, 395; Herbert, *Inside Christie's*, pp. 84–85.

32. Herrmann, *Sotheby's*, pp. 398, 402.

33. Ibid., pp. 425–426.

34. In the 1960s and 1970s, 20 percent of Sotheby's business was with individual collectors, 80 percent with dealers. By the 1990s these proportions had shifted to 70 and 30 percent. See Woolley, *Going Once*, pp. 54–55.

35. "Going, Going . . . Gone to New York?" *Economist,* Oct. 17, 1981, pp. 90–91.

36. Peter Watson, *From Manet to Manhattan: The Rise of the Modern Art Market* (New York: Random House, 1992), pp. 362–363.

37. Alexandra Peers, "Market for Art Is Strongest in Seven Years," *WSJ,* Nov. 21, 1997, pp. C1, C27.

38. Carol Vogel, "Over the Top in an Auction Catalogue," *NYT,* Mar. 6, 1996, pp. C11, C14.

39. Alexandra Peers, "Christie's Bids for Art-World Dominance as It Sets to Raise Gavel on Ganz Sale," *WSJ,* Nov. 10, 1997, p. B16A.

40. Bias in auction estimates is a recurrent issue. If buyers believe estimates to be unbiased market values, the auctioneer has an incentive to inflate them and thereby raise hammer prices and commissions. Consigners, believing in estimates' signal value, shop for high estimates. One statistical test reported that hammer prices actually exceed the mean of high and low estimates, but that leaves out the unsold lots for which the mean estimate necessarily exceeded buyers' top reservation price. See M. A. Louargand and J. R. McDaniel, "Price Efficiency in the Art Auction Market," *JCE* 15 (December 1991): 53–65.

41. Ann E. Berman, "The Auctions: Guarantees, Yes; Sure Things, No," *WSJ,* Nov. 25, 1997, p. A20.

42. Carol Vogel, "At the Wire, Auction Fans, It's, It's . . . Christie's!" *NYT,* Feb. 11, 1997, pp. C11, C18; Wooley, *Going Once,* pp. 54–55.

43. Rita Reif, "Christie's Reverses Stand on Price Guarantees," *NYT,* Mar. 12, 1990, pp. C13, C16.

44. Andrew Decker, "Big Art Buyers Avoid the Auction Room," *WSJ,* Sept. 11, 1998, p. W10.

45. See Raymonde Moulin, *The French Art Market: A Sociological View,* trans. Arthur Goldhammer (New Brunswick, N.J.: Rutgers University Press, 1987), pp. 38–44, on the Paris art market.

46. John Russell Taylor and Brian Brooke, *The Art Dealers* (New York: Scribner's, 1969), p. 43.

47. This property has shown itself on occasions when collectors relying on Old Master dealers have died suddenly, exposing their recent purchases to much lower estate valuations based on auction prices. Joseph Duveen occasionally bought up such collections or took other measures to keep the valuation discrepancy concealed. See Watson, *From Manet to Manhattan,* pp. 220–224; Simpson, *Partnership,* pp. 182–186; Moulin, *French Art Market,* pp. 41–44.

48. Joseph Duveen's maneuvers, including his clandestine association with the leading certifier Bernard Berenson (see Chapter 12), were chronicled by Simpson in *Partnership.*

49. Germain Seligman, *Merchants of Art: 1880–1960* (New York: Appleton-Century-Crofts, 1961), pp. 19–21. The history of Seligmann's galleries documents the large scales of outlay on opulent premises and costly public shows as investments in credence and reputation assets (especially pp. 30–35, 181–182).

50. A similar ecology of secondary dealers in the London antiques trade was documented by Jeremy Cooper, *Dealing with Dealers: The Ins and Outs of the London Antiques Trade* (London: Thames and Hudson, 1985).

51. Ray Jackson, "A Museum Cost Function," *JCE* 12 (June 1988): 41–50. Jackson found that the unit cost declines with museum attendance for small museums, but claimed that it increases for museums with more than 100,000 annual attendance. This increase is almost surely due to "quality" differences—the higher-value works and more opulent presentations being found in the largest museums—and not to technical diminishing returns. Jackson's own results show this, in that compensation per employee increases significantly with museum size (total cost).

52. Nathaniel Burt, *Palaces for the People: A Social History of the American Art Museum* (Boston: Little, Brown, 1977); Karl E. Meyer, *The Art Museum: Power, Money, Ethics* (New York: William Morrow, 1979); Calvin Tomkins, *Merchants and Masterpieces: The Story of the Metropolitan Museum of Art*, rev. ed. (New York: Henry Holt, 1989). On the diffusion of museums from city to city, see Joshua C. Taylor, "The Art Museum in the United States," in Sherman E. Lee, ed., *On Understanding Art Museums* (Englewood Cliffs, N.J.: Prentice-Hall, 1975), pp. 34–67.

53. See Walker, *Self-Portrait with Donors*, on the National Gallery; on the Museum of Modern Art, consult Russell Lynes, *Good Old Modern: An Intimate Portrait of The Museum of Modern Art* (New York: Atheneum, 1973).

54. Edward P. Alexander, *Museum Masters: Their Museums and Their Influence* (Nashville, Tenn.: American Association for State and Local History, 1983). Although the founding of European government-supported museums shows a good deal of entrepreneurial effort, their innovative record as ongoing institutions strikes many observers as inferior to that of donor-supported NPOs, which are freer to experiment with the scope and financing of their operations. See Daniel M. Fox, *Engines of Culture: Philanthropy and Art Museums* (New Brunswick, N.J.: Transaction Books, 1995), pp. 50–51.

55. A central theme in Tomkins's history of the Metropolitan Museum *(Merchants and Masterpieces)* is its continuing effort to upgrade the standards of the material that it acquired.

56. Philip Fisher, *Making and Effacing Art: Modern American Art in a Culture of Museums* (New York: Oxford University Press, 1991).

57. See Meyer, *Art Museum*, especially pp. 36–44.

58. Stephen E. Weil, *Beauty and the Beasts: On Museums, Art, the Law, and the Market* (Washington: Smithsonian Institution Press, 1983), especially pp. xiv, 6, 11, 30–55.

59. A conspicuous example was Thomas Hoving as director of the Metropolitan Museum. See his *Making the Mummies Dance: Inside the Metropolitan Museum of Art* (New York: Simon & Schuster, 1993).

60. Paul J. DiMaggio, "Constructing an Organizational Field as a Professional Project: U.S. Art Museums, 1920–1940," in Walter W. Powell and Paul J. DiMaggio, eds., *The New Institutionalism in Organizational Analysis* (Chicago: University of Chicago Press, 1991), pp. 267–292.

61. For a treatment of the museum's set of choices and governance arrangements in a European context, see Bruno S. Frey and Werner W. Pommerehne, "An Economic Analysis of the Museum," in William S. Hendon, James L. Shanahan, and

Alice J. MacDonald, eds., *Economic Policy for the Arts* (Cambridge, Mass.: Abt Books, 1980), pp. 248–259.

62. Meyer, *Art Museum*, pp. 131, 134, 146–148, 161.

63. Lynes, *Good Old Modern*, pp. 399, 408; ibid., pp. 148–159. This dilemma caught up with a number of arts organizations that inherited performing-arts centers, which were popular cultural trappings in the 1960s and 1970s. While such centers provided attractive venues, their sizes frequently exceeded the best operating scales (optimal audience capacities) for the organizations they were intended to serve. They either sank the arts organizations with inflated operating costs or forced the center's manager to displace the intended performers in favor of lower-minded but more lucrative entertainment such as touring Broadway musicals. See Edward Rothstein, "Classical Arts Lose Their Stages to Broadway," *NYTNE*, May 31, 1998, p. 1, 16.

64. Edwin C. Banfield, *The Democratic Muse: Visual Arts and the Public Interest* (New York: Basic Books, 1984), ch. 4.

65. Judith H. Dobrzynski, "Museums Paint Prosperity by Numbers," *NYTNE*, Feb. 26, 1998, pp. B1, B6. The Philadelphia Museum of Art's Cezanne exhibit raised its membership from 30,000 to 48,000.

66. Judith H. Dobrzynski, "Glory Days for the Art Museum," *NYTNE*, Oct. 5, 1997, sec. 2, pp. 1, 44; Victoria Newhouse, *Toward a New Museum* (New York: Monacelli, 1998). Between 1992 and 1997, gallery space at 185 U.S. museums increased by 3.3 percent, while space devoted to museum stores increased by 28.2 percent. No aggregate figures are available on stores' net profits (gross revenues run 18 to 26 percent of museums' earned income), but they are apparently substantial. Judith H. Dobrzynski, "Art(?) to Go: Museum Shops Broaden Wares, at a Profit," *NYTNE*, Dec. 10, 1997, pp. A1, A26.

67. The argument makes two assumptions about the supply of donations: (1) that a person's voluntary contribution increases with the surplus of the value of benefits from museum attendance over the out-of-pocket cost of the visit; (2) the average museum visitor enjoys some such surplus, so the surplus available to motivate donations strictly increases with the museum's number of visitors.

68. Tomkins, *Merchants and Masterpieces,* pp. 225–226, 230, 235, 250–261, 277–278; Lynes, *Good Old Modern*, pp. 415, 416.

69. Plattner, *High Art Down Home*, pp. 60–68.

70. As with other donor-supported NPOs, board membership gives some measure of governance rights in exchange for financial support. Museums seem notably successful in devising affiliate organizations that appear to have a governance role but in reality have a donor function (see, for example, Lynes, *Good Old Modern*, pp. 75–76, 133, 259–260, 380–382).

71. Meyer, *Art Museum*, pp. 222, 231–238.

72. Daniel Catton Rich, "Management, Power, and Integrity," in Lee, *On Understanding Art Museums*, pp. 131–162.

73. Deborah Solomon, "As Art Museums Thrive, Their Directors Decamp," *NYTNE*, Aug. 2, 1998, sec. 2, pp. 1, 35.

74. One example of outright institutional competition is the displacement of the longstanding New York Historical Society (founded 1804) by the Metropolitan

Museum (1870). When Gertrude Vanderbilt Whitney in 1929 offered the Met her collection of then-contemporary American art, however, she was turned down flat and went off to found the Whitney Museum. In 1942 the Met attempted unsuccessfully to incorporate the Whitney. See Tomkins, *Merchants and Masterpieces,* p. 38, ch. 22; Paul Goldberger, "To the Rescue of a Grande Dame of Museums," *NYTNE,* June 2, 1997, pp. B1, B2.

75. See Fox, *Engines of Culture,* pp. 454–6; Tomkins, *Merchants and Masterpieces,* pp. 153–164, 169–174, 189, 234.

76. Meyer, *Art Museum,* ch. 6; Rich, "Management, Power, and Integrity," p. 154; Walker, *Self-Portrait with Donors,* pp. 134–140; Weil, *Beauty and the Beasts,* pp. 56–68.

77. Judith H. Dobrzynski, "Have Show, Will Travel (within Limits)," *NYT,* Feb. 25, 1996, sec. 2, pp. 1, 26; Terry Pristin, "The Art behind the Art Show," *NYTNE,* Oct. 2, 1997, pp. B1, B3.

78. Judith H. Dobrzynski, "Masterminding an Epic Show," *NYT,* June 9, 1996, sec. 2, pp. 1, 39.

79. William D. Grampp, *Pricing the Priceless: Art, Artists, and Economics* (New York: Basic Books, 1989), pp. 178–184; J. Michael Montias, "Are Museums Betraying the Public's Trust?" in Mark Blaug, ed., *The Economics of the Arts* (Boulder, Colo.: Westview, 1976), pp. 205–217. For a thoughtful critique, see Peter Cannon-Brookes, "Cultural-Economic Analyses of Museums: A British Curator's Viewpoint," in Victor A. Ginsburgh and Pierre-Michel Menger, eds., *Economics of the Arts: Selected Essays* (Amsterdam: Elsevier, 1996), pp. 255–274.

80. Peter Temin, "An Economic History of American Art Museums," in Martin Feldstein, ed., *The Economics of Art Museums* (Chicago: University of Chicago Press, 1991), pp. 182–183.

81. Patti Hartigan, "Reception for Nagoya Museum Dampened by Injured Economy," *BG,* Apr. 9, 1999. pp. D1, D4.

22. New versus Old Art

1. Geraldine Keen, *Money and Art: A Study Based on the Times-Sotheby Index* (New York: G. P. Putnam's Sons, 1971), p. 48.

2. Ibid., pp. 49–50.

3. For example, Francis Haskell, *Rediscoveries in Art: Some Aspects of Taste, Fashion, and Collecting in England and France* (Ithaca, N.Y.: Cornell University Press, 1980).

4. Ibid., especially pp. 51, 71–74, 77–82, 142, 154–160.

5. Keen, *Money and Art,* pp. 58, 230, and ch. 4 generally; John Walker, *Self-Portrait with Donors: Confessions of an Art Collector* (Boston: Atlantic–Little, Brown, 1974), pp. xi–xvii.

6. Joseph Alsop, *The Rare Art Traditions: The History of Art Collecting and Its Linked Phenomena Wherever These Have Appeared* (London: Thames and Hudson, 1982), especially pp. 95–100.

7. Robert Woolley, *Going Once: A Memoir of Art, Society, and Charity* (New York: Simon & Schuster, 1995), pp. 62–63, 87–93.

8. Christie's recently sought (unsuccessfully) to abet this substitution by reorganizing the time periods used to subdivide their painting auctions: it placed earlier nineteenth-century art cheek by jowl with the ever-costlier and scarcer Impressionists, and grouped modern art to 1970 with works of the early twentieth century to suggest alternatives to collectors frustrated in the pursuit of Picasso and Mondrian. Ann E. Berman, "Auction Season Makes a New Impression," *WSJ*, May 21, 1998, p. A15.

9. Russell Lynes, *Good Old Modern: An Intimate Portrait of the Museum of Modern Art* (New York: Atheneum, 1973), pp. 180–181, 319.

10. Terry Smith, *Making the Modern: Industry, Art, and Design in America* (Chicago: University of Chicago Press, 1993).

11. Liah Greenfeld, *Different Worlds: A Sociological Study of Taste, Choice, and Success in Art* (Cambridge: Cambridge University Press, 1989), ch. 5.

12. Walter Darby Bannard, "The Art Museum and the Living Artist," in Sherman E. Lee, ed., *On Understanding Art Museums* (Englewood Cliffs, N.J.: Prentice-Hall, 1975), pp. 163–184.

13. Michael Kimmelman, "At Dia, Fresh Wounds and a Fresh Start," *NYT*, Sept. 15, 1996, sec. 2, p. 36; Roberta Smith, "More Spacious and Gracious, Yet Still Funky at Heart," *NYTNE*, Oct. 31, 1997, pp. B1, B34.

14. Carol Vogel, "Four Prized Drawings, No Longer Modern, Have Left MOMA," *NYTNE*, Oct. 26, 1998, pp. A1, A23.

15. Michael Kimmelman, "A Renewed Modern: More of a Museum or More Modern?" *NYT*, Nov. 22, 1994, pp. C15, C21; Lynes, *Good Old Modern*, ch. 15; Calvin Tomkins, *Merchants and Masterpieces: The Story of the Metropolitan Museum of Art*, rev. ed. (New York: Henry Holt, 1989), ch. 22.

16. Lynes, *Good Old Modern*, pp. 432–433, 442–443.

17. Peter Temin, "An Economic History of American Art Museums," in Martin Feldstein, ed., *The Economics of Art Museums* (Chicago: University of Chicago Press, 1991), pp. 179–193.

18. Unless, of course, some economy of scale or agglomeration gives it first pick of all newly ensconced masterpieces.

19. John Walsh in Feldstein, *Economics of Art Museums*, pp. 23–30.

20. Diana Crane, *The Transformation of the Avant-Garde: The New York Art World, 1940–1985* (Chicago: University of Chicago Press, 1989), ch. 7.

21. Wilhelm Treue, *Art Plunder: The Fate of Works of Art in War and Unrest*, trans. Basil Creighton (New York: John Day, 1961).

22. Haskell, *Rediscoveries in Art*, ch. 2.

23. American collecting actually did get something of a jump-start from favorable prices that greeted Americans on the Grand Tour during the period of the Napoleonic wars. See Neil Harris, *The Artist in American Society: The Formative Years, 1790–1860* (New York: George Braziller, 1966), pp. 103–106.

24. Tomkins, *Merchants and Masterpieces*, pp. 36–37.

25. Walker, *Self-Portrait with Donors*, pp. 110–111.

26. Hector Feliciano, *The Lost Museum: The Nazi Conspiracy to Steal the World's Greatest Works of Art* (New York: Basic Books, 1997).

27. Judith H. Dobrzynski, "For What Nazis Stole, a Longtime Art Hound,"

NYTNE, Nov. 29, 1997, pp. A17, A22. On the general problem of titles to art objects, see William M. Landes and Richard A. Posner, "The Economics of Legal Disputes over the Ownership of Works of Art and Other Collectibles," in Victor A. Ginsburgh and Pierre-Michel Menger, eds., *Economics of the Arts: Selected Essays* (Amsterdam: Elsevier, 1996), pp. 177–219.

28. Judith H. Dobrzynski, "Wary Hong Kong Collectors Send Art Abroad for Safety," *NYTNE,* May 27, 1997, pp. A1, B2.

29. If the *nobody knows* principle applies, the opportunity cost for a new composition turns on the subjective probability that it will excel a rehearing of a familiar work. Clearly, it matters whether a skilled musician can determine at low cost—by reading the score—whether a new piece can achieve viable entry into the performed stock.

30. Sonia S. Gold, "Consumer Sovereignty and the Performing Arts," in William S. Hendon and James L. Shanahan, eds., *Economics of Cultural Decisions* (Cambridge, Mass.: Abt Books, 1983), pp. 207–218.

31. Aspects of this reasoning were developed by Michael O'Hare, "A Malthusian Nightmare for the Composer and His Audience," in William S. Hendon, James L. Shanahan, and Alice J. MacDonald, eds., *Economic Policy for the Arts* (Cambridge, Mass.: Abt Books, 1980), pp. 114–120; and Philip Hart, *Orpheus in the New World: The Symphony Orchestra as an American Cultural Institution* (New York: Norton, 1973), ch. 17. On the contrast between music and visual arts, see Vera L. Zolberg, "Displayed Art and Performed Music: Selective Innovation and the Structure of Artistic Media," *Sociological Quarterly* 21 (Spring 1980): 219–231.

32. William J. Baumol and Hilda Baumol, "On the Economics of Musical Composition in Mozart's Vienna," in James M. Morris, ed., *On Mozart* (Cambridge: Cambridge University Press, 1994), pp. 72–101.

33. William Weber, *The Rise of Musical Classics in Eighteenth-Century England: A Study in Canon, Ritual, and Ideology* (Oxford: Clarendon Press, 1992), especially pp. 1–20, chs. 5, 6.

34. Ibid., p. 196.

35. John H. Mueller, *The American Symphony Orchestra: A Social History of Musical Taste* (Bloomington: Indiana University Press, 1951), ch. 4; Kate Hevner Mueller, *Twenty-Seven Major American Symphony Orchestras: A History and Analysis of Their Repertoires* (Bloomington: Indiana University Press, 1973); Hart, *Orpheus,* ch. 17.

36. Norman Lebrecht, *Who Killed Classical Music? Maestros, Managers, and Corporate Politics* (Secaucus, N.J.: Birch Lane Press, 1997), pp. 397, 408.

37. Marianne Victorius Felton, "The Economics of the Creative Arts: The Case of Composers," *JCE* 2 (June 1978): 41–61.

38. In Henry Swoboda, ed., *The American Symphony Orchestra* (New York: Basic Books, 1967), p. 181. On the economics of commissioning new music, see John Rockwell, "Commissions: Where Patron Meets Composer," *NYT,* Apr. 5, 1987, sec. 2, pp. 24, 38.

39. Felton, "Economics of the Creative Arts"; see also Ernst Roth, *The Business of Music: Reflections of a Music Publisher* (London: Cassell, 1969), pp. 99–102;

Deena Rosenberg and Bernard Rosenberg, *The Music Makers* (New York: Columbia University Press, 1979), pp. 51–52, 387, 406.

40. K. Robert Schwarz, "Bag Full of Operas: Anyone Want One?" *NYTNE*, July 12, 1998, sec. 2, pp. 27, 30. Even Broadway musicals show repertory congestion. See Anthony Tommasini, "A Crowd of Old Musicals Squeezes the New," *NYTNE*, Aug. 16, 1998, sec. 2, pp. 1, 24–25.

41. Alan Peacock and Ronald Weir, *The Composer in the Market Place* (London: Faber Music, 1975), p. 160; Roth, *Business of Music*, pp. 57–58. Gustav Mahler had to pay a Viennese firm to publish his gigantic symphonies, and publishers rejected Wagner's scores while busily issuing those of Lindpaintner and Halevy (Roth, *Business of Music*, pp. 54–55). On attempts to escape the problem of publishing costs, see Anthony Tommasini, "Mom and Pop Jolt Music Publishing," *NYTNE*, Oct. 11, 1998, sec. 2, pp. 29, 31.

42. Rosenberg and Rosenberg, *Music Makers*, pp. 14–15, 66–67, 120, 245–246.

43. Ibid., pp. 382–386.

44. For example, Henry Pleasants, *The Agony of Modern Music* (New York: Simon & Schuster, 1955).

45. Ibid., pp. 56, 125–126, 380, 385.

46. Paul Griffiths, "For Future Mozarts, No Place to Shine?" *NYTNE*, May 24, 1998, sec. 2, p. 25.

47. Jesse Green, "The Song Is Ended," *New York Times Magazine*, June 2, 1996, pp. 28–61.

Epilogue

1. This is Howard S. Becker's felicitous phrase for the agents and institutions participating on both demand and supply sides of a creative-goods market. See his *Art Worlds* (Berkeley: University of California Press, 1982).

2. Noël Carroll, *A Philosophy of Mass Art* (Oxford: Clarendon Press, 1998).

Index

449

452 | Index

sMontgomery, Sarah S., 80, 82
Morgan, J. P., 332, 339
Motley crew property: defined, 5–6; movies,
106–108, 367; stage plays, 116, 119–120;
nonprofit organizations, 236–237, 263;
record royalties, 300, 313
Mott, Frank, 76
Moulin, Raymonde, 28
Movie studios: studio contract system, 88–
92; organization of production, 90–92,
141; disintegration, 96–102, 134;
distribution services, 112, 165–167;
accounting practices, 113–114
Mueller, John, 245
Mueller, Kate, 249
"Muscle" (influence), 5, 92, 119, 128
Museum of Fine Arts (Boston), 249, 341,
347
Museum of Modern Art, 217, 220, 272,
341–342, 351, 352–353
Museums: origins, 340–341, 353; policies,
342–345, 346, 351–353, 354; competition
among, 345–347; deaccessioning, 346–
347
Music Corporation of America (MCA), 70
Musicians, classical: training, 24–25, 35;
contests, 35–36; concert booking, 69–72
Musicians, popular: apprenticeship, 34–35;
managers of, 35, 63; recording contracts,
61–67

National Gallery of Art, 341, 346, 355
Navarro, Peter, 252
Networking, 60, 125
Newman, Barnett, 27
New York Philharmonic Orchestra, 239–240,
241–242
Nobody knows property: defined, 3; TV
programs, 3; visual artists' contracts, 39–
40; record label contracts, 61–62; movie
financing, 111; failed projects, 137–141;
movie distribution, 167; record
distribution, 209; toys and games, 212;
theatre flop rates, 254–255; business
decisionmaking, 315–316
Nonprofit organizations: fixed costs, 225–
226, 340; governance conditions, 226–
228, 345; prevalence, 230–233; policies,
233–237; performance quality, 239–242;
free-riding problem, 247–250

Opera companies, 235
Option contracts: defined, 15; record labels

and artists, 62–64; actors and movie
studios, 88–89; movie scripts, 90–91, 104–
106; movie PFD agreements, 112–113;
stage plays, 116
Ostrower, Francie, 250
Ovitz, Michael, 70, 99

Pace Gallery, 46, 48
Paramount case, 89, 93–95
Parsons, Betty, 45, 49
Partch, Harry 204
Passman, Donald, 62
Peterson, Richard A., 207
Photography, 25
Picasso, Pablo, 42–43
Picker enterprises: art galleries, 47–48, 340;
books, records, 158, 159, 209
Piracy, 284–285
Plagiarism suits, 89–90, 212–213, 298
Plattner, Stuart, 32
Play-or-pay contracts, 107, 140
Playwrights, 116–118
Plunder, 354–356
Poggi, Jack, 263
Pollock, Jackson, 49, 194, 217
Pop Art, 49, 50
Price discrimination, 168, 224, 278
Prices, conventionalized, 55, 57–58, 117–
119, 286–287, 310–311
Prizes, literary, 198–199
Producers: movie, 91, 104–106, 110–112;
stage play, 116–117, 120
Production Code (Hollywood), 100
Product placement, 294–295
Promoter enterprises: art galleries, 47–48,
340; book publishers, 151; record
companies, 158–159, 209; governance
problems, 316–317
Publishers, book: contracts with authors, 56–
59; editors' roles, 59–60; failed projects,
142–145; sales promotion, 143–144, 150–
152
Publishers, music: payola, 288; promotion,
288, 298–299; movie studio ownership,
304, 307; songwriter ownership, 310–311;
copyright administration, 311; fixed costs,
360

Radio broadcasting, playlist selection, 153–
154
Radway, Janice, 200
Rates of return, art holdings, 330–331
Rational addiction, 175–178